MEGA-REGIONAL TRADE AGREEMENTS: CETA, TTIP, AND TISA

INTERNATIONAL ECONOMIC LAW

Series Editors
Andrew D. Mitchell is Professor at Melbourne Law School, The University of Melbourne
Tania Voon is Professor at Melbourne Law School, The University of Melbourne

The International Economic Law series, established by the late Professor John H Jackson, addresses a range of issues in international economic law, which includes international trade law, international investment law, and the global financial order. The Series aims to encourage interest in the broad contours of international economic law, heightening awareness of its significance across the globe as well as its continuous interactions with other areas. The Series Editors encourage quality submissions from a wide range of perspectives, including doctrinal, theoretical, empirical, and interdisciplinary. Novel and cutting edge research is particularly welcome, as are contributions from both emerging and established scholars from around the world.

ALSO PUBLISHED IN THIS SERIES

Small and Medium-Sized Enterprises in International Economic Law
Edited by Thilo Rensmann

Domestic Law in International Investment Arbitration
Jarrod Hepburn

Treaty Shopping in International Investment Law
Jorun Baumgartner

Good Faith and International Economic Law
Edited by Andrew D. Mitchell, M Sornarajah, and Tania Voon

Mega-Regional Trade Agreements: CETA, TTIP, and TiSA

New Orientations for EU External Economic Relations

Edited by
STEFAN GRILLER
WALTER OBWEXER
ERICH VRANES

OXFORD
UNIVERSITY PRESS

OXFORD
UNIVERSITY PRESS

Great Clarendon Street, Oxford, OX2 6DP,
United Kingdom

Oxford University Press is a department of the University of Oxford.
It furthers the University's objective of excellence in research, scholarship,
and education by publishing worldwide. Oxford is a registered trade mark of
Oxford University Press in the UK and in certain other countries

First Edition published in 2017

Published in the United States of America by Oxford University Press
198 Madison Avenue, New York, NY 10016, United States of America

British Library Cataloguing in Publication Data
Data available

Library of Congress Control Number: 2017945337

ISBN 978–0–19–880889–3

Series Editors' Preface

In *Mega-Regional Trade Agreements: CETA, TTIP, and TiSA*, Professors Griller, Obwexer and Vranes have assembled an impressive group of international authors to address some of the most complex questions facing the global economy and the international community today. While appropriately focused on the European Union ('EU'), the authors in this volume have a range of connections with countries around the globe, including the United States and the United Kingdom, as well as an in-depth understanding of international perspectives and their intersection with EU priorities. Leading experts on international economic law (particularly international trade law and international investment law) share their insights alongside eminent scholars in related and overlapping fields including public law, EU law, public international law, and intellectual property rights. Moreover, this ambitious volume goes beyond legal questions to place these mega-regional trade agreements in the broader context of economics and political science, through both dedicated chapters by subject matter experts and cross-cutting consideration of a range of economic and policy issues.

The book targets three trade and investment treaties of critical importance to the EU and the wider landscape of international economic law: the EU–Canada Comprehensive Economic and Trade Agreement ('CETA') (signed after a tumultuous final period of internal EU wrangling but not yet in force); the Transatlantic Trade and Investment Partnership ('TTIP') under negotiation between the United States ('US') and the EU; and the negotiations among twenty-three Members of the World Trade Organization ('WTO') (including the EU representing its twenty-eight Member States) towards a Trade in Services Agreement ('TiSA'), which have been conducted outside the WTO and jointly led by the US, the EU, and Australia. As the Editors and other contributors discuss, each of these three agreements has suffered setbacks and raised community concerns in a range of areas, including the impact of investor–State dispute settlement on sovereign regulatory autonomy, the accountability deficit associated with confidential treaty negotiations, and the effect of heightened intellectual property protections on access to essential medicines. Moreover, even as we write, the future of TTIP and TiSA is beset by uncertainties following the election of US President Donald Trump and his ongoing revision of US trade and investment policy.

The problems faced by these mega-regional trade agreements may be partially understood as arising from their increased breadth and depth of liberalization in comparison to previous bilateral, regional, or even multilateral agreements. For example, as explored further in this volume, the negotiators of these treaties are grappling with cutting edge aspects of trade in services such as financial regulation and cross-border data transfer, which generate a complicated web of issues across technology, logistics, and social and regulatory preferences. The treaties must also address perennial tensions between economic and non-economic objectives and, correspondingly, interconnecting areas of domestic, regional, and international law—including in relation to human rights and labour and environmental standards—all while recognising economic, political, and cultural differences between the negotiating parties.

The importance of the drafting, conclusion, and implementation of CETA, TTIP and TiSA is heightened by other recent developments, most notably the 2017 withdrawal by the US from the Trans-Pacific Partnership ('TPP') already signed by it and 11 other countries a year before (precluding its entry into force in its current form). In the absence of the TPP and the apparent end to the US 'pivot to Asia', the ongoing negotiations towards the Regional Comprehensive Economic Partnership ('RCEP') have taken on greater significance, particularly given their inclusion of China and India, which were not part of the TPP. The stalemate in multilateral trade negotiations at the WTO also increases the need to look critically at current approaches to international economic law to determine new pathways towards consensus-building and fairer distribution of the gains of liberalization. Against this background, CETA has the potential to lead the way in reforming the investment treaty regime through the investment court system, while TiSA negotiating parties have the opportunity to improve on the TPP's provisions directed at electronic commerce. The EU itself may have the ability through the TTIP negotiations to revive US interest in the national and international benefits of liberalization and openness. This book makes a valuable and timely contribution to all of these debates.

Andrew D Mitchell
Tania Voon
April 2017

Preface

This book examines three 'mega-regional' treaty projects that have aroused academic and public interest to an unquestionably greater extent than most other international agreements concluded by the EU so far: the Comprehensive Economic and Trade Agreement between the EU and Canada (CETA), the Transatlantic Trade and Investment Partnership between the EU and the US (TTIP), and the plurilateral Trade in Services Agreement (TiSA) currently being negotiated between the EU and twenty-two other Member States of the World Trade Organization (WTO).

These agreements are exceedingly complex in legal terms and decidedly controversial in terms of legitimacy. Their legal complexity stems from a series of factors. On the one hand, there is their sheer regulatory extent. CETA alone accounts for almost 1,600 pages. TTIP and TiSA will hardly be less voluminous. On the other hand, all three treaties are designed to function as 'WTO-plus' agreements that reconfirm, improve, and complement the trade rules of the WTO. Hence, it is impossible to understand, implement, apply, and teach these agreements without a thorough understanding of the core principles, and many technical details, of WTO law. Moreover, all three agreements try to cover new ground by deepening and extending trade disciplines to additional fields in trade in goods and services, by increasing the country-specific commitments in trade in services, and by establishing new mechanisms such as enhanced frameworks for regulatory cooperation. Also, CETA and TTIP comprise elaborate rules on investment protection and investor-state dispute settlement (ISDS) that surpass existing investment protection regimes in many respects.

However, these agreements have also proven to be highly controversial. This, too, is due to a series of reasons. First, there is the 'regulatory ambition' of these agreements, which will further reduce domestic regulatory autonomy despite repeated confirmations, in the treaty texts, of a 'right to regulate' on the domestic level. Second, this ambition may be felt more acutely in the future due to an increased dynamism in a bilateral and plurilateral context of 'like-minded' countries and mechanisms such as ISDS that are to be included in CETA and TTIP. While many other reasons could be cited, mention should also be made of the fact that, despite some attempts to increase transparency in the negotiation process of TTIP in particular, these agreements have been negotiated in a manner that has been regarded by many as insufficiently transparent and responsive to democratic, societal, and legitimacy concerns more generally.

This volume is the outcome of a conference held in Salzburg in March 2016. Leading experts of universities from eight countries and both sides of the Atlantic address significant parts of the aforementioned issues in sixteen chapters. Eleven of these, grouped in Parts I and II of this book, deal with the wider background and selected sectoral issues of these mega-regional projects. Four chapters stem from an extensive panel discussion closing the conference. These have been grouped as shorter contributions, together with a concluding chapter, in Part III of this volume. All contributions have been finalized between the autumn and winter of 2016. As organizers of the 2016 conference, and as editors of this volume, we wish to express our sincere gratitude for the thoroughness with which all contributors have accepted the challenge of examining these intricate topics.

Also, we would like to express our profound gratefulness to the Austrian National Bank (OeNB), the Austrian Ministry of Science, Research and Economy, the City of Vienna, the European Community Studies Association Austria (ECSA Austria), and the Province of the Tyrol for their generous support of this project. We would also like to sincerely thank Merel Alstein, Emma Endean-Mills, and Nicole Leyland (all of Oxford University Press) as well as Vignesh Kannan and his colleagues at Newgen Knowledge Works for their effective support and advice. Last but not least, we would like to thank MMag Daniela Führer; Johannes Hartlieb, LLM, BSc; Dr Andreas Orator, BA, LLM (NYU), diplômé (Sciences-Po); Mag Roman Puff; and Mag Maria-Theresia Rappersberger for their invaluable assistance in the various stages of this project.

Stefan Griller, Walter Obwexer, and Erich Vranes
Salzburg, Innsbruck, Vienna, January 2017

Contents

Table of Cases

WTO

GATT and WTO Panel Reports

Appellate Body Reports

WTO Arbitration Reports

EU

CJEU Cases

Opinions of Advocates-General

OTHER

ECtHR

ICJ

ICSID

UNCITRAL

OTHER INTERNATIONAL DECISIONS

NATIONAL COURT DECISIONS

Legal Materials

WTO DOCUMENTS

EU DOCUMENTS

UN DOCUMENTS

OTHER DOCUMENTS

List of Abbreviations

AB	Appellate Body
ACTA	Anti-Counterfeiting Trade Agreement
AG	Attorney General
Am J Finance & Accounting	*American Journal of Finance and Accounting*
Am J Int L	*American Journal of International Law*
Am Soc'y Int'l L Proc	American Society of International Law Proceedings
APEC	Asia–Pacific Economic Cooperation
Arb Int'l	*Arbitration International*
Art/Arts	Article/s
ASEAN	Association of Southeast Asian Nations
ASIL	American Society of International Law
BCBS	Basel Committee of Banking Supervision
BIT	bilateral investment treaty
BRICS	Brazil, Russia, India, China, and South Africa
BVerfGE	Bundesverfassungsgerichtsentscheidung (decision by the German Constitutional Court)
CAFTA	Central America Free Trade Agreement
CAFTA–DR	Dominican Republic–Central America Free Trade Agreement
CBTS	cross-border trade in services
cCh/cChs	chapter/s
CCP	common commercial policy
CES	Center for Economic Studies
CETA	Comprehensive Economic and Trade Agreement
cf	confer, compare
CFSP	Common Foreign and Security Policy
Chicago JIL	*Chicago Journal of International Law*
CISDL	Centre for International Sustainable Development Law
CJEU	Court of Justice of the European Union
CLEER	Centre for the Law of EU External Relations
CML Review	*Common Market Law Review*
Col J Eur L	*Columbia Journal of European Law*
Colum J Transnat'l L	*Columbia Journal of Transnational Law*
COREPER	Committee of Permanent Representatives of the EU
COSAC	Conference of Parliamentary Committees for Union Affairs of Parliaments of the European Union
CPC	UN Central Product Classification
DG Trade	Directorate-General for Trade
DSB	Dispute Settlement Body
DSU	Dispute Settlement Understanding
EC	European Communities
ECHR	European Convention on Human Rights
ECI	European Citizens' Initiative

ECJ	European Court of Justice
ECON Committee	Committee on Economic and Monetary Affairs (European Parliament)
ECSA Austria	European Community Studies Association Austria
ECT	Energy Charter Treaty
ECtHR	European Court of Human Rights
ed/eds	editor/s
EEA	European Economic Area
EEC	European Economic Community
EFTA	European Free Trade Area
EJIL	*European Journal of International Law*
EMU	Economic and Monetary Union
EP	European Parliament
ERC	European Research Council
ERTA	European Road Transport Agreement
EU	European Union
EU–CARIFORUM Agreement	EU–Caribbean Forum Agreement
EU CARIFORUM EPA	EU–Caribbean Forum Economic Partnership Agreements
EUCFR	Charter of Fundamental Rights of the EU
EUI	European University Institute
EU–Moldova AA	EU–Moldova Association Agreement
EUSFTA	EU–Singapore Free Trade Agreement
FAO	Food and Agriculture Organization
FATF	Financial Action Task Force on Money Laundering
FCC	German Federal Constitutional Court
FDI	foreign direct investment
FET	fair and equitable treatment
ff	and the following
fn	footnote
Fordham L Rev	*Fordham Law Review*
FSB	Financial Stability Board
FTA	free trade agreement
G8	Group of Eight (Canada, France, Germany, Italy, Japan, Russia, the UK, and the US)
G20	Group of Twenty (an international forum for the governments and central bank governors from twenty major economies)
Ga J Int'l & Comp L	*Georgia Journal of International and Comparative Law*
GATS	General Agreement on Trade in Services
GATT	General Agreement on Tariffs and Trade 1994
GDP	gross domestic product
Georgetown Int'l Envir L Rev	*Georgetown International Environmental Law Review*
GIs	geographical indications
GMO	genetically modified organism
GPA	Government Procurement Agreement
HRC	Human Rights Council
HRL	human rights law
IAIS	International Association of Insurance Supervisors

ICJ	International Court of Justice
ICS	investment court system
ICSID Convention	Convention on the Settlement of Investment Disputes between States and Nationals of Other States
ICT	information and communications technology
IEL	international economic law
ifo Institute	Institut für Wirtschaftsforschung
IIA	international investment agreement
IIA on Better Law-Making	Inter-Institutional agreement between the EP, the Council of the EU and the European Commission on Better Law-Making
IIED	International Institute for Environment and Development
IISD	International Institute for Sustainable Development
ILA	International Law Association
ILC	International Law Commission
IILJ	Institute for International Law and Justice
ILM	International Legal Materials
ILO	International Labour Organization
IMF	International Monetary Fund
INTA	European Parliament's Committee on International Trade
IO	International Organization
IOSCO	International Organization of Securities Commissions
IP	intellectual property
IPR law	intellectual property rights law
IPRs	iIntellectual property rights
ISDS	investor-stated dispute settlement
ISIC	International Standard Industrial Classification of all Economic Activities
J Int Econ L	*Journal of International Economic Law*
J World Inv & Trade	*Journal of World Investment & Trade*
JIDS	*Journal of International Dispute Settlement*
LDC	less-developed country
Leiden J Int L	*Leiden Journal of International Law*
lit	litera
MA	market access
MAI	Multilateral Agreement on Investment
Max Planck YB of UN L	*Max Planck Yearbook of United Nations Law*
MEP	Member of the European Parliament
MFN	most-favoured nation
n	note
NAAEC	North American Agreement on Environmental Cooperation
NAALC	North American Agreement on Labor Cooperation
NAFTA	North American Free Trade Agreement
Nat'l LJ	*National Law Journal*
NATO	North Atlantic Treaty Organization
NGO	non-governmental organization

NSA	National Security Agency
NT	national treatment
NTB	non-tariff barrier to trade
Nw J Int'l L & Bus	*Northwestern Journal of International Law & Business*
NYU IILJ	New York University Institute for International Law and Justice
NYU J Int'l L & Pol	*New York University Journal of International Law and Politics*
NYU L Rev	*New York University Law Review*
OECD	Organisation for Economic Co-operation and Development
OHCHR	Office of the High Commissioner on Human Rights
Ox J Int Econ L	*Journal of International Economics*
para/paras	paragraph/s
PCA	Permanent Court of Arbitration
PCT	Patent Cooperation Treaty
PGs	public goods
PR	performance requirements
PA	Plurilateral Agreement
PTA	preferential trade agreement
RCEP	Regional Comprehensive Economic Partnership
RTA	regional trade agreement
S2B	Seattle to Brussels Network
SCC	Stockholm Chamber of Commerce
SCEUS	Salzburg Centre of European Union Studies
SEPA	Single Euro Payments
SIA	sustainability impact assessment
SME	small and medium-sized enterprise
SPA	EU–Canada Strategic Partnership Agreement
SPS Agreement	Agreement on the Application of Sanitary and Phytosanitary
SPS Measures	Sanitary and Phytosanitary Measures
TBT	technical barrier to trade
TBT Agreement	Agreement on Technical Barriers to Trade
TDM	*Transnational Dispute Management*
TELC	Transnational Economic Law Research Centre
TEU	Treaty on European Union
TFEU	Treaty on the Functioning of the European Union
TILEC	Tilburg Law and Economics Center
TiSA	Trade in Services Agreement
TK	Traditional Knowledge
TPP	Trans-Pacific Partnership
TPSEP Agreement	Trans-Pacific Strategic Economic Partnership Agreement
TRIPs Agreement	Agreement on Trade-Related Aspects of Intellectual Property Rights
TTIP	Transatlantic Trade and Investment Partnership
UDHR	Universal Declaration of Human Rights
UK	United Kingdom
UN	United Nations
UNCITRAL	UN Commission on International Trade Law
UNCLOS	UN Convention on the Law of the Sea
UNESCO	UN Educational, Scientific and Cultural Organization

UNTS	UN Treaty Series
UPOV	International Union for the Protection of New Varieties of Plants
US	United States
US–EU HLWG	US–European Union High Level Working Group on Jobs and Growth
USTR	US Trade Representative
v/vs	versus
Vand J Transnat'l L	*Vanderbilt Journal of Transnational Law*
VCLT	Vienna Convention on the Law of Treaties
VCLTIO	Vienna Convention on the Law of Treaties between States and International Organizations or Between International Organizations
WCT	WIPO Copyright Treaty
WHO	World Health Organization
WIPO	World Intellectual Property Organization
WPDR	Working Party on Domestic Regulation
WPPT	WIPO Performances and Phonograms Treaty
WTO	World Trade Organization
Yale LJ	*Yale Law Journal*

Notes on Editors and Contributors

***Lorand Bartels*, Cambridge University, UK (Chapter 9)**
Lorand Bartels is a University Senior Lecturer in Law in the Faculty of Law and a Fellow of Trinity Hall at the University of Cambridge, where he teaches international law, WTO law, and EU law. He holds degrees in English literature and law from the University of New South Wales and a PhD in law from the European University Institute. Dr Bartels is a member of the ILA's study group on free trade agreements and helped to establish the Society of International Economic Law. He is a general editor of the Cambridge International Trade and Economic Law Series (Cambridge University Press) and an editorial board member of several journals, including the *Journal of International Economic Law*, the *Journal of International Dispute Settlement*, the *Journal of World Trade*, and *Legal Issues of Economic Integration*.

***Walter Berka*, University of Salzburg, AT (Chapter 7)**
Walter Berka is Full Professor of Constitutional and Administrative Law and General Theory of the State at the University of Salzburg. He is Full Member of the Austrian Academy of Sciences, Deputy Judge at the Liechtenstein State Court, and he served as Dean of the Law School from 1998 to 2004. His main research areas include fundamental freedoms and human rights, media law, education law, planning law, and data protection law. He is active in several scientific organizations, for example, as chairperson and board member of the Research Institute for the Law of Electronic Media (Vienna) and as board member of the European Association for Education Law and Policy (Antwerp). He was Faculty Member of the Institute for International Judges Brandeis University (2004) and Distinguished Visiting Professor at McGeorge School of Law (2004). Professor Berka has received several research awards, inter alia, the Austrian Prize for Constitutional Law and the International Science Prize of the City of Salzburg. As to his publications, see <http://www.uni-salzburg.at/vvr/berka>.

***Thomas Cottier*, University of Berne, CH (Chapter 6)**
Thomas Cottier is Emeritus Professor of European and International Economic Law at the University of Bern, a senior research fellow at the World Trade Institute, and adjunct professor at the University of Ottawa, Faculty of Law. He was educated at the University of Bern, University of Michigan Law School, and was a visiting fellow at Cambridge University, UK. He taught at several universities in Switzerland and abroad and was a member of the Swiss National Research Council. He served on the Swiss negotiating team of the Uruguay Round from 1986 to 1993, first as Chief Negotiator on dispute settlement and subsidies for Switzerland and subsequently as Chief Negotiator on TRIPs when he was the Deputy-Director General of the Swiss Intellectual Property Office. He served as a member or chair of several GATT and WTO panels. He acted as Of Counsel to Baker McKenzie and a board member of several NGOs. He was the founder and managing director of the World Trade Institute, University of Berne, from 1999 to 2015.

***Kevin Crow*, University of Halle-Wittenberg, DE (co-author Chapter 4)**
Kevin Crow is a lecturer, researcher, and doctoral candidate at Transnational Economic Law Research Centre (TELC) at the Law School of the University of Halle-Wittenberg, and

a Research Associate at the Asia School of Business: a collaboration with the MIT Sloan School of Management. A US lawyer with international practice experience, his scholarship has appeared in US, European, and Asian law journals. His current research focuses on the role of 'belief' and 'judgment' in international law, and most recently, on the private sector's role in 'authoring' public international law. Kevin holds a BA from the University of Washington, a JD from the University of Southern California, and a LLM from the London School of Economics, all with honors. He is licensed to practise law in the State of California.

***Panagiotis Delimatsis*, Tilburg University, NL/Harvard University, US (Chapter 10)**
Panagiotis Delimatsis is Professor of EU and International Trade Law at Tilburg University. He also is the Director of the Tilburg Law and Economics Center (TILEC), an interdisciplinary Center of Excellence, the biggest of its kind in Europe, studying the governance of economic activity. In the academic year 2015–16, Panagiotis was a visiting Scholar at Harvard Law School and a Fellow with the Program on International Financial Systems, on research leave from Tilburg University. In December 2016, he was awarded an ERC Consolidator Grant of €2 million for his research project on the resilience of non-state regulatory bodies and the role of the law. Panagiotis' research focuses on the comparative regulation of services industries, issues of transnational governance, and the regulation of international trade. Currently, he is interested in the institutional and substantive aspects of standardization, financial regulation, and energy, using interdisciplinary methods. His work has appeared in top refereed international and European journals. He is the author of *International Trade in Services and Domestic Regulations: Necessity, Transparency, and Regulatory Diversity* (International Economic Law Series, Oxford University Press, 2007). He also co-edited two collective volumes, the first on *The Prospects of International Trade Regulation* (Cambridge University Press, 2011) and the second on *Financial Services at the Crossroads: Implications for Supervision, Institutional Design and Trade* (Kluwer Law International, 2011). His most recent work includes *The Law, Economics and Politics of International Standardization*, published by Cambridge University Press in 2015, and the *Research Handbook on Climate Change and Trade Law*, published by Edward Elgar in 2016.

***Stefan Griller*, University of Salzburg, AT (Chapters 1, 14, and 16)**
Stefan Griller was appointed Professor for Public Law with special regard to European Law at the Vienna University of Economics and Business in 1991. Teaching and research assignments led him to Maastricht (1994–9), Tamkang University, Taipeh (1994), the EUI in Florence (2007–8), and the Bratislava School of Law (2009–10). In 1995, he was appointed Jean Monnet-Professor for Legal Problems of European Integration. Since 2008, he is President of ECSA Austria. At the University of Salzburg, he has been Vice President of the Salzburg Centre of European Union Studies (SCEUS) since 2011, and since 2013 holds the chair for EU Law. In the same year, he became the chairperson of the university's Senate. Professor Griller has published widely on European public law, with a special focus on its constitutional dimension at the interface with economic law, and acts as a counsel for public administration, parliamentary committees, and civil society actors at the Austrian and EU levels.

***Verena Madner*, Vienna University of Economics and Business, AT (Chapter 15)**
Verena Madner is Professor of Public Law, Environmental Law, Public and Urban Governance at WU, Vienna University of Economics and Business (Department of Socio-Economics). Her research and teaching focuses on environmental, planning, and infrastructure law,

globalization, multi-level policy, and governance. As head of WU's Research Institute for Urban Management and Governance, she explores issues of sustainable urban development and concepts of governance in an urban context, as well as the framework and conditions for the provision of public services at the municipal level. Verena Madner recently co-authored a study on the impact of CETA on the legal framework for the provision of public services in Austria.

***Stefan Mayr*, Vienna University of Economics and Business, AT (Chapter 11)**
Stefan Mayr is a researcher at the Research Institute for Urban Management and Governance at the Vienna University of Economics and Business. He earned a LLM in comparative constitutional law from Central European University, Budapest, in 2009, and holds a doctoral degree in law from the Vienna University of Economics and Business. His research interests include international trade and investment law, systemic questions of the interactions between international law, EU law, and national law, and the law of public services. Mayr has published papers in a number of national and international journals, including *Europarecht* and the *European Journal of Legal Studies* and co-authored a study on the impact of CETA on the legal framework for the provision of public services in Austria. His dissertation deals with legal issues of remunicipalizations in the light of the national economic constitution, the European single market, and new generation FTAs.

***Christoph Moser*, University of Salzburg, Salzburg Centre of European Union Studies (SCEUS), AT (Chapter 12)**
Christoph Moser is Professor of Economics at the University of Salzburg and Deputy Director at the Salzburg Centre of European Union Studies (SCEUS) since October 2015. He is also a Research Affiliate at the CESifo, Munich, and a Research Professor at ETH Zurich, KOF Swiss Economic Institute, where he has worked for the last couple of years. Professor Moser received his PhD in Economics from the University of Mainz, after studying International Economic and Business Studies at the University of Innsbruck. As a visiting scholar at UC Berkeley, he worked on the impact of regional trade agreements on the stock market. His research focus is on international economics, trade and labour, international macroeconomics, political economy, and applied econometrics. Professor Moser has published in international peer-review journals such as the *Journal of International Economics, European Economic Review*, and the *Journal of Public Economics*.

***Walter Obwexer*, University of Innsbruck, AT (Chapters 1 and 16)**
After legal studies in Innsbruck and Padua, *Walter Obwexer* was appointed Full Professor for EU Law, Public International Law, and International Relations at the University of Innsbruck in 2012. Apart from his university functions, since the 1990s Professor Obwexer has served as a legal counsel of government institutions in Austria (among them the Ministries for Innovation, Transport, and Technology; Education, Economy, Science and Research; and Europe, Integration, and Foreign Affairs) and Italy (Provincial Government of South Tyrol). Professor Obwexer serves as Vice Dean in Innsbruck and is the author of numerous books and articles in European and international law.

***Christoph Ohler*, University of Jena, DE (Chapter 8)**
Christoph Ohler holds a chair in public law, European law, public international law, and international economic law at the Friedrich-Schiller University of Jena. He received his PhD from the University of Bayreuth (1997) and his venia legendi from the Ludwig-Maximilians University Munich (2005). In 1998 and 1999, he worked as an associate in the banking

department of an international law firm in Frankfurt/Main. From 2008 to 2014, he was the spokesperson of the interdisciplinary graduate programme 'Global Financial Markets' at the universities of Jena and Halle. It dealt with the issue of financial market stability from the perspective of law and economics. Christoph Ohler publishes extensively on German and EU constitutional law, European Monetary Union, and the regulation of financial markets in international and European law. *Bankenaufsicht und Geldpolitik in der Währungsunion* (*Banking Supervision and Monetary Policy in EMU*) (2015) is his most recent book.

***Ernst-Ulrich Petersmann*, European University Institute, Florence, IT (Chapter 2)**
Ernst-Ulrich Petersmann is Emeritus Professor of International and European Law and former head of the Law Department of the European University Institute at Florence. He previously taught constitutional law at the Universities of Hamburg and Heidelberg and was a Professor of International Law and European Law at the Universities of St Gallen, Fribourg, Geneva, and the Geneva Graduate Institute of International Relations. As a visiting professor, he taught international economic law at The Hague Academy of International Law, the EUI Academy of European Law, the Xiamen Academy of International Law, and at numerous universities throughout Europe, North and Latin America, Africa, and Asia. He published some thirty books and more than 300 contributions to books and journals in German, English, French, and other languages focusing on international law, European law, and comparative constitutional law. In parallel to his academic career, Professor Petersmann worked as legal counsel for the German Government representing Germany in European and UN institutions (1978–80), as well as legal counsel/consultant in GATT and the WTO (1981–2016). He was a secretary, member, or chairman of numerous GATT and WTO dispute settlement panels and participated actively in numerous academic associations, for instance, as rapporteur (1993–99) and chairman of the International Trade Law Committee of the International Law Association (2000–14).

***Sonja Puntscher Riekmann*, University of Salzburg, AT (Chapter 13)**
Sonja Puntscher Riekmann is Professor of Political Theory and European Politics at the University of Salzburg. She is also academic director of the Centre of European Union Studies of the University of Salzburg (SCEUS), and member of the Austrian Academy of Sciences, the Board of the Austrian Science Fund (FWF), and the editorial board of the *Austrian Journal of Political Science*. She is vice-president of the European Forum Alpbach. She was the founder of the Institute of European Integration Research at the Academy of Sciences and served as its director from 2002 to 2008. She taught at the Universities of Vienna, Innsbruck, Humboldt University of Berlin, and Florence. Her research fields are European integration, European institutional development, parliamentarism, and theory of democracy, constitutionalism, and legitimacy. She is coordinator of the Horizon 2020 project EMU-Choices, entitled 'The Choice for Europe since Maastricht. Member States' Preferences for Economic and Fiscal Integration' (2015–19), in which eminent political science and legal scholars from nine European universities participate to study the preferences of all Member States with regard to the development of the Eurozone and the EU since Maastricht and in the financial and fiscal crisis. She published in high-ranking journals such as the *Journal of Common Market Studies, West European Politics*, the *European Law Journal*, the *Journal of European Integration*, and *Contemporary Politics*. Among her work are the following: 'Constitutionalism and Representation: European Parliamentarism in the Treaty of Lisbon' in Petra Dobner and Martin Loughlin (eds), *The Twilight of Constitutionalism?* (Oxford University Press, 2010) 120–37; *Is There a European Common Good?* (Nomos, 2013) (co-edited with A Somek and D Wydra); 'Representation in the European State of

Emergency: Parliaments against Governments', Special Issue on Representation, edited by R Bellamy and S Kröger, (2013) 35(5) *Journal of European Integration* 565–82 (with D Wydra); and '"Obligations of Good Faith": On the Difficulties of Building US-Style EU Federalism' (2015) 21(2) *Contemporary Politics* 201–19 (with D Wydra).

***Stephan W Schill*, University of Amsterdam, NL (Chapter 5)**
Stephan W Schill (Dr iur (Frankfurt am Main, 2008); LLM (New York University, 2006); LLM (Augsburg, 2002)) is Professor of International and Economic Law and Governance at the University of Amsterdam and Principal Investigator in the ERC project on 'Transnational Private-Public Arbitration as Global Regulatory Governance: Charting and Codifying the Lex Mercatoria Publica' (LexMercPub, Grant agreement no 313355). He is admitted to the Bar as a German Rechtsanwalt and as Attorney-at-Law (New York), is a Member of the List of Conciliators of the International Centre for Settlement of Investment Disputes, and serves as Editor-in-Chief of the *Journal of World Investment and Trade*.

***Christian Tietje*, University of Halle-Wittenberg, DE (co-author Chapter 4)**
Christian Tietje is Professor (tenure) for European Law and International Economic Law, director of the Institute for Economic Law, and director of the Transnational Economic Law Research Centre (TELC) at the Law School at Martin-Luther-University Halle-Wittenberg, Germany. His primary research interests lie in the areas of EU common commercial policy and international economic law (world trade law, investment protection and arbitration, global financial markets). Professor Tietje received his legal education at the Universities of Kiel/Germany, Paris V, and University of Michigan Law School, Ann Arbor. He holds two German law degrees with distinction and is a Professor of Law since 2001. He has published several books and more than 150 articles and has advised governments, international organizations, non-governmental organizations, business associations, and multilateral companies in the above-mentioned research areas. He has been appointed legal expert and arbitrator in several investment arbitrations, was leading a working group of the investment law committee of the German branch of the International Law Association (ILA) dealing with the relationship of international investment law and general public international law, and is a member of the 'ILA Study Group on the Role of Soft Law Instruments in International Investment Law'. He has been appointed by the EU on the roster of panelists for financial services under the EU–Korea free trade agreement.

***Erich Vranes*, Vienna University of Economics and Business, AT (Chapters 1, 3, and 16)**
Erich Vranes is Professor of International Law, European Law, Public Law, and International Economic Law at the WU Vienna (Vienna University of Economics and Business). His research focuses on international economic law, fundamental issues of international law, European law, EU external economic relations, and legal theory. Professor Vranes has studied law at the Universities of Graz, Lausanne, and Geneva. He was an APART scholar of the Austrian Academy of Sciences and serves as head of the Institute for European and International Law and deputy head of Department at WU Vienna, and as secretary general of the European Community Studies Association Austria.

PART I

FUNDAMENTAL AND INTRODUCTORY ISSUES

1

Mega-Regional Trade Agreements

New Orientations for EU External Relations?

Stefan Griller, Walter Obwexer, and Erich Vranes

I. Economic Policy as Foreign Policy

'Foreign policy today is more than ever economic policy.'[1] With these words, then US Secretary of State John Kerry has explained why the US and other states should work intensively to advance the negotiations on mega-regional trade agreements.[2] Prime examples of a growing number of mega-regional trade agreements that have been negotiated in the last decade are the Trans-Pacific Partnership (TPP) negotiated by the US and a series of Asia-Pacific states, the Transatlantic Trade and Investment Partnership (TTIP) being negotiated by the European Union and the US at the time of writing, the Comprehensive Economic and Trade Agreement (CETA) having been negotiated between the EU and Canada between 2009 and 2016 and signed in 2016, and the Trade in Services Agreement (TiSA), which is still under negotiation and should complement TTIP and CETA not only from a trade perspective, but also from a strategic economic and foreign policy viewpoint.[3]

These mega-regional initiatives are meant to transform and shape the international economic order and also to promote more far-reaching geopolitical goals. Both the EU and the US are key players in these bilateral and plurilateral attempts. From the viewpoint of the EU, CETA, TTIP, and TiSA constitute central instruments in this regard. This is why this book, which is written primarily from an EU point of view, focuses on these three projects in particular.

[1] US Secretary of State John Kerry, 'Remarks at the APEC CEO Summit' (Asia-Pacific Economic Cooperation CEO Summit, Bali, Indonesia, 7 October 2013) <https://2009-2017.state.gov/secretary/remarks/2013/10/215176.htm> accessed 11 April 2017. The present chapter was drafted in September 2016 and updated at the beginning of January 2017.

[2] On this, see also Daniel S Hamilton, 'America's Mega-Regional Trade Diplomacy: Comparing TPP and TTIP' (2014) 49(1) *The International Spectator* 81 (hereafter Hamilton, 'America's Mega-Regional Trade Diplomacy').

[3] cf in the following text.

Mega-Regional Trade Agreements: New Orientations for EU External Relations? Stefan Griller, Walter Obwexer, Erich Vranes.

II. The New Regionalism: Motivations and Context

Mega-regional trade agreements have been defined as 'deep integration partnerships between countries or regions with a major share of world trade and foreign direct investment', which 'beyond simply increasing trade links ... aim to improve regulatory compatibility and provide a rules-based framework for ironing out differences in investment and business climates'.[4] The new global trend to negotiate such agreements can be attributed to four main reasons at least.

A first major motivation is the stalemate from which the Doha Round of trade negotiations among the World Trade Organization (WTO) membership has been suffering for several years by now. This round, which was launched in 2001, was intended to reform the WTO system by lowering trade barriers and amending trade rules.[5] It got stuck early, however, in particular due to the complexity of its topics, antagonistic interests, and the WTO's cumbersome consensus-based decision-making process.[6] A second reason for the move towards regional approaches to international trade and investment is that, even if the Doha Round had not failed, existing WTO rules and Member-specific obligations are perceived as being unsatisfactory, as they often tend to reflect the lowest common denominator, are said to not really impact on actual trade,[7] and are said to be still imbued by the General Agreement on Tariffs and Trade (GATT) 1947 philosophy of 'making it here, selling it there', instead of today's motif of 'making it in many places, selling it to the world'.[8] This is particularly troublesome in the field of trade in services, where it has been pointedly submitted that the General Agreement on Trade in Services (GATS) is 'getting older without growing up', as the WTO Members' schedules of country-specific commitments are regarded as having become outdated.[9] Negotiations on improved rules on trade in services became a victim of the failing Doha Round, as it had been agreed to deal with services disciplines only after a consensus on trade in agriculture and other issues would be achieved—an intermediate goal that was never reached. This in turn has contributed to undermining the credibility of the

[4] Thomas Hirst, 'What Are Mega-Regional Trade Agreements?' (World Economic Forum, 9 July 2014) <http://www.weforum.org/agenda/2014/07/trade-what-are-megaregionals> accessed 27 March 2017 (hereafter Hirst, 'Mega-Regional Trade Agreements').

[5] On this and the background and developments of the Doha Round, cf the official WTO website, <http://www.wto.org/english/tratop_e/dda_e/dda_e.htm> accessed 27 March 2017.

[6] cf, eg, Frank Altemöller, 'Perspektiven für das Welthandelssystem' (2016) 10 *Europäische Zeitschrift für Wirtschaftsrecht* 376.

[7] Andrew L. Stoler, 'Will the WTO have Functional Value in the Mega-regional World of FTAs?' (E15 Expert Group on Regional Trade Agreements and Plurilateral Approaches, World Economic Forum, December 2013) 2, <http://e15initiative.org/wp-content/uploads/2015/09/E15-Regional-Trade-Agreements-Stoler-FINAL.pdf> accessed 27 March 2017 (hereafter Stoler, 'WTO Functional Value').

[8] Gary Clyde Hufbauer and Cathleen Cimino-Isaacs, 'How Will TPP and TTIP Change the WTO System?' (2015) 18 *Journal of International Economic Law* 681ff (hereafter Hufbauer and Cimino-Isaacs, 'TPP and TTIP').

[9] Shin Yi Peng, 'Is the Trade in Services Agreement (TiSA) a Stepping Stone for the Next Version of GATS?' (2013) 43(2) *Hong Kong Law Journal* 612 (hereafter Peng, 'TiSA').

WTO, both as regards its substantive disciplines and its role as a global negotiation forum.[10] These developments have also been seen as contrasting sharply with the dynamism and importance of international trade in services.[11]

Third, the WTO is today seen as not being the most adequate place for negotiating regulatory issues—that is, behind-the-border measures that today often constitute economically more important obstacles to international trade than tariffs. Many such non-tariff barriers result from different domestic risk preferences and national regulatory cultures, and quite often from the pursuance of legitimate goals through different means. Cooperative strategies for overcoming such barriers—such as mutual recognition and equivalence, regulatory coherence, and regulatory cooperation—are particularly difficult to negotiate in the multilateral WTO context.[12] Therefore, discussions on such initiatives have shifted to the regional context.

Furthermore, the current trend towards mega-regional trade agreements can be seen, to some extent, as a secondary reaction to the expectations that were not fulfilled by the WTO Doha Round. As a primary reaction, many states started to negotiate large numbers of bilateral trade agreements, a trend which has—together with many bilateral agreements that have been concluded for diplomatic and geopolitical reasons[13]—contributed to the existence of about 800 preferential trade agreements today.[14] As these factors have led to an intransparent web of bilateral trade agreements, which is similar to the maze of bilateral investment treaties (BITs) and often comprises weak and sometimes conflicting obligations, some countries, in particular in the Asia-Pacific region, have felt a need to 'plurilateralize' these bilateral obligations in order to increase the consistency of their trade commitments on a regional level.

The EU and US turn to bilateralism and regionalism needs to be seen in this broader context, too. Both started to negotiate deep and comprehensive free trade agreements in the last ten to fifteen years. Thus, the US has concluded free trade agreements with Australia, Bahrain, Chile, Costa Rica, the Dominican Republic, El Salvador, Guatemala, Honduras, Korea, Nicaragua, and Singapore since 2001. Likewise, the EU announced in its 2006 'Global Europe' strategy that it would increasingly negotiate free trade agreements besides remaining committed to multilateralism.[15] The EU has since then concluded the EU–CARIFORUM agreement

[10] ibid, 612–13.

[11] Juan A. Marchetti and Martin Roy, 'The TiSA Initiative: An Overview of Market Access Issues' (2014) 48(4) *Journal of World Trade* 683 (hereafter Marchetti and Roy, 'TiSA Initiative').

[12] See Chapter 3 in this volume.

[13] Hamilton, 'America's Mega-Regional Trade Diplomacy', 81; Jeffrey D Wilson, 'Mega-Regional Trade Deals in the Asia-Pacific: Choosing between the TPP and RCEP?' (2015) 45(2) *Journal of Contemporary Asia* 345–6; see also Thomas Cottier, 'The Common Law of International Trade and the Future of the World Trade Organization' (2015) 18 *Journal of International Economic Law* 3ff (hereafter Cottier, 'Common Law').

[14] Cottier, 'Common Law' (n 13).

[15] European Commission, 'Global Europe Competing in the World: A Contribution to the EU's Growth and Jobs Strategy' (European Commission, 2006), <http://trade.ec.europa.eu/doclib/docs/2006/october/tradoc_130376.pdf> accessed 27 March 2017 (hereafter European Commission, 'Global Europe Competing in the World').

(between the EU and the Caribbean Group of the African, Caribbean and Pacific Forum), as well as agreements with Colombia, Peru, Singapore, South Korea, and the CETA agreement with Canada. It is also negotiating BITs with China and Myanmar, and trade agreements with Algeria, Japan, India, Libya, and Vietnam, and the TTIP agreement with the US.[16]

It is the TTIP, TPP, CETA, and TiSA initiatives—together with the rival project of an Asian Regional Comprehensive Economic Partnership (RCEP)[17]—that stand out as mega-regional trade agreements from this rising tide of bilateralism and regionalism. This is due to their economic impact, their functions, and their political and geopolitical implications, to which we will turn next. In the following sections, the TPP and RCEP plans will also briefly be dealt with, since all of these mega-regional projects have been distinctly influencing each other.

III. Economic Impact

It goes without saying that the purely economic dimensions of these mega-regional initiatives are significant. Even if the following figures are, contrasting to the impression sometimes raised, mere estimations, the overall positive welfare effects seem to be beyond doubt. TPP would comprise twelve initial contracting parties from the Asia-Pacific region, which have a combined GDP of $278 trillion, accounting for 37 per cent of world GDP. Intra-TPP exports amount to 13 per cent of world exports, and intra-TPP foreign direct investment (FDI) flows total 9 per cent of world outward investment.[18] The TPP negotiating partners together account for more than a third of US trade in goods.[19] However, as tariffs are low among TPP parties, export gains from tariff reductions are expected to be comparatively small, whereas investment gains should be significant.[20] TPP is estimated to lead to $295 billion in annual global gains by 2025.[21] Economically speaking, TPP may perhaps be 'a North American story rather than a Pacific story' due to the intensive trade relations between the US, Canada, and Mexico.[22] However, geopolitically speaking, TPP would have a clear Asia-Pacific dimension unmistakably promoting US interests.[23]

[16] Marc Bungenberg, 'EU-Freihandelsabkommen in der Entwicklung' in Peter-Christian Müller-Graff (ed), *Europäische Union und USA—Europas nordatlantische Aufgaben* (Nomos, 2016) 91 (hereafter Bungenberg, 'EU-Freihandelsabkommen'); and Billy A Melo Araujo, 'Regulating Services through Trade Agreements' (2014) 6(2) *Trade, Law and Development* 393ff (hereafter Melo Araujo, 'Regulating Services').

[17] On this, cf below, section IV.B.2.

[18] Hufbauer and Cimino-Isaacs, 'TPP and TTIP' (n 8) 680.

[19] Hamilton, 'America's Mega-Regional Trade Diplomacy' (n 2) 82.

[20] Hufbauer and Cimino-Isaacs, 'TPP and TTIP' (n 8) 680.

[21] Ming Du, 'Explaining China's Tripartite Strategy Toward the Trans-Pacific Partnership Agreement' (2015) 18 *Journal of International Economic Law* 408 (hereafter Du, 'China's Strategy').

[22] Hamilton, 'America's Mega-Regional Trade Diplomacy' (n 2) 82. Under these circumstances, the scepticism of incoming US president Trump vis-à-vis TPP and his announcement to block US membership in TPP is far from being evidence-based.

[23] See below, section IV.B.1.

On the other hand, the TTIP parties would account for a combined GDP of $34 trillion, goods and services exports of about 6 per cent of world exports, and FDI flows of about 16 per cent of world outward investment. As in the case of TPP, tariff barriers among the TTIP partners are very low already. Therefore, the significant gains associated with TTIP are to be expected rather from investment and regulatory cooperation.[24] TTIP was estimated to boost the EU economy by some €120 billion and the US economy by some €90 billion annually.[25] Furthermore, it has been projected that TTIP would increase real per capita income in the EU by 3.9 per cent and by 4.9 per cent in the US, whereas it would decrease by 0.9 per cent in the rest of the world. Within the EU, Member States in the EU periphery would profit more than Member States whose economy is more open already. Furthermore, it is expected that third countries with currently comparatively strong economic ties to the EU and/or the US, such as Canada, Mexico, and Turkey, would lose in terms of economic welfare in the future.[26]

TPP and TTIP would each affect at least a quarter of world trade in goods and services and global FDI.[27] As the US will be a party to both agreements (and TiSA), it will enjoy significant economic and political leverage.[28]

While CETA is of strategic importance for the EU in that it is meant to help in transforming the international economic order,[29] economically speaking, CETA has been said to be a higher priority for Canada than the EU.[30] This is due to the facts that Canada would gain preferential access to the largest market in the world and that the EU is already Canada's second-largest trade and investment partner. A joint study by Canada and the EU concluded that CETA would increase Canadian income by $12 billion annually and bilateral trade by 20 per cent, which is the economic equivalent of adding almost 80,000 new jobs to the Canadian economy.[31]

As regards the economic import of TiSA, it has been observed that services are the 'sleeping giant' in international trade. Hence, even modest progress in TiSA's negotiations would lead to substantial economic gains,[32] which have been estimated as totalling $1 trillion, given that national barriers to trade in services amount to

[24] Hufbauer and Cimino-Isaacs, 'TPP and TTIP' (n 8) 681.

[25] Hirst, 'Mega-Regional Trade Agreements' (n 4).

[26] Gabriel Felbermayr, Benedikt Heid, and Mario Larch, 'TTIP: Geringe Chancen, hohe Risiken?' in Peter-Christian Müller-Graff (ed), *Europäische Union und USA—Europas nordatlantische Aufgaben* (Nomos, 2016) 69ff.

[27] Hirst, 'Mega-Regional Trade Agreements' (n 4).

[28] See Hamilton, 'America's Mega-Regional Trade Diplomacy' (n 2) 91; see also below, section IV.B.

[29] cf above, II.

[30] Christian Deblock and Michèle Rioux, 'From Economic Dialogue to CETA: Canada's Trade Relations with the European Union' (2010/11) 66(1) *International Journal* 39ff (hereafter Deblock and Rioux, 'Economic Dialogue'); see also below, section IV.B.3.

[31] cf the official information by the Government of Canada, available at <http://www.international.gc.ca/trade-agreements-accords-commerciaux/agr-acc/ceta-aecg/benefits-avantages/canadians-canadiens.aspx?lang=eng> accessed 27 March 2017.

[32] Hamilton, 'America's Mega-Regional Trade Diplomacy' (n 2) 87ff.

a tariff equivalent of 40 per cent or more and that the TiSA negotiating parties account for about two-thirds of global trade in services.[33]

In sum, this means that if these mega-regional trade agreements, and perhaps also the Asia-Pacific RCEP, were to enter into force, then most important goods, services, and investment transactions would in the near future be covered by these regional agreements.[34]

IV. A Closer Look at the 'Mega-Regional' Landscape

A. The functions of mega-regional trade agreements

It is often overlooked in the wider public debate that these mega-regional initiatives are not merely meant to increase trade and investment on a bilateral or regional level. Through TTIP, TTP, CETA, and TiSA, the US and the EU have also been pursuing considerably more far-reaching strategic goals. On the one hand, the EU and the US aim to establish the core of future global standards on issues such as trade in services, investment, intellectual property, discriminatory industrial policies, and state-owned enterprises.[35] It is hoped that these legal standards will spill over into other trade relations due to the economic pull of these mega-regional trade agreements and the negotiating leverage of the EU and the US, in particular. Some observers envisage a potential domino effect that could take place when further countries join mega-regional treaties such as TPP.[36] In a related vein, others assume that the sheer economic clout of the transatlantic market to be promoted by TTIP, and to some extent by CETA, will make producers from other countries adhere to these standards and press their governments to align their domestic and trade rules.[37] On the basis of optimistic forecasts, this might even spark multilateral progress within the WTO.[38] Furthermore, it is expected that TTIP and TPP norms may be taken up by international organizations and in private codes, and may also, for example, become conditional standards for development assistance.[39]

Another rationale behind the rush to conclude mega-regional trade agreements such as TPP, TTIP, and to some extent CETA clearly is the aim of defining such standards before other countries, in particular rising economic powers such as China, can do so. These states would then face a strengthened international economic order that would be more difficult to challenge for them.[40] From the EU perspective, another

[33] Hufbauer and Cimino-Isaacs, 'TPP and TTIP' (n 8) 689ff.

[34] Stoler, 'WTO Functional Value' (n 7) 7.

[35] Hamilton, 'America's Mega-Regional Trade Diplomacy' (n 2) 85.

[36] ibid, 84; and Du, 'China's Strategy' (n 21) 412.

[37] See, eg, Marise Cremona, 'Negotiating the Transatlantic Trade and Investment Partnership (TTIP)' (2015) 52 *Common Market Law Review* 358 (hereafter Cremona, 'Negotiating TTIP').

[38] Hamilton, 'America's Mega-Regional Trade Diplomacy' (n 2) 84.

[39] Reeve T Bull, Neysun A Mahboubi, Richard B Stewart, and Jonathan B Wiener, 'New Approaches to International Regulatory Cooperation' (2015) 78(4) *Law and Contemporary Problems* 7.

[40] Hamilton, 'America's Mega-Regional Trade Diplomacy' (n 2) 85; and Cremona, 'Negotiating TTIP' (n 37) 355.

motivation underlying TTIP and CETA is that these agreements are intended as steps in developing the EU *acquis* for investment protection and to ultimately replace the more than 1,400 BITs that have been concluded by EU Member States so far. These initiatives represent EU attempts to improve investment standards, by serving as a model in particular for an improved right to regulate, clearer definitions of indirect expropriation and the fair and equitable treatment (FET) standard, an improved ISDS system, and a joint interpretation mechanism.[41] Furthermore, mega-regional trade and investment disciplines can serve as internationally entrenched obligations for domestic reforms that may have important economic springboard effects—as those experienced by China after its WTO accession[42] or Canada after the start of the North American Free Trade Agreement (NAFTA)[43]—which might otherwise be impossible to implement.

B. The (geo-)political implications of today's prime mega-regional projects

1. *The Trans-Pacific Partnership*

The TPP must be seen in the broader context of economic integration in the Asia-Pacific region. Under the impression of the deadlock of the Uruguay Round on the one hand and quickly progressing regional economic integration in the EC/EU and NAFTA, Asia-Pacific states founded the Asia-Pacific Economic Cooperation (APEC) in 1989. However, economic integration in this regional context remained difficult due to the institutional weakness of APEC, which is based on consensus and non-binding activities. While this 'soft' approach to economic integration may have been attractive for some (in particular developing country) members, it has resulted in considerable inertia. However, an important impetus was given to regional economic integration in 2002, when Brunei, Chile, New Zealand, and Singapore started negotiations on the Trans-Pacific Strategic Economic Partnership Agreement (TPSEP or P4 agreement), which entered into force in 2006. In 2008, the US began negotiations with the P4 countries, which led to negotiations on the TPP project.[44] The TPP was signed on 4 February 2016 and still needs to be ratified.

The TPP undertaking has been central to the US 'pivot to East Asia'—that is, its rebalancing of military, political, and economic interests towards the Asia-Pacific region that was announced by then President Obama in 2012.[45] It has also been regarded as a 'grand institutional shift' from the former US containment policy against China to an approach of building defence, trade, and investment alliances that exclude China.[46] This geopolitical aim of containing China and its economic

[41] Cremona, 'Negotiating TTIP' (n 37) 355.
[42] Du, 'China's Strategy' (n 21) 414ff.
[43] Deblock and Rioux, 'Economic Dialogue' (n 30) 39ff.
[44] cf, eg, Du, 'China's Strategy' (n 21) 407ff with further references.
[45] See also Hamilton, 'America's Mega-Regional Trade Diplomacy' (n 2) 86.
[46] Eric Yong Joong Lee, 'Trans-Pacific Partnership (TPP) as a US Strategic Alliance Initiative under the G2 System: Legal and Political Implications' (2015) 2 *Journal of East Asia and International Law* 324 (hereafter Lee, 'TPP').

rise becomes obvious, for example, in the US stance not to admit new countries to the TPP negotiations before the latter are concluded, a position which is viewed as an attempt to coerce China to unilaterally accept these rules in the future, should it want to become part of this regional integration project.[47] Moreover, the US interest in TPP must also be seen against the backdrop that all of the many other free trade agreements in the Asia-Pacific had so far excluded the US.[48]

From the US perspective, besides these strategic political interests, the TPP is of course meant to enhance US economic growth, as the TPP countries together amount to the largest market for US exports, surpassing even the EU. Furthermore, as the US would be a party to the TPP as well as TTIP and TiSA, it has considerable negotiating leverage, which it may use to influence standards or to even transfer them from one agreement to the other. Furthermore, as TPP is open for future accessions, perhaps reaching even beyond the Asia-Pacific region, it would potentially become highly influential. On the other hand, ratifying TPP may prove difficult due to its highly ambitious WTO-plus agenda and the perspective of US leadership in the Asia-Pacific region, which may be perceived as problematic by some potential contracting parties.[49]

2. *The Regional Comprehensive Economic Partnership*

Of course, the ambitious TPP project has already had perceptible repercussions in East Asia, and has in particular prompted China to adopt a multi-part strategy, consisting especially in a wait-and-see attitude towards TPP, the conclusion of twelve, and the negotiation of further, free trade agreements, the pursuance of the 'One Belt, One Road' initiatives,[50] and China's joining the negotiations on the RCEP.[51]

Negotiations on the RCEP started in 2013 between the Association of South-East Asian Nations (ASEAN) states (Brunei, Burma (Myanmar), Cambodia, Indonesia, Laos, Malaysia, the Philippines, Singapore, Thailand, and Vietnam) on the one hand, and Australia, China, India, Japan, South Korea, and New Zealand, on the other. The RCEP is an ASEAN-led initiative which constitutes an alternative to TPP and pursues the primary goal of multilateralizing the regional trading system by combining existing free trade agreements into a single agreement in order to render the so-called 'spaghetti bowl' of conflicting trade agreements in the Asia-Pacific region more consistent. Hence, whereas TPP can be seen as a response to the insufficient quality of existing free trade agreements in the Asia-Pacific area,

[47] Du, 'China's Strategy', (n 21) 408. [48] ibid, 411ff.

[49] Hamilton, 'America's Mega-Regional Trade Diplomacy', (n 2) 87ff.

[50] The 'One Belt, One Road' initiatives comprise the projects of building a 'Silk Road Economic Belt' and the '21st-Century Maritime Silk Road' (see Lee, 'TPP' (n 46) 326ff; see also David Dollar, 'China's Rise as a Regional and Global Power: The AIIB and the "One Belt, One Road"' (The Brookings Institution, 15 July 2015), <http://www.brookings.edu/research/chinas-rise-as-a-regional-and-global-power-the-aiib-and-the-one-belt-one-road> accessed 27 March 2017.

[51] Lee, 'Trans-Pacific Partnership' (n 46) 326ff.

RCEP is rather regarded as a means to address the problems resulting from regional legal fragmentation.[52] Its ambitions are sizeably more moderate than those of the TPP, as it is meant to be a WTO-consistent rather than a WTO-plus agreement.[53] By contrast with the TPP, the RCEP also includes China and offers more flexibility for developing countries. Despite its lower ambitions, the gains from RCEP may be higher than those expected from TPP, due to RCEP's focus on larger pre-existing trade barriers. However, the RCEP may turn out difficult to realize due to weak ASEAN leadership, historical conflicts, and current territorial disputes.[54] It is expected that the outcome of the 'race' between the negotiations of TPP and RCEP will have significant economic and political ramifications, as both are meant to shape the regional economic and political architecture, and the agreement concluded first may lead to a long-lasting lock-in.[55]

3. *TTIP and CETA as reactive and proactive devices*

TTIP, too, to some extent constitutes a reaction both to the US rebalance towards Asia and the TPP agreement. To some degree, it serves as a reassurance for Europe in view of this US 'pivot' and as a second transatlantic anchor besides NATO.[56] It has also been observed that whereas EU–US relations have so far essentially been governed by the WTO most-favoured-nation (MFN) disciplines, some mutual recognition agreements, and—often not overly successful[57]—attempts of regulatory cooperation,[58] TTIP is meant to establish a more holistic and dynamic EU–US relationship that should also strengthen the basic rules of the international order.[59] It thus also has a clear proactive strategic thrust and has therefore even been referred to as an 'Economic NATO'.[60]

CETA, on the other hand, can be regarded as a reaction to both TPP and TTIP. This must be seen against the backdrop that while Canada had traditionally seen the EU as a partner to counterbalance US influence, since the inception of NAFTA, Canada had been strengthening its ties with the US and loosening those with Europe. When the initial economic springboard effects of NAFTA started to weaken and multilateralism in the WTO got bogged down in the Doha Round, Canada like many other countries tried to adopt a bilateral approach to trade and investment relations. As Canada was said to not have found 'worthy interlocutors' and as the US had already started pursuing greater ambitions than deepening

[52] Wilson, 'Mega-Regional Trade Deals' (n 13). [53] ibid, 349ff.

[54] Du, 'China's Strategy' (n 21) 420ff.

[55] Wilson, 'Mega-Regional Trade Deals' (n 13) 349ff; and Hamilton, 'America's Mega-Regional Trade Diplomacy' (n 2) 86.

[56] Hamilton, 'America's Mega-Regional Trade Diplomacy' (n 2) 87.

[57] See, eg, Peter Chase and Jacques Pelkmans, 'This Time It's Different: Turbo-Charging Regulatory Cooperation in TTIP' (Centre for European Policy Studies, June 2015), <https://www.ceps.eu/system/files/SR110%20Regulatory%20Cooperation%20in%20TTIP.pdf> accessed 27 March 2017.

[58] Cremona, 'Negotiating TTIP' (n 37) 352.

[59] Hamilton, 'America's Mega-Regional Trade Diplomacy' (n 2) 86ff.

[60] Clayland Boyden Gray, 'Upgrading Existing Regulatory Mechanisms for Transatlantic Regulatory Cooperation' (2015) 78(4) *Law and Contemporary Problems* 31.

NAFTA, Canada turned to the EU to begin negotiations on CETA.[61] While initially Canada may not have been a top priority for the EU,[62] the CETA project has meanwhile turned into a cardinal project in the EU's external economic relations. This can be inferred, for example, from its efforts to win the support of sceptical Member States such as Germany and Austria and the Belgian region Wallonia in 2016. Their resistance has been overcome especially through the adoption of an 'Interpretative Instrument' of questionable legal status and effect.[63] Most parts of CETA will be provisionally applied.[64] Had the EU not been able to sign the CETA agreement, its role as a major player in international trade and investment politics would have been seriously damaged.

4. *The Trade in Services Agreement*

Like TTIP, TiSA must also be seen as a US and EU attempt to reform international trade governance in the light of the failing Doha Round by plurilateralizing, among like-minded countries, trade rules that have been developed by the EU and the US in their more recent 'deep and comprehensive' bilateral free trade agreements.[65] The agreement to prepare TiSA negotiations was reached in 2012. Similarly to TTIP, CETA, etc, TiSA is often also regarded as a mega-regional trade agreement, even as one the three major ones besides TPP and TTIP.[66] In any case, it is a complement

[61] Deblock and Rioux, 'Economic Dialogue' (n 30) 39ff. [62] ibid.

[63] The Joint Interpretative Instrument on the Comprehensive Economic and Trade Agreement (CETA) was adopted at the moment of signature of CETA (cf Council of the European Union, document 13541/16, 27 October 2016). While this document was referred to as an 'interpretative declaration' in the lead-up to the signature of CETA, it was eventually renamed 'Interpretative Instrument'. According to its preamble, '[t]his interpretative instrument, provides, *in the sense of Article 31 of the Vienna Convention on the Law of Treaties*, a clear and unambiguous statement of what Canada and the European Union and its Member States agreed in a number of CETA provisions that have been the object of public debate and concerns and provides an agreed interpretation thereof. This includes, in particular, the impact of CETA on the ability of governments to regulate in the public interest, as well as the provisions on investment protection and dispute resolution, and on sustainable development, labour rights and environmental protection' (emphasis added).

The italicized reference to the Vienna Convention on the Law of Treaties aims to clarify this 'instrument's' legal status. Whether this aim has been achieved remains doubtful (on this, cf, eg, Gus Van Harten, 'The EU-Canada Joint Interpretive Declaration/Instrument on the CETA' (25 October 2016) <http://ssrn.com/abstract=2850281> accessed 4 January 2017). Moreover, as this 'instrument' partly uses 'promotional language' and partly merely restates CETA provisions in a more condensed form, it is questionable whether it actually clarifies CETA provisions (cf ibid; see also Simon Lester, 'Interpreting the CETA Joint Interpretative Instrument' (posted on 1 November 2016), <http://worldtradelaw.typepad.com/ielpblog/2016/11/the-ceta-joint-interpretative-instrument.html> accessed 27 March 2017).

[64] cf Council of the European Union, document 10974/16 of 5 October 2016; on several questions raised by the provisional application of CETA, cf Guillaume Van der Loo, 'CETA's Signature: 38 Statements, a Joint Interpretative Instrument and an Uncertain Future' (31 October 2016), <https://www.ceps.eu/system/files/GVdL%20CETA%20%20II.pdf> accessed 27 March 2017.

[65] Melo Araujo, 'Regulating Services' (n 16) 410ff.

[66] Dan Ciuriak, 'Mega Regionals and the Developing Countries' (Social Science Research Network, 19 June 2014) 7, <http://papers.ssrn.com/sol3/papers.cfm?abstract_id=2460501> accessed 30 August 2016.

to TTIP and CETA in the sense just referred to.[67] While there have been almost no preferential trade in services agreements before the year 2000, since then such agreements have proliferated, yielding a dense net of such agreements among the states currently negotiating TiSA.[68]

TiSA's economic and strategic significance is considerable, as it would bring about preferential commitments on trade in services between the three largest services markets in the world, that is, the US, the EU, and Japan. Moreover, no single TiSA negotiating party has pre-existing preferential trade in services agreements with all of these three economies.[69] Nonetheless, it has been critically observed that if the TiSA participants exchanged the best commitments they have undertaken in their preferential trade agreements,[70] then this would not necessarily yield great economic benefits for two reasons in particular: on the one hand, several TiSA negotiating parties have already exchanged significant concessions in their bilateral preferential trade agreements; on the other hand, plurilateralizing these concessions in the TiSA context will not *eo ipso* meet these countries' most important export interests, as these have often remained unaddressed so far and as relevant markets are sometimes situated in non-participating states.[71]

The rules and commitments laid down in TiSA should, according to the EU at least, eventually be incorporated into the WTO GATS agreement.[72] Integration of TiSA into the WTO framework could be accomplished in at least three different ways: first, it would be possible for the TiSA parties to integrate their TiSA commitments into the GATS schedules on a MFN basis.[73] The idea underlying this approach, which has already been adopted, for example, for financial services in the past, is that if a 'critical mass' of WTO Members participates in TiSA, then multilateralization would be economically conceivable. In this first approach, commitments on regulatory issues could also be incorporated into the GATS schedules as additional commitments. Second, TiSA parties could theoretically incorporate their TiSA concessions in the GATS individually—that is, independently of 'critical mass' considerations. Third, following the example of the WTO Government Procurement Agreement, TiSA commitments could be integrated into the WTO framework in the form of a plurilateral agreement. This would shield TiSA's GATS-plus concessions against the MFN commitment and free riders; additionally, it would also make the WTO's dispute settlement disciplines available for TiSA disciplines. Alternatively, TiSA could be concluded as a preferential trade agreement outside the WTO framework. It would then have to comply with the conditions for preferential trade agreements set forth in Article V of the GATS.[74]

[67] Hufbauer and Cimino-Isaacs, 'TPP and TTIP' (n 8) 689ff; see also Monika Ermert, 'Trade Outlook in 2015: The Race of the Mega-Regionals' (Intellectual Property Watch, 4 March 2015) 3ff, <http://www.ip-watch.org/2015/03/04/trade-outlook-in-2015-the-race-of-the-mega-regionals> accessed 27 March 2017.

[68] Marchetti and Roy, 'TiSA Initiative' (n 11) 687ff.

[69] ibid, 691.

[70] This step is also expected by Hufbauer and Cimino-Isaacs, 'TPP and TTIP' (n 8) 689ff.

[71] Marchetti and Roy, 'TiSA Initiative' (n 11) 683ff.

[72] cf Chapter 3 in this volume.

[73] On the functioning of the MFN clause and GATS schedules, cf Chapter 3 in this volume.

[74] These alternatives are discussed in Marchetti and Roy, 'TiSA Initiative' (n 11) 717ff; and Peng, 'TiSA' (n 9) 614ff.

All of these alternatives may cause problems, however.[75] Thus, it has been questioned whether TiSA, once negotiations will be concluded, will really comply with Article V of the GATS.[76] Furthermore, it has been submitted that transatlantic initiatives are no longer automatically sufficiently attractive for other WTO Members; therefore, it should not be taken for granted that a critical mass of countries will join the TiSA initiative.[77] Also, it has been indicated that it is doubtful whether WTO Members not participating in TiSA, such as China or India, for example, would agree to the incorporation of TiSA into WTO structures.[78]

As will be shown below,[79] the EU has proposed the first of the aforementioned alternatives for TiSA. Accordingly, once a critical mass is achieved, then TiSA should be incorporated into the WTO GATS framework.

V. New Orientations for EU External Economic Relations

A. The attempted reorientation

The last decade has clearly witnessed a fundamental reorientation of EU external economic relations. This new positioning became obvious already in the ambivalent tone of the EU's 2006 'Global Europe' strategy. There, the EU maintained on the one hand that 'there will be no European retreat from multilateralism'. On the other hand, however, it emphasized more cautiously that 'we ... are prepared to pay, *reasonably*, to keep the [multilateral] system thriving' (emphasis added). Furthermore, the EU went on to explicitly point out that free trade agreements building on WTO and other international rules should be used in the future to tackle 'issues which are not ready for multilateral discussion and by preparing the ground for the next level of multilateral liberalisation'. [80]

This shift towards bilateralism and regionalism is not a completely new orientation for the EU, which had for many years already entertained an ever-increasing network of bilateral and regional agreements spanning large parts of the world. However, this shift clearly constitutes a new prioritization within the EU's foreign and external economic policies. This reweighting of bilateralism and regionalism on the one hand and multilateralism on the other is due in particular to the factors outlined above: in order to remain a key player in shaping the future international economic order despite the disappointments of the Doha Round, the EU felt that it had to turn to bilateral approaches and to enter into negotiations on mega-regional trade agreements such as TTIP, CETA, and TiSA. This was seen as necessary, in particular, as regards issues that appear most important to the EU, such as

[75] Peng, 'TiSA' (n 9) 618ff.

[76] In principle, at least, TiSA members could accept, in that case, a MFN effect via Art II GATS, which would almost equal (unilateral) incorporation into the national schedules.

[77] Melo Araujo, 'Regulating Services' (n 16) 415–16.

[78] Peng, 'TiSA' (n 9) 618ff, 628ff.

[79] cf Chapter 3 in this volume.

[80] European Commission, 'Global Europe Competing in the World' (n 15) 10 (emphasis added). On all of this, see also Bungenberg, 'EU-Freihandelsabkommen' (n 16) 98ff.

trade in services, investment, and regulatory cooperation—that is, issues on which economically meaningful progress was perceived as unmanageable on the multilateral WTO level.[81]

As regards regulatory cooperation, it bears noting that the TTIP and CETA initiatives not only constitute attempts to bypass multilateral inertia and resistance: both agreements also represent efforts to overcome long-standing bilateral impasses between the EU on the one hand and the US and Canada, respectively, on the other hand, as within these bilateral relations substantial progress on regulatory cooperation has only rarely occurred in several decades.[82]

Regarding FDI, the interests of the EU and its Member States are manifold. While the EU Commission and several Member States are clearly interested in advancing FDI standards at the international level, the EU Commission is also interested in modernizing the standards of the BITs concluded by EU Member States with third states, and, especially, in ultimately replacing these BITs by investment treaties concluded by the EU.[83] In this regard, CETA and TTIP also constitute principal test cases for the distribution of powers among the EU and its Member States in EU external relations.

A further notable feature of the EU's reorientation in recent years is its treatment, or rather denial, of direct effect of agreements concluded by it with non-European partners. Whereas originally the determination of the (non-)existence of direct effect of international agreements within the EU legal order was left to the European Court of Justice, in more recent agreements the EU has expressly excluded direct effect. CETA is a case in point in this respect, as well.[84]

B. A need to re-evaluate the new orientation?

Paradoxically to some extent, while CETA, TTIP, and TiSA indeed constitute prime examples of the EU's reorientation in its external economic relations, the experiences made during the negotiations of these agreements will certainly require the EU and its Member States to question, or at least re-evaluate, this attempted new positioning.

Thus, the negotiations on CETA and TTIP have not only become new culmination points in the 'traditional' anti-globalization movement, which began in the 1990s and was originally aimed at the WTO and other multilateral fora, but the negotiations on these two mega-regional initiatives of the EU have also turned into crystallization points for a much broader public unease with European integration and globalization, where responsibilities have become diffuse, leaving growing parts of the population with an anxious feeling that they are not in a position to democratically influence fundamental settings of the course in the present-day 'multilevel' system that is perceived as constantly becoming more complex.[85] The

[81] cf also Bungenberg, 'EU-Freihandelsabkommen' (n 16) 98ff.
[82] cf Chapter 3 in this volume. [83] Cremona, 'Negotiating TTIP' (n 37) 355ff.
[84] ibid; on this see also Chapters 2, 11, and 14 in this volume.
[85] On this, cf also Chapter 13 in this volume.

intransparent negotiations of these agreements, their potentially highly transformative character, and other debatable features—such as the lack of direct effect for citizens coupled with special procedural (ISDS) rights for foreign investors—risk making citizens feel increasingly alienated from EU and global economic integration.[86] The fact that international and (mega-)regional economic integration creates not only winners, but also losers, has obviously been a major factor contributing to the Brexit vote. The underlying apprehensions of considerable parts of the population can hardly be 'cured' permanently by 'sedative' devices such as the Interpretative Instrument adopted on the occasion of the signature of CETA. Moreover, should the envisioned mega-regional initiatives fail, then a renewed emphasis on the WTO as the primary forum for negotiating multilateral trade—and possibly investment—issues will become compulsory for the EU as well.

Finally, the impasses in the lead-up to the signature of CETA and the fact that CETA—and similar 'mixed' agreements to be concluded by the EU and its Member States—may still fail to be ratified not only in the EU Parliament, but also in the national and regional parliaments of the EU's twenty-eight Member States, have made it abundantly clear for any observer that the division of competences in the EU creates heightened, and at times not entirely foreseeable, hurdles for the EU and its Member States and tends to cast shadows over their perceived reliability in external relations.

These new orientations in international economic law and the EU's external economic relations are analysed in the following chapters of this volume.

[86] See Chapter 2 in this volume.

2

CETA, TTIP, and TiSA

New Trends in International Economic Law

Ernst-Ulrich Petersmann

I. Introduction and Overview

Politics, the economy, science, and law are described by sociologists as the four—out of altogether ten—major sub-systems governing societies in order to cope with the overall complexity of human interactions.[1] Each of these social sub-systems uses different 'media' and 'codes' for promoting different social functions. For instance, *politics* refers to the governance of citizens in a community and focuses on power, ideologies, and the 'code' of 'government/opposition' in order to promote social order and peace inside and among communities. The *economy* focuses on money, prices, and the 'code' of 'payment/non-payment (efficiency)' in order to coordinate economic activities, distribute scarce resources, and satisfy consumer demand for goods and services. *Sciences* focus on truth, theories, and verification or falsification of knowledge. *Law* focuses on governance through rules, principles, and institutions for a 'just' and 'lawful social order' inside and among communities. These and other social sub-systems (like religion, education, art, health systems, mass media, sports) are driven by different rationalities and values such as: religious faith; education through transfer of knowledge and character formation; creation of innovative arts, fashions, and styles; restoration from illness to health; media diffusion of information; and 'fair sports competitions'; yet they overlap and interact—also in international economic law (as illustrated by new fields such as 'Islamic finance', 'sports law', and 'internet law'). Trade and investment regulation can transform international relations by inducing billions of people to cooperate in the global division of labour.

Law as an instrument of politics historically evolved through the emergence of property, governance, and justice systems. Long before the scientific demonstration of the mutually beneficial effects of division of labour through trade (eg by A Smith in the eighteenth century), international commerce developed on the basis

[1] cf Steffen Roth and Anton Schutz, 'Ten Systems. Toward a Canon of Function Systems' (2015) 22(3) *Cybernetics and Human Knowing* 88–102.

CETA, TTIP, and TiSA: New Trends in International Economic Law. Ernst-Ulrich Petersmann.

of private transaction law, public regulation (eg monetary law, the Roman *lex mercatoria*, colonial preferences), and international trade and investment agreements. Globalization and its transformation of most *national* 'public goods' (PGs)[2] into *transnational* 'aggregate PGs'—such as human rights, rule of law, democratic peace, mutually beneficial monetary, trading, development, environmental, communication, and legal systems promoting 'sustainable development'—require reviewing legal methodologies enabling citizens and people to increase their social welfare through global cooperation and international economic law (IEL). The subject of this book—the Comprehensive Economic and Trade Agreement (CETA) between Canada and the European Union (EU), the Transatlantic Trade and Investment Partnership (TTIP) Agreement between the EU and the US, and the Trade in Services Agreement (TiSA) among almost fifty members of the World Trade Organization (WTO)—raises complex legal, political, economic, and methodological questions over the relationships between free trade agreements (FTAs), other 'plurilateral agreements' (PAs), WTO law, and trade governance. All these agreements aim at liberalizing market access and regulating 'market failures' (eg to supply PGs) and 'governance failures' (like use of welfare-reducing border restrictions). The regulatory standards of CETA, TTIP, and TiSA tend to be based on WTO law (eg Arts XXIV GATT and V GATS), but their regulatory treaty objectives aim at liberalizing and regulating trade beyond what is politically possible in the WTO, partly by using innovative, new regulatory standards for trade in goods, services, and investments. Section II briefly explains why 'legal fragmentation' (eg of WTO law through mega-regional FTAs like CETA and TTIP) and 'methodological pluralism' (eg negotiation of diverse kinds of PAs and FTAs) are inevitable in the world trading system. Section III broadens the analysis by discussing competing conceptions of 'IEL' resulting from the diverse conceptions of 'principles of justice' and from diverse methods for further developing IEL. Section IV evaluates CETA, TTIP, and TiSA not only from economic 'utilitarian perspectives', but also from legal and political, regional and global perspectives.

II. 'Legal Fragmentation' and Disagreements over 'Methodology' in Economic Law and Governance

The General Agreement on Tariffs and Trade (GATT 1947), the eight GATT Rounds of multilateral trade negotiations, and the GATT dispute settlement practices (eg the 115 panel reports under GATT Art XXIII and the corresponding provisions of the 1979 Tokyo Round Agreements from 1948 to 1995) were dominated by the industrialized countries in Europe, North America, and Asia. Decolonization entailed that—since the 1960s—less-developed countries (LDCs)

[2] Pure 'PGs' (like sunshine, clean air, and inalienable human rights) tend to be defined by their non-rival and non-excludable use that prevents their production in private markets. Most PGs are 'impure' in the sense of being either non-rival (eg 'club goods') or non-excludable (like common pool resources).

became the majority of GATT contracting parties and insisted on certain adjustments of GATT law (eg by adding Part IV on 'Trade and Development' and the 1979 'enabling clause' providing for preferential treatment of LDCs). Yet, it was only due to the 'grand bargain' in the Uruguay Round negotiations (1986–94) that agreement was reached on the progressive phasing-out of systemic discrimination against exports from LDCs (eg of cotton, textiles, agricultural products) and on more comprehensive 'preferential and differential treatment' of LDCs in most areas of GATT/WTO law. In exchange, the 'legal fragmentation' of the GATT legal system resulting from the separate Kennedy Round and Tokyo Round Agreements (usually ratified by only twenty to thirty GATT contracting parties) was overcome by the conclusion of the Uruguay Round and WTO agreements as a 'single undertaking' integrating more than sixty different trade agreements, including accession protocols and other trade agreements negotiated in the WTO since 1995.

A. 'Fragmentation' and dialectic evolution of international law

The sovereign freedom of the 193 UN Member States to choose which international treaties they wish to ratify makes 'legal fragmentation' (eg the coexistence of thousands of international treaty regimes) a defining feature of modern international law. Legal fragmentation often reflects not only intergovernmental power politics (eg 'voluntary export restraint agreements' imposed by powerful importing countries); it is also promoted by attempts of countries to reform international law and governance by transforming agreed 'principles of justice' (eg fundamental rights, democracy, judicial remedies, rule of law) into legislation, administration, adjudication, and international law. For instance:

- The 1967 Kennedy Round, 1979 Tokyo Round and 1994 Uruguay Round Agreements were approved by national parliaments and implemented through parliamentary legislation in most democratic countries, thereby enhancing the democratic legitimacy of GATT/WTO law (GATT 1947 had not been approved by parliaments in most countries due to its 'provisional application' based on an intergovernmental 'Protocol on provisional application of GATT').
- The more than 600 FTAs notified to the WTO (415 of which are in force) often aim at promoting consumer welfare, transnational rule of law, non-discriminatory conditions of competition, and judicial remedies far beyond WTO disciplines.
- The PAs concluded among some WTO members (like the 1994 Government Procurement Agreement (GPA)) aim at liberalizing and regulating trade and promoting economic welfare beyond the general WTO rules (eg by liberalizing government procurement procedures and protecting individual access to domestic courts that review the compliance with the GPA, cf Art XX GPA).

B. Limitation of legal fragmentation through multilateralism

International cooperation among 193 UN Member States can be promoted most efficiently through multilateral agreements on common rules and principles justifying mutually beneficial cooperation (eg economic principles of efficiency for mutually beneficial trade, legal principles of procedural, constitutional, distributive, corrective, commutative justice, and equity in social cooperation). The ambitious 'Doha Round' objective of 2001 to further improve the multilateral trading system through negotiations aimed at a 'single undertaking' on about twenty different subjects of trade regulation could so far not be realized. Yet, this failure did not prevent the successful conclusion of other WTO agreements such as:

- Accession Protocols with forty new WTO Members (such as China and Russia);
- WTO agreements on liberalization of trade in goods like the WTO Information Technology Agreements of 1997 and 2015, and the revised WTO Government Procurement Agreement (in force since 2015);
- WTO agreements on liberalization of trade in services like the WTO Agreement on Basic Telecommunications (in force since 1998) and the WTO Agreement on Financial Services (in force since 1999);
- the 2001 WTO Declaration on the TRIPS Agreement and Public Health, and the related 2003 WTO 'waiver' and 2005 amendment of the TRIPS rules on compulsory licences for essential medicines; and
- the 2014 Trade Facilitation Agreement.

Hence, in spite of disagreements on many Doha Round agenda subjects, the WTO system remains the most successful multilateral trading system in history covering now more than 90 per cent of world trade, including an increasing share of LDCs (now over 53 per cent).

Intergovernmental trade negotiations inside and outside the WTO remain 'member-driven' and dominated by the relative power of trading countries (eg their 'market power', and financial and legal resources). The more than 500 invocations of the compulsory WTO dispute settlement system follow a different paradigm of rules-based, third-party adjudication and progressive clarification of the often contested meaning of WTO rules and principles. The political differences over how to pursue the Doha Round negotiations—and the increasing differences over the legitimate authority and methodologies of the WTO dispute settlement bodies—reflect far-reaching disagreements among the 164 WTO Members about political, legal, and judicial methodologies in WTO governance, as illustrated by politically motivated refusals to appoint WTO Appellate Body judges in 2016 and the inconclusive WTO negotiations about improvements of the WTO Dispute Settlement Understanding (DSU). Due to disagreements on how to conclude the Doha Round negotiations, FTAs and PAs continue to proliferate; especially mega-regional FTAs (like TTIP) could assume geopolitical importance in view of the possibility of a future merger of mega-regional FTAs. For instance, similar to the replacement of GATT 1947 by the 1994 WTO Agreement, the more than fifty WTO members participating in CETA, TTIP, the Trans-Pacific Partnership (TPP) Agreement (including twelve WTO/TPP members), and the Regional Comprehensive Economic Partnership (including sixteen WTO/RCEP members) account for almost 80 per cent of world gross domestic product (GDP); they could decide to merge their mega-regional FTAs into a new 'WTO 2020' if consensus-based negotiations inside the WTO fail to reform the WTO rules on trade liberalization, regulation, and adjudication.

The Trade Facilitation Agreement of 2014 and the Undertaking by developed countries of December 2015 to remove export subsidies have been among the most important results of the Doha Round negotiations so far. In view of the limited 2013 'Bali package' and 2015 'Nairobi package' on liberalization and regulation of world trade, the 2015 WTO Ministerial Declaration at Nairobi acknowledged that WTO Members 'have different views' on the future of the Doha Round negotiations, notwithstanding their 'strong commitment ... to advance negotiations on the remaining Doha issues'. The consensus practices and 'single undertaking principle' governing the Doha Round negotiations render the outcome of these negotiations uncertain. The stockpile of trade restrictions introduced by WTO Members since the financial crises of 2008 continues to grow. The successful legal challenges of non-discriminatory safeguard measures (Art XIX GATT) in now ten WTO dispute settlement proceedings entailed that WTO Members increasingly resort to discriminatory anti-dumping and countervailing duties as 'selective safeguard measures', many of which have been found in WTO dispute settlement rulings to violate the pertinent WTO Agreements on anti-dumping measures and subsidies. The economic rationale of these WTO Agreements on Art VI GATT and on subsidies remains contested, as illustrated by their lack of Preambles justifying the vague and incoherent 'fair trade principles' underlying these often indeterminate treaty provisions. Similarly, the role of the WTO and of its legal disciplines in implementing other policy goals—like the UN agreements on climate change prevention and the 2030 UN Agenda for Sustainable Development—remains controversial and to be clarified.

Over 500 disputes have been submitted to the WTO dispute settlement system since 1995; about 90 per cent of the more than 300 panel, appellate, and arbitration reports have been implemented. Yet, the only prospective remedies (termination of the illegal measures following a 'reasonable period of time' after a WTO dispute settlement finding), the non-application of the customary rules on reparation of injury, and the widespread disregard for the WTO guarantees of effective judicial remedies in domestic jurisdictions entail that WTO Members sometimes engage in temporary treaty violations as 'politically efficient' responses to domestic interest group pressures, albeit without effective judicial remedies of adversely affected citizens and trading partners. The more legal clarification of indeterminate WTO rules and of under-theorized WTO principles—like 'sustainable development', 'fair price comparison' in calculating dumping margins, 'green subsidies', 'non-violation', and 'situation complaints' pursuant to Art XXIII GATT—is left to WTO dispute settlement bodies, the stronger become the controversies among WTO Members about the legal and judicial methodologies used in WTO panel, appellate, and arbitration proceedings and in the political control of judicial dispute settlement institutions by the intergovernmental Dispute Settlement Body (DSB).

C. Methodological pluralism in multi-level trade law and governance

The term 'legal methodology' is used here as the 'best way' for identifying the 'sources' of legal systems, the methods of legal interpretation, the 'primary rules of conduct', and 'secondary rules of recognition, change and adjudication', the relationship between 'legal positivism', 'natural law', and 'social theories of law', and the 'dual nature' of modern legal systems. The etymological origins of the word methodology—ie the Greek word '*meta-hodos*', referring to 'following the road'—suggest that the reality of 'legal fragmentation' is driven by the diversity of legal conceptions over how private and public, national and international interests should be pursued most effectively and legitimately in the three regulatory functions of legal systems:

- first, as a normative ordering of social cooperation (eg the inadequate limitation of power politics and 'veto powers' through GATT/WTO law and the failures in WTO governance to successfully conclude the WTO Doha Round negotiations since 2001);
- second, as a coherent system of 'primary rules of conduct' and 'secondary rules' of recognition, change, and adjudication (eg the controversies over the legitimate 'judicial functions' of the 'dispute settlement system' of the WTO); and
- third, as social facts ('living law') based on 'legal socialization' and compliance by legal subjects with legal rules and principles (eg the often inadequate implementation of WTO legal obligations in domestic jurisdictions preventing a 'WTO compliance culture' enabling transnational rule of law).

Mega-regional FTAs (like CETA and TTIP) and PAs (like TiSA) are political responses to 'governance failures' in WTO practices; they illustrate the need to review methodological challenges in IEL. The legal design of multi-level governance arrangements depends on how, and at what level of regulation, the ubiquity of conflicts between rational private interests and reasonable public interests can be resolved. For instance, *private economic actors* are confronted with 'market failures' (like restrictive business practices) and 'governance failures' (like governmental market distortions through subsidies) that are inadequately regulated in WTO law. *Reasonable citizens* have self-interests in 'institutionalizing public reason' through constitutional, legislative, administrative, and judicial rules and institutions protecting 'principles of justice' (like human rights, judicial remedies, and accountability mechanisms) and limiting 'market failures' as well as 'governance failures'. *Public choice theory* explains why—in responding to private conflicts of interests (eg between 'Wall Street' and 'main street')—*politicians* also pursue political self-interests (eg in satisfying protectionist interest groups in exchange for their political support); legal regulation is often politically easier through reciprocal agreements (eg limiting competing subsidies) than through unilateral, national regulation. Even if economic regulations are allegedly based on purely economic considerations, their distributive and competitive effects may give rise to legal and judicial challenges. Art 3 DSU emphasizes the need for following the customary rules of treaty interpretation (as prescribed in the Vienna Convention on the Law of Treaties (VCLT)). Yet, Arts 31–33 VCLT set out ambiguous principles rather than rules without offering a precise legal methodology for clarifying indeterminate treaty texts, contexts, objects, and purposes (eg through 'systemic' and 'dynamic interpretations' pursuant to Art 31:3 VCLT) that often remain contested among the parties to the dispute. In May 2016, the opposition by the US to reappointing the Korean judge in the WTO Appellate Body—based on the US allegation that he had exceeded his limited, judicial powers (eg in participating in certain Appellate Body findings and posing certain questions to the disputing parties)—revealed the diverse conceptions among WTO Members of the legitimate scope of judicial powers of WTO dispute settlement bodies.

III. Changing Conceptions of IEL and of Its 'Principles of Justice'

Up until the Second World War, international law was justified primarily in terms of power-oriented concepts like state sovereignty and colonialism. Due to UN human rights law (HRL), the universal recognition of 'inalienable' and 'indivisible' human rights entails increasing legal protection of civil, political, economic, social and cultural rights of citizens and economic actors, like legal and judicial protection of rights of producers, investors, traders and consumers in trade, investment, and regional integration agreements. While 'constitutionalism 1.0' (like the democratic American and French Constitutions during the eighteenth century) focused on *democratic emancipation of people* in nation states, the 'constitutionalism 2.0' following the Second World War (eg the 'human rights constitutions' in European and decolonized countries like India) also focused on *human emancipation* from other abuses of public and private power (like 'market powers'). European integration prompted adjustments of many national Constitutions ('cosmopolitan constitutionalism 3.0') aimed at protecting and emancipating citizens vis-à-vis abuses of national foreign policy powers through *multi-level constitutionalism* constituting, limiting, regulating, and justifying multi-level governance of transnational PGs (like common markets, transnational rule of law, and multi-level legal and judicial protection of cosmopolitan rights), with far-reaching repercussions on IEL as illustrated by European constitutional and common market law and EU membership in worldwide organizations (like the WTO and Food and Agriculture Organization (FAO)).[3]

[3] cf Alexander Somek, *The Cosmopolitan Constitution* (Oxford University Press, 2014); and my criticism of Somek's misconception of 'cosmopolitan constitutionalism' in Ernst-Ulrich Petersmann, *Multilevel Constitutionalism for Multilevel Governance of Public Goods—Methodology Problems in International Law* (Bloomsbury, 2016) ch 3 (hereafter Petersmann, *Multilevel Constitutionalism*).

A. Five competing conceptions of IEL

Governments, intergovernmental and non-governmental organizations, and citizens conceptualize IEL from diverse perspectives and value premises. For instance:

- Governments insisting on 'state sovereignty' and prioritizing 'national interests' tend to perceive *IEL as public international law regulating the international economy* (eg the 1944 Bretton Woods Agreements, GATT 1947, the WTO Agreement).
- Private economic actors using their private legal and economic autonomy in the global division of labour perceive *IEL* primarily *as private international transaction law, commercial, corporate, and 'conflicts law'*.
- Citizens, democratic institutions, and courts of justice in constitutional democracies tend to perceive *IEL* from a republican perspective *as multi-level democratic regulation of PGs* and of related 'market failures' and 'governance failures' (eg through national competition, trade, environmental, labour, and social legislation as preconditions for the proper functioning of a 'social market economy') that must remain consistent also with principles of economic efficiency.
- EU citizens, their twenty-eight EU Member States, and representative EU institutions view *European economic law as multi-level constitutional regulation* of their common market and of multi-level governance of other European PGs (like transnational rule of law, multi-level protection of human and constitutional rights of EU citizens), even if third European countries insist on maintaining their diverse constitutional traditions in designing IEL, like the European Free Trade Area (EFTA) countries participating in the European common market on the basis of the European Economic Area (EEA) Agreement of 1993.
- UN Specialized Agencies, the WTO, and ever more regional economic organizations recognize that their primary and 'secondary' treaty law is increasingly limited by 'global administrative law' principles protecting transparency, legal accountability, and rule of law in multi-level governance of transnational PGs (like monetary stability, the world trading system, world food security, public health protection).[4]

Academic analyses of IEL also often disagree on how these five competing conceptions of IEL ((1) international law based on state sovereignty; (2) private international law based on private autonomy rights; (3) multi-level economic regulation based on 'law and economics'; (4) multi-level constitutional law; or (5) global administrative law) should be evaluated and reconciled with each other. The customary rules of treaty interpretation (as codified in Arts 31–33 VCLT) require not only that 'a treaty shall be interpreted in good faith in accordance with the ordinary

[4] For a discussion of these competing conceptions of IEL, see Ernst-Ulrich Petersmann, *International Economic Law in the 21st Century* (Hart, 2012) ch 1 (hereafter Petersmann, *International Economic Law*).

meaning to be given to the terms of the treaty in their context and in the light of its object and purpose' (Art 31 para 1), but Art 31:3(c) also clarifies that '[t]here shall be taken into account, together with the context ... (c) any relevant rules of international law applicable in the relations between the parties'. As all UN Member States have accepted human rights obligations as well as other 'principles of justice' under the UN Charter and under additional UN conventions, the Preamble to the VCLT emphasizes:

> ... that disputes concerning treaties, like other international disputes, should be settled by peaceful means and in conformity with the principles of justice and international law ...
>
> *Recalling* the determination of the peoples of the United Nations to establish conditions under which justice and respect for the obligations arising from treaties can be maintained ...
>
> *Having in mind* the principles of international law embodied in the Charter of the United Nations such as the principles of the equal rights and self-determination of peoples, of the sovereign equality and independence of all States, of non-interference in the domestic affairs of States, of the prohibition of the threat or use of force and of universal respect for, and observance of, human rights and fundamental freedoms for all.[5]

B. Political disagreements on legal and economic principles in IEL reflect power struggles

How should these state-centred 'principles of justice' (like sovereign equality of states), peoples-centred 'principles of justice' (like democratic self-determination of peoples), human rights, and fundamental freedoms for all be reconciled with each other in multi-level economic regulation? Since Aristotle, procedural, distributive, corrective, commutative justice and equity continue to be recognized as diverse 'spheres of justice' in the design and justification of legal and dispute settlement systems (eg for 'violation complaints', 'non-violation complaints', and 'situation complaints' pursuant to Art XXIII GATT). Post-colonial IEL also includes 'principles of transitional justice' based on preferential treatment of less-developed countries (eg in Part IV of GATT and in the dispute settlement system of the WTO), as well as 'cosmopolitan principles of justice' based on the universal human rights obligations of all UN Member States. The different kinds of 'principles of justice' reflect human struggles for emancipation and liberation from subjugation to abuses of public and private powers. The failure of WTO Members to conclude their 'Doha Development Round' negotiations and the more than 500 WTO disputes since 1995 illustrate disagreements among governments and non-governmental actors on how 'principles of justice' should guide and limit trade regulation and adjudication inside and outside the WTO. EU citizens have insisted on 'constitutionalizing' their national and European legal systems by linking fundamental rights of citizens to multi-level governance duties to protect PGs. Yet, similar 'constitutional approaches' (eg deriving the legitimacy also of international law from

[5] Emphases in the original.

'constitutional contracts' among citizens and from respect for their 'inalienable' constitutional rights) are resisted by many UN and WTO diplomats, for instance if they defend authoritarian, foreign policy discretion by the need for 'realism' in intergovernmental power politics.

Similar to the diverse *political theories* on governance inside states and on designing 'private–public partnerships' (eg for supplying PGs such as financial stability and public health), views on multi-level trade and economic regulation differ depending on the diverse conceptions of foreign policies and international relations. For instance:[6]

- *'Realist' theories* continue to perceive states as key actors in world affairs and focus on 'national interests' in terms of power, security, and separation of national from international law. The more hegemonic 'intergovernmental power politics' fails to protect international PGs demanded by citizens (such as protection of consumer welfare), the more reason citizens and democratic parliaments have to insist on multi-level, constitutional safeguards limiting abuses of public and private power in order to protect common, reasonable self-interests of citizens, also beyond states.
- *Liberal regime theories* explain why international rules, procedures, and institutions can help overcome 'collective action problems' in international relations, for instance through: (a) formation of clubs excluding 'free-riders'; (b) monitoring of rule-compliance (eg as a disincentive for 'cheating'); (c) institutionalized, long-term cooperation promoting trust and predictability; (d) rules-based reduction of transaction costs; and (e) sanctions imposed on countries violating their 'duties to protect' human rights and other PGs.
- *Functional integration theories* offer additional strategies for depoliticising and transforming 'high politics' into mutually beneficial 'low politics' (eg inside FTAs, customs, and monetary unions) based on rational self-interests of subnational and supranational actors, as illustrated by the multi-level 'common market freedoms' of EU citizens and their multi-level, legal protection by independent institutions (like national and EU competition, monetary and judicial authorities). Reliance on citizen-driven market integration has increased the need for standard-setting bodies (such as the Basel Committee for Banking Supervision and the International Standards Organization) aimed at promoting transparency and integrity of product and production standards, market transactions, and related government regulations (eg of money laundering and consumer protection).
- *Public choice theories* explain the ubiquity of 'market failures' and 'governance failures' in terms of the rational egoism of 'rent-seeking' individuals, interest groups, and periodically elected politicians. For instance, national trade

[6] For an application of the following international relations theories to the GATT/WTO system, see Ernst-Ulrich Petersmann, *The GATT/WTO Dispute Settlement System: International Law, International Organizations and Dispute Settlement* (Kluwer, 1997) 10ff.

policy discretion risks being distorted unless interest group politics is legally constrained by multi-level safeguards of common reasonable interests of citizens (eg GATT/WTO law protecting non-discriminatory market competition). Similarly, the abuses of national fiscal, debt, and economic policies in over-indebted Eurozone member countries (like Greece) required the EU to introduce ever more multi-level, legal, and institutional disciplines, surveillance mechanisms, and financial assistance in order to contain the financial crises since 2010. In order to avoid systemic risks, multi-level governance must coordinate the 'horizontal' and 'vertical' interdependencies among international movements of goods, services, persons, capital, payments, related rules, and institutions at the national and transnational levels.

- *Constitutional theories* emphasize that legitimate and effective governance of PGs depends on mutually coherent constitutional, legislative, administrative, judicial, and international rules and institutions for the benefit of citizens and their constitutional rights as ultimate constitutional values and guarantees of constitutional, parliamentary, 'deliberative', and 'participatory democracy'. *Multi-level constitutionalism* aims at integrating legitimately diverse regulatory approaches in order to promote coherent and legitimate, multi-level governance of 'aggregate PGs'. Just as morality requires limiting rational egoism by reasonableness, *cosmopolitan constitutionalism* aims at institutionalizing 'public reason' (eg in terms of human rights and 'courts of justice' limiting majority politics) so as to protect constitutional rights of citizens and decentralized enforcement of rule of law by individuals as 'constituent powers', 'democratic principals' of governance agents, and 'agents of justice' entitled to cosmopolitan rights (as 'intermediate PGs').

Economic theories remain crucial for efficient design of multi-level governance institutions and for understanding the *rationale* of many economic rules and institutions. For instance:

- The *economic theory of 'optimal intervention'* explains how alternative policy instruments for correcting 'governance failures' as well as 'market failures' should be regulated and 'legally ranked' (eg trade policy instruments in GATT/WTO law) in order to achieve their policy goals most efficiently.
- The *economic theory of 'separation of policy instruments'* explains why UN law and IEL allocate the multi-level governance of diverse international PGs (eg monetary, trade, and public health governance, labour market regulation) to different international institutions. Central banks have been given legal independence in ever more countries in order to protect monetary and financial stability efficiently.
- *Economic theories of PGs* explain why the 'supply strategies' for the different types of PGs—such as 'best shot PGs' (like a medical invention), 'weakest link PGs' (like nuclear non-proliferation), and 'aggregate PGs' (like monetary and trading systems)—vary depending on their particular characteristics and the preferences of the citizens and governments involved (eg for

'internalizing external effects' by means of taxes, subsidies, or a change in property rights).

- *Welfare economics* explains why market regulation (eg in order to protect financial stability) must also provide for independent supervision of micro- and macro-policies (eg competition authorities protecting undistorted competition, IMF and EU surveillance of monetary policies) and for crisis management (eg national central banks as lenders of last resort for governments and banks).

C. Democratic, republican, and cosmopolitan constitutionalism as 'emancipatory struggles' for limiting power politics

The universal recognition—albeit often only ineffective implementation—by UN Member States of human rights, rule of law, and democratic governance reflects the constitutional insight that the ubiquity of conflicts among rational self-interests of individuals requires 'constitutional principles, rules, and institutions' of a higher legal rank that:

- constitute, limit, regulate, and justify multi-level governance powers of PGs for the benefit of all citizens;
- transform the agreed 'principles of justice' (eg in the 1776 US Declaration of Independence and the 1948 Universal Declaration of Human Rights (UDHR)) into democratic constitutions, legislation, administration, adjudication, and 'PGs treaties' protecting equal rights of citizens; and
- institutionalize 'public reason' so as to enhance the democratic capability of citizens to protect PGs.

Authoritarian rulers and diplomats pursue rational self-interests in defending 'path-dependent, foreign policy discretion' and other 'diplomatic privileges' (like diplomatic secrecy) limiting their legal, democratic, and judicial accountability vis-à-vis citizens.[7] Citizens have reasonable self-interests in limiting abuses of foreign policy discretion through constitutional restraints and protection of equal rights of citizens. Like the construction of a multi-storey house accommodating diverse people under a common roof,[8] and similar to the 'plywood principle' (ie using complementary layers of wood reinforcing each other), the collective construction of transnational 'aggregate PGs'—like multi-level regulation of monetary, trading,

[7] See, eg, Robert D Putnam, 'Diplomacy and Domestic Politics: The Logic of Two-Level Games' (1988) 42 *International Organization* 427 (the diplomatic power to conceal from the public and parliaments essential information 'disconnects' intergovernmental rule-making from democracy and enables diplomats to manipulate domestic decision-making by misrepresenting at the national level the negotiation situation—for instance, regarding intergovernmental exclusion of private rights) (hereafter Putnam, 'Diplomacy and Domestic Politics').

[8] cf Thomas Cottier, 'Towards a Five Storey House' in Christian Joerges and Ernst-Ulrich Petersmann (eds), *Constitutionalism, Multilevel Trade Governance and International Economic Law* (Hart, 2011) 495–532.

investment, and competition systems—must build on local, state, federal, regional, and global levels of legal and political protection; mutually coherent 'constitutional principles' and other 'intermediate PGs' (like human rights and rule of law) must protect diversity and the overall legal, political, social, and economic consistency and resilience of multi-level regulation and governance. UN and WTO governance of transnational PGs remain 'disconnected'—and often ineffective—due to their domination by politicians prioritizing their own rights and power politics over equal rights of citizens and related constitutional principles (like subsidiarity, limited delegation of powers, and judicial protection of rule of law). The cosmopolitan rights protected in some of the UN 'treaty constitutions'—such as labour rights protected by the International Labor Organization (ILO), health rights protected by the World Health Organization (WHO), rights to food protected by the FAO, rights to education protected by the UN Educational, Scientific and Cultural Organization (UNESCO), and other human rights protected by UN law—are not effectively protected inside many UN Member States. The success of many FTAs and PAs is due to their comparatively more effective domestic implementation mechanisms protecting equal freedoms and other rights of citizens.

The more than 2,000 years of political struggles—from the 'democratic Constitution' of the ancient Athenian democracy and the 'republican Constitution' of the Ancient Roman republic up to modern 'cosmopolitan democracies' in the EU—empirically confirm the normative claim that democratic and republican constitutionalism are the most legitimate and effective 'legal methodologies' for protecting equal rights and other PGs for the benefit of citizens.[9] *Democratic constitutionalism* explains why—in order to be legitimate—law and governance must not only be justified by 'principles of social justice' of a higher legal rank to be agreed in 'constitutional contracts' supported by citizens as 'constituent powers' and 'democratic principals' of all governance agents; constitutionalism is even more necessary for transforming the agreed 'principles of justice' into socially effective 'living law' based on democratic legislation, administration, adjudication, and multi-level international regulation of transnational cooperation institutionalizing 'public reason' supported by civil society as 'just' (eg in the sense of sufficiently justified). *Republican* and *cosmopolitan constitutionalism* explain why equal rights and 'republican virtues' of citizens are the most powerful incentives for limiting arbitrary power and domination of citizens by holding governments accountable for protecting constitutionally agreed PGs (*res publica*). The EU is explicitly 'founded on the values of respect for human dignity, freedom, democracy, equality, the rule of law and respect for human rights' (Art 2 of the Treaty on European Union (TEU)). This 'constitutional foundation' builds on that of UN law which—in the 1945 UN Charter and in the 1948 UDHR—is based on 'recognition of the inherent dignity and of the equal and inalienable rights of all members of the human family (as) the foundation of freedom, justice and peace in the world' (Preamble to the UDHR).

[9] cf Petersmann, *Multilevel Constitutionalism* (n 3).

National and EU courts interpret the Lisbon Treaty as a 'constitutional instrument' promoting fundamental rights and emancipation of citizens throughout the EU: it constitutes, limits, regulates, and justifies legislative, executive, and judicial governance powers for the collective supply of enumerated transnational PGs; EU powers remain subject to, inter alia, fundamental rights of EU citizens (eg as codified in the EU Charter of Fundamental Rights (EUCFR)), multi-level democratic governance, and republican, constitutional 'checks and balances' (eg between political and judicial EU institutions, national and EU jurisdictions) based on principles of conferral of limited powers, subsidiarity, proportionality (cf Art 5 TEU), and respect for the diverse constitutional identities of Member States (Art 4 TEU). Many courts in many countries construe treaties as deferring the clarification of 'direct effects' of treaty obligations to national courts; the EU courts, however—in cooperation with national courts—have progressively protected rights and remedies of citizens derived from EU law obligations. They recognize 'direct effect' and legal supremacy as matters of EU law and fundamental rights of EU citizens derived from precise and unconditional EU legal obligations. Comparative institutional research confirms that also other international 'PGs regimes'—if national and international courts cooperated in protecting equal rights of citizens by construing 'PGs treaties' as 'protectors of citizens' without being dependent on prior implementing legislation pertaining to that particular right, for instance in regional FTAs, human rights regimes, commercial, investment, intellectual property, or criminal law regimes—have protected PGs more effectively than state-centred 'Westphalian regimes' treating citizens as mere objects of discretionary, intergovernmental power politics.[10]

D. Competing judicial approaches to promoting legal coherence in IEL

Whether, and under what legal conditions, national or international courts of justice have jurisdiction to construe international rules as a 'sword' protecting legal integration, individual rights, and 'emancipation' (eg liberating migrant foreigners and other individuals from abuses of public and private power)—rather than as a 'shield' protecting legislative discretion—often remains contested among citizens and political and judicial powers. In order to develop a coherent *theory of IEL* and clarify the legal interrelationships among different principles and legal systems, one can use the distinction by the American legal philosopher R. Dworkin of the following 'four stages of legal theory':

- at the *semantic stage* of law, many legal terms (like 'IEL', human rights, and trade and investment law standards like non-discrimination and 'fair and equitable treatment') remain indeterminate 'interpretive concepts' that may be used by different actors with different meanings;

[10] cf Petersmann, *International Economic Law* (n 4) 145ff.

- at the *jurisprudential stage*, IEL requires justification in terms of 'principles of justice' (eg state-centred vs cosmopolitan, constitutional, and global administrative law conceptions of IEL) and elaboration of a convincing theory of 'rule of law' that citizens can accept as legitimate;
- at the *doctrinal stage*, the 'truth conditions' have to be constructed of how particular fields of law-making and administration can best realize their values and justify their practices and ideals (eg European insistence on competition, environmental, and social law limiting 'market failures' so as to legally construct a well-functioning 'social market economy'); and
- *judicial administration of justice* must apply, clarify, and enforce the law in concrete disputes through independent and impartial rule-clarification that institutionalizes 'public reason' and protects equal rights and social peace.[11]

Modern HRL is based on the universal recognition that '[a]ll human beings are born free and equal in dignity and rights. They are endowed with reason and conscience and should act towards one another in a spirit of brotherhood' (Art 1 UDHR). Yet, such legal assumptions of *human reasonableness* may conflict with economic models of a selfish *homo economicus* maximising individual preferences through cost-benefit calculations. Also, 'public choice analyses' of rational behaviour in 'political markets' acknowledge the psychological, social, and cultural influences on decision-making and human behaviour, such as the 'three principles' of:

- 'thinking automatically' (eg 'fast' and 'spontaneous' rather than 'deliberative' and 'reasonable slow thinking');
- 'thinking socially' (eg adjusting to social contexts of corruption); and
- 'thinking with mental models' that depend on the situation and the culture (eg in under-regulated financial industries profiting from tax-avoidance and circumvention of the law).[12]

The search for the 'sources' of IEL, the best methods of legal interpretation, the 'primary rules of conduct', and 'secondary rules of recognition, change, and adjudication' of IEL is usually approached from the point of view of *legal positivism* as a discovery of legal facts in the sense of authoritative law-making and effective law-enforcement. For example, Art 38 of the Statute of the International Court of Justice (ICJ) codifies the sources of international law in terms of 'international conventions', 'international custom, as evidence of a general practice accepted as law', and 'general principles of law recognized by civilized nations'. The same article defines the 'rules of recognition' not only in terms of recognition by states; the references to 'civilized nations' and to 'judicial decisions and the teachings of the most highly qualified publicists ... as subsidiary means for the determination of rules of law' qualify state consent in conformity with the customary rules of treaty interpretation as codified in the VCLT. The customary law duties of interpreting

[11] cf Ronald Dworkin, *Justice in Robes* (Harvard University Press, 2006) 9ff.
[12] cf 'World Development Report 2015: Mind, Society and Behavior' (World Bank, 2015).

treaties 'in conformity with the principles of justice' refer to the dynamically changing 'public reason' prevailing among citizens and in their democratic institutions and 'courts of justice'. In contrast to the 'freedoms of the ancient' (B. Constant) which protected only limited freedoms of a privileged class of male property owners (eg in the democratic constitutions of Athens and the republican constitution of Rome some 2,500 years ago), modern HRL (eg UN, regional, and national human rights instruments) and constitutional democracies proceed from equal, 'inalienable', and 'indivisible' human rights and 'fundamental freedoms for all' as preconditions for individual and democratic self-determination and 'constitutional justice'.[13] As all UN Member States have accepted legal obligations to respect, protect, and fulfil 'inalienable' human rights as integral parts of modern legal systems, HRL requires 'critical legal positivism' reconciling the 'constitutional premises' of HRL (eg its recognition of citizens as 'agents of justice', 'constituent powers', and 'democratic principals' who delegate only limited governance powers subject to inalienable human rights and democratic and judicial remedies) with the path-dependent, power-oriented conceptions of international law; conceptions of 'Hobbesian social contracts' delegating unlimited powers to 'states' and 'absolute rulers' so as to transform the civil 'war of everybody against everybody else' into peace and order have become inconsistent with modern HRL. Even if citizens are often 'rationally ignorant' vis-à-vis distant international treaty negotiations and—also during the secretive CETA negotiations—the 'democratic sovereign slept', the emancipatory function of human rights and constitutional democracy in the EU argue for protecting individual autonomy rights and equal cosmopolitan rights vis-à-vis path-dependent, power-oriented claims of rulers and their diplomats.

Globalization entails that traditional legal distinctions (eg in European legal systems) between private law (sub-divided into regulation of persons, things and actions, contract law, property law, family law, and inheritance law), national public law (sub-divided into constitutional law and administrative law), and international law are increasingly challenged by the emergence of transnational law and multi-level regulatory systems; the latter are driven no longer only by states, but increasingly also by non-governmental and international actors, as illustrated by transnational regulation of global supply chains, of the internet (*lex digitalis*) and of global 'sports law'.[14] The new 'legal pluralism' based on *functional* rather than only *territorial* legal sub-systems is illustrated by the WTO membership of states, sub-national and supranational customs territories like Hong Kong and the EU; it entails conflicts of jurisdiction which challenge the boundaries and cultures of national, transnational, and international legal and judicial systems and related legal preconceptions (*Vorverständnis*) of legal actors. These and other 'collective action problems' of the diverse kinds of PGs differ depending on their diverse

[13] cf Ernst-Ulrich Petersmann, 'Human Rights, International Economic Law and "Constitutional Justice"' (2008) 19 *European Journal of International Law* 769–98.

[14] cf Miguel Maduro, Kaarlo Tuori, and Suvi Sankari (eds), *Transnational Law: Rethinking European Law and Legal Thinking* (Cambridge University Press, 2014).

regulatory contexts.[15] Understanding worldwide legal regimes (like WTO law) and multi-level governance institutions (like the WTO dispute settlement bodies, regional and national economic courts) requires interdisciplinary studies that often explain the choices of political actors in different ways—for instance, depending on whether international relations theories focus on *states* (like realism, institutionalism, functionalism) or on *individual* and *non-governmental actors* in order to disaggregate the 'black box' of 'states' (like 'public choice', constitutional, or other constructivist theories).[16]

IV. How to Evaluate CETA, TTIP, and TiSA?

CETA, TTIP, and TiSA reflect the previously described trends of 'legal fragmentation' and 'methodological disagreements' over how to liberalize and regulate trade if the 'consensus-' and 'single-undertaking-practices' of the WTO do not enable successful conclusion of the Doha Round negotiations. The parties to mega-regional FTAs and TiSA continue to actively participate in the 2013 'Bali-' and 2015 'Nairobi-agreements' advancing the Doha Round agenda 'piecemeal' (ie departing pragmatically from the 'single-undertaking principle' of the 2001 Doha Round Declaration). So far, they present their agreements as 'WTO consistent FTAs' and complementary PAs rather than as 'counter-multilateralism'[17] aimed at contesting and changing the WTO—for instance, by evolving into a 'building block' for replacing the existing 'WTO 1994' by a revised 'WTO 2020' based on a merger of mega-regional FTAs and PAs. From an economic perspective, CETA, TTIP, and TiSA are likely to enhance consumer welfare, productivity, competition,

[15] For instance, while 'best-shot PGs' (like invention of pharmaceuticals against global diseases) may be promoted unilaterally through private–public partnerships in a single country, transnational 'aggregate PGs' may require universal participation of states in a worldwide 'global administrative law regime' (like the Universal Postal Union) or 'constitutional regime' (like enforcement of international criminal law through the UN Security Council and international criminal courts, and multi-level legal and judicial protection of transnational rule of law and human rights in the EU). On the promotion of PGs through preferential trade agreements, see Joost Pauwelyn, 'Taking the Preferences out of Preferential Trade Agreements: TTIP as a Provider of Public Goods?' in Jean-Frédéric Morin, Tereza Novotná, Frederik Ponjaert, and Mario Telò (eds), *The Politics of Transatlantic Trade Negotiations: TTIP in a Globalized World* (Ashgate, 2015) 187.

[16] On 'realist challenges' of international law and of the 'idealism' associated with inter-war legal and political scholarship, and the emergence of alternative political science conceptions of international law (notably 'liberalism', 'institutionalism', and 'constructivism') overcoming realism's hostility to international law by explaining the mutual advantages of international rules and institutions and of 'legal constructivism', see Jeffrey L Dunoff and Mark A Pollack (eds), *Interdisciplinary Perspectives on International Law and International Relations: The State of the Art* (Cambridge University Press, 2012). The '*status quo* bias' of American international relations theories and their frequent neglect of international HRL are often criticized by Europeans as 'an American crusade' aimed at justifying hegemonic US power politics without offering convincing strategies or leadership for collective supply of many international PGs (like transnational rule of law and protection of human rights, climate change prevention) beyond national US interests driven by domestic interest-group politics.

[17] cf Robert O Keohane and Julia C Morse, 'Counter-Multilateralism' in Morin et al, *The Politics of Transatlantic Trade Negotiations*, 17.

and transatlantic 'economic convergence' through liberalization and regulation of markets (section A). From the perspective of the EU's 'cosmopolitan trade policy constitution' and its disregard by EU trade politicians, CETA and TTIP risk undermining protection of fundamental rights of EU citizens and the 'emancipatory functions' of EU law (section B). Even if CETA, TTIP, and TiSA should succeed in liberalizing and regulating international trade and investments—and in harmonizing international trade and investment rules—beyond the current level of WTO rights and obligations, their 'geopolitical leadership' for reforming international trade and investment law remains uncertain—for instance, in view of the 'intergovernmental' rather than 'constitutional paradigms' underlying most CETA, TTIP, and TiSA rules and their inadequate protection of equal rights of citizens as primary sources of legal and 'social justice' in IEL in the twenty-first century (section C).

A. CETA, TTIP, and TiSA promote economic welfare gains and transatlantic policy convergence

The CETA and TTIP negotiations aim at 'transformative FTAs' that—similar to other mega-regional FTAs like the TPP agreement signed in February 2016 by twelve pacific trading countries producing more than 40 per cent of global GDP—will liberalize and regulate trade in goods, services, and investments far beyond WTO rules. The primary objective of TTIP is economic: to liberalize trade and investment barriers and, thereby, to create additional jobs, reduce transaction and production costs, and enhance productivity and consumer welfare. The exclusion of audio-visual services, and of general free movement of workers and of other citizens illustrates that TTIP remains less ambitious than the EEA agreement. The EU's regulatory paradigm of a 'highly competitive social market economy' (Art 3 TEU) differs from the neo-liberal economic paradigm of North American Free Trade Agreement (NAFTA) countries; yet, CETA and TTIP reflect increasing economic policy convergence, for instance by promoting regulatory product, production and investment standards, and limiting 'market failures' by competition, labour, and environmental policy cooperation. Due to the 'bounded rationality' of macroeconomic 'trade impact assessments' (eg regarding future public procurement at local and national levels of governments) and the dynamic function of CETA and TTIP as 'living agreements' providing for institutionalized regulatory cooperation, the precise gains from trade to be expected from CETA and TTIP—and their distribution among economic actors (eg among labour and capital, workers employed in the import-competing sector, and new job opportunities in export sectors)—remain contested. Civil society opposition against TTIP is increasing (eg in Austria, Germany, and the US) in spite of promises by trade negotiators that TTIP:

- will not lower consumer protection, labour, and environmental standards; and
- the protection of sovereign 'rights to regulate' will prevent foreign investors and powerful business lobbies from abusing their legal and judicial privileges (eg in investor-state arbitration, business participation in US 'notice and

comment' procedures in regulatory decision-making) for 'rent-seeking' at the expense of taxpayers.

The more citizens contest ideologies of 'perfectly competitive markets', 'sovereign consumers', and 'morally justified competition', the more TTIP negotiators had to concede that the procedures of the future TTIP Regulatory Cooperation Body for legal harmonization, mutual recognition agreements, and common minimum (equivalence) standards will duly respect the need for democratic legislation in Europe and the US. Economists warn that TTIP is likely to prioritize mutual recognition of product and production standards rather than elaborate global standards for world trade.[18] US regulators tend to use less international standards than the EU, and the US federal government has limited control over the testing of products in the seventeen privately owned test centres in the US (which are not obliged to recognize each other's results). Hence, it remains unpredictable to what extent TTIP may succeed in lowering the high product certification costs in the US and in enhancing the compatibility of regulatory regimes through a permanent system of regulatory cooperation (eg avoiding bureaucratic duplication of procedures by means of sectorial agreements for textiles, chemicals, pharmaceuticals, cosmetics, medical devices, cars, electronics/ICT, machinery/engineering, and pesticides).

B. Disregard in transatlantic FTAs for the EU's 'cosmopolitan foreign policy constitution'

In contrast to utilitarian concepts of 'economic justice' (eg in terms of consumer welfare and poverty reduction), constitutional democracies and the Lisbon Treaty justify law and governance in terms of equal constitutional and cosmopolitan rights (eg as codified in the EUCFR) as 'first principle of justice' justifying the 'constitutional contracts' among citizens recognizing each other as bearers of 'inalienable' human rights, 'constituent powers', and 'democratic principals' delegating only limited governance powers to national governments and EU institutions; democratic governance, rule of law, and other 'secondary constitutional principles' derive from the human and constitutional rights mutually recognized among citizens in their 'social contracts'.[19] The Lisbon Treaty prescribes (eg in Arts 3 and 21 TEU) 'protection of the citizens' through fundamental rights, 'strict observance of international law', and legal coherence between domestic and international market regulations and policies also for the *external relations powers* of the EU. Most of the fundamental rights protected in the EUCFR are rights of 'everybody' that constitutionally limit all EU powers, including trade policy powers. The EU Treaty provisions on

[18] cf Ferdi de Ville and Gabriel Siles-Brügge, *TTIP: The Truth about the Transatlantic Trade and Investment Partnership* (Cambridge Polity, 2016) 48ff.

[19] On 'social contract' theories as constitutional foundation of democratic legal systems, 'development as freedom' (Amartya Sen), for example, in Amartya Sen, *Development as Freedom* (Oxford University Press, 2001), and the derivation of utilitarian values from protecting equal civil, political, economic, and social rights of citizens, see Petersmann, *International Economic Law* (n 4) chs III and VII.

'democratic principles' (Arts 9ff TEU), on conferral of limited EU powers subject to constitutional restraints (like the principles of conferral, subsidiarity, proportionality, and rule of law set out in Arts 2 and 5 TEU), and on multi-level judicial protection of fundamental rights confirm the EU's multi-level constitutionalism and institutional 'checks and balances': citizens—individually and collectively—are the 'democratic sovereigns'; the democratic legitimacy of EU institutions derives from protecting fundamental rights, democracy, rule of law (ie the 'democratic trias' governing EU Member States), and other transnational PGs which—due to globalization—no EU state can protect unilaterally without international law and multi-level governance institutions.

1. Fundamental rights as constitutional restraints of EU competences

Fundamental rights permeate and limit EU law and EU competences as 'primary rules' without any limitation by a territorial jurisdiction clause (cf Art 51 EUCFR) or 'reciprocity clause'. The Court of Justice of the EU (CJEU) emphasizes that 'respect for human rights is a condition of the lawfulness of Community acts'[20] also in the external relations of the EU. EU law (eg the EUCFR) protects fundamental rights as constitutional restraints on the exercise of all public authority by EU institutions, including also fundamental rights to effective judicial remedies (Art 47 EUCFR). Are transatlantic FTAs consistent with the constitutional EU mandate of 'protection of citizens' and of their fundamental rights (eg under the EUCFR) in the exercise of internal and external EU policy powers? For instance, did the EU Commission—in its negotiations of CETA and TTIP—protect the fundamental rights to privacy and data protection (Arts 7 and 8), 'the freedom to conduct a business in accordance with Union law' (Art 16), private property rights (Art 17), and rights to effective judicial remedies (Art 47 EUCFR) with due regard to the constitutional requirement that limitations 'on the exercise of the rights and freedoms recognized by this Charter' are lawful 'only if they are necessary and genuinely meet objectives of general interest recognised by the Union or the need to protect the rights and freedoms of others' (Art 52 EUCFR)? Even if third countries may legitimately oppose inclusion of EU fundamental rights and of corresponding 'general principles of the Union's law' (cf Art 6:3 TEU) into FTAs on political and legal grounds (eg in view of the different constitutional traditions of NAFTA countries): did the EU Commission comply in its FTA negotiations with its constitutional mandate to 'be guided by the principles which have inspired its own creation, development and enlargement, and which it seeks to advance in the wider world'? As Art 52 EUCFR protects (eg

[20] Opinion 2/94, *Avis* [1996] ECLI:EU:C:1996:140, para 34. On the '*Kadi*-jurisprudence' annulling 'smart sanctions' of the EU on grounds of human rights violations even though these sanctions were ordered by the UN Security Council against alleged terrorists, see Matej Avbelj, Filippo Fontanelli, and Giuseppe Martinico (eds), *Kadi on Trial: A Multifaceted Analysis of the Kadi Trial* (Routledge, 2014). The relevance of the EUCFR and of Art 21 TEU as constitutional restraints on EU trade agreements was recognized by the General Court in the recent case T-512/12, *Front Polisario v Council* [2015] ECLI:EU:T:2015:953.

in conformity with Arts 29 UDHR and 6 and 13 of the European Convention on Human Rights (ECHR)) a fundamental right of everybody to justification of the necessity and proportionality of EU restrictions of fundamental rights as well as corresponding duties of EU institutions to justify such restrictions: did the EU Commission convincingly justify the legal necessity of CETA and TTIP provisions denying EU citizens and corporations the judicial remedies provided for Canadian and US investors vis-à-vis national and EU governance institutions (cf Arts 8.18 and 8.23 CETA)?

2. Disregard for the EU's 'cosmopolitan foreign policy mandate' in FTAs

It is mainly in view of the multi-level legal and judicial protection of fundamental rights under EU law that the EU rules constituting, limiting, regulating, and justifying the conferral of limited EU foreign policy powers (eg in Arts 3 and 21 TEU, Arts 205ff TFEU, the EUCFR) for multi-level protection of transnational PGs can be construed as a 'cosmopolitan foreign policy constitution' based, inter alia, on:

(1) EU Treaty commitments to 'protection of its citizens' and of their human and constitutional rights in the EU's external relations (cf Arts 3, 21 TEU), as illustrated by the 'human rights clauses' in more than 130 EU agreements with third countries;[21]

(2) multi-level legal commitments to the 'rule of law' (Art 2 TEU), to effective judicial remedies at national and European levels of governance (cf Arts 47 EUCFR, 19 TEU) and also in the external relations beyond the EU, as illustrated in regional and worldwide 'PGs treaties' limiting EU powers by judicial remedies (eg by the EFTA Court, WTO dispute settlement adjudication, the International Tribunal for the Law of the Sea) aimed at 'strict observance of international law' (Art 3 TEU)—without delegation of EU powers to violate international treaties approved by parliaments for the benefit of EU citizens;

(3) multi-level parliamentary, participatory, and deliberative democracy in internal and external policy-making (cf Arts 9–12 TEU), as illustrated by parliamentary co-decision powers (eg of the directly elected European Parliament) and individual rights that go far beyond the more limited parliamentary and democratic principles in other multilateral treaties; the European Parliament has used its powers also for rejecting international draft agreements negotiated by EU executives without adequate involvement of the European Parliament;[22]

[21] cf Ernst-Ulrich Petersmann, 'Integrating Human Rights into EU Trade Relations—The EU as a Global Role Model?' in Tamara Takács, Andrea Ott, and Angelos Dimopoulos (eds), *Linking Trade and Non-Commercial Interests: The EU as a Global Role Model?* (2013) 4 CLEER Working Papers.

[22] cf Marise Cremona, 'International Regulatory Policy and Democratic Accountability: The EU and the ACTA' in Marise Cremona, Peter Hilpold, Nikos Lavranos, Stefan Staiger Schneider, and

(4) EU membership in worldwide and regional 'PGs organizations' has led to the incorporation into EU law of related 'PGs treaties' (like the WTO Agreement, the UNCLOS) as 'integrating parts of the Community legal system', thereby justifying legal presumptions that precise and unconditional treaty obligations of the EU (eg under the EEA Agreement) approved by parliaments for the benefit of citizens can be invoked by adversely affected citizens in domestic courts as relevant legal constraints of EU powers.

EU politicians oppose such judicial protection of individual rights (eg based on EU trade agreements with EFTA countries, Russia and Turkey) in FTAs with non-European countries in order to limit their own legal and judicial accountability vis-à-vis citizens in external relations.[23] Parliaments in the EU apparently never discussed or challenged such 'anti-citizen clauses'—for instance, in Art 30.6 CETA ('[n]othing in this Agreement shall be construed as conferring rights or imposing obligations on persons other than those created between the Parties under public international law, nor as permitting this Agreement to be directly invoked in the domestic legal systems of the Parties'). Are such limitations of legal and judicial remedies of EU citizens justifiable as 'necessary' and 'proportionate' (eg in terms of Art 52 EUCFR) for protecting fundamental rights and general interests of EU citizens? Is the power-oriented WTO jurisprudence of the CJEU denying rights of citizens to invoke WTO legal obligations of the EU in domestic courts convincing and relevant in the very different context of FTAs among constitutional democracies?[24] Arguably, the intergovernmental 'disempowerment' of EU citizens and prioritization of rights of EU institutions over the fundamental rights and remedies of EU citizens is neither 'necessary' nor 'proportionate' in terms of Art 52 EUCFR, inter alia on the following grounds:

- without individual rights to invoke FTA provisions in domestic courts inside the EU, citizens have no effective remedies to hold national and EU institutions accountable for FTA violations that adversely affect citizens (eg their liberties, property rights, judicial remedies, and democratic responsibilities as protected by the EUCFR and related FTA legal disciplines);

Andreas R Ziegler (eds), *Reflections on the Constitutionalisation of International Economic Law: Liber Amicorum for Ernst-Ulrich Petersmann* (Nijhoff, 2014) 155ff.

[23] cf Aliki Semertzi, 'The Preclusion of Direct Effect in the Recently Concluded EU Free Trade Agreements' (2014) 51 *Common Market Law Review* 1125–58.

[24] The term 'freedom of manoeuvre' continues to be used by both the political EU institutions and the CJEU (eg in Case C-120/06 P, *FIAMM* [2008] ECLI:EU:C:2008:476, para 119) as the main justification for their disregard of legally binding UN conventions, WTO rules, and WTO dispute settlement rulings. The most recent CJEU judgment (Case C-21/14 P, *Rusal* [2015] ECLI:EU:C:2015:494) justifies 'the settled case-law of the Court that, given their nature and purpose, those (WTO) agreements are not in principle among the rules in the light of which the Court is to review the legality of measures adopted by the EU institutions', essentially on utilitarian grounds such as the 'lack of reciprocity' by the EU's most important trading partners (paras 38–9). Yet, as recognized by the CJEU in its *Kupferberg* judgment of 1982, 'the fact that the courts of one of the parties consider that certain of the stipulations in the agreement are of direct application whereas the courts of the other party do not recognise such direct application is not in itself such as to constitute a lack of reciprocity in the implementation of the agreement' (Case C-104/81, *Kupferberg* [1982] ECLI:EU:C:1982:362, para 18).

- EU institutions have not given any convincing reasons for why EU citizens should receive less legal and judicial protection in FTAs with constitutional democracies outside Europe than under FTAs with European countries; 'PGs treaties' approved by parliaments for the benefit of EU citizens and incorporated into EU law must be legally presumed to justify 'consistent interpretations' aimed at 'protection of citizens', as prescribed in Art 3 TEU;
- 'negative discrimination' of EU citizens by legal and judicial privileges for foreign investors (eg under investor-state arbitration pursuant to CETA chapter 8) is neither 'necessary' nor 'proportionate' in terms of Art 52 EUCFR in view of the alternative of non-discriminatory, more comprehensive legal and judicial remedies in domestic courts inside the EU.[25]

Hence, the 'disempowerment' of citizens through intergovernmental trade and investment rules, the lack of effective parliamentary and democratic control of FTA negotiation, the one-sided influence of 'stakeholder interests' in these FTA negotiations, and the lack of protection of fundamental rights (eg those in the EUCFR) and of effective judicial remedies justify popular fears that intergovernmental trade agreements—even among constitutional democracies—risk curtailing constitutional rights of EU citizens through non-transparent 'executive governance' and interest group politics.[26] As explained by public choice theory, 'diplomatic privileges' risk being abused for circumventing constitutional rights through 'intergovernmental collusion' to the detriment of EU citizens, especially if EU citizens remain 'rationally ignorant' of FTAs and the 'democratic sovereign sleeps'.[27] In a judgment of 6 October 2015, the CJEU annulled the EU Council decision to conclude the EU–US agreements on the transfer of private data in view of their inadequate protection of privacy and data protection rights (Arts 7 and 8 EUCFR) vis-à-vis spying practices by US National Security agencies.[28] In Opinions 1/2009 (European Patent Court) and 2/2013 (ECHR), the CJEU emphasized the constitutional

[25] The legal controversies over whether 'negative discrimination' of EU investors inside the EU is consistent with EU law (eg Arts 18, 267, and 344 TFEU) are illustrated by the request of 3 March 2015 (I ZB 2/15) by the German *Bundesgerichtshof* for a preliminary ruling by the CJEU on whether investor-state arbitration inside the EU is consistent with EU law (*Slovakia v Achmea* [2016] OJ C 296/19).

[26] Similar fears are cited by US politicians as justification of their rejection of the one-sided focus of the TPP Agreement (eg its provisions on investor protection—without judicial remedies for other adversely affected citizens, trade unions, and environmental and other civil society groups).

[27] cf Putnam, 'Diplomacy and Domestic Politics' (n 7). On the distinction (going back to Thomas Hobbes) between the 'sovereign' and 'government' and the criticism (already by Jean-Jacques Rousseau) that popular delegation of sovereign powers and election of representatives are not enough to make government democratic, see Richard Tuck, *The Sleeping Sovereign: The Invention of Modern Democracy* (Cambridge University Press, 2016). Since John Locke and Immanuel Kant, constitutional contract theories recognize equal rights of citizens and their constitutional protection as 'first principle of justice' (John Rawls). Democratic constitution-making, 'constitutional plebiscites', and participatory and 'deliberative democracy' are illustrations of how democratic people must remain responsible also in representative, parliamentary democracies, as recognized in the 'democratic principles' prescribed for EU governance in Arts 9–12 TEU.

[28] *Schrems* [2015] ECLI:EU:C:2015:650.

prohibition of unnecessarily limiting the EU guarantees of interpreting and protecting fundamental rights within the particular structures and restraints of EU law (eg cooperation between national and EU courts through preliminary rulings subject to multi-level constitutional restraints). A legal opinion by the German Association of Judges inferred from this jurisprudence as well as from other EU and German constitutional law arguments that the CETA limitations of the jurisdiction of national and EU courts for investor-state disputes are neither necessary nor consistent with EU law in view of the alternative of more effective and more comprehensive legal and judicial remedies in European courts.[29] Arguably, the EU's 'cosmopolitan foreign policy constitution' is disregarded by transatlantic FTA provisions which impede the fundamental rights of 'everybody' to 'conduct a business in accordance with Union law' (Art 16 EUCFR), protect his or her property rights (Art 17 EUCFR), and enjoy 'an effective remedy and fair trial' in domestic courts if the FTA does not permit 'this Agreement to be directly invoked in the domestic legal systems' (cf Art 30.6 CETA) inside the EU without any 'necessity' (in terms of Art 52 EUCFR) of such a restriction of fundamental rights and remedies. Insistence by foreign trading partners on maintaining their different legal and policy traditions (eg of providing for ICSID procedures for investment disputes in NAFTA countries) does not justify undermining more comprehensive fundamental rights inside the EU. Alleged judicial deficiencies in some EU states must be corrected and brought into conformity with EU law; they cannot justify undermining fundamental rights and rule of law inside the EU through FTAs and foreign arbitrators that risk ignoring EU constitutional law.

C. Transatlantic leadership for reforming international trade and investment law?

Prior to the election of US President Trump in 2016, American and European politicians described CETA, TTIP, TPP, and TiSA as Western initiatives of 'geopolitical importance' for setting new standards—through 'regime-shifting' and 'regulatory competition'—for multilateral trade, investment, environmental and labour law, and consumer protection. Since 2017, however, the new Trump government prioritizes bilateral over multilateral trade agreements and refused to ratify the TPP Agreement; even though TTIP is essentially a bilateral EU–USA agreement, the US position on whether to finalize the TTIP remained unclear by April 2017. The more than fifty WTO members participating in these and other mega-regional FTAs—like the RCEP between the ten Association of Southeast Asian Nations countries and six countries with whom ASEAN has a FTA (Australia, China, India, Japan, South Korea, and New Zealand)—make up almost 80 per cent of global

[29] cf Deutscher Richterbund, 'Stellungnahme zur Errichtung eines Investitionsgerichts für TTIP', <http://www.drb.de/fileadmin/docs/Stellungnahmen/2016/DRB_160201_Stn_Nr_04_Europaeisches_Investitionsgericht.pdf> accessed 31 March 2017.

GDP and world trade. If the WTO continues to fail to realize its treaty objectives, a merger of these FTAs could be used as a blueprint for creating a new 'WTO 2020' in order to reform the 'Westphalian principles' impeding the WTO 1994 (like veto powers preventing consensus-based trade regulation). The preceding analyses suggest, however, that also CETA and TTIP—in spite of their 'issue-linkages' going far beyond WTO law—remain driven by 'power-oriented regulatory paradigms' (such as 'negative discrimination' and 'disempowerment' of domestic citizens, legal and judicial privileges for foreign investors, disregard for fundamental rights and judicial remedies, and inadequate democratic accountability) that are rightly criticized and resisted by civil societies.

Evaluations of CETA and TTIP may differ from the different 'constitutional perspectives' of NAFTA countries. In Canada, for instance, most of the thirty-one NAFTA investor-state arbitration complaints against Canada might have received lesser legal and judicial protection (eg due to the constitutional protection of 'parliamentary sovereignty' and the lack of constitutional guarantees of investor rights) if they had been decided in Canadian courts;[30] as Canadian courts construe Canadian constitutional law as protecting provincial powers to retain trade barriers fragmenting the internal market inside Canada, CETA's trade and investment rules could contribute to reforming trade and investment law and judicial remedies in Canada. In the EU, by contrast, CETA and TTIP risk undermining fundamental rights (like Arts 7, 8, 16, 17, and 47 EUCFR) and non-discriminatory treatment of EU citizens; for instance, even though the 2016 CETA text 'reaffirms' and 'recognizes' human rights in two Preamble paragraphs, it makes no effort at complying with the individual 'freedom to conduct a business in accordance with Union law' (Art 16 EUCFR) by providing 'an effective remedy before a tribunal' (Art 47 EUCFR) enabling citizens to challenge violations of CETA rules in domestic courts or CETA investment tribunals (whose 'applicable law' is limited to international law without EU law, cf Art 8.31 CETA). Human rights require that 'everyone shall be subject only to such limitations as are determined by law solely for the purpose of securing due recognition and respect for the rights and freedoms of others and of meeting the just requirements of morality, public order and the general welfare in a democratic society' (Art 29 UDHR, similarly Art 52 EUCFR). The EU's 'cosmopolitan foreign policy constitution' could be implemented more effectively if FTAs among democracies would protect legal and judicial remedies of citizens to hold EU institutions legally, democratically, and judicially more accountable for violations of FTAs. TiSA, likewise, seems to prioritize rights of governments over rights of citizens without protection of cosmopolitan rights in international services trade. As the intergovernmental 'disempowerment' of citizens is neither 'necessary' (eg in terms of Art 52 EUCFR) nor in conformity with the 'legal consistency'

[30] cf Armand de Mestral, 'Investor-State Arbitration between Developed Democratic Countries' (2015) 1 *Investor-State Arbitration Series* (September 2015), <https://www.cigionline.org/sites/default/files/isa_paper_series_no.1.pdf> accessed 31 March 2017.

requirements of Art 21 TEU, citizens have good reasons to insist that EU diplomats comply with their legal duties (eg in Art 3:5 TEU) to act as 'protectors of citizens' by protecting fundamental rights coherently in internal and external market regulations; limitations of fundamental rights and judicial remedies and 'negative discrimination' of EU citizens are not 'necessary' (eg in terms of Art 52 EUCFR).

The broad definition of the 'applicable law' in Art 42 of the World Bank Convention on the Settlement of Investment Disputes between States and Nationals of other States illustrates that investor-state arbitration involves all three dimensions of international investment law, ie national laws, investor-state contracts, and international law rules applicable in the relations among the home and host states involved.[31] The EU proposals for new FTA investment rules 're-fragment' these complex interactions among the interdependent 'three levels of investment regulation' and related adjudication; this risks harming investors, other citizens and rule of law (including national law, EU law, and international treaty obligations of the EU), for instance if EU investors cannot invoke FTA guarantees in domestic courts and foreign investors cannot invoke their fundamental rights (eg under the EUCFR) in investment courts. Again, EU law does not authorize trade negotiators to use FTAs to curtail national and European constitutional law and judicial remedies of citizens in order to limit the judicial accountability of EU institutions (eg on grounds of 'reciprocity' in international trade).

The CETA provisions on the 'right to regulate' and on 'exceptions' do not secure that national and EU trade and investment measures remain consistent with EU law (eg fundamental rights). Nor does CETA secure that legally binding rulings of CETA's investment tribunal do not adversely affect EU law (eg the autonomy of EU law and domestic implementation of FTAs as an 'integral part' of EU law);[32] even though CETA will improve *arbitration procedures* and the *composition* of investment tribunals, CETA's often vague investment rules may run counter to higher, procedural, and substantive standards of EU law (cf Arts 47 and 52 EUCFR) and of the ECHR (cf Arts 6:1 and 13 ECHR). Rather than providing for legal and 'judicial privileges' for foreign investors that discriminate against domestic investors and citizens inside the EU and risk circumventing EU constitutional law, Arts 3 and 21 TEU and the EUCFR require EU trade negotiators to protect the fundamental rights of *all EU citizens* through—comparatively more effective and constitutionally more constrained—domestic and EU judicial remedies. Even if many WTO countries outside Europe continue to prioritize rights of governments over rights of citizens, it is to be regretted that the democratic EU and NAFTA countries do not use transatlantic FTAs as strategic opportunities for reforming international trade and investment law for the benefit of citizens and of their constitutional rights. Without such leadership, the cosmopolitan ideal of 'development as equal

[31] cf Jeswald W Salacuse, *The Three Laws of International Investment: National, Contractual, and International Frameworks for Foreign Capital* (Oxford University Press, 2013).

[32] CETA provides not only for the possibility of judicial awards of monetary damages, but also of restitution of property (cf Art 8.39), interim measures of protection (Art 8.34), and domestic enforcement of awards (Art 8.41).

freedoms' of citizens, the republican ideal of limiting arbitrary domination of citizens in the collective supply of PGs, and democratic self-government of citizens in their mutually beneficial, international cooperation risk remaining ineffective in the twenty-first century. Authoritarian 'disempowerment' of citizens by EU institutions also risks alienating citizens by undermining constitutional and democratic protection of PGs and 'public reason' inside the EU.

On 30 October 2016, the CETA was finally signed by the EU and Canada as a 'mixed agreement' (ie involving Canada, the EU, and all twenty-eight EU Member States) after the Belgian region of Wallonia had finally given up its opposition to authorizing the federal Belgian Government to sign the deal. This consent by the regional government of Wallonia had been conditional, inter alia, on the formal adoption of a legally binding 'Joint Interpretative Declaration on the CETA between Canada and the EU and its Member States', as well as on a commitment by the Belgian federal government to request the CJEU for a legal Opinion (pursuant to Art 218(11) TFEU) on the compatibility of CETA's 'investment court system' with EU law.[33] In a 'Namur Declaration' of 5 December 2016, a large number of academics and politicians justified the civil society challenges of the CETA by, inter alia, the need 'to ensure that European economic and trade agreement negotiations respect the civil society's legitimate demands for transparency and the democratic parliamentary control procedures' and 'guarantee public interests in the dispute resolution mechanism'.[34] In a competing Declaration of 25 January 2017 on 'Trading Together—For strong and democratically legitimized EU international agreements',[35] an even larger number of academics warned of the dangers of making EU Agreements covering principally issues falling within the EU's exclusive competence 'artificially mixed', thereby 'allowing a particular local interest to veto the interests of all other EU citizens even in areas where EU Member States have decided to act collectively'. Both Declarations criticized, inter alia, that: '(a)ll private stakeholders (not just foreign investors) should have access to effective surveillance mechanisms regarding the compliance of the signatories with their obligations under these international trade agreements'; and 'national and regional parliaments should engage more with the positions taken by their governments in the EU institutions'. Following the approval of CETA by the European Parliament on 15 February 2017, parts of CETA will be 'provisionally applied' by Canada and the EU in view of the fact that the approval of CETA by all national parliaments—and CETA's legal entry into force—risk requiring many additional years. Yet, the provisional application is limited to areas of exclusive EU competences and does not include CETA's investment court system, whose legal consistency with EU constitutional law (eg Arts 47, 52 EUCFR) remains contested.

[33] cf G Van der Loo, 'CETA's Signature: 38 Statements, a Joint Interpretative Instrument and an Uncertain Future', CEPS Commentary (31 October 2016), <http://www.ceps.eu> accessed 18 May 2017.

[34] For the Déclaration de Namur, see <http://www.declarationdenamur.eu> accessed 18 May 2017.

[35] For the Declaration on 'Trading Together', see <http://www.trading-together-declaration.org> accessed 18 May 2017.

PART II

SELECTED SECTORAL ISSUES

3

The Contents of CETA, TTIP, and TiSA

The (Envisaged) Trade Disciplines

Erich Vranes

I. Introduction

Few, if any, international agreements negotiated by the EU and its Member States have aroused public and academic interest to such an extent as three current treaty projects:[1] the Comprehensive Economic and Trade Agreement (CETA) between the EU and Canada; the Transatlantic Trade and Investment Partnership (TTIP) between the EU and the US; and the plurilateral Trade in Services Agreement (TiSA) presently being negotiated by the EU and twenty-two Member States of the World Trade Organization (WTO). While CETA and TTIP have attracted a great deal of this attention due to their rules on investment protection, most parts of both agreements are in fact devoted to trade. The negotiations on CETA had even started as negotiations on a pure trade agreement, and most of its forty-two chapters and protocols deal with trade issues. Likewise, despite an investment dimension,[2] TiSA is predominantly a trade agreement. Furthermore, all three initiatives are meant to constitute 'WTO-plus' agreements, ie comprehensive trade treaties that clearly go beyond the law of the WTO. Therefore, whereas most academic writings on CETA and TTIP so far have focused on the investment aspect of these agreements, the present chapter highlights the trade disciplines of these two treaty projects, taking into account the closely related trade rules in TiSA.

However, these mega-regional trade agreements of course not only deal with 'classic' trade issues such as tariffs and quotas; on the contrary, a great part of these treaties is devoted to 'measures behind the borders', ie domestic regulations which may have effects on trade (non-tariff barriers to trade). The fact that many disciplines in these agreements deal with such regulatory issues (under catchwords such as 'regulatory cooperation', 'regulatory coherence', and 'good regulatory practices') has also

[1] This chapter was written in 2016 and updated in October 2016. The author would like to thank Mag Martina Almhofer, LLM (WU) BSc (WU) and MMag Daniela Führer for their research assistance.

[2] cf below, section IV.

The Contents of CETA, TTIP, and TiSA: The (Envisaged) Trade Disciplines. Erich Vranes.

contributed to this public and academic attention. This chapter will also address these regulatory issues.

Whereas in the case of CETA, the negotiated treaty text has been available since September 2014,[3] at the time of writing TTIP and TiSA were still being negotiated. However, as regards TTIP, CETA is often seen as its blueprint. Furthermore, the EU has already officially published a series of textual proposals for, and background papers on, TTIP. As regards TiSA, the EU and other official sources, such as the Swiss Government, have made relevant information available.[4] Therefore, unlike in the case of other treaty projects, regarding TTIP and TiSA there is an unusually broad range of information available during the negotiation stage, which has already given rise to academic analysis.

Against this background, this chapter gives an overview of these three treaty projects. In view of their considerable regulatory extent (the CETA text alone accounting for 1,598 pages), this overview has to concentrate on the essential structures, contents, and core questions that have become visible so far. Given that the negotiated text of CETA is accessible, the focus will preponderantly be on CETA. TTIP and TiSA will be dealt with in a comparative, and comparatively shorter, manner.

Finally, whereas some trade-related aspects of these agreements will be addressed in other chapters of this volume, some special trade issues cannot be covered due to space restraints in this chapter.[5]

II. The Trade Disciplines Envisaged in CETA

A. General remarks

CETA is the outcome of negotiations between the EU and Canada that ended on 26 September 2014. The provisional CETA text was officially published in September 2014. Having undergone legal scrubbing, the finalized text was published in February 2016.[6] During this phase, there have also been modifications of its contents.[7] CETA now comprises forty-two chapters, annexes, appendices, protocols, declarations, and understandings.

On the one hand, CETA will create a free trade area between the EU and Canada, which is meant to be compatible with the WTO General Agreement on Tariffs and

[3] Consolidated CETA Text (published on 26 September 2014), <http://trade.ec.europa.eu/doclib/docs/2014/september/tradoc_152806.pdf> accessed 3 April 2017.

[4] cf below, section IV.

[5] Financial services, trade-related aspects of intellectual property, data protection, labour, the environment, and human rights, and transparency are addressed in Chapters 8, 6, 7, 9, and 10, respectively.

[6] Consolidated CETA Text (published on 29 February 2016), <http://trade.ec.europa.eu/doclib/docs/2016/february/tradoc_154329.pdf> accessed 3 April 2017 (hereafter draft CETA February 2016).

[7] A much-discussed modification concerns the introduction of an investment court system for investor-state disputes (see Chapter 4 in this volume). A less noticed, but highly important modification of the CETA text has clarified that decisions by the CETA Joint Committee shall be binding on the parties only subject to the completion of any necessary internal requirements and procedures (on this see below, section II.D.1).

Trade (GATT) and the WTO General Agreement on Trade in Services (GATS). In this regard, the CETA agreement cross-refers to the relevant provisions in the GATT and GATS, namely Art XXIV GATT and Art V GATS, which constitute the benchmarks that are relevant for determining whether a free trade area is in conformity with the GATT and GATS.[8] A main legal consequence of such conformity would be that the trade preferences applying within CETA need not be extended, on the basis of the GATT and GATS most-favoured nation (MFN) clauses, to other 'free-riding' WTO Members.

On the other hand, CETA can be characterized as a 'WTO-plus' agreement in three respects at least. First, as regards trade in goods and services, it comprises provisions that often can already be found in similar form in WTO law. These WTO disciplines are reconfirmed in principle[9] and incorporated into CETA in several central provisions.[10] Second, in many instances, such WTO disciplines are developed further, complemented, and rendered more precise.[11] Furthermore, CETA introduces new trade rules in areas not covered by the WTO so far.[12] Third, CETA also constitutes a 'WTO-plus' agreement in that it comprises a series of investment protection rules that clearly surpass existing WTO law, which contains few substantive rules on investor protection[13] and no investor-state dispute settlement mechanism.

CETA also aims to promote labour rights and environmental protection, and to preserve the parties' 'right to regulate' as well as their autonomy to achieve legitimate policy objectives, which are referred to in a non-exhaustive manner in the preamble, such as public health, safety, and the promotion and protection of cultural diversity.[14] Furthermore, CETA goes beyond WTO law, and most other forms of international economic integration, in that it provides for institutionalized mechanisms of 'regulatory cooperation' concerning future domestic regulatory initiatives that might affect bilateral trade.[15]

B. Trade in goods

Trade in goods is primarily covered in chs 2 to 7 in CETA. In addition, other chapters, such as those on trade and sustainable development, regulatory cooperation, and dispute settlement, are relevant for trade in goods as well.

[8] cf Art 1.4 in ch 1 ('General Definitions and Initial Provisions').

[9] cf, eg, the very first para of the preamble ('build[ing] on their respective rights and obligations under the Marrakesh Agreement Establishing the World Trade Organization …'); cf also initial provisions such as Art 1.5 in ch 1, where the parties 'affirm their rights and obligations with respect to each other under the WTO Agreement and other agreements to which the Parties are party'.

[10] cf, eg, the cardinal WTO provisions on national treatment and import and export restrictions for goods, which are incorporated into CETA in ch 2 (discussed below, in section II.B.1).

[11] Regarding trade in goods, cf the examples below, in section B.

[12] eg international maritime transport services in CETA ch 14.

[13] cf, eg, Christoph Herrmann, Wolfgang Weiss, and Christoph Ohler, *Welthandelsrecht* (2nd edn, Beck, 2007) 360ff.

[14] cf in particular paras 6, 10, and 11 of the preamble as well as chs 22 (Trade and Sustainable Development), 23 (Trade and Labour), and 24 (Trade and Environment).

[15] See below, section II.D.2.

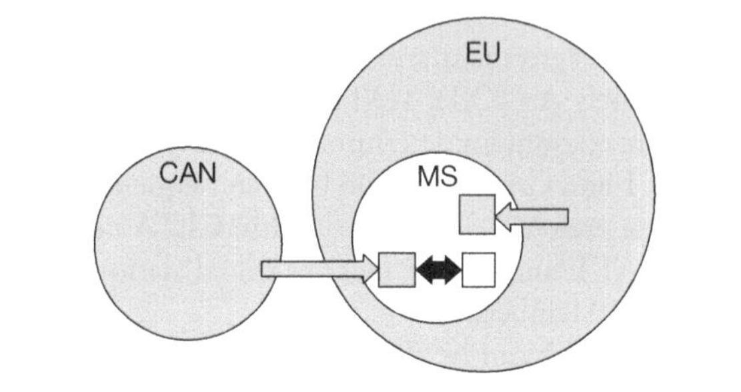

Fig. 3.1 CETA clarification on national treatment (goods)

1. Core principles

Chapter 2 lays down the fundamental principles of national treatment and market access for goods. The national treatment clause in CETA explicitly incorporates the national treatment clause of the WTO GATT Agreement, which has become a central building block in today's trade relations. Pursuant to CETA, each party 'shall accord national treatment to the goods of the other Party in accordance with Art III of the GATT 1994'.[16] Importantly, this CETA provision also clarifies the reach of the national treatment clause within the federal system of Canada and the EU: accordingly, the obligation to accord national treatment means:

> ... with respect to a measure taken by a government *in* Canada other than at the federal level or by a government *of or in a European Member State*, treatment no less favourable than that accorded by that government to like, directly competitive or substitutable goods ... of Canada or *the Member State* respectively.[17]

This implies that where an EU Member State, by virtue of EU Internal Market law, accords more favourable treatment to goods imported from another EU Member State than to domestic products, Canada could not request such more favourable treatment for its own products. It can merely require that treatment for Canadian products in a given EU Member State that is granted by that Member State to its own domestic products (see Figure 3.1). In other words, if there is a case of 'reverse discrimination' by a Member State against its own products as compared to products of other EU Member States (which is permissible in terms of EU law), it is merely this lower level of treatment that can be invoked by Canada.

A second cornerstone of WTO law—Art XI GATT, dealing with quantitative restrictions—is incorporated by reference into CETA as well: accordingly, import and export restrictions on goods are prohibited. Unfortunately, an issue of systemic importance is not very clearly regulated in this context. It is the question of how non-discrimination disciplines, such as, in particular, the requirement of national

[16] cf Art 2.3 (National Treatment) in ch 2 (National Treatment and Market Access for Goods).

[17] cf Art 2.3 para 2 (National Treatment) in ch 2 (National Treatment and Market Access for Goods) (emphases added).

treatment (which is usually understood as dealing with *qualitative* requirements for products) and the prohibition of restrictions on imports and exports (which is usually seen as dealing with *quantitative* restrictions), relate to each other.

This question concerns the issue as to whether a legal regime of economic integration such as CETA is to be understood merely as a non-discrimination regime or as a market access regime, which may be distinctly more intrusive for domestic regulatory autonomy. This question, which is one of the most important in the regulation of international trade,[18] is regulated, in the GATT, in the so-called *Note ad Article III*. Pursuant to it, if a national measure applies to an imported product and is enforced at the border, it must not be regarded as an import restriction, but needs to be scrutinized under the more lenient national treatment provision of the GATT, *if* like domestic products are subject to analogous domestic regulations. Hence, the GATT is to be understood primarily as a non-discrimination regime.[19]

As there is no such provision in CETA, as this *Note* in the GATT, it is important that a clause in the CETA 'Initial Provisions' Section stipulates that where CETA refers to or incorporates by reference other agreements, such references include related explanatory notes. Hence, as the CETA provisions relevant in this context explicitly incorporate Arts III and XI of the GATT, the *Note ad Article III* of the GATT must be read as having been *implicitly incorporated* into CETA. It follows that national measures establishing conditions for imported products ought not to be scrutinized under the CETA prohibition on import restrictions, but under the more lenient disciplines laid down in CETA's national treatment provision. In other words, this central CETA chapter on trade in goods is to be understood, like the GATT, as a non-discrimination regime.

A third cornerstone of ch 2 of CETA is its mechanism for reducing customs duties. Pursuant to it, tariffs on imports must be reduced or eliminated during a transitional period of up to eight years, which is subdivided into several product categories, some of which require tariffs to be eliminated on the date of entry into force of CETA, whereas others require a gradual removal of tariffs over four, six, or eight years, respectively.[20]

[18] Joseph H H Weiler, 'Epilogue: Towards a Common Law of International Trade' in Weiler (ed), *The EU, the WTO, and the NAFTA: Towards a Common Law of International Trade?* (Oxford University Press, 2000) 201, 205; Joost Pauwelyn, 'Rien ne Va Plus? Distinguishing Domestic Regulation from Market Access in GATT and GATS' (2005) 2(4) *World Trade Review* 131ff, <http://scholarship.law.duke.edu/cgi/viewcontent.cgi?article=1725&context=faculty_scholarship> accessed 3 April 2017 (hereafter Pauwelyn, 'Rien ne Va Plus?'); Erich Vranes, 'The WTO and Regulatory Freedom' (2010) 12(4) *JIEL* 953ff (hereafter Vranes, 'The WTO and Regulatory Freedom'); and Panagiotis Delimatsis, 'Don't Gamble with GATS—The Interaction between Articles VI, XVI, XVII and XVIII GATS in the Light of the *US-Gambling* Case' (2006) 40(6) *Journal of World Trade* 1059.

[19] cf Vranes, 'The WTO and Regulatory Freedom' (n 18) 953ff with further references; on the conceptual background; cf also Jan Wouters and Dominic Coppens, 'GATS and Domestic Regulation: Balancing the Right to Regulate and Trade Liberalization' in Alexander Kern and Mads Andenas (eds), *The World Trade Organization and Trade in Services* (Brill, 2008) 207, 209–10.

[20] cf Art 2.4 and Annex 2-A (Tariff Elimination) to ch 2 (National Treatment and Market Access for Goods).

2. Anti-dumping, safeguard measures, and subsidies

A very short ch 3 deals with anti-dumping and countervailing measures on the one hand and safeguarding measures on the other. With the exception of provisions on increased transparency and informal consultations in particular, this chapter essentially confines itself to reconfirming existing rights and obligations under WTO law and excludes any dispute settlement under CETA.[21]

A similar approach is taken in the chapter on subsidies, which reaffirms relevant rules of WTO law that are laid down in Art VI GATT, the WTO Agreement on Subsidies and Countervailing Measures, and the Agreement on Agriculture.[22] It sets forth additional provisions on transparency and consultations, which go beyond WTO disciplines. However, dispute settlement proceedings under CETA are excluded for the main disciplines of this chapter.[23] An issue that is regarded as crucial by both Canada and several EU Member States,[24] namely the protection and promotion of cultural diversity, is addressed in Art 7.7: accordingly, for the EU, subsidies for audiovisual services and, for Canada, subsidies for cultural industries are exempted from the scope of CETA altogether.

3. Technical barriers to trade

Technical barriers to trade are regulated in ch 4, which has a broad scope of application, as it applies to any technical regulations, (voluntary) standards,[25] and conformity assessment procedures that 'may affect' trade.[26] This chapter, too, incorporates basic WTO provisions on technical barriers to trade, namely Arts 2 to 9 and Annexes 1 and 3 of the WTO Technical Barriers to Trade (TBT) Agreement.[27] It is noteworthy, however, that only Arts 3, 4, 7, 8, and 9 are subjected to the dispute settlement system of CETA, but not Art 2, which is the WTO TBT Agreement's central provision that sets out the principles of national and MFN treatment on the one hand, and the requirement that technical regulations must not create unnecessary obstacles to international trade, on the other.[28] Chapter 4 also refers to the controversial obligations of regulatory cooperation, which are laid down in the general chapter on regulatory cooperation.[29] In addition, it also sets forth special duties of cooperation of its own in order to enhance

[21] cf Arts 3.1 and 3.4 in ch 3 (Trade Remedies), respectively.

[22] Art 7.8 of ch 7 (Subsidies).

[23] ibid, Art 7.9.

[24] European Commission, 'TTIP and Culture' (16 July 2014), <http://trade.ec.europa.eu/doclib/docs/2014/july/tradoc_152670.pdf> accessed 21 March 2016.

[25] Standards are defined as any 'document approved by a recognised body, that provides, for common and repeated use, rules, guidelines or characteristics for product or related processes and production methods, with which compliance is not mandatory'—see Art 2 of Annex 1 to the WTO TBT Agreement (Agreement on Technical Barriers to Trade (15 April 1994)), <http://docsonline.wto.org> accessed 3 April 2017; relevant WTO TBT definitions are incorporated by reference into the CETA chapter on Technical Barriers to Trade through Art 1 of this chapter.

[26] Art 4.1 of ch 4 (Technical Barriers to Trade).

[27] ibid, Art 4.2.

[28] ibid, Art 4.2 para 3.

[29] To be discussed below, section II.D.2.

the recognition of the equivalence of foreign technical regulations: pursuant to them, a party may request the other party to recognize those of its own standards which it considers to be equivalent to those of the importing party. It is incumbent on the party making such a request to set out detailed reasons. If the other party does not agree, it must provide reasons for its decision.[30] Hence, under CETA, it is the *exporting* party that bears the initial burden of proving equivalence as a pre-condition of recognition in the importing party.

Furthermore, ch 4 contains additional provisions on conformity assessment, transparency, marking and labelling, and cooperation in the field of motor vehicle regulations, which go beyond WTO law. In particular, a protocol on the mutual acceptance of the results of conformity assessment deals not only with the recognition of conformity assessment results, but also with the recognition of conformity assessment bodies that are established in the other CETA party.[31]

4. *Sanitary and phytosanitary measures*

Similarly to ch 4, ch 5 on sanitary and phytosanitary measures (SPS) on the one hand affirms the rights and obligations of the CETA parties under the corresponding WTO SPS Agreement[32] and, on the other, goes well beyond WTO law. Like the WTO SPS Agreement, CETA's SPS chapter is meant to protect human, animal, and plant life or health while ensuring that SPS measures do not create unjustified barriers to trade.[33]

However, CETA's SPS disciplines reach beyond WTO law in particular through the introduction of specific rules on adaptation to regional conditions, and on equivalence and technical issues such as audits and consultations, which are regulated in Arts 5.5 to 5.12 and no less than ten annexes. As regards 'adaptation to regional conditions', CETA in particular establishes the concept of zoning, according to which import restrictions, which are motivated by outbreaks of specific diseases in the exporting country, should not affect all imports of a given type of product from the other party, when such diseases only have a small geographical range. Therefore, according to Art 5.5, the importing party shall in principle base its SPS measures regarding animals and animal products imported from the other party on 'zoning decisions' made by the *exporting* party, if they are based in particular on international standards. This applies without prejudice to the importing party's right to apply additional protective measures.[34] Furthermore, the importing party shall accept the SPS measure of the exporting party as equivalent to its own, if the latter party 'objectively demonstrates ... that its measure achieves the

[30] Art 4.4 para 2 of ch 4 (Technical Barriers to Trade).

[31] See the Protocol on the Mutual Acceptance of the Results of Conformity Assessment (695ff of CETA).

[32] Art 5.4 of ch 5 (Sanitary and Phytosanitary Measures).

[33] cf ibid, Art 5.2.

[34] cf ibid, Art 5.5 para 1 lit (d); further details are to be included in Annex 5-C to ch 5, if the parties agree on them in the future.

importing Party's appropriate level of protection'.[35] This to some extent constitutes an 'inverted principle of origin', as the burden of proving that the exporting party's measures are suitable for achieving the importing party's legitimate policy goal is borne by the exporting party.

5. *Further disciplines*

Chapter 6 on customs and trade facilitation is based on three leitmotifs: cooperation, necessity (least trade-restrictiveness), and the use of international standards. This means, first, that the parties agree to enhanced cooperation bilaterally and in international fora. Second, ch 6 confirms that export and transit requirements shall not be more burdensome or trade restrictive than necessary to achieve legitimate objectives. Third, the parties agree to base their import, export, and transit requirements on international instruments and standards.[36] These principles are regulated in more detail in the specific rules of ch 6, which lay down in particular requirements for transparency, simplification of customs procedures, risk management, the use of information technologies to expedite domestic procedures, advance rulings, and prompt review of administrative action.[37] As regards customs valuation, the corresponding special WTO Agreement[38] is confirmed and complemented by a duty of cooperation to reach a common approach to issues relating to customs valuation.[39]

A protocol on rules of origin and origin procedures and seven annexes lay down detailed provisions regarding rules of origin on more than 140 pages.[40] These rules go well beyond the rather rudimentary provisions in the WTO Rules of Origin Agreement, which, moreover, are not applicable to preferential trading regimes such as the free trade area envisaged by CETA.[41] The provisions in CETA are based on standard EU rules to a considerable extent. Regarding some areas, in which Canada would have faced problems meeting EU standards, a compromise in the form of less stringent derogations for certain quantities of imported Canadian products was found. Reciprocal derogations were granted by Canada to EU exports of textiles.[42]

C. Trade in services

1. *Introductory remarks*

Trade in services is of evident importance for Canada and the EU, given that their economies and external trade are dominated to a great extent by trade in services. As in the field of trade in goods, CETA builds upon and further

[35] ibid, Art 5.6. [36] See Art 6.1 of ch 6 (Customs and Trade Facilitation).
[37] ibid, Arts 6.2–6.13. [38] Agreement on the Implementation of Art VII GATT.
[39] Art 6.4 of ch 6 (Customs and Trade Facilitation).
[40] Protocol on rules of origin and origin procedures (549ff of CETA).
[41] See above, section II.A.
[42] See also European Commission, 'CETA—Summary of the Final Negotiating Results' (February 2016) 7, <http://trade.ec.europa.eu/doclib/docs/2014/december/tradoc_152982.pdf> accessed 3 April 2017.

develops WTO rules. However, while there are similarities in the regulatory approaches taken in the WTO GATS agreement and the CETA chapters dealing with trade in services, there are also a series of essential structural differences. These concern in particular the respective scopes of application, substantive disciplines, and country-specific commitments and exceptions.

2. Regulatory approach

The WTO GATS agreement defines four so-called modes of supplying services. According to this approach, a service is supplied

1. from the territory of one Member into the territory of any other Member (mode 1; 'cross-border trade in services' (CBTS));
2. in the territory of one Member to the service consumer of any other Member (mode 2; 'consumption abroad');
3. by a service supplier of one Member, through commercial presence in the territory of any other Member (mode 3; 'commercial presence'); and
4. by a service supplier of one Member, through presence of natural persons of a Member in the territory of any other Member (mode 4; 'presence of natural persons').[43]

It is characteristic for these GATS modes, first, that aspects of investment protection are addressed as an aspect of 'trade in services' within mode 3 ('commercial presence'). Second, whereas under mode 1 it is only the service that crosses the frontier, there is movement of persons under modes 2, 3, and 4.

By contrast, CETA takes a different approach and deals with investment protection and 'other' trade in services in separate chapters: whereas investment ('commercial presence' in the sense of the GATS) is regulated in ch 8, 'other' trade in services is treated in chs 9 to 16, in particular. Chapter 9 deals with CBTS, which is defined as the supply of a service

1. from the territory of a Party into the territory of the other Party (which corresponds to GATS mode 1); and
2. in the territory of a Party to the service consumer of the other Party (which corresponds to GATS mode 2).[44]

The temporary entry and stay of natural persons for business purposes is dealt with in ch 12. Chapters 11 to 16 address the mutual recognition of professional qualifications, domestic regulation, international maritime transport services, telecommunications networks and services, electronic commerce, and financial services,[45] respectively.

[43] cf Art I.2(c) General Agreement on Trade in Services (15 April 1994) LT/UR/A-1B/S/1, <http://docsonline.wto.org> accessed 3 April 2017 (hereafter GATS).

[44] Art 9.1 of ch 9 (Cross-Border Trade in Services).

[45] cf Chapter 8 in this volume.

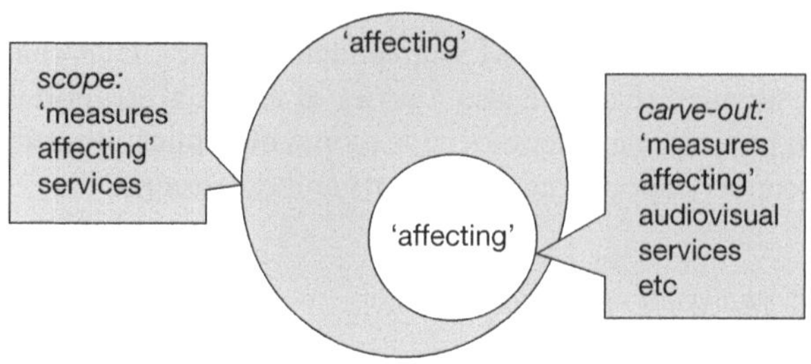

Fig. 3.2 Chapter 9: scope and carve-out

3. Cross-border trade in services

a) Scope of application

The central chapter dealing with trade in services is ch 9 (Cross-Border Trade in Services). Like the GATS, its scope is defined in a very comprehensive manner, as it is meant to apply to any measures '*affecting* cross-border trade in services'.[46] However, ch 9 also uses the pivotal term 'affecting' to establish exceptions from this chapter's scope, as this chapter is not intended to apply to measures 'affecting' services supplied in the exercise of governmental authority, audiovisual services (for the EU), cultural services (for Canada), financial services, air services, government procurement, and subsidies.[47]

This regulatory approach is bound to create a series of problems. First, it seems problematic to define both the scope of these disciplines and the exemption thereof by using the concept of 'affecting' trade in services (see Figure 3.2). This can be illustrated by the example of audiovisual services. Regarding such services, it seems undue to exempt any measures 'affecting' audiovisual services from the scope of the CETA disciplines on CBTS in ch 9: this approach would seem to imply that even measures that are meant to regulate *other* services, and which would therefore fall under ch 9 in principle, would have to be regarded as being exempted from ch 9 as a whole if they inadvertently or incidentally also 'affect' audiovisual services. Analogous problems arise as regards the other exceptions mentioned above.[48]

Second, it has been submitted that the aforementioned carve-out for subsidies relating to services might be circumvented by a party which invokes disciplines under the CETA chapter on investment protection to challenge a subsidy arguing that the subsidy for domestic service suppliers amounts to 'indirect expropriation' of foreign investors or a violation of the 'fair and equitable treatment' standard. Similarly, it has been argued that private investors could rely on these standards under the investor-state dispute settlement system in ch 8.[49] In this regard, it

[46] Emphasis added. [47] cf Art 9.2 of ch 9 (Cross-Border Trade in Services).

[48] On the problem of using the concept of 'affecting trade' for delimiting the scopes of application of overlapping trade rules, cf Erich Vranes, 'The Overlap between GATT and GATS: A Methodological Maze' (2009) 36(3) *Legal Issues of Economic Integration* 215–38.

[49] cf Thomas Fritz, 'Analyse und Bewertung des EU-Kanada Freihandelsabkommens CETA' (2015) 20, <https://www.boeckler.de/pdf_fof/91420.pdf> accessed 21 March 2016 (hereafter Fritz, 'Analyse CETA').

should be noted, however, that a systematic-teleological interpretation might militate against circumventing the effect of the explicit exemption of subsidies for services from ch 9 by relying on the provisions of ch 8. Furthermore, the standards of indirect expropriation and fair and equitable treatment have been drafted in comparatively narrow terms in CETA ch 8.[50]

Third, two problematic issues arise as regards services supplied in the exercise of governmental authority, which, as indicated, are also meant to be exempted from the services disciplines of ch 9. Such governmental services are defined as any services that are 'supplied neither on a commercial basis, nor in competition with one or more service suppliers'.[51] In this regard, it remains unclear, on the one hand, when services such as educational or medical services, which are supplied by the state but for which the receiver pays a contribution, and which may be lower or higher, are to be regarded as not being supplied on a 'commercial basis'. On the other hand, as soon as any service which is offered by the state is also offered by a private competitor, the exemption would appear to lapse, as the governmental service could no longer be seen as not being 'supplied ... in competition with one or more service suppliers'.[52] Hence, the 'protective effect' of this exemption may be subject to coincidental developments in given services sectors.

Finally, it must be stressed that the scope of application of these services disciplines can be modified in country-specific schedules, which allow the parties to CETA to individually adapt their commitments in specific services sectors and subsectors.[53]

b) Substantive disciplines

The main substantive disciplines of ch 9 are laid down in Arts 9.3 to 9.6. Numerous interpretative issues arise in this context.

The national treatment clause (Art 9.3) requires the contracting parties to 'accord to service suppliers and services of the other Party treatment no less favourable than that it accords, *in like situations*, to its own service suppliers and services'.[54] The national treatment clause being a non-discrimination provision, the two main elements are the criteria of likeness and less favourable treatment.

Regarding the criterion of likeness, this CETA provision differs in a crucial aspect from the GATS model, given that the corresponding core provision in the GATS (Art XVII) does not rely on the concept of *like situations*, but on the concepts of *like*

[50] cf Annex 8-A (Expropriation) to ch 8 (Investment). See also Hans-Georg Dederer, 'Neujustierung der Balance von Investorenschutz und "right to regulate"', *Verfassungsblog/On Matters Constitutional* (2014), <http://thomas-fritz.org/studien/Analyse-und-Bewertung-des-EU-Kanada-Freihandelsabkommens+CETA> accessed 15 May 2017 (hereafter Dederer, 'Balance von Investorenschutz').

[51] Art 9.1 of ch 9 (Cross-Border Trade in Services).

[52] This is also pointed out by Fritz, 'Analyse CETA' (n 48) 18ff; on the analogous problem in the GATS, see Markus Krajewski, *National Regulation and Trade Liberalization in Services* (Kluwer, 2003) (hereafter Krajewski, 'National Regulation'); and Marcus Klamert, *Services Liberalization in the EU and WTO: Concepts, Standards and Regulatory Approaches* (Cambridge University Press, 2014) (hereafter Klamert, *Services Liberalization in the EU and WTO*).

[53] cf below, section c). [54] Emphasis added.

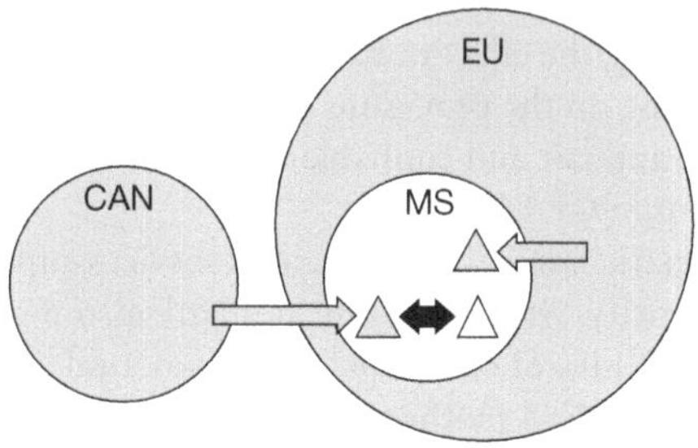

Fig. 3.3 CETA clarification on national treatment (services)

services and *like service suppliers*. The CETA approach may prima facie help to avoid crucial problems that have arisen under these GATS criteria in WTO jurisprudence, where like suppliers were merely defined as suppliers of like services, which has resulted in a scope of the concept of like suppliers that has been criticized as being overly encompassing.[55] The CETA approach, however, remains problematic to the extent that the dispute settlement organs of CETA are obligated to take into account interpretations of corresponding GATS provisions in reports of panels and the Appellate Body of the WTO,[56] as it is not evident how interpretations can be transferred from the GATS text to the diverging CETA text.

Regarding the second criterion of 'no less favourable treatment', the national treatment discipline is further concretized in several provisions. Thus, as under the CETA national treatment clause in the field of trade in goods,[57] it is made clear that in the case where a measure affecting services is taken by a government in Canada other than at the federal level or where a measure is taken by a 'government *of or in a European Member State*', it is the (discriminatory) treatment accorded by that government to its own service suppliers and services which is relevant.[58] Accordingly, there is no violation of the national treatment principle, if a central or regional government of an EU Member State accords more favourable treatment to services or service suppliers from another EU Member State, to the extent that such more favourable treatment is accorded pursuant to EU fundamental freedoms, such as EU free movement of persons and services, or is accorded by 'any other measure adopted pursuant to' the Treaty on the Functioning of the European Union (TFEU) (cf Figure 3.3).[59]

Furthermore, this chapter makes it clear that formal requirements—such as the requirement to obtain a licence, registration, or language certification—do not

[55] cf Werner Zdouc, 'Dispute Settlement Practice Relating to the GATS' (1999) 1 *Journal of International Economic Law* 285; and Werner Zdouc, 'WTO Dispute Settlement Practice Relating to the General Agreement on Trade in Services' in Federico Ortino and Ernst-Ulrich Petersmann (eds), *The WTO Dispute Settlement System 1995–2003* (Kluwer, 2004) 381.

[56] See Art 29.17 of ch 29 (Dispute Settlement).

[57] cf above, section II.B.1.

[58] Art 9.3 para 2 of ch 9 (Cross-Border Trade in Services) (emphasis added).

[59] cf Annex 9-A (Understanding on National Treatment) to ch 9 (Cross-Border Trade in Services).

amount to less favourable treatment prohibited in terms of the national treatment clause, if such requirements are not applied 'in a manner which would constitute a means of arbitrary or unjustifiable discrimination'.[60] This clarification thus secures important policy space to domestic regulators, thereby considerably contributing to the much-debated 'right to regulate'.[61]

Chapter 9 also sets forth a requirement of MFN treatment. Just as the national treatment principle, the MFN clause is not based on the criteria of *like services* and *like suppliers*, but relies on the concept of *like situations*,[62] which mutatis mutandis raises the same problems as those just indicated under the CETA national treatment principle.

The third main substantive discipline, market access, is laid down in Art 9.6. It prohibits certain forms of quantitative restrictions, thereby clearly, but not completely, following the example of the corresponding principle of Art XVII GATS, which prohibits even further types of quantitative restrictions. Thus, the CETA market access provision prohibits limitations on:

1. 'the *number* of service suppliers, whether *in the form* of numerical quotas, monopolies, exclusive service suppliers or the requirements of an economic needs test';
2. 'the *total value* of service transactions or assets in the *form* of numerical quotas or the requirement of an economic needs test'; and
3. 'the *total number* of service operations or the *total quantity* of services output expressed in terms of designated *numerical units* in the *form* of quotas or the requirement of an economic needs test'.[63]

Crucially, the interplay between the market access clause, the national treatment principle, and the CETA chapter on domestic regulation is not explicitly regulated in CETA. As under the GATS, where the interrelationships between these disciplines are not expressly defined, this raises a series of issues going to the heart of the extent of national regulatory autonomy that is left for the contracting parties.[64] In this regard, the relationship between the national treatment and market access principles is of particular importance. If the market access clause were interpreted as prohibiting national regulatory measures that merely (incidentally) *affect* the market access of imported services, then the scope of the market access provision would be overly broad: it might then be read as prohibiting domestic regulatory measures that merely lay down *qualitative minimum* requirements (as opposed to *quantitative maximum* requirements) for the provision of services, even if they are not discriminatory in the sense of the national treatment clause.

[60] Art 9.4 of ch 9 (Cross-Border Trade in Services).

[61] On the right to regulate, cf Dederer, 'Balance von Investorenschutz' (n 50).

[62] Art 9.5 of ch 9 (Cross-Border Trade in Services).

[63] Emphases added.

[64] cf Pauwelyn, 'Rien ne Va Plus?' (n 18) 131ff; and Vranes, 'The WTO and Regulatory Freedom' (n 18) 953ff.

It is of fundamental importance for the reach of CETA, therefore, that its central market access provision for services is drafted in very narrow terms: as indicated, according to its wording, it does not apply to each and every measure *affecting* imported services, but merely to measures 'in the *form*' of numbers, numerical units etc. This clearly indicates that national regulatory measures, which merely (incidentally) *affect* market access, should *not* be seen as being per se *prohibited* under the market access clause. On the contrary, they ought to be examined under the more lenient national treatment and MFN clauses, which do not contain per se prohibitions, but under which national measures must be scrutinized for eventual discriminatory effects.

As regards the GATS, a similar reading of the corresponding provisions has been proposed in the literature.[65] However, in the first relevant case in WTO dispute settlement, the Appellate Body had taken the opposite approach,[66] which had been severely criticized.[67] As the dispute settlement fora under CETA are required to take into account WTO rulings, it will be interesting—and highly important for domestic regulatory autonomy (ie the 'right to regulate')—to see how CETA dispute settlement bodies will deal with this fundamental issue.

c) Scheduling in CETA

i) Background

Trade in services, and the regulation of it, touches upon a series of sensitive issues. First, in terms of services *sectors*, several areas, such as medical, media, educational services, etc, are politically delicate. Likewise, the modes of supplying services differ in their sensitivity: whereas cross-border supply of services will often be regarded as being unproblematic, the other aforementioned modes involve movement of persons and will therefore frequently be perceived as more problematical, when it comes to liberalizing international trade.

This is an experience that has also been made in trade liberalization efforts within the EU, where it has proven impossible, for example, to establish a uniform approach to trade in services under the EU Services Directive.[68] Likewise, the WTO GATS example has shown that it is necessary to take a considerably more flexible approach to trade in services than to trade in goods. In the GATS context, this has meant that it was necessary to allow WTO Members to vary their commitments under the GATS, on a country-specific basis, as regards the different services sectors and subsectors and as regards the modes of supplying services. This has been accomplished, in the GATS, through so-called schedules of country-specific

[65] ibid.

[66] WTO, Appellate Body Report, *United States: Measures Affecting the Cross-Border Supply of Gambling and Betting Services* (20 April 2005) WT/DS285/AB/R.

[67] cf Pauwelyn, 'Rien ne Va Plus?' (n 18) 131ff; and Vranes, 'The WTO and Regulatory Freedom' (n 18) 953ff.

[68] Directive 2006/123/EC of the European Parliament and of the Council of 12 December 2006 on services in the internal market [2006] OJ L 376, 36ff. For an analysis, cf Klamert, 'Services Liberalization in the EU and WTO' (n 52).

Box 3.1 GATS schedules

Scheduling in GATS	
MFN	negative
NT	positive
MA	positive

commitments, permitting WTO Members to inscribe exemptions from the GATS MFN clause ('negative scheduling') in country-specific lists and to schedule commitments, on a sector-by-sector basis, under the GATS national treatment (NT) and market access (MA) disciplines ('positive scheduling'; see Box 3.1).[69]

ii) The approach in CETA

CETA takes a scheduling approach as well, which, however, differs in important respects from the GATS. The CETA system consists of two types of annexes. Both annexes apply to the CETA chapter on CBTS discussed presently. However, they also apply to the CETA chapters on investment, financial services, and maritime transport services.

Annex I permits the contracting parties to inscribe reservations taken by a party with respect to *existing* measures that do not comply with:

1. the national treatment clauses in the chapters on investment, CBTS, or, for the EU, financial services;
2. the MFN clauses in the chapters on investment, CBTS, or, for the EU, financial services;
3. the market access clauses in the chapters on investment, CBTS, or, for the EU, financial services;
4. performance requirements (PR) in the chapter on investment;
5. requirements for senior management and boards of directors in the chapters on investment or financial services;
6. disciplines for the cross-border supply of financial services in the chapter on financial services;
7. obligations in the chapter on international maritime transport services (see Box 3.2).[70]

[69] Arts II, XVI, and XVII GATS, respectively. On this scheduling approach, cf Krajewski, *National Regulation* (n 52).

[70] cf Art 9.7 of ch 9 (Cross-Border Trade in Services) and para 1 of the Headnote to Annex I (728 of CETA).

Box 3.2 CETA Annex I

Annex I – existing measures: negative scheduling			
discipline	**chapters**		
NT	CBTS	fin. services (EU)	investment
MFN	CBTS	fin. services (EU)	investment
MA	CBTS	fin. services (EU)	investment
PR			investment
etc	...	...	...

plus:
- standstill
- ratchet

Under Annex I, CETA thus in principle takes a so-called 'negative scheduling' approach: this means that a contracting party must schedule measures that do not conform to the disciplines just mentioned. In other words, if a party omits to inscribe a non-conforming measure into Annex I, it can be challenged by the other contracting party.

Moreover, under Annex I, a 'standstill effect' and a so-called 'ratchet clause' apply. This means on the one hand that upon entry into force of Annex I, only those CETA-inconsistent domestic measures may be maintained that have been inscribed in Annex I (standstill). According to the ratchet clause, on the other hand, an amendment to any national non-conforming measure must not 'decrease the conformity of the measure' with the national treatment, MFN treatment, and market access clauses in ch 9. It is submitted, however, that it will prove difficult to assess, in many instances, whether an amended measure is 'less' in conformity with these CETA clauses, as there is no clear yardstick for 'measuring' degrees of conformity. It might have been more adequate to focus on the concept of trade restrictiveness, ie on the question of whether an amendment is likely to increase negative trade effects, than on 'decreases of conformity'.[71] Overall, however, the effect of this ratchet clause is that a party's level of commitments that exists upon entry into force of CETA is guaranteed in the future, which considerably restricts the room for domestic regulatory action in the future.

Annex II serves to enable the contracting parties to set out the reservations taken by that party with regard to specific sectors, subsectors, or activities for which it may maintain existing, or adopt *new or more restrictive*, measures that do not conform with

[71] cf the experience in the jurisprudence on Art XX GATT (dealing with national measures not conforming with the GATT): initially, in determining whether a measure prima facie inconsistent with the GATT could be justified under Art XX, GATT dispute settlement panels inter alia inquired into whether the contracting party had used the measure which 'entails the least degree of inconsistency' with the GATT (cf the GATT panel report, *US—Section 337*, para 5.26). Later GATT rulings have focused on the least degree of trade restrictiveness, however. On this, see Erich Vranes, *Trade and the Environment* (Oxford University Press, 2009) 270 with further references (hereafter Vranes, *Trade and the Environment*).

Box 3.3 CETA Annex II

Annex II—new or more restrictive measures: negative scheduling ('policy space')			
discipline	**chapters**		
NT	CBTS	fin services (EU)	investment
MFN	CBTS	fin services (EU)	investment
MA	CBTS	fin services (EU)	investment
PR			investment
etc	...	...	...

the obligations just enumerated under bullet points 1 to 7 above (see Box 3.3).[72] As Annex II thus deals with reservations for *future* measures in these sectors, this Annex, which is sometimes also called the *Policy Space* Annex,[73] is of pivotal importance for the scope of regulatory autonomy that is secured by the contracting parties.[74]

Reservations in Annexes I and II must set out the general sector, specific subsector, and type of reservation (eg reservation to the national treatment or market access obligations). As under the GATS, CETA reservations can be based on international codes such as the UN Central Product Classification (CPC).[75] In reservations under Annex I, the national measure and its non-conforming aspects must be described.[76] In a reservation under Annex II, the scope of the sector, subsector, or activities covered by the reservation for future measures must be described.[77]

iii) Example: reservations relating to water

This can be illustrated by the example of the EU reservation, inscribed in Annex II, regarding services relating to water.[78] This reservation takes the form shown in Box 3.4.

[72] Annex II (1192ff of CETA).

[73] cf, eg, Delimatsis and Sauvé, 'The Treatment of Services and Investment in the EU—Canada Comprehensive Economic and Trade Agreement (CETA)' (INTA Workshop, European Parliament Brussels, 9 December 2015) 4 (on file with the author).

[74] Verena Madner, Stefan Mayr, and Dragana Damjanovic, 'Die Auswirkungen des Comprehensive Economic and Trade Agreement (CETA)' (Arbeiterkammer Wien, 2015) 55ff, 67ff, <https://media.arbeiterkammer.at/wien/PDF/studien/Ceta_studie_2015.pdf> accessed 3 April 2017 (hereafter Madner et al, 'Auswirkungen CETA').

[75] Central Product Classification (CPC) numbers set out in the Statistical Office of the United Nations, 'Provisional Central Product Classification' (1991) Statistical Papers, Series M, No 77, <http://unstats.un.org/unsd/cr/registry/regcst.asp?cl=9&lg=1> accessed 3 April 2017.

[76] cf para 3 of the Headnote to Annex I (728 of CETA).

[77] cf para 3 of the Headnote to Annex II (1193 of CETA).

[78] cf Annex II, Schedule of the European Union (1297 of CETA).

Box 3.4 Reservation in Annex II

Sector:	Collection, purification and distribution of water
Sub-sector:	
Industry Classification:	ISIC rev. 3.1: 41
Type of Reservation:	Market Access National Treatment
Description:	Cross-Border Services and Investment The EU reserves the right to adopt or maintain any measures with respect to the provision of services relating to the collection, purification, and distribution of water to household, industrial, commercial, or other users, including the provision of drinking water, and water management

This entry concerns a reservation regarding future and existing measures. It is therefore inscribed in Annex II. The reservation relates to the sector of collection, purification, and distribution of water. 'ISIC rev. 3.1' means the UN International Standard Industrial Classification of all Economic Activities;[79] '41' refers to ISIC section E subsection 41, which comprises the collection, purification, and distribution of water. The heading 'Type of Reservation' refers to the obligations from which the reservation is taken, in this case the market access and national treatment obligations. The heading 'Description' makes it clear that the reservations apply to these types of obligation both under the chapters on CBTS and on investment. The description further clarifies that the reservation covers regulatory measures with regard to the provision of services relating to the collection, purification, and distribution of water to household and other users, etc.

Hence, this reservation does not apply to MFN treatment and certain standards encompassed in the CETA investment chapter. Likewise, it does not cover wastewater disposal. For the purpose of further illustration, it is important, therefore, that, for example, Germany has added a reservation on market access in Annex II, in which it reserves 'the right to maintain or adopt any measure prohibiting the cross-border provision of services and requiring establishment with regard to the supply of waste management services, other than advisory services. Germany reserves the right to adopt or maintain any measure relating to the designation, establishment, expansion, or operation of monopolies or exclusive suppliers providing waste management services'. As this reservation concerns market access, but does not relate to national treatment, etc, a service supplier, who has acquired market access in Germany, can thereafter invoke national treatment under CETA if it feels discriminated against.[80]

[79] International Standard Industrial Classification of all Economic Activities as set out in Statistical Office of the United Nations (2002) Statistical Papers, Series M, No 4, ISIC REV 3.1, <http://unstats.un.org/unsd/cr/registry/regcst.asp?Cl=17> accessed 3 April 2017.

[80] This example is discussed in Fritz, 'Analyse CETA' (n 48) 32–3.

Likewise, it has been submitted that it might be possible for supply companies established in Canada to invoke the obligation of fair and equitable treatment or the prohibition on indirect expropriation in the CETA investment chapter. As the German reservation is confined to monopolies and exclusive service suppliers, it might not apply to disposal companies, which are not exclusive suppliers of service.[81] Other problematic examples, which may contain unintended gaps, can arguably be found in the EU schedule.[82] Such gaps obviously risk inadvertently restricting future regulatory autonomy.

4. *Further obligations regarding trade in services*

Chapter 10 deals with the temporary entry and stay of natural persons for business purposes in order to facilitate trade in services and investment activities. This chapter's rules apply to measures of the contracting parties that regulate the entry and stay of key personnel, contractual services suppliers, independent professionals, and short-term business visitors. Chapter 10 does not apply to measures affecting natural persons seeking access to the employment market, nor to measures regarding citizenship, residence, or employment on a permanent basis. It sets out obligations of its own, but also incorporates, by reference, obligations laid down in the chapter on CBTS that were described above.[83] Several details are regulated in a series of annexes.

Chapters 11 to 16 also deal with trade in services. Chapter 11, in particular, establishes a framework for the negotiation of future agreements on the mutual recognition of professional qualifications. Chapter 12 applies to licensing requirements and procedures and qualification requirements and procedures that affect the cross-border supply of services, and the supply of services through commercial presence and by natural persons. It requires the parties to comply with standards of due process, to simplify and accelerate relevant procedures, and to preclude competent authorities from exercising their powers in an arbitrary manner. Chapters 13 to 16 are concerned with financial services, maritime transport services, telecommunications, and e-commerce.[84]

D. Related aspects, in particular institutional structure and regulatory cooperation

This section deals with the related chapters on administrative and institutional provisions on the one hand and regulatory cooperation on the other. CETA also contains chapters on trade and sustainable development, trade and labour, and trade and the environment. These are dealt with in separate contributions in

[81] See ibid, 33. [82] ibid, 29ff; and Madner et al, 'Auswirkungen CETA' (n 74) 64ff.

[83] cf, eg, Art 5 para 2 of ch 12.

[84] While the latter, as indicated, will not be dealt with in this contribution, financial services are examined in Chapter 8 in this volume.

this book.[85] The same holds for the government-to-government dispute settlement disciplines that apply to trade in goods and services.[86]

1. Institutional aspects

CETA's principal institutional provisions are set forth in a very short chapter on administrative and institutional provisions. Its main body, to be co-chaired by the Canadian Minister for International Trade and the EU's Commissioner for Trade, is the so-called 'CETA Joint Committee' that is responsible for all questions concerning the CETA agreement. Thus, it is empowered in particular to supervise and facilitate the implementation and application of the CETA and the work of all bodies established under the CETA, and to adopt interpretations that shall be binding for the government-to-government and investor-to-state dispute settlement tribunals.[87]

Furthermore, the CETA Joint Committee may agree on 'amendments as provided in this Agreement', adopt interpretations of CETA provisions which shall be binding on the CETA dispute settlement bodies, and take decisions 'in respect of all matters in the cases provided by the Agreement', which 'shall be binding for the Parties'.[88] Importantly, during the legal scrubbing phase, it has been explicitly added that the decisions made by the CETA Joint Committee shall be binding 'subject to the completion of any necessary *internal requirements and procedures*'.[89] This reference to domestic ratification settles an essential criticism, namely that it was unclear in the provisional September 2014 text of CETA[90] whether there actually was such a requirement.[91] It is evident that it would have been highly problematic in terms of democratic legitimation if decisions, for example, on amendments of CETA's schedules, could have been taken without the possibility of parliamentary ratification.

On the other hand, however, as regards the Joint Committee's power to take binding decisions 'in respect of all matters in the cases provided in [CETA]', it remains unclear whether this means merely that the Joint Committee can take decisions with binding effect, if a power to take a binding decision is *explicitly* laid down in a *specific* provision in CETA; or whether this means that the Committee can take binding decisions in any cases where provisions simply speak of decisions. It is evident that the second reading might grant very broad competences to the Joint Committee of CETA.[92]

Further committees are foreseen in several CETA chapters, such as the Joint Management Committee for Sanitary and Phytosanitary Measures and the Committee for Trade in Goods, which shall also be competent for technical

[85] cf Chapter 9 in this volume.

[86] cf Chapter 5 in this volume.

[87] cf Art 26.1 of ch 26 (Administrative and Institutional Provisions).

[88] cf ibid, Arts 26.1 and 26.3.

[89] ibid, Art 26.3 para 2 (emphasis added).

[90] On this text, cf above, section II.A.

[91] See Peter-Tobias Stoll, Till Patrik Holterhus, and Henner Gött, 'Die geplante Regulierungszusammenarbeit zwischen der Europäischen Union und Kanada sowie den USA nach den Entwürfen von CETA und TTIP' (2015) 9ff, <https://media.arbeiterkammer.at/wien/PDF/studien/Regulierungszusammenarbeit_ttip_ceta.pdf> accessed 3 April 2017 (hereafter Stoll et al, 'Regulierungszusammenarbeit EU, Kanada und USA').

[92] See ibid.

barriers to trade.[93] Additional specialized committees can be established by the Joint Committee, which can also delegate responsibilities to such specialized committees.[94]

2. *Regulatory cooperation*

During the negotiations on CETA and TTIP, there have been intense public debates on the disciplines on 'regulatory cooperation' in both agreements. In this context, regulatory cooperation means bilateral cooperation, between the parties, on regulatory projects to be undertaken in the future.[95] In CETA, relevant provisions can be found in a general chapter entitled 'Regulatory Cooperation',[96] as well as in special provisions in the chapters on sanitary and phytosanitary measures, TBT, services, mutual recognition of professional qualifications,[97] financial services,[98] and sustainable development.[99] Such cooperation inter alia pursues the objectives of contributing to the protection of human life, health or safety, and the environment, as well as of contributing to the base of information for managing risks, for reducing unnecessary differences in regulation, and administrative requirements.[100]

The need to include rules on international regulatory cooperation into trade agreements stems from the rapidly changing nature of today's trade policy agenda, in which domestic regulations (measures 'behind the border') have become greater impediments to international trade than tariffs, which have been reduced to very low levels in particular by industrialized countries during GATT tariff rounds in the past decades.[101] Despite many efforts dating back to the 1970s, the EU, the US, and Canada have not so far been able to establish sufficiently effective bilateral regulatory cooperation.[102] As the WTO has not proved to be an effective forum for negotiating regulatory issues (due to insufficient trust among its more than 160 Members and due to the difficulty of measuring and predicting the effects of international disciplines on regulatory cooperation[103]), and given that economic gains from trade agreements among industrialized countries are largely expected to flow from regulatory cooperation on such non-tariff barriers, Canada and the EU have devoted large parts of CETA to regulatory issues.

[93] cf Art 5.14 of ch 5 (Sanitary and Phytosanitary Measures) and Art 4.7 of ch 4 (Technical Barriers to Trade).

[94] cf Art 26.2 of ch 26 (Administrative and Institutional Provisions).

[95] On this and the following, see also Stoll et al, 'Regulierungszusammenarbeit EU, Kanada und USA' (n 91) 9ff.

[96] Ch 21 (Regulatory Cooperation).

[97] On these chapters, see above, section II.B.

[98] On this, see Chapter 8 in this volume.

[99] On this, see Chapter 9 in this volume.

[100] Art 21.3 of ch 21 (Regulatory Cooperation).

[101] cf Bernard Hoekman, 'Multilateral Cooperation in a World of Preferential Trade Agreements' (2015) XXI(2) *Brown Journal of World Affairs* 131.

[102] cf, eg, Bernard Hoekman, 'Fostering Transatlantic Regulatory Cooperation and Gradual Multilateralization' (2015) 18 *JIEL* 611ff (hereafter Hoekman, 'Fostering'); Alberto Alemanno, 'The Regulatory Cooperation Chapter' (2016) 18 *JIEL* 625ff (hereafter Alemanno, 'Regulatory Cooperation'); and Gregory Shaffer, 'Alternatives for Regulatory Governance under TTIP' (2016) 22(3) *Columbia Journal of European Law* 403ff (hereafter Shaffer, 'Alternatives').

[103] cf Patrick Messerlin, 'Negotiating Mega-Regional Agreements: Lessons from the EU' (2014) EUI Working Paper RSCAS 2014/112, 1, <http://cadmus.eui.eu/bitstream/handle/1814/33776/RSCAS_2014_112.pdf?sequence=1> accessed 3 April 2017.

However, effective regulatory cooperation requires going beyond binding treaties. As regulation is often highly technical and dynamic, involving many actors with different degrees of autonomy and decentralization, mutual trust among the parties and these actors is indispensable. This implies, for example, that regulatory agencies must adjust their regimes together and that there must be sufficient incentives for them to cooperate. Likewise, there has to be sufficient (high-level) political leadership and stakeholder involvement, and it is necessary for trade agreements establishing regulatory cooperation to be designed as living instruments endowed with adequate institutions.[104] In any case, regulatory cooperation is a long-term project whose benefits depend on sustained cooperation in the long run.[105]

According to CETA's general chapter on regulatory cooperation, such cooperation appears to be possible in any fields that might affect trade in goods and services.[106] This general chapter stresses that such regulatory cooperation activities may be undertaken 'on a *voluntary* basis';[107] consequently, 'neither Party is obliged' to take part in, and may withdraw from, such activities. If a party refuses cooperation, 'it should be prepared to explain the reasons for its decision'.[108] Furthermore, the regulatory cooperation activities in this general chapter are subject to an 'endeavours clause': accordingly, the parties are to endeavour to fulfil the aforementioned objectives through activities that may include, for example, bilateral discussions, exchanges of experiences, and sharing proposed regulations as early as possible so that comments and proposals for amendments may be taken into account.[109] This CETA chapter also establishes a 'Regulatory Cooperation Forum', which inter alia has the functions of serving as a discussion forum, reviewing regulatory initiatives, and encouraging cooperation activities.[110]

In the light of these rather weak disciplines, the question arises as to why the related CETA negotiations have occasioned such fierce debates in the public and, to some extent, in the academia. On the one hand, this general chapter on cooperation indeed provides a framework for voluntary activities only. On the other hand, however, it seems that it is feared by some that such a framework may also 'institutionalize' pathways for, and increase, political or lobbyist pressures. Furthermore, while such regulatory cooperation may be voluntary legally speaking, it would seem to potentially cover any fields and measures that might indirectly and potentially affect trade. Moreover, it should be taken into account that more concrete obligations of cooperation could be inferred from more specific provisions in the special chapters just mentioned.[111]

[104] cf, eg, Hoekman, 'Fostering' (n 102) 613.

[105] Richard W Parker, 'Four Challenges for TTIP Regulatory Cooperation' (2015) 22(1) *Col J Eur L* 3ff.

[106] cf Art 21.1 of ch 21 (Regulatory Cooperation), which refers to the national regulatory measures covered by it in a non-exhaustive manner ('This chapter applies to the development, review and methodological aspects of regulatory measures … that are covered by, inter alia …').

[107] Emphasis added.

[108] Art 21.2 para 6 of ch 21 (Regulatory Cooperation).

[109] Art 21.4 of ch 21 (Regulatory Cooperation).

[110] cf ibid, Art 21.6.

[111] See also Stoll et al, 'Regulierungszusammenarbeit EU, Kanada und USA' (n 91) 6–7.

Hence, the future reach and effects of the mechanism of regulatory cooperation are difficult to predict. In the case of the EU, these problems are compounded by the fact that these issues would seem to come within the competence of the EU to a considerable extent at least,[112] that the EU and its Member States would probably be represented by the EU Commission, and that relevant CETA bodies would be presided over by members or officials of the EU Commission. According to EU primary law, however, the influence of the EU Council, EU Member States, and the EU Parliament would be rather restricted.[113]

3. *General exceptions*

Chapter 28 returns to key questions of substantive law in that it lays down general exceptions from several CETA chapters. Regarding trade in goods, the general exceptions clause of the GATT (Art XX), a cornerstone of WTO law, is incorporated into CETA and made applicable, in particular, to the chapters on national treatment and market access for goods, rules of origin, customs and trade facilitation, and sanitary and phytosanitary measures. The relevant CETA clause[114] sets forth additional clarifications that build upon relevant WTO dispute settlement rulings.[115]

With regard to trade in services, on the other hand, this CETA chapter does not explicitly incorporate the analogous general exceptions clause of the GATS (Art XIV), but lays down disciplines that are clearly inspired by the latter. Thus, as regards the CETA chapters on CBTS, telecommunications, and temporary entry and stay of natural persons, a party may take measures that are necessary for an exhaustive list of legitimate objectives, which includes, for example, public security, public morals, human, animal or plant life, or health and safety.[116]

Furthermore, as regards the EU, this chapter creates an additional exception for temporary safeguard measures with regard to capital movements and payments, when the latter risk causing serious difficulties for the operation of the EU Economic and Monetary Union (EMU). Such safeguard measures must be strictly

[112] On this, see Franz C Mayer, 'Stellt das geplante Freihandelsabkommen der EU mit Kanada (Comprehensive Economic and Trade Agreement, CETA) ein gemischtes Abkommen dar?' (expert opinion 28 August 2014) 24 et *passim*, <https://www.bmwi.de/BMWi/Redaktion/PDF/C-D/ceta-gutachten-einstufung-als-gemischtes-abkommen,property=pdf,bereich=bmwi2012,sprache=de,rwb=true.pdf> accessed 3 April 2017.

[113] cf Art 218 para 9 TFEU, according to which the Council shall adopt a decision establishing the positions to be adopted on the Union's behalf in a body set up by an agreement, when that body 'is called upon to adopt acts *having legal effects*, with the exception of acts supplementing or amending the institutional framework of the agreement' (emphasis added); on this see also Stoll et al, 'Regulierungszusammenarbeit EU, Kanada und USA' (n 91) 7ff et *passim*.

[114] Art 28.3 para 1 of ch 28 (Exceptions).

[115] Thus, it is clarified that, for the purposes of CETA, the measures referred to in Art XX(b) GATT include *environmental* measures necessary to protect human, animal, or plant life or health. Furthermore, CETA makes it clear that Art XX(g) GATT applies to measures for the conservation of living and non-living exhaustible natural resources. For an overview of relevant GATT/WTO rulings, see Vranes, *Trade and the Environment* (n 71) 256ff.

[116] Art 28.3 para 2 of ch 28 (Exceptions).

necessary for protecting the operation of the EMU and must not be maintained for a period exceeding six months.[117] These requirements match the corresponding ones laid down in EU law (Art 66 TFEU), but are now subjected under CETA to an *external* review by CETA dispute settlement bodies.

In addition, this CETA chapter includes exceptions permitting Canada and EU Member States that have not so far introduced the Euro to enact restrictions with regard to capital movements and payments in cases of serious balance-of-payment difficulties. Such restrictions must in particular be consistent with IMF rules. Moreover, the parties may restrict trade in goods and services to safeguard their balance-of-payments or external financial position. It is worth noting that in assessing the legality of such measures, the relevant yardsticks are the GATT and the GATS and not the corresponding CETA chapters.[118] Moreover, in this chapter, CETA sets out further exceptions allowing the parties to take actions necessary for protecting national security and detailed provisions regarding taxation.

As regards these fundamental exceptions that are highly relevant for determining the actual reach of the substantive disciplines of CETA, it must be recalled that these exceptions, too, have to be interpreted in line with relevant WTO dispute settlement rulings, as is underlined by CETA itself.[119] This fact—and the facts that CETA's general exception disciplines are clearly inspired by WTO law and that in assessing the legality of safeguard measures in balance-of-payments crises it is WTO law that is the relevant yardstick—once more confirms the high relevance of WTO law for the CETA agreement.

III. The Trade Disciplines Envisaged in TTIP

The TTIP agreement, which at the time of writing was being negotiated by the EU Commission and the US Trade Representative, is expected to comprise twenty-four chapters that would be grouped together in four parts:[120]

1. 'market access' (comprising chapters on trade in goods, trade in services, public procurement, and rules of origin);
2. 'regulatory cooperation' (dealing, for example, with regulatory coherence, technical barriers to trade, food safety and animal and plant health (SPS), medical devices, textiles, and vehicles);
3. 'rules' (including chapters on, for example, sustainable development, customs and trade facilitation, investment, and government-to-government dispute settlement); and
4. 'institutional provisions'.

[117] Art 28.4 of ch 28 (Exceptions).

[118] Art 28.5 of ch 28 (Exceptions).

[119] Art 29.17 of ch 29 (Dispute Settlement). On the dispute settlement system in CETA, cf Chapter 5 in this volume.

[120] See the introduction to TTIP by the EU Commission, <http://trade.ec.europa.eu/doclib/press/index.cfm?id=1230#market-access> accessed 3 April 2017.

For reasons of transparency,[121] the EU has published a series of negotiating texts, namely textual proposals on parts 2 and 3 of TTIP, as well as position papers that set out the EU's general approach on given topics in the negotiation process.[122] The documents published by the EU so far show that the EU Commission has indeed regarded CETA as a model for TTIP. Thus, a series of parallels are evident, which result from the fact that the EU, in its textual proposals for TTIP, has built on the concepts and structures of both CETA and WTO law. At the time of writing, the EU has in particular published textual proposals on trade in goods,[123] trade in services,[124] investment,[125] regulatory cooperation,[126] small and medium enterprises, competition, intellectual property, trade, and sustainable development,[127] as well as government-to-government dispute settlement.[128]

This section will analyse and compare the TTIP disciplines proposed by the EU with those of CETA that have been discussed above. Since these EU documents constitute proposals from which an eventual TTIP agreement may diverge, this section will deliberately be kept comparatively shorter.

A. Trade in goods

In the field of trade in goods, the EU Commission has—at the time of writing—released textual proposals on national treatment and market access, technical barriers to trade, sanitary and phytosanitary measures, customs and trade facilitation, and subsidies.

1. National treatment and market access

Similarly to CETA, the EU's proposal provides for a transitional period for further trade liberalization in conformity with Art XXIV GATT. Like CETA, it incorporates the GATT rules on national treatment, import and export restrictions, and general exceptions (Arts III, XI, and XX GATT, respectively). As regards customs duties, whereas duties on imports are to be reduced and subjected to a standstill obligation, duties and taxes on exports are prohibited per se.[129]

2. Technical barriers to trade

The EU's proposal for a TTIP chapter on technical barriers to trade (TBT) contains some clear parallels to the corresponding CETA chapter, but also some important

[121] On the issue of transparency in the negotiations on TTIP, CETA, and TiSA, cf Chapter 7 in this volume.

[122] These documents are available at <http://ec.europa.eu/trade/policy/in-focus/ttip/documents-and-events/index_en.htm#eu-position> accessed 3 April 2017.

[123] See below, section III.A.

[124] See below, section III.B.

[125] See Chapter 4 in this volume.

[126] See below, section III.C.

[127] See Chapter 9 in this volume.

[128] See Chapter 5 in this volume. As indicated in the introduction, intellectual property and competition are not covered in this chapter due to space constraints.

[129] cf EU Commission, 'Textual Proposal on National Treatment and Market Access for Goods' (made public on 21 March 2016), <http://trade.ec.europa.eu/doclib/docs/2016/march/tradoc_154369.pdf> accessed 3 April 2017.

deviations. Like the CETA chapter on TBT, the TTIP chapter envisaged by the EU is to apply to technical regulations, standards, and conformity assessment procedures 'that may *affect*' trade in goods.[130] By contrast with the CETA chapter, which incorporates a series of relevant provisions of the WTO TBT Agreement, the EU's textual proposal for TTIP would incorporate the WTO TBT Agreement in its entirety.[131] Both the CETA and TTIP chapters would contain an analogous general article on cooperation[132] and more specific provisions on closer cooperation relating to standardization and conformity assessment procedures.[133] However, unlike its CETA counterpart,[134] the EU proposal for TTIP does not contain rules on the recognition of foreign technical regulations. Moreover, unlike CETA, the textual proposal for TTIP does not aim to establish an institutional body for dealing with technical barriers to trade. However, it appears possible that the TTIP parties may avail themselves in this regard of the institutional structures of the proposed general TTIP chapter on Regulatory Cooperation.[135]

3. *Sanitary and phytosanitary measures*

The text proposed by the EU for sanitary and phytosanitary (SPS) measures under TTIP shows clear substantive and structural affinities to CETA. Like the CETA SPS chapter, the textual proposal for SPS disciplines in TTIP reaffirms the parties' rights under the WTO SPS Agreement and is governed by the guiding principle that SPS measures should not create unnecessary barriers to trade.[136] This implies in particular that SPS procedures are to be simplified and expedited. Furthermore, trade is to be facilitated by the requirements that each party apply its SPS import conditions to the entire territory of the other party and that products in conformity with these conditions can circulate freely on the basis of a single authorization.[137] Moreover, the importing party is obligated to recognize the zoning decisions of the exporting party,[138] that is, decisions regarding the health status with regard to animal diseases to be specified in an Annex to the SPS chapter, and decisions on pest-free areas, determined by the exporting party with regard to plants and plant products.[139] Furthermore, pursuant to the EU's textual

[130] Emphasis added.

[131] cf EU Commission, 'Textual Proposal on Technical Barriers to Trade' (made public on 7 January 2015) Art 2, <http://trade.ec.europa.eu/doclib/docs/2015/january/tradoc_153025.pdf> accessed 3 April 2017.

[132] cf EU Commission, 'Textual Proposal on TBT' (n 127) Art 3.

[133] cf ibid, Arts 6–7.

[134] cf above, section II.B.3.

[135] On this, cf below, section III.C.

[136] cf EU Commission, 'Textual Proposal on Sanitary and Phytosanitary Measures' (made public on 7 January 2015) Arts 1 and 2, <http://trade.ec.europa.eu/doclib/docs/2015/january/tradoc_153026.pdf> accessed 3 April 2017.

[137] EU Commission, 'Textual Proposal on Sanitary and Phytosanitary Measures' (n 132) Art 6.

[138] On this concept, see above, section II.B.4; see also EU Commission, 'TTIP and Regulation: An Overview' (10 February 2015) 12, <http://trade.ec.europa.eu/doclib/docs/2015/february/tradoc_153121.pdf> accessed 3 April 2017.

[139] EU Commission, 'Proposal on Sanitary and Phytosanitary Measures' (n 132) Art 10.

proposal, international standards on tolerances and maximum residue levels that were originally created as non-binding guidelines by the international Codex Alimentarius Commission[140] would be transformed into binding obligations, unless the importing party had signalled a reservation in the Codex Alimentarius Commission.[141]

The EU's SPS proposal also contains a series of requirements relating to the recognition of foreign standards. Thus, it is incumbent on the *exporting* party to ensure that the levels of protection of the importing party are met. The importing party may, however, require the exporting party to 'objectively demonstrate, to the satisfaction of the importing party', that the import requirements are met.[142] Furthermore, the parties are obligated to *recognize* each other's competent authorities as responsible to ensure that establishments, facilities, and products to be exported meet the SPS standards of the importing party.[143] Also, similarly to CETA, the SPS measures of the exporting party must be accepted as equivalent to its own by the importing party, if the exporting party 'objectively demonstrates' the suitability of its measures. However, the 'final determination' in this regard rests 'solely with the importing party'.[144] Finally, in order to protect human, animal, and plant health, the importing party may, 'on serious grounds', provisionally take necessary emergency measures.[145]

It should be noted that this clause is restricted to *provisional* measures and to the objective of protecting health, but does not cover other legitimate policy grounds. Hence, as there is no other general exceptions clause in the EU's textual proposal for SPS measures under TTIP, it will be of particular importance whether the TTIP treaty framework will comprise, like CETA,[146] a *horizontal general exceptions* clause applying to all or most TTIP chapters, including its SPS chapter.

4. *Customs and trade facilitation*

Similarly to the corresponding CETA chapter, the proposed TTIP chapter on customs and trade facilitation is inspired by the principles of necessity (least trade-restrictiveness) and the use of international standards. Accordingly, import and export formalities and other requirements are to be designed in particular to constitute the least trade-restrictive measure among possible alternatives. In the same vein, a series of provisions require the parties to expedite and simplify relevant procedures and to adopt risk management systems for border and customs controls. The parties' respective rules and procedures are to be based on international

[140] The Codex Alimentarius Commission is responsible for making proposals to the Food and Agriculture Organization and the World Health Organization on all matters pertaining to the implementation of the Joint FAO/WHO Food Standards Programme, the purpose of which is, in particular, to initiate and guide the development of food standards (cf Art 1 of the Statutes of the Codex Alimentarius Commission, <http://www.fao.org/fao-who-codexalimentarius/codex-home/en/> accessed 3 April 2017).

[141] EU Commission, 'Proposal on Sanitary and Phytosanitary Measures' (n 132) Art 7 para 7.

[142] ibid, Art 7 para 13. [143] ibid, Art 8. [144] ibid, Art 9. [145] ibid, Art 16.

[146] cf above, section II.D.3.

instruments and standards.[147] Unlike the corresponding CETA chapter, the EU's textual proposal for TTIP does not incorporate the respective special WTO agreement.[148] Furthermore, this TTIP chapter is less ambitious than CETA in an institutional perspective: whereas the CETA chapter on trade facilitation aims for enhanced bilateral cooperation,[149] this leitmotif is missing in the EU's textual proposal for TTIP.

5. *Subsidies*

The EU's proposals also comprise a chapter on subsidies. Subsidies are defined as under the WTO Agreement on Subsidies and Countervailing Measures. Unlike the latter and unlike the CETA chapter on subsidies, the EU's textual proposal covers subsidies granted to enterprises manufacturing goods or supplying *services*. Therefore, the scope of application of this textual proposal is considerably broader than its CETA counterpart. On the other hand, however, the intensity of its obligations is equally weak, as it is proposed that subsidies will not be subjected to dispute settlement, but merely to consultations, which, at most, require a TTIP party to use its *best endeavours* to eliminate or minimize the adverse trade effects of given subsidy.[150]

B. Trade in services

1. *Regulatory approach*

As indicated above, services and trade in services have become vital for the EU and US economies. As the US is the main importer of EU services and vice versa, the significance of TTIP disciplines on trade in services is self-evident. The rules for trade in services suggested by the EU Commission for TTIP are contained in a 2015 proposal covering trade in services, investment, and e-commerce. Similarly to the CETA approach to services, the EU proposal for TTIP in principle contains different chapters for investment on the one hand and trade in services on the other. Thus, the EU's proposal consists of a text laying down general provisions and definitions for investment and trade in services (ch I of the 2015 proposal), rules relating to investment (ch II), obligations relating to cross-border supply of services (ch III), the entry and temporary stay of natural persons for business purposes (ch IV), the regulatory framework (ch V), and exceptions (ch VII).[151] Three annexes further

147 cf EU Commission, 'Textual Proposal on Customs and Trade Facilitation' (made public on 7 January 2015) Arts 1ff, <http://trade.ec.europa.eu/doclib/docs/2015/january/tradoc_153027.pdf> accessed 3 April 2017.

148 Agreement on the Implementation of Art VII of the GATT, <https://www.wto.org/english/docs_e/legal_e/20-val.pdf> accessed 3 April 2017.

149 See above, section II.B.5.

150 EU Commission, 'Textual Proposal on Subsidies' (made public on 7 January 2015), in particular Arts X.1, X.4, and X.7, <http://trade.ec.europa.eu/doclib/docs/2015/january/tradoc_153031.pdf> accessed 3 April 2017.

151 Chs II and VI deal with investments and electronic commerce, respectively. The TTIP's investment obligations are analysed in Chapter 4 in this volume.

specify these obligations and reservations, sector by sector, for the contracting parties. Financial services are not covered by this EU proposal, as the EU has made a separate offer in this field.[152]

2. *Cross-border supply of services*

a) Scope of application

Like the CETA chapter on cross-border trade in services, the proposed TTIP chapter on cross-border supply of services has a broad scope of application, as it is meant to apply to any measures *affecting* the cross-border supply of services in all services sectors. It is important, in a political and practical perspective, that this TTIP chapter would not apply to subsidies. Likewise, state measures regulating audio-visual services, which are perceived as particularly sensitive by some EU Member States,[153] are to be exempted from the disciplines in this chapter. In contradistinction to CETA, the TTIP proposal does not try to establish this carve-out by using the CETA wording of 'measures *affecting* ... audio-visual services',[154] but by clarifying that the provisions of this TTIP chapter 'shall not apply to audio-visual services'. While this wording is imprecise,[155] it at least avoids the problems, discussed above, that stem from the questionable CETA technique of defining both rule and exception by twice relying on the concept of '*affecting* trade'.[156]

b) Substantive disciplines

The main substantive obligations are laid down in Arts 3-2 to 3-4 of ch III. According to the proposed national treatment obligation, each party 'shall accord to services and service suppliers of the other Party ... treatment no less favourable than the treatment it accords, *in like situations*, to its own services and service suppliers'.[157] Hence, with regard to this fundamental provision, the EU's TTIP proposal, like CETA, diverges from the GATS, which is based on equal treatment of *like services* and *like suppliers*, as opposed to the TTIP and CETA concept of *like situations*. Since the TTIP dispute settlement panels, just as CETA panels, would be required to take into account relevant interpretations in reports of the WTO

152 On trade in financial services, cf Chapter 8 in this volume.

153 cf, eg, Hans-Georg Dederer, 'TTIP und Kultur' (expert opinion 9 February 2015) with further references, <http://www.miz.org/dokumente/2015_Gutachten_TTIP_Kultur.pdf> accessed 3 April 2017; see also Jean-Paul Philippot, 'TTIP, Public Service Media and Cultural Diversity' (19 October 2015), <https://www.euractiv.com/section/languages-culture/opinion/ttip-public-service-media-and-cultural-diversity/> accessed 3 April 2017.

154 Emphasis added.

155 It is imprecise, as the drafters clearly did not want to exempt 'audio-visual services' from this chapter, but *state measures regulating* such services.

156 cf above, section II.C (emphasis added).

157 EU Commission, 'Textual Proposal on Trade in Services' (made public on 31 July 2015) Art 3-3 para 1 of ch III (Cross Border Supply of Services), <http://trade.ec.europa.eu/doclib/docs/2015/july/tradoc_153669.pdf> accessed 3 April 2017 (hereafter EU Commission, 'Proposal on Trade in Services') (emphasis added).

dispute settlement bodies,[158] making the national treatment obligations depend, in a central aspect, on a different key concept appears problematical.

These difficulties are compounded by the fact that the proposed TTIP provision, after the next paragraph, returns to a WTO GATS-type approach, when it goes on to state that 'formally identical or formally different treatment shall be considered to be less favourable if it modifies the conditions of competition in favour of services or service suppliers of the Party compared to *like services or service suppliers* of the other Party'.[159] Hence, two different approaches are used within the same central provision. The fact that the EU's proposal appears inconsistent in this essential aspect is underlined also by the fact that the very next fundamental provision in this principal chapter, the MFN clause, is then based on the 'like situations' concept again.[160]

The third cornerstone of the EU's textual proposal, ie its market access clause, is drafted like its CETA counterpart. In clear contrast to the latter, however, the market access clause proposed by the EU for TTIP would function on the basis of a *positive* scheduling approach,[161] which tends to leave more regulatory space for the domestic legislators. As in the case of CETA,[162] the fundamental question of the interplay between the obligations of national treatment, market access, and domestic regulation (ch V) remains unregulated in the EU's TTIP proposal. Hence, it remains unclear how intrusive this chapter's disciplines would actually be for domestic regulatory autonomy.[163]

c) Scheduling in TTIP

Similarly to the WTO GATS agreement and CETA, the EU's proposal for TTIP is based on a scheduling approach. Like in CETA, this scheduling approach would be applicable not only to the cross-border supply of services, but also to investment.[164] As in CETA and the GATS, the scheduling approach is to be based on annexes that are used for the purpose of establishing country-specific commitments and reservations on a sector-by-sector basis.

Regarding the national treatment and MFN treatment obligations described in the preceding section, a *negative scheduling* approach is proposed.[165] This means first that these basic obligations would merely not apply to those *existing* non-conforming measures that are set out, for the EU and national or regional governments of EU Member States, in a so-called Annex I (see Box 3.5). Furthermore,

158 See EU Commission, 'Textual Proposal: Dispute Settlement' (made public on 7 January 2015) Art 20, <http://trade.ec.europa.eu/doclib/docs/2015/january/tradoc_153032.pdf> accessed 3 April 2017.

159 EU Commission, 'Proposal on Trade in Services' (n 152) Art 3-3 para 3 of ch III (Cross Border Supply of Services) (emphasis added).

160 ibid, Art 3-4 of ch III.

161 cf the next section below.

162 cf above, section II.C.3.

163 On the related structural problem in the CETA and GATS, cf already above, section II.C.3.

164 On investment and scheduling, see Chapter 4 in this volume.

165 On scheduling, see already above, section II.C.3; see also EU Commission, 'Reading Guide: Publication of the EU Proposal on Services, Investment and E-commerce for the Transatlantic Trade and Investment Partnership' (31 July 2015), <http://trade.ec.europa.eu/doclib/press/index.cfm?id=1230&serie=866&langId=en> accessed 3 April 2017.

Box 3.5 TTIP Annex I

Annex I – existing measures: negative scheduling		
discipline	**chapters**	
NT	CBTS	investment
MFN	CBTS	investment
MA	CBTS	investment
PR		investment
etc	…	…

plus:
• ratchet

Box 3.6 TTIP Annex II

Annex II – new measures: negative scheduling		
discipline	**chapters**	
NT	CBTS	investment
MFN	CBTS	investment
MA	CBTS	investment
PR		investment
etc	…	…

policy space

reservations for public utilities and new services

measures existing on the level of a local government would be exempted from these disciplines,[166] which is important for many communal activities. Similarly to CETA, measures inscribed in Annex I or maintained at the local level are subject to a 'ratchet effect', pursuant to which amendments of such measures must not 'decrease the conformity of the measure' with the national and MFN treatment principles. Regarding this ambiguous concept of 'decreasing conformity', the same interpretative problems are bound to arise as under CETA.[167]

Second, the national and MFN treatment obligations do not apply to measures that a party adopts or maintains with regard to sectors or activities set out in the so-called Annex II (see Box 3.6).[168] The aforementioned ratchet mechanism does *not* apply under Annex II. Thus, similarly to the approach in CETA, this annex is meant to safeguard policy space that is essential for *future* national measures.

[166] cf EU Commission, 'Proposal on Trade in Services' (n 152) Art 3-5 of ch III (Cross Border Supply of Services) and Annex I (Reservations for Existing Measures).

[167] cf above, section II.C.3.

[168] EU Commission, 'Proposal on Trade in Services' (n 152) Art 3-5 para 2 of ch III (Cross Border Supply of Services).

In contradistinction to CETA, the TTIP proposal envisages a *positive scheduling* approach for market access commitments. This means that the market access obligation is meant to apply only to those sectors (or subsectors) that a TTIP party sets out in its Annex III. By contrast, any measures existing at the level of a *local* government are exempted per se from the market access obligation, but are subjected to a ratchet clause.[169]

In terms of EU political sensitivities, it is important that the EU proposes to protect public services and sectors such as public health, public education, social services, and services relating to water in the EU by inserting a 'public utilities reservation' in Annex III and other relevant reservations in Annex II.[170] Likewise, by scheduling yet another exception, the EU aims to secure room for manoeuvre as regards so-called 'new services' that may come into existence due to technological advances in the future.[171]

Regarding these critical policy spaces, it should be noted, however, that the EU proposes the establishment of a body, whose name would have to be defined in the eventual agreement, which would have the power to decide to amend these annexes.[172] It goes without saying that it would be exceedingly problematic if the sector-specific commitments and reservations in any sector, many of which are politically quite sensitive, could indeed be amended by a treaty organ alone.

3. Further obligations regarding trade in services

Similarly to CETA, the EU proposal contains further chapters on the entry and temporary stay of natural persons for business purposes, the 'regulatory framework' (dealing, like the GATS and CETA, with licensing requirements and procedures, qualification requirements and procedures that affect trade in services), mutual recognition of professional qualifications, international maritime services, electronic commerce, and financial services.[173] A concluding chapter contains a general exceptions clause that is modelled on the GATS and would permit the parties to adopt measures that are necessary to pursue legitimate policy objectives such as the protection of public security, human, animal, or plant life, or health. Further exceptions relating to balance-of-payment crises and security concerns are to be inserted in the course of the negotiations.[174]

C. Regulatory cooperation

As mentioned above, on the global level, there have been attempts to establish regulatory cooperation since the 1970s. The same holds true for the bilateral

[169] cf ibid, Art 3-5 para 3 of ch III.

[170] cf reservations 17, 18, and 20; see also EU Commission, 'Reading Guide' (31 July 2015) 2.

[171] cf reservation 26.

[172] EU Commission, 'Proposal on Trade in Services' (n 152) Art 3-6 of ch III (Cross Border Supply of Services).

[173] ibid, chs IV and V. As indicated above, while the former issues will not be dealt with in this contribution, the TTIP obligations relating to financial services are analysed in Chapter 8 in this volume.

[174] ibid, ch VII.

relationship between the US and the EU. With some sectoral exceptions, most of these efforts have been largely unsuccessful, however.[175] Nonetheless, as has been indicated, effective international cooperation on regulatory issues has the greatest potential for gains in the economic relations between industrialized countries. The joint aim of the EU and the US to institute a permanent framework for regulatory cooperation in TTIP must be seen against this background.

Yet, the economic benefits expected from such cooperation are only part of a far larger picture, as the US and the EU were said to pursue ambitious strategic and geo-political goals with this part of the TTIP project, in particular. Effective bilateral regulatory cooperation should restore US and EU primacy in the WTO and other international fora through setting de facto global standards, which other countries would have to accept in the future due to the economic weight of the EU and the US. Furthermore, standards developed by the US and the EU in the TTIP context might come to be used in international organizations and as a condition for development assistance. TTIP, and regulatory cooperation in TTIP, are therefore also seen as an attempt to meet the challenge of China and other emerging economies.[176]

The EU's TTIP approach to regulatory cooperation consists of five basic components, namely SPS-plus and TBT-plus dimensions (comprising improved dialogues, cooperation, and rules going beyond the WTO-SPS and WTO-TBT Agreements), sectoral annexes for specific goods and services, cross-cutting disciplines on regulatory coherence and transparency ('good regulatory practices'), and a bilateral framework including an institutional basis for future progress on regulatory cooperation.[177]

The last two elements are most noteworthy. While the framework for future progress is laid down in a first horizontal chapter on 'Regulatory Cooperation', the disciplines on regulatory coherence are defined in a second horizontal chapter on 'Good Regulatory Practices' in the EU's proposals.[178] Institutionally speaking, the EU proposed to create a 'Transatlantic Regulators' Forum' in July 2016.[179] Further obligations applying on a horizontal basis should be included in more specific chapters, such as, in particular, those on technical barriers to trade and sanitary and phytosanitary measures that were discussed above. On the other hand, there should also

[175] cf Hoekmann, 'Fostering' (n 102) 611ff; Alemanno, 'Regulatory Cooperation' (n 102) 625ff; and Shaffer, 'Alternatives' (n 102) 403.

[176] Reeve T Bull, Neysun A Mahboubi, Richard B Stewart, and Jonathan B Wiener, 'New Approaches to International Regulatory Cooperation: The Challenge of TTIP, TPP, and Mega-Regional Trade Agreements' (2015) 78(4) *Law and Contemporary Problems* 2–3, 8ff (hereafter Bull et al, 'New Approaches'); and Clayland Boyden Gray, 'Upgrading Existing Regulatory Mechanisms for Transatlantic Regulatory Cooperation' (2015) 78(4) *Law and Contemporary Problems* 31ff.

[177] See also Alemanno, 'Regulatory Cooperation' (n 102) 625ff.

[178] EU Commission, 'TTIP—EU Proposal for Chapter: Regulatory Cooperation' (made public on 21 March 2016), <http://trade.ec.europa.eu/doclib/docs/2015/april/tradoc_153403.pdf> accessed 3 April 2017; and EU Commission, 'TTIP—Proposal for Chapter: Good Regulatory Practices' (made public on 21 March 2016), <http://trade.ec.europa.eu/doclib/docs/2016/march/tradoc_154380.pdf> accessed 3 April 2017.

[179] EU Commission, 'EU Proposal for Institutional, General and Final Provisions' (made public on 14 July 2016), <http://trade.ec.europa.eu/doclib/docs/2016/july/tradoc_154802.pdf> accessed 3 April 2017.

be sectoral parts governing specific economic sectors; in this regard, at the time of writing, the EU had made proposals with regard to the sectors of chemicals, cosmetics, medical devices, motor vehicles, pharmaceuticals, and textiles.[180] The US and the EU were also working on the sectors of information and communications technology, engineering, and pesticides.[181] Taken together, these elements have been regarded as a new model of international regulatory cooperation comprising permanent regulatory cooperation through horizontal disciplines, which are complemented by a number of sectoral disciplines, and through a light institutional structure.[182]

The horizontal chapter on regulatory cooperation proposed by the EU Commission should enable EU and US regulators to cooperate when they develop new technical regulations or review existing ones that relate to both goods and services. It establishes a framework to accommodate regulatory exchanges, which are based on *voluntary* cooperation.[183] While the preamble of the proposed chapter affirms the right to regulate, this chapter's first article confirms that the parties are to pursue high levels of protection of non-economic goals such as the environment, consumers, health, and life, in particular. It is clarified, furthermore, that the framework for cooperation to be established in this chapter 'does not entail any obligation to achieve any particular regulatory outcome'. Moreover, services of general interest should be exempted from this chapter.[184]

The EU proposal requires the parties to periodically update each other on upcoming regulatory measures and to provide each other with opportunities for cooperation and information exchange at the earliest possible stage and to take account of regulatory approaches of the other party. Cooperation activities should promote regulatory compatibility through, inter alia, mutual recognition of equivalence or harmonization of regulatory measures and mutual recognition or reliance on each other's implementing tools to avoid unnecessary duplication of regulatory requirements.[185] The proposal emphasizes that none of the obligations set forth in this general chapter obliges a party to suspend or delay steps foreseen under its domestic regulatory procedures.[186] The disciplines of cooperation set out in this general chapter, due to their specific nature, would not be subjected to regular dispute settlement.[187]

In March 2016, the EU also published the aforementioned second horizontal chapter dealing with 'good regulatory practices', which requires the parties to foster good regulatory practices, including transparent planning, stakeholder

[180] For an introduction, see EU Commission, 'TTIP and Regulation: An Overview' (n 134) 12ff.

[181] cf World Trade Online, 'EU Wants Political Officials to Prod Bilateral Regulatory Cooperation' (25 February 2016), <http://insidetrade.com> accessed 3 March 2016.

[182] Alemanno, 'Regulatory Cooperation' (n 102) 629.

[183] cf EU Commission, 'Detailed Explanation on the EU proposal for a Chapter on Regulatory Cooperation' (6 May 2015) 6, <http://trade.ec.europa.eu/doclib/docs/2015/may/tradoc_153431.1.1%20Detail%20explanation%20of%20the%20EU%20proposal%20for%20a%20Chapter%20of%20reg%20coop.pdf> accessed 3 April 2017. On these elements, see also in the following text.

[184] EU Commission, 'TTIP—EU Proposal for Chapter: Regulatory Cooperation' (n 173) Art x.1.

[185] ibid, Arts x.4 and x.5. [186] ibid, Art x.1. [187] ibid, Art x.9.

consultation, impact assessments, and retrospective evaluations of regulatory acts; to make publicly available a description of regulatory processes; to provide early information on planned major regulatory acts; to offer any persons a reasonable opportunity for providing input on planned regulatory acts, to consider the contributions received, and to make publicly available any comments received; and to offer the opportunity for any persons to submit views on improvements on existing regulatory frameworks.[188] Furthermore, the parties affirm their intention to carry out regulatory impact assessments for planned regulatory acts that include an analysis of their impact on international trade or investment, and commit themselves also to promote periodic retrospective evaluations of regulatory frameworks.[189]

As regards the third element mentioned above, that is, the creation of an institutional mechanism, the EU intended to submit detailed provisions on the institutional set-up to support regulatory cooperation under TTIP after the round of negotiations in February 2016. According to the EU Commission, this body should not have the power to adopt legal acts.[190] In 2016, the EU also proposed to create a ministerial-level mechanism that would oversee the envisaged regulatory cooperation also to the extent it is carried out by independent regulators.[191] It was reported that the EU separated the proposal for such an oversight mechanism from earlier proposals on substantive disciplines, as it expected US resistance against such political oversight.[192] The 2016 proposal also aims to improve stakeholder involvement by suggesting that 'any natural or legal persons' can submit proposals for regulatory measures so that no class of stakeholders would be accorded privileged treatment.[193]

In sum, the proposed principles for cooperation go well beyond those to be found in particular in the WTO TBT and SPS agreements and the GATS. However, due to the features just mentioned, this form of cooperation, if compared with the EU in particular, is only lightly institutionalized. Its success would evidently depend on whether there would be sufficient stakeholder input and political will to cooperate on these issues. Past experiences have been sobering, as domestic regulators may not have had sufficient incentives for engaging in international regulatory cooperation and producers have not necessarily been interested in increased international competition resulting from regulatory cooperation. It has therefore

188 EU Commission, 'TTIP—Proposal: Good Regulatory Practices' (n 173) Art 3-7.

189 ibid, Art 8.

190 cf EU Commission, 'TTIP—EU Proposal for Chapter: Regulatory Cooperation' (n 173) Annex; see also EU Commission, 'Detailed Explanation on Regulatory Cooperation' (n 178) 12; and EU Commission, 'TTIP and Regulation: An Overview' (n 134) 9.

191 cf EU Commission, 'TTIP—EU Proposal for Chapter: Regulatory Cooperation' (n 173) Annex.

192 cf World Trade Online, 'EU Wants Political Officials to Prod Bilateral Regulatory Cooperation' (n 176); and World Trade Online, 'EU Will Hold Off on Tabling Second Regulatory Cooperation Text' (22 February 2016), <http://insidetrade.com> accessed 3 March 2016.

193 cf EU Commission, 'TTIP—EU Proposal for Chapter: Regulatory Cooperation' (n 173) Art x.5; see also World Trade Online, 'EU Wants Political Officials to Prod Bilateral Regulatory Cooperation' (n 176).

been suggested that agenda-setting must be better coordinated, and backed by high-level political leadership, in the future, in particular as regards retrospective regulatory cooperation, that is, cooperation that is meant to critically review existing domestic regulations.[194]

IV. The Trade Disciplines Envisaged in TiSA

A. Background

TiSA is a project of a plurilateral agreement that is to be based on the GATS. It is meant to advance the largely stalled multilateral negotiations of the Doha Development Round. When it was officially acknowledged at the 8th WTO Ministerial Conference in 2011 that there was an impasse in the negotiations, WTO Members were officially allowed to attempt to reach bi- or plurilateral agreements earlier.[195] Against this background, the EU and twenty-two other WTO Members started negotiations on TiSA in 2012.

Whereas CETA and TTIP can be regarded as 'WTO-plus' agreements, TiSA, being restricted to services, is meant to function as a 'GATS-plus' agreement. In addition, it is meant to build upon the more than 100 bilateral agreements on trade in services that have been notified to the WTO since its coming into existence in 1995.[196] For the EU, this initiative is not only important in general economic but also in strategic terms, given that only very few bilateral free trade agreements concluded by the EU contain chapters on trade in services.[197]

Like the GATS, TiSA would consist of a framework agreement and schedules of country-specific commitments and exceptions. It has been reported that the negotiating parties agreed in November 2013 that the draft text of the agreement was sufficiently elaborated for initial offers to be exchanged by the parties. While the US and Switzerland did so in November 2013 and January 2014, respectively, an exchange of revised offers was scheduled for May 2016.[198]

[194] cf Bull et al, 'New Approaches' (n 176) 21ff.

[195] cf WTO, Ministerial Conference, Eighth Session 2011, *Elements for Political Guidance* (1 December 2011) WT/MIN(11)/W/2; see also EU Commission, 'The Trade in Services Agreement', 1 ff, <http://trade.ec.europa.eu/doclib/docs/2016/september/tradoc_154971.doc.pdf> accessed 15 May 2017 (hereafter EU Commission, 'TiSA').

[196] cf the document entitled 'Media Release: Advancing Negotiations on Trade in Services', which is attributed to the participants of the TiSA negotiations and which can be found on the website of the Swiss Government, <http://www.seco.admin.ch> accessed 3 April 2017.

[197] EU Commission, 'TiSA' (n 190) 2.

[198] cf the official chronology provided by the Swiss Government, State Secretariat for Economic Affairs SECO, 'Chronology of the Negotiation Process' (updated 1 March 2016), <http://www.seco.admin.ch> accessed 3 April 2017; see also Inside US Trade, World Trade Online, 'USTR Trade Agenda Silent on TPP Next Steps; Seeks TTIP, TiSA Deals in 2016' (2 March 2016), <http://insidetrade.com/daily-news/ustr-trade-agenda-silent-tpp-next-steps-seeks-ttip-tisa-deals-2016> accessed 3 April 2017.

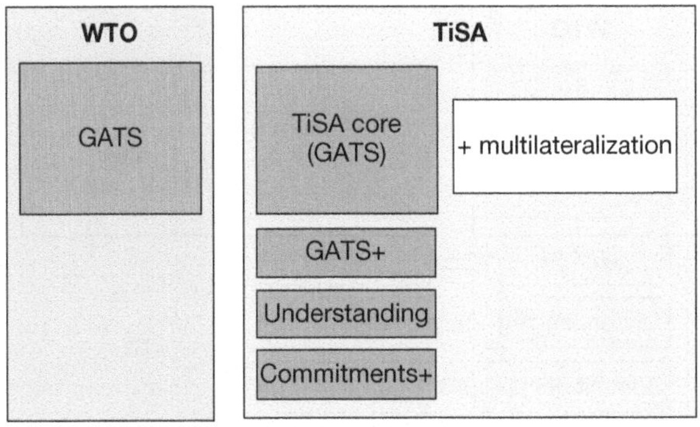

Fig. 3.4 TiSA regulatory approach (I)

B. Objectives and potential scope

The scope of TiSA should in principle be as comprehensive as that of the GATS;[199] as under the GATS, however, the TiSA parties would be able to modify their commitments in schedules annexed to the TiSA framework agreement ('scheduling approach'; see in the following text[200]). The TiSA project is flagged as a trade agreement, not as an investment agreement. However, just as the GATS, it has a clear investment dimension, in that it is expected to cover the supply of services through commercial presence (the so-called GATS 'mode 3'[201]).[202]

According to the EU Commission, the TiSA negotiations should legally bind the currently existing autonomous levels of liberalization, improve market access, and lead to new and enhanced disciplines for fields such as domestic regulation (eg authorization and licensing procedures), international maritime transport services, e-commerce, postal services, financial services, and temporary movement of natural services.[203]

C. Regulatory approach

A modular approach has been proposed for the treaty architecture of TiSA by the EU Commission (see Figure 3.4). This means that some GATS core articles—such as the principles of market access and national treatment—should be incorporated

[199] EU Commission, 'Memo: Negotiations for a Plurilateral Agreement on Trade in Services' (15 February 2013) 2, <http://trade.ec.europa.eu/doclib/press/index.cfm?id=1133> accessed 3 March 2016.

[200] See below, section C. [201] On 'mode 3', see above, section II.C.3.

[202] See the model schedule tabled by the EU Commission during the TiSA negotiations: <http://trade.ec.europa.eu/doclib/docs/2014/july/tradoc_152690.pdf> accessed 3 April 2017; see also the initial offer tabled by the EU in November 2013, <http://trade.ec.europa.eu/doclib/docs/2014/july/tradoc_152689.pdf> accessed 3 April 2017; and EU Commission, 'How to Read the TiSA Initial Offer of the European Union?', <http://trade.ec.europa.eu/doclib/docs/2014/july/tradoc_152691.pdf> accessed 3 April 2017.

[203] EU Commission, 'TiSA' (n 190) 2–3. These principles are also set forth in the draft TiSA negotiating directives for the European Commission; cf EU Council, Draft Directives for the negotiation of a plurilateral agreement on trade in services, 6891/13 ADD 1 DCL 1 (10 March 2015).

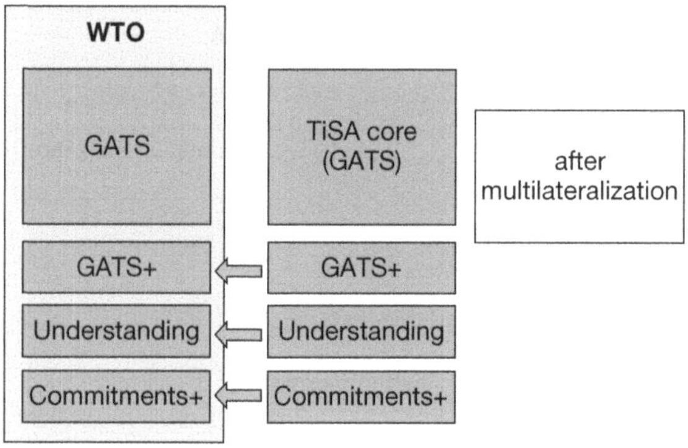

Fig. 3.5 TiSA regulatory approach (II)

into TiSA as a first pillar, or module, of TiSA. This would facilitate a future integration of TiSA into the GATS. A second 'GATS plus' module would comprise a series of chapters dedicated to sectors and/or to specific rules; a third module would be an understanding on country-specific commitments (dealing with issues such as standstill and ratchet effects); and a fourth module would comprise specific commitments inscribed into GATS-type schedules.[204]

The TiSA negotiating parties obviously share the understanding that the plurilateral TiSA agreement should be multilateralized and brought back to the WTO and GATS in the future, when the agreement will have attracted a critical mass of WTO Members (see Figure 3.5).[205]

As some important trading partners such as Brazil, China,[206] India, and the Association of Southeast Asian Nations countries do not participate in the negotiations, but would reap the benefits due to the automatic extension of the contents of TiSA via the GATS MFN clause,[207] the negotiating parties of TiSA will apparently try to prevent such free-riding. This is to be achieved by ensuring that TiSA meets the requirements of Art V GATS, which shields against such unwanted MFN effects, if an agreement has substantial sectoral coverage and provides for the elimination of substantially all discrimination. Importantly, however, it has been

[204] cf EU Commission, 'A Modular Approach to the Architecture of a Plurilateral Agreement on Services' (distributed in September 2012) 1ff, <http://trade.ec.europa.eu/doclib/press/index.cfm?id=1133> accessed 3 April 2017.

[205] EU Commission, 'TiSA' (n 190) 2; see also EU Commission, 'Memo: Negotiations for a Plurilateral Agreement on Trade in Services' (n 194) 2.

[206] China had expressed its interest to join the TiSA negotiations; its application was, however, rejected by Japan and the US (see euractiv, 'European Parliament is gearing up for TiSA' (16 January 2015), <http://www.euractiv.com/section/trade-society/news/european-parliament-is-gearing-up-for-tisa> accessed 3 April 2017).

[207] According to the GATS MFN clause, each WTO Member 'shall accord immediately and *unconditionally* to services and service suppliers of any other Member treatment no less favourable than that it accords to like services and service suppliers of any other country' (Art II GATS) (emphasis added).

Box 3.7 Scheduling in TiSA

Scheduling in TiSA	
MFN	negative
NT	negative
MA	positive

ratchet

reported that it was agreed among the negotiating parties that an accession clause for other interested WTO Members should be included in TiSA.[208]

Like the GATS, CETA, and TTIP, the TiSA agreement would rely on a scheduling system (see Box 3.7). It is expected that regarding market access, a positive scheduling approach would apply as under the GATS, that is, the TiSA market access obligation would apply only in those services sectors where a contracting party has inscribed a commitment into its schedule. By contrast with the GATS, the national treatment obligation could be subjected to a negative scheduling approach, which means that it would apply horizontally to all sectors in principle. Sectors to be exempted from the horizontal national treatment obligation would have to be enshrined as exceptions in the respective country-specific schedule. It is also expected that the national treatment obligation in TiSA would contain standstill and ratchet clauses, which are to apply unless an exemption is scheduled. As regards the MFN clause in TiSA, a negative scheduling approach is likely to be pursued, which would neither introduce a standstill nor a ratchet effect.[209]

V. Concluding Remarks

This chapter has attempted to give an overview of the trade disciplines envisaged in CETA, TTIP, and TiSA, concentrating on the essential structures, contents, and core questions that have become visible so far. Legally speaking, it is the most characteristic common feature of these treaty projects that all three represent 'WTO-plus' agreements: they are agreements that are meant to go beyond the corpus of WTO trade disciplines in terms of substance.

To what extent CETA, TTIP, and TiSA will actually do so is very difficult to assess. While the CETA and TTIP projects clearly reconfirm central WTO disciplines, and establish new ones in additional areas, these initiatives attempt to

[208] EU Commission, 'TiSA' (n 190) 2; see also EU Commission, 'Memo: Negotiations for a Plurilateral Agreement on Trade in Services' (n 194) 3–4.

[209] See also the official description of TiSA by the Swiss Government, <https://www.seco.admin.ch/seco/en/home/Aussenwirtschaftspolitik_Wirtschaftliche_Zusammenarbeit/Wirtschaftsbeziehungen/Internationaler_Handel_mit_Dienstleistungen/TISA/Schweiz_und_TiSA.html> accessed 15 May 2017.

surpass the status quo of WTO law, inter alia, by introducing rules such as those on regulatory cooperation, which are meant to be non-binding. Although regulatory cooperation, as indicated, may have especially great potential in economic terms, the success of this approach, which is based on a voluntary framework, will inherently depend on the political will to cooperate and on future economic and political contingencies.

As regards TiSA, on the other hand, the intention to outpace the notoriously slow WTO reform processes is equally clear. To what extent this will happen depends largely on the contents of the individual schedules of TiSA commitments, which will be country-specific. As in the case of the GATS, the 'truth' of TiSA will lie in its schedules, therefore, which will have to be analysed as they become available and will necessarily be subject, in future dispute settlement, to interpretative uncertainties.

Whereas CETA, TTIP, and TiSA are meant to function as 'WTO-plus' agreements in terms of substance, they constitute 'WTO-minus' agreements in terms of membership. All three projects are restricted to like-minded WTO Members: while the CETA and TTIP initiatives will be confined to bilateral transatlantic trade (and investment) partnerships, the TiSA project at least officially offers a perspective of future multilateralization and reintegration into the WTO system. This might, in the long run, reinforce the WTO framework substantively and institutionally.

Whether this plan will work in the medium or, more realistically, long term is everything but clear. From today's perspective, being prime examples of a renewed bilateralism and plurilateralism in international economic law, CETA, TTIP, and TiSA rather risk contributing to a fragmentation of the multilateral WTO system.

4

The Reform of Investment Protection Rules in CETA, TTIP, and Other Recent EU FTAs: Convincing?

Christian Tietje and Kevin Crow

I. Introduction

In recent years, the law and politics surrounding international investment protection, including investment arbitration, have triggered a flurry of debates more divisive than any other topic in international economic law.[1] Indeed, other topics—such as the World Trade Organization's (WTO) Doha-Round, the International Monetary Fund's (IMF) Policy for Exceptional Access Lending reform,[2] the February 2016 Argentinian hedge funds deal to absolve its multi-billion dollar debt,[3] or the fundamental challenges to anti-dumping law due to the upcoming legal transition of China from a so-called non-market to a market economy[4]—wield a far greater potential for global economic impact and create considerable systemic challenges to the international economic system. Nevertheless, legal scholars and the general

[1] See eg Catharine Amirfar and Julian Fouret, 'The Current State and Future of International Arbitration: Regional Perspectives', IBA Arb 40 Subcommittee (2015); Michele Potestà, 'Legitimate Expectations in Investment Treaty Law: Understanding the Roots and the Limits of a Controversial Concept' (2013) 28(1) *ICSID Rev* 88; Anthea Roberts, 'Power and Persuasion in Investment Treaty Interpretation: The Dual Role of States' (2010) 104(2) *Am J Int L* 179; and Susan D Franck, 'The Legitimacy Crisis in Investment Treaty Arbitration: Privatizing Public International Law through Inconsistent Decisions' (2005) 73 *Fordham L Rev* 1521 (hereafter Franck, 'The Legitimacy Crisis in Investment Treaty Arbitration').

[2] International Monetary Fund Report, 'The Fund's Lending Framework and Sovereign Debt—Further Considerations' (International Monetary Fund, 9 April 2015) 1–3; see also International Monetary Fund Survey, 'IMF Reforms Policy for Exceptional Access Lending' (International Monetary Fund, 29 January 2016), <http://www.imf.org/external/pubs/ft/survey/so/2016/POL012916A.htm> accessed 3 April 2017.

[3] Alexandra Stevenson and Jonathan Gilbert, 'Argentina Reaches Deal with Hedge Funds Over Debt', *New York Times* (29 February 2016), <http://www.nytimes.com/2016/03/01/business/dealbook/argentina-reaches-deal-with-hedge-funds-over-debt.html?_r=0> accessed 3 April 2017.

[4] See, eg, Laura Puccio, 'Granting Market Economy Status to China: An Analysis of WTO Law and of Selected WTO Members' Policy' (European Parliamentary Research Service, November

The Reform of Investment Protection Rules in CETA, TTIP, and other Recent EU-FTAs: Convincing? Christian Tietje, Kevin Crow.

public alike concentrate their debates to a large degree on the single topic of international investment law.

Any attempt to identify the exact reasons for this almost overwhelming interest would be speculative at best. However, it is fair to assume that to a large degree, public debate is setting the agenda, and much of that debate is fostered and conducted by non-governmental organizations (NGOs), such as IIED,[5] IISD,[6] S2B,[7] and CISDL.[8] Indeed, many of these same organizations have influenced the trajectory for certain academic writing.[9] Whether this is a development to welcome or to criticize shall be left open at this juncture. Instead, this chapter seeks to elucidate the dilemma of the current reform debate in the context of what we will refer to as 'vagueness' in international law generally and international investment law specifically. Vagueness in any legal text is somewhat of a double-edged sword. On the one hand, vagueness is necessary to keep law flexible, especially with regard to unforeseen disputes or political challenges, but on the other hand, it can leave stakeholders uncertain of what the law prescribes, and can be exploited by the clever lawyers of special interest groups.[10]

The aim of this chapter is not, however, to engage too thoroughly in a discussion of the pros and cons of investment protection and its respective reform proposals.

2015, PE 571.325), <http://www.europarl.europa.eu/RegData/etudes/IDAN/2015/571325/EPRS_IDA(2015)571325_EN.pdf> accessed 3 April 2017.

[5] Foundation for International Institute for Environment and Development. See, eg, Maidan K Suleimenov and Yerlan B Osipov, 'Governance for Oil and Gas Contracts in Kazakhstan' (International Institute for Environment and Development, 2010), <http://pubs.iied.org/G02760/> accessed 3 April 2017.

[6] International Institute for Sustainable Development. See, eg, Harm Schepel, 'Recasting Rules and Exceptions? On the Relationship between Regulatory Sovereignty and International Investment Law' (2016) 7(3) *Investment Treaty News* 9, <http://www.iisd.org/sites/default/files/publications/iisd-itn-august-2016-english.pdf> accessed 9 October 2016.

[7] Seattle to Brussels Network. See, eg, Cecilia Olivet, Marc Maes, Pia Eberhardt et al, 'ISDS: Courting Foreign Investors: Why the Commission's Proposal for an "Investment Court System" Still Fails to Address the Key Problems of Foreign Investors' Privileges' (Analysis by the S2B Seattle to Brussels Network, 29 September 2015), <https://www.tni.org/files/publication-downloads/s2b_isds.pdf> accessed 3 April 2017.

[8] Centre for International Sustainable Development Law. See, eg, Marie-Claire Cordonier Segger, Markus W Gehring, and Andrew Newcombe (eds), *Sustainable Development in World Investment Law* (Kluwer Law International, 2010); Michael Kerr, Richard Janda, and Chip Pitts, *Corporate Social Responsibility: A Legal Analysis* (LexisNexis, 2009); Kishan Khoday and Usha Natarajan, 'Fairness and International Environmental Law from Below: Social Movements and Legal Transformations in India' (2012) 25 *Leiden J Int L* 415; Andrew Newcombe and Luis Paradell, *Law and Practice of Investment Treaties: Standards of Treatment* (Kluwer Law International, 2009).

[9] See, eg, Marie-Claire Cordonier Segger and Markus W Gehring, 'Making Progress? Climate Change, Sustainable Development, and International Trade and Investment Law' in Charlotte Streck and David Freestone (eds), *Legal Aspects of Carbon Trading: Kyoto, Copenhagen and Beyond* (Oxford University Press, 2009); Martin Endicott, 'Investment in ICSID: Development Lessons for the WTO?' in Markus W Gehring and Marie-Claire Cordonier Segger (eds), *Sustainable Development in World Trade Law* (Kluwer Law International, 2005); Mario Prost, 'Is the European Union Becoming More Sustainable?' in Gehring and Cordonier Segger, *Sustainable Development*; see generally Andrea K Bjorklund and August Reinisch, *International Investment Law and Soft Law* (Edward Elgar, 2012).

[10] See generally Pia Eberhardt and Cecilia Olivet, 'Profiting from Injustice: How Law Firms, Arbitrators, and Financiers are Fuelling an Investment Arbitration Boom', Corporate Europe Observatory and Transnational Institute Report (November 2012), <https://www.tni.org/files/

Instead, this chapter's primary aim is to explore the systemic problems that plague provision-dependent proposals themselves, so long as they operate within the current international investment system. After beginning with a background on 'vagueness' in law, both generally and in the international investment system (section II), this chapter will address the fundamental question of why we need new investment disciplines in the first place (section III). It will then analyse the most prominent reforms in the current international investment landscape (section IV) before drawing preliminary conclusions on the degree of effectiveness these reforms may have in addressing the concerns of stakeholders while maintaining congruency within the existing international investment system (section V). The chapter will then elucidate the structural problems with the current reform proposals (section VI) and demonstrate that a symmetrical approach could alleviate these problems (section VII) before concluding that current reform proposals cannot stand because they run counter to the logic of the existing international investment system (section VIII).

II. Background

Overall, and leaving details aside for a moment, the landscape of current reform proposals on substantial investment protection and investor-state dispute settlement (ISDS) is dominated by the following concerns: ensuring policy space for states (and the EU); clarifying vague legal terms such as fair and equitable treatment; restricting the possibility for investors to rely on indirect expropriation in order to gain compensation; and abolishing the current mechanism of arbitration in favour of a more democratically legitimate and accountable court system, which would include an appeals mechanism. Vagueness in the law plays a role in all of these concerns, and, accordingly, this section will provide a background on the problem of vagueness in free trade agreements (FTAs) and bilateral investment treaties (BITs) (section A), and the use of vagueness in law more generally (section B).

A. Vagueness of BIT provisions

Traditionally, the vast majority of BIT and FTA investment provisions have neglected to incorporate specific details for what may constitute, for example, an infringement on a state's right to regulate,[11] an unfair or unequitable treatment,[12] or an indirect expropriation.[13] Instead, these concerns (and resulting concerns about how to assess the foreseeability of a tribunal's interpretation of a given BIT provision) have been a mainstay in the arguments of both states and investors in a

download/profitingfrominjustice.pdf> accessed 3 April 2017 (hereafter Eberhardt and Olivet, 'Profiting from injustice').

[11] See section IV.A of this chapter. [12] See section IV.E. [13] See section IV.B.

long list of investment arbitral tribunal awards.[14] In many cases, ambiguities have given rise to problematic and controversial decisions. For example, the ICSID tribunal in *CMS v Argentine Republic*, while ultimately rejecting Argentina's interpretation of the fair and equitable treatment standard, explicitly stated that the Argentina–United States BIT, 'like most bilateral investment treaties, does not define the standard of fair and equitable treatment and to this extent Argentina's concern about it being somewhat vague is not entirely without merit'.[15]

The concerns about the unpredictability of ambiguity have been echoed by commentators, such as Olivet and Eberhardt, who cite Gus Van Harten's work on procedural fairness in investment arbitration in arguing that investment rules are '[c]ertainly ... too broad in scope, vaguely phrased, and contain provisions that allow corporations the right to sue governments even when their actions are meant to protect people's basic rights or the environment'.[16] Nevertheless, vagueness in international investment law is also somewhat of a necessity; it manifests a well-known contract theory problem regarding how to best deal with uncertainty.[17] In investment treaty law, the state gives up ex ante a commitment to protect investments in its territory in exchange for ex post flexibility, through vague provisions, in order to uphold the efficiency of the treaty.[18] As Anne van Aaken puts it, states essentially 'trade credibility for sovereignty' in transactions necessary in order to attract investment.[19]

Moreover, it is crucial to understand that the original purpose of the most frequently arbitrated BIT and FTA provision, the fair and equitable treatment standard,[20] was

[14] See, eg, *BG Group plc v The Republic of Argentina*, UNCITRAL, Final Award, 24 December 2007; *TSA Spectrum de Argentina SA v Argentine Republic*, ICSID Case No ARB/05/5, Award, 19 December 2008; *SUAR International SA v Republic of Argentina*, ICSID Case No ARB/04/4, Award, 22 May 2014; *Philip Morris Brands Sàrl, Philip Morris Products SA and Abal Hermanos SA v Oriental Republic of Uruguay*, ICSID Case No ARB/10/7, Award, 8 July 2016; *Mondev International Ltd v United States of America*, ICSID Case No ARB(AF)99/2, Award, 11 October 2002; *InterTrade Holding GmbH v The Czech Republic*, PCA Case No 2009-12, Final Award, 23 May 2012; *Bernard Friedrich Arnd Rüdiger Von Pezold et al v Republic of Zimbabwe*, ICSID Case No ARB 10/15, Award, 28 July 2015; *Plama Consortium Ltd v Republic of Bulgaria*, ICSID Case No ARB/03/24, Award, 27 August 2008; *EnCana Corp v Republic of Ecuador*, LCIA Case No UN3481, UNCITRAL, Award, 3 February 2006; and *ADC Affiliate and ADC & ADMC Management Ltd v Republic of Hungary*, ICSID Case No ARB/03/16, Award, 27 September 2006. These are just some of the examples used in this chapter; there are many others.

[15] *CMS v Argentine Republic*, ICSID Case No ARB/01/8, Award, 12 May 2005, para 273.

[16] Cecilia Olivet and Pia Eberhardt, 'Arbitrators' Role in the Recent Investment Arbitration Boom' (2013) 3(3) *Investment Treaty News*, <http://www.iisd.org/sites/default/files/publications/iisd_itn_march_2013_en.pdf> accessed 3 April 2017, citing Eberhardt and Olivet, 'Profiting from Injustice' (n 10) ch 4. This source ultimately bases Olivet and Eberhardt's assertion on Gus Van Harten, 'Investment Treaty Arbitration, Procedural Fairness, and the Rule of Law' in Stephan W Schill (ed), *International Investment Law and Comparative Public Law* (Oxford University Press, 2012) ch 20.

[17] See Robert E Scott and Paul B Stephan, *The Limits of Leviathan: Contract Theory and the Enforcement of International Law* (Cambridge University Press, 2006).

[18] See Anne van Aaken, 'International Investment Law between Commitment and Flexibility: A Contract Theory Analysis' (2009) 12 *J Int Econ L* 2, 507–38 (hereafter Aaken, 'International Investment Law').

[19] ibid, 509.

[20] The FET standard has been around almost as long as investment treaty arbitration and is still a frequently litigated 'evolving' standard. Marcela Klein Bronfman, 'Fair and Equitable Treatment: An Evolving Standard' (2006) 10 *Max Planck YB of UN L* 609, 613–15. See also The Havana Charter,

to 'fill the gaps' that might occur should the guarantees of compensation evade applicability in a case of expropriation or discrimination.[21] Accordingly, vague provisions such as the fair and equitable treatment standard, properly understood, are legal mechanisms designed to adopt to changing circumstances and situations. The 'vagueness' of such provisions can perhaps be most adequately justified by general considerations of 'treaties over time'. As Georg Nolte, the Rapporteur of the International Law Commission on the project *Treaties over Time*, explains:

> The general question of 'treaties over time' reflects the tension between the requirements of stability and change in the law of treaties. On the one hand, it is generally the purpose of the law of treaties to provide stability in the face of evolving circumstances. On the other hand, legal systems must also leave room for the consideration of subsequent developments in order to ensure meaningful respect for the agreement of the parties and identification of its limits.[22]

Any assessment of the new proposals for international investment reform, including but not limited to the fair and equitable treatment standard, should be based on these general considerations.

B. Law and 'vagueness'

In the broader context of law as both a domestic and international discipline, vagueness with regard to legal terms is not at all unusual. To the contrary, by the very nature of the medium through which it exists (language), law inevitably contains an element of vagueness. As H L A Hart puts it: 'In all fields of experience, not only that of rules, there is a limit, inherent in the nature of language, to the guidance which general language can provide.'[23] Naturally, the inherent vagueness in the medium of language affects all proposed reforms to standard investment treaty practice because all proposed reforms utilize the same medium.

The inherent vagueness of law as a medium also generates an inherent necessity for interpretation if law is to have efficacy. This necessity—classically embodied by Montesquieu's description of a judge as 'the mouth that pronounces the words of the law'[24]—begs the question of whether the power of the arbitrator in the international investment system is appropriately balanced by other traditional sources of law, namely, a legislator and an executive.[25] As such, the democratic

April 1948, Art 11(2) (stating that foreign investments should be granted 'just and equitable treatment'), <https://www.wto.org/english/docs_e/legal_e/havana_e.pdf> accessed 3 April 2017; and 'OECD Draft Convention on the Protection of Foreign Property' (1968) 2(2) *Int Lawyer* 331–53.

21 See Sabrina A Bandali, 'Understanding FET: The Case for Protecting Contract-Based Legitimate Expectations' in Ian A Laird, Borzu Sabahi, Frédéric G Sourgens, and Todd J Weiler (eds), *Investment Treaty Arbitration*, vol 7 (Juris, 2014) 133–64.

22 Georg Nolte, Special Rapporteur of the International Law Commission (ILC), *Treaties Over Time In Particular: Subsequent Agreement and Practice*, Annex I, 152 (ILC, 2008).

23 H L A Hart, *The Concept of Law* (Oxford University Press, 1961) 126.

24 '[L]a bouche qui pronونce les paroles de la loi.' Charles de Secondat, Baron de Montesquieu, *De l'Esprit des Lois* (1748) (hereafter Baron de Montesquieu, *De l'Esprit des Lois*).

25 Baron de Montesquieu, *De l'Esprit des Lois* (n 24).

legitimacy of arbitration as a method for dispute settlement can be called into question: unlike the domestic judicial systems of most democracies—wherein a legislator draws its legitimacy through public vote and the judiciary interprets the laws of the legislator, which can then in turn be altered again by the legislator after judicial interpretation—an international investment tribunal interprets a trade agreement which is the joint product of two or more legislators, acting on behalf of two or more peoples, and, as such, precludes the option of quick adjustment should judicial interpretation run awry of legislative intent.[26] (This problem could be alleviated through a symmetrical investment protection system, discussed later in this chapter, because it would recalibrate the balance of motives between states in renegotiating BITs by allowing for counterclaims against investors based on damage caused to the public's interests.)

Nevertheless, the structure and rationale of the international investment protection system requires that the legal terms used in BITs remain rather broad. This is because, as a legal system, investment protection is inherently cross-sectional. Indeed, investment protection applies potentially to any state measure for any purpose in any economic sector.[27] Specifics in BITs are therefore sparse not by design so much as by necessity; most specific applications of treaty terms are precluded by mere potentialities. Indeed, although treaty provisions on fair and equitable treatment, indirect expropriation, and national treatment appear to be gaining greater degrees of specificity in recent drafts,[28] even the comparatively specific language in recent draft plurilateral investment treaties such as the TPP,[29] CETA,[30]

[26] To explain in further detail: within a typical democratic domestic system with power divided between executive, judicial, and legislative branches, legislation draws its legitimacy from the will of the people through democratic vote to accord the responsibility of drafting and enacting laws to the legislative branch. If the judicial branch within that system then interprets the legitimate action of the legislature in a way that is incongruent with the will of the people within that system, the legislature can quickly act to remedy the offending interpretation through further legislation, or the people can act by electing a legislature who will remedy the offending interpretation. In the international investment system, however, unlike in the domestic process, remedying an arbitral award that is incongruent with the will of the people of one state through the legislature of that state is impossible without a joint effort and consent from the people and by extension the legislature of the other international investment treaty party. Thus, although a common theoretical justification for the international investment system is that it draws its legitimacy from the legitimate action of democratically elected legislators, the function of democracy within the system is, in fact, far more limited post-arbitral interpretation.

[27] See, eg, Omar Al Farooque and Subba Reddy Yarram, 'Corporate Governance and Foreign Direct Investment Inflows: Cross-sectional International Evidence' (2010) 2(1) *Am J Finance & Accounting* 1–15.

[28] See generally, eg, TPP, CETA, and TTIP, fully cited at nn 29, 30, and 31.

[29] US Trade Representative, 'Trans-Pacific Partnership Agreement', <https://ustr.gov/trade-agreements/free-trade-agreements/trans-pacific-partnership/tpp-full-text> accessed 3 April 2017. The TPP has been signed by all parties, but is not yet ratified. The twelve potential Member States are, in alphabetical order, Australia, Brunei, Canada, Chile, Japan, Malaysia, Mexico, New Zealand, Peru, Singapore, the United States, and Vietnam.

[30] Comprehensive Economic and Trade Agreement (CETA), cf Consolidated CETA Text (published on 26 September 2014), <http://trade.ec.europa.eu/doclib/docs/2014/september/tradoc_152806.pdf> accessed 3 April 2017. CETA, a free trade agreement between Canada and the EU's twenty-eight Member States, has not yet entered into force, and may be compromised by the exit of the United Kingdom from the European Union. See, eg, Mike Blanchfield, 'CETA in Jeopardy after Brexit Referendum, Experts Say', *Huffington Post Canada* (Ottawa, 24 June 2016), <http://www.

and TTIP[31] is curbed by the use of evaluative terms such as 'manifestly arbitrary', 'rare circumstances', 'excessive', and 'necessary'.[32] Such terms call for an inevitable degree of subjective evaluation that tilts interpretative power squarely back towards the arbitral tribunal.

Thus, as far as vagueness is concerned, international investment law finds itself in what might be described as a 'Catch-22'[33]—all options appear to carry equally damning consequences. If the law remains vague, the arbitral tribunals retain an arguably illegitimate degree of power over terms that cannot be easily adjusted by either of the participating democracies. However, if the law veers too far towards specificity, the law again loses legitimacy by failing to mirror the cross-sectional nature of international investment, which requires flexible (vague) treaty language.

III. Why Do We Need 'New' or 'Better' Investment Disciplines?

As one may imagine based on the sections above, legitimacy and power concerns brought on by the inherent vagueness of language as a medium and investment law as a field have ushered in the onset of what might be called a 'crisis of legitimacy' in international investment law.[34] In recent years in particular, arbitral awards have contributed to growing concerns regarding the balance and fairness of claims in international investment law. Specifically, a large part of the debate considers the single directionality, or 'asymmetry', of claims that fall within the jurisdiction of arbitral tribunals.[35] That is, international investment law provides a cause of action for investors against states to protect investments in a host state, but does not provide a cause of action for host states against investors, and generally refutes attempts by states to bring counterclaims against investors.[36] (An alternative to this structure will be proposed in section VII of this chapter.) Indeed, ICSID decisions over the past years have all but eliminated the use of counterclaims in international

huffingtonpost.ca/2016/06/24/canada-u-s-free-trade-deals-imperilled-by-british-vote-to-leave-eu-experts_n_10660236.html> accessed 3 April 2017.

31 Transatlantic Trade and Investment Partnership (TTIP). For a chapter-by-chapter guide to TTIP provisions, see European Commission, 'The Transatlantic Trade and Investment Partnership: Toward an EU-US Trade Deal' (Report 2015), <http://trade.ec.europa.eu/doclib/docs/2015/july/tradoc_153635.pdf> accessed 3 April 2017. The TTIP, like CETA, is signed but not yet ratified by both the EU and the US. Like CETA, the UK's exit from the EU may put the agreement at jeopardy.

32 Caroline Henckels, 'Protecting Regulatory Autonomy through Greater Precision in Investment Treaties: The TPP, CETA, and TTIP' (2016) 19 *Ox J Int Econ L* 27, 30.

33 A difficult situation for which there is no easy or possible solution. The phrase is based on Joseph Heller's satirical novel of the same name: *Catch-22* (Simon & Schuster, 1961).

34 See Franck, 'The Legitimacy Crisis in Investment Treaty Arbitration' (n 1) 1521.

35 See, eg, Anne K Hoffmann, 'Counterclaims' in Meg Kinnear, Geraldine Fischer, Jara Minguez Almeida et al (eds), *Building International Investment Law: The First 50 Years of ICSID* (Wolters Kluwer, 2015) ch 36 (hereafter Hoffmann, 'Counterclaims').

36 This is a general rule, but in rare circumstances, tribunals have found jurisdiction to hear counterclaims. See, eg, *Saluka Investments BV v The Czech Republic*, UNCITRAL, Decision on Jurisdiction over the Czech Republic's Counterclaim, 7 May 2004.

investment arbitration,[37] that is, unless an investor consents to a counterclaim, the state has exhausted domestic remedies, and the counterclaim is sufficiently linked to the claim.[38]

This asymmetry presents a troubling dilemma. On the one hand, the interpretative power of arbitrators in international tribunals is potentially immense, and many of the provisions in the treaties that arbitrators interpret are vague by necessity.[39] Insofar as the terms of a given investment treaty embody a degree of ambiguity, arbitrators are concretely bound in their tools of interpretation by little more than the rules of the given tribunal and the basics of treaty interpretation in international law, as codified in the Vienna Convention on the Law of Treaties (VCLT).[40] On the other hand, states require a degree of ambiguity to maintain regulatory freedom or policy space. Especially recent arbitral decisions have propelled protections on the state's right to regulate to the spotlight, particularly the framing of the right to regulate as opposed to the interpretative power accorded to arbitrators.[41] Indeed, states and regional organizations, including the US and the EU, have sought means through which to safeguard their regulatory power to pursue public policy objectives—a sometimes daunting challenge given that the international investment system's *raison d'être* is to protect and promote investments, not the public.[42]

As a result of the concerns and criticisms addressed above, a slew of 'reform' language has emerged in a variety of investment treaties since 2004. Nevertheless, no matter how nobly-intended these provisions may be, we suggest that the nature of 'reform' as opposed to novelty fails to address the systemic problems inherent in the investment protection system itself, and that is why 'new' investment disciplines might be needed.

On the forefront of the reformed investment treaties of 2004 were the new model BITs established by the US and Canada.[43] Both model treaties included greater specificity

[37] ibid, at 506–18. See also, eg, *Spyridon Roussalis v Romania*, ICSID Case No ARB/06/01, Award, 7 December 2011; *Limited Liability Co AMTO v Ukraine*, SCC Case No 080/2005, Final Award, 26 March 2008; *RSM Production Corp v Grenada*, ICSID Case No ARB/05/14, Award, 13 March 2009; *Antoine Goetz & Consorts and SA Affinage des Metaux v Burundi*, ICSID Case No ARB/01/2, Award, 21 June 2012; and *Occidental Petroleum Corp and Occidental Exploration and Production Co v Republic of Ecuador*, ICSID Case No ARB/06/11, Award, 5 October 2012.

[38] See Hoffman, 'Counterclaims' (n 35) ch 36.

[39] This argument is demonstrated in section II.B of this chapter.

[40] Opened for signature 23 May 1969, entered into force 27 January 1980, 1155 UNTS 331, Arts 31–2, 8 ILM 689.

[41] See, eg, *Philip Morris Brands Sàrl, Philip Morris Products SA and Abal Hermanos SA v Oriental Republic of Uruguay*, ICSID Case No ARB/10/7 (formerly *FTR Holding SA, Philip Morris Products SA and Abal Hermanos SA v Oriental Republic of Uruguay*), Award, 8 July 2016; see also *CMS Gas Transmission Co v The Republic of Argentina*, ICSID Case No ARB/01/8, Award, 12 May 2005; *BG Group plc v The Republic of Argentina*, UNCITRAL Final Award, 24 December 2007; *TSA Spectrum de Argentina SA v Argentine Republic*, ICSID Case No ARB/05/5, Award, 19 December 2008; and *SUAR International SA v Republic of Argentina*, ICSID Case No ARB/04/4, Award, 22 May 2014.

[42] See, eg, Catharine Titi, *The Right to Regulate in International Investment Law* (Hart, 2014).

[43] US 2004 Model BIT, US Dep't of State, <http://www.state.gov/documents/organization/117601.pdf> accessed 3 April 2017; and Canada 2004 Model BIT, <http://www.italaw.com/documents/Canadian2004-FIPA-model-en.pdf> accessed 3 April 2017.

with regard to fair and equitable treatment and indirect expropriation. The next major reform came through the European Parliament's Resolution of 8 July 2015, which was concerned with the investment dispute settlement in TTIP.[44] That Resolution stated that 'standards of protection and definitions of investor and investment should be drawn up in a precise legal manner protecting the right to regulate in the public interest, clarifying the meaning of indirect expropriation and preventing unfounded or frivolous claims'.[45] These trends and ambitions take on varied incarnations in the recent CETA, Singapore, and Vietnam agreements, and in the draft versions of several pending agreements, both bilateral and unilateral.[46] The following section and its subsections will provide a brief analysis of each of the pending proposals.

IV. Proposed New Provisions

Probably the most advanced reform language in negotiated legal texts is contained in the draft free trade agreements of the EU with Canada, Singapore, and Vietnam. Broadly speaking, and drawing provisions not necessarily included in all of the treaties, one can identify the following reform elements: reaffirmation efforts on the right to regulate, greater specificity in enumerating situations that amount to indirect expropriation, the inclusion of full protection and security clauses, the inclusion of so-called umbrella clauses, greater specificity in defining fair and equitable treatment, and efforts to enumerate specific exceptions to investment treaty provisions, *à la* Art XX of the General Agreement on Tariffs in Trade 1994 (GATT).[47] The following subsections will explore each of these reform elements as they appear in TTIP, CETA, the EU–Vietnam FTA,[48] and the EU–Singapore FTA.[49]

A. Right to regulate

A 'reaffirmation' of the right to regulate has taken a prominent role in reform language, and at least from a political perspective, it is a highly important reform.[50]

[44] European Parliament, 'Negotiations for the Transatlantic Trade and Investment Partnership (TTIP)' (8 July 2015) P8 TA(2015)0252, <http://www.europarl.europa.eu/sides/getDoc.do?pubRef=-//EP//NONSGML+TA+P8-TA-2015-0252+0+DOC+PDF+V0//EN> accessed 3 April 2017. (hereafter TTIP resolution of 8 July 2015).

[45] ibid, s S(2)(d)(14).

[46] See, eg, CETA, EU–Vietnam, EU–Singapore, US–Belarus, US–El Salvador, and US–Uzbekistan, inter alia, according to information posted on the US Department of State's website, <http://www.state.gov/e/eb/ifd/bit/117402.htm> accessed 3 April 2017.

[47] General Agreement on Tariffs and Trade 1994 (15 April 1994), Marrakesh Agreement Establishing the World Trade Organization, Annex 1A, The Legal Texts: The Results of the Uruguay Round of Multilateral Trade Negotiations, 17 (1999), 1867 UNTS 187, 33 ILM 1153 (1994).

[48] European Commission, 'EU–Vietnam Free Trade Agreement: Agreed Text As of January 2016' (1 February 2016), <http://trade.ec.europa.eu/doclib/press/index.cfm?id=1437> accessed 9 October 2016 (hereafter EU–Vietnam FTA).

[49] European Commission, 'EU–Singapore Free Trade Agreement' (negotiations completed 17 October 2014, not yet entered into force) Text of ch 9, Investment, <http://trade.ec.europa.eu/doclib/docs/2014/october/tradoc_152844.pdf> accessed 3 April 2017 (hereafter EU–Singapore FTA).

[50] Art 8.9 CETA.

Indeed, the EU–Vietnam FTA Art 13bis(1) explicitly states that '[t]he Parties reaffirm the right to regulate within their territories to achieve legitimate policy objectives', and continues to give an open list of acceptable objectives including cultural diversity, public health, and public morals.[51] Art 13(2) and (3) lay out provisions '[f]or greater certainty' that clarify that the treaty's language cannot be interpreted as a commitment by either party not to change its current regulatory framework in a way that may negatively affect a given investment, and cannot require a party to discontinue a subsidy.[52] These reforms appear to answer concerns respecting both specificity and the sovereignty of the states.

Nevertheless, it is questionable whether such reform provisions, including similar provisions in CETA,[53] really carry any legal significance. For one thing, it is already well established in arbitral practice that investment treatment standards that favour the investor must be balanced against the legitimate regulatory interests of the host state.[54] One need look no further than the ICSID Tribunal's 8 July 2016 Award in *Philip Morris v Uruguay* to encounter a firm declaration that, in international arbitral practice, state action that interferes 'with foreign property in the valid exercise of police power [(ie regulatory power)] is not considered expropriation and does not give rise to compensation'.[55] Moreover, the finding of a public purpose for regulation is already an explicit prerequisite of a non-compensable expropriation, as has been affirmed and reaffirmed by a number of tribunals.[56] Thus, the new provisions on the right to regulate that appear in CETA and EU–Vietnam have at least

[51] EU–Vietnam FTA Art 13bis.

[52] EU–Vietnam FTA Art 13(2) and (3).

[53] cf Art 19.3(2) CETA.

[54] See, eg, *Plama Consortium Ltd v Republic of Bulgaria*, ICSID Case No ARB/03/24, Award, 27 August 2008; *EnCana Corp v Republic of Ecuador*, LCIA Case No UN3481, UNCITRAL, Award, 3 February 2006; and *ADC Affiliate and ADC & ADMC Management Ltd. v Republic of Hungary*, ICSID Case No ARB/03/16, Award, 27 September 2006. See also Ursula Kriebaum, 'Regulatory Takings: Balancing the Interests of the Investor and the State' (2007) 8(5) *J of World Inv & Trade* 717–44.

[55] *Philip Morris Brands Sàrl, Philip Morris Products SA and Abal Hermanos SA v Oriental Republic of Uruguay*, ICSID Case No ARB/10/7 (formerly *FTR Holding SA, Philip Morris Products SA and Abal Hermanos SA v Oriental Republic of Uruguay*), Award, 8 July 2016, para 188. This paragraph paraphrases the Respondent's submission. The Tribunal agreed in paras 290–1: '[The treaty] must be interpreted in accordance with Art 31(3)(c) of the VCLT requiring that treaty provisions be interpreted in the light of "[a]ny relevant rules of international law applicable to the relations between the parties," a reference "which includes customary international law" ... as [it] has evolved. Protecting public health has since long been recognised as an essential manifestation of the State's police power, as indicated also by Art 2(1) of the BIT which permits contracting States to refuse to admit investments "for reasons of public security and order, public health and morality"' (ibid, at 290–1). This language essentially enshrines the state's right to regulate in arbitral practice as a component of customary international law in accordance with Art 31 VCLT. Ibid at 288–91. See also, eg, *InterTrade Holding GmbH v The Czech Republic*, PCA Case No 2009-12, Final Award, 23 May 2012; *Nykomb Synergetics Technology Holding AB v The Republic of Latvia*, SCC Arbitration No 118/2001, Opinion of Prof Ove Bring and Dr Richard Happ; and *Bernard Friedrich Arnd Rüdiger Von Pezold et al v Republic of Zimbabwe*, ICSID Case No ARB 10/15, Award, 28 July 2015.

[56] Art 8.12(1)(a) CETA codifies this practice, but the prerequisite is already well established. See, eg, *Tidewater Investment SRL and Tidewater Caribe, CA v The Bolivarian Republic of Venezuela*, ICSID Case No ARB/10/5, Award, 13 March 2015; *Saipem SpA v The Peoples Republic of Bangladesh*, ICSID Case No ARB/05/7, Award, 30 June 2009; and *Marvin Feldman v Mexico*, ICSID Case No ARB(AF)/99/1, Award, 16 December 2002.

the potential of being tautologies.[57] Even if one would not follow this rather critical assessment on the value of the explicit recognition of the right to regulate, its legal significance would still probably be limited to informing an arbitral tribunal on the necessity to assess the value of the public interest of the host state in a given case.

New in CETA, but applicable only in very specific situations, is the provision that a host state remains free—subject to certain conditions—not to issue, renew, or maintain a subsidy or to withdraw an existing subsidy based on a respective decision of a court, tribunal, or other competent authority.[58] This provision is a direct reaction to cases like *Micula v Romania*[59] and the numerous cases against Spain[60] concerning the withdrawal of subsidies in the renewable energy sector. These new provisions cannot be said to reflect tribunal decisions in those cases, as many of those cases are still pending.[61] However, it can be said that the new CETA provisions would restrict the flexibility of tribunals in related subsidy disputes.

B. Indirect expropriation

Provisions regarding indirect or creeping expropriation are responsible for some of the most publicly controversial awards issued in international economic law.[62] The EU–Vietnam FTA exhibits stringent language in response, answering calls for greater specificity in provisions related to indirect expropriation. To that end, the Expropriation Annex to the EU–Vietnam FTA, paragraph 3, confirms both parties' 'shared understanding' that:

> For greater certainty, except in rare circumstances where the impact of a measure or series of measures is so severe in light of its purpose that it appears manifestly excessive, non-discriminatory measures or series of measures by a Party that are designed to protect legitimate public policy objectives do not constitute indirect expropriation.[63]

One question to consider is whether this language, through its specificity, too severely limits the situations in which arbitrators can find an indirect expropriation has occurred. For example, one might imagine a variety of situations in which a state acts to protect a legitimate public policy objective but does so in a manner that is more restrictive than necessary upon foreign investments within its territory. In

57 See EU–Vietnam FTA Art 13bis; cf Art 19.3(2) CETA.

58 Art 8.9(3) and (4) CETA.

59 *Ioan Micula, Viorel Micula, SC European Food SA, SC Starmill SRL and SC Multipack SRL v Romania* ('*Micula v Romania*'), ICSID Case No ARB/05/20, Final Award, 11 December 2013.

60 See, eg, *NextEra Energy Global Holdings BV and NextEra Energy Spain Holdings BV v Kingdom of Spain*, ICSID Case No ARB/14/11, Notice of Arbitration, 23 May 2014; *Charanne BV and Construction Investments SARL v The Kingdom of Spain*, SCC Arbitration No 062/2012, Final Award, 21 January 2016; and *RREEF Infrastructure (GP) Limited and RREEF Pan-European Infrastructure Two Lux SARL v Kingdom of Spain*, ICSID Case No ARB/13/30, Notice of Arbitration (not public), 22 November 2013.

61 See ibid.

62 See, eg, *National Grid plc v Argentine Republic*, UNCITRAL Arbitration Case 1:09-cv-00248-RBW, Award, 3 November 2008; and *BG Group plc v The Republic of Argentina*, UNCITRAL Final Award, 24 December 2007.

63 EU–Vietnam FTA, Expropriation Annex, 22, para 3, <http://trade.ec.europa.eu/doclib/docs/2016/february/tradoc_154210.pdf> accessed 3 April 2017.

such a situation, it might be preferable to adopt a proportionality standard similar to the ones applied by other international courts, for example, the European Court of Human Rights (ECtHR).[64] Indeed, such an approach has been applied to questions of indirect expropriation resulting from political regulatory action at least since the ICSID Tribunal's decision in *Tecmed v Mexico* in 2003.[65] In that case, the arbitral tribunal cited several ECtHR decisions[66] in setting out its approach to balancing a state's duties to the public against an investor's right to his or her investment. That tribunal found that:

> ... in order to determine if they are to be characterized as expropriatory, [the Tribunal must consider] whether such actions or measures are proportional to the public interest presumably protected thereby and to the protection legally granted to investments, taking into account that the significance of such impact has a key role upon deciding the proportionality.[67]

Indeed, reflecting these evolutions, language that indicates a proportionality-based approach was suggested during the TTIP negotiations;[68] specifically, the Modified EU Draft Proposals on Trade in Services, Investment, and Electronic Commerce suggested the following language:

> For greater certainty, non-discriminatory measures of general application taken by a Party that are designed to protect legitimate public policy objectives do not constitute indirect expropriation, if they are necessary and appropriate in light of the above mentioned factors and are applied in such a way that they genuinely meet the public policy objectives for which they are designed.[69]

This language places interpretative power back in the hands of the arbitral tribunal in at least two ways. First, rather than meeting the EU–Vietnam BIT's high threshold of 'manifestly excessive', the proposed TTIP language would require an evaluative assessment of whether the measures are 'necessary and appropriate' in light of certain factors. Second, while the EU–Vietnam BIT requires only that the measures be designed to protect a legitimate public policy objective, the TTIP

64 See *Handyside v United Kingdom*, App no 5493/72 (ECtHR, 7 December 1976) 24, <http://hudoc.echr.coe.int/eng?i=001-57499> accessed 3 April 2017; Report of 11 May 1984, B 88; *Engel and Others v The Netherlands*, App no 5100/71 (ECtHR, 8 July 1976) 22, <http://hudoc.echr.coe.int/eng?i=001-57478> accessed 3 April 2017; *Case of the Sunday Times v United Kingdom*, App no 6538/74 (ECtHR, 26 April 1979), 30, <http://hudoc.echr.coe.int/eng?i=001-57583> accessed 11 December 2016; and *Lingens v Austria*, App no 9815/82 (ECtHR, 8 July 1986) 103, <http://hudoc.echr.coe.int/eng?i=001-57523> accessed 11 December 2016.

65 *Tecnicas Medioambientales Tecmed SA v The United Mexican States*, ICSID Case No ARB (AF)/00/2, Award, 29 May 2003 (hereafter *Tecnicas Medioambientales v Mexico*).

66 *Case of Matos e Silva, Lda, and Others v Portugal*, App no 15777/89 (ECtHR, 16 September 1996) 19, <http://hudoc.echr.coe.int/eng?i=001-58063> accessed 11 December 2016; and *Case of James and Others v United Kingdom*, App no 8793/79 (ECtHR, 21 February 1986) 19–20, <http://hudoc.echr.coe.int/eng?i=001-57507> accessed 11 December 2016.

67 *Tecnicas Medioambientales v Mexico* (n 65) para 122.

68 'TTIP Negotiations: Modified EU Draft Proposals on Trade in Services, Investment and Electronic Commerce' (2 July 2013) TRADE B1, B2/asc/2557028.

69 ibid.

language additionally requires that the measures be applied in a way that meets those objectives. Thus, while the EU–Vietnam language answers calls for greater specificity, the TTIP proposals more closely resemble proportionality approaches taken by other international courts,[70] and, accordingly, the reform language regarding indirect expropriation again appears to merely codify emerging standards in international practice.

C. Full protection and security

Greater specificity can also be seen in the protection and security clauses of the CETA and the EU–Vietnam FTA. The CETA, reacting to cases such as *Mondev v United States*,[71] clarifies that 'full protection and security' refers to the party's obligations relating to 'physical security of investors and covered investments.'[72] Such language surely restricts interpretative scope by limiting the clause's protection *only* to physical security, but ensuring that security is extended to both investments and people.[73]

Curiously, the EU–Vietnam BIT embellishes upon this language. That treaty states: 'For greater certainty, "full protection and security" relates to the Party's obligations to act as may be *reasonably necessary* to protect physical security of investors and covered investments.'[74]

The added 'reasonably necessary' requirement highlights a broader systemic problem that is the subject of the next section of this chapter, namely, the lack of state ability to bring counterclaims against investors. Nevertheless, the 'reasonably necessary' requirement may incorporate interpretative leeway to safeguard states against excessive claims from investors whose physical security (or the physical security of investments) has been compromised by circumstances wholly unforeseeable to and

[70] See, eg, the ECtHR cases cited at n 64. See also, eg, Military and Paramilitary Activities in and against Nicaragua (*Nicaragua v United States of America*) (Merits, Judgment) [1986] ICJ Rep 14; Oil Platforms (*Islamic Republic of Iran v United States of America*) (Judgment) [2003] ICJ Rep 161; Armed Activities on the Territory of the Congo (*Democratic Republic of the Congo v Uganda*) (Judgment) [2005] ICJ Rep 168; WTO, Decision by the Arbitrators, *European Communities—Regime for the Importation, Sale and Distribution of Bananas—Recourse to Arbitration by the European Communities under Art 22.6 of the DSU* (9 April 1999) WT/DS27/ARB, para 6.16; WTO, Appellate Body Report, *United States–Transitional Safeguard Measure on Combed Cotton Yarn from Pakistan* (8 October 2001) WT/DS192/AB/R, para 120; WTO, Decision by the Arbitrators, *Brazil—Export Financing Programme for Aircraft—Recourse to Arbitration by Brazil under Art 22.6 of the DSU and Art 4.11 of the SCM Agreement* (28 August 2000) WT/DS46/ARB, para 3.51.

[71] *Mondev International Ltd v United States of America*, ICSID Case No ARB(AF)99/2, Award, 11 October 2002, paras 115–16. *Mondev* broke with the 1920s *Neer* application of full faith and security, finding that a breach of 'security' need not be 'egregious' or 'outrageous' by modern standards. It distinguished its finding by emphasizing that *Neer* articulated the standard in application to a physical person, not to physical property.

[72] Art 8.10 para 5 CETA.

[73] This application of 'full protection and security' was first articulated in *USA (LF Neer) v United Mexican States*, Decision of the General Claims Commission, United States–Mexico, 15 October 1926, *Opinions of Commissioners, 1927*, reproduced in *The American Journal of International Law*, 555–6; 3 ILR 213.

[74] EU–Vietnam FTA ch 8 Art 14 para 4 (emphasis added).

unpreventable by the state. Such language does not go to great lengths to answer calls for greater specificity in FTAs; to the contrary, the EU–Vietnam language appears to accord a new realm of interpretative authority to arbitrators. Moreover, in observing the ICSID's decisions in cases such as *Asian Agricultural Products*,[75] which used the 'reasonably necessary' qualifier to assess regulatory actions even where that language was absent from a BIT, we can again observe that the new EU–Vietnam language merely codifies existing practice rather than truly addressing any call for reform.

D. Umbrella clauses

Most umbrella clauses contain broad and simple form language[76] that has been interpreted since 2003 to allow investors to claim a breach of contract or other agreement as a violation of the BIT containing the clause.[77] This essentially elevates contractual agreements of the state to judgment in international tribunals. While CETA's proposed umbrella clause is relatively classic,[78] the Vietnam and Singapore agreements contain certain embellishments. The EU–Vietnam FTA Art 14 reads:

> Where a Party has entered into a written agreement with investors of the other Party or their investments referred to in Article 13 [Scope of section II Investment Protection] that satisfies all of the following conditions, that Party shall not breach the said agreement through the exercise of governmental authority. The conditions are:
>
> (a) the written agreement is concluded and takes effect after the date of entry into force of this Agreement;

[75] *Asia Agricultural Products Ltd (AAPL) v Republic of Sri Lanka*, ICSID Case No ARB/87/3, Final Award, 27 June 1990, para 8. The Tribunal stated that with regard to 'Art. 4(2) [of the UK-Sri Lanka BIT], the Government's liability thereunder would not arise except in the case that Claimant succeeds in providing the proof that the counter-insurgency actions were not *reasonably necessary* or that the governmental security forces caused excessive destruction' (emphasis added). However, Art 4(2) of the Sri Lanka BIT makes no mention of the 'reasonably necessary' standard. Paragraph 2(b) of Art 4 likely provides the basis of the Tribunal's interpretation. That subparagraph requires compensation for losses suffered resulting from the government's 'destruction of their property by its forces or authorities which was not caused in combat action or was not required by the necessity of the situation'. UK–Sri Lanka Agreement for the Promotion and Protection of Investments, Art 4(2)(b), entered into force on 18 December 1980, <http://investmentpolicyhub.unctad.org/Download/TreatyFile/2293> accessed 3 April 2017.

[76] A comprehensive version of an umbrella clause typically reads: 'Each Contracting Party shall observe any obligation it may have assumed with regard to investments.' See, eg, Katia Yannaca-Small, 'Interpretation of the Umbrella Clause in Investment Agreements' in Organization for Economic Cooperation and Development, *International Investment Law: Understanding Concepts and Tracking Innovations* (OECD, 2008).

[77] *Société Générale de Surveillance SA v Islamic Republic of Pakistan*, ICSID Case No ARB/01/13, Decision of the Tribunal on Objections to Jurisdiction, 6 August 2003, paras 166–7; and *Société Générale de Surveillance SA v Republic of the Philippines*, ICSID Case No ARB/02/6, Decision of the Tribunal on Objections to Jurisdiction, 29 January 2004, paras 115 and 119. The *SGS v Philippines* tribunal commented that the umbrella clause of the Swiss–Pakistan BIT is 'formulated in different and rather vaguer terms' and is 'less clear and categorical' (ibid, at para 119).

[78] Although the CETA umbrella clause largely mirrors the umbrella clause in the EU Model BIT, some have criticized the wording of the umbrella clause for failing to address all uncertainties regarding

(b) the investor relies on that written agreement in deciding to make or maintain an investment referred to in article Article 13 … other than the written agreement itself and the breach causes actual damages to that investment;
(c) the written agreement creates an exchange of rights and obligations in connection to the said investment, binding on both parties; and
(d) the written agreement does not contain a clause on the settlement of disputes between the parties to that agreement by international arbitration.[79]

Footnote 18 clarifies that 'written agreement' refers to 'an agreement in writing, entered into by a Party with an investor of the other Party or their investment, referred to in Article 13 … and negotiated and executed by both Parties, whether in a single instrument or multiple instruments'.[80]

The EU–Vietnam FTA language frames the umbrella clause positively: if a given agreement to which a government is bound fulfils the predefined conditions in Art 14, that party to the FTA cannot breach that agreement. If it does, it brings that breach within the jurisdiction of an international arbitral tribunal. By contrast, the EU–Singapore FTA, enacted just a year earlier, frames the triggering of its umbrella clause negatively. Art 9.4 of that FTA reads:

Where a Party, itself or through any entity mentioned in paragraph 5 of Article 9.1 (Definitions), had given a specific and clearly spelt out commitment in a contractual written obligation towards a covered investor of the other Party with respect to the covered investor's investment or towards such covered investment, that Party shall not frustrate or undermine the said commitment through the exercise of its governmental authority either:

(a) deliberately; or
(b) in a way which substantially alters the balance of rights and obligation in the contractual written obligation unless the Party provides reasonable compensation to restore the covered investor or investment to a position which it would have been in had the frustration or undermining not occurred.[81]

Notably, the EU–Singapore FTA introduces a 'substantial alteration' standard for determining whether a party frustrated or undermined a commitment. It moreover places interpretative power in the hands of the arbitrator to balance the 'rights and obligations' that amount to a frustration or an undermining of a commitment. Again, this language can be seen as a codification of existing practice, particularly with regard to the ICSID Argentina cases.[82]

the effects and scope of application of umbrella clauses still existing in arbitral jurisprudence. See, eg, Anna De Luca, 'Umbrella Clauses and Transfer Provisions in the (Invisible) EU Model BIT' (2014) *J World Inv & Trade* 506, 512.

[79] Footnotes excluded. EU–Vietnam FTA ch 8, Art 14.

[80] EU–Vietnam FTA ch 8, Art 14, fn 18.

[81] Footnotes excluded. EU–Singapore FTA ch 9, Art 9.4.

[82] See, eg, *El Paso Energy International Co v The Argentine Republic*, ICSID Case No ARB/03/15, Decision on Jurisdiction of 27 April 2006; arguments of the parties in *Siemens AG v The Argentine Republic*, ICSID Case No ARB/02/8, Award, 6 February 2007.

E. Fair and equitable treatment

At first glance, far-reaching reforms have been adopted with regard to the fair and equitable treatment standard. Instead of only referring to 'fair and equitable treatment' as a rather vague legal term, a list of specific measures constituting a breach of fair and equitable treatment is included in the investment protection chapter of the recent FTAs of the EU. This list includes the following measures: denial of justice; fundamental breach of due process and similar measures; manifest arbitrariness; target discrimination based on gender, race, and the like; and abusive treatment of investors.[83] Specifically, Art 8.10 paragraph 2 CETA stipulates that:

[a] Party breaches the obligation of fair and equitable treatment referenced in paragraph 1 if a measure or series of measures constitutes:

(a) denial of justice in criminal, civil or administrative proceedings;
(b) fundamental breach of due process, including a fundamental breach of transparency, in judicial and administrative proceedings;
(c) manifest arbitrariness;
(d) targeted discrimination on manifestly wrongful grounds, such as gender, race or religious belief;
(e) abusive treatment of investors, such as coercion, duress and harassment; or
(f) a breach of any further elements of the fair and equitable treatment obligation adopted by the Parties in accordance with paragraph 3 of this Article.[84]

These provisions might appear to stand in contrast to the 1920s *Neer* standard, which required a stringent 'egregious and shocking' threshold for state behaviour to amount to a breach of fair and equitable treatment.[85] However, more recent decisions have distinguished certain elements of *Neer* while upholding its core standard in flexible terms.[86] In *Glamis Gold v United States*, a UNCITRAL Tribunal adjudicating the fair and equitable treatment standard found:

... although situations may be more varied and complicated today than in the 1920s, the level of scrutiny is the same. The fundamentals of the *Neer* standard thus still apply today: to violate the customary international law minimum standard of treatment codified in Article 1105 of the NAFTA, an act must be sufficiently egregious and shocking—a gross denial of justice, manifest arbitrariness, blatant unfairness, a complete lack of due process, evident discrimination, or a manifest lack of reasons—so as to fall below accepted international standards and constitute a breach of Article 1105(1). The Tribunal notes that one aspect of evolution from *Neer* that is generally agreed upon is that bad faith is not required to find a

[83] Art 8.10(2) CETA. [84] Art 8.10(2) CETA, footnotes omitted.

[85] *USA (LF Neer) v United Mexican States*, Decision of the General Claims Commission, United States–Mexico, 15 October 1926, *Opinions of Commissioners, 1927*, reproduced in *The American Journal of International Law*, 555–6; 3 ILR 213. See also *Mondev International Ltd v United States of America*, ICSID Case No ARB(AF)99/2, Award, 11 October 2002, paras 115–16. *Mondev* broke with the 1920s *Neer* application of full faith and security, finding that a breach of 'security' need not be 'egregious' or 'outrageous' by modern standards. It distinguished its finding by emphasizing that *Neer* articulated the standard in application to a physical person, not to physical property.

[86] *Mondev International Ltd v United States of America*, ICSID Case No ARB(AF)99/2, Award, 11 October 2002, paras 115–16.

violation of the fair and equitable treatment standard, but its presence is conclusive evidence of such. Thus, an act that is egregious or shocking may also evidence bad faith, but such bad faith is not necessary for the finding of a violation. The standard for finding a breach of the customary international law minimum standard of treatment therefore remains as stringent as it was under *Neer*; it is entirely possible, however that, as an international community, we may be shocked by State actions now that did not offend us previously.[87]

With this decidedly flexible reaffirmation of *Neer*'s fundamentals in mind, and turning back to the provisions of Art 8.10 CETA, one can observe several evolving (post-*Neer*) principles of customary international law reflected in that Article's sub-paragraphs. For example, Art 8.10(2)(a) CETA's reference to the 'denial of justice in criminal, civil or administrative proceedings' mirrors the European Convention on Human Rights' Art 6, which protects an individual's right to a fair trial '[i]n the determination of his civil rights and obligations or of any criminal charge against him'.[88] However, Art 8.10(2)(b) appears to limit the customary interpretation of this right by limiting a finding of FET breaches to 'a *fundamental* breach of due process'.[89] This language implies that only serious or even grave breaches of due process can be considered violations, whereas an interpretation abiding only by *Glamis Gold* and customary international law could include any breach of due process rights. Similarly, Art 8.10(2)(c) CETA requires 'manifest arbitrariness', which limits the scope of arbitrary discrimination that can fall under the FET provisions. And for better or for worse, Art 8.10(2)(d) brings into the scope of investment treaty tribunals an element previously reserved to human rights law by forbidding discrimination based on 'manifestly wrongful grounds, such as gender, race or religious belief'. Finally, after restricting the interpretative power of arbitral tribunals by limiting 'vagueness' through specificity in Art 8.10(2), CETA opens up the interpretative landscape via Art 8.10(4):

> When applying the above fair and equitable treatment obligation, a Tribunal may take into account whether a Party made a specific representation to an investor to induce a covered investment, that created a legitimate expectation, and upon which the investor relied in deciding to make or maintain the covered investment, but that the Party subsequently frustrated.[90]

Notably, the tribunal is accorded discretion as to whether to consider representations a state made to an investor in courting the investor prior to an investment in deciding whether the FET standard was violated. The tribunal is also accorded interpretative power in determining what constitutes a 'legitimate expectation' on the part of the investor in light of those representations.

Overall, as with so many other reforms, the reforms in FET codification appear generally to reflect standards that already exist in customary international law. Indeed, in actual practice, there are no arbitral cases indicating that the FET

[87] *Glamis Gold v United States*, UNCITRAL, Award, 8 June 2009, <http://www.italaw.com/sites/default/files/case-documents/ita0378.pdf> accessed 3 April 2017.
[88] European Convention on Human Rights (ECHR), Art 6.
[89] Emphasis added. Ch 8, Art 8.10(2)(b) CETA.
[90] Ch 8, Art 8.10(4) CETA.

standard undermines a government's legitimate right to regulate in the public interest or chills regulatory activity.[91] However, it would appear that codification of these standards provides less protection for investors through terms requiring that arbitrary treatment be 'manifest' or that breaches of due process be 'fundamental'. Moreover, actually codifying arbitral practice in treaty language restricts the interpretative flexibility of arbitral tribunals.

F. General exceptions

Art 9.3 of the EU–Singapore FTA[92] sets out general exceptions to the non-discrimination requirements similar to those found in Art XX GATT. Both treaties set out general exceptions that allow states to accord less favourable treatment to international interests than to domestic ones. While Art XX GATT applies to restrictions on trade, Art 9.3 EU–Singapore FTA applies to covered investments.[93]

At first glance, the Singapore FTA indeed accords greater regulatory freedom to states by allowing domestic lawmakers to privilege domestic investors in situations where it is necessary to protect domestic interests—for example, regarding public morals or human life or health. However, the EU–Singapore FTA's adoption of some GATT language in no way implicates a shift towards the dispute settlement process employed to bring claims under the GATT and its sister treaties in the WTO system. That system, at least as far as directionality of claims are concerned, presents a truly symmetrical system of liability between parties to a given dispute, because any WTO member can initiate proceedings against any other WTO member.[94] Granted, the WTO system has other problems of asymmetry,[95] especially asymmetry between parties to treaty negotiations, but because those are asymmetries in establishing procedure (and substance),[96] not in procedure itself, those debates are outside the scope of this chapter. The important point at this juncture is that, although general exceptions to non-discrimination have been introduced in international investment law as so-called 'reforms', in practice, they do not reform

[91] See, eg, Christian Tietje and Freya Baetens, 'The Impact of Investor-State Dispute Settlement (ISDS) in the Transatlantic Trade and Investment Partnership' (2015), <https://www.rijksoverheid.nl/documenten/rapporten/2014/06/24/the-impact-of-investor-state-dispute-settlement-isds-in-the-ttip> accessed 3 April 2017; and Gary H Sampliner, 'Arbitration of Expropriation Cases Under U.S. Investment Treaties—A Threat to Democracy or the Dog That Didn't Bark?' (2003) 18 *ICSID Rev* 1.

[92] EU–Singapore FTA ch 9, Art 9.3.

[93] ibid.

[94] Any state party can bring a complaint under any of the WTO's covered agreements pursuant to the DSU, Dispute Settlement Rules: Understanding on Rules and Procedures Governing the Settlement of Disputes, Marrakesh Agreement Establishing the World Trade Organization, Annex 2, The Legal Texts: The Results of the Uruguay Round of Multilateral Trade Negotiations, 354 (1999), 1869 UNTS 401, 33 ILM 1226 (1994).

[95] See, eg, Joost Pauwelyn, 'A Typology of Multilateral Treaty Obligations: Are WTO Obligations Bilateral or Collective in Nature?' (2003) 14 *European J Int L* 907–51; see also J Langille, 'Neither Constitution nor Contract: Understanding the WTO by Examining the Legal Limits on Contracting Out through Regional Trade Agreements' (2011) 86 *NYU L Rev* 1482–518.

[96] See ibid. Pauwelyn argues that WTO law is essentially a multilateralization of bilateral negotiations between states, and that because the initial bilateral negotiations that eventually become 'multilateralized' are often asymmetrical in terms of state bargaining power, the multilateral system too exhibits an asymmetrical character.

the directionality of investment claims, and, accordingly, do not address the asymmetry of the system. As a result, the transplant of existing international standards through the inclusion of well-known GATT-inspired provisions again represents a continuation of existing international arbitration practice rather than any genuine reform to the existing system.

V. Conclusions on Current State of Reform

As demonstrated in the sections above, there are varying degrees of success in the reform proposals and provisions put forth in international investment law since 2004. On the one hand, states have adopted some welcome clarifications addressing investment treaty provisions that placed too great an interpretative power in the hands of arbitrators—for example, with regard to fair and equitable treatment.[97] On the other hand, the reforms have not addressed or given rise to new problematic restrictions on investment protection—for example, with regard to indirect expropriation provisions.[98] Overall, the proposed and enacted reforms have clarified within the limits of what can be clarified. Perhaps more than anything, the reform provisions since 2004 have clarified the limits of using greater specificity in treaty drafting as a tool to curb the interpretative power of arbitrators. That is, they elucidated the boundaries of what can be addressed through specificity alone. Moreover, the reforms do not appear to actually reform anything about how the system functions: interpretative power for arbitrators remains vast, and as can be seen especially through existing right-to-regulate and FET reforms, most of the language bringing greater specificity to investment treaties merely codifies established arbitral practice.

Finally, while greater specificity may address some of the problems with the current international investment system, it is inadequate to address a more systemic problem that plagues the project of reform itself: state-investor claim directionality. That is, simply put, the lack of investor liability to the state. Accordingly, the next section of this chapter will illustrate the dilemma of the current reforms proposals and attempt to explain that all of those proposals are inadequate to alleviate the dilemma. This will lead to the final part of this chapter, which will present a somewhat radical new approach to investment protection which is in line with the so-called UN protect, respect, and remedy framework.

VI. Structural Problem of Current Reform Attempts

Much of what the reforms in international investment agreements since 2004 have tried to achieve is greater protection for a state that finds itself caught between a potential financial obligation to an investor and a public policy obligation to

[97] See section IV.E of this chapter.

[98] See section IV.B of this chapter.

its citizens. However, reforms that merely attempt to provide predictability through specificity fail to address the greater systemic problem that leads to this dilemma: namely, the fact that the international investment system only imposes obligations on states, not on investors. Indeed, as the ICSID in *Spyridon Roussalis v Romania* put it:

The Tribunal ... considers that the ... BIT limit[s] jurisdiction to claims brought by investors about obligations of the host State. The meaning of the 'dispute' is the issue of compliance by the State with the BIT ... *the BIT imposes no obligations on investors, only on contracting States.*[99]

The evolution of ICSID jurisdictional decisions since *Roussalis* has shown a very limited universe of situations in which states can actually bring counterclaims against investors after investors initiate proceedings against states.[100] Moreover, as *Roussalis* makes clear, the state has no opportunity to initiate claims against investors because the international investment system as such imposes no positive obligations on investors vis-à-vis states.[101] Thus, limitations on counterclaims and the absence of a right to bring a claim as such for states present a glaring dilemma in light of the current dominant reform proposals.

This dilemma may best be highlighted by conceptualizing the three primary possibilities for reform to the current international investment system. First, because the system exists to address the necessity of protecting international investors in situations in which they are legally weak (ie investing in foreign states subject to foreign legal systems in which investments are legally subject only to the domestic dispute settlement system), the system could be reformed to limit the rights of states. However, this is not a realistic option, at the very least for political reasons.[102]

Second, because the state is conceptualized as an equal partner in an international investment agreement but as a sovereign entity, the system could be reformed to limit the rights of investors. However, as we have shown in previous sections, reforms to the current system that attempt to emphasize state equality run counter to the logic of a system in which investment agreements pose obligations only on states and counterclaims by states are permitted only where investors agree to permit them. The reform attempts in this area, at best, codify existing international arbitral practice and provide greater predictability, but they do not address the systemic inequality of the structure.

The third possibility for reforming the system is addressing the inherently asymmetrical structure of investment treaties. While the first two options (investor

[99] *Spyridon Roussalis v Romania*, paras 869 and 871 (emphasis added).

[100] See, eg, *Antoine Goetz & Consorts and SA Affinage des Metaux v Burundi*; and *Occidental Petroleum Corp and Occidental Exploration and Production Co v Republic of Ecuador*. See also older decisions, eg, *Saluka Investments BV v The Czech Republic; Limited Liability Co AMTO v Ukraine*, Final Award; and *RSM Production Corp v Grenada*, Award.

[101] See *Spyridon Roussalis v Romania*, paras 869 and 871; see generally ibid.

[102] See, eg, Philipp Harms, *International Investment, Political Risk and Growth* (Kluwer Academic Publishing, 2000) 72; and Multilateral Investment Guarantee Agency, *World Investment and Political Risk 2010* (World Bank, 2011) 19.

protection and state equality/sovereignty) cast treaty language as culprit and attempt to ensure predictability through specificity, the third possibility addresses the structure of the system and therefore allows for recognition that some degree of vagueness is not only inherent in treaty language, but also provides necessary flexibility. Rather than limiting the rights of the state or limiting the rights of the investor as a general matter, reforming the asymmetrical structure to one that allows both investors and states to bring claims would enshrine the interests of both parties and limit rights only as necessary where obligations are breached or infringed. It would also live up to Professor Ruggie's Guiding Principles on Business and Human Rights enshrined in the UN's 2011 Protect, Respect and Remedy Framework.[103]

VII. Towards a Symmetrical System of International Investment Law

Establishing a symmetrical system in international investment law would foster the common reform goals of coherence and cooperation of the stakeholders within the system. While the current asymmetrical system provides rights only for investors and imposes obligations only on states, a symmetrical system would provide rights and impose obligations on both states and investors.

Attempts to mitigate the asymmetry of investment law are already emerging in international investment treaties, although no comprehensive counterclaim provision has yet gone into force. Indeed, India's 2015 Draft Model BIT included language that would have altered the established arbitral practice in Art 14.11:

> A Party may initiate a counterclaim against the Investor or Investment for a breach of the obligations set out under Articles 9, 10, 11 and 12 of Chapter III of this Treaty [corruption, disclosure, taxation, compliance with host state law] before a tribunal established under this Article and seek as a remedy suitable declaratory relief, enforcement action or monetary compensation.[104]

For reasons beyond the scope of this chapter, this language was later dropped in India's new 2016 Draft Model BIT.[105] However, a provision that has not been dropped but has yet to enter into force can be found in the Investment Chapter of

[103] United Nations, Office of the High Commissioner on Human Rights (OHCHR), 'Guiding Principles on Business and Human Rights: Implementing the United Nations "Protect, Respect and Remedy" Framework' (United Nations, 2011) HR/PUB/11/04, <http://www.ohchr.org/Documents/Publications/GuidingPrinciplesBusinessHR_EN.pdf> accessed 3 April 2017 (hereafter OHCHR, 'Guiding Principles'); see also John Ruggie for the Human Rights Council (HRC), 'Protect, Respect and Remedy: A Framework for Business and Human Rights' (7 April 2008) A/HRC/8/5, <https://business-humanrights.org/sites/default/files/reports-and-materials/Ruggie-report-7-Apr-2008.pdf> accessed 3 April 2017 (hereafter Ruggie, HRC, 'Protect, Respect and Remedy').

[104] 2015 Indian Draft Model BIT, ch 14, Art 14.11, <https://www.mygov.in/sites/default/files/master_image/Model%20Text%20for%20the%20Indian%20Bilateral%20Investment%20Treaty.pdf> accessed 3 April 2017.

[105] 2016 Model Text for the Indian Bilateral Investment Treaty, <http://indiainbusiness.nic.in/newdesign/upload/Model_BIT.pdf> accessed 10 October 2016.

the proposed Trans-Pacific Partnership Agreement (TPP).[106] TPP Chapter 9, Art 9.19(2) reads: 'When the claimant submits a claim pursuant to [TPP Chapter 9], the respondent may make a counterclaim in connection with the factual and legal basis of the claim or rely on a claim for the purpose of a set off against the claimant.'[107] Footnote 32 to that provision reads: 'In the case of investment authorisations, this paragraph shall apply only to the extent that the investment authorisation, including instruments executed after the date the authorisation was granted, creates rights and obligations for the disputing parties.'[108]

This language more or less mirrors existing treaty practice, which all but precludes the possibility of state counterclaims against investors. Under footnote 32, like the ICSID found in *Roussalis v Romania* and other cases,[109] a state could bring a counterclaim only where an investor has agreed a priori to a justiciable obligation.[110] There are no broad categories for justiciable counterclaims in TPP Art 9.19(2) or footnote 32, such as those present in the 2015 Indian Draft Model BIT—that is, corruption, disclosure, taxation, and compliance with host state law.[111] Rather than allowing for a revival of state ability to counterclaim, as an initial glance at TPP Art 9.19 might indicate, footnote 32 would essentially limit the ability of a state party to the TPP to the same limitations set out in *Roussalis*: the state could only bring a counterclaim where the investor agrees that the counterclaim can be brought beforehand.[112] Once again, the alleged 'reforms' to the existing system merely codify established arbitral practice: even the TPP's effort to re-establish counterclaims are rendered nominal by footnote 32. Accordingly, while TPP Art 9.19(2) may represent an effort to move towards greater symmetry, it does not go far enough. Only a provision like the discarded one in the 2015 Indian Model BIT could take significant steps towards a more symmetrical system.

Moreover, and more generally, efforts to restore the state's ability to bring counterclaims still fail to impose positive obligations on investors and create investor liability only after an investor has already initiated a claim against the state. Thus, although reform provisions such as those in the TPP and the 2015 Indian Model BIT may increase liability for investors, they do not go far enough to encourage investor responsibility before the arbitral stage.

Indeed, all of the challenges so far identified to the legitimacy of the international investment system could be addressed through a new symmetrical international investment structure that establishes a cause of action for both states and investors based on rights and obligations recognized in accordance with public international law. To this end, John Ruggie, the UN Special Representative on Business and Human Rights, proposed a set of Guiding Principles on Business and Human Rights, which were endorsed by the UN Human Rights Council

[106] TPP (n 29) ch 9. [107] ibid, Art 9.19(2). [108] TPP, fn 32.

[109] *Spyridon Roussalis v Romania*, paras 869 and 871; see also *Antoíne Goetz & Consorts and SA Affinage des Metaux v Burundi*; and *Occidental Petroleum Corp and Occidental Exploration and Production Co v Republic of Ecuador*. See also older decisions, eg, *Saluka Investments BV v The Czech Republic; Limited Liability Co AMTO v Ukraine,* Final Award; and *RSM Production Corp v Grenada*, Award.

[110] ibid. [111] See 2015 Indian Draft Model BIT, ch 14, Art 14.11.

[112] *Spyridon Roussalis v Romania*, paras 869 and 871.

in June 2011.[113] Paragraph 1, which sets out the grounding assumptions of the Guiding Principles, grants explicit recognition to:

(a) States' existing obligations to respect, protect and fulfil human rights and fundamental freedoms;
(b) The role of business enterprises as specialized organs of society performing specialized functions, required to comply with all applicable laws and to respect human rights;
(c) The need for rights and obligations to be matched to appropriate and effective remedies when breached.[114]

Adherence to the Guiding Principles would necessitate a symmetrical structure of the international investment regime that employed a combination of obligations for states and responsibility requirements for business partners. In accordance with the Principles, it should be recognized that, as articulated in the 1948 UN Universal Declaration on Human Rights, businesses are 'specialized organs of society' and they must 'comply with all applicable laws and ... respect human rights',[115] just like the language of the defunct 2015 Indian Draft Model BIT suggested (eg through its allowance of counterclaims in international tribunals for investor non-compliance with domestic laws).[116] Moreover, paragraph 1(a) refers to 'existing obligations' set out already in the 2008 'Respect, Protect and Remedy' Framework proposed by UN Special Representative John Ruggie and endorsed by the UN Human Rights Council.[117] That document rests on three essential pillars:

> [T]he state duty to protect against human rights abuses by third parties, including business, through appropriate policies, regulation, and adjudication; the corporate responsibility to respect human rights, which means to act with due diligence to avoid infringing on the rights of others and to address adverse impacts that occur; and greater access by victims to effective remedy, both judicial and non-judicial.[118]

Notably, while this language imposes a positive duty on states to protect human rights through state policy and action, it imposes only a 'responsibility' rather than a 'duty' on business enterprises to protect human rights, likely in recognition of the fact that states, not private enterprises, are bound by international human rights obligations.[119] Accordingly, reform of the international investment regime could not impose one-way obligations on business enterprises and remain congruent with the UN Guiding Principles for Businesses. To the contrary, reforms must also incorporate the right of access to remedies in the Framework as well as the Guiding

[113] OHCHR, 'Guiding Principles' (n 103). [114] ibid.
[115] Universal Declaration of Human Rights, Preamble, 217 A (III), 10 December 1948.
[116] 2015 Indian Draft Model BIT, ch 14, Art 14.11.
[117] Ruggie, HRC, 'Protect, Respect and Remedy' (n 103).
[118] UN Special Representative John Ruggie, 'The UN "Protect, Respect and Remedy" Framework for Business and Human Rights' (United Nations, September 2010) 1, <https://business-humanrights.org/sites/default/files/reports-and-materials/Ruggie-protect-respect-remedy-framework.pdf> accessed 3 April 2017.
[119] ibid.

Principles paragraphs 1(b) and 1(c), which emphasize the need for business enterprises to cooperate with states in ensuring that victims of human rights violations have traditional due process guarantees (ie the right to 'effective remedy, both judicial and non-judicial'[120]).[121]

Thus, a symmetrical international investment regime, pursuant to the UN Guiding Principles and arguably existing international law, should ensure the rule of law by the state as an essential component through the imposition of good governance obligations on states, but should also ensure 'responsibility' of enterprises as 'organ[s] of society', pursuant to the Guiding Principles and the Preamble to the Universal Declaration of Human Rights.[122] While the current asymmetrical system discourages investor-state cooperation by imposing obligations only on states, a symmetrical system that accomplishes a balanced system of rights and obligations of states and business enterprises would foster cooperation by restoring bargaining power to both stakeholders.

VIII. Conclusion

As we have demonstrated in the sections above, current discussions on reform disregard the logic of the system. The reform proposals attempt to limit investors' rights and accord greater protection to states in international investment disputes, but they only do so by codifying existing arbitral practice or by shifting the interpretative power of arbitrators from one flexible wording to another within a given BIT. Attempts to protect the right of states to regulate, then, run counter to the logic of an asymmetric system which, by design, assigns only rights to investors and only obligations to states. Therefore, current reform proposals that remain within an asymmetrical structure fail to convince as they are in contradiction to the system: the only existing international legal system that accords rights without obligations to one party and obligations without rights to another. Accordingly, 'replacing the current system' —for example, with a twenty-one-member investment court as proposed for the TTIP by the EU Commission and Parliament[123] and the other investment courts already contained in the text of CETA[124] and the EU–Vietnam FTA[125]—would require a change of the system. Whether or not this is advisable is a question we will leave for another juncture.

[120] ibid. [121] See OHCHR, 'Guiding Principles' (n 103).

[122] Universal Declaration of Human Rights, Preamble, 217 A (III), 10 December 1948: '[E]very individual and *every organ of society*, keeping this Declaration constantly in mind, shall strive by teaching and education to promote respect for these rights and freedoms and by progressive measures, national and international, to secure their universal and effective recognition and observance, both among the peoples of Member States themselves and among the peoples of territories under their jurisdiction' (emphasis added).

[123] European Parliament resolution of 8 July 2015 containing the European Parliament's recommendations to the European Commission on the negotiations for the Transatlantic Trade and Investment Partnership (TTIP) (2014/2228(INI)).

[124] European Commission, 'Investment Provisions in the EU–Canada Free Trade Agreement (CETA)', <http://trade.ec.europa.eu/doclib/docs/2013/november/tradoc_151918.pdf> accessed 3 April 2017.

[125] EU–Vietnam FTA ch 13, Art 23.

5

Authority, Legitimacy, and Fragmentation in the (Envisaged) Dispute Settlement Disciplines in Mega-Regionals

Stephan W Schill

I. Innocence Lost in International Dispute Settlement Design

Dispute settlement mechanisms have always been an important component of trade and investment agreements.[1] This holds true for the trading system established by the World Trade Organization (WTO), as well as for preferential trade and investment agreements, including traditional bilateral investment treaties (BITs) and, more recently, so-called mega-regionals. The existence and design of dispute settlement provisions can make the difference between a (relatively) inconsequential expression of political intentions concerning the future conduct of contracting parties in respect of an agreement's content and an effective legal regime that provides a mechanism for enforcing substantive obligations and instilling mutual compliance. In addition, dispute settlement mechanisms are important for resolving disagreement between contracting states about the interpretation of (necessarily) indeterminate and incomplete treaty terms and for allowing, within the limits of permissible interpretation, their further development. The juridification connected to both of these functions makes dispute settlement disciplines an important tool for contracting states to achieve the objectives of trade and investment agreements.[2]

Yet, for a long time, dispute settlement mechanisms have been seen not only primarily, but almost exclusively, as mere enforcement mechanisms that facilitate compliance of states with substantive economic law disciplines. The WTO Appellate

[1] The research leading to this chapter has received funding from the European Research Council (ERC) under ERC Grant Agreement No 313355, as part of the research project on 'Transnational Private-Public Arbitration as Global Regulatory Governance: Charting and Codifying the Lex Mercatoria Publica' (LexMercPub) carried out at the University of Amsterdam. The chapter was finalized based on material available as of 30 September 2016.

[2] See John H Jackson, *Sovereignty, the WTO, and Changing Fundamentals of International Law* (Cambridge University Press, 2006) 148; see also Joel P Trachtman, 'The WTO Cathedral' (2007) 43 *Stanford Journal of International Law* 127, 131.

Authority, Legitimacy, and Fragmentation in the (Envisaged) Dispute Settlement Disciplines in Mega-Regionals. Stephan Schill.

Body, for example, has been conceived by its founders as 'part of the enforcement wing of the WTO institution'.[3] More recently, this innocence, if not naivety, has been lost. Among scholars and states, an increasingly critical view has taken hold of the analysis of international dispute settlement as they have come to realize that the creation and design of these mechanisms can raise their own problems, problems, namely, that are not of a technical nature, but concern the multiple functions of dispute settlement disciplines, including in the further development of the law they apply and expound, their increasingly deep impact on domestic governance, and their evasiveness to control by states. In other words: their legitimacy, including from a democratic perspective, is at stake.[4]

Two concerns have proven to be particularly prominent in this respect. First, the creation of international dispute settlement mechanisms introduces a new class of actors (judges or arbitrators) that exercise interpretative authority over the governing law independently of the contracting parties. Dispute resolvers not only mechanically enforce pre-agreed substantive obligations and make them effective, but actively shape the governing law through interpretation, potentially even against the will of the contracting parties.[5] Dispute resolvers are thus able to serve as important lawmakers in international economic law and contribute to shaping the behaviour of states, including the manner in which they regulate in the public interest, as well as that of other actors, such as traders, investors, workers, and the population more generally. This concern has been particularly prominent with regard to Investor-State Dispute Settlement (ISDS) under international investment agreements (IIAs),[6] but has also been raised in relation to the WTO Appellate Body.[7] It involves questions about the scope of authority of dispute resolvers and the way in which they are controlled and legitimised.

[3] See generally on the development of the WTO Appellate body from its conceptualization as an enforcement tool towards the central actor in further developing WTO law, Robert Howse, 'The World Trade Organization 20 Years On: Global Governance by Judiciary' (2016) 27 *EJIL* 9, 31 (hereafter Howse, 'The World Trade Organization 20 Years On').

[4] See generally on the issue of legitimacy of international dispute settlement, Armin von Bogdandy and Ingo Venzke, *In Whose Name?: A Public Law Theory of International Adjudication* (Oxford University Press, 2014); see also Armin von Bogdandy and Ingo Venzke (eds), *International Judicial Lawmaking* (Springer, 2012).

[5] See generally Ingo Venzke, *How Interpretation Makes International Law* (Oxford University Press, 2012) (hereafter Venzke, 'How Interpretation Makes International Law').

[6] Charles N Brower, 'A Crisis of Legitimacy' *Nat'l LJ* (7 October 2002) B9; Charles N Brower, Charles H Brower, and Jeremy K Sharpe, 'The Coming Crisis in the Global Adjudication System' (2003) 19 *Arb Int'l* 415; Charles H Brower, 'Structure, Legitimacy, and NAFTA's Investment Chapter' (2003) 36 *Vand J Transnat'l L* 37; Ari Afilalo, 'Towards a Common Law of International Investment: How NAFTA Chapter 11 Panels Should Solve Their Legitimacy Crisis' (2004) 17 *Georgetown Int'l Envir L Rev* 51; Ari Afilalo, 'Meaning, Ambiguity and Legitimacy: Judicial (Re-)construction of NAFTA Chapter 11' (2005) 25 *Nw J Int'l L & Bus* 279, 282; Susan D Franck, 'The Legitimacy Crisis in Investment Treaty Arbitration: Privatizing Public International Law through Inconsistent Decisions' (2005) 73 *Fordham L Rev* 1521; Charles N Brower and Stephan W Schill, 'Is Arbitration a Threat or a Boon to the Legitimacy of International Investment Law?' (2009) 9 *Chicago JIL* 471 (hereafter Brower and Schill, 'Is Arbitration a Threat or a Boon'); and David Schneiderman, 'Legitimacy and Reflexivity in International Investment Arbitration: A New Self-Restraint?' (2011) 2(2) *JIDS* 471.

[7] See, eg, Howse, 'The World Trade Organization 20 Years On' (n 3); Venzke, 'How Interpretation Makes International Law' (n 5) 135ff; and Ingo Venzke, 'Making General Exceptions: The Spell of

Second, concerns have been raised about the fragmentation of international economic law resulting from the proliferation of bilateral and plurilateral trade and investment agreements with dispute settlement mechanisms.[8] This concern is particularly pressing in light of the question of whether these agreements interfere with, or even undermine, multilateralism in international economic relations, most importantly as regards the functioning of the WTO's multilateral trading system.[9] In this respect, the interaction of dispute settlement disciplines under mega-regionals with the WTO Dispute Settlement Body (DSB) as envisaged by these agreements becomes key. Do they threaten the authority of WTO multilateralism and the authority of the WTO Appellate Body? Or are dispute settlement disciplines in mega-regionals crafted in a way to minimise possible interference with the multilateral trading regime? Another aspect of fragmentation that has plagued both international trade and investment law is the relationship between economic and non-economic concerns, given that international dispute settlement disciplines tend to be asymmetric to the benefit of specific economic interests.[10]

Despite the fundamental questions that are connected to dispute settlement design in international economic law, these questions have, for a long time, drawn relatively little attention in trade and investment negotiations. Negotiators wring hard about the substantive commitments, in particular the extent of liberalization,

Precedents in Developing Article XX GATT into Standards for Domestic Regulatory Policy' in Armin von Bogdandy and Ingo Venzke (eds), *International Judicial Lawmaking* (Springer, 2012) 179.

[8] On fragmentation resulting from the proliferation of international dispute settlement bodies see, eg, Laurence R Helfer and Anne-Marie Slaughter, 'Toward a Theory of Effective Supranational Adjudication' (1997) 107 *Yale LJ* 273; Benedict Kingsbury, 'Foreword: Is the Proliferation of International Courts and Tribunals a Systemic Problem?' (1999) 31 *NYU J Int'l L & Pol* 679; Jonathan I Charney, 'The Impact on the International Legal System of the Growth of International Courts and Tribunals' (1999) 31 *NYU J Int'l L & Pol* 697; Cesare P R Romano, 'The Proliferation of International Judicial Bodies: The Piece of the Puzzle' (1999) 31 *NYU J Int'l L & Pol* 709; Roger P Alford, 'The Proliferation of International Courts and Tribunals: International Adjudication in Ascendance' (2000) 94 *Am Soc'y Int'l L Proc* 160; Shane Spelliscy, 'The Proliferation of International Tribunals: A Chink in the Armor' (2001) 40 *Colum J Transnat'l L* 143; and Lucy Reed, 'Great Expectations: Where Does the Proliferation of International Dispute Resolution Tribunals Leave International Law?' (2002) 96 *Am Soc'y Int'l L Proc* 219. See also the other contributions to a symposium held at New York University School of Law in October 1998 on the proliferation of international courts and tribunals, in (1999) 31 *NYU J Int'l L & Pol* 679–933. See generally also Martti Koskenniemi, 'Fragmentation of International Law: Difficulties Arising from the Diversification and Expansion of International Law', Report of the Study Group of the International Law Commission (International Law Commission, 13 April 2006) UN Doc A/CN.4/L.682.

[9] For the view that free trade agreements (FTAs) undermine multilateralism in international trade law, see Jagdish Bhagwati, *Termites in the Trading System: How Preferential Agreements Undermine Free Trade* (Oxford University Press, 2008). For a positive view on the relationship between FTAs and multilateralism, see, eg, Richard E Baldwin, 'Multilateralising Regionalism: Spaghetti Bowls as Building Blocs on the Path to Global Free Trade' (2006) 29(11) *The World Economy* 1451; and Adrian M Johnston and Michael J Trebilcock, 'Fragmentation in International Trade Law: Insights from the Global Investment Regime' (2013) 12(4) *World Trade Review* 621.

[10] Jochen von Bernstorff, 'Reflections on the Asymmetric Rule of Law in International Relations' in James Crawford and Sarah Nouwen (eds), *Select Proceedings of the European Society of International Law*, vol III: 2010 (Hart, 2012) 381; and Benedict Kingsbury, 'International Courts: Uneven Judicialisation in Global Order' in James Crawford and Martti Koskenniemi (eds), *The Cambridge Companion to International Law* (Cambridge University Press, 2012) 203.

whether to follow a negative list-approach or a positive list-approach, what substantive standards to base such agreements on, and what exceptions to maintain. Dispute settlement issues, by contrast, have normally only entered relatively late in the game, and with comparatively little academic or prior public discussion. In the Uruguay Round leading up to establishment of the WTO, for example, the creation of a dispute settlement system with a standing appellate body, which was to authoritatively interpret and apply WTO law, rather than a diplomatic mechanism as previously provided for under the General Agreement on Tariffs and Trade (GATT), was left for the later parts of the negotiations.[11] Still, it made all the difference in subjecting international trade relations to independent and effective legal disciplines and in creating institutions that could administer and further develop international trade law independently of the WTO members and their respective political and economic power.[12]

Meanwhile, by contrast, public attention to questions of dispute settlement design in mega-regionals abounds. While inter-state dispute settlement attracts very little attention, the intended inclusion of ISDS provisions in the Transatlantic Trade and Investment Partnership (TTIP) has brought hundreds of thousands of protesting citizens to the streets in Europe,[13] and led the European Commission to initiate a public consultation that resulted in almost 150,000, mostly critical, responses.[14] ISDS has also caused public outcry in the US and made the ratification of the Trans-Pacific Partnership (TPP) into a topic of US presidential elections; in fact, one of Donald Trump's first acts in office as US President has been the formal withdrawal from TPP, even though this decision was not motivated by criticism of ISDS.[15] Academic attention to these issues has equally increased tremendously.[16] In line with the emerging focus on international courts and

[11] See Peter Van den Bossche, 'From Afterthought to Centerpiece: The WTO Appellate Body and Its Rise to Prominence in the World Trading System' Maastricht Working Papers 2015/1,<http://pub.maastrichtuniversity.nl/bcde67e0-2775-4ab7-bb0d-9b89c1ca99d5> accessed 12 June 2017. See also John Croome, *Reshaping the World Trading System: A History of the Uruguay Round* (WTO, 1995) 264 (stating that 'the idea of an appellate body ... was discussed in detail from late 1989 onwards'); Ernst-Ulrich Petersmann, 'The Uruguay Round Negotiations 1986–1991' in Ernst-Ulrich Petersmann and Meinhard Hilf (eds), *The New GATT Round of Multilateral Trade Negotiations: Legal and Economic Problems* (2nd edn, Kluwer, 1991) 501, 555; and, generally, Terence P Stewart (ed), *The GATT Uruguay Round: A Negotiating History (1986–1992)*, vol II: *Commentary* (Kluwer, 1993) 2663ff ('Dispute Settlement Mechanisms').

[12] See also JHH Weiler, 'The Rule of Lawyers and the Ethos of Diplomats: Reflections on the Internal and External Legitimacy of WTO Dispute Settlement' (2001) 35(2) *Journal of World Trade* 191.

[13] Chris Johnston, 'Berlin Anti-TTIP Trade Deal Protest Attracts Hundreds of Thousands', *The Guardian* (10 October 2015), <https://www.theguardian.com/world/2015/oct/10/berlin-anti-ttip-trade-deal-rally-hundreds-thousands-protesters> accessed 4 April 2017.

[14] European Commission, 'Report: Online Public Consultation on Investment Protection and Investor-to-State Dispute Settlement (ISDS) in the Transatlantic Trade and Investment Partnership Agreement (TTIP)' SWD (2015) 3 final (13 January 2015) 3.

[15] See US Trade Representative, Letter to the Trans-Pacific Partnership Depositary (30 January 2017), <https://ustr.gov/sites/default/files/files/Press/Releases/1-30-17%20USTR%20Letter%20to%20TPP%20Depositary.pdf> accessed 8 May 2017. The importance of TPP in the presidential elections is noted by José E Alvarez, 'Is the Trans-Pacific Partnership's Investment Chapter the New "Gold Standard"?' IILJ Working Paper 2016/3 (2016) 1, <http://iilj.org/wp-content/uploads/2016/08/Alvarez_IILJ_2016_3-MegaReg.pdf> accessed 5 April 2017 (hereafter Alvarez, 'New Gold Standard').

[16] See, eg, Armand de Mestral (ed), *Second Thoughts: Investor State Arbitration between Developed Democracies* (CIGI Press, 2017); Ingo Venzke, 'Investor-State Dispute Settlement in TTIP from the

tribunals as lawmakers, the driving motivation of criticism of ISDS is its tension with constitutional principles, in particular the principle of democracy, the rule of law, and the protection of fundamental and human rights, in light of the far-reaching decisions tribunals can reach based on relatively indeterminate standards.[17] In parallel, as the assessment of dispute settlement disciplines morphed from a technical question to a highly political concern, negotiations on this issue have become more difficult.

It is therefore little surprising that making decisions on dispute settlement in ongoing trade and investment negotiations is happily deferred to the later parts of negotiations, although state parties regularly already table proposals about dispute settlement at an early stage of the negotiations, and although questions of dispute settlement are usually addressed in the negotiators' mandates.[18] Thus, negotiations on questions of dispute settlement in both the plurilateral Trade in Services Agreement (TiSA) and the TTIP have not proceeded beyond their incipient phases at the time of writing, without agreed textual proposals being available on either state-to-state or investor-state dispute settlement.[19] This, together with the fact that negotiations largely take place behind closed doors, despite efforts

Perspective of a Public Law Theory of International Adjudication' (2016) 17 *J World Inv & Trade* 374; Stefanie Schacherer, 'TPP, CETA and TTIP Between Innovation and Consolidation—Resolving Investor-State Disputes under Mega-Regionals' (2016) 7 *JIDS* 628; Philip Hainbach, 'The EU's Approach to Investor-State Arbitration in the Comprehensive Economic and Trade Agreement (CETA)' (2016) 13(1) *TDM*; Catharine Titi, 'The European Union's Proposal for an International Investment Court: Significance, Innovations and Challenges Ahead' (2017) 14(1) *TDM*; Kyle Dickson-Smith, 'Does the European Union Have New Clothes?: Understanding the EU's New Investment Treaty Model' (2016) 17 *J World Inv & Trade* 773; Rob Howse, 'Courting the Critics of Investor-State Dispute Settlement: The EU Proposal for a Judicial System for Investment Disputes' (2015) <https://cdn-media.web-view.net/i/fjj3t288ah/Courting_the_Criticsdraft1.pdf> accessed 4 April 2017; Piergiuseppe Pusceddu, 'State-to-State Dispute Settlement Provisions in the EU–Canada Comprehensive Economic and Trade Agreement' (2016) 13(1) *TDM*; and Alvarez, 'New Gold Standard' (n 15).

[17] See Stephan W Schill, 'International Investment Law and Comparative Public Law: An Introduction' in Stephan W Schill (ed), *International Investment Law and Comparative Public Law* (Oxford University Press, 2010) 3, 6–7 (hereafter Schill, 'International Investment Law and Comparative Public Law: An Introduction').

[18] See, eg, negotiation mandate for the European Commission for CETA, Council of the European Union, 'EU–Canada Trade Negotiating Mandate Made Public' (15 December 2015), <http://www.consilium.europa.eu/en/press/press-releases/2015/12/15-eu-canada-trade-negotiating-mandate-made-public/> accessed 4 April 2017. For TTIP, see Council of the European Union, 'Directives for the Negotiation on a Comprehensive Trade and Investment Agreement, Called the Transatlantic Trade and Investment Partnership, Between the European Union and the United States of America', ST 11103/13 (17 June 2013) paras 22ff, <http://data.consilium.europa.eu/doc/document/ST-11103-2013-DCL-1/en/pdf> accessed 28 August 2016. For TiSA, see Council of the European Union, 'Draft Directives for the Negotiation of a Plurilateral Agreement on Trade in Services', 6891/13 ADD 1 (8 March 2013).

[19] For the latest state of play on the negotiations of these agreements regarding dispute settlement at the time of writing, see the reports by the European Commission. On TiSA, see European Commission, 'Report of the 19th TiSA Negotiation Round 8–18 July 2016' (27 July 2016) 2, <http://trade.ec.europa.eu/doclib/docs/2016/july/tradoc_154824.pdf> accessed 4 April 2017 (hereafter European Commission, 'TiSA 27 July 2016'). On TTIP, see European Commission, 'Public Report of the 14th Round of Negotiations for the Transatlantic Trade and Investment Partnership' (July 2016) 15–16, <http://trade.ec.europa.eu/doclib/docs/2016/august/tradoc_154837.pdf> accessed 4 April 2017 (hereafter European Commission, 'Public Report of the 14th Round').

namely of the European Commission to introduce greater transparency,[20] makes meaningful analysis of dispute settlement disciplines as a matter of positive law in these mega-regionals complicated and speculative. What is more, as the case of the Canada–EU Comprehensive Economic and Trade Agreement (CETA) shows, provisions on dispute settlement can still change quite radically even after negotiations are formally concluded. Thus, the ISDS provisions originally agreed on in CETA in September 2014 were altered during so-called 'legal scrubbing' from a system of reformed investor-state arbitration to include a version of the 'investment court system' (ICS) that the EU first proposed as part of the TTIP negotiations in November 2015.[21]

While the text of CETA, which reflects the EU's position on dispute settlement in trade and investment agreements more generally, can therefore be analysed, no texts exist, at the time of writing, that would reflect agreed positions of the parties negotiating TiSA and TTIP. With regard to TiSA, we know little more than the contours of its envisaged dispute settlement mechanism, namely that it will likely include state-to-state arbitration with provisions largely mirroring those of the WTO Dispute Settlement Understanding (DSU), but no provisions on ISDS.[22] With regard to TTIP, whose future has become questionable after Donald Trump taking office, proposals of the EU on inter-state and ISDS have been made public,[23] but no US proposal is publicly known. Reports on the negotiation indicate, however, that the positions of the EU and the US on inter-state dispute settlement are relatively close, reflecting differences in detail rather than principle.[24] With regard

[20] For information provided by the EU, see European Commission, 'In Focus: Trade in Services Agreement (TiSA)', <http://ec.europa.eu/trade/policy/in-focus/tisa/> accessed 4 April 2017; and European Commission, 'In Focus: Transatlantic Trade and Investment Partnership (TTIP)', <http://ec.europa.eu/trade/policy/in-focus/ttip/> accessed 4 April 2017. Similar efforts from other negotiating parties, including above all the US, are sparse. See Office of the US Trade Representative, 'Transatlantic Trade and Investment Partnership (T-TIP)', <https://ustr.gov/ttip> and 'Trade in Services Agreement', <https://ustr.gov/TiSA> both accessed 4 April 2017. In addition, documents relating to mega-regional negotiations are regularly leaked and published, inter alia, on <https://wikileaks.org/tisa/> and <https://wikileaks.org/ttip/> both accessed 4 April 2017.

[21] Compare Comprehensive Economic and Trade Agreement (CETA) Between Canada, of the One Part, and the European Union, of the Other Part (Final Text) (2016) ch 8 ('Investment'), <http://trade.ec.europa.eu/doclib/docs/2014/september/tradoc_152806.pdf>, to Comprehensive Economic and Trade Agreement (CETA) Between Canada, of the One Part, and the European Union, of the Other Part (Consolidated Text as of 26 September 2014) ch 10 ('Investment'), <www.bmwfw.gv.at/Aussenwirtschaft/investitionspolitik/Documents/CETA-Text.pdf> both accessed 12 June 2017.

[22] See European Commission, 'TiSA 27 July 2016' (n 19) 2.

[23] Proposal of the European Union for Investment Protection and Resolution of Investment Disputes (12 November 2015), <http://trade.ec.europa.eu/doclib/docs/2015/november/tradoc_153955.pdf> accessed 4 April 2017 (hereafter EU Commission, 'Proposal 12 November 2015'); and Proposal of the European Union on Dispute Settlement (Government to Government) (7 January 2015), <http://trade.ec.europa.eu/doclib/docs/2015/january/tradoc_153032.pdf> accessed 4 April 2017 (hereafter EU Commission, 'Proposal 7 January 2015').

[24] See European Commission, 'Public Report of the 14th Round' (n 19) (stating that 'there is a large extent of convergence in this area' and listing issues that are still subject to discussion, including questions of timing, compliance, and post-retaliation, the possibility or not of non-violation complaints, publication of dissenting opinions, and some questions linked to retaliation).

to ISDS, by contrast, the positions still appear further apart, as the EU is seeking the creation of a permanent tribunal for settling investor-state disputes, while the US, at least before Trump, appears to aim at a reformed version of investor-state arbitration as is reflected in the investment chapter included in TPP.[25] Consequently, CETA and TPP not only illustrate the transatlantic struggle about different approaches to dispute settlement, but are (still) good indicators of how the future structural features of dispute settlement disciplines in international economic agreements will be shaped, given that the EU and the US are still the most important global rule-shapers.

Against this background, the present chapter engages in a critical analysis of CETA and TPP as indicators of how mega-regional trade agreements more generally are likely going to deal with dispute settlement. Dealing with both inter-state dispute settlement and ISDS, it argues that dispute settlement disciplines rightly assume a pivotal role in trade and investment negotiations as they raise fundamental questions about the authority and legitimacy of dispute resolution and concerns of fragmentation. Addressing these concerns arguably explains the developments and reforms in dispute settlement design, some rather minor, others more significant, that we are seeing in mega-regional trade agreements. The comparison between CETA and TPP shows that inter-state dispute settlement in mega-regionals builds largely on existing dispute settlement features that developed in the WTO, and only cautiously innovate. They do make use, however, of arbitration rather than permanent judicial bodies. Inter-state dispute resolution mechanisms in these agreements aim at striking a balance between the need for effective compliance, on the one hand, and ensuring control of states over dispute resolution and minimising negative effects of fragmentation, in particular in respect of the WTO, on the other.

In respect of ISDS, in turn, both CETA and TPP innovate as compared to classical investment-treaty-based arbitration and adapt to the constitutional challenges and legitimacy critique by ensuring that policy space is safeguarded, that control by contracting parties over dispute settlement is tightened, and that internal and external fragmentation is limited. However, notwithstanding common trajectories in ISDS reform, stark differences arise as US opposition (already before Trump) against the push of the EU for the creation of permanent judicial bodies, both at the bilateral and multilateral level, crystallizes. The position of the EU, on the one hand, and that taken by the parties to TPP, on the other, likely mark the poles between which the global structure of ISDS design will oscillate in the future.

A big question mark, of course, is connected to how the US position will develop since Trump's taking office and given his withdrawal from TPP. Some see this, together with Brexit, as a sign for a renewed and enduring trend of protectionism and nationalism taking hold of international economic goveranance. Others are inclined to see these phenomena as transitory regressions in the process of international economic integration. After all, the US under Trump as well as the UK

[25] See Trans-Pacific Partnership Agreement (adopted 4 February 2016, not yet in force) Arts 9.19–9.30, <https://ustr.gov/sites/default/files/TPP-Final-Text-Investment.pdf> accessed 4 April 2017.

after Brexit will have to find a stance on issues of international dispute settlement design even if they will not push or participate in mega-regional trade agreements of the sort discussed here. Yet, whether their positions will diverge fundamentally from either what the EU is currently pursuing, or what the US has pursued before Trump, is doubtful, as the current mega-regionals projects, above all CETA and TPP, are likely going to serve as models even for Trump's US and for post-Brexit UK. Despite all of these uncertainties, what is more certain is that, to the extent the major actors in global economic governance can agree, we may witness a constitutional moment in international economic law at some point in the future.

II. Inter-State Dispute Settlement in Mega-Regionals

Mega-regionals all provide for state-to-state dispute settlement mechanisms. This holds true for CETA and TPP, as well as for TTIP[26] and TiSA.[27] What is more, although differences in detail exist, TPP and CETA show a great level of commonality and convergence in their structural approaches and at the level of principle. This convergence is, to a large extent, due to the fact that the state-to-state dispute settlement provisions in both agreements build on well-established practices enshrined in the WTO DSU and in the dispute settlement chapters of existing FTAs. Moreover, the inter-state dispute settlement disciplines in CETA and TPP share the concern of minimising friction with the authority of the WTO DSB, particularly the Appellate Body. This is achieved both through the choice for arbitration and a low level of institutionalization, but also through a number of other features that clarify that the purpose behind the creation of inter-state dispute settlement disciplines in mega-regionals is not to challenge the authority of the WTO (see section II.A). Still, contracting states are clearly concerned about transferring too much authority to dispute settlement mechanisms. For these reasons, various features in CETA and TPP cater to the interest of contracting states to control the authority of inter-state dispute resolution bodies (see section II.B). Both aspects contribute to what parties to mega-regionals consider to be a legitimate role for international dispute settlement that helps to enforce substantive obligations, without becoming too independent from contracting parties (see section II.C).

A. Building on and minimising friction with the WTO

Inter-state dispute settlement mechanisms under mega-regionals are, to a large extent, inspired by the dispute settlement mechanism in the WTO. Often enough, they even copy provisions from the DSU verbatim or at least build on them. In other aspects, CETA and TPP codify practices that the WTO Appellate Body

[26] See EU Commission, 'Proposal 12 November 2015' (n 23); EU Commission, 'Proposal 7 January 2015' (n 23); and EU Commission, 'Public Report of the 14th Round' (n 19).

[27] See European Commission, 'TiSA 27 July 2016' (n 19) 2.

has developed in its dispute settlement experience, based on wide interpretations of its governing law and inherent powers. Like in the WTO, inter-state dispute settlement mechanisms in CETA and TPP aim at providing effective compliance mechanisms that allow contracting parties to enforce the substantive obligations undertaken in the respective agreement. This is crucial as alternative fora for the settlement of disputes under these agreements are not available, or of limited use. The WTO DSB, for example, can only be called on for disputes under the WTO; it is unavailable to enforce obligations in mega-regionals as these are not 'covered agreements' in the sense of Art 1(1) DSU. Other international courts or tribunals, such as the International Court of Justice (ICJ), are not specifically tailored to resolve international economic disputes, above all in terms of the need for speedy dispute resolution in economic matters, and hence are not satisfactorily efficient.[28] Domestic courts, finally, are often equally unavailable for the enforcement of rights and obligations under mega-regionals as the treaties often lack direct effect within the domestic legal order.[29] Besides, domestic courts pose a greater risk to incoherent interpretation of the agreements and may be subject to home bias, therefore putting a truly neutral and independent application and enforcement of these agreements into question.

The most important difference with the WTO, however, is the fact that mega-regionals do not opt for institutionalized dispute settlement, but rely on ad hoc inter-state arbitration. No secretariats are established to support the settlement of mega-regional disputes, no appeal mechanisms are created in the inter-state dispute settlement realm. The low level of institutionalization connected with the choice for arbitration is a mechanism to minimise the authority of dispute settlement and ensure a high level of control by contracting parties. After all, as compared to a standing judicial body, one-off dispute settlement mechanisms are structurally in a much weaker situation to develop a coherent jurisprudence and ensure that this jurisprudence is carried forward independently of the active support of contracting states. A standing judicial body, by contrast, can develop its own jurisprudence and

[28] General inter-state dispute resolution mechanisms may also lack the necessary expertise in trade and investment matters and are procedurally poorly adapted to the resolution of international economic disputes, inter alia, in respect of the mechanisms for implementing their decisions.

[29] Both CETA and TPP contain provisions that exclude such direct effect and preclude parties from using domestic courts to enforce rights and obligations under mega-regionals. See Art 30.6 CETA ('Private rights'), which provides:

> 1. Nothing in this Agreement shall be construed as conferring rights or imposing obligations on persons other than those created between the Parties under public international law, nor as permitting this Agreement to be directly invoked in the domestic legal systems of the Parties.
> 2. A Party shall not provide for a right of action under its domestic law against the other Party on the ground that a measure of the other Party is inconsistent with this Agreement.

Similarly, Art 28.22 TPP ('Private rights') provides:

> No Party shall provide for a right of action under its law against any other Party on the ground that a measure of that other Party is inconsistent with its obligations under this Agreement, or that the other Party has otherwise failed to carry out its obligations under this Agreement.

implement its interpretation of the governing law more easily and at times even against the preference of contracting states.

Moreover, the choice of arbitration has the effect of protecting the authority of the WTO DSB, and particularly that of the Appellate Body, as it is less likely that a jurisprudential counterweight to its authority develops under the cloak of inter-state dispute settlement in mega-regionals. Certainly, mega-regionals generally grant the parties a choice among different available fora for the enforcement of the substantive obligations contained in TPP and CETA, including those norms that TPP and CETA copy or incorporate from other international agreements, including WTO law (so-called multi-sourced equivalent norms); however, mega-regionals do not establish hierarchies or priorities among different available fora.[30] Instead, any dispute settlement mechanism created by mega-regionals is considered as an alternative, not an additional forum to those already in existence elsewhere. After all, a choice for a specific forum once made under a mega-regional cannot be undone to the benefit of another forum. This rule excludes parallel and subsequent dispute settlement in multiple fora and suggests that dispute settlement disciplines in mega-regionals do not intend to siphon disputes away from other fora or the respective forum's applicable law, nor to multiply dispute settlement possibilities for one and the same dispute by opening up an additional avenue for dispute resolution.

Yet, the structural features of inter-state dispute settlement under mega-regionals cannot only be explained by states' desire to curtail the authority of independent third-party participation, but also by the desire to reduce friction with WTO dispute settlement and to avoid undermining the authority of the WTO DSB. Thus, the low level of institutionalization of inter-state dispute settlement under mega-regionals certainly also accounts for the parties' desire to allow a future reintegration of the substantive disciplines of mega-regionals into the WTO. This is not only the goal of TiSA, but also the desire with other WTO+ commitments undertaken in mega-regionals, such as TPP or CETA, which the parties may ultimately hope to multilateralize (within the WTO) in the future.

Avoiding fragmentation between mega-regionals and the WTO is also the purpose of specific rules of interpretation included in mega-regionals. Thus, both CETA and TPP make consideration of WTO precedent expressly into a rule of interpretation. Article 28.12(3)2 TPP provides that: 'With respect to any provision of the WTO Agreement that has been incorporated into this Agreement, the panel shall also consider relevant interpretations in reports of panels and the WTO Appellate Body adopted by the WTO Dispute Settlement Body.' Article 29.17 CETA even makes it into a general rule of interpretation that '[t]he arbitration panel shall also take into account relevant interpretations in reports of Panels and the Appellate Body adopted by the WTO' without limiting this rule to norms that are equivalent to WTO obligations.

[30] An exception is Art 10.2(7) TPP with regard to dispute settlement provisions provided in respect of air services agreements, which have to be exhausted before recourse is possible under the state-to-state dispute settlement chapter under TPP.

Only in some areas do the dispute settlement disciplines in mega-regionals go beyond WTO disciplines. This holds true, to different degrees, with regard to concerns other than the interests of traders and investors, including in the context of chapters on labour and the environment.[31] In this respect, the differences between CETA and TPP, and hence the general approaches taken by the US and the EU respectively, are somewhat greater than in other areas of state-to-state dispute settlement. CETA, for once, excludes matters arising under the chapters on labour and environment from formal inter-state dispute resolution completely.[32] Instead, in order to implement the respective chapters and settle disagreement between the contracting parties, it provides for recourse to cooperation mechanisms at the intergovernmental level[33] and to panels of experts, whose composition and procedures resemble those of state-to-state arbitration, but whose determinations are not binding.[34] In addition, inter-state mediation is encouraged to settle labour and environmental disputes.[35]

TPP, by contrast, allows recourse to inter-state arbitration, but foresees some modifications, in particular as regards the necessary qualification of arbitrators in labour, respectively environmental, law and practice.[36] TPP equally requires enhanced cooperative efforts by the disputing parties to settle labour and environment disputes amicably.[37] In the case of disputes under the chapter on labour, prior inter-governmental consultations are required, including if necessary involvement of the Labour Council, a treaty organ established under TPP and composed of senior governmental representatives.[38] The chapter on environment even provides a three-step consultation procedure prior to state-to-state arbitration, involving simple inter-governmental environmental consultations, senior representative consultations within the Environmental Committee established under TPP, and ministerial consultations.[39] In case no agreement can be reached among contracting parties to settle disputes about labour or environmental concerns, these concerns are given a better enforcement mechanism under TPP, and other US-led FTAs,[40] as

[31] See chs 23 ('trade and labour') and 24 ('trade and environment') of CETA and chs 19 ('labour') and 20 ('environment') of TPP.

[32] See Arts 23.11(1) and 24.16(1) CETA.

[33] See Arts 23.9 and 24.14 CETA.

[34] See Arts 23.10 and 24.15 CETA. Similarities with arbitration exist particularly in respect of: the requirement of experts to be independent and impartial; the rules on transparency; and their task to determine how measures in question have to be judged according to the legal standards contained in the chapters on labour and environment.

[35] See Arts 23.11(2) and 24.16(2) CETA.

[36] See Art 28.9(5) TPP.

[37] See Arts 19.15(12) and (13) and 20.23(1) TPP.

[38] For the procedures of labour consultations, see Art 19.15 TPP. Establishment, composition, and competences of the Labour Council are provided for in Art 19.12 TPP.

[39] See Arts 20.20, 20.21, and 20.22 TPP for the three-step procedure. Establishment, composition, and competences of the Environmental Committee are provided for in Art 20.19 TPP.

[40] US-led agreements allow binding inter-state dispute settlement in order to make states comply with their obligation to enforce domestic environmental and labour legislation. See, eg, Dominican Republic–Central America–United States FTA (signed 5 August 2004, entered into force 1 January 2009) Arts 16.7 (concerning disputes under the labour chapter) and 17.11 (concerning environmental matters), both in connection with the inter-state dispute settlemenet mechanisms laid down in ch 20, <https://ustr.gov/trade-agreements/free-trade-agreements/cafta-dr-dominican-republic-central-america-fta/

compared to CETA and the approach the EU generally takes in its trade and investment agreements,[41] which overall provide for weaker compliance tools for labour and environmental concerns.

All of this suggests that the inter-state dispute settlement provisions in mega-regionals aim at preserving, not undermining, the authority of the WTO DSB. The low level of institutionalization and careful crafting of the scope of inter-state dispute settlement in mega-regionals achieves to limit the authority of dispute resolvers under mega-regionals to the necessary minimum for making it into an effective compliance mechanism, while at the same time maximising state control over dispute settlement, and preventing the emergence of a serious counterweight to the WTO and its dispute settlement mechanism. Areas where dispute settlement are further-reaching than under the WTO, such as with regard to labour and environmental disputes, in turn, are areas outside the current competence of the WTO. In these areas, dispute settlement under mega-regionals could cautiously develop ideas for future reforms of the WTO, in particular as regards the incorporation of labour and environmental disciplines.

B. Controlling the authority of inter-state dispute settlement

The experience with dispute settlement in the WTO has not only influenced the contracting parties of mega-regionals in building dispute settlement disciplines that minimise friction with the WTO. It has also provided them with a suitable example for how powerful dispute settlement bodies can become and how much they can take control of a certain international legal regime. It is therefore little surprising that both CETA and TPP contain a variety of features—beyond the choice for arbitration with its low institutionalization—that aim at limiting the impact of dispute resolution bodies and ensuring the authority of contracting states. This includes a selective judicialization of subject matters covered by mega-regionals and the modification of the general dispute settlement regime for specifically sensitive

final-text> accessed 4 April 2017; and United States–Bahrain FTA (signed 14 September 2004, entered into force 11 January 2006) Arts 16.8(5) (concerning environmental matters) and 15.6(5) (concerning disputes under the labour chapter), each in connection with ch 19, <https://ustr.gov/trade-agreements/free-trade-agreements/bahrain-fta/final-text> accessed 4 April 2017. See also Michele Potestà, 'From Mutual Supportiveness to Mutual Enforcement? The Contribution of US Preferential Trade and Investment Agreements to the Effectiveness of Environmental Norms' in Rainer Hofmann, Stephan W Schill, and Christian J Tams (eds), *Preferential Trade and Investment Agreements: From Recalibration to Reintegration* (Nomos, 2013) 167.

[41] For the EU's approach, see Lorand Bartels, 'The EU's Approach to Social Standards and the TTIP' in Sangeeta Khorana (ed), *The Transatlantic Trade and Investment Partnership (TTIP) Negotiations between the EU and the USA* (Barcelona Centre for International Affairs, 2015) 83, 89f, <https://www.cidob.org/en/articulos/monografias/ttip/part_2_chapter_7> accessed 4 April 2017; Lorand Bartels, 'Social Issues in Regional Trade Agreements: Labour, Environment and Human Rights', Cambridge University Faculty of Law Legal Studies Research Paper No 57/2014 (2014) 17, <http://papers.ssrn.com/sol3/papers.cfm?abstract_id=2463246> accessed 4 April 2017; see also Amelia Porges, 'Dispute Settlement' in Jean-Pierre Chauffour and Jean-Christophe Maur (eds), *Preferential Trade Agreement Policies for Development* (World Bank, 2011) 482f.

areas of law and policy (see section II.B.1), the inclusion of a number of procedural safeguards (see section II.B.2), and the encouragement of alternative dispute resolution mechanisms, in particular mediation (see section II.B.3).

1. Selective judicialization

First of all, contracting parties control the authority of inter-state arbitral tribunals by circumscribing what the tribunals are competent to decide on. For this purpose, contracting parties limit the applicable law to claims for breach of the agreement in question, thereby excluding the possibility to enforce norms from outside the agreement through the dispute settlement mechanisms under mega-regionals. Both CETA and TPP thus provide that inter-state dispute settlement must concern a 'dispute concerning the interpretation or application of the provisions of this Agreement'.[42]

Yet, unlike in the WTO, inter-state dispute settlement under mega-regionals is not comprehensive in the sense that every dispute under the respective agreements could be submitted to third-party adjudication. Instead, mega-regionals regularly contain a number of carve-outs that exclude recourse to inter-state dispute settlement for certain subject matters. Mega-regionals therefore follow a model of selective judicialization by only making certain subject matters justiciable.

Under CETA, the following are excluded from recourse to inter-state dispute settlement:

- antidumping and countervailing duties (Art 3.7 CETA);
- subsidies (Art 7.9 CETA);
- decisions under the Investment Canada Act (Art 8.45 CETA and Annex 8-C);
- competition policy (Art 17.4 CETA);
- trade and labour (Art 23.11(1) CETA); and
- trade and environment (Art 24.16(2) CETA).

TPP contains an even greater list of subject matters that are excluded from state-to-state dispute settlement, including disputes about:

- antidumping and countervailing duties (Art 6.8(3) TPP);
- the equivalence of sanitary or phytosanitary measures of exporting and importing parties and about the conformity of the measures risk assessment with scientific standards (Art 7.8(6) fn 2 and Art 7.9(2) fn 3 TPP);
- violation of the provisions of the TBT Agreement incorporated into the TPP (Art 8.4(2) TPP);
- competition policy (Art 16.9 TPP);
- cooperation and capacity building (Art 21.6 TPP);

[42] Art 29.2 CETA; see further for limitation on dispute settlement to such disputes Arts 29.4(1) and 29.6(2) CETA. For the parallel provisions in TPP, see Arts 28.3(1), 28.5(1), and 28.8 TPP.

- cooperation in respect of competitiveness and business facilitation (Art 22.5 TPP);
- cooperation under the chapter on development (Art 23.9 TPP);
- cooperation on small and medium enterprises (Art 24.2 TPP);
- regulatory coherence (Art 25.11 TPP); and
- the refusal to grant temporary entry except if such refusal involved a pattern of practice (Art 12.10(1) TPP).

Several of these carve-outs have the function of making obligations in mega-regionals softer by excluding them from judicialization. This preserves policy space of contracting parties and allows them to further develop the law in the covered areas cooperatively rather than under the shadow of arbitral control. This is the case, for example, with the obligations on competition policy, movement of personnel of traders and investors,[43] taxation,[44] or anti-corruption laws and policies.[45] Preserving policy space, albeit in very specific policy contexts, can also be found in country-specific exceptions that allow certain contracting states a transitory period for adaptation as regards specific measures.[46] Other carve-outs have the function to protect the authority of the WTO. This is the case, for example, with the exclusion of recourse under TPP for breach of the rules on technical barriers to trade or sanitary and phytosanitary measures that are incorporated into TPP from the WTO—and thereby become independent obligations under TPP—or the rules on antidumping and countervailing measures.

Apart from carve-outs that exclude dispute settlement with regard to a specific subject matter completely, mega-regionals, such as TPP and CETA, also contain certain self-judging exceptions for the protection of core areas of public policy that, while not excluding dispute settlement altogether, expressly modify the standard of review to be applied. With regard to the issues covered by self-judging exceptions, the dispute settlement body cannot conduct a full *de novo* review, but only assess whether the discretion granted was exercised contrary to good faith.[47] Thus, Art 28.6(b) CETA contains a narrowly tailored self-judging clause relating to the protection of national security. It allows the contracting states to take measures they consider necessary to protect essential security interests connected to the production of and traffic in goods and technology relevant for military activity, actions taken in times of war and other emergency in international relations, and measures relating to fissionable material. The self-judging exception in TPP is slightly broader and includes, inter alia, measures the contracting state considers necessary for the protection of its own essential security interests, without the specific

[43] Art 12.10 TPP. [44] Art 29.4(2) TPP. [45] Art 26.12(3) TPP.

[46] See Art 14.18 TPP (exempting Malaysia and Vietnam from dispute settlement in respect of certain measures regarding electronic commerce for a period of two years); and Art 17.2(5) TPP fn 10 (exempting Malaysia from dispute settlement with regard to certain state-owned enterprises for a period of two years in light of the ongoing process of developing new legislation concerning state-owned enterprises).

[47] See generally on the good faith standard of review under self-judging clauses: Stephan W Schill and Robyn Briese, '"If the State Considers": Self-Judging Clauses in International Dispute Settlement' (2009) 13 *Max Planck Yearbook of United Nations Law* 61.

subject-matter restrictions found in CETA.[48] Both agreements show, however, that for certain areas limits are set up to reduce the depth of review in dispute settlement.

Furthermore, the agreements regularly provide for certain modifications to the general inter-state dispute settlement regime with regard to specifically sensitive subject matters in order to limit the authority of dispute settlement mechanisms and to ensure the contracting parties' control. The most important area in this respect concerns provisions on financial services that are regularly included in mega-regionals in a specific chapter.[49] While not excluding state-to-state dispute settlement altogether, the chapters on financial services regularly contain stricter safeguards against arbitral scrutiny, in particular in order to protect government measures for 'prudential reasons'.[50]

For this purpose, arbitrators in disputes arising under the financial services chapter are required to have a more specific expertise, namely 'expertise or experience in financial services law or regulation or in the practice thereof, which may include the regulation of financial service suppliers'.[51] This ensures that decisions in such proceedings are taken in full knowledge of their implications on financial services regulation and the financial system more generally. Noteworthy are also limitations on enforcement options in order to protect the financial system of contracting states, such as the exclusion of cross-sector suspension of benefits.[52] TPP aims to achieve the same purpose by requiring the involvement of financial experts in non-implementation proceedings.[53]

2. *Inclusion of procedural safeguards*

Contracting parties to mega-regionals not only take pains in tailoring the scope of dispute settlement, but they also include a number of procedural safeguards to ensure that the authority of inter-state dispute settlement disciplines remains limited and subject to adequate state control. This includes, inter alia, provisions on arbitrator qualifications, rosters of arbitrators, rules on transparency, third-party and *amicus curiae* participation, notice and comment procedures before the issuance of reports by the tribunals, a stronger role for the parties in the implementation of reports, and a formalized role of the parties in interpreting the respective agreement.

First, contracting parties to mega-regionals exercise tighter control over the qualifications and attributes of arbitrators in inter-state disputes. For this purpose,

[48] Art 29.2(b) TPP. [49] See ch 13 CETA and ch 11 TPP.

[50] See Arts 13.16(1) CETA and 11.11(1) TPP for the 'prudential measures' exceptions for financial regulation.

[51] Art 13.20(4) CETA. Accordingly, a specific list of arbitrators may be established for disputes under the financial services chapter (Art 13.20(3) CETA). See also Art 11.21(3) TPP (requiring 'expertise or experience in financial services law or practice, which may include the regulation of financial institutions').

[52] See Art 13.20(5) CETA (providing that benefits in the financial sector can only be suspended in order to induce compliance with a finding of non-compliance by a state-to-state tribunal if the measure in question related to the financial services sector).

[53] Art 11.21(5) TPP.

mega-regionals provide that arbitrators have to have relevant expertise in international trade law and the matters covered by the agreement in question.[54] This aims to ensure that arbitrators are able to interpret the agreement properly and thereby remain within the textual confines agreed to by the contracting parties. Compared to situations where just anybody could serve as arbitrator, this gives contracting parties more control over the concrete settlement of mega-regionals disputes and the future direction of the interpretation of the agreements because states' intentions when concluding the agreement in question are arguably better reflected in interpretations by experts chosen by the parties, rather than interpretations by individuals without the requisite expertise.

Building on existing WTO rules,[55] mega-regionals also aim at ensuring that arbitrators are not subject to undue influence in their adjudicatory task. For this purpose, both CETA and TPP require that arbitrators are independent from the parties and do not take instructions from any organization or government.[56] They also have to abide by a specific Code of Conduct that sets out specific ethical obligations and provides for compliance mechanisms, in particular through disclosure and challenge procedures.[57] While such a Code does not yet exist under TPP,[58] CETA already includes a more elaborate, three-page Code of Conduct for Arbitrators and Mediators,[59] which is likely to serve as a guidepost for similar rules in other mega-regionals, including perhaps TPP. According to CETA's Code:

> [an] arbitrator shall avoid impropriety and the appearance of impropriety, shall be independent and impartial, shall avoid direct and indirect conflicts of interests and shall observe high standards of conduct so that the integrity and impartiality of the dispute settlement mechanism is preserved.[60]

The Code also provides for disclosure obligations,[61] which include, inter alia, not only financial interests in the proceedings, but also 'public advocacy or legal or other representation concerning an issue in dispute in the proceeding or involving the same matters'.[62] Once appointed, arbitrators must avoid not only actual conflicts of interests,[63] but already the 'appearance of bias and shall not be influenced

[54] See Art 29.8(2) CETA (requiring arbitrators to have 'specialised knowledge of international trade law'; chairpersons must, in addition, have 'experience as counsel or panellist in dispute settlement proceedings on subject matters within the scope of this Agreement'); Arts 28.10(1)(a) and 28.11(2)2 TPP (requiring all arbitrators to 'have expertise or experience in law, international trade, other matters covered by this Agreement or the resolution of disputes arising under international trade agreements').

[55] See Arts 8(2) and 17(3) DSU. See further Rules of Conduct for the Understanding on Rules and Procedures Governing the Settlement of Disputes, 11 December 1996, WT/DSB/RC/1 (96-5267).

[56] See Art 29.8(2)3 CETA; and Art 28.10(1)(c) TPP.

[57] See Art 29.8(2)3 CETA; and Art 28.10(1)(d) TPP.

[58] The Code of Conduct stills need to be developed as part of the Rules of Procedure by the TPP Commission, a treaty organ composed of government representatives of each contracting party. The establishment of the Commission is provided for in Art 27.1 TPP. Its competence to establish the Rules of Procedure for inter-state dispute settlement is contained in Art 27.2(f) TPP.

[59] See Annex 29-B CETA.

[60] Annex 29-B CETA para 2.

[61] Annex 29-B CETA paras 3 and 4.

[62] Annex 29-B CETA para 4(4).

[63] eg by incurring obligations or accepting benefits that interfere with their impartiality; see Annex 29-B CETA para 12.

by self-interest, outside pressure, political considerations, public clamour, loyalty to a Party, or fear of criticism'.[64] Likewise, '[a]n arbitrator may not use her or his position on the arbitration panel to advance any personal or private interests'[65] or allow 'financial, business, professional, family or social relationships or responsibilities to influence her or his conduct or judgement'.[66] Finally, arbitrators are also bound by strict confidentiality requirements in respect of the proceeding.[67] All of this is to ensure the independence and impartiality of persons fulfilling adjudicatory functions in inter-state dispute settlement under mega-regionals. While being a sign of increased judicialization of inter-state arbitration, the rules on independence of arbitrators from the parties and other external influences are also a way to limit extraneous motivations or incentives for certain interpretations by arbitrators. These rules thus have the purpose of ensuring that the respective agreement is interpreted, as much as possible, in line with the original intentions of the contracting parties.

Second, contracting parties to mega-regionals set out to determine the persons who can serve as arbitrators in inter-state disputes individually. For this purpose, contracting parties typically agree on the establishment of rosters of arbitrators for appointment in inter-state disputes. While parties in both TPP and CETA inter-state disputes remain free to appoint any arbitrator that meets the necessary criteria in terms of independence and expertise, the parties agree to the establishment of rosters that are binding for appointments by an appointing authority, for example, if one party fails to make an appointment, or for appointments of the chair by the co-arbitrators.[68] The establishment of rosters not only ensures better control of parties over which individuals are acting as arbitrators, it also increases the democratic legitimacy of the dispute settlement body, as arbitrators under TPP and CETA are more directly linked to domestic democratic processes as compared to institutional appointments that are not bound to rosters established by consensus of the contracting parties.

Third, building on the practice that developed over the past decade in WTO dispute settlement with the judicial activity—some say activism—of the Appellate Body,[69] mega-regionals, such as TPP and CETA, formally put down rules on transparency, third-party participation, and interventions of *amicus curiae* in inter-state proceedings. Subject to an agreement of the disputing parties to the contrary, as well as an exception for the protection of confidential (business) information, both TPP

[64] Annex 29-B CETA para 11.

[65] Annex 29-B CETA para 13.

[66] Annex 29-B CETA para 14.

[67] Annex 29-B CETA paras 17 and 19.

[68] For the establishment of Rosters of Panel Chairs and Party Specific Lists under TPP, see Art 28.11 TPP. The roster becomes binding in certain situations (see Art 28.9 TPP). Under CETA, the CETA Joint Committee is tasked with establishing a roster for arbitrators (see Art 29.8(1) CETA). This roster becomes binding for certain appointments pursuant to Art 29.7(2) CETA.

[69] For a concise summary of the development and state of law and practice on these issues in WTO dispute settlement, see Christiane Ahlborn and James Headen Pfitzer, 'Transparency and Public Participation in WTO Dispute Settlement' (Center for International Environmental Law, 2009) 5–25, <http://www.ciel.org/Publications/Transparency_WTO_Dec09.pdf> accessed 4 April 2017. See also Panagiotis Delimatsis, 'Institutional Transparency in the WTO' in Andrea Bianchi and Anne Peters (eds), *Transparency in International Law* (Cambridge University Press, 2013) 112, 118ff.

and CETA provide for public hearings in inter-state disputes.[70] Likewise, parties to a dispute are under an obligation to make their submissions public.[71] The final report of the panel is equally to be made public by the parties.[72] Furthermore, *amicus* participation is allowed for under both TPP and CETA.[73] TPP, as a multilateral treaty, also contains express provisions permitting non-disputing third-party intervention, that is, participation of governments not involved in the dispute at hand.[74]

All of these rules aim at ensuring that the dispute settlement process can take place under the eyes of all contracting parties, the affected public, academic observers, and non-governmental organizations (NGOs). This not only has the purpose of increasing the legitimacy of inter-state dispute settlement; transparency and third-party participation are also ways to increase the accountability of dispute resolvers. In transparent proceedings, they are under increased, albeit informal, pressure to render decisions, and reason them accordingly, that are understandable to all involved constituencies, and in principle acceptable to them as a proper construction of the agreement. In addition to being a sign of judicialization of inter-state arbitration, transparency, third-party, and *amicus* participation are mechanisms that tighten control over the authority of arbitral tribunals in inter-state dispute settlement and help to legitimise dispute settlement better.

Fourth, the dispute settlement procedures in mega-regionals are cast in a way that allows disputing parties to influence the outcome of an arbitral award and ensure its correctness from their point of view. Similar to existing WTO rules for panel proceedings,[75] both CETA and TPP provide that panels in inter-state dispute settlement do not immediately issue a final and binding report, but in a first step produce an 'interim' or 'initial' report which is submitted to the disputing parties for comments.[76] This procedure gives the parties additional control over the outcome of the dispute and allows them to provide input in order to correct what they see as incorrect or illegitimate decision-making by inter-state arbitral tribunals in mega-regionals, including potentially unacceptable further development of the law of the agreement itself.

Fifth, as compared to the WTO, where the DSB is responsible for the supervision of the implementation of panel and Appellate Body reports,[77] contracting parties

[70] For the requirement of public hearings in CETA, see Annex 29-A CETA para 38 (providing that 'unless the Parties decide otherwise, the hearings of the arbitration panel shall be open to the public'). An exception for the protection of 'confidential business information' is provided for in Annex 29-A CETA para 39. For the parallel provisions in TPP, see Art 28.13(b) TPP (requiring public hearings except if the parties agree otherwise); for an exception for the protection of 'confidential information', see Art 28.13(f) TPP. This exception arguably is broader than the exception under CETA, as it is not limited to 'business' information.

[71] See Annex 29-A CETA para 38 ('each Party shall make its submissions publicly available'). TPP contains a 'best efforts'-obligation to make submissions public 'as soon as possible after those documents are filed' and an unqualified obligation to release documents once the final panel report is issued (see Art 28.13(d) TPP).

[72] See Art 29.10(3) CETA; and Art 28.18(1)2 TPP.

[73] See Annex 29-A CETA para 43; and Art 28.13(e) TPP.

[74] See Art 28.14 TPP.

[75] See DSU, app 3 ('Working Procedures') para 12.

[76] See Art 29.9 CETA ('interim panel report'); and Art 28.17 TPP ('initial report').

[77] Art 2(1)(2) DSU.

to mega-regionals maintain a comparatively stronger role in the implementation of inter-state arbitral awards. Both under CETA and TPP, the implementation of such awards is to take place primarily through voluntary inter-state cooperation. The parties are to agree on a 'reasonable period of time' for the losing party to eliminate any non-conformity with the agreement.[78] Failing such elimination, the parties are to agree on compensation of the prevailing party, and only when no agreement can be reached can the prevailing party suspend concessions.[79] Resulting disputes about the implementation of reports, in turn, are relegated to the arbitral tribunal.[80] Likewise, the arbitral tribunal can be asked to conduct an independent compliance review.[81] CETA also involves the CETA Joint Committee in the implementation of arbitral awards.[82] Given the lack of a proper institutional enforcement mechanism, the contracting parties have an important role in implementing awards, and potentially have room for efficient breach, but also resisting enforcement unilaterally. This comparatively strong role of the parties in implementing inter-state awards means a relative reduction of the authority of arbitral tribunals as compliance with their awards depends to a large extent on the goodwill of the disputing parties, certainly more so than in the WTO context.

Finally, both TPP and CETA institutionalize the power of the contracting parties to interpret the respective agreement authoritatively through joint interpretations. Under TPP, the TPP Commission, inter alia, has the function to 'issue interpretations of the provisions of this Agreement'.[83] Similarly, the CETA Joint Committee may 'adopt interpretations of the provisions of this Agreement, which shall be binding on tribunals established under ... Chapter Twenty-Nine (Dispute Settlement)'.[84] This express power of a treaty organ serves to control the interpretative power of arbitral tribunals by allowing the parties to react to a tribunal decision or its reasoning, thereby undoing any possible effect of arbitral awards as precedent in future cases. Together with the other procedural safeguards discussed in this subsection, it constitutes one of several elements through which contracting parties in mega-regionals try to control and constrain the powers of inter-state dispute settlement bodies and ensure that the parties remain masters of the treaties.

3. Encouraging mediation

Contracting parties to mega-regionals also attempt to exercise more control over dispute settlement by encouraging cooperative dispute resolution and alternative means of dispute settlement, above all inter-state mediation. Not only is access to

[78] Art 29.13 CETA; and Art 28.19(3) TPP. [79] See Art 29.14 CETA; and Art 28.20 TPP.
[80] See Art 29.14(5) CETA; and Art 20.20(5) TPP.
[81] Art 29.15 CETA; and Art 28.21 TPP. [82] See Arts 29.12–29.15 CETA.
[83] Art 27.2(2)(f) TPP. This requires agreement of all parties (see Art 27.3(2)1 TPP). This considerable hurdle in a multilateral agreement is slightly alleviated, however, as '[a] decision shall be deemed to be reached if a Party which does not indicate agreement when the Commission considers the issue does not object in writing to the interpretation considered by the Commission within five days of that consideration' (see Art 27.3(2)2 TPP).
[84] Art 26.1(5)(e) CETA.

formal inter-state arbitration dependent on prior inter-governmental consultations in order to arrive at an agreed solution,[85] some contracting parties, in particular the EU, seek to channel dispute resolution away from adjudicatory dispute resolution into inter-state mediation.[86] Mediation gives parties additional control over both the outcome and mechanism of dispute settlement as compared to dispute settlement through adjudication. For this reason, strengthening inter-state mediation is also a means to limit the authority of inter-state arbitration in dispute resolution.

As illustrated by CETA, mediation is provided for as a mechanism for dispute resolution that can take place at any time, prior to, but also in parallel with, formal inter-state arbitration.[87] Furthermore, the EU aims at formalizing mediation as an alternative mechanism for inter-state dispute settlement not just by making passing reference to mediation, as is the case under TPP,[88] but by including an elaborated four-page annex for the administration of inter-state mediation proceedings in the agreement.[89] This annex contains detailed rules on the initiation and implementation of mediation proceedings, including the process for selecting mediators, rules on independence and impartiality of mediators,[90] the procedure to follow with time limits, the powers and instruments available to mediators, provisions on implementation of an agreed result, and costs.

All of this enhances the status of mediation compared to the WTO, where mediation receives only passing mention as one form of aiming to settle disputes prior to, and exceptionally in parallel with, adjudication by panels and the Appellate Body,[91] without detailed regulation. Other mega-regionals, such as the TPP, follow the same lax approach and copy almost verbatim the provision on mediation from the WTO DSU.[92]

Yet, mediating inter-state disputes, instead of arbitrating them, stresses the authority of states because a settlement reached through mediation is, unlike in third-party adjudication, always dependent on the consent of both disputing states. What is more, mediation proceedings are confidential,[93] therefore shielding the dispute from public scrutiny. As transparency increases in formal inter-state and investor-state dispute settlement, mediation may serve as an exit valve for disputes that neither state wants to see resolved under public scrutiny. Mediation would then serve as a device for flexibility and preservation of certain policy concerns.[94] Either way, efforts to promote mediation coincide with giving disputing parties additional control over the resolution of the dispute at hand.

[85] See Art 29.6(1) in connection with Art 29.4 CETA; and Art 28.1(1) in connection with Art 28.5(1) TPP.

[86] See Art 29.5 and Annex 29-C CETA.

[87] See Annex 29-C ETA, Arts 2(1) and 6(2) and (3).

[88] TPP only mentions inter-state mediation in Art 28.6 TPP.

[89] Annex 29-C CETA.

[90] With regard to mediators, the same Code of Conduct applies as the one applicable to arbitrators. See Annex 29-C ETA, Art 3(3)2.

[91] See Art 5 DSU.

[92] See Art 28.6 TPP.

[93] Annex 29-C ETA, Art 6(1).

[94] See generally for the connection between confidentiality and flexibilty in dispute resolution, Emilie M Hafner-Burton, Zachary C Steinert-Threlkeld, and David G Victor, 'Predictability Versus Flexibility' (2016) 68 *World Politics* 413.

C. Evaluation

The inter-state dispute settlement provisions in mega-regionals are carefully crafted to balance the need of contracting parties for an effective compliance mechanism with the desire to limit any overreach of the dispute settlement body into sensitive areas of public policy. With the low level of institutionalization, various carve-outs, modifications for specific subject matters, and encouragement of mediation, contracting parties maintain much greater levels of control in dispute settlement under mega-regionals as compared to WTO dispute settlement. They seek to contain the authority of inter-state dispute settlement to the minimum necessary for serving as an effective compliance mechanism, while also minimizing negative effects for the multilateral trading system and WTO dispute settlement. This also serves to ensure the legitimacy of inter-state dispute under mega-regionals as the control exercised by contracting states in relation to inter-state arbitral tribunals links dispute settlement under mega-regionals closer to domestic democratic decision-making. Ensuring the authority of the WTO and avoiding fragmentation in turn preserves the legitimatory value of multilateralism and fosters predictability and the continued observance of the rule of law in international economic relations.

Yet, there is overall relatively little remarkable about the developments in inter-state dispute settlement in mega-regionals when compared to the debates surrounding ISDS. At the most, developments in the inter-state regime may be interpreted as an example of the renewed interest of states in arbitration and possible hesitation towards permanent judicial bodies under international law. Whether this is truly the case will depend, however, on the actual use made of the inter-state dispute settlement provisions in these agreements. If past experience with the dispute settlement under FTAs is any indicator, the contracting parties to mega-regionals are likely to continue settling trade-related disputes in the WTO rather than outside of it. Reasons for this are the WTO DSB's track record and the support by the WTO Secretariat, both of which make dispute settlement in the WTO predictable and efficient.[95] This notwithstanding, dispute settlement under mega-regionals, albeit still cautiously, develops some features that could feed into future reforms at the WTO. The enhanced rules on transparency, stronger emphasis on mediation, and the establishment of enforcement mechanisms for labour and environmental rules could be seen as precursors of a future multilateralization of these issues within the WTO.

In any event, the more remarkable developments as regards dispute settlement in mega-regionals undoubtedly take place in the realm of ISDS, to which the next section turns.

[95] William J Davey, 'Dispute Settlement in the WTO and RTAs: A Comment' in Lorand Bartels and Federico Ortino (eds), *Regional Trade Agreements and the WTO Legal System* (Oxford University Press, 2006) 343, 344ff. See also Patrick Specht, 'The Dispute Settlement Systems of WTO and NAFTA—Analysis and Comparison' (1998) 27 *Ga J Int'l & Comp L* 57, 127; and Rafael Leal-Arcas, 'Comparative Analysis of NAFTA's Chapter 20 and the WTO's Dispute Settlement Understanding' (2011) 8(3) *TDM*.

III. Investor-State Dispute Settlement in Mega-Regionals

Increasing control by contracting parties over dispute settlement and avoiding fragmentation by restricting the possibility of parallel, subsequent, and overlapping proceedings, and thereby enhancing the legitimacy of dispute settlement, are also the main factors that drive the provisions on ISDS in mega-regionals, as illustrated by the investment chapters in CETA and TPP. More so than in the context of inter-state dispute settlement, ISDS had become a contested, publicly scrutinized, and highly political issue in the negotiation of mega-regionals. It takes places against the background of the intense criticism that investor-state arbitration under BITs has attracted over the past year, which is widely associated with what is often called a 'legitimacy crisis' of the field. This crisis takes issue with the constitutional implications of ISDS on the principle of democracy, the concept of the rule of law, and the protection of human and fundamental rights, and hence challenges the legitimacy of investor-state arbitration from a constitutional law perspective (see section III.A). This constitutional challenge determines the evaluation of ISDS and explains many of the elements of reform that are being introduced to ISDS in modern trade and investment treaty practices on both sides of the Atlantic in order to safeguard contracting states' right to regulate and increase consistency in dispute settlement (see section III.B). Despite the many commonalities that emerge from an analysis of the ISDS provisions in CETA and TPP, a major dissonance remains with regard to the question of whether ISDS should continue to take place in the form of loosely institutionalized, one-off investor-state arbitration, as has been the preference of the US, or whether it should be further institutionalized by creating either an appeals mechanism or, as proposed by the EU, a permanent international investment court (see section III.C).

A. Legitimacy crisis of investment law as a constitutional challenge

From the perspective of foreign investors, investment treaty arbitration, which is offered in addition to, or as an alternative for, the host state's domestic courts, has been successful in making host states comply with their IIA obligations in an effective, neutral, and independent forum for the settlement of investment disputes.[96] In particular, in countries with weak government and judicial institutions, ISDS is considered to be a crucial safeguard to allow foreign investors to sanction illegitimate government conduct, such as arbitrary conduct or expropriations without compensation, without the need to being subject to the vagaries of litigating against the host government in its own courts.[97] In addition, direct recourse to ISDS replaces

[96] The text of this subsection is adapted from Stephan W Schill, 'Reforming Investor-State Dispute Settlement (ISDS): Conceptual Framework and Options for the Way Forward', E15 Task Force on Investment Policy Think Piece (International Centre for Trade and Sustainable Development/World Economic Forum, July 2015) 2–4.

[97] Problems with domestic courts may involve a lack of personal or institutional independence of the domestic judiciary, including in some cases problems of corruption, or major shortcomings in the length of judicial proceedings. Furthermore, ISDS can serve as a mechanism to make states comply

the otherwise available mechanism for the investor's home state to exercise diplomatic protection, thus preventing an investor-state dispute from becoming a diplomatic incident that can strain inter-governmental relations.[98]

At the same time, the success of ISDS has created its own problems and generated vocal criticism, which is often said to have resulted in a 'legitimacy crisis' of the system.[99] Signs of this crisis are seen in the withdrawal of some Latin American states from the Convention on the Settlement of Investment Disputes Between States and Nationals of Other States (ICSID Convention) (Bolivia, Ecuador, and Venezuela); the withdrawal of some states from IIAs or entire IIA programmes (including Ecuador, Venezuela, South Africa, the Czech Republic, and Indonesia); abstaining from including ISDS in new IIAs (which was Australia's policy for a time); or recrafting the substance and procedure of IIAs to increase state control and ensure government policy space. Further, ISDS has become the focal point of criticism in IIAs by public interest groups, in particular in Europe and North America, by scholars from various disciplines, including constitutional law, international law, and economics, in the general media, and by the general public.[100]

Claims for the lack of legitimacy are the common denominator of the current critique of ISDS. Recurring concerns in this context include the following.

- First, the increasing number of conflicting and inconsistent interpretations by arbitral tribunals of standard principles of investment protection, not only under different treaties, but also in virtually identical cases brought under the same treaty.
- Second, the wide latitude investment treaties give to arbitrators to interpret broadly formulated principles of investment protection, which creates uncertainty and unpredictability in arbitral decision-making and gives arbitrators significant powers in further developing IIA disciplines.

with their obligations in IIAs, given that these are not necessarily directly applicable in domestic courts and cannot always be vindicated there. In such a case, a dispute settlement mechanism under international law is the only option for invoking breaches of the international legal obligations involved.

[98] O Thomas Johnson and Jonathan Gimblett, 'From Gunboats to BITs: The Evolution of Modern International Investment Law' in Karl P Sauvant (ed), *Yearbook on International Investment Law and Policy 2010–2011* (Oxford University Press, 2012) 649.

[99] See, eg, Brower and Schill, 'Is Arbitration a Threat or a Boon' (n 6); Gus Van Harten, *Investment Treaty Arbitration and Public Law* (Oxford University Press, 2007); Gus Van Harten et al, 'Public Statement on the International Investment Regime' (31 August 2010), <http://www.osgoode.yorku.ca/public-statement-international-investment-regime-31-august-2010/> accessed 4 April 2017; and Muthucumaraswamy Sornarajah, *Resistance and Change in the International Law on Foreign Investment* (Cambridge University Press, 2015).

[100] For contributions dealing with the different symptoms of the crisis and state reactions to it, see Michael Waibel, Asha Kaushal, Kyo-Hwa Liz Chung, and Claire Balchin (eds), *The Backlash against Investment Arbitration: Perceptions and Reality* (Kluwer, 2010); Steffen Hindelang and Markus Krajewski (eds), *Shifting Paradigms in International Investment Law: More Balanced, Less Isolated, Increasingly Diversified* (Oxford University Press, 2016); and Andreas Kulick (ed), *Reassertion of Control over the Investment Treaty Regime* (Cambridge University Press, 2016).

- Third, the insufficient regard paid by some tribunals to the need for host states to regulate in the public interest, for example, to protect public health, labour standards, the environment, or to react to economic and financial crises.
- Fourth, the misalignment between governance effects of ISDS that go beyond the disputing parties and private law-inspired procedural maxims of arbitration, in particular confidentiality of proceedings, the understanding of independence and impartiality of arbitrators, and the idea that dispute settlement under investment treaties constitutes a party-owned process, in which non-parties, even if affected, are voiceless.
- Fifth, the lack of mechanisms to ensure 'correct' interpretations of IIA obligations in line with the intentions of the contracting parties and to control the further development of investment law by arbitral tribunals.
- Sixth, the high costs and considerable length of many arbitral proceedings, including in cases that manifestly are lacking of merits or are even frivolous or abusive.

Common to all these aspects of criticism is that they do not principally concern the outcome of individual decisions rendered in ISDS, but concern ISDS as a system. Moreover, the criticism does not focus primarily on the function of arbitral tribunals to settle past disputes, but rather on the impact the ISDS system has on the future conduct of governments. ISDS, in other words, is analysed and criticized as a system of governance in which individual tribunals exercise public authority by: (1) reviewing government conduct under IIA disciplines in place of, or in addition to, administrative or constitutional courts at the domestic level; and (2) further developing applicable IIA standards and effectively making investment law.[101] In sum, the criticism focuses on ISDS's public governance function, not its private function to settle individual disputes, and the tension it causes with constitutional standards that are customarily used to assess the legitimacy of public authority.

While any adjudicatory mechanism, including domestic courts, has governance functions, the ISDS system as structured so far under BITs and investment chapters in FTAs lacks the institutional infrastructure in which courts that exercise judicial review are usually embedded. In ISDS, there is no hierarchical court system that

[101] On the understanding of ISDS as a system of governance and the legitimacy concerns raised from a public law perspective, see Stephan W Schill, 'International Investment Law and Comparative Public Law: An Introduction' (n 17) 3–37. In many cases, ISDS proceedings deal with matters that are customarily considered as public law disputes dealt with in ISDS. Claims concerning environmental conditions for the operation of power plants, the legality of subsidies, or the prohibition of harmful substances are examples of what are in essence administrative law disputes. Claims against Uruguay and Australia on cigarette packaging, or the claim concerning Germany's nuclear power phase-out, are examples of genuinely constitutional law disputes settled in ISDS. In this context, law-making occurs, notwithstanding a considerable number of inconsistent decisions, because arbitral tribunals generally operate in a strongly precedent-oriented fashion in which they further develop and concretize the vague standards of treatment, such as fair and equitable treatment or the concept of indirect expropriation. See further Stephan W Schill, *The Multilateralization of International Investment Law* (Cambridge University Press, 2009) 321–61.

could control judicial errors and ensure consistency and coherence in adjudication, nor is there a legislative body that could control the law-making activities of arbitral tribunals. Instead, ISDS so far is composed of one-off tribunals that decide individual cases only, usually without the possibility of appeal or comparable control mechanisms. In addition, ISDS procedures follow largely private law rationales that most domestic systems consider inadequate for settling private–public disputes. ISDS is based on the idea of a party-owned and party-controlled process that has few, if any, public repercussions and is often conducted based on confidentiality, rather than on transparent and open procedures. Finally, several arbitrators, unlike tenured judges, also take up other professional roles in the system, including as counsel in other ISDS proceedings.

In sum, the current ISDS system conceptually suffers from a tension between its public governance functions and its set-up as a private dispute settlement mechanism that is modelled on, and breathes the intellectual and epistemic spirit of, how private–private disputes are settled in commercial arbitration. Against this background, ISDS comes as a challenge to core constitutional law values, such as the principle of democracy, the concept of the rule of law, and the protection of fundamental or human rights. Inconsistencies in arbitral jurisprudence are a problem from a constitutional perspective because they undermine the value of predictability inherent in the idea of the rule of law. Concerns about possible conflicts of interests of arbitrators pose a challenge to the independence of decision-makers, which forms part of the rule of law. High costs and overly lengthy proceedings limit the parties' access to justice, an aspect that also follows from the concept of the rule of law.

Other points of criticism concern challenges to the principle of democracy. Thus, disregard for domestic policy space can limit a host state's democratic choices. Further, creative interpretations of arbitral tribunals, or even the further development of investment law, are in essence legislative functions that require decision-makers' democratic legitimation. Yet, arbitrators do not dispose of a solid democratic mandate to further develop investment disciplines. On the contrary, arbitral tribunals are on the whole far removed from democratic processes, both in the appointment of arbitrators and in the control of their decisions. Arbitrators' democratic legitimacy is limited to the state's one-time consent to the governing IIA and the appointment of some members of a tribunal in a concrete dispute. Moreover, there is no functioning separation of power between adjudicatory and legislative institutions, as required by the principle of democracy.

ISDS also poses a problem for the principle of equality, which is part of the democratic principle, because it only grants standing to foreign investors, while denying access to domestic investors who are limited to accessing domestic courts. Similarly, the lack of transparency and of third-party participation poses a challenge to the openness and transparency required by the principle of democracy of the exercise of public authority and the possibility for everyone affected to have a voice in decision-making through participatory rights.

Finally, the protection of fundamental or human rights is affected by ISDS to the extent that arbitral tribunals extend investor rights to the detriment of competing non-investment concerns, such as the right to public health, the right to water, or the rights of indigenous people. It is to these challenges that mega-regionals, such as CETA and TPP, react in the design of ISDS provisions.

B. Public law responses common to CETA and TPP

Both CETA and TPP formulate responses to, and include reform elements for, at least some of the above challenges to ISDS. While adhering to the principle that foreign investors, and only foreign investors, have recourse to a specialized jurisdiction independently of domestic courts, and hence rejecting more radical reform options that would consist in a return to the system of diplomatic protection coupled with recourse to domestic courts, CETA and TPP particularly aim at addressing problems relating to a lack of consistency in ISDS and strengthening the control of contracting states over dispute resolvers. Overall, both CETA and TPP aim at implementing a system for ISDS that is more legitimate and less problematic than the system of investor-state arbitrations under BITs that we have seen so far.

In pursuing the aim of creating a more legitimate system of ISDS, both CETA and TPP include many elements that are also present in the agreements' state-to-state dispute settlement provisions discussed in Part II, but also add features that are specific to ISDS. Some of these features are relatively novel and can only been found so far in a few IIAs; others build on reform efforts that have be present more widely in the IIA practice of the past decade and in reforms that have already taken place at the level of arbitration rules. This includes in particular the revisions of the ICSID Arbitration Rules in 2006, which already contained some elements of transparency and mechanisms to reject frivolous and spurious claims more expeditiously,[102] and the reform of the UNCITRAL Arbitration Rules in 2013, which introduced comprehensive rules for transparency and third-party participation for treaty-based investor-state arbitration.[103]

First, both CETA and TPP confine the scope of possible investor-state claims to breaches of the investment chapter of the respective agreement. Breaches of provisions of other chapters generally remain in the realm of state-to-state dispute settlement. Under TPP, access to ISDS is limited to claims for breach of all treaty provisions in the investment chapter, as well as claims for breach of 'investment agreements' and 'investment authorizations'.[104] This includes claims for breach of market access provisions and performance requirements. The governing law in ISDS under TPP may therefore include both the TPP as such and the law governing

[102] For analysis of the changes introduced to the ICSID Rules in 2006, see Aurélia Antonietti, 'The 2006 Amendments to the ICSID Rules and Regulations and the Additional Facility Rules' (2006) 21 *ICSID Review—FILJ* 427; Jarrod Wong and Jason W Yackee, 'The 2006 Procedural and Transparency-Related Amendments to the ICSID Arbitration Rules: Model Intentions, Moderate Proposals, and Modest Returns' in Karl P Sauvant (ed), *The Yearbook on International Investment Law & Policy 2009–2010* (2010) ch 6.

[103] United Nations, 'Report of the United Nations Commission on International Trade Law of its Forty-Sixth Session (8–26 July 2013)', Official Records of the General Assembly, Sixty-Eighth Session, Supplement No 17 (A/68/17) (2013) para 128 and Annex I, <http://www.un.org/en/ga/search/view_doc.asp?symbol=A/68/17> accessed 4 April 2017 (hereafter UN, 'Report 8–26 July 2013').

[104] Art 9.19(1)(a)(i) and (b)(i) TPP.

an investment agreement or investment authorization, that is, either the law chosen by the parties, or by default the law of the respondent state.[105] CETA is even more limited and only allows claims for breach of investment protection standards related to established investments; it excludes claims relating to alleged violations of market access rights or to unlawful performance requirements.[106] CETA also excludes claims for breach of domestic law entirely,[107] and provides that fraudulently obtained investments are not protected.[108] Similar to state-to-state dispute settlement, both CETA and TPP thus adhere to a principle of selective judicialization that aims at ensuring control of the contracting parties over the type of disputes that can end up in ISDS.

Second, both CETA and TPP provide for specific carve-outs and modifications for subject matters that are specifically sensitive for public policy-making, be it for all countries involved, or for individual contracting parties. TPP, for example, contains a number of country-specific limitations on ISDS,[109] as well as specific limitations for claims relating to sensitive areas of government conduct, such as the restructuring of public debt.[110] Likewise, CETA excludes access to ISDS for certain areas of government action, including notably procurement and subsidies, but also services supplied in the exercise of governmental authority and air services, as well as audio-visual services for the EU and cultural services for Canada.[111] Similar to the TPP, CETA also provides limitations on claims relating to public debt.[112]

Furthermore, both TPP and CETA provide special dispute settlement regimes for ISDS in the financial services sector.[113] This includes not only the need for dispute resolvers to have specific expertise in financial services law and regulation,[114] but also the involvement of the Financial Services Committees established under the agreements in limiting the authority of the ISDS system.[115] Thus, if the respondent state relies on certain defences for financial measures, in particular the prudential carve-out, it can refer the question of whether the exception applies for determination to the respective Financial Services Committee, which is binding on an investor-state tribunal.[116] Similarly, with regard to taxation, both CETA and TPP ensure

[105] Art 9.25(2) TPP. [106] Art 8.18(1) CETA.

[107] Art 8.31(2) CETA. [108] Art 8.18(2) CETA.

[109] See, eg, the exceptions for certain claims against Mexico for breach of investment agreements of investment authorizations, listed in Annex 9-L(C) TPP, or the exceptions for claims against Malaysia for breach of specific government procurement contracts under Annex 9-K TPP.

[110] See Annex 9-G TPP, which excludes investor-state proceedings in case of 'negotiated restructurings' of public debt.

[111] Access to ISDS here is excluded because the scope of application of the entire investment chapter is subject to certain carve-outs. See the list in Art 9.2(2) CETA.

[112] See Art 8.18(4) CETA and Annex 8-B (excluding, inter alia, dispute settlement in case it concerns a negotiated restructuring and imposing a time-bar of 270 days on claims in order to ensure more policy space).

[113] For modifications of the general ISDS regime, see Art 13.21 CETA and Art 11.22 TPP.

[114] See Art 13.21(2) in connection with Art 13.20.3 and 4 CETA; and Art 11.22(1) TPP.

[115] See Art 13.18 CETA and Art 11.19 TPP.

[116] See Art 11.22(2)(a) and (b)(3) TPP. Almost identical provisions exist under Art 13.21(3) CETA, which provides for referral to the Committee. If the Committee accepts the respondent's reliance on

additional policy space by providing for enhanced involvement of the contracting parties who can, through inter-state consultations requested by the respondent, decide, with binding effect for the tribunal, inter alia, on whether the measure in question is a taxation measure and whether it breached the substantive standards of protection.[117] All of these features provide nuanced reactions to square the contracting states' need for policy space to govern effectively in the public interest with the interest in ensuring effective protection and fair treatment of foreign investors.

Third, just as in the context of state-to-state dispute settlement, recourse to ISDS is dependent on attempts at prior amicable settlement. Both TPP and CETA require consultations between the disputing parties for six months prior to formal recourse to ISDS.[118] Likewise, both TPP and CETA mention mediation in order to settle investor-state disputes under the agreements amicably, with CETA going slightly further in putting emphasis on the fact that mediation can take place at any time during the course of a dispute, including in parallel to adjudication, and providing for the development of formalized rules for investor-state mediation by the CETA Committee on Services and Investment.[119] The need for amicable dispute settlement and encouragement of mediation puts a check on the unregulated escalation of investor-state disputes and thereby limits the authority of adjudication in ISDS.

Fourth, both CETA and TPP contain a variety of provisions that aim at reducing, if not excluding, parallel, overlapping, and subsequent proceedings, thereby ensuring more consistency in ISDS. TPP, while much less systematic in this respect than CETA, prohibits recourse to domestic courts by requiring a waiver of such proceedings when ISDS proceedings are initiated.[120] Fork-in-the-road provisions that would exclude recourse to ISDS once domestic proceedings have been initiated, by contrast, are only provided for under TPP with regard to Chile, Mexico, Peru, and Vietnam.[121] Parallel and subsequent proceedings are further excluded to the extent that TPP provides for the primacy of forum selection clauses in relation to claims involving breach of an investment agreement.[122] Finally, more

the prudential carve-out, the ISDS mechanism is discontinued (Art 13.21(4)3 CETA); in case of partial acceptance of the defence, this decision is binding on the tribunal (Art 13.21(4)4 CETA). Under TPP, in case no determination by the Committee can be reached, the respondent can initiate state-to-state arbitration under the financial services chapter whose decision on whether an exception applies, in particular whether it was covered as a prudential measure, is equally binding on an investor-state tribunal. See Art 11.22(3) TPP; see also Art 11.11(1)1 TPP fn 11 (clarifying that an ISDS tribunal has to accept the determination pursuant to Art 11.22 TPP by the Committee that a measure was for prudential reasons).

[117] See Art 28.7(7) CETA. Under TPP, the involvement of the respondent state and the investor's home state is slightly more limited. Still, the two parties can determine whether the measure in question constituted an expropriation (Art 29.4(8) TPP). However, the scope of application of TPP to taxation measures is more limited. It excludes taxation matters generally from the scope of coverage of the treaty, except for those causes of action specifically permitted. See Art 29.4(2) TPP.

[118] See Art 8.23(1)(b) CETA and Art 9.19(1) TPP.

[119] See Art 8.20 CETA and Art 9.18(1) TPP.

[120] See Art 9.21(2)(b) TPP. [121] See Annex 9-J TPP. [122] See Annex 9-L(A) TPP.

consistency is achieved by the possibility of consolidating claims[123] if two or more proceedings have a 'question of law or fact in common and arise out of the same facts or circumstances'.[124] In such a case, the constitution of a consolidation tribunal can be requested, which decides the dispute(s) in question instead of the original tribunal(s), thereby excluding inconsistent and contradictory decisions.

CETA, in turn, is stricter and more systematic when it comes to limitations on parallel, overlapping, and subsequent proceedings. It contains a version of a fork-in-the-road clause under which parallel domestic and international proceedings are prohibited.[125] When submitting a claim under CETA's investment chapter, investors are required to waive any future recourse to domestic or other international proceedings.[126] Where a claim is pending under the ISDS disciplines of CETA and under another international agreement, which would affect the remedies due, CETA requires the tribunal to stay its proceedings or ensure through other means that the outcome of the other proceeding is taken into account.[127] Furthermore, CETA, in principle, excludes inter-state proceedings in parallel to ISDS, unless measures of general application are at issue; in this case, inter-state arbitration may contribute to limiting the number of claims as it creates an incentive for investors to refrain from initiating investor-state claims, thereby shifting the cost risks to their home state.[128] Finally, CETA includes provisions on the consolidation of investor-state claims that are rather similar to those under TPP.[129] Hence, both TPP and CETA aim at ensuring consistency by limiting the possibilities for parallel, subsequent, and overlapping proceedings that could create inconsistencies.

Fifth, both CETA and TPP establish requirements for the qualifications and ethical obligations of dispute resolvers. This not only enhances the control of contracting parties over ISDS, but also contributes to making decision-making more coherent, namely by limiting the pool of appointable persons, thus leading to a more uniform mindset and epistemic outlook of the individuals involved in investor-state dispute resolution. CETA requires dispute resolvers to possess the qualifications needed for appointment to judicial office, or being a jurist of recognized competence, and hold demonstrated expertise in public international law and desirable expertise in international investment law, in international trade law, and the resolution of disputes arising under international investment or trade agreements.[130] TPP, in turn, stipulates that expertise in the governing law is desirable.[131] Likewise, tighter and more concrete ethical standards for dispute resolvers will help ensure a more coherent habitus and adjudicatory posture, which will arguably translate into more coherent interpretations. Under CETA,[132] decision-makers must be independent and comply with the International Bar Association Guidelines on Conflicts of Interest in International Arbitration or any supplemental rules adopted later by the

[123] See Art 9.28 TPP. [124] Art 9.28(1) TPP. [125] Art 8.22(1)(f) CETA.

[126] Art 8.22(1)(g) CETA. Turning back to dispute settlement before domestic courts is only possible if the claim under CETA's investment chapter is not successful on procedural grounds; see Art 8.22(5) CETA.

[127] Art 8.24 CETA. [128] See Art 8.42(1) CETA. [129] See Art 8.43 CETA.

[130] See Art 8.27(4) CETA. [131] Art 9.22(5) TPP. [132] Art 8.30(1) CETA.

CETA Services and Investment Committee; decision-makers are also excluded from 'double-hatting', that is, acting as counsel or experts in other investment disputes under CETA or any other international agreement.[133] CETA further requires expressly the disclosure of third-party funding arrangements in order to ensure that any possible conflict of interests is avoided.[134] Under TPP, the same Code of Conduct as in inter-state disputes applies to arbitrators in investor-state proceedings.[135]

Sixth, both CETA and TPP provide for largely identical rules on transparency of proceedings as well as participation of *amici curiae* and non-disputing parties. Building on the UNCITRAL Transparency Rules,[136] CETA and TPP foresee public hearings[137] and the publication of relevant documents,[138] while ensuring the protection of 'confidential or protected information'.[139] Both agreements also permit the participation of non-disputing parties[140] and that of *amici*.[141] These provisions not only ensure better knowledge of the public about the existence, administration, outcome, and implementation of investor-state disputes, and allow for the participation of everybody who is affected by such proceedings, but will also increase the consistency of decisions, as the greater number of participating actors is likely to insist on coherent and consistent decision-making once a proper and widely acceptable construction of the respective agreement is settled. Transparency of proceedings, in turn, will create an incentive for dispute resolvers to render their decisions so as to correspond with the expectations of all actors involved in consistent decision-making and take account of interpretations of the same and similar agreements by other dispute settlement bodies.

Seventh, both CETA and TPP contain a number of procedural features that react to the constitutional challenges and make ISDS both more effective and expedient, and ultimately more legitimate. Thus, CETA and TPP allow for the expedient dismissal of frivolous and spurious claims at the stage of preliminary objections.[142] Both agreements also provide for temporal limitation for bringing claims in ISDS of three, respectively three-and-a-half years.[143] The agreements further limit the available remedies to monetary damages and restitution, provided that the state maintains the possibility to substitute restitution for the payment of compensation;[144]

133 Art 8.30(1) CETA.

134 See Art 8.27(2) CETA.

135 See Art 9.22(6) TPP.

136 See Art 8.36 CETA. For the UNCITRAL Transparency Rules, see UN, 'Report 8–26 July 2013' (n 103) para 128 and Annex I. TPP contains a transparency regime that does not expressly mention the UNCITRAL Transparency Rules, but matches them by and large in terms of content. See Art 9.24 TPP.

137 Art 8.36(5)1 CETA and Art 9.24(2) TPP.

138 Art 8.36(2)–(4) CETA and Art 9.24(1) TPP.

139 Art 8.36(4) and (5)(3) CETA (covering 'confidential or protected information'); and Art 9.24(3) TPP (covering 'protected information ... that it may withhold in accordance with Art 29.2 (Security Exceptions) or Art 29.7 (Disclosure of Information)').

140 Art 8.38 CETA and Art 9.23(2) TPP.

141 See Art 8.36(1) CETA in connection with Art 4 of the UNCITRAL Transparency Rules; Art 9.23(3) TPP.

142 See the provisions on preliminary objections under Art 8.32 CETA for claims that are 'manifestly without legal merit' and under Art 8.33 CETA for claims that are 'unfounded as a matter of law'. For the parallel provision in TPP, see Art 9.23(4) TPP.

143 See Art 8.19(6) CETA and Art 9.21(1) TPP.

144 Art 8.39(1) CETA and Art 9.29(1) TPP.

punitive damages, in turn, are excluded.[145] Furthermore, the provisions on costs are adapted in order to limit effectively the bringing of unmeritorious claims, with CETA expressly incorporating the 'loser pays' principle,[146] and TPP containing a clause that permits to shift costs, including attorney fees.[147] Both agreements also provide that no enforcement of investor-state awards is conceivable until a possible annulment or set-aside proceeding is completed.[148]

All of these provisions limit the use of ISDS for illegitimate purposes and aim at ensuring that it does not reduce the policy space states need to govern in the public interest. TPP even goes further and requires, in mirroring the provisions on state-to-state dispute settlement, the submission of draft decisions by the investor-state tribunal to the disputing parties for comments.[149] At the same time, CETA and TPP also clarify that ISDS has the powers and the duty to settle disputes effectively and expeditiously. For this purpose, both agreements clarify that tribunals can render interim measures;[150] CETA even requires that decisions in ISDS are rendered, in principle, within twenty-four months.[151] All of this ensures efficient dispute settlement, but also limits the authority of the ISDS mechanism so that contracting parties possess the policy space they need.

Finally, as with inter-state dispute resolution, both CETA and TPP put in place treaty organs that can render authoritative interpretations of the investment chapter with binding effect on ISDS. This allows the contracting parties to effectively react to unwanted interpretations and further development of the governing agreement through ISDS. CETA provides for the authority of the CETA Joint Committee to issue binding interpretations of CETA's investment chapter in cases '[w]here serious concerns arise as regards matters of interpretation that may affect investment';[152] under TPP, interpretations by the TPP Commission are binding on ISDS tribunals.[153]

Unlike often feared, these provisions do not allow the treaty organs in question to resolve a specific dispute in a binding fashion. They are only empowered to interpret the agreements, that is, to give an abstract and general concretization of the meaning of its terms without applying this interpretation to the facts of a specific dispute. The latter would transcend the realm of interpretation and enter into the field of adjudication. By establishing the treaty organs in question, the contracting parties maintain better control of ISDS, in particular as it relates to the potential for law-making through interpretation. In addition, the CETA Joint Committee and the TPP Commission have competences to adapt the dispute settlement provisions to changing circumstances, if needed, without the need to formally renegotiate the agreements.[154] This also ensures that parties can react to deficits in dispute settlement that may become apparent over time.

145 Art 8.39(4) CETA and Art 9.29(6) TPP. 146 Art 8.39(5) CETA.
147 Art 9.29(3) TPP. 148 Art 8.41(3) CETA and Art 9.29(9) TPP.
149 See Art 9.23(10) TPP. 150 Art 8.34 CETA and Art 9.23(9) TPP.
151 Art 8.39(7) CETA. 152 Art 8.31(3) CETA.
153 Art 9.25(3) TPP; regarding the interpretation of annexes, see also Art 9.26(2) TPP.
154 Under CETA, the CETA Joint Commission and the Committee on Services and Investment work jointly in this respect: see Art 8.44(3) CETA. Under TPP, the competences of the TPP Commission are arguably more restricted than those of the CETA Joint Committee, but include the

All of the features discussed in this section react to (at least some of) the challenges ISDS poses for constitutional values, in particular the principle of democracy, the concept of the rule of law, and the protection of fundamental and human rights. By making proceedings more transparent, allowing the participation of non-disputing parties and *amici curiae*, establishing control bodies for interpretations of the agreements, imposing stricter limits on the type of claims that can be submitted to ISDS, and limiting the remedies that are available, CETA and TPP aim both at limiting the authority of ISDS and ensuring that the agreements do not unnecessarily limit the policy space needed for the implementation of public interests. Moreover, the different features enabling more consistency in decision-making aim at increasing the predictability of the operation of the investment chapter, for both states and investors, therefore contributing to a better alignment of ISDS with the rule of law.

At the same time, both CETA and TPP maintain access to ISDS as a form of access to justice that allows investors to enforce the rights granted to them. This redeems the promise of the rule of law that rights must correspond to remedies. Yet, they only fulfil this promise for foreign, not domestic, investors, and equally do not directly enhance access to justice for affected third parties. Finally, both CETA and TPP aim at making dispute settlement under their respective investment chapters more efficient and effective by clarifying certain competences of the dispute resolution body and trying to ease the financial burden of the proceedings on parties by making them more efficient. To this end, it bears noting that CETA also takes first steps to enhance the usefulness of the investment protection provisions for small and medium-sized enterprises (SMEs), for whom ISDS so far has often been too expensive. Thus, CETA includes provisions that try to make the system more attuned to the special needs of SMEs, in particular by stating a preference for sole arbitrators, instead of a three-member tribunal, for such disputes,[155] and through an opening clause that allows the CETA Joint Committee to develop other rules to deal with the special needs of SMEs, including perhaps even the establishment of an advisory centre or some other legal aid mechanism.[156]

All of these measures will contribute to making ISDS not only more palatable to constitutional values; on the contrary, they use ISDS decisively to further constitutional values in times of globalization and take them seriously as a yardstick for ISDS design. To a great extent, TPP and CETA are therefore aligned in implementing public law reforms of ISDS. They both aim to implement similar principles for how investor-state relations should be regulated in a global economy and how investor-state disputes should be settled. Notably, there seems to be little difference

monitoring of the implementation of the agreements and its interpretation, issuing binding interpretations and proposing amendments or changes if needed, and of its competences (see ch 27 TPP). Matters relating to dispute settlement that fall short of an amendment of TPP can be implemented under Art 27.2(1)(a) TPP.

[155] See Arts 8.23(5) and 8.27(9) CETA.

[156] See Art 8.39(6) CETA: 'The CETA Joint Committee shall consider supplemental rules aimed at reducing the financial burden on claimants who are natural persons or small and medium-sized enterprises. Such supplemental rules may, in particular, take into account the financial resources of such claimants and the amount of compensation sought.'

on both sides of the Atlantic about the principle that ISDS mechanisms need to be designed in a way that they are democratically legitimate, do not intrude illegitimately into states' policy space, and live up to the requirements set up by the idea of the rule of law. Similarly, many of the responses that follow from criticizing ISDS provisions from the perspective of constitutional law standards are shared by CETA and TPP and hence by two of the major actors in international investment governance, namely the EU and the US. This is promising for global ISDS reform efforts and initiatives that are under way in different fora. The broad agreement on matters of principle notwithstanding, there is greater divergence when it comes to the institutional structures for ISDS that are preferred on either side of the Atlantic.

C. The transatlantic gap on further institutionalization of investor-state dispute settlement

Both TPP and CETA take a common approach to the procedure applicable to ISDS. Under both agreements, investors have a choice between the arbitral rules under ICSID, ICSID Additional Facility, UNCITRAL Arbitration Rules, or any other rules as may be agreed between the disputing parties.[157] Similarly, the enforcement of awards is to take place under either the ICSID or the New York Conventions.[158] These similarities notwithstanding, there are fundamental differences in the organizational rules for ISDS under CETA and TPP, in particular as regards the question of who decides disputes under the respective investment chapters, and what remedies are available against an ISDS award. In this respect, a transatlantic gap exists that may not only complicate the successful conclusion of TTIP, wherever this project may stand after Trump's taking office, but may also ultimately hamper the development of a global consensus on ISDS in ongoing reform discussions.

TPP is by far the more traditional agreement in this respect. Notwithstanding the integration of the reform features discussed above, TPP continues to build on arbitration, with party-appointed arbitrators as the method of choice for settling investor-state disputes under the agreement's investment chapter. It does not engage in fundamental institutional reform of the ISDS system, and does not even pursue or build on earlier positions held by the US on creating an appeals facility for investor-state disputes under IIAs.[159] All that TPP contains is an 'opening clause' concerning the creation of an appellate mechanism in the future, which provides:

> In the event that an appellate mechanism for reviewing awards rendered by investor-State dispute settlement tribunals is developed in the future under other institutional arrangements, the Parties shall consider whether awards rendered under Art 9.29 (Awards) should be subject to that appellate mechanism. The Parties shall strive to ensure that any such appellate

[157] See Art 8.23(2) CETA and Art 9.19(4) TPP.

[158] See Art 8.41(5) and (6) CETA and Art 9.29(12) TPP.

[159] See Art 28(10) 2004 US Model BIT, <http://www.state.gov/documents/organization/117601.pdf> accessed 4 April 2017; Art 10.19(10) United States–Chile FTA (signed 6 June 2003, entered into force 1 January 2004), <https://ustr.gov/trade-agreements/free-trade-agreements/chile-fta/final-text> accessed 4 April 2017; and Art 10.20(10) Dominican Republic–Central America–United States FTA (n 40).

mechanism they consider adopting provides for transparency of proceedings similar to the transparency provisions established in Art 9.24 (Transparency of Arbitral Proceedings).[160]

TPP therefore continues to trust in arbitration as an appropriate mechanism for settling investor-state disputes under international trade and investment agreements. In the eyes of its contracting parties, the inclusion of a reformed version of investor-state arbitration seemingly strikes an appropriate balance between the protection of foreign investors, consistency in decision-making, and control of contracting parties, and reacts sufficiently to the legitimacy concerns posed by ISDS.

The EU, by contrast, as illustrated by CETA, wants to go beyond the innovations in access conditions, procedural law, and increased state control of ISDS, and build entirely new dispute settlement institutions. Although the September 2014 version of CETA still contained a reformed version of investor-state arbitration, the final text of February 2016, which resulted from 'legal scrubbing', contains a version of the 'investment court system' that the European Commission had developed for TTIP and introduced formally into the TTIP negotiations in November 2015. Similar provisions are also contained in the EU–Vietnam FTA of 2 December 2015. The EU–Singapore FTA from May 2015, by contrast, still contains a reformed version of investor-state arbitration.

Departing starkly from the model of reformed investor-state arbitration contained in TPP, CETA's 'investment court system' consists of a permanent two-tiered dispute settlement body for investor-state disputes; it comprises a (first instance) Tribunal and an Appellate Tribunal.[161] In CETA, the first instance is composed of fifteen members, who are appointed jointly by the EU and Canada, rather than by the disputing parties (investor and host state).[162] The Tribunal's members decide in chambers of three, which are staffed following a system to be established by the President of the Tribunal that has to ensure a random composition and give equal opportunity to all members.[163] The Tribunal is, however, not a standing court or treaty organ. It does not have a courthouse or seat, nor does it have judges as members. Instead, its fifteen members are remunerated with a monthly retainer to secure their availability; they only exercise adjudicatory functions ad hoc as disputes may arise under CETA's investment chapter, in which case the same fees as for a regular investor-state arbitration accrue. ICSID, in turn, serves as the Tribunal's Secretariat. Challenges to members are to be decided by the President of the ICJ.[164]

The Appellate Tribunal, in turn, which consists of a yet unspecified number of members, can review the (first instance) Tribunal's awards for: '(a) errors in the application or interpretation of applicable law; (b) manifest errors in the appreciation of the facts, including the appreciation of relevant domestic law; (c) the grounds set out in Art 52(1)(a) through (e) of the ICSID Convention, in so far as they are not covered by paragraphs (a) and (b).'[165] Recourse to the Appellate Tribunal excludes control of the outcome of dispute settlement under CETA's investment chapter by ICSID Annulment Committees or domestic courts, depending on the choice of forum and procedure.

[160] Art 9.23(11) TPP.
[161] Arts 8.27 and 8.28 CETA.
[162] Art 8.27(2) CETA.
[163] Art 8.27(6) and (7) CETA.
[164] Art 8.30(2) CETA.
[165] See Art 8.28(2) CETA.

All in all, the 'investment court system' now included in CETA, and proposed for TTIP, is somewhat of a hybrid that combines features of international arbitration and of permanent judicial institutions. Yet, whether it is a true court or just another form of arbitration arguably matters little for most practical purposes. What is crucial, instead, is that it represents the EU's vision of how to ensure legitimacy and consistency in ISDS beyond a reformed version of investor-state arbitration that will remedy some, but not all, shortcomings identified as part of the constitutional challenge to ISDS. It is the EU's answer to the criticism of ISDS among Europe's population and the values of democracy, the rule of law, and the protection of fundamental rights enshrined in its own constitution.[166] Above all, the permanent features of the 'investment court system' are likely to create a greater degree of consistency in the interpretation and application of the agreement concerned, as the number of decision-makers is much lower compared to TPP's system of arbitration and because the creation of an Appellate Tribunal will no doubt lead to the development of a highly consistent jurisprudence on the interpretation of CETA, comparable to how the WTO Appellate Body has interpreted WTO law consistently.

[166] Art 21 of the Treaty on European Union (TEU) draws a direct connection between the EU's own constitutional principles and the formulation of a constitutional response to the constitutional challenges that international dispute settlement under mega-regionals pose to democracy, the rule of law, and the protection of fundamental and human rights in a global economy. Art 21 TEU provides in relevant part as follows:

1. The Union's action on the international scene shall be guided by the principles which have inspired its own creation, development and enlargement, and which it seeks to advance in the wider world: democracy, the rule of law, the universality and indivisibility of human rights and fundamental freedoms, respect for human dignity, the principles of equality and solidarity, and respect for the principles of the United Nations Charter and international law.

   The Union shall seek to develop relations and build partnerships with third countries, and international, regional or global organisations which share the principles referred to in the first subparagraph. It shall promote multilateral solutions to common problems, in particular in the framework of the United Nations.
2. The Union shall define and pursue common policies and actions, and shall work for a high degree of cooperation in all fields of international relations, in order to:
   (a) safeguard its values, fundamental interests, security, independence and integrity;
   (b) consolidate and support democracy, the rule of law, human rights and the principles of international law;
   (c) preserve peace, prevent conflicts and strengthen international security, in accordance with the purposes and principles of the United Nations Charter, with the principles of the Helsinki Final Act and with the aims of the Charter of Paris, including those relating to external borders;
   (d) foster the sustainable economic, social and environmental development of developing countries, with the primary aim of eradicating poverty;
   (e) encourage the integration of all countries into the world economy, including through the progressive abolition of restrictions on international trade;
   (f) help develop international measures to preserve and improve the quality of the environment and the sustainable management of global natural resources, in order to ensure sustainable development;
   (g) assist populations, countries and regions confronting natural or man-made disasters; and
   (h) promote an international system based on stronger multilateral cooperation and good global governance. ...

CETA does not, however, only envisage the bilateral creation of more permanent structures for ISDS. Widening the transatlantic gap on ISDS even further, the EU's approach as contained in CETA also envisages and actively encourages the creation of a permanent multilateral investment court in the future. For this purpose, Art 8.29 CETA (entitled 'Establishment of a multilateral investment tribunal and appellate mechanism') provides:

> The Parties shall pursue with other trading partners the establishment of a multilateral investment tribunal and appellate mechanism for the resolution of investment disputes. Upon establishment of such a multilateral mechanism, the CETA Joint Committee shall adopt a decision providing that investment disputes under this Section will be decided pursuant to the multilateral mechanism and make appropriate transitional arrangements.

The establishment of a multilateral court is the EU's policy for the reform of international investment law more generally. Its approach has the potential to constitute a watershed in international investment law and increase differences with the US preference for merely reforming ISDS without structural change. While many tricky details remain, the European Commission's political courage and craftsmanship merit applause. It clearly breaks with a private law conceptualization of international investment law and takes the long-called-for 'public law approach' to ISDS to its logical conclusion[167] by aiming at building new dispute settlement institutions and ultimately envisaging even the creation of a multilateral investment court. This allows not only an increase in the consistency of decision-making in ISDS—it also allows building the investment court system into a system of checks and balances that lives up in all nuances to the challenges of a dispute settlement framework that takes constitutional principles, in particular democracy, the rule of law, and the protection of fundamental and human rights, to heart. The system of reformed investor-state arbitration contained in TPP, by contrast, is less likely to produce the same level of consistency and would be viewed with more suspicion by the populations in many important host and home countries, in particular in many quarters in Europe.

Yet, whether the predominantly bilateral set-up of permanent investment courts in the EU's new trade and investment agreements is the best way towards more consistency in international investment law generally is more than questionable.[168] While investment courts included in bilateral agreements would eliminate inconsistent interpretations of that agreement, it is less likely that treaty-overarching inconsistencies will equally be reduced, unless largely identical individuals will sit on different investment

[167] For one example of this approach, see the contributions in Stephan W Schill (ed), *International Investment Law and Comparative Public Law* (Oxford University Press, 2010). For a critical discussion of this, and other proponents' public law approaches to ISDS, see José E Alvarez, '"Beware: Boundary Crossings"—A Critical Appraisal of Public Law Approaches to International Investment Law' (2016) 17 *J World Inv & Trade* 171.

[168] See on this and the following, Stephan W Schill, 'The European Commission's Proposal of an "Investment Court System" for TTIP: Stepping Stone or Stumbling Block for Multilateralizing International Investment Law?' (2016) 20(9) *ASIL Insights*, <https://www.asil.org/insights/volume/20/issue/9/european-commissions-proposal-investment-court-system-ttip-stepping> accessed 4 April 2017.

courts within a broader network of investment courts. Instead, if permanent investment courts were to proliferate on a bilateral basis as a result of the European Commission's approach, inconsistencies in the approaches of different investment courts to essentially identical issues and treaty provisions are likely to persist.

What is more, the inclusion of permanent investment courts in important mega-regionals, such as TTIP or CETA, may further entrench bilateralism in international investment law, rather than constitute a stepping stone towards a genuine multilateralization with more global outreach. After all, the more effectively a TTIP- or CETA-Tribunal functions, the more difficult it will become to replace them later with a multilateral mechanism whose functioning will still be unknown. Such an effect can only be avoided if permanent investment courts in important mega-regionals, such as TTIP, are structured so as to morph easily into a multilateral institution, with third states being able to simply join the Tribunal's statute. This could be achieved if judges on such an investment court were appointed not by the contracting parties (eg the EU and the US under TTIP), but by a multilateral body representing the entire international community, such as the UN General Assembly and the UN Security Council (as with the ICJ).[169] Although the contracting parties to a mega-regional would thereby relinquish their appointment powers as an instrument to influence the interpretation of the agreement, the jurisprudence of that Tribunal would still be controlled by the contracting parties through the type of treaty committees that CETA and TPP envisage, which allow contracting parties to issue interpretations that are binding upon the Tribunal. Either way, all of this would require concerted efforts of the US and the EU to become reality.

The big question, however, is whether the US is going to be amenable to the creation of such, or any other, permanent investment court. While it has signalled, at least prior to the Trump administration, its openness towards an appellate mechanism, in TPP as well as other FTAs and its model BIT, the creation of a fully fledged, two-tier permanent court system as envisaged by the EU is less certain, given the critical stance the US has for a long time taken towards the creation of new international courts, as well as the submission to the jurisdiction of existing ones. For this reason alone, continuing to pursue the creation of an appellate mechanism, rather than a fully fledged court system, may be the more feasible way forward for an ISDS system in which participation of the US is envisaged. After all, an appellate mechanism would have benefits that are similar to a multilateral investment court in terms of creating coherence and ensuring an appropriate balance in ISDS jurisprudence. Its great advantage, by contrast, would be that it is potentially more easily agreeable for a greater number of states. An appellate mechanism could also be combined more easily with the existing arbitral system serving as a first instance. This would allow an appellate mechanism to build on the trust the existing system has earned with investors, while the creation of a two-tiered investment court system is seen with suspicion among many in the business community.

[169] See Art 4 Statute of the International Court of Justice, 24 October 1945, 59 Stat 1031; TS 993.

This notwithstanding, it is also important to remember that the establishment of a multilateral appellate mechanism or a permanent investment court comes with its own problems. Notably, the introduction of centralized dispute resolution institutions, whether an appellate mechanism or permanent court, could raise its own legitimacy concerns. Apart from the question of who sits as decision-makers, and who appoints or elects them, permanent institutions may display stronger dynamics in enlarging their jurisprudential powers than a system of one-off arbitral tribunals. After all, a permanent institution could develop international investment law much more consistently, including in ways governments may not agree with. In addition, the influence of individual states on who gets to sit as decision-makers in a permanent institution is likely going to be lower compared to the current arbitral system, where the majority of the arbitrators on a tribunal generally require support of the state party to the dispute. Both aspects arguably move a standing appellate mechanism or permanent court further away from democratic processes and the democratic influence of individual states than the present arbitral system.[170]

Either way, given the importance of the EU and the US as global rule-makers in international investment law, the question of whether the transatlantic gap on ISDS can be overcome, in TTIP or any other setting, is likely to influence the future architecture of global investment governance. Whose approach will succeed, that of the EU or of the US, is not only a matter of bargaining power on both sides of the Atlantic; it will be key, too, whose vision for governing international investment relations is more persuasive to third parties.

IV. Conclusion: Constitutional Moments in International Economic Governance

Mega-regionals, such as CETA and TPP, will influence the debates about the modes and structures of dispute settlement disciplines in international economic law. They also show that concerns for fragmentation, the authority of dispute settlement bodies, their control by states, and their overall legitimacy have become important topics in scholarly analysis, dispute settlement design, and treaty negotiation. In many regards, they build on, refine, and reform pre-existing experiences made with dispute settlement, above all in the multilateral trading system, without introducing fundamentally new approaches or bringing about major change. This is the case with state-to-state dispute settlement disciplines in CETA and TPP. They are relatively unremarkable and follow practices that are fairly established in WTO dispute settlement and in the crafting of preferential trade and investment agreements. While generally seeking to avoid conflict with, or worse undermining the authority of, the WTO DSB, their most important contribution could be in consolidating and approving practices the

[170] For the argument that arbitration may be closer to domestic democratic decision-making processes than permanent international courts or tribunals, see Stephan W Schill, 'The Overlooked Role of Arbitration in International Adjudication Theory' (2015) 4(2) *ESIL Reflections* 4–5, <http://www.esil-sedi.eu/sites/default/files/Schill%20Reflection%20PDF_0.pdf> accessed 12 June 2017.

WTO Appellate Body has developed jurisprudentially on legally shaky grounds, such as opening dispute settlement to the public and allowing *amicus* participation, and in providing impetus for reforms of the WTO dispute settlement mechanism.

In other regards, however, mega-regionals are likely going to function as a catalyst for more fundamental change and potentially bring about a constitutional moment in international economic law. This is particularly true for ISDS, which is at a historic juncture, as starkly diverging positions of the US and the EU have emerged on the institutional structure for ISDS, as expressed in CETA and TPP respectively. While largely agreeing on the need to ensure regulatory space, the inclusion of widespread transparency rules, and tighter state control of ISDS—thus reforming ISDS in light of constitutional challenges—the US, at least prior to Trump, prefers a reform of investor-state arbitration, whereas the EU aims at a proper institutionalization, with the creation of permanent international investment courts with appellate divisions, first at the bilateral level, and later ideally multilaterally. If the EU's Proposal were accepted by the US and beyond, the establishment of a permanent investment court system will embody a constitutional moment in international economic governance and mark the beginning of a new era for international investment law, and international economic law generally. If it meets with insurmountable resistance by the US, the EU will need to consider its reactions and either settle on a reformed version of investor-state arbitration *à la* TPP or develop a permanent international investment court without the US.

Which vision will ultimately prevail on a global scale is also a reflection of different philosophies in international politics. The US so far has taken a pragmatic and realistic approach, at least prior to Trump taking office. Concerns about ISDS and regulatory space are taken into account as one element in the much broader endeavour to integrate different national economies, including between developed economies, in order to create more open markets that benefit all participating actors. The EU, by contrast, takes a much more cautious and still too introverted approach that focuses more on the question of how to preserve regulatory space at home and too little on how to shape the international economic order according to its own needs and ideals. If the proposal to establish a permanent investment court does not hold sufficient global appeal, Europe may lose global rule-making power to a considerable extent. This does not necessarily mean that the idea of a permanent investment court should not be pursued. On the contrary, this idea is likely better suited to deal with the problems in investment governance than the current system of one-off arbitration. But it certainly needs to be better sold.

What the EU should focus on is to link its proposal for a permanent investment court to its own constitutional ideals and its vision for the future legal infrastructure of the global economy. For this purpose, it would be most critical to overcome the emphasis on shortcomings with investor-state arbitration as the justification for the establishment of a permanent investment court. This court, just like the EU's entire approach, is sold mainly as a cure to an ill, rather than as the foundation and lodestar of a new paradigm for global economic governance. However, if a permanent investment court is no more than medicine, there are less fundamental ways of curing the ills produced by investor-state arbitration, namely by reforming it along the lines of TPP, rather than abolishing it altogether. As a consequence, in order to make a stronger case for a permanent investment court as an independent global public good, more is needed than thinking of it only as medicine for introverted European sensitivities. It needs to be seen—and sold—as an entirely different ball game that can attract attention and excitement on both sides of the Atlantic (and beyond). It could be presented as what it actually is: a means to shape the future institutional infrastructure of the global economy in ways that are more in line with fundamental constitutional values, such as democracy, the rule of law, and the protection of economic and non-economic concerns, than the present system. It is in emphasizing these constitutional elements in an outward-looking perspective that Europe can develop a decidedly value-oriented and perhaps idealistic vision that is not only in line with its own constitutional mandate in the Lisbon Treaty, but shared both across the Atlantic as well as with a great number of important players in international trade and investment relations across the globe. Further developing and aiming to implement such a constitutional vision for international economic governance could be the EU's most important contribution in the age of mega-regionals and their quest for building the legal infrastructure of the global economy.

6

Intellectual Property and Mega-Regional Trade Agreements

Progress and Opportunities Missed

Thomas Cottier

I. The Common Law of Intellectual Property Protection

For industrialized countries and thus the EU, adequate protection of intellectual property (IP) is of paramount importance.[1] The process of globalization increased division of labour and the importance of global value chains, calling for legal security in foreign trade and investment abroad. Products developed and engineered in Europe often are produced elsewhere, while marketing again takes place out of Europe, adding value and mainly service sector jobs. The effort to enhance international IP protection commenced by the US at the end of the General Agreement on Tariffs and Trade 1994 (GATT) Tokyo Round equally stimulated efforts on the part of the Commission and the EU ever since. It has been high on the agenda of external economic relations since the 1990s and has remained so, translating also into new powers to regulate IP in the internal market and in trade policy.[2] It amounts to an important part of preferential trade agreements (PTAs) negotiated ever since in the wake of regime shifting,[3] and thus also of emerging mega-regional trade agreements depicting the most recent development of a long history.

Indeed, intellectual protection amounts to the oldest field of multilateral trade regulation. The 1883 Paris Convention on the Protection of Industrial Property and the 1896 Berne Convention on the Protection of Literary and Artistic Works provide the foundation[4] which a century later was taken up by the Agreement on Trade-Related Aspects of Intellectual Property Rights (TRIPs Agreement) of the

[1] I am most grateful to Dannie Jost, Senior Research Fellow WTI, and Henning Grosse Ruse-Kahn, University Lecturer, King's College, University of Cambridge, for valuable comments and suggestions.

[2] Arts 118 and 207 TFEU.

[3] Laurence R Helfer, 'Regime Shifting: The TRIPs Agreement and the New Dynamics of International Intellectual Property Law Making' (2004) 29 *Yale Journal of International Law* 1–26.

[4] For these and other treaties administered under the auspices of WIPO, see 'WIPO-Administered Treaties', <http://www.wipo.int/treaties/en/> accessed 4 April 2017.

Intellectual Property and Mega-Regional Trade Agreements: Progress and Opportunities Missed. Thomas Cottier.

WTO.[5] Subsequently, developments moved to PTA.[6] Since the TRIPs Agreement explicitly included intellectual property rights (IPRs) in the trade agreement, all EU PTAs concluded since then contain an extensive chapter on IPRs, partly repeating TRIPs obligations, partly expounding additional and increased levels of protection, so-called TRIPs+ standards.[7] The chapters on IPRs in PTAs follow the structure of TRIPs, and build upon it, not necessarily in the same order. They are highly detailed and complex, culminating in the EU—Canadian Comprehensive Economic and Trade Agreement (CETA) concluded in 2015.[8] The most recent phase of continued forum shifting relates to mega-regional trade agreements. Negotiations on the Trans-Pacific Trade Partnership (TPP) were concluded in the same year.[9] Negotiations on the Transatlantic Trade and Investment Partnership Agreement (TTIP)[10] and the China–ASEAN Regional Comprehensive Economic Partnership Agreement (RCEP)[11] are under way. For TTIP, no comprehensive negotiating text on IPRs has been made available, either officially[12] or informally.[13] At the time of writing, outcomes for TTIP still remain a matter of speculation. Given the focus on the impact of the EU's commercial policy, we briefly compare the main IP provisions of CETA with TPP, taking into account also EU proposals on TTIP.

From the point of view of the EU, the most advanced agreement as of today in this respect is ch 22 of CETA, serving as a reference point for the state of the art in a world of fragmentation and varied standards. It is likely to influence TTIP negotiations, albeit results will not be identical due to diverging US concerns. These, in turn, are mainly reflected in TPP. Globally, ch 18 of this Agreement amounts to the most important recent document as it includes relations among industrialized as well as relations among and with developing countries.

Importantly, the new standards are not limited to the parties to these Agreements, but also benefit third parties. They globally raise levels of protection and enforcement. It is recalled that Art 3 of the TRIPs Agreement extended most-favoured

[5] 'WTO Legal Texts', <https://www.wto.org/english/docs_e/legal_e/legal_e.htm> accessed 4 April 2017.

[6] See Andreas Dür and Manfred Elsig (eds), *Trade Cooperation: The Purpose, Design and Effects of Preferential Trade Agreements* (Cambridge University Press, 2015).

[7] See Josef Drexl, Henning Grosse Ruse-Khan, and Souheir Nadde-Phlix (eds), *EU Bilateral Trade Agreements and Intellectual Property: For Better or Worse?* (Springer, 2014).

[8] See European Commission, 'In Focus: Comprehensive and Economic Trade Agreement (CETA)', <http://ec.europa.eu/trade/policy/in-focus/ceta/> accessed 4 April 2017.

[9] For the text, see, eg, New Zealand, Foreign Affairs and Trade, Trans-Pacific Partnership Agreement (not yet in force), <https://www.tpp.mfat.govt.nz/> accessed 23 May 2017.

[10] European Commission, 'In Focus: Transatlantic Trade Investment Partnership', <http://ec.europa.eu/trade/policy/in-focus/ttip/> accessed 4 April 2017.

[11] See Government of Australia, Department of Foreign Affairs and Trade, 'Regional Comprehensive Economic Partnership', <http://dfat.gov.au/trade/agreements/rcep/pages/regional-comprehensive-economic-partnership.aspx> accessed 4 April 2017.

[12] See European Commission, 'EU Negotiating Texts in TTIP', <http://trade.ec.europa.eu/doclib/press/index.cfm?id=1230> accessed 4 April 2017.

[13] See Inside US Trade's World Trade Online, 'Collection of All Leaked and Publicly Released EU TTIP Documents', <https://insidetrade.com/daily-news/collection-all-leaked-and-publicly-released-eu-ttip-documents> accessed 4 April 2017.

nation (MFN) treatment to IP protection. Absent under the Berne and Paris Conventions, MFN obligations relate to any advantage and privilege granted to any other country, subject to certain exceptions. In other words, TRIPs+ obligations incurred under a PTA or mega-regional trade agreements are not limited to the parties to that agreement. They extend to all Members of the WTO. They create, subject to specific exceptions, equal conditions for all right-holders operating in a particular market. WTO Members negotiating PTAs and mega-regional trade agreements are aware that additional rights and obligations incurred provide the basis for domestic IPR law applicable *erga omnes* within the WTO Membership. While standards of protection within countries vary, they are equally applied to all 164 WTO Members (2016). Other WTO members thus benefit from spill-over effect, without reciprocal obligations.

To the extent that enhanced standards are granted to nationals on the basis of national treatment, these effects already result from the national treatment obligations of Art 3 TRIPs Agreement, Art 2 Paris Convention, and Art 5 para 1 Berne Convention. To the extent, however, that additional protection is granted to foreign right-holders, MFN triggers additional levels of protection. This is of particular importance in investment protection to the extent that it falls under the jurisdiction of the TRIPs Agreement. Overall, national treatment and the MFN clause of the TRIPs Agreement thus creates what may be called the common law of IPR protection, adding up layers of norms eventually created in different fora and instruments, from the Berne and Paris Conventions and related agreements under the auspices of the World Intellectual Property Organization (WIPO), the GATT, and the TRIPs Agreement of the WTO, to subsequent preferential trade and mega-regional trade agreements.

II. Great Expectations

In the process of legal developments in different fora, one would expect that impending systemic problems are subsequently taken up and addressed. It would be expected that the mega-regionals, in particular TPP and TTIP, and perhaps RCEP, while creating new standards of the common law, address problems identified and discussed post the adoption of the TRIPs Agreement and its remaining lacunae and issues. The IP system consists of many agreements, and their interrelationship awaits clarification on various and complex issues.[14] Are they incorporated into agreements or merely referred to? The incorporation of IPRs into the multilateral trading system and the dispute settlement mechanism of the WTO is not a formality. It does not remain without implications in defining the relationship of exclusive rights, freer trade and market access, but also non-trade issues in particular human

[14] See, in particular, Henning Grosse Ruse-Kahn, *The Protection of Intellectual Property in International Law* (Oxford University Press, 2016) chs 5 and 6 (hereafter Ruse-Kahn, *The Protection of Intellectual Property*).

rights.[15] These interfaces are expected to be addressed in subsequent agreements. There is no shortage of unresolved problems waiting to be addressed with a view to deepen and enhance the long-term legitimacy of international IP and trading and investment law. They in particular include the following issues, widely discussed in the literature over the last twenty years.[16]

Parallel trade, that is, the lawful importation of IP-protected products lawfully placed on third markets, amounts to the most important trade-related issue of IPRs in a free trade context. Article 6 TRIPs Agreement leaves the matter essentially to WTO Member States. At the same time, parallel trade—depending on the origin of the product and not the right-holder—also falls under the disciplines of GATT 1994; restrictions call for particular justification. While leaving the regulation of parallel trade to domestic policy space—commensurate with industrial and economic conditions—is appropriate for patents and copyright, international exhaustion in trademarks and geographical indications (GIs) is appropriate in a system promoting and protecting free trade. The International Law Association adopted a report and resolution to this effect in 2000.[17]

This issue also bears on the relationship of IPRs and competition law and investment protection and trade. The TRIPs Agreement is limited to setting minimum standards. Domestic law may, with limited exceptions on enforcement, freely adopt higher, more stringent levels of protection. Extending exclusive rights may unduly restrict competition and equal opportunities on the market. Yet, no disciplines exist in international economic law restraining the extension of protection domestically.[18] In investment law, the contours and scope of protection of IPRs remains controversial and unsettled.[19] What restrictions amount to regulatory taking? Do IPRs also oblige governments to allow usage, or are they limited to horizontal relations among competitors?

Much of the debate on IPRs relates to the needs of developing countries and emerging economies.[20] While these countries generally opt for lower levels of

[15] See generally Thomas Cottier, 'The Agreement on Trade-Related Aspects of Intellectual Property Rights' in Patrick F J Macrory, Arthur E Appleton, and Michael G Plummer (eds), *The World Trade Organization* (Springer, 2005); and Thomas Cottier, *Trade and Intellectual Property Protection in WTO Law: Collected Essays* (Cameron May, 2005).

[16] Keith E Maskus and Jerome H Reichman (eds), *International Public Goods and Transfer of Technology under a Globalized Intellectual Property Regime* (Cambridge University Press, 2005); Christoph Geiser (ed), *Research Handbook on Human Rights and Intellectual Property* (Edward Elgar, 2015); and Daniel Gervais, *International Intellectual Property: A Handbook of Contemporary Research* (Edward Elgar, 2015).

[17] Frederick M Abbott, 'Second Report (Final) to the Committee on International Trade Law of the International Law Association on the Subject of the Exhaustion of Intellectual Property Rights and Parallel Importation' (69th Conference of the International Law Association, July 2016, prepared 6 September 2000), <http://papers.ssrn.com/sol3/papers.cfm?abstract_id=1921856> accessed 4 April 2017.

[18] Annette Kur and Henning Gosse Ruse-Khan, 'Enough Is Enough—The Notion of Binding Ceilings in International Intellectual Property Protection' in Annette Kur (ed), *Intellectual Property Rights in a Fair World Trade System: Proposals for Reform of TRIPs* (Edward Elgar, 2011) 359–407.

[19] See, in particular, the special issue edited by Henning Grosse Ruse-Kahn, 'Intellectual Property and International Investment Law' (2016) 19 *Journal of International Economic Law* 87–277.

[20] Daniel Gervais (ed), *Intellectual Property, Trade and Development* (Oxford University Press, 2014).

protection, areas of genuine interests to them have remained underdeveloped. IP essentially is an offspring of industrialization. It has not catered to agriculture and rural populations. As up to 70 per cent of the population in developing countries relate to farming and rural life forms, an effort should be made to render the international IP system more beneficial to their economic and cultural interests. The promotion of GIs for specialized agricultural products and the protection of traditional knowledge (TK) and of genetic resources in the context of biodiversity are pressing needs. One would expect new rules on obligations to indicate the indication of origin of an invention, or efforts to catalogue TK electronically with a view to identify prior art. One would expect, beyond negative protection, the evolution of new types of IPRs addressing TK. This is less a matter of introducing appropriate disciplines in domestic law of developing countries, but much more an effort among industrialized countries to offer appropriate forms of protection which need coordination, if not harmonization, among themselves. Transfer of state-of-the-art technology and know-how and capacity building perhaps are the most urgent issues in the context of climate change mitigation and adaption. Governments are unable to honour even weak obligations as they do not possess the technology and cannot freely dispose of it. Companies, on the other hand, depend upon income, are interested to preserve first-mover advantages, and thus are reluctant to license state-of-the-art technology. Particular efforts are required to bring about improvements. Again, this is primarily a matter among industrialized countries in keeping level playing fields among competitors. It requires coordination on tax incentives and subsidies; all matters to be addressed in international trade agreements with a view to bring first-hand technologies combating greenhouse gas emissions or facilitating climate change adaption to countries of production. We would expect answers to these fundamental questions in new agreements. To this effect, fundamental principles, objectives, and goals are expected to be further developed beyond the provisions of Arts 7 and 8 of the TRIPs Agreement, also in light of the experiences made with facilitating access to essential drugs under the 2001 Doha Declaration on the TRIPs Agreement and Public Health on access to essential drugs and its implementing instruments.[21] One would expect efforts to graduate obligations at IP, commensurate with the level of social and economic development of countries and hence also the need to imitate technologies which has since been a major driver of development in economic history.[22]

It will be seen that these issues are only partly and marginally addressed, if at all, in recent PTAs and mega-regional trade agreements. Great expectations of the kind indicated have barely been met and progress has been slow and arduous. Public policy interests in achieving an overall balanced, workable, and fully legitimate system are recognized, but hardly translate in operational terms. Efforts at bringing about

[21] WTO, 'TRIPS and Public Health', <https://www.wto.org/english/tratop_e/trips_e/pharmpatent_e.htm> accessed 4 April 2017.

[22] Thomas Cottier, 'From Progressive Liberalization to Progressive Regulation in WTO Law' (2006) 4 *Journal of International Economic Law* 779–821; and Thomas Cottier, 'International Economic Law in Transition from Trade Liberalization to Trade Regulation' (2014) 17 *Journal of International Economic Law* 671–7.

new disciplines on TK on the basis of unfair competition rules have not made progress in WIPO and the concern has not been taken up in detail in PTAs beyond improving the assessment of prior art in patent law. Considerations of risks of excessive protection for innovation, competition, and free trade are still largely absent. Instead, negotiations have been defined and driven by specific sectoral demands of the industries concerned, as they were translated in negotiating positions of industrialized country governments.[23] Neither civil society nor academia was sufficiently involved in setting the agendas. PTAs, in their chapters on IPRs, are essentially TRIPs+ agreements which, in the case of TPP, developing country partners are willing to accept because they are interested in the overall package, reluctantly willing to take into account IPR obligations beyond the TRIPs Agreement. Moreover, the erosion of tariff preferences granted to developing countries due to the proliferation of PTAs further reduces such trade-offs. All this is unlikely to improve the legitimacy and effectiveness of the multilateral system and of voluntary implementation of its various disciplines. Efforts to tailor the system to the particular needs of countries while building at the same time the rule of law in the field are still largely lacking in international trade diplomacy. CETA, it will be seen, is more balanced, but equally fails taking up issues relating to parallel trade and competition.

III. Objectives and Basic Principles

In terms of objectives, TPP essentially restates Art 7 of the TRIPs Agreement, but adds the goal of a balance of rights and obligations in Art 18.2:

> The protection and enforcement of intellectual property rights should contribute to the promotion of technological innovation and to the transfer and dissemination of technology, to the mutual advantage of producers and users of technological knowledge and in a manner conducive to social and economic welfare, and to a balance of rights and obligations.

Article 18.4 adds an interesting provision entitled 'Understanding in Respect of this Chapter' and thus all the provisions on IP:

> Having regard to the underlying public policy objectives of national systems, the Parties recognise the need to:
>
> (a) promote innovation and creativity;
> (b) facilitate the diffusion of information, knowledge, technology, culture and the arts; and
> (c) foster competition and open and efficient markets, through their respective intellectual property systems, while respecting the principles of transparency and due process, and taking into account the interests of relevant stakeholders, including right holders, service providers, users and the public.

[23] Katrina Moberg, 'Private Industry's Impact on U.S. Trade Law and International Intellectual Property Law: A Study of Post-TRIPs U.S. Bilateral Agreements and the Capture of the USTR' (2014) 96 *Journal of the Patent and Trademark Office Society* 228.

Paragraph (c) renders the perception of balance of rights and obligations somewhat more specific. It emphasizes the need to foster competition and open and efficient markets—both potentially limiting IP rights. Finally, it adds the interests of the public at large, beyond right-holders and users. Article 15 particularly emphasizes the importance of public and open space:

1. The Parties recognise the importance of a rich and accessible public domain.
2. The Parties also acknowledge the importance of informational materials, such as publicly accessible databases of registered intellectual property rights that assist in the identification of subject matter that has fallen into the public domain.

The public interest thus is particularly emphasized and needs to be taken into account in interpreting the provisions of ch 18. The recognition of TK is perceived as a matter of public domain and main protection is sought by means of improving information of prior art in Art 16. The overall system, however, remains one of establishing minimal standards, and Members remain free under Art 18.5 TPP to establish higher levels of protection; it will be a matter of detailed examination to see whether some of the provisions also entail maximum standards and ceilings, in particular in the field of enforcement.

These provisions reflect the debate between developed and developing countries in TPP negotiations. They are absent in CETA, which modestly states in ch 20, Art 1:

The objectives of this Chapter are to:

(a) facilitate the production and commercialisation of innovative and creative products, and the provision of services, between the Parties; and
(b) achieve an adequate and effective level of protection and enforcement of intellectual property rights.

Both agreements restate Art 8 TRIPs in Arts 18.6 TPP and 20.3 CETA and in particular add references incorporating the instruments adopted in implementing the decision on public health within the TRIPs Agreement which thus has become part of the common law of IPRs. The need to provide an appropriate balance of rights and obligations, however, has not translated into more specific provisions fostering competition. Articles 18.11 TPP and 20.4 CETA explicitly exclude any implications on exhaustion of rights and thus parallel trade and competition, even the minimal standards of national treatment and MFN treatment contained in Art 6 TRIPs Agreement. One of the most important trade issues thus waits to be dealt with in the future. We also note that the relationship of IPRs and human rights—beyond public health—is explicitly addressed in the new agreements, and is left to the application and interpretation of the various provisions. Nor do we find the idea of graduation reflected. TPP adopts in Art 18.83 a varied geometry for implementing provisions in different countries strictly on the basis of time, without taking into account factors reflecting levels of social and economic development.

IV. General Provisions, Other Agreements, and Linkages

Beyond objectives and goals, general provisions relate to cooperation, other IPR agreements forming part of the overall system, and the linkages to other parts of the agreement, in particular investment and competition law.

A. Trans-Pacific Trade Agreement

Article 18.9 TPP provides for enhanced transparency by means of internet publication of laws and regulations and in Art 12 by means of contact points allowing rapid information in rights and obligations for right-holders and users. In particular, Art 18.13 provides the basis for enhanced cooperation among the IP Offices of Members, and particularly addresses the issue of transfer of technology and patent search cooperation.

Article 18.7 obliges Members to 'ratify or adhere' to the Paris and Berne Conventions and PCT, and in the future to the Madrid Protocol, the Budapest Treaty, the Singapore Treaty, the International Union for the Protection of New Varieties of Plants (UPOV) 1991, the WIPO Copyright Treaty (WCT), and the WIPO Performances and Phonograms Treaty (WPPT). The TRIPs Agreement is referred to in ch 1, Art 1.2(2) and is deemed to 'coexist' with TPP, yet without prejudging the status of these agreements in dispute settlement. The relationship of these Agreements to TPP remains somewhat unclear. Are they incorporated, as Berne and Paris are in the TRIPs Agreement, or existing independently? Assessing obligations under TPP without due regard to TRIPs, Paris and Berne will hardly be possible and substantive provisions can be taken into account under Art 31(3)(c) of the Vienna Convention on the Law of Treaties (VCLT). But will TPP panels have jurisdiction or not to assess potential violations of these other Agreements under the new mega-regional trade Agreement, or will jurisdiction be limited to assess compliance with the obligation to join the Agreements?[24] At any rate, the obligation to join these Agreements even independently strongly contributes to the common law of international IP, moving WIPO agreements towards universality.

The agreement addresses the linkage to investment protection in Art 9.1(f) and recognizes IP in terms of property rights eligible for investment protection; in case of conflict between investment protection and IPRs, the latter is deemed to prevail in accordance with Art 9.16 TPP.

TPP, however, does not establish minimal standards on competition policy in ch 16 as a counterbalance to strong IP protection of ch 20. While the treaty obliges parties to maintain national competition laws, the provisions do not set out detailed provisions comparable to IP standards; they focus on procedural obligations and international cooperation, presumably within the international competition law network. Specific issues relating to IPRs, in particular limitations on voluntary

[24] See, in particular, Grosse Ruse-Kahn, *The Protection of Intellectual Property* (n 14) ch 5.

licensing on grounds of anti-trust, are not addressed. Article 16.3 addresses consumer protection and contains an obligation to proscribe fraudulent and deceptive commercial practices, essentially building upon Art 10bis of the Paris Convention. The provision may thus be able to serve as a basis to protect TK on a case-by-case basis where such knowledge is being used without letting consumers and holders of that knowledge participate.[25] Regrettably, Art 19.9 excludes competition policy from dispute settlement and thus bars the development of linkages to IPRs and competition policy in case.

B. Comprehensive Economic and Trade Agreement

In comparison, CETA shows only few horizontal provisions beyond TRIPs obligations. Article 20.25 provides for cooperation in enforcement and among collecting societies and for a dialogue on matters relating to protection, enforcement, and any other issues pertaining to IP. Article 20.50 addresses bilateral cooperation. It is open to what extent this will lead to regulatory cooperation beyond the soft law provisions of ch 21, as this chapter does not list IP among its subject matters in Arts 21.1 and 21.2 CETA.[26]

Beyond TRIPs+, CETA also refers to, or incorporates, other international agreements of the overall multilateral IP system. Article 20.2 states that this chapter complements the TRIPs Agreement, the status of the most important instrument remaining unclear. Article 20.7 obliges to comply with the substantive provisions of the Paris and Berne Conventions, thus also restating TRIPs standards. In addition, however, CETA incorporates in this provision the WCT, the WIPO Performers and Phonogram Treaty, and even the Rome Convention, focusing on the protection of authors and collecting societies. Reasonable efforts to comply with the Protocol relating to the Madrid Agreement (trademarks) and the Hague Agreement (designs) are made in Arts 20.13 and 20.24 of the Agreement, respectively. Article 22.26 refers in the same way to the Patent Law Treaty and Art 22.31 to the 1991 UPOV Convention, thus reducing flexibilities under Art 27 TRIPs Agreement. While some of the Agreements are incorporated, the standard of making reasonable efforts leaves the relationship to this group of Agreements unclear. It would seem that the later obligations are merely procedural and do not go beyond the obligation to make an effort towards joining these Agreements.

The relationship of IPRs with investment protection is more elaborate in CETA than in TPP. Article 8.1 defines IPRs to be included in investment protection as follows:

> Intellectual property rights means copyright and related rights, trademark rights, rights in geographical indications, rights in industrial designs, patent rights, rights in layout designs

[25] See, for a detailed analysis and comprehensive review, Christoph Riffel, *Protection against Unfair Competition in the WTO TRIPs Agreement* (Brill Nijhoff, 2016); Thomas Cottier and Ana Jevtic, 'The Protection against Unfair Competition in WTO Law: Status, Potential and Prospects' in Josef Drexl, Reto M Hilty, Laurence Boy et al (eds), *Technology and Competition: Contributions in honour of Hanns Ullrich* (Larcier, 2009) 669–95.

[26] See below, section VIII.

of integrated circuits, rights in relation to protection of undisclosed information, and plant-breeders' rights; and, if such rights are provided by a Party's law, utility model rights. The CETA Joint Committee may, by decision, add other categories of intellectual property to this definition.

For the purposes of investment law, determination, validity, and scope of IPRs are to be exclusively defined by domestic courts (in accordance with domestic law) and not subject to review by CETA panels for the time being.[27]

Expropriation under Art 8.12(5) does not apply to compulsory licensing in accordance with the TRIPs Agreement. Paragraph 6 of this provision further states:

> For greater certainty, the revocation, limitation or creation of intellectual property rights, to the extent that these measures are consistent with the TRIPs Agreement and Chapter Twenty (Intellectual Property), do not constitute expropriation. Moreover, a determination that these measures are inconsistent with the TRIPs Agreement or Chapter Twenty (Intellectual Property) does not establish an expropriation.

Equally following from the Canadian experience of *Eli Lilly v Canada* filed under NAFTA ch 11,[28] formal revocation on the basis of domestic law and compulsory licensing of IPRs consistent with international obligations is excluded under the Agreement and remedies available essentially focus on fair and equitable treatment and possibly regulatory taking. Moreover, exceptions relating to transfer of technology in terms of performance requirements, national treatment, and MFN are provided for under Art 8.15(4) to the extent that these exceptions are compatible with current or future provisions under the TRIPs Agreement or a waiver granted under WTO law. The same exceptions also apply under Art 13.10(6) in relation to performance requirements on IPRs in the field of services. CETA amounts to the most elaborate relationship of IPRs and investment protection as of today, standing for progress in the law.

A general exception for the protection of IPRs is further provided for in government procurement under Art 19.3(c) of the Agreement, disclosure requirements under Art 19.16(3)(c), and under the general exception clause of Art 28.3(1), which incorporates Art XX GATT in respect of trade in goods, while IP is not explicitly mentioned for exceptions for services, but may be covered by recourse to

[27] Annex 8-D Joint Declaration concerning Art 8.12.6 states: 'Mindful that investor-State dispute settlement tribunals are meant to enforce the obligations referred to in Art 8.18.1, and are not an appeal mechanism for the decisions of domestic courts, the Parties recall that the domestic courts of each Party are responsible for the determination of the existence and validity of intellectual property rights. The Parties further recognise that each Party shall be free to determine the appropriate method of implementing the provisions of this Agreement regarding intellectual property within their own legal system and practice. The Parties agree to review the relation between intellectual property rights and investment disciplines within three years after entry into force of this Agreement or at the request of a Party. Further to this review and to the extent required, the Parties may issue binding interpretations to ensure the proper interpretation of the scope of investment protection under this Agreement in accordance with the provisions of Art 8.31.3.'

[28] *Eli Lilly and Co v The Government of Canada*, UNCITRAL, ICSID Case No UNCT/14/2, <http://www.italaw.com/cases/1625> accessed 4 April 2017.

Art 28(3)(2) providing, as under Art XIV of the General Agreement on Trade in Services (GATS), for measures to secure compliance with laws or regulations which are not inconsistent with the provisions of this Agreement.

The chapter on competition policy recognizes in Art 17.2 the importance of competition law:

1. The Parties recognise the importance of free and unrestricted competition in their trade relations. The Parties acknowledge that anti-competitive business conduct has the potential to distort the proper functioning of markets and undermine the benefits of trade liberalisation.
2. The Parties shall take appropriate measures to proscribe anti-competitive business conduct, recognising that such measures will enhance the fulfilment of the objectives of this Agreement.

Cooperation, however, is limited to enforcing domestic competition law in Art 17.4.3, and the chapter is excluded from dispute settlement in Art 17.4. The relationship to IPRs is not addressed. This is yet another opportunity missed, going even behind the competition policy chapter in previous generations of the EU's free trade agreements (FTAs).[29]

In conclusion, TPP and CETA are used to incorporate or relate to other IPR agreements forming part of the global IP system. They essentially contribute to the enlargement of membership which often has remained limited so far to WIPO-administrated agreements. The policy of incorporating the Paris and Berne Conventions in the TRIPs Agreement thus is continued and extrapolated. This may also be expected for TTIP. The proposal published in July 2015 confirms TRIPs, Paris, Berne, Rome, WIPO, Phonograms, Budapest, UPOV, Madrid, and PCT, and provides for reasonable efforts to comply with the Patent Law Treaty, Trademark Law Treaty, Singapore Treaty on Law of Trademarks, Hague Agreement on Industrial Designs, Beijing Treaty on Audiovisual Performances, and the Marrakesh Treaty to facilitate access to published works to visually impaired people.[30]

Linkages to other parts of the Agreement, however, remain without sufficient elaboration. While the status of IPRs as property in investment protection is included, levels of protection against government intervention are left open in TPP or are subject to significant exceptions in CETA, and obligations of governments to allow the use of IPRs will need to be defined in case law. Finally, linkages to competition policy remain vague and weak, and depend on existing domestic law. In substance, the Agreements do not offer guidance in addressing the abuse of IPRs and thus fail to contribute to a better balance, despite objectives to this effect in TPP expounded above. The exclusion of competition law from government-to-government dispute settlement under the two Agreements is an opportunity missed

[29] See, eg, Art 23 of the 1972 EC–Switzerland Free Trade Agreement [1972] OJ L 300/189.

[30] 'Draft Provisions on International Agreements relating to Intellectual Property' (tabled April 2015), <http://trade.ec.europa.eu/doclib/docs/2015/july/tradoc_153673.pdf> accessed 4 April 2017.

to overcome the fragmentation between integrated trade policies and decentralized competition policy.

V. Main TRIPs+ Standards

Some of the TRIPs+ standards are necessary complements to the TRIPs Agreement in filling existing lacunae. This is particularly true for defining periods of exclusivity of test data in Art 39(3) TRIPs Agreement. The provision, without such periods, is hardly workable. In most other areas, however, TRIPs+ standards reflect new technological or commercial needs of industries and reinforce the level and scope of protection of right-holders. They are closely based upon the TRIPs Agreement and build upon it.

The main template for TRIPs+ standards was set by the US–Central America FTA (CAFTA), shortly upon completing the TRIPs Agreement.[31] This Agreement provided the basis for TRIPs+ disciplines in subsequent PTAs.

Within this chapter, it is impossible to assess the implications of each and every of the detailed provisions as to what extent they go beyond TRIPs, and to what extent they merely reflect existing levels of protection. The chapter is limited to a brief survey, highlighting the most important and obvious TRIPs+ obligations without claiming to be complete. We group the respective provisions of CETA and TPP in tandem and in comparison.

TPP and CETA comprise a number of important TRIPs+ elements relating to substantive standards. A detailed analysis is beyond the scope of this chapter, which merely indicates the areas of prime interest. They essentially build upon TRIPs+ obligations developed in a number of PTAs concluded since 1995, mainly pioneered in CAFTA. These obligations all build upon the disciplines of the TRIPs Agreement.

A. Patent law and protection of undisclosed information

TPP contains a number of important TRIPs+ obligations relating to patent protection and procedures, largely discussed in the WIPO Patent Law Treaty. Article 18.39 provides for revocation of patents, 18.42 deals with patent filings, 18.43 with amendments and corrections of applications, and 18.44 sets minimal standards on publication of patent applications. Article 18.46 addresses delays caused by Patent Offices, essentially defining a reasonable period to amount to no more than five years after filing or three years following the request for a patent examination.

[31] Office of the US Trade Representative, 'CAFTA–DR (Dominican Republic–Central America FTA)', <http://www.ustr.gov/trade-agreements/free-trade-agreements/cafta-dr-dominican-republic-central-america-fta> accessed 4 April 2017; and Thomas Cottier, Dannie Jost, and Michelle Schupp, 'Setting the Scene: The Prospects of TRIPs-plus Protection in Future Mega Regionals' in Thilo Rensmann (ed), *Mega-Regional Trade Agreements and the Future of International Trade and Investment Law* (Springer, 2017).

Article 18.48 provides for an application to adjust and extend the patent term due to unreasonable curtailment of the marketing approval procedures, yet without defining a particular timeframe.

Article 18.38 introduces a grace period for publication of patents of twelve months, thus facilitating prior publication in scientific journals. Article 18.47 defines an exclusive period of ten years for agricultural chemical products. The exclusivity for pharmaceuticals is five years in accordance with Art 18.50, plus five years' exclusivity under a Supplementary Protection Certificate of at least five years offsetting time spent for regulatory approval. Article 18.52 introduces a requirement to protect biologics with eight years of exclusivity within or outside of patent protection, a provision subject to review after ten years upon entry into force of the Agreement. In pharmaceuticals, the term of biologics in not legally defined in the agreement and leaves uncertainties for the time being.

The protection of trade secrets is reinforced as Art 18.78 requires parties to provide for penal sanctions beyond Art 39(1) of the TRIPs Agreement.

The TPP does not further define the impact on biotechnology and genetic engineering. As to plant variety protection, Art 18.37 obliges Members to adhere to UPOV 1991, which in effect reduces the options for *sui generis* protection under Art 27 of the TRIPs Agreement.

The Agreement recognizes the importance of protecting TK in Art 18.16, which, at this stage in operational terms, is mainly linked to patent protection and the determination of prior art. The provision of Art 18.48 provides for international cooperation and better understanding of the issues. It allows, but does not oblige, Members to take into account TK in prior art determination, the participation of NGOs, and recourse to electronic database and digital libraries. It is regrettable that these provisions are not mandatory. They could offer a balance to extensive TRIPs+ obligations in patent law.

CETA on patents essentially focuses on pharmaceuticals. A TRIPs+ definition is adopted, extending patent protection beyond processes and substances to diagnostics and methods of treatment, including biologics. Article 20.6 provides:

> For the purposes of this Section:
>
> pharmaceutical product means a product including a chemical drug, biologic drug, vaccine or radiopharmaceutical, that is manufactured, sold or represented for use in:
>
> (a) making a medical diagnosis, treating, mitigating or preventing disease, disorder, or abnormal physical state, or its symptoms, or
> (b) restoring, correcting or modifying physiological functions.

CETA obliges the parties to maintain a system of supplementary or *sui generis* protection of pharmaceuticals beyond the duration of the patent. Article 20.27(5) provides for supplementary protection *sui generis* from filing to marketing minus five years, but in accordance with Art 20.27(6) overall not extending more than two to five years beyond the maximum patent term. This is one of the few provisions imposing a ceiling to protection. Article 20.28 allows for a patent-linking mechanism, essentially limiting market approvals to patented products. Finally, Art 20.29 provides for exclusivity of test data protection for pharmaceuticals for six years. Article 20.30 extends test data for plant protection to ten years. Article 20.31 obliges parties to implement the 1991 UPOV Convention and thus limit the options under Art 27 of the TRIPs Agreement. The implications of these provisions on health care costs remain to be seen. The extension of protection will limit recourse to generic products; the same is likely to be the case under TTIP, despite assurances by the Commission as regards neutrality of the Agreement for the health sector.[32]

B. Copyright and neighbouring rights

TPP essentially builds on the TRIPs Agreement. Only a detailed assessment will show to what extent its general provisions contain TRIPs+ elements beyond extending protection to seventy years post mortem in Art 18.63. Article 18.66 provides for an interesting provision seeking a proper balance between right-holders, users, and the public at large, which is of importance in relation to human rights protection:

> Balance in Copyright and Related Rights Systems
>
> Each Party shall endeavour to achieve an appropriate balance in its copyright and related rights system, among other things by means of limitations or exceptions that are consistent with Art 18.65 (Limitations and Exceptions), including those for the digital environment, giving due consideration to legitimate purposes such as, but not limited to: criticism; comment; news reporting; teaching, scholarship, research, and other similar purposes; and facilitating access to published works for persons who are blind, visually impaired or otherwise print disabled.[33]

This novel provision is of particular interest as it is binding, thus requiring a binding system, albeit subject to the three-step test of Art 18.65 which it may modify in due course.[34]

The main focus is on technical protection measures of works and performances in Art 18.68 and on Rights Management Information in Art 18.69. The Agreement provides, inter alia, for penal sanctions in cases of wilful circumventions of technological measures of protection for the purpose of commercial advantage or financial gain, subject to certain exceptions. Article 18.70 stresses the importance of collecting societies and of fair, efficient, and accountable procedures thereof.

TPP stresses improvements on enforcing copyright and related rights protection. Article 18.72 establishes a presumption in favour of copyright and related right-holders, strongly reinforcing their position in penal and administrative proceedings. Article 18.74 provides for additional damages in copyright, and Art 18.74 prescribes criminal penalties and prosecution *ex officio* for infringements on a commercial scale, as defined by the provision.

[32] European Commission, 'Pharmaceuticals in TTIP', 3, <http://trade.ec.europa.eu/doclib/docs/2015/january/tradoc_153010.4.7%20Pharmaceuticals.pdf> accessed 15 May 2017: 'We won't negotiate anything in TTIP which would upset this delicate balance [in EU and US IP law] or increase the costs for EU countries.'

[33] Footnotes omitted.

[34] See, in particular, Grosse Ruse-Kahn, *The Protection of Intellectual Property* (n 14) ch 12.

New and detailed provisions relate to the protection of encrypted programme-carrying satellites and cable signals in Art 18.79. Article 18.80 addresses government use of software and obliges governments to respect licensing, thus combating illicit use in public administrations. Article 18.81 introduces detailed disciplines on internet service providers, carving out safe harbour rules and exceptions on liability for providers in dealing with copyright and related rights-protected materials.

CETA is less detailed on copyright and related rights protection than TPP. Articles 20.9 and 20.10 similarly stress technical protection measures and rights management information, yet without imposing penal sanctions. Article 20.11 requires, under certain conditions, restrictions of liability of intermediary internet service providers. Moreover, Art 20.12 establishes a prohibition of camcording of live events, and may subject such conduct to penal sanctions. By fully referring to the Berne Convention, CETA also entails the protection of moral rights and removes the exception under Art 9 of the TRIPs Agreement. Article 20.42 also establishes a presumption in favour of the right-holder of copyright and related rights, reinforcing their procedural position.

C. Trademarks and geographical indications

TPP builds upon disciplines of the TRIPs Agreement and requires in Art 18.19 the recognition of collective and certification marks. Article 18.22 refers to the 1999 Joint Recommendation of WIPO on well-known trademarks. A number of additional procedural requirements are set forth in Art 18.23, including an obligation to provide for electronic applications in Art 18.24, recourse to classifications of the WIPO Nice Agreement concerning the classification of trademarks in Art 18.25, a term of protection of no less than ten years in Art 18.26, and a ban on registration of trademark licences in Art 18.27 of the Agreement. TPP also addresses Internet Domain Names and obliges parties to submit to the WIPO Internet Domain Name dispute resolution mechanism which evolved informally and is being incorporated into the TPP Agreement. Finally, TPP provides in Art 18.29 new protection for country names to the extent that recourse to them is misleading and contrary to principles of unfair competition and consumer protection.

TPP addresses GIs in Arts 18.30 to 18.36 in great detail. The Agreement requires direct applications without interposition of parties, and expounds in particular the relationship to trademarks to which we return below in greater detail.[35]

CETA incorporates the Singapore Treaty on Trademarks in Art 20.14 and introduces fair use exemptions so far not mentioned in the TRIPs Agreement in Art 20.15, in particular descriptive terms of geographical origin. The bulk of the chapter is dedicated to the protection of GIs in Arts 20.16 to 20.23 and Annex 20, A listing of specific GIs (A: EU) (B: Canada). Protection extends beyond TRIPs,

[35] See below, section VI.B.

catching up to the level of protection granted for alcoholic beverages under Art 23 of the TRIPs Agreement under Art 20.19(3):

> The protection referred to in subpara 2(a) shall be provided even where the true origin of the product is indicated or the geographical indication is used in translation or accompanied by expressions such as 'kind', 'type', 'style', 'imitation' or the like.

Foundations, exceptions, and the relationship to trademarks are set out in great detail, reflecting one of the EU's main goals and concerns.

D. Enforcement of IPRs

TPP sets out a comprehensive section on enforcement, the difference of which from the TRIPs Agreement would require detailed analysis beyond the scope of this chapter. Beyond the measures already discussed for enhancing copyright protection, the main TRIPs+ component can be found in increasing penal measures and sanctions for wilful trademark and copyright violations on a commercial scale. Reinforcing penal law obligations, in particular in trademark and copyright infringements, were generally reinforced for commercial operations—the notion of commercial scale being defined more precisely after the US had lost a complaint before the WTO against China on such grounds.[36] The Agreement defines the threshold in Art 18.77, also including non-commercial activities:

> In respect of wilful copyright or related rights piracy, 'on a commercial scale' includes at least:
> (a) acts carried out for commercial advantage or financial gain; and
> (b) significant acts, not carried out for commercial advantage or financial gain, that have a substantial prejudicial impact on the interests of the copyright or related rights holder in relation to the marketplace.[37]

CETA equally entails a comprehensive chapter on enforcement, building on the TRIPs Agreement. Again, a detailed analysis beyond this chapter would be required to assess TRIPs+ elements. Other than TPP, CETA, however, does not provide for enhanced penal remedies and sanctions, and provisions inspired by the Anti-Counterfeiting Trade Agreement (ACTA) were not included in this Agreement.

Additional elements are proposed by the EU for TTIP rules on customs enforcement. They entail interesting proposals on risk analysis and international cooperation, drawn from other agreements:[38]

> ...
>
> 7. In respect of goods subject to customs control, the customs authorities shall carry out adequate controls in accordance with risk analysis criteria with a view to preventing acts in breach of intellectual property laws applicable in their territories and in order to cooperate

[36] WTO, Panel Report, *China—Measures Affecting the Protection and Enforcement of Intellectual Property Rights* (26 January 2009) WT/DS362/R.

[37] Footnote omitted.

[38] 'Art XX—Customs Enforcement of Intellectual Property Rights', proposal tabled April 2015, published 31 July 2015, <http://trade.ec.europa.eu/doclib/docs/2015/july/tradoc_153672.pdf> accessed 4 April 2017.

on the customs enforcement of intellectual property rights. Those controls, other than random checks, shall primarily be based on risk analysis using electronic data-processing techniques.

14. The Parties agree to cooperation in respect of international trade in goods suspected of infringing intellectual property rights. In particular, the Parties agree to share data and information on trade in goods suspected of infringing intellectual property rights affecting both Parties. In addition to exchanging general information regarding seizures, trends and risk analysis, the customs administrations of each Party shall provide available specific information allowing the customs administration of the other Party to swiftly enforce intellectual property rights against shipments destined to its territory. The information shall be provided in full respect of the provisions on protection of personal data applicable in the territories of the Parties.

VI. Potentially Conflicting Rules

Most of the TRIPs+ rights and obligations in different PTAs complement each other and levels of protection in a country are defined on the basis of MFN for all WTO Members alike. Yet, norms may also be conflicting for countries belonging to more than one preferential agreement. Canada being a member of TPP and CETA faces such problems of consistency and coherence, creating challenges for domestic regulation of IPRs. Such configurations arise where levels of protection are subject to ceilings in one or the other Agreement. Supplementary protection for agricultural chemicals and pharmaceuticals, and protection of test data and of GIs are examples in point.

A. Exclusive marketing right and supplementary protection

TPP requires, as indicated above, to provide for supplementary protection of patented agricultural chemical products and pharmaceuticals due to temporal suspension of effective patent protection by virtue of regulatory approval for at least ten years in Art 18.47, and at least five years in Art 18.50, respectively, from the date of the marketing approval. The period is at least three years for evergreens, that is, new clinical information as applied to a previously applied pharmaceutical (Art 18.50). CETA, on the other hand, requires a *sui generis* system to be installed for protection of pharmaceuticals following marketing approvals granted. The period of supplementary patent protection is calculated as follows in Art 20.27:

5. Each Party shall provide that the period of *sui generis* protection be for a period equal to the period which elapsed between the date on which the application for the basic patent was filed and the date of the first marketing authorisation, reduced by a period of five years.
6. Notwithstanding para 5 and without prejudice to a possible extension of the period of *sui generis* protection by a Party as an incentive or a reward for research in certain target populations, such as children, the duration of the *sui generis* protection may not exceed a period of two to five years, to be established by each Party.

Under CETA, the maximum duration may thus be limited to two years, while under TPP the period extends to at least five years. In implementing the provisions, Canada will need to combine the two and provide supplementary protection for pharmaceuticals for five years, notwithstanding the right to limit such protection to two years under CETA. The example shows the need for global harmonization of supplementary protection and test data protection under a revised TRIPs Agreement.

B. Geographical indications

GI protection is of paramount importance to the EU, while it has been reluctantly accepted in North America, which prefers protection by means of collective and certified marks. The difference translates into a potentially conflicting relationship of GIs and trademarks in CETA and TPP. Similar conflicts also arise under other configurations, in particular between CAFTA and the EU—Caribbean Forum Economic Partnership Agreements (EU CARIFORUM EPA) as applied in the Dominican Republic.[39] They are largely amplified by CETA and TTP.

CETA clearly grants a preference to GI protection over trademarks in case of conflict with new trademarks in Art 20.19(5):

> The registration of a trademark which contains or consists of a geographical indication of the other Party listed in Annex 20-A shall be refused or invalidated, ex officio if a Party's legislation so permits or at the request of an interested party, with respect to a product that falls within the product class specified in Annex 20-A for that geographical indication and that does not originate in the place of origin specified in Annex 20-A for that geographical indication.

The Agreement, however, protects previously filed and protected trademarks as follows in Art 20.21(5):

> If a trademark has been applied for or registered in good faith, or if rights to a trademark have been acquired through use in good faith, in a Party before the applicable date set out in para 6, measures adopted to implement this Subsection in that Party shall not prejudice the eligibility for or the validity of the registration of the trademark, or the right to use the trademark, on the basis that the trademark is identical with, or similar to, a geographical indication.

The TPP Agreement, on the other hand, establishes a priority of trademark protection over GIs. It essentially allows the latter only to the extent that they are compatible with trademark protection in Art 18.32:

> Grounds of Opposition and Cancellation
>
> 1. If a Party protects or recognises a geographical indication through the procedures referred to in Art 18.31 (Administrative Procedures for the Protection or Recognition

[39] cf Josef Drexl, 'Intellectual Property and Implementation of Recent Bilateral Trade Agreements in the EU' in Josef Drexl, Henning Grosse Ruse-Khan, and Souheir Nadde-Phlix (eds), *EU Bilateral Trade Agreements and Intellectual Property: For Better or Worse?* (Springer, 2014) 265–91.

of Geographical Indications), that Party shall provide procedures that allow interested persons to object to the protection or recognition of a geographical indication and that allow for any such protection or recognition to be refused or otherwise not afforded, at least, on the following grounds:

(a) the geographical indication is likely to cause confusion with a trademark that is the subject of a pre-existing good faith pending application or registration in the territory of the Party;
(b) the geographical indication is likely to cause confusion with a pre-existing trademark, the rights to which have been acquired in accordance with the Party's law; and
(c) the geographical indication is a term customary in common language as the common name for the relevant good in the territory of the Party.

2. If a Party has protected or recognised a geographical indication through the procedures referred to in Art 18.31 (Administrative Procedures for the Protection or Recognition of Geographical Indications), that Party shall provide procedures that allow for interested persons to seek the cancellation of a geographical indication, and that allow for the protection or recognition to be cancelled, at least, on the grounds listed in para 1. A Party may provide that the grounds listed in para 1 shall apply as of the time of filing the request for protection or recognition of a geographical indication in the territory of the Party (footnote omitted).
3. No Party shall preclude the possibility that the protection or recognition of a geographical indication may be cancelled, or otherwise cease, on the basis that the protected or recognised term has ceased meeting the conditions upon which the protection or recognition was originally granted in that Party.

TPP also seeks to pre-empt geographical indications recognized by other international agreements in Art 18.36 by imposing equivalent procedures and objections under this Agreement. The provision only applies to subsequently concluded agreements.

International Agreements

1. If a Party protects or recognises a geographical indication pursuant to an international agreement, as of the applicable date under para 6, involving a Party or a non-Party and that geographical indication is not protected through the procedures referred to in Art 18.31 (Administrative Procedures for the Protection or Recognition of Geographical Indications) or Art 18.32.4 (Grounds of Opposition and Cancellation), that Party shall apply at least procedures and grounds that are equivalent to those in Art 18.31(e) (Administrative Procedures for the Protection or Recognition of Geographical Indications) and Art 18.32.1 (Grounds of Opposition and Cancellation) ...

TPP intends to oblige Canada and other Members entering into subsequent agreements on GIs with the EU to respect the principles and procedures set out in TPP. They establish obligations of TPP Members vis-à-vis other Members and a commitment to take such obligations into account in negotiating third-party agreements, such as CETA. Disrespect of such obligations may incur state responsibility vis-à-vis other TPP parties. While in CETA the EU respects pre-existing trademarks, the opposition procedures in TPP may impair the protection of GIs listed in Annex 20-A of the CETA Agreement and remove legal security for the listed European GI products in North America. Provided that the US becomes a party to the the

TPP Agreement, protected GIs may be challenged in particular by US trademark owners under TPP rules. In practical terms, tension may eventually primarily arise in respect of US trademarks sold in Canada while protecting European GIs in Canada on grounds that the GI amounts to a generic term under Art 18.32(1)(c) TPP. Liability of parties under international law would be subject to Art 30 para 4 of the VCLT, that is, in accordance with respective bilateral treaty relations. In other words, Canada would be liable both to the US and the EU under different Agreements. The question arises to what extent TPP violates the principle of *pactum tertiis nec nocent nec prosunt* in that respect. TPP may oblige its Members to comply with such rules, but cannot expect that third parties fully agree to these terms in future agreements. The configuration shows that it will be important to achieve, eventually, harmonization of GI rules and principles in the WTO.

VII. Dispute Settlement

TPP dispute settlement applies to IPRs, potentially including non-violation complaints once adopted for TRIPs under WTO law under Art 28.3.2. The scope of dispute settlement in Art 28.12-16, largely following the patterns of WTO law, yet short of appeals and a permanent secretariat, relates to the provisions of the Agreement and those incorporated in it, arguably the substantive provisions of the TRIPs Agreement. It remains open to what extent jurisdiction extends to other international agreements referred to in ch 20, albeit excluding competition law which leaves important remedies against the abuse of IPRs outside the scope of TPP dispute resolution. Jurisdiction of TPP is not exclusive, and parties have the choice of forum and may continue to submit disputes to the WTO dispute settlement system under Art 28.4. Disputes before the WTO, however, cannot be based on TPP provisions, but need to rely on those of the WTO and TRIPs. The WTO panel and Appellate Body may take into account TPP provisions in interpreting TRIPs provisions under Art 31(3)(c) VCLT; TRIPs+ claims, however, cannot be heard before the WTO. Additional reasons to take recourse to TPP panel proceedings are that Art 28.19(3) provides for temporary financial compensation, which has been absent in WTO law unless the parties agree to it. What remains unclear is whether dispute settlement is mandatory prior to taking unilateral measures against a Member allegedly violating its obligations under the TPP Agreement. Other than Art 2 DSU, ch 28 does not provide for an equivalent requirement and provision and may allow for unilateral action in response to alleged violations. TPP excludes direct effect in Art 28.21 and thus the invocation of IPR provisions before domestic courts in terms of direct effect, but not consistent interpretation:

> No Party may provide for a right of action under its domestic law against any other Party on the ground that a measure of the other Party is inconsistent with its obligations under this Agreement, or that the other Party has otherwise failed to carry out its obligations under this Agreement.

However, recourse to the TPP disciplines on IP, as well as investment protection, can be heard under alternative dispute resolution mechanisms under Art 28.22 and by recourse to enforceable international commercial arbitration:

1. Each Party shall, to the maximum extent possible, encourage and facilitate the use of arbitration and other means of alternative dispute resolution for the settlement of international commercial disputes between private parties in the free trade area.
2. To this end, each Party shall provide appropriate procedures to ensure observance of agreements to arbitrate and for the recognition and enforcement of arbitral awards in such disputes.
3. A Party shall be deemed to be in compliance with para 2 if it is a party to and is in compliance with the 1958 United Nations Convention on the Recognition and Enforcement of Foreign Arbitral Awards.

CETA similarly coexists with WTO dispute settlement, and the same principles and questions apply as set out above for TPP. Article 28.4 allows for choice of forum. Panel proceedings, short of appeal and a permanent secretariat, are largely modelled after DSU rules of the WTO in Arts 29.7–11 and 29.16–19. CETA also offers the choice of forum, but excludes recourse to multiple fora in Art 29.3:

1. Recourse to the dispute settlement provisions of this Chapter is without prejudice to recourse to dispute settlement under the WTO Agreement or under any other agreement to which the Parties are party.
2. Notwithstanding para 1, if an obligation is equivalent in substance under this Agreement and under the WTO Agreement, or under any other agreement to which the Parties are party, a Party may not seek redress for the breach of such an obligation in the two fora.
3. Nothing in this Agreement shall preclude a Party from implementing the suspension of obligations authorised by the WTO Dispute Settlement Body. A Party may not invoke the WTO Agreement to preclude the other Party from suspending obligations pursuant to this Chapter.

The two fora are thus separate, but panels are obliged to take into account the case law of the WTO law and thus the interpretation and application of the TRIPs Agreement in accordance with Art 29.17:

The arbitration panel shall interpret the provisions of this Agreement in accordance with customary rules of interpretation of public international law, including those set out in the *Vienna Convention on the Law of Treaties*. The arbitration panel shall also take into account relevant interpretations in reports of Panels and the Appellate Body adopted by the WTO Dispute Settlement Body.

Similar to TPP and other PTAs, CETA excludes direct effect and does not allow domestic courts to override domestic law in Art 30.6:

1. Nothing in this Agreement shall be construed as conferring rights or imposing obligations on persons other than those created between the Parties under public international law, nor as permitting this Agreement to be directly invoked in the domestic legal systems of the Parties.

2. A Party shall not provide for a right of action under its domestic law against the other Party on the ground that a measure of the other Party is inconsistent with this Agreement.

Finally, it is recalled that for the interpretation of IPRs in the context of investment dispute settlement, domestic courts remain fully responsible for determining the validity and scope of IPRs.[40]

VIII. Regulatory Cooperation

Regulatory cooperation has a long tradition in WIPO and among leading patent offices, in particular the US, Japan, and the European Patent Organization. This tradition is extended to other TPP members. TPP provides for best endeavours to cooperate in the field of IP protection. Article 18.12 establishes contact points. Article 18.13–16 provides for cooperation in particular in the fields of transfer of technology, patent administration, and development of TK protection. The engagement is promising, but not compelling, as it is subject to resources available in Art 18.17. TPP further provides for capacity building in ch 21 and for cooperation in ch 25 on mainly domestic regulatory coherence with emphasis on domestic interagency cooperation within governments and economic impact assessment; both areas do not exclude IP, and it remains to be seen to what extent TPP will eventually develop regulatory cooperation in the long run also in the field of IPRs.

CETA provides in Art 20.50 for cooperation, in particular in the fields of enforcement, geographical indications, and cooperation of collecting societies, committing to 'establish and maintain an effective dialogue' on any relevant issue under the Agreement. The relationship to the general ch 21 on Regulatory Cooperation mainly deals with protection of human and plant health and life and safety and environmental concerns; IP is not included, but could be equally suitable to be dealt with along the principles of cooperation set out in this chapter of the Agreement. The Regulatory Cooperation Forum could equally operate in the field of IP and its linkages to other chapters of the Agreement, in particular on technical barriers to trade. The same holds true for Art 21.5 on mutually assessing the compatibility of domestic measures. It should be recalled, however, that regulatory cooperation under ch 21 is voluntary and may be withdrawn upon notice to the other party in accordance with Art 21.2.6. While ch 21 thus remains soft law, obligations under Art 20.50 are more committing in establishing an effective dialogue.

IX. Conclusions

The review of TPP and CETA allows for a number of conclusions and lessons to be learned in the field of IP protection. Future agreements, including TTIP and

[40] Annex 8-D Joint Declaration concerning Art 8.12.6.

RCEP, should further build upon modest, but interesting, commitments to establish a proper balance between exclusive rights and the public domain, and turn these commitments into operational provisions largely lacking so far. In a free trade context, at least trademarked products should be subject to international exhaustion. Linkages to investment law in the Agreements amount to important progress, in particular in CETA, but linkages should also be established with competition policy. The lack of substantive standards in anti-trust and minimal standards and the exclusion from dispute settlement undermines the goals of establishing a proper balance and combatting and preventing the abuse of exclusive rights often controlled by strong market participants. Linkages should also be made to the rules on technical barriers to trade and to regulatory cooperation and coherence. There is no reason why IP should be exempted from impact assessment in different policy fields, in particular the health sector and communications, and from seeking harmonization in an ongoing regulatory process. Linkages to human rights should be made explicit, allowing arbitration to take them into account in shaping an appropriate balance of exclusive rights, the public domain, and integrity of individuals. Climate change mitigation and adaption calls for new rules on technology transfer and adjustment of technologies suitable for the terrain in which they are applied, taking into account taxation and subsidies and the linkages to these fields. It is important to use negotiations to overcome long-standing fragmentation of different regulatory fields, negotiated by different communities and driven by different interests.

Greater coherence and careful attention should also be sought in relation to the multilateral system of the WTO. Both TPP and CETA do not explicitly incorporate the substantive provisions of the TRIPs Agreement, while on substance strongly relying upon this foundation. The status of WTO law and TRIPs needs clarification and should not be left entirely to dispute settlement. Agreements should be clear as to whether these norms are incorporated, like the Paris and Berne Conventions in TRIPs, or are merely operating in the process of interpreting PTA norms under the VCLT. From a substantive point of view, TRIPs+ obligations cannot be separated and considered in isolation from the TRIPs Agreement. Explicit incorporation would thus be suitable, on the one hand, from a substantive point of view. Incorporation, on the other hand, bears the risk of diverging interpretations and the loss of clear guidance by WTO panels and the Appellate Body, comparable to the situation in investment protection. The configuration confirms the insight that jurisdiction under the WTO DSU should be extended to include PTAs and mega-regional trade agreements. Instead of operating a separate system, as expounded in TPP and CETA, yet short of a centre and the expertise of a secretariat staff, future litigation in the framework of PTAs should take place before the WTO law operating as world trade court.[41] It would allow bringing greater coherence, in particular in

[41] James Flett, 'Referring PTA Disputes to the WTO Dispute Settlement System' in Andreas Dür and Manfred Elsig (eds), *Trade Cooperation: The Purpose, Design and Effects of Preferential Trade Agreements* (Cambridge University Press, 2015) 555–79; Agnes Forere Malebakeng, *The Relationship of WTO Law and Regional Trade Agreements in Dispute Settlement* (Kluwer Law International, 2015)

the field of the IP system, which is composed of a considerable number of different agreements, including those administered by WIPO.

The implications of ever-increasing TRIPs+ standards deserve careful examination. To some extent, they are necessary to bring about legal security. To some extent, they essentially result from sectorial pressures, regulatory capture, and highly specialized negotiating structures which are not sufficiently inclusive. General levels of education in IPRs in the legal profession and in non-specialized sectors has remained low. Issues identified only on completion of the TPP—and to some extent, CETA—rule-making processes confirm traditional patterns, but also show the rise of increasing awareness.[42] All interests at stake need to be on the table and considered. The structure of TTIP negotiations on the European side has made substantial progress in terms of transparency and inclusiveness, and it will be interesting to learn how this will translate into transatlantic IP regulation. Maximum levels of protection are not optimal levels of protection. IP agreements should thus include ceilings to protection. Even if competition policy is fully integrated, it is not in a position to establish a proper balance to the current minimal standards approach.[43] Ever-increasing levels tend to clog the system, and are detrimental to research, development, consumers, and welfare.[44]

Both the US and the EU have extensive IP systems. Instead of developing a fully comprehensive gold standard, negotiations may focus on and be limited to contentious issues, and also focus on issues where changes in respective domestic legislations are a necessity. Finally, the potential conflicts of norm between TPP and CETA show that negotiations on future IP standards in the context of the international trading system should return to the WTO. For the time being, PTA negotiators should bear this in mind in shaping the building blocks of future multilateralism and the global common law of IP.

Universities and law schools, finally, should also draw lessons: a better balance in the field, in the long run, depends on enhanced legal and economic education and training. IPRs, protecting modern property in the age of globalization, should move centre-stage in legal education and be taken seriously as an important chapter of public international law by non-specialized scholars and students alike.

161–222; and Thomas Cottier, 'The Common Law of International Trade and the Future of the World Trade Organization' (2015) 18 *Journal of International Economic Law* 3–20. Specific IP-related aspects are discussed by Grosse Ruse-Kahn, *The Protection of Intellectual Property* (n 14) ch 4.

[42] Kimberlee Weatherall, 'The TPP as a Case Study of Changing Dynamics for International Intellectual Property Negotiations' in Tania Voon (ed), *Trade Liberalisation and International Cooperation: A Legal Analysis of the Trans-Pacific Partnership Agreement* (Edward Elgar, 2013) 50–74.

[43] Eleanor M Fox, 'Can Antitrust Policy Protect the Global Commons from the Excesses of IPRs?' in Keith E Maskus and Jerome H Reichman (eds), *International Public Goods and Transfer of Technology under a Globalized Intellectual Property Regime* (Cambridge University Press, 2005) 758–69.

[44] See Keith E Maskus, *Private Rights and Public Problems: The Global Economics of Intellectual Property in the 21st Century* (Peterson Institute, 2012); and Keith E Maskus, *Globalizing Information: The Economics of International Technology Trade* (World Scientific Publishing, 2014).

7

CETA, TTIP, TiSA, and Data Protection

Walter Berka

I. Introduction

If we talk about transatlantic trade relations and the protection of data, it is utterly impossible not to mention the Snowden revelations. The legitimate outrage of Europeans about massive surveillance by US secret services forms the background theme for this chapter. However, that is not a recent issue. Data protection has been a sensitive matter between Europe and the US for many years. Transatlantic privacy policy entered a particular tense stage some twenty years ago, after the adoption of the EU Data Protection Directive of 1995.[1] Because the directive restricted the transfer of data to countries outside the EU, the US were considerably concerned about possible detrimental effects on their business interests.[2] It was in those days that the godfather of European data protection, Spiros Simitis, used to say 'personal data are not bananas'.[3] By this reference to the banana war, he firmly reminded us of the European position that personal data are something quite different from goods, and that data protection is not merely a simple trade barrier. It is the dual perception of personal data that we have to bear in mind, since we cannot overlook that data are goods as well.

In the digitized global economy, the flow of data is the backbone of trade, and is of critical importance for the economy as a whole. In particular, digital services in finance or trade make up an important segment of the transatlantic economy. Cross-border data flows between the US and Europe are the highest in the world, almost double the data flows between the US and Latin America, and 50 per cent higher than those between the US and Asia. Over half of the EU–US cross-border

[1] cf Directive 95/46/EC of the European Parliament and of the Council of 24 October 1995 on the protection of individuals with regard to the processing of personal data and on the free movement of such data, OJ L 281/31.

[2] See Lee A Bygrave, 'International Agreements to Protect Personal Data' in James B Rule and Graham Greenleaf (eds), *Global Privacy Protection* (Edward Elgar, 2010) 15 (hereafter Bygrave, 'International Agreements').

[3] ibid, 15.

trade in services depends on the Internet. The US and the EU are the two largest net exporters of digital goods and services to the rest of the world.[4]

Therefore, trade agreements cannot avoid dealing with digital services and data sharing, although another layer of complexity is added to an already complex business, once we begin to consider the issue of data protection. Data protection is a delicate matter in many respects. The cases of the Comprehensive Economic and Trade Agreement (CETA), the Transatlantic Trade and Investment Partnership (TTIP), and the Trade in Services Agreement (TiSA) are especially touchy, because of the deep Atlantic divide regarding privacy protection. This divide comes from diverse principles and flows from the different traditions in the US and Europe. With this collision of different privacy protection concepts, there is the fear on the European side that the EU's *acquis* on data privacy could be compromised through the liberalization of data flows. If one would agree with the alleged role of the EU as the 'privacy cop to the world',[5] this would indeed be worrying.

In this chapter, I will first briefly highlight the differences between the US and Europe in their approach to data protection. I will continue with an analysis of the three agreements, based on the information available. Finally, in dealing with these issues, one has to bear in mind that the EU and the US are discussing data transfers and data protection in other fora as well, namely on the tracks of the new Safe Harbor Agreement and the Data Protection Umbrella Agreement. These subjects I will touch at the end.

II. Two Concepts on Privacy

The Atlantic divide, when it comes to data protection, is great, both in detail and the underlying philosophy: the US approach is linked to the American tradition of privacy protection and is, therefore, focused on the concept of personal privacy. America's first Privacy Act was triggered by the fear of inappropriate government surveillance. A general, overarching regulation of the collection and processing of personal data was and is not aspired. Data privacy legislation for the private sector takes the form of sectoral regulations dealing with special issues like health care or finance data. A high degree of trust is put in measures of self-regulation and contractual agreements.

On our side of the Atlantic, we protect personal data, and not only privacy, by means of an overarching data protection framework, which is a kind of 'omnibus legislation' compared to the US 'piecemeal legislation'. Personal data encompass

[4] See, inter alia, Martin A Weiss and Kristin Archick, 'U.S.–EU Data Privacy: From Safe Harbor to Privacy Shield', Congressional Research Service 7-5700, CRS Report prepared for Members and Committees of Congress (19 May 2016) 4, with further references, <https://www.fas.org/sgp/crs/misc/R44257.pdf> accessed 5 April 2017.

[5] David Scheer, 'Europe's New High-Tech Role: Playing Privacy Cop to World', *Wall Street Journal* (10 October 2003) A 1; cited according to Paul M Schwartz and Daniel J Solove, 'Reconciling Personal Information in the United States and European Union' (2014) 102(4) *California Law Review* 880 (hereafter Schwartz and Solove, 'Reconciling Personal Information').

all information of an identifiable person, which is a very broad definition. In the US, the definition of protected data is often particularly narrow and focuses on persons that have already been identified.[6] Most notably, data protection is hailed as a fundamental right in Europe that can trump over other interests. Let me express the fundamental consequences of these two frameworks in a nutshell: in Europe, processing of data is prohibited unless there is an explicit legal basis that allows it. In the US, by contrast, it is allowed unless it causes harm or is expressly limited by US law. When it comes to a balancing of interests, data protection in Europe is more or less predominant, while US law considers it as a right among others. Finally, given that data protection is a human right in Europe, everybody can rely on it regardless of their origin, whereas only US citizens are protected in the US.[7]

Other significant differences can be found with regard to the legal remedies for alleged breaches of data protection provisions, the public authorities involved, and the overall effectiveness of privacy protection. Without going into too much detail, data protection regulation in the US and Europe differs as to *what* data are protected, *how* they are protected, and the *effectivity* of the remedies available.

Necessarily, these differences have a critical impact on transatlantic data flows. Viewed from the European point of view and its approach to data protection, personal data may be transferred only to countries with an 'adequate level of protection' of privacy. Thereby, the level for 'adequateness' corresponds to the European data protection law.[8] From the US side, barriers to the flow of data affect and harm legitimate business interests involved in cross-border trade. From this point of view, data protection is a trade barrier that could serve as a camouflage for protectionism. Therefore, conflict rules are imperative, rules that decide whether free flow of information or data protection deserves priority and, if data protection law applies, which level of protection is relevant. If one tries to analyse the trade agreements in question, these are the critical yardsticks.

[6] As to this difference see Schwartz and Solove, 'Reconciling Personal Information' (n 5) 877.

[7] As to the differences between US privacy protection and European data protection, see Ioanna Tourkochoriti, 'The Snowden Revelations, the Transatlantic Trade and Investment Partnership and the Divide Between U.S.–EU in Data Privacy Protection' (2014) 36 *University of Arkansas at Little Rock Law Review* 161, 164f (hereafter Tourkochoriti, 'The Snowden Revelations'); Schwartz and Solove, 'Reconciling Personal Information' (n 5) 880–1; Priscilla M Regan, 'The United States' in James B Rule and Graham Greenleaf (eds), *Global Privacy Protection* (Edward Elgar, 2010) 50; Alexander Dix, *Datenschutz und transatlantische Freihandelszone* (KIT Scientific Publishing, 2013) 6f; and Walter Berka, 'Das Grundrecht auf Datenschutz im Spannungsfeld zwischen Freiheit und Sicherheit (Gutachten)' (2012) I/1 18. Österreichischer Juristentag 58f (hereafter Berka, 'Das Grundrecht auf Datenschutz').

[8] Directive 95/46/EC on the protection of individuals with regard to the processing of personal data and on the free movement of such data [1995] OJ L 281, Art 25; see also the recently adopted Regulation (EU) 2016/679 on the protection of natural persons with regard to the processing of personal data and on the free movement of such data, etc [2016] OJ L 119/1 (General Data Protection Regulation), Art 45.

III. Data Protection and Trade Agreements

A. CETA

I will start with CETA, mainly because I can refer to an officially published text.[9] If one wades through the roughly 1,600 pages of this agreement, the first finding will be (if I have not overlooked something) that there is no general provision regulating the flow of information. To my understanding, this would mean that in the absence of any general provision, the transfer of data will be governed by the relevant principles and requirements of the respective national law on either side. Once the EU Data Protection Regulation is in effect, directly applicable EU law would also be involved.[10]

References to data protection can be found in CETA only with regard to two special industry sectors, namely financial services (ch 13) and—not surprisingly—electronic commerce (ch 16).

Regarding financial services, the parties agree on a free flow of information by stipulating: 'Each Party shall permit a financial institution or a cross-border financial service supplier of the other Party to transfer information in electronic or other form, into and out of its territory, for data processing if such processing is required in the ordinary course of business' (ch 13 Art 13.15 § 1). Nevertheless, restrictions on the transfer and processing of information are permitted to maintain adequate safeguards to protect privacy: 'If the transfer of financial information involves personal information, such transfers should be in accordance with the legislation governing the protection of personal information of the territory of the Party where the transfer has originated' (ch 13 Art 13.15 § 2). With this reference to a principle of origin, national or regional standards of data protection are reserved, including the restrictive European standards of protection. Under these conditions, any transatlantic data transfer will have to meet the 'adequate protection' standard in the sector of finance.

With regard to electronic commerce, CETA seems to follow another approach. Under the headline 'Trust and Confidence in Electronic Commerce', the parties agreed that they should 'adopt or maintain laws, regulations or administrative measures for the protection of personal information of users engaged in electronic commerce and, when doing so, shall take into due consideration international standards for data protection of relevant international organisations of which both Parties are a member' (ch 16 Art 16.4). In this case, beside an obligation to have a kind of data protection, a certain level of protection is fixed, namely by the reference to certain international standards. Although the text leaves open which standards it refers to, there is some evidence that its primary targets are the respective

[9] See draft CETA February 2016, consolidated version published by the EU Commission on 29 February 2016, <http://trade.ec.europa.eu/doclib/docs/2016/february/tradoc_154329.pdf> accessed 5 April 2017.

[10] See General Data Protection Regulation (n 8).

Organisation for Economic Co-operation and Development (OECD) Guidelines for data protection.

These 'Privacy Guidelines', adopted by the OECD in 1980 and revised in 2013, introduce a set of principles that are not legally binding, but can serve as a benchmark for adequate privacy data protection.[11] They were inspired by the corresponding efforts of the Council of Europe, which led to the Council of Europe's Data Protection Convention, although the Guidelines are much less strict and less specific than those of the Convention. Considering that Canada and most of the European countries are members of the OECD,[12] the substantial principles of the OECD Code, together with its enforcement mechanism, could constitute the 'international standards' CETA parties to the treaty would have to take into 'due consideration'.[13] What could this mean in the context of a trade agreement such as CETA? On one hand, the Guidelines give the free flow of information considerable weight by imposing duties on states not to restrict cross-border flow of data without justification (Art 17). Commercial concerns about restrictions on the free flows of information were indeed a trigger for the OECD Guidelines. On the other hand, the Guidelines describe themselves as 'minimum standards ... capable of being supplemented by additional measures for the protection of privacy' (para 6). Therefore, states can realize a higher standard of data protection even if such additional measures may impact transborder flows of personal data, as the Guidelines make explicitly clear.[14]

Considering this clause in the OECD Guidelines, the reference to international standards in CETA would, as far as I can see, not hinder a state to apply its national data protection law even with regard to cross-border electronic commerce in the sense of chapter 18 of CETA.

To sum up, there is no indication that CETA has restricted the application of national or regional regulations even if they might interfere with the free flow of information in fields covered by the agreement.

[11] Recommendation of the Council concerning Guidelines governing the Protection of Privacy and Transborder Flows of Personal Data (2013), C(80)58/FINAL, as amended on 11 July 2013 by C(2013)79; the Guidelines and additional documents are published as 'The OECD Privacy Framework' (2013), <http://www.oecd.org/sti/ieconomy/oecd_privacy_framework.pdf> accessed 5 April 2017; as to the Guidelines from 1980, see Bygrave, 'International Agreements' (n 2) 26f.

[12] As the Council of Europe's Convention may be ratified by states not belonging to the Council of Europe, its standards would also be applicable after an accession of Canada; see Art 23 of the (European) Convention for the Protection of Individuals with regard to Automatic Processing of Personal Data (1 October 1995) ETS 108 (Data Protection Convention).

[13] One could, further, consider the UN Guidelines on privacy and data protection, adopted by the General Assembly in resolution 45/95 of 14 December 1990. However, compared with the OECD Code, the UN document is less substantial and concrete, especially when it comes to regulations on data flow; as to the UN code, see Bygrave, 'International Agreements' (n 2) 29.

[14] Paragraph 17 of the Guidelines (n 11) specifies two circumstances in which a Member country should refrain from imposing restrictions on transborder flows of personal data. As the Supplementary Explanatory Memorandum to the Revised OECD Privacy Guidelines makes clear, this does not exclude the application of para 6 and the authorization to enact 'additional measures'; see 'OECD Privacy Framework' (n 11) 30.

B. TiSA

Moving on to TiSA, the picture changes, although we cannot be as concrete due to the limited publicity of TiSA. If we refer to the information from some leaked documents, the worst fears of data protection experts do not appear to be unfounded. For example, according to the draft Financial Services Annex of TiSA, published by WikiLeaks in June 2014, the US have proposed a clause stating that parties to the agreement must not prevent financial service suppliers from data processing 'in and out' of the territory of a party to the treaty.[15] One background of this proposal is to promote cloud-based technology and other sectors including insurance or credit card industries that seek for a right to hold data offshore. Further, the US advocates to apply this principle of free cross-border data flows to the entire agreement by placing it in the core text.[16] Another document leaked in December 2014, the 'Proposal of New Provisions Applicable to All Services etc', seems to confirm this suspicion: according to Art X.4 of this proposal, 'no Party may prevent a service supplier of another Party from transferring, accessing, processing or storing information, including personal information, within or outside the Party's territory, where such activity is carried out in connection with the conduct of the service supplier's business'.[17] A provision like this comes near to a *carte blanche* for the transmission of personal data without any condition or any reference to data protection, and there is no provision to allow any state to protect personal privacy and data at all.[18]

Of course, we are talking about proposals made in ongoing negotiations, but the thrust is evident: data protection constrains the commercial flow of information and, therefore, privacy seems to be obliged to give way. Even if privacy safeguards cannot be completely avoided, their impact has to be minimized. This shift towards a minimum privacy standard can be best illustrated if we have a look into the text of the Trans-Pacific Partnership (TPP) Agreement, whose final text is already available. At first glance, Art 14.8 of this agreement seems to recognize privacy protection by stipulating that each party shall adopt or maintain a legal framework that provides for the protection of the personal information of the users of electronic commerce. However, this provision is subject to a footnote, and that is the snag, because the footnote practically weakens the requirements for the alleged privacy protection by referring, inter alia, to voluntary undertakings by enterprises concerning data protection.[19] Therefore,

[15] Art X.11 (Transfers of Information and Processing of Information) of the Financial Services Annex of TiSA according to the leaked text (3 June 2015), <https://wikileaks.org/tisa/financial/02-2015/TiSA%20Financial%20Services%20Negotiating%20Text.pdf> accessed 9 May 2017.

[16] See the US-proposed Art X.6 (Movement of Information) of the Electronic Commerce Annex according to the leaked text of TiSA (20 February 2015), <https://wikileaks.org/tisa/ecommerce/TiSA%20Annex%20on%20Electronic%20Commerce.pdf> accessed 5 April 2017.

[17] See the articles of the Associated Whistleblowing Press, 'Proposal of New Provisions Applicable to All Services of the Secret TiSA Negotiations' (17 December 2014), <https://data.awp.is/filtrala/2014/12/17/19.html> accessed 5 April 2017.

[18] See the critical analysis by Jane Kelsey, 'Memorandum on Leaked TISA Financial Services Text' (14 April 2014), <https://wikileaks.org/tisa-financial/Analysis-of-secret-tisa-financial-annex.pdf> accessed 9 May 2017.

[19] Footnote 6 concerning Art 14.8 reads as follows: 'For greater certainty, a Party may comply with the obligation in this paragraph by adopting or maintaining measures such as a comprehensive privacy,

it practically falls under those moderate standards codified in international guidelines, and disregards the higher standards of the European data protection law.

It is open what the outcome of the TiSA negotiation will be—it could be a *carte blanche* for the transfer of personal data, like in the proposals I have cited, a minimum privacy standard as in TPP, or a decision not to touch the delicate question of data protection. Most recently, the European Parliament gave its opinion on the TiSA negotiations and took a firm stand:[20] the US proposals on movement of information should 'immediately and formally' be opposed. Data protection and the right to privacy should have to be recognized as fundamental rights, not as a trade barrier. Full compliance with the European Court of Justice's (ECJ's) ruling regarding Safe Harbor has to be achieved and so on.[21] This shows that the Parliament is unafraid to use strong language when it comes to the issue of data protection. It leads to a concrete suggestion, 'to incorporate a comprehensive, unambiguous, horizontal, self-standing and legally binding provision based on GATS Art XIV which fully exempts the existing and future EU legal framework for the protection of personal data from the scope of this agreement, without any conditions that it must be consistent with other parts of the TiSA'.[22]

A provision like this would imply a horizontal exception for EU data protection law. I will come back to this, but first we finally need to look at TTIP.

C. TTIP

As far as we know, data protection standards are not part of the ongoing negotiations on TTIP—at least, this is claimed by European officials.[23] As the former Vice-President of the Commission Viviane Reding had stated, with some amount of pathos: 'Data protection is not red tape or a tariff. It is a fundamental right and as such it is not negotiable.'[24] On the other side, it is no secret that advocates of US business interests are vigorously demanding measures in TTIP that would prevent restrictions on data flows.

personal information or personal data protection laws, sector-specific laws covering privacy, or laws that provide for the enforcement of voluntary undertakings by enterprises relating to privacy.' cf Text of the TPP (26 January 2016), <http://tpp.mfat.govt.nz/text> accessed 5 April 2017.

[20] European Parliament, 'Report 25 January 2016 Containing the European Parliament's Recommendations to the Commission on the Negotiations for the Trade in Services Agreement (TiSA)' (2015/2233(INI), [A8-0009/2016]) (25 January 2016), <http://www.europarl.europa.eu/sides/getDoc.do?pubRef=-//EP//TEXT+REPORT+A8-2016-0009+0+DOC+XML+V0//EN> accessed 5 April 2017.

[21] ibid, s 1(c)iii. [22] ibid.

[23] See the Press Release of the European Commission, 'European Commission Calls on the U.S. to Restore Trust in EU–U.S. Data Flows' (27 November 2013), <http://europa.eu/rapid/press-release_IP-13-1166_en.htm> accessed 5 April 2017; see further Art 7-1 (General exceptions) of the EU's proposal for a 'services, investment and e-commerce text' of TTIP, <http://trade.ec.europa.eu/doclib/press/index.cfm?id=1230> accessed 5 April 2017; see also Greenpeace, 'TTIP Leaks', <https://www.ttip-leaks.org> accessed 5 April 2017.

[24] Viviane Reding, 'Towards a More Dynamic Transatlantic Area of Growth and Investment', European Commission Press Release Database (29 October 2013) <http://europa.eu/rapid/press-release_SPEECH-13-867_de.htm> accessed 5 April 2017.

Again, the outlook for these negotiations remains uncertain. In any case, the European Parliament is insisting on the 'European standard' of data protection, as in the case of TiSA. In its TTIP recommendation to the Commission, the Parliament asks to incorporate, 'as a key point', a 'comprehensive and unambiguous horizontal self-standing provision, based on Art XIV of the General Agreement on Trade in services (GATS), that fully exempts the existing and future EU legal framework for the protection of personal data from the agreement without any condition that it must be consistent with other parts of the TTIP'.[25] As can be clearly seen, this is literally the same claim as for TiSA.

Both recommendations of the Parliament refer to Art XIV GATS. This provision contains a general exception for national regulations regarding the protection of the privacy of individuals. It stipulates that nothing of this agreement prevents the application of data protection law, if it is applied without arbitrary or unjustifiable discrimination.[26] This provision serves as a justification for what is intended by the European Parliament: a horizontal and self-standing exception for EU data protection law in the context of the trade agreements.

In practical terms, an exception to allow for EU data protection law would back the 'adequate protection clause' as the main yardstick for cross-border data transfer. Because the exemption refers to the 'existing and future' EU legal framework, it also encompasses the standards of the new EU General Data Protection Regulation, which replaces the 1995 Data Protection Directive.[27] Although the new Regulation adheres to the 'adequacy standard' for transnational data flows, it realizes a higher standard in certain other respects, such as the right to be forgotten or stricter requirements for consent. Thus, convincing the non-European parties to agree on the proposed exemption clause has not become easier with the new Regulation.[28]

IV. The EU–US Privacy Shield and the Data Protection Umbrella Agreement

However, things may be decided in another arena anyway. Therefore, I will now move to the new Safe Harbor Agreement and the Data Protection Umbrella Agreement.

[25] See s 2(b)xii of the Report from 1 June 2015 containing the European Parliament's 'recommendations to the European Commission on the negotiations for the Transatlantic Trade and Investment Partnership (TTIP)' (2014/2228(INI)) (1 June 2015), <http://www.europarl.europa.eu/sides/getDoc.do?type=REPORT&reference=A8-2015-0175&language=EN> accessed 5 April 2017.

[26] It is not by chance that the Parliament refers to Art XIV GATS: after the adoption of the EU Data Protection Directive of 1995, the US had questioned the legality of the 'adequate protection' clause for cross-border flow of data under international trade law. Because Art XIV GATS allows restrictions on data flow when necessary to secure compliance with rules relating to data protection, it was soon recognized that there is 'little if any solid evidence' indicating that Arts 25–26 of the Directive have been or are being applied in breach of the GATS; in this sense, see Bygrave, 'International Agreements' (n 2) 40f.

[27] See General Data Protection Regulation (n 8).

[28] Similarily Tourkochoriti, 'The Snowden Revelations' (n 7) 173.

The former Safe Harbor Agreement has created a voluntary self-certification programme for US firms to meet the requirements of an 'adequate level of protection'. It was a pragmatic solution to make transatlantic data transfer easier, and a compromise with many loopholes and flaws.[29] With the deep mistrust against US privacy protection after the Snowden revelations, there came a growing call to reform this arrangement, which had obviously missed its aim to provide for an adequate protection of personal data for European citizens. The *Schrems* decision of the ECJ from October 2015, which invalidated the Safe Harbor Agreement, was the legal manifestation of this criticism.[30] After this finding, Safe Harbor could no longer provide a legal basis for data transfers between Europe and US companies. Legal actions against further data transfers by the national European Data Protection Agencies could have been expected.[31] To prevent the blocking of data transfers to the US and to provide leeway to find solutions, a kind of moratorium was proclaimed by the Art 29 working group (an important assembly of EU national data protection commissioners trying to coordinate the application of national data protection law in Europe).[32]

After the expiry of the moratorium, and after the original 31 January 2016 deadline was missed, a last-minute deal between the Commission and the US was announced at the beginning of February. The underlying agreements between the US and the Commission were presented some weeks later, together with a draft of the new adequacy decision by the Commission, which was adopted in July 2016.[33] Does the new agreement really provide for 'adequate protection', or is it just another placebo? In the official language, it is labelled as the 'EU–US Privacy Shield' that should prepare for 'a renewed and safe framework for transatlantic data

[29] Beside the legal deficits disclosed in the *Schrems* decision, there were other structural shortcomings of the former Safe Harbor scheme in the way in which it was applied. Therefore, there were already earlier calls for the suspension of Safe Harbor, eg, European Parliament, 'Communication from the Commission to the European Parliament and the Council: Rebuilding Trust in the EU–US Data Flows' (27 November 2013), <http://ec.europa.eu/justice/data-protection/files/com_2013_846_en.pdf> accessed 5 April 2017, 6 COM 846 final. According to Heisenberg, already from its start the main goal of Safe Harbor has been to maintain transatlantic data flow, whereas privacy protection was very much a secondary concern; see Dorothee Heisenberg, *Negotiating Privacy: The European Union, the United States, and Personal Data Protection* (Lynne Rienner, 2005) 160.

[30] *Schrems* [2015] ECLI:EU:C:2015:650.

[31] To legitimize transatlantic data transfer, there are alternatives to the Safe Harbor protection, namely Model Contract Clauses, Binding Corporate Rules (for intra-company data transfer), and explicit consent.

[32] For the current state of the suggestions of the Art 29 working group, see Article 29 Data Protection Working Party, 'Working Document 01/2016 on the Justification of Interferences with the Fundamental Rights to Privacy and Data Protection through Surveillance Measures When Transferring Personal Data (European Essential Guarantees)' (adopted on 13 April 2016), <http://ec.europa.eu/justice/data-protection/article-29/documentation/opinion-recommendation/files/2016/wp237_en.pdf> accessed 5 April 2017.

[33] The EU–US Privacy Shield was adopted by the European Commission on 12 July 2016 following the approval by a majority of EU Member States in the so-called Art 31 Committee. See European Commission, 'Commission Implementing Decision of 12.7.2016 Pursuant to Directive 95/46/EC of the European Parliament and of the Council on the Adequacy of the Protection Provided by the EU–U.S. Privacy Shield', <http://ec.europa.eu/justice/data-protection/files/privacy-shield-adequacy-decision_en.pdf> accessed 5 April 2017.

flows'. A serious assessment is not easy, because the agreement is complex both in substance and in terms of its legal relevance. The Commission praises it as putting 'main achievements' into effect.[34] However, European privacy watchers branded it as a 'joke' the day it was announced and the Art 29 working group also articulated its concerns.[35] So what does it really accomplish? There is a commitment of the US Government and its law enforcement and national security authorities, notably from the National Security Agency (NSA), to limit and safeguard access to data. Nevertheless, the privacy principles of the agreement are subject to far-reaching limitations to meet national security and other public interests. There should be dispute settlement mechanisms for European citizens claiming that their data has been misused. In this respect, the agreement refers to means of alternative dispute resolution with an arbitration mechanism and the installation of an ombudsman in the area of national security.

Whatever difference weak commitments and non-formal remedies really can make, from a legal perspective the crucial question will be whether the new agreement lives up to the requirements of the ECJ. In this respect, I am not sure that this is the case, and it might very well be that the fundamental right for data protection, as the European side sees it, is again scuttled in an unsafe harbour. To prove this scepticism, I have to enter one further, and last, arena: the negotiations of an 'Umbrella Agreement'.

Whereas the new Safe Harbor Agreement deals with the commercial data flow and affects companies, the EU–US Umbrella Agreement tries to secure a high level of data protection where personal information is transferred to the US for the purpose of law enforcement, including the fight against terrorism. This agreement goes beyond my theme, and I only touch on it because it is linked to the safe harbour issue in one important respect, namely the US Judicial Redress Act.[36] As a part of the new EU–US privacy shield, the US harbours should become safer for Europeans, inter alia, because privacy rights and remedies available to US citizens must be extended to them. This is what the Judicial Redress Act should provide for. However, there is a drawback: foreigners can only benefit from these privacy remedies if they belong to a country that has an agreement with the US (like the Umbrella Agreement) and which is sharing data with the US. If the US authorities hold that a country is no longer 'effectively' sharing data with the US or 'impedes the transfer of information', the particular EU Member State could be removed from the list of covered countries. Thus, US authorities could deny the citizens of such a country the protection granted by the Judicial Redress Act. This gives the US authorities a stick they can wave at countries that are slow to respond to US law

[34] Justice Commissioner Jourová, 'Speaking Points at the Press Conference' (2 February 2016), <http://europa.eu/rapid/press-release_SPEECH-16-221_en.htm> accessed 5 April 2017.

[35] Article 29 Data Protection Working, 'Opinion 01/2016 on the EU–U.S. Privacy Shield Draft Adequacy Decision' (adopted on 13 April 2016), <http://ec.europa.eu/justice/data-protection/article-29/documentation/opinion-recommendation/files/2016/wp238_en.pdf> accessed 5 April 2017.

[36] HR 1428—114th Congress (2015–16), passed the House of Representatives on 20 October 2015 and the Senate on 9 February 2016.

enforcement demands,[37] even if they decline to fulfil such demands in compliance with local data protection law.

As the lack of judicial remedies for EU citizens was decisive for the *Schrems* judgment, this and other flaws of the Judicial Redress Act show that there are still significant shortcomings in the US data protection law, which may influence the legal assessment of a renewed Safe Harbor Agreement.

V. Conclusions

Let me conclude with final observations.

The Europeans are gallantly defending their approach to data protection in the ongoing negotiations. Nobody really knows what the outcome will be. Considering the complexities of trade negotiations, it might very much be the case that the issues of transatlantic data transfer are decided very fast: either in the context of special talks, such as the Safe Harbor Agreement, or during the ongoing trade negotiations. Whether in the context of TTIP or TiSA, or in special arrangements on data transfer, past experience has shown that the US often have more pull when data protection competes with sturdy economic interests. What is referred to as the new 'EU–US Privacy Shield', agreed on by the European Commission and the US Trade Ministry on 2 February 2016, might very well be further proof for this thesis.[38] European advocates for a strong data protection will probably resort to the ECJ. The Court might indeed become a counterbalance once again, especially if one bears in mind that it has interpreted the 'adequacy clause' in the EU Data Protection Directive as demanding a level of protection that is 'essentially equivalent to that guaranteed within the European Union'.[39]

Whatever the outcome will be, it will be difficult, if not impossible, to bridge the current gap between EU and US privacy law. Since both sides are deeply committed to their respective approaches, attempts to harmonize the diverging bodies of law are unlikely to succeed. For me, if I may conclude with a personal opinion, it is anything but clear which approach is actually the privacy concept of the future. The European data protection law was a trendsetter for privacy protection for some decades, not only in Europe, but worldwide. What we have gained is a strong protective shield for any data based on an ambitious 'right to informational self-determination' ('*Recht auf informationelle Selbstbestimmung*'). To grant this right effectively, we accept a high level of data bureaucracy and a complicated bulk of data protection law, although there is a feeling that our privacy is eroded

[37] See Jens-Henrik Jeppesen and Greg Nojeim, 'The EU–US Umbrella Agreement and the Judicial Redress Act: Small Steps Forward for EU Citizens' Privacy Rights' (5 October 2015), <https://cdt.org/blog/the-eu-us-umbrella-agreement-and-the-judicial-redress-act-small-steps-forward-for-eu-citizens-privacy-rights/> accessed 5 April 2017.

[38] See, eg, Michael M Pachinger, 'Der transatlantische Datenschutzschild ("EU-US-Privacy-Shield")' (2016) 2 *Zeitschrift für Informationsrecht* 135–8.

[39] *Schrems* (n 30).

anyway. As it is sometimes said: we have gained much data protection law and less data protection.

Therefore, one can wonder whether the 'success story' of the European data protection law can be continued. Adverse winds are strong and they are not only blowing from the West. The growing importance of China and other Asian states will also have an impact on data protection law. It is not by chance that Google is touting the APEC privacy framework (the privacy framework of the Asia–Pacific Economic Cooperation) as an appropriate baseline for global privacy standards.[40] This could lead to the question of whether something like a new design of data protection is preferable, even for Europe.[41]

This is clearly a question that goes far beyond the issue of trade negotiations discussed in this chapter. But I wanted to close with this outlook on developments that are looming on the horizon in a somehow broader context.

[40] In this sense, see Bygrave, 'International Agreements' (n 2) 48.
[41] See Berka, 'Das Grundrecht auf Datenschutz' (n 7) 54–7.

8

CETA, TTIP, TiSA, and Financial Services

Christoph Ohler

I. Introduction

Financial services are considered as a sector that is particularly suited for trade liberalization. The underlying economic factor, capital,[1] is highly mobile. In the era of digitalization and internet technologies, effecting a transaction between two business partners does not require more than a mouse-click.[2] The technical development has been boosted by a far-reaching, unilateral liberalization of capital movements in leading financial centres, including the EU.[3] Starting in the early 1990s, many states, in particular members of the Organisation for Economic Co-operation and Development (OECD), renounced domestic legislation that so far had restricted capital movements to and from other countries. The commitments undertaken in the General Agreement on Trade in Services (GATS) typically locked in this level of market opening.[4] As a consequence, financial industries and the share of financial services in international trade grew considerably in the decades thereafter. In the years of the financial crisis from 2007 to 2009, the trade volume fell sharply, yet the international trade regime remained intact.[5]

While, in principle, financial services markets in many countries are relatively open, financial institutions are at the same time subject to strict domestic regulation and supervision. Regulatory provisions typically refer to minimum

[1] International law distinguishes between capital flows and current transactions, cf Art XXX(d) IMF Articles of Agreement; on this distinction and its relevance for Art XI GATS, see Bart de Meester, 'Liberalization of financial flows and trade in financial services under the GATS' (2012) 46 *Journal of World Trade* 733.

[2] cf WTO, Council for Trade in Services, Committee on Trade in Financial Services, Background Note by the Secretariat, S/C/W/312S/FIN/W/73, 3 February 2010, para 47 (hereafter Committee on Financial Services, Background Note 3 February 2010).

[3] See Art 63 of the Treaty on the Functioning of the European Union (TFEU). The provision was originally inserted into EU law by the Treaty of Maastricht.

[4] Eric Leroux, 'Trade in Financial Services in the World Trade Organization' (2002) 36 *Journal of World Trade* 413, 427 (hereafter Leroux, 'Trade in Financial Services').

[5] Thomas Cottier and Markus Krajewski, 'What Role for Non-Discrimination and Prudential Standards in International Financial Law?' (2010) 13 *Journal of International Economic Law* 817, 818 (hereafter Cottier and Krajewski, 'Role for Non-Discrimination').

requirements for solvency, liquidity, and risk management. Their purpose is to protect consumers and other customers, to ensure the proper functioning of the respective firms, and to prevent risks for the stability of the wider financial system.[6] Generally, the provisions are non-discriminatory in nature, but they lead to financial and organizational burdens for service suppliers which may have an effect similar to trade barriers.[7] Under the pressure of the financial crisis, the regulatory grip was considerably tightened. Following the recommendations adopted by the G20 since 2009, many countries extended their prudential supervision to markets and industries unregulated so far, like, for example, trade in derivatives and alternative investment funds, and intensified the requirements for all sectors that traditionally had been under public supervision, like, for example, banks and insurance companies.

The majority of regulatory standards were, as in the years before, adopted within international fora, most of them situated in Basel.[8] Yet, more visible than ever, the new rounds of financial market regulation since 2009 demonstrated a complete absence of coordination between the multilateral trade policy forum of the WTO in Geneva and the regulatory fora in Basel.[9] A similar lack of coordination between these areas can be identified today in transatlantic bilateral negotiations. What are the reasons for this situation? It was argued that in particular the Basel Committee of Banking Supervision is a club with limited membership which excludes recognition of its standards under Art VII GATS.[10] Other organizations, like IAIS and IOSCO, however, are open to members from all over the world which makes this explanation less convincing. The club argument also does not apply in the context of bilateral negotiations where the parties are at the same time members of these clubs. It seems more probable that the true reasons for this reluctance are political ones. The states do not want to be restricted in their flexibility to regulate and supervise the financial markets under their jurisdiction.[11] They accept the practice of international standard setting as an instrument to create minimum standards, but they do not want to establish a conclusive and legally binding system of regulation

[6] General Agreement on Trade in Services (15 April 1994) LT/UR/A-1B/S/1, <http://docsonline.wto.org> accessed 5 April 2017, Annex on Financial Services, eg, para 5(a) (hereafter GATS Annex on Financial Services).

[7] Panagiotis Delimatsis and Pierre Sauvé, 'Financial Services after the Crisis: Policy and Legal Conjectures' (2010) 13 *Journal of International Economic Law* 837, 851 (hereafter Delimatsis and Sauvé, 'Financial Services after the Crisis').

[8] These are the Financial Stability Board (FSB), the Basel Committee of Banking Supervision (BCBS), and the International Association of Insurance Supervisors (IAIS). The general secretariat of the International Organization of Securities Commissions (IOSCO) is located in Madrid. The secretariat of the Financial Action Task Force on Money Laundering (FATF) is located at the OECD headquarters in Paris.

[9] cf Cottier and Krajewski, 'Role for Non-Discrimination' (n 5) 829; Delimatsis and Sauvé, 'Financial Services after the Crisis' (n 7) 837; and Régis Bismuth, 'Financial Sector Regulation and Financial Services Regulation at the Crossroads: The Relevance of International Financial Standards in WTO Law' (2010) 44 *Journal of World Trade* 489 (hereafter Bismuth, 'Financial Sector Regulation').

[10] Bismuth, 'Financial Sector Regulation' (n 9) 501.

[11] cf Delimatsis and Sauvé, 'Financial Services after the Crisis' (n 7) 850.

and supervision. In terms of distribution of responsibilities between home country and host country of financial service suppliers, both home and host countries want to retain the possibility to exercise full control over the firms operating within their territories.[12]

Against this backdrop, it would be completely unrealistic to aim at an international harmonization of financial market regulation and at a distribution of powers between home and host countries similar to the internal market of the EU. Yet, bilateral and multilateral trade negotiations could be used as a means to re-establish mutual trust between the trading partners[13] that was lost during the last financial crisis—and even before. Accordingly, the main thesis of this chapter is that any international attempt for further liberalization in the financial services sector will be limited in its effect as long as regulatory issues are not integrated in these negotiations.[14]

In order to analyse the interplay between trade liberalization on the one hand and regulatory cooperation on the other, this chapter will discuss first the status quo under the GATS (in section II). New approaches in the draft chapters of the Comprehensive Economic and Trade Agreement (CETA), the Transatlantic Trade and Investment Partnership (TTIP), and Trade in Services Agreement (TiSA) will be identified against this background (in section III). The right to regulate is enshrined in the so-called prudential carve-out provisions of these texts, the content of which will be analysed in section IV. The chapter concludes with an outlook on future possibilities for increased regulatory cooperation (section V).

II. The Status Quo of Liberalization under WTO Law

A. Scope

The GATS is based on a very broad understanding of financial services.[15] The Annex on Financial Services which is an integral and binding part of the Agreement defines them as 'any service of a financial nature offered by a financial service supplier of a Member'. They include all insurance and insurance-related services, banking services, and other financial services (excluding insurance).[16] The list detailing the various kinds of services is comprehensive and its wording is sufficiently general

[12] cf Basel Committee on Banking Supervision, 'Core Principles for Effective Banking Supervision', Principle 13: Home-host-relationships, revised version September 2012, <http://www.bis.org/publ/bcbs230.pdf> accessed 23 August 2016.

[13] On this core problem, see Bernard Hoekman, 'Fostering Transatlantic Regulatory Cooperation and Gradual Multilateralization' (2015) 18 *Journal of International Economic Law* 609, 613 (hereafter Hoekman, 'Fostering Transatlantic Regulatory Cooperation').

[14] For an early analysis of this problem, see Joel Trachtman, 'Trade in Financial Services under GATS, NAFTA and the EC: A Regulatory Jurisdiction Analysis' (1995) 34(1) *Columbia Journal of Transnational Law* 37.

[15] Michael J Trebilcock and Robert Howse, *The Regulation of International Trade* (3rd edn, Routledge, 2005) 380.

[16] GATS Annex on Financial Services (n 6) para 5(a).

so that future market developments can be encompassed. From a legal point of view, however, it is arguable whether the list is exhaustive or non-exhaustive. If it would be understood as being exhaustive, this could pose problems when future technical developments or changes of business models fall outside the scope of the list. The wording of para 5 subpara (a) of the Annex which refers to 'any service of a financial nature' indicates, however, that the list has the function to specify the meaning of the term 'financial services', but not to restrict the scope of the Annex to these activities.[17] In legal practice, however, WTO Members will not liberalize financial services in general, but use the list as a blueprint for their schedules of specific commitments. This can be easily explained by the fact that the various subtypes of financial services pose very different risks and require, accordingly, very different regulatory approaches.

As in the GATS in general, the Annex on Financial Services excludes services supplied in the exercise of governmental authority.[18] They are defined as activities conducted by a central bank or monetary authority or by any other public entity in pursuit of monetary and exchange rate policies or activities forming part of a statutory system of social security or public retirement plans or other activities conducted by a public entity for the account or with the guarantee or using the financial resources of the government. This is a much narrower and clearer definition than the one in Art I subpara 3(c) GATS, which refers to the non-commercial character of an activity or the absence of market competition.[19] The Annex expressly provides that in the area of financial services Art I subpara 3(c) GATS does not apply.[20] This approach is also reflected in the definition of public entity, which is excluded from the definition of financial service supplier.[21]

As regards the modes of supply, the Annex on Financial Services does not alter the general scheme under Art I subparas 2(a)–(d) GATS.[22] This mirrors economic reality since financial services are supplied in all of the four modes recognized by the GATS. Legal practice of the Members in the area of prudential law, however, mainly refers to mode 1 (cross-border supply) and mode 3 (establishment).[23] In contrast to that, mode 2 (consumption abroad) does not play any significant role in domestic law, as usage of this mode normally does not affect any regulatory objectives in the country of origin of the customer.[24] Rare legal problems could only arise when a Member wishes to protect its consumers abroad.

[17] Armin von Bogdandy and Joseph Windsor, 'Annex on Financial Services' in Rüdiger Wolfrum, Peter-Tobias Stoll, and Clemens Feinäugle (eds), *Max Planck Commentaries on World Trade Law: WTO—Trade in Services* (Nijhoff, 2008) 632, para 19 (hereafter Bogdandy and Windsor, 'Annex'); and Leroux, 'Trade in Financial Services' (n 4) 428. See also Committee on Financial Services, Background Note 3 February 2010 (n 2) para 23: 'non-exhaustive'.

[18] GATS Annex on Financial Services (n 6) para 1(b).

[19] But see also the exemption under para 1(c) of the GATS Annex on Financial Services (n 6).

[20] GATS Annex on Financial Services (n 6) para 1(d). [21] ibid, para 5(c).

[22] ibid, para 1(a). [23] cf Arts 33–46 Directive 2013/36, [2013] OJ L 176/338.

[24] Leroux, 'Trade in Financial Services' (n 4) 436.

B. Positive-list approach for market access and national treatment

The GATS is based on the distinction between general obligations, conditional general obligations, and specific commitments.[25] General obligations have an automatic legal effect on the Members and include most-favoured nation (MFN) treatment (Art II) and transparency requirements[26] (Art III). Contrary to that, Members must assume specific commitments on an individual basis by inscribing them in their schedules of specific commitments.[27] Thus, the schedules represent the positive-list approach, that is, only commitments expressly inscribed lead to a legal obligation of a Member.[28] The scope of these lists encompasses market-access guarantees (Art XVI) and national treatment (Art XVII). Conditional general obligations, like, for example, the rules on domestic regulation (Art VI), have an intermediate legal effect. Their application depends on a Member undertaking specific commitments.

If a Member agrees to grant full market access, it is prohibited from taking the six measures that are defined in Art XVI para 2 GATS.[29] They are mainly of quantitative nature referring to maximum numbers of suppliers, monopolies, exclusive service suppliers, economic needs tests, value of service transactions, and so on. The only commitment which is of qualitative nature is that a service supplier may freely choose the type of legal entity or joint venture through which it will supply its service. This list is exhaustive, which means that market entry barriers resulting from other forms of domestic regulation are not covered by market access obligations under the GATS.[30] These measures fall under the right of domestic regulation which the GATS recognizes in its Art VI and, specifically with a view to prudential supervision, in para 2(a) of the Annex on Financial Services. Once a Member has undertaken specific commitments, the right of domestic regulation is only subject to some due process requirements reflecting procedural and substantive elements of the rule of law.[31] As a further consequence of taking specific commitments, a Member must not restrict transfers and payments for current transactions and capital transactions relating to its specific commitments.[32]

[25] On this distinction see WTO, *A Handbook on the GATS Agreement* (2005) 13–17(hereafter WTO, *Handbook GATS*).

[26] For a broad overview of transparency requirements, see Alexander Kern, 'The GATS and Financial Services: The Role of Regulatory Transparency' (2007) 20 *Cambridge Review of International Affairs* 111.

[27] GATS Annex on Financial Services (n 6) Art XX. For an overview, cf Leroux, 'Trade in Financial Services' (n 4) 422.

[28] See, eg, Andreas Lowenfeld, *International Economic Law* (2nd edn, Oxford University Press, 2008) 129; Erich Vranes, 'The Single Euro Payments Area (SEPA) and Its Compatibility with the GATS Disciplines on Financial Services' (2008) 42 *Journal of World Trade* 509, 515 (hereafter Vranes, 'SEPA').

[29] cf WTO, Appellate Body Report, *United States—Measures Affecting the Cross-Border Supply of Gambling and Betting Services* (7 April 2005) WT/DS285/AB/R, para 215.

[30] Committee on Financial Services, Background Note 3 February 2010 (n 2) para 5.

[31] Art VI paras 1–3, 5, and 6 GATS. See also Markus Krajewski, 'Article VI GATS' in Wolfrum et al, *WTO—Trade in Services* (n 17) 168, para 4.

[32] Art 11 paras 1 and 2 GATS.

The structure of the GATS grants Members a high degree of flexibility when undertaking specific commitments. They can assume different legal obligations, depending on the various service sectors and subsectors and the four modes of supply. The flexibility is furthered by the right to make the specific commitments subject to terms, limitations, and conditions. These qualifications may reflect the status quo under domestic law, or more generally, aim at reserving the right to operate measures inconsistent with full market access and/or national treatment.[33] As a consequence, the specific commitments vary considerably between different sectors, modes of supply, and, of course, Members. The practical result is a strong fragmentation of international legal obligations in these areas or, to put it otherwise, a very complex and uneven matrix of liberalization approaches.

C. Understanding on Commitments in Financial Services

The Understanding on Commitments in Financial Services is an alternative approach to the Member-specific schedules and aims at standardizing international commitments in the area of financial services. It is not binding as such, but constitutes a boilerplate—or model schedule[34]—to be used voluntarily by Members when inscribing in their schedules.[35] In 1999, the EU adopted the Understanding as a basis for its financial sector commitments.[36] Beside the EU-28, a further twelve Members, including Australia, Canada, Japan, Switzerland, and the US, adhere to the Understanding.[37]

Other than the GATS, the document focuses mainly on two modes—cross-border trade and commercial presence, but deals also with mode 2 and the temporary entry of personnel, that is, natural persons employed by a service supplier. In terms of negotiating modalities, the Understanding maintains the positive-list approach for cross-border trade, consumption abroad, and presence of natural persons, while abolishing it for mode 3.

Market access in mode 1 (cross-border trade) shall be permitted in some subsectors of insurance services only,[38] whereas trade in mode 2 (consumption abroad) is unrestricted for practically all subsectors,[39] which is in line with domestic practice in most jurisdictions. The Understanding grants a general right to establish a commercial presence for all subsectors of financial services.[40] The meaning of 'commercial presence' is very broad and includes subsidiaries, branches, agencies, and representative offices.[41] Members shall also permit service providers established in

[33] WTO, *Handbook GATS* (n 25) 8.

[34] Vranes, 'SEPA' (n 28) 518.

[35] cf Committee on Financial Services, Background Note 3 February 2010 (n 2) para 35; and Leroux, 'Trade in Financial Services' (n 4) 432.

[36] WTO, GATS/SC/31/Suppl.4/Rev.1 of 18 November 1999.

[37] cf Committee on Financial Services, Background Note 3 February 2010 (n 2).

[38] Understanding on Commitments in Financial Services (15 April 1994) LT/UR/U/1 s B para 3, <http://docsonline.wto.org> accessed 5 April 2017 (hereafter Understanding).

[39] ibid, s B para 4.

[40] ibid, s B para 5; see also Committee on Financial Services, Background Note 3 February 2010 (n 2) para 42.

[41] ibid s D para 2.

their territory to offer 'any new financial services'. These are defined as services that are not supplied in the territory of the respective Member, but which are supplied in the territory of another Member.[42]

In contrast to the market-access commitments, the Understanding is more restrained as far as non-discrimination commitments are concerned. National treatment shall be accorded to all financial service suppliers established in the territory of a Member with regard to the access to payment and clearing systems operated by public entities and to official funding and refinancing facilities available in the normal course of business.[43] This provision refers mainly to standard services supplied by national central banks in the course of monetary policy[44]—even if they are not considered as suppliers of financial services in the meaning of the GATS.

III. New approaches in CETA, TTIP, and TiSA

A. CETA

The draft CETA between Canada and the EU combines existing legal conceptions derived from the North American Free Trade Agreement (NAFTA) and the GATS, with some new approaches. This is also the case with ch 13 of CETA on financial services. Its most outstanding feature is that it puts the obligations of the parties in the context of investment protection.[45] In this way, it deviates from the GATS and follows the example of ch 14 of the NAFTA. This involves two consequences: first, even if the obligations of the parties under CETA have no direct effect on service suppliers,[46] their violation may lead to claims that can be enforced by a private investor within an investment dispute. Second, investment protection under CETA does not relate to the supply of financial services, but to investors and investment in financial service suppliers and in financial institutions.[47] Financial institutions are defined as financial service suppliers that are regulated and supervised under the law of the party in whose territory they are located.[48] As a further consequence, the substantive provisions of CETA distinguish clearly between the establishment of a financial institution and cross-border supply of services.

The scope of application of the financial services chapter follows mainly the traces of GATS and NAFTA. CETA defines financial services in the same way as the Annex on Financial Services,[49] but uses a slightly narrower understanding of

[42] ibid s D para 3. [43] ibid s C para 1. [44] cf Art 127 TFEU.

[45] Art 13.2 paras 2–4 draft CETA. All references refer to the consolidated version published by the EU Commission on 29 February 2016, <http://trade.ec.europa.eu/doclib/docs/2016/february/tradoc_154329.pdf> accessed 5 April 2017 (hereafter 'draft CETA February 2016').

[46] ibid, Art 30.6.1. [47] ibid, Art 13.2, subparas 2(a) and (b).

[48] ibid, Art 13.1. See also European Parliament, Directorate-General for Internal Policies, Policy Department A: Economic and Scientific Policy, *Financial Services in EU Trade Agreements—Study for the ECON Committee* (European Parliament, 2014) 13 (hereafter European Parliament, *Financial Services in EU Trade Agreements—Study for the ECON Committee*).

[49] Art 13.1 draft CETA February 2016 (n 45).

the term 'financial services supplier' by requiring that the person is already engaged in this activity.[50] Services supplied in the exercise of governmental authority are exempt under the same terms as under the GATS Annex on Financial Services, but on the basis of a different technical solution.[51] A further, rather formal, deviation from the GATS can be found with regard to the definition of cross-border supply. Under CETA, this term refers to both modes 1 and 2 in the meaning of the GATS.[52] From the point of view of substantive obligations, however, CETA differentiates again between these two modes.[53]

As regards market-opening obligations for financial services, the draft agreement distinguishes clearly between investment or establishment on the one hand and cross-border trade on the other. In the area of establishment of financial institutions, CETA goes slightly further than the GATS. First, all disciplines, including MFN treatment, national treatment, and market access, are unconditional and not subject to a separate scheduling.[54] Second, these obligations cover all subsectors of financial services. Compared to the GATS Understanding, this leads to an extension of obligations on national treatment, whereas market-access standards are not higher since the Understanding also grants full market access for all subsectors in mode 3. With regard to the content of market access obligations, CETA pursues the GATS approach and simply duplicates the exhaustive categories provided by Art XVI para 2 GATS.[55] Authorization requirements under domestic law for the establishment and expansion of a commercial presence are still exempt from market access obligations as it is expressly clarified in the agreement.[56] CETA also provides that a party may impose a legal separation of certain business activities from the supply of other financial services.[57] This reflects a current discussion on whether proprietary trading of securities and derivatives should be separated from the deposit-taking business.[58]

In the area of cross-border trade, national treatment and market access obligations apply only to financial services that are expressly inscribed in schedules for each party.[59] *Ratione materiae*, they cover the few subsectors already liberalized under the GATS Understanding, plus portfolio management services. The EU Member States that had acceded after 1999 adopt, however, obligations for further subsectors reflecting their additional specific commitments under the GATS. The content of market-access obligations is limited to an exhaustive list of quantitative

[50] ibid.

[51] See the definition of 'public entity' under Arts 13.1 and 13.17 draft CETA February 2016 (n 45).

[52] See the definition under Art 13.1 draft CETA February 2016 (n 45).

[53] cf ibid, Art 13.7.1 vs Art 13.7.6.

[54] See ibid, Arts 13.3, 13.4, and 13.6. On this negative list approach, see European Parliament, *Financial Services in EU Trade Agreements—Study for the ECON Committee* (n 48) 16.

[55] Art 13.6.1 draft CETA February 2016 (n 45).

[56] ibid, Art 13.6.3(a).

[57] ibid, Art 13.6.3(b).

[58] See High-level Expert Group on reforming the structure of the EU banking sector, chaired by Erkki Liikanen, Final Report of 2 October 2012, 100; Commission 'Proposal for a regulation on structural measures improving the resilience of EU credit institutions' COM (2014) 43 final.

[59] Art 13.7.1 in combination with Annex 13-A draft CETA February 2016 (n 45).

measure.[60] Again, registration or licensing requirements for suppliers of cross-border services are expressly permitted.[61]

The market-opening obligations in all sectors and all modes are subject to extensive reservations which are annexed to the draft CETA. Under these reservations, the parties may maintain, continue, or renew existing non-conforming measures.[62] Parties may also amend non-conforming measures to the extent that the amendment does not decrease the conformity of the measure, as it existed immediately before the amendment, with the treaty obligations. Yet, reservations also extend to future amendments of domestic law as specified in Annexes II and III. Thus, CETA creates limited standstill obligations only. More important is that the broad spectrum of domestic regulation which falls neither under market access nor under national treatment obligations is still left to the discretion of the parties. Accordingly, the wording of the prudential carve-out clause is more detailed as regards legitimate objectives than the version used in the GATS Annex on Financial Services.[63] It is also broader, in that it permits expressly the prohibition for prudential reasons of a particular service, subject only to non-discrimination obligations.[64] It is, however, slightly narrower than the Annex in requiring that prudential measures must be 'reasonable'. In an extensive annex, the parties agreed on high-level principles for the interpretation of the provision.[65]

Finally, CETA pursues a new approach for the admissibility of investment disputes with regard to financial institutions—the so-called filter mechanism.[66] When the respondent, that is, the state party of a dispute, invokes the prudential carve-out clause, the matter may be referred to the Financial Services Committee for a decision on the validity of this defence.[67] The Committee is composed of representatives of authorities in charge of financial services policy with expertise in this field.[68] Its members decide by mutual consent. Their determination, that the prudential carve-out is a valid defence, is binding on the claimant who is deemed to have withdrawn its claim.[69] Still, the respondent may request the tribunal to decide as a preliminary matter whether and to what extent the prudential carve-out is a valid defence to the claim.[70]

B. TTIP

The outcome of the negotiations between the EU and the US on the Agreement on TTIP is particularly uncertain. So far, official documents reflecting a final common position do not exist. The EU published a proposal for a text on services, investment, and e-commerce on 31 July 2015 that is suggested to form part of the future

[60] ibid, Art 13.7.1 in combination with Art 9.6.

[61] ibid, Art 13.7.1 in combination with Arts 9.4 and 13.16.2.

[62] ibid, Art 13.10.

[63] cf ibid, Art 13.16.

[64] ibid, Art 13.16.3.

[65] ibid, Annex 13-B; Understanding on the Application of Arts 13.16.1 and 13.21.

[66] European Parliament, *Financial Services in EU Trade Agreements—Study for the ECON Committee* (n 48) 19.

[67] Art 13.21.3 draft CETA February 2016 (n 45).

[68] ibid, Art 13.18.1.

[69] ibid, Art 13.21.4.

[70] ibid, Art 13.21.6.

TTIP.[71] Like CETA, it builds on the fundamental distinction between investment and cross-border trade. As regards the scope of financial services and the exceptions for services supplied in the exercise of governmental authority, the EU uses practically the same structure and wording as the GATS Annex.[72] For both modes, market-access commitments must be separately undertaken in a schedule of specific commitments.[73] The EU announced that its ambition to submit offers is 'closely linked to progress of discussions on regulatory co-operation'.[74] In the negotiating round of 11 to 15 July 2016, the EU tabled an offer that was made public on 14 July 2016.[75] Its content is limited to an extensive list of reservations on national treatment and unambitious market-access obligations which are based on the same exhaustive list used in GATS and CETA. TTIP is also expected to use a broad prudential carve-out clause[76] that is practically identical to the GATS version.

In the draft proposed by the EU, the provisions on regulatory cooperation in financial services are the most outstanding feature.[77] They read:

1. The Parties recognise that prudential measures strengthen domestic financial systems; encourage sound, efficient and robust institutions, markets, and infrastructure; and promote international financial stability by facilitating better-informed lending and investment decisions, improving market integrity, and reducing the risks of financial distress and contagion.
2. The Parties undertake to use their best endeavours to achieve mutual compatibility of their respective regulatory and supervisory frameworks for financial services in a way that supports the objectives mentioned in paragraph 1. Furthermore, the general objectives and principles of the Chapter [Regulatory Cooperation] apply to regulatory cooperation on financial services.
3. The Parties agree to consult each other at the earliest stage of the regulatory process.
4. The Parties agree, wherever possible, defer to the rules of the other Party if they achieve comparable outcomes, for the purpose of assessing compliance with domestic regulations.
5. The Parties shall conduct their cooperation in respect of financial services through a Joint EU/US Financial Regulatory Forum ('the Forum'), which is hereby established. The Forum shall be composed of representatives of regulators, supervisors and competent

[71] cf European Commission, 'TTIP—EU Proposal Trade in Services, Investment and E-Commerce' (made public on 31 July 2015), <http://trade.ec.europa.eu/doclib/docs/2015/july/tradoc_153669.pdf> accessed 5 April 2017.

[72] ibid, Arts 5-30 and 5-34.

[73] ibid, Arts 2-2 and 3-2.

[74] 'Transatlantic Trade and Investment Partnership—Services and Investment Offer of the European Union' (made public on 31 July 2015) 3, para 6, <http://trade.ec.europa.eu/doclib/docs/2015/july/tradoc_153670.pdf> accessed 5 April 2017.

[75] European Commission, 'TTIP—Services and Investment Offer of the European Union. Financial Services' (made public on 14 July 2016), <http://trade.ec.europa.eu/doclib/docs/2016/july/tradoc_154794.pdf> accessed 5 April 2017.

[76] Art 5-31 EU Commission, 'TTIP—EU Proposal Trade in Services' (n 71).

[77] ibid, Art 5-38. For an initial assessment, see Brett Bickel, 'Harmonizing Regulations in the Financial Services Industry through the Transatlantic Trade and Investment Partnership' (2014–15) *Emory International Law Review* 557, 577; Laura Puccio, *TTIP and Regulation of Financial Markets* (European Parliamentary Research Service, June 2015—PE 559.494) 21. Cf also Marise Cremona, 'Guest Editorial: Negotiating the Transatlantic Trade and Investment Partnership (TTIP)' (2015) 52 *Common Market Law Review* 351.

authorities responsible for financial regulation. In the area of financial services it shall carry out the functions of the Regulatory Cooperation Council established in Article 14 par. 1 of the Chapter [on Regulatory Cooperation].

6. The detailed arrangements of regulatory cooperation shall be set out in a [Memorandum of Understanding on Regulatory Cooperation in Financial Services].

C. TiSA

Under the planned, multilateral TiSA, financial services are dealt with in a separate Annex[78] that is based on the GATS Annex on Financial Services. The main characteristics of TiSA are, contrary to the GATS, a negative list approach for market-opening obligations of the parties, including national treatment and market access.[79] The practical legal effects, however, do not go beyond the Understanding on Financial Services. The mode of commercial presence is identical in both documents and the mode of cross-border supply is limited to an exhaustive list of financial services under TiSA leading to a similar result as the GATS Understanding. Also the dividing line between market access and domestic regulation is drawn according to the example given by the GATS.

IV. The Impact of the 'Prudential Carve-Out'

As already discussed, neither the GATS nor the services agreements currently negotiated by the EU restrict the right of the parties to adopt domestic regulation. In the field of financial services, this underlined by the so-called 'prudential carve-out'. The provision in para 2 of the GATS Annex on Financial Services reads:

> Notwithstanding any other provisions of this Agreement, a Member shall not be prevented from taking measures for prudential reasons, including for the protection of investors, depositors, policy holders or persons to whom a fiduciary duty is owed by a financial service supplier, or to ensure the integrity and stability of the financial system. Where such measures do not conform with the provisions of the Agreement, they shall not be used as a means of avoiding the Member's commitments or obligations under the Agreement.

The exception has three functions: first, it clarifies the legitimation of prudential regulation and supervision for the proper functioning of individual institutions and financial markets as a whole. The list of specific prudential reasons given in the first sentence is not exhaustive, but illustrative.[80] They demonstrate that the

[78] This and all further references refer to the draft released by WikiLeaks and dated 25 September 2015, <https://wikileaks.org/tisa/document/20150925_Annex-on-Financial-Services/20150925_Annex-on-Financial-Services.pdf> accessed 5 April 2017.

[79] Arts X.3, X.4, X.7, and X.8 Wikileaks, 'Draft TiSA Financial Services Annex' (n 78).

[80] WTO, Panel Report, *Argentina—Measures Relating to Trade in Goods and Services* (30 September 2015) WT/DS453/R, paras 7.819 and 7.869 (hereafter WTO, Panel Report *Argentina*); Bismuth, 'Financial Sector Regulation' (n 9) 496; Carlo Cantore, 'Shelter from the Storm: Exploring the Scope of Application and Legal Function of the GATS Prudential Carve-Out' (2014) 48 *Journal of World*

Members typically[81] protect the consumers and other customers of banks, securities firms, and insurance companies from losses of their assets. The integrity and stability of the financial system mentioned in the second part of the first sentence involves micro-prudential and macro-prudential objectives. On the micro-prudential level, regulation and supervision aim at individual institutions. On the macro-prudential level, states may also attempt to shield their economies from a breakdown of the financial system as it happened in the Great Depression of 1929 to 1932 and again during the financial crisis of 2007 to 2009. In order to achieve these objectives, the prudential carve-out leaves the WTO Members with broad regulatory autonomy[82] to assess relevant risks, to attribute them to specific financial institutions or markets, and to choose the means they consider appropriate to reduce these risks. Second, the prudential carve-out clarifies that this field belongs to the wider field of domestic regulation which, in principle, is not covered by the market-opening commitments of non-discrimination and market access. Third, the provision constitutes an exception to the Agreement. Even if, in an individual case, prudential measures would not conform with the provisions of the GATS, that is, also with specific commitments undertaken by a Member, this would be justified as far as the prudential carve-out applies.[83] CETA and TTIP pursue an identical approach, even if their wording diverges slightly from the GATS Annex. Both agreements provide that they do 'not prevent a Party from adopting or maintaining reasonable measures for prudential reasons ...'.[84] This means that in the case of a conflict between treaty obligations and domestic regulatory law, the latter shall prevail under the GATS.

The primacy of prudential regulation is only restrained by the requirement that the measures must be reasonable. The GATS Annex does not explicitly make use of this word, but provides that the measures 'shall not be used as a means of avoiding the Member's commitments or obligations'. While this does not entail a necessity test in a strict sense,[85] it is at least understood by most authors as prohibiting arbitrary or protectionist measures, similar to the chapeau in Art XX GATT.[86] The EU

Trade 1223, 1227 (hereafter Cantore, 'Shelter from the Storm'); and Leroux, 'Trade in Financial Services' (n 4) 430.

[81] cf WTO, Panel Report *Argentina* (n 80) para 7.873: 'evolutionary nature of the concept'.

[82] ibid, para 7.849; Bogdandy and Windsor, 'Annex' (n 17) 634, para 22; and Cottier and Krajewski, 'Role for Non-Discrimination' (n 5) 827; see also Cantore, 'Shelter from the Storm' (n 80) 1225.

[83] WTO, Panel Report, *Argentina* (n 80) para 7.814; confirmed by Appellate Body Report, WT/DS453/AB/R, 14 April 2016, para 6.254; see also Inu Barbee and Simon Lester, 'Financial Services in the TTIP: Making the Prudential Exception Work' (2014) 45(4) *Georgetown Journal of International Law* 953, 956 (hereafter Barbee and Lester, 'Financial services in the TTIP'). For an even wider view, see Cantore, 'Shelter from the Storm' (n 80) 1242.

[84] Art 13.16.1 draft CETA February 2016 (n 45); and Art 5-31 EU Commission, 'TTIP—EU Proposal Trade in Services' (n 71).

[85] For a different view, see Puccio, 'TTIP and Financial Markets' (n 77) 11.

[86] Barbee and Lester, 'Financial Services in the TTIP' (n 83) 960; Bogdandy and Windsor, 'Annex' (n 17) 632, para 24; Delimatsis and Sauvé, 'Financial Services after the Crisis' (n 7) 850; and Leroux, 'Trade in Financial Services' (n 4) 431. See also Kalypso Nicolaidis and Joel Trachtman, 'From Policed Regulation to Managed Recognition in GATS' in Pierre Sauvé and Robert M Stern (eds), *GATS 2000* (The Brookings Institution, 2000) 241, 255.

proposal for TTIP goes a considerable step further by saying that 'these measures shall not be more burdensome than necessary to achieve their aim'.[87] CETA also develops further the GATS Annex by specifying in Annex 13-B several high-level principles for the application of the prudential carve-out. According to them, a 'party may determine its own appropriate level of prudential regulation'.[88] Other factors are 'the urgency of the situation and the information available to the party at the time when the measure was adopted'.[89] A measure is deemed to conform with the prudential carve-out if it has a prudential objective and is not so severe in the light of its purpose that it is manifestly disproportionate to the attainment of its objective.[90] Furthermore, a measure is deemed to meet the requirements of the clause if it is in line with international prudential commitments that are common to the parties.[91]

V. The Interface between Trade and Regulation

In practical terms, however, the number of unsolved issues on the interface between trade and regulation is growing constantly. On the regulatory plane, the G20 cooperate in various fora for the supervision of financial industries and produce international standards the volume and complexity of which grows constantly in each negotiation round.[92] Their work is expert-driven and, accordingly, highly technical. Yet, these approaches do not solve the fundamental problem that behind the technical surface of international standard-setting, the states still do not trust each other.[93] Differences in regulatory philosophy and national interests are deeply rooted.[94] After the experiences of the financial crisis, most states aim at protecting 'their' financial system more than ever from risks—be they of internal or external origin.

Also unsolved is the fundamental problem that issues of regulatory standard-setting are not linked at all to international trade issues. This separation is due to the fact that the trade fora and the various regulatory fora act completely detached from each other. A further problem is that the international standards agreed upon in Basel and elsewhere are not legally binding on the participants. Even if it is widely acknowledged today that international soft law matters,[95] in practice, the states enjoy full discretion whether and to what extent they implement the standards in domestic law. This means that, on a case-by-case basis, states could fully stick to

[87] Art 5-31 para 2 EU Commission, 'TTIP—EU Proposal Trade in Services' (n 71).

[88] Para 8(a) of Annex 13-B draft CETA February 2016 (n 45).

[89] ibid, para 8(b) of Annex 13-B.

[90] ibid, para 8(d) of Annex 13-B.

[91] ibid, para 8(e)(i) of Annex 13-B.

[92] See, eg, the current version of the international regulatory framework for banks, 'Basel III' of 11 June 2011, <http://www.bis.org/bcbs/basel3.htm?m=3|14|572> accessed 5 April 2017.

[93] See Daniel Tarullo, *Banking on Basel: The Future of International Financial Regulation* (Peterson Institute for International Economics, 2008).

[94] Chris Brummer, *Soft Law and the Global Financial System* (Cambridge University Press, 2012) 270.

[95] For an excellent overview, see ibid, 115ff.

these standards, go beyond them, or disregard them fully or in part. Another point on the interface of trade and regulation is that many jurisdictions, including the EU and the US, make extensive use of legislation with extraterritorial effect.[96] For the financial services industries, this can lead to double or even multiple prudential requirements, depending on the number of jurisdictions which demand the observance of their laws. In the worst case scenario, these requirements could contradict each other. A newer development is that states attempt to ring-fence the companies which are active in their territories and detach them effectively from the international group to which they belong. A salient example is the banking regulation under the US Dodd–Frank Act. Under s 165 of this Act, the Federal Reserve System as the competent regulatory authority is empowered to adopt enhanced prudential standards for large banking groups. In 2014, the Federal Reserve adopted a final rule requiring foreign banking organizations with a significant US presence to establish an intermediate holding company over their US subsidiaries.[97] The intermediate holding company must fully observe regulatory requirements for supervision on a consolidated basis. As a practical consequence, an internationally operating group is split into a fully fledged American sub-group and the group companies in the rest of the world.[98]

VI. Towards Regulatory Cooperation?

Against this backdrop, the question arises as to whether international regulatory cooperation would contribute to solving the problems on the interface between trade and regulation. The answer is clearly positive. However, there exists no convincing one-fits-all model for this kind of cooperation so far.[99] The WTO does not offer an appropriate framework, as had been already observed.[100] Under the GATS, this is reflected in the fact that the mechanism for mutual recognition under Art VII has never become operative in the area of financial services. The proposal by the EU for a chapter on regulatory cooperation within TTIP is a first step forward, but it does not clarify the relationship with existing international standards. From a substantive point of view, only the CETA high-level principles for the application of the prudential carve-out include an explicit reference to international standards. Combining both approaches, that is, the procedural and the substantive, could help to close the gap between trade and regulatory issues. All bilateral approaches,

[96] See, eg, Arts 11 para 12, 25, and 77 Regulation (EU) 648/2012 on OTC derivatives, central counterparties and trade repositories, [2012] OJ L 201/1.

[97] Federal Reserve System, Enhanced Prudential Standards for Bank Holding Companies and Foreign Banking Organizations, Final Rule, Federal Register/Vol 79, No 59/Thursday, 27 March 2014/Rules and Regulations, <https://www.gpo.gov/fdsys/pkg/FR-2014-03-27/pdf/2014-05699.pdf> accessed 5 April 2017.

[98] See Puccio, 'TTIP and Financial Markets' (n 77) 14.

[99] cf Hoekman, 'Fostering Transatlantic Regulatory Cooperation' (n 13) 611; and Barbee and Lester, 'Financial Services in the TTIP' (n 83) 863.

[100] Cottier and Krajewski, 'Role for Non-Discrimination' (n 5) 827.

however, must decide how they deal with the fact that standard-setting is a multilateral business which is dealt with in international expert fora with a different mandate and different membership.

In order to bridge the gap between these two worlds, it would be necessary to amend the respective mandates of trade and regulatory fora and coordinate them with each other. In particular, this would mean widening the mandate of the international regulatory fora, requiring them to consider also the trade implications of their recommendations. The general focus should be on the question of which measures could be a basis for building up mutual trust between national competent supervisors. As a first step, an in-depth analysis of open issues in home/host country relations would be indispensable. This would help to clarify the relationship between home and host regulators and supervisors and contribute to a better understanding of why national jurisdictions impose double or contradictory regulatory requirements on financial services suppliers. In a further step, practical modes of international cooperation between home and host country supervisors could be developed. It is on the basis of mutual trust generated in these forms of cooperation that the *political* decision could be adopted to recognize the regulations and the supervisory practice of a trading partner and renounce additional requirements in domestic law.

9

Human Rights, Labour Standards, and Environmental Standards in CETA

Lorand Bartels

I. Introduction

Like the US and certain other countries, Canada and the EU have for some years included provisions in their free trade and, latterly, investment agreements establishing rights and obligations with regard to the protection of labour and environmental standards and, for the EU, human rights.[1] It is therefore unsurprising that their recently signed Comprehensive Economic and Trade Agreement (CETA) contains provisions on these matters reflecting their respective recent treaty practices.[2] However, CETA also contains a number of innovations, not only for each party, but also for free trade agreements (FTAs) more generally.

This chapter explores these provisions, and remarks on certain of their innovations, both for each of the parties, and for trade and investment agreements more generally. It begins by outlining the obligations of the parties to protect labour and environmental standards, human rights, and democratic principles. Next, it discusses certain means by which the economic obligations of the parties may be interpreted, either expressly or by implication, to reflect these values. Third, it analyses the rights of the parties, in the context of exceptions, to adopt measures to protect labour and environmental standards and human right obligations, and the extent to which CETA's obligations might expand the ordinary jurisdictional scope of these rights.

[1] For a recent survey, see Lorand Bartels, 'Social Issues: Labour, Environment and Human Rights' in Simon Lester, Bryan Mercurio, and Lorand Bartels (eds), *Bilateral and Regional Trade Agreements: Commentary and Analysis* (2nd edn, Cambridge University Press, 2016) 364–84.

[2] Comprehensive Economic and Trade Agreement between Canada, of the one part, and the European Union and its Member States, of the other part, Council Doc 10973/16, <http://data.consilium.europa.eu/doc/document/ST-10973-2016-INIT/en/pdf> accessed 6 April 2017. CETA was signed on 30 October 2016. It is envisaged that those parts of the agreement within EU competence will be provisionally applied once these parts of the agreement are approved by the European Parliament (Art 30.7.3 CETA). All references to Arts in this contribution are to CETA unless specified otherwise.

II. Obligations

A. Labour and environmental standards

Since 1993 (for Canada) and 2008 (for the EU), both of the CETA parties have included broadly similar obligations to respect labour and environmental standards in their trade and, more recently, investment agreements.[3] It was therefore no surprise that CETA would, broadly speaking, follow these precedents, which it does by including the following three types of obligations: (1) obligations to implement certain multilateral obligations; (2) obligations requiring the parties not to reduce their existing levels of protection; and (3) best endeavours obligations encouraging the parties to raise their levels of protection of labour and environmental standards. There are, however, some variations and compromises on certain issues, particularly enforcement, on which the partners still have different approaches.

1. Multilateral standards

The baseline for labour and (in some cases) environmental obligations in recent trade agreements is usually set by reference to multilateral standards. CETA does this for labour standards, but not for environmental standards.

CETA first of all requires its parties to comply with the minimum standards set out in the 1998 International Labour Organization (ILO) Declaration on Fundamental Principles and Rights at Work and its Follow-up.[4] According to these instruments, all ILO Members are obliged to respect four 'core labour standards': freedom of association and collective bargaining; elimination of all forms of forced or compulsory labour; abolition of child labour; and elimination of discrimination with regard to employment and occupation. CETA effectively incorporates these as hard obligations insofar as it lists these four core labour standards and requires that '[e]ach Party shall ensure that its labour law and practices embody and provide protection for the[se] fundamental principles and rights at work'.[5]

CETA also requires the promotion of: (a) health and safety at work; (b) acceptable minimum employment standards for wage earners, including those not

[3] For Canada, this began with the NAFTA Side Agreements on Labor and Environmental Cooperation (NAALC and NAAEC) 32 ILM 1499 (1993) and 32 ILM 1480 (1993); for the EU, this began with the EU–CARIFORUM Economic Partnership Agreement [2008] OJ L 289/I/3. See, further, Lorand Bartels, 'Human Rights and Sustainable Development Obligations in the EU's Free Trade Agreements' (2013) 40 *Legal Issues of Economic Integration* 297–314.

[4] ILO Declaration on Fundamental Principles and Rights at Work and its Follow-up adopted by the International Labour Conference at its Eighty-sixth Session, Geneva, 18 June 1998 (Annex revised 15 June 2010), <http://www.ilo.org/declaration/info/publications/WCMS_467653/lang--en/index.htm> accessed 6 April 2017.

[5] Art 23.3.1 CETA.

covered by a collective agreement; and (c) non-discrimination in respect of working conditions, including—notably—for migrant workers.[6] In addition, CETA requires, as a hard obligation, each of the parties to 'ensure that its labour law and practices embody and provide protection for working conditions that respect the health and safety of workers'.[7] If 'the measures may affect trade or investment between the Parties', this must be done 'taking into account existing relevant scientific and technical information and related international standards, guidelines or recommendations',[8] but 'in case of existing or potential hazards or conditions that could reasonably be expected to cause injury or illness to a person, a Party shall not use the lack of full scientific certainty as a reason to postpone cost-effective protective measures'.[9]

In addition, CETA also contains a number of redundant—or close to redundant—provisions referencing multilateral obligations, each of which would arguably have been better left to a political declaration. Each party 'reaffirms its commitment to effectively implement ... the fundamental ILO Conventions that Canada and the Member States of the European Union have ratified respectively'.[10] It is the same for environmental protection: each party 'reaffirms its commitment to effectively implement in its law and practices, in its whole territory, the multilateral environmental agreements to which it is party'.[11] Such 'reaffirmations' have little or no meaning. Just as pointless, though for different reasons, is the statement that '[t]he Parties affirm their commitment to respect, promote and realise [core labour] principles and rights'.[12] These commitments are already the subject of hard obligations. There is also an obligation to 'make continued and sustained efforts to ratify the fundamental ILO Conventions if they have not yet done so',[13] directed at Canada's non-ratification of ILO Convention No 98 on the Right to Organise and Collective Bargaining.[14] The practical salience of this obligation is elusive.

2. *Beyond minimum standards*

CETA also contains a number of obligations based on the parties' existing labour and environmental laws. These are significant, and come in two main variations.

a) Obligations to implement labour and environmental laws

Most importantly, CETA contains two sets of obligations requiring the implementation of existing labour and environmental laws. The first set requires each party not to 'waive or otherwise derogate from, or offer to waive or otherwise derogate

[6] Art 23.3.2 CETA. [7] Art 23.3.3 CETA. [8] ibid. [9] ibid.
[10] Art 23.3.4 CETA. [11] Art 24.4.2 CETA. [12] Art 23.3.1 CETA.
[13] Art 23.3.4 CETA.
[14] Joint Interpretative Instrument on the Comprehensive Economic and Trade Agreement (CETA) between Canada and the European Union and its Member States, 27 October 2016, para 8(b), Annexed to EU Council Doc 13541/16, <http://data.consilium.europa.eu/doc/document/ST-13541-2016-INIT/en/pdf> accessed 6 April 2017 (hereafter CETA Joint Interpretative Instrument).

from its labour law and standards [its environmental law], to encourage trade or the establishment, acquisition, expansion or retention of an investment in its territory'.[15] A second set requires that each party 'shall not, through a sustained or recurring course of action or inaction, fail to effectively enforce its labour law and standards [environmental law] to encourage trade or investment'.[16] CETA goes on to specify what enforcement means in practice, setting out positive rules on inspections, and domestic enforcement remedies with due process guarantees and a right of appeal.[17]

This second obligation is in certain significant respects similar to a provision subject to litigation in *Guatemala—Article 16.2.1(a) CAFTA–DR*. That provision states:

> A Party shall not fail to effectively enforce its labor laws, through a sustained or recurring course of action or inaction, in a manner affecting trade between the Parties, after the date of entry into force of this Agreement.

While the panel report is not yet available, the submissions of the parties have clarified a number of pertinent interpretative issues,[18] and even where these issues are not, strictly speaking, relevant to the equivalent CETA obligations, due to their difference in wording,[19] some are of interest to the equivalent CETA provision.

One issue is when the failure to enforce labour (or environmental) standards 'affects trade'. The US argues that what is important is an effect on conditions of competition in either the domestic or export markets for products of the type produced by the entities not in compliance with domestic labour law. It argues, further, that the actual products produced by the entities at issue do not need to be sold in either market, as the effects of non-compliance spread throughout the industry. Guatemala argues that actual trade effects must be demonstrated, in the sense of a demonstrated reduction in market access, and moreover that these must be related to the prices of the actual products produced by the entities not in compliance with domestic labour law.[20] It points in this regard to the fact that, as in the WTO, CAFTA–DR provides for monetary penalties that 'take into account', inter

[15] Arts 23.4.2 and 24.5.2 CETA. [16] Arts 23.4.3 and 24.5.3 CETA.

[17] CETA Art 23.5-7 and, less elaborately, Art 24.6.

[18] 'In the Matter of Guatemala—Issues Relating to the Obligations under Article 16.2.1(a) of the CAFTA–DR' (*Guatemala—Article 16.2.1(a) CAFTA–DR*), <https://ustr.gov/issue-areas/labor/bilateral-and-regional-trade-agreements/guatemala-submission-under-cafta-dr> accessed 6 April 2017.

An interim report was issued in early October 2016, and a final report is expected early in 2017. See World Trade Online, 'Settlement Panel Completes Initial Report In U.S.–Guatemala Labor Dispute' (14 October 2016) Vol 34 No 40, 156176, <http://insidetrade.com> accessed 6 April 2017.

[19] The parties disagree on the relevance of the definition in Art 16.8 CAFTA–DR of 'labor laws' as being enforceable by the executive. There is no equivalent provision in CETA. They also disagree on whether affected trade must be between all of the parties to the CAFTA–DR or merely bilateral trade suffices. This is not relevant to a bilateral agreement, such as CETA, in relation to trade.

[20] 'Comments of Guatemala to the United States' Supplementary Written Submission and Responses to the Panel's Questions', 1 July 2015, para 66, <https://ustr.gov/sites/default/files/files/Issue_Areas/Labor/Comments%20of%20Guatemala%20July%201.pdf> accessed 6 April 2017.

alia, 'the bilateral trade effects of the Party's failure to effectively enforce the relevant law'.[21] The US responds that, as in the WTO, the questions of violation and remedy are separate, and in any event 'taking account' of such effects is only one of a number of relevant factors in determining the penalty.

In CETA, this issue is directly relevant to the obligation, noted above, 'to ensure that ... labour law and practices embody and provide protection for working conditions that respect the health and safety of workers'.[22] But CETA's structurally similar enforcement obligations require the parties not 'to encourage trade or investment'. This is materially different, because any price depression in that party's domestic market as a result of non-enforcement of labour or environmental laws would tend rather to restrict imports rather than encourage them. This means that the CETA equivalent is necessarily limited to trade effects in that party's export market.

A second issue concerns the intent of the delinquent party. The US argues that effects are sufficient; Guatemala disagrees. Again, the CETA language—'[inaction] to encourage trade or investment'—is different. If anything, this wording tends to favour intention. The WTO Appellate Body has read the phrase 'so as to afford protection to domestic production' in terms of 'objective intention'.[23] But even if this is the case, this does not necessarily exclude a test also based on mere effects. Finally, there is a dispute in the Guatemala case as to the meaning of a 'sustained or recurring' course of action or inaction. The US emphasizes that the term is disjunctive, and argues that repeated incidences will suffice to trigger the obligation. Guatemala responds that any intervening event or interruption falls beneath the requisite standard, and that the inaction must be country-wide. On balance, given the bare text of the phrase, the US would appear to have the more persuasive approach.

b) Obligation to 'seek to ensure' high labour and environmental standards

Less importantly, CETA contains a pair of obligations stating that 'each Party shall seek to ensure that ... [its labour and environmental] laws and policies provide for and encourage high levels of [labour and environmental] protection and shall strive to continue to improve such laws and policies with the goal of providing high levels of [labour and environmental] protection'.[24] One might be tempted to think that a best endeavours provision of this type can have no meaning. But laws and policies that manifestly fail to protect labour or environmental standards would violate such an obligation. Thus, the US commenced consultations with Bahrain under an equivalent provision on labour standards.[25] It should be noted, however, that in the EU's TTIP proposal (as in other trade agreements) the wording is much stronger, stating that '[e]ach Party *shall ensure* that its domestic policies and laws provide for and encourage high levels of protection in the labour and environmental areas and

[21] CAFTA–DR Art 20.17.2(a). [22] CETA Art 23.3.2.

[23] The phrase is found in Art III:1 GATT 1994. See WTO, Appellate Body Report, *Japan—Alcoholic Beverages II* (1 November 1996) WT/DS8/AB/R, para 32.

[24] Arts 23.2 and 24.3 CETA.

[25] Letter requesting consultations under Art 15.6.1 of the US–Bahrain FTA (6 May 2013), <https://www.dol.gov/ilab/reports/pdf/20130506BahrainLetter.pdf> accessed 6 April 2017.

shall strive to continue to improve those policies and laws and their underlying levels of protection'.[26]

B. Implementation

1. Organs

CETA establishes a Committee on Trade and Sustainable Development to monitor the implementation of the CETA provisions on labour and environmental protection.[27] This Committee is to be composed of high-level representatives responsible for those matters—although it is unclear whether they are already to be expert in these areas—and its role is to oversee the implementation of the trade and environment chapters of the agreement, through regular meetings,[28] which will include a session open to the public (unless the parties decide otherwise).[29] In addition, the parties are to 'facilitate' a 'Civil Society Forum' composed of representatives of civil society organizations established in their territories, which is to be convened once a year, and is to 'conduct a dialogue' on the sustainable development aspects of this Agreement.[30] This forum is to include participants in yet another set of bodies established by CETA, namely national 'domestic advisory groups' comprising stakeholders from a range of affected sectors.[31] These groups are able to submit opinions and make recommendations on any matter related to the labour and environmental chapters on their own initiative,[32] and, at least in relation to disputes on compliance with labour obligations, are also to be consulted on dispute settlement proceedings.[33]

C. Dispute settlement

Typically, Canadian FTAs establish mechanisms by which individuals of one party (which, in practice, tends to mean organized civil society groups, especially labour unions) may make submissions to the other party in relation to matters arising under the agreement, and this is then linked to the treaty parties invoking consultation and dispute settlement proceedings.[34] This is very much watered down in CETA. Instead, '[e]ach Party shall be open to receive and shall give due consideration to submissions from the public on matters related to this Chapter, including communications on implementation concerns'.[35] If this occurs, '[e]ach Party shall

[26] EU Textual Proposal, Trade and Sustainable Development, Transatlantic Trade and Investment Partnership, 6 November 2015, Art 3.2, <http://trade.ec.europa.eu/doclib/html/153923.htm> accessed 6 April 2017 (emphasis added).

[27] Art 26.2(g) CETA.

[28] Arts 23.8.3 and 24.13.3 CETA.

[29] Art 22.4.3 CETA.

[30] Art 22.5 CETA.

[31] ibid, referring to Art 28.8.3 CETA (which should be 28.3.4) and Art 24.13 (which should be 24.13.5).

[32] ibid.

[33] Arts 23.9.4 and 23.10.12 CETA.

[34] eg Canada–Korea Free Trade Agreement (in force 1 January 2015), Art 18.10, <http://international.gc.ca/trade-commerce/trade-agreements-accords-commerciaux/agr-acc/korea-coree/fta-ale/index.aspx?lang=eng> accessed 17 January 2017 (hereafter Canada–Korea FTA).

[35] Arts 23.8.5 and 24.7.3 CETA.

inform its respective domestic labour or sustainable development advisory groups [or civil society organisations] of those communications'.[36]

The system that is adopted for CETA is instead a traditional state–state dispute settlement system. A party may request consultations 'in relation to any matter arising under this chapter' and if this does not satisfactorily address the matter, that party may request a 'Panel of Experts'.[37] The crucial point, however, concerns the consequences of a finding of a violation. This, following recent EU treaty practice,[38] is decidedly weak. If the panel determines that 'a Party has not conformed with its obligations under this Chapter, the Parties shall engage in discussions and shall endeavour, within three months of the delivery of the final report, to identify an appropriate measure or, if appropriate, to decide upon a mutually satisfactory action plan. In these discussions, the Parties shall take into account the final report.'[39] In other words, there is no real enforcement at all. Lest there be any doubts as to this conclusion, it is further stipulated in each chapter that '[f]or any dispute that arises under this Chapter, the Parties shall only have recourse to the rules and procedures provided in this Chapter'.[40]

This differs significantly from standard Canadian practice in relation to labour obligations. These are subject to a monetary penalty equal to any adverse effects resulting from the violation, the amount being adjustable in light of good faith and any aggravating factors.[41] This sum is to be spent on implementing an action plan remedying the violation.[42] Standard Canadian enforcement of environmental obligations, on the other hand, is in line with that in CETA.[43] On the enforcement of environmental obligations, at least, both the EU and Canada lag behind the US, which operates under a legislative negotiating objective 'to ensure that enforceable labor and environment obligations are subject to the same dispute settlement and remedies as other enforceable obligations under the agreement'.[44]

III. Human Rights Obligations

A. Background

Unlike the labour and environmental provisions just discussed, the human rights obligations in the EU–Canada Strategic Partnership Agreement originate in EU

[36] ibid. [37] Arts 23.9-11 and 24.14-16 CETA.

[38] eg Free Trade Agreement between the European Union and its Member States, of the one part, and the Republic of Korea, of the other part [2011] OJ L 127/6, Art 13.15(2) (hereafter EU–Korea FTA); Association Agreement between the European Union and the European Atomic Energy Community and their Member States, of the one part, and the Republic of Moldova, of the other part [2014] OJ L 260/4, Art 379.

[39] Arts 23.10.12 and 24.15.11 CETA. [40] Arts 23.11.1 and 24.16.1 CETA.

[41] eg Canada–Korea FTA (n 34) Annex 18-E para 3. For an overview, see International Labour Organization (ILO), *Assessment of Labour Provisions in Trade and Investment Arrangements* (ILO, 2016) 47–52.

[42] eg Agreement on Labour Cooperation between Canada and the Republic of Honduras (Canada–Honduras FTA), in force 1 October 2014, <http://www.international.gc.ca/trade-agreements-accords-commerciaux/agr-acc/honduras/labour-travail.aspx?lang=eng> accessed 6 April 2017, Annex 3 para 3.

[43] eg Canada–Korea FTA (n 34) Art 17.13. [44] 19 USC 4201(b)(10)(H).

practice.[45] Since the early 1990s, the EU's trade agreements (and, more recently, its investment agreements) have included or otherwise been governed by a 'human rights clause' requiring the parties to respect human rights and democratic principles. This practice is anchored in a policy formally adopted by the EU in 1995 that all cooperation and trade agreements would henceforth include human rights clauses that would permit the partial or full suspension of an agreement in the event that either party violated human rights norms.[46] A domestic mechanism for such suspension was included in Art 218(9) TFEU. In 2009, the EU amended its policy such that trade agreements can be subject to a human rights clause in a parallel framework cooperation agreement between the same parties,[47] this being effected by means of a cross-reference (sometimes by implication).[48] The human rights clause in the EU–Canada Strategic Partnership Agreement (SPA) is an example, although in other respects an unusual one.

B. Obligations

Article 2(1) of the SPA states, relevantly, as follows:

> Respect for democratic principles, human rights and fundamental freedoms, as laid down in the Universal Declaration of Human Rights and existing international human rights treaties and other legally binding instruments to which the Union or the Member States and Canada are party, underpins the Parties' respective national and international policies and constitutes an essential element of this Agreement.

This is a standard 'essential elements' clause, with essentially the same wording that is found in all of the EU's trade agreements since the early 1990s.

Normatively, the reference point of this essential elements clause is the 1948 Universal Declaration of Human Rights. The Universal Declaration contains obligations covering civil, political, economic, social, and cultural rights. Some of the most significant are rights of non-discrimination on grounds of race, sex, and religion, as well as the right to life, liberty and security of the person, freedom from arbitrary arrest and torture, access to justice and a fair trial, privacy, rights to work, leisure and social security, the right to education, and rights of political participation. The potential scope of Art 2(1) is therefore extensive, even if, on the twenty-five or so occasions over the past twenty years in which they have been invoked, the situations at issue were almost all situations of major political instability, such as

[45] EU/MS–Canada Strategic Partnership Agreement [2016] OJ L 329/45, signed 30 October 2016, provisional application of part within EU competence envisaged once approved by the European Parliament (Art 30.2 SPA) (hereafter SPA).

[46] European Commission, 'Communication on the Inclusion of Respect for Democratic Principles and Human Rights in Agreements between the Community and Third Countries', COM (1995) 216 and EU Council Conclusions of 29 May 1995 (reported in EU Bulletin 1995-5, point 1.2.3).

[47] EU Council, 'Reflection Paper on Political Clauses in Agreements with Third Countries', Doc 7008/09, 27 February 2009 (partially derestricted).

[48] EU–Korea FTA (n 38) Art 15.14 states that: 'Unless specified otherwise, previous agreements between the Member States of the European Union and/or the European Community and/or the European Union and Korea are not superseded or terminated by this Agreement.'

coups d'état, flawed elections[49] or, in the case of Syria, grave crimes that threaten the peace, security, and well-being of the international community.[50]

The SPA is, however, much more limited than standard human rights clauses in several respects. First, it expressly limits the application of the essential elements clause to CETA to extreme situations. Article 28(7) states:

> [T]he Parties recognise that a particularly serious and substantial violation of human rights or non-proliferation, as defined in paragraph 3, could also serve as grounds for the termination of the EU–Canada Comprehensive Economic and Trade Agreement (CETA) in accordance with Art 30.9 of that Agreement.

The threshold for such a violation is high, being defined thus: 'its gravity and nature would have to be of an exceptional sort such as a coup d'État or grave crimes that threaten the peace, security and well-being of the international community'.[51] This threshold is therefore higher than the situation of 'special urgency' that allows one party to suspend the SPA (but not CETA).[52] Moreover, the reference to Art 30.9.1 CETA appears to be redundant, as this provision permits termination in any case. It states:

> A Party may denounce this Agreement by giving written notice of termination to the General Secretariat of the Council of the European Union and the Department of Foreign Affairs, Trade and Development Canada, or their respective successors. This Agreement shall be terminated 180 days after the date of that notice. The Party giving a notice of termination shall also provide the CETA Joint Committee with a copy of the notice.

As far as CETA is concerned, then, the human rights clause in the SPA is of an entirely political value, and this reflects an important shift in the EU's treaty practice. Traditionally, these clauses were intended to enable the EU (and, in theory, the other party) to suspend or terminate obligations under the agreement which it could not otherwise do. In practice, it is the possibility of suspension that has been important, because suspension is an act that can be reversed. That cannot be said of termination, which, in practice, is irreversible. Such a 'nuclear' option would also weaken the practical utility of the human rights clause, on the assumption that it might be necessary to base a termination on such a clause (which is not the case here).

[49] See Johanne Døhlie Saltnes, 'The EU's Human Rights Policy: Unpacking the Literature on the EU's Implementation of Aid Conditionality' (2013) Arena Working Paper 2/2013, 7 (Table 1), <http://www.sv.uio.no/arena/english/research/publications/arena-working-papers/2013/wp2-13.pdf> accessed 6 April 2017.

[50] The EEC–Syria cooperation agreement was suspended in 2011 because of a statement in its preamble that the agreement was 'based on the common desire of the Parties to maintain and strengthen friendly relations in accordance with the principles of the United Nations Charter'. This was treated as an essential elements clause. See Council of the European Union, Council Decision of 2 September 2011 partially suspending the application of the Cooperation Agreement between the European Economic Community and the Syrian Arab Republic 2011/523/EU [2011] OJ L 228/19.

[51] SPA (n 45) Art 28(3).

[52] ibid, Art 28(6)(a). Moreover, this provision states, for the first time, that the suspension of an agreement under a human rights clause requires unanimity on the EU side.

IV. Interpretations of Rights and Obligations

CETA contains two of the most controversial obligations in international investment agreements—the obligation not to expropriate investments by indirect means and the obligation to accord fair and equitable treatment to investors—but confines their scope.

As a general matter, CETA states, with reference to Section D ('Investment protection'):

For greater certainty, the mere fact that a Party regulates, including through a modification to its laws, in a manner which negatively affects an investment or interferes with an investor's expectations, including its expectations of profits, does not amount to a breach of an obligation under this Section.[53]

In relation to the fair and equitable treatment obligation, it adds that 'the fact that a measure breaches domestic law does not, in and of itself, establish a breach of this Article'.[54] The obligation not to expropriate, directly or indirectly, is also given a further interpretation, relevantly:

For greater certainty, except in the rare circumstance when the impact of a measure or series of measures is so severe in light of its purpose that it appears manifestly excessive, non-discriminatory measures of a Party that are designed and applied to protect legitimate public welfare objectives, such as health, safety and the environment, do not constitute indirect expropriations.[55]

Following an early objection to ratification by Wallonia, the parties agreed to a Joint Interpretative Instrument.[56] Mostly, this document reiterates the provisions of the agreement. However, it does also add some clarifications of material legal value. Relevantly, Art 2 of the Instrument states as follows:

CETA preserves the ability of the European Union and its Member States and Canada to adopt and apply their own laws and regulations that regulate economic activity in the public interest, to achieve legitimate public policy objectives such as the protection and promotion of public health, social services, public education, safety, the environment, public morals, social or consumer protection, privacy and data protection and the promotion and protection of cultural diversity.

A concordance table at the end of the Instrument specifies that this paragraph is to assist in the interpretation of a non-exhaustive list of provisions, of which the following are relevant to the present chapter: Art 8.9 (right to regulate—investment); Annex 8-A (Expropriation); Art 23.3 (multilateral labour standards and agreements); Art 23.4 (upholding rights of protection—labour); Art 24.4 (multilateral environmental agreements); Art 24.5 (upholding rights of protection—environment); and

[53] Art 8.9.2 CETA. [54] Art 8.10.7 CETA.

[55] Art 3 of Annex 8-A CETA ('Expropriation'), defining further Art 8.12 ('Expropriation').

[56] CETA Joint Interpretative Instrument (n 14).

Art 28.3 (General Exceptions). It is difficult to see what this paragraph has to do with labour or environmental standards. But it may add some interpretative value to the provisions on investment, for example, on the meaning of a manifestly excessive non-discriminatory measure for the purposes of the prohibition on indirect expropriation.

V. Rights to Protect Labour and Environmental Standards and Human Rights

A final way in which CETA treats labour and environmental standards and human rights is by either establishing or recognizing an existing right to regulate to protect these values. This is done by means of exceptions and the inclusion of reference to the parties' right to regulate for public policy measures.

A. Exceptions

The first of these mechanisms establishes an express right to adopt measures for public policy reasons, including those at issue. CETA does this by incorporating by reference Art XX of the General Agreement on Tariffs and Trade (GATT) 1994 in relation to many (but not all) of its obligations relating to trade in goods.[57] It applies to traditional market access and discrimination obligations, as well as trade facilitation obligations, rules of origin procedures, specific bilateral agreements on alcohol that are incorporated into CETA, and obligations with regard to sanitary and phytosanitary measures.[58] It does not cover obligations in relation to trade remedies (unlike, probably, in the WTO), technical barriers to trade (other than sanitary and phytosanitary measures), subsidies, or regulatory cooperation. Interestingly, Art 28.3.1 also states that Art XX GATT applies to the establishment and non-discrimination obligations concerning investment in goods. This is novel. Article 28.3.2 contains another exception, this time based on Art XIV of the General Agreement on Trade in Services (GATS), and restricted to services, for obligations on cross-border services (except for those on mutual recognition of professional qualifications), as well as the establishment and non-discrimination investment obligations.

It is becoming increasingly clear, from recent WTO jurisprudence, that these provisions offer the parties great scope for regulating to protect human rights and the environment, both domestically and, depending on the measure at issue, also beyond the scope of their ordinary jurisdictional rights under international law. Article XX(a) GATT 1994 and Art 28.3.2(a) CETA (on services) permit the adoption of measures necessary to the protection of 'public morals'. In *EC—Seal*

[57] Art 28.3.1 CETA.

[58] ibid. It is odd that Art XX GATT 1994 should be incorporated in relation to sanitary and phytosanitary obligations, given that these obligations are themselves elaborations of that provision.

Products, Art XX(a) was held to cover animal welfare even in another country's territory;[59] so one could assume that this exception also covers human rights in all territories.[60] Moreover, the fact that the CETA parties have agreed to a human rights clause in the SPA means that it can be taken for granted that the parties' 'public morals' include the protection of human rights in each other's territories, as well as their own.

The measure must also be 'necessary' to protect public morals, which means first of all that it must be 'not incapable' of achieving this goal,[61] and beyond that there must be an assessment of whether an alternative measure can achieve the same objective in a less trade-restrictive manner. If there is any discrimination, that must also be justified as necessary, and this can (most likely) be for different reasons.[62]

The right to protect a party's own environment is permitted under Art XX(g) GATT, although, interestingly, there is no equivalent in the GATS. This provision permits measures 'relating to the conservation of exhaustible natural resources'. Article 28.3.1 adds that '[t]he Parties understand that Art XX(g) of the GATT 1994 applies to measures for the conservation of living and non-living exhaustible natural resources', essentially incorporating the ruling in *US—Shrimp*. This exception does not require that the adopted measure be 'necessary' to its environmental objective, although it does require that it be taken in conjunction with restrictions on domestic production or consumption, in order to make sure that the measure is genuine, and any discrimination needs to be justified separately.

There is an important question whether environmental concerns outside of the jurisdiction of the regulating party can be protected under this exception. The Appellate Body refused to say in *US—Shrimp*, while at the same time justifying that measure on the basis that the turtles being protected had a sufficient 'jurisdictional nexus' with the US because they were migratory and their species sometimes passed through US waters. This is an unsettled question.[63] However, the existence of environmental obligations in CETA may change the picture if these can be taken as permitting a party to regulate activities occurring in the territory of the other party.[64] In addition, it would appear from *US—Tuna II*, which involved labels designed to protect dolphins beyond US jurisdiction, that market-based measures, at least of this type, are exempt from this possible restriction.[65]

[59] WTO, Appellate Body Report, *EC—Seal Products* (18 June 2014) WT/DS400/AB/R, para 5.195.

[60] One might be tempted to refer to the human rights clause in the SPA in support of such an interpretation, given that. However, SPA (n 45) Art 28(8) specifies: 'This Agreement shall not affect or prejudice the interpretation or application of other agreements between the Parties.'

[61] WTO, Appellate Body Report, *Colombia—Textiles* (22 June 2016) WT/DS461/AB/R, para 5.89.

[62] The legal tests applicable to Arts XX GATT and XIV GATS are discussed in Lorand Bartels, 'The Chapeau of the General Exceptions in the WTO GATT 1994 and GATS Agreements: A Reconstruction' (2015) 109 *American Journal of International Law* 95.

[63] Erich Vranes, *Trade and the Environment: Fundamental Issues in International Law, WTO Law, and Legal Theory* (Oxford University Press, 2009) ch 1.

[64] For an argument to similar effect, see Lorand Bartels, 'Article XX of GATT and the Problem of Extraterritorial Jurisdiction: The Case of Trade Measures for the Protection of Human Rights' (2002) 36 *Journal of World Trade* 353.

[65] WTO, Appellate Body Report, *US—Tuna II* (13 June 2012) WT/DS381/AB/R.

The protection of the environment is also possible under Art XX(b) GATT and Art 28.3.2(b) CETA, which permits measures necessary to protect human, animal, or plant life or health. Indeed, CETA contains two parallel provisions stating that '[t]he Parties understand that the measures referred to in Art XX(b) of the GATT 1994 [the measures referred to in sub-paragraph (b)] include environmental measures necessary to protect human, animal or plant life or health'.[66] The obvious limitation to these provisions is the need to meet the stricter standard of 'necessity' for measures directed at environmental protection. This is, however, only an issue for measures involving services.

What is missing from these exceptions is any reference to the right to protect labour standards. Here, one needs to draw an important distinction. Core labour standards are also human rights, and to that extent would be covered by the exceptions on public morals. In other circumstances, other labour standards are unlikely to be covered. However, once again, the fact that CETA includes obligations in relation to labour standards that go beyond core labour standards is significant. As mentioned, CETA requires the parties to promote the objectives in the ILO Decent Work Agenda and the 2008 ILO Declaration on Social Justice for a Fair Globalization, and that could be taken as an indication that the parties agree that these values are part of their respective 'public morals'. Beyond this, however, the extent to which labour standards are seen as a matter of common values, and how much a matter of each party's comparative advantage, remains to be determined.

B. Right to regulate

In addition, and specifically in the context of certain of its investment obligations, CETA contains a 'reaffirmation' of a right to regulate, applicable to Section D ('Investment Protection') of Chapter 8 ('Investment'), which is concerned with the substantive investment protection obligations concerning fair and equitable treatment, full protection and security, and expropriation. Article 8.9.1 states that:

> For the purpose of this Chapter, the Parties reaffirm their right to regulate within their territories to achieve legitimate policy objectives, such as the protection of public health, safety, the environment or public morals, social or consumer protection or the promotion and protection of cultural diversity.

It is questionable whether this provision has any legal effect. By 'reaffirming' a right to regulate within their territories, by its own wording this paragraph is limited to rights that already exist for both parties.[67] It is weaker than formulations by which the parties 'recognize' a right to regulate, which might at least support an interpretation that the right exists because of the treaty. On the other hand, the

[66] Art 28.3.1 and fn 32 (on services) CETA.

[67] Catherine Titi, *The Right to Regulate in International Investment Law* (Nomos, 2014) discusses some of these provisions, with similar conclusions, at 106–15.

Interpretative Instrument, described above, could be seen as implicitly 'recognizing' such a right. But that also does not change anything.

VI. Conclusions

In relation to obligations directed at the protection of labour and environmental standards, as well as human rights, CETA represents a mixture of the familiar and the novel. Its substantive standards on labour and the environment are relatively typical, when seen against recent FTAs concluded by both parties. For the EU, the fact that these obligations are enforced only by means of an (at most) morally suasive report is also standard; for Canada, this represents somewhat of a regression. More interesting is what has been done with the human rights clause located in the EU–Canada SPA, insofar as this clause applies to CETA. This clause refers directly to the termination clause in CETA, meaning that it does precisely nothing. For Canada, at least in operative legal terms, this means that there has been no change to its treaty practice. For the EU, however, this represents such a watering down of its policy on human rights clauses that one can legitimately ask whether this agreement is in compliance with the EU's stated policy that all economic agreements must be subjected to an operative human rights clause. Finally, CETA also establishes certain rights to adopt measures to protect human rights and environmental standards, albeit not labour standards (except for those comprising human rights). Importantly, these rights apply for the first time to market access and non-discrimination investment obligations. Moreover, CETA contains certain provisions directed at the interpretation of substantive investment obligations, especially fair and equitable treatment and expropriation, which sets a new standard for these obligations.

10

TTIP, CETA, and TiSA Behind Closed Doors

Transparency in the EU Trade Policy

Panagiotis Delimatsis

I. Introduction

Amid increasing fears that the European integration is at peril in view of the result of the UK referendum to leave the EU; the most severe refugee crisis the European continent has seen in decades; and a protracted attempt by the Eurozone to stand on its feet, the expansion of the EU trade policy continues apace. The President of the European Commission, Jean-Claude Juncker, and his administration have prioritized the conclusion of comprehensive economic agreements with strategic partners, including Canada, the US, Japan, and China. These negotiations that showcase the dramatic change of global trade politics in the last ten years are currently conducted by the EU Commission on behalf of the EU. In recent times, a clear shift away from the World Trade Organization (WTO) as the predominant trade-negotiating forum has taken place. The fact that the recent WTO Ministerial Conference in Nairobi expressly recognized not only the centrality, but also the primacy, of the WTO system does not seem to affect these dynamics.[1]

Focusing on the future EU trade policy, the European Commission made clear what the EU agenda in the coming years would look like:[2] it will seek to become more effective and transparent, and will attempt to export the EU values to the rest of the world. These three elements constitute the three pillars of the revitalized EU trade policy. Effectiveness means that the EU trade policy will become more results-oriented, focusing on the facilitation of value chains, the inclusion of digital trade in prospective negotiations, and the easing of rules governing movement of high-skilled professionals.

The second pillar of the new EU trade policy focuses on transparency as an important component of an effort to increase the legitimacy of and confidence in

[1] See WTO, *Nairobi Ministerial Declaration* (adopted on 19 December 2015) WT/MIN(15)/DEC, 19.

[2] See European Commission Communication, 'Trade for all: Towards a More Responsible Trade and Investment Policy', COM (2015) 497 final, 19 October 2015.

TTIP, CETA, TiSA Behind Closed Doors: Transparency in the EU Trade Policy. Panagiotis Delimatsis.

the EU in dealing with important national interests of the EU Member States.[3] Transparency has been a recurring theme in trade negotiations and the EU institutions have been the recipients of numerous calls for increased access to documents previously regarded as confidential. In a significant policy turn towards more openness vis-à-vis civil society and the public in general (which, admittedly, was also the result of a more hands-on approach on the issue of access to confidential documents by the Court of Justice of the European Union (CJEU), the EU's highest court), the EU started publishing key negotiating texts shortly after they were discussed at the negotiating table with the EU's partners. This is in stark contrast with the policy adopted by the US administration, turning a deaf ear to the demands for more transparency in the negotiations for a Trans-Pacific Partnership (TPP) or in the Transatlantic Trade and Investment Partnership (TTIP) negotiations.[4]

The third pillar of the EU new approach in trade matters resides on the idea that EU values could be 'exported' through trade negotiations. In EU foreign policy, this has previously included the exportation of concepts relating to public services (so-called 'services of general interest') to the EU's partners in Eastern Europe, but also concepts relating to competition law. In its new trade-related strategy, the EU aspires to enrich this agenda with new concepts such as enhanced corporate social responsibility to ensure: a high level of protection for European consumers; increased legitimacy for investment arbitration systems used by the EU in its international agreements; or a more targeted system of autonomous preferences given to developing and least developed countries.

Against this backdrop, the present chapter chronicles the quest and turning moments relating to transparency during the negotiations conducted by the EU within the framework of the concluded Comprehensive Economic Trade Agreement (CETA) with Canada, the currently negotiated trade deals with the US (TTIP), and the Trade in Services Agreement (TiSA) at the plurilateral/WTO level. As is well known from the WTO realm, transparency in trade negotiations mainly relates to access to negotiating documents, position papers, and consolidated draft texts. The recent TTIP leaks by Greenpeace Netherlands dramatically exemplified just that.[5] As much of the discussion relating to transparency in negotiations revolves around the conditions under which public access to negotiating documents exchanged among the trading partners, this chapter focuses on the conditions, extent, and limits of such access to documents of or received by EU institutions acting in the broader area of negotiating and concluding trade agreements.

[3] cf Case C-615/13 P, *ClientEarth and PAN Europe v EFSA* [2015] ECLI:EU:C:2015:489, para 56.

[4] This same approach dominated on the EU side during the previous administration of the European Commission under the leadership of Trade Commissioner Karel de Gucht.

[5] See Arthur Neslen, 'Leaked TTIP Documents Cast Doubt on EU–US Trade Deal', *The Guardian* (1 May 2016), <https://www.theguardian.com/business/2016/may/01/leaked-ttip-documents-cast-doubt-on-eu-us-trade-deal> accessed 6 September 2016 (hereafter Neslen, 'Leaked TTIP Documents').

II. Transparency as a Principle of EU Law

Transparency in diplomatic negotiations and political discussions is an oxymoron. Rather, secrecy and informality traditionally reign trade negotiations at the bilateral, regional, and multilateral levels. Having said this, transparency ranks among the most essential *desiderata* in the grammar of contemporary global governance and has been regarded as positively related to legitimacy.[6] And yet, transparency is still an elusive concept, meaning different things to different people.[7] It comes as no surprise that, to date, transparency is not a universal principle: it matters for certain countries more than for others, depending on each country's constitutional tradition and legal culture. In international law, transparency is a rule which operates at the interstices of primary rules and which is doomed never to acquire the status of primary rule absent courts with compulsory jurisdiction that could take care of enforcing such obligation of unfettered flows of information.[8]

Transparency started becoming a pressing issue for the EU since its creation in Maastricht and the deepening of European integration, leading to a growing Europeanization of a broad array of policies. Together with 'more Europe', a reflection about the legitimacy and accountability of EU institutions, notably the Council and the Commission, quickly turned into a discussion about increased transparency of EU decision-making. At the time (and, for all practical purposes, this is still the case), more transparency was regarded as the most appropriate means to counterweigh the agency costs associated with the growing supranational institutions and the ensuing claims about the democratic deficit. Before that, for several decades, transparency did not belong among the general principles of EU law expressly set out in the EU treaties.

This process culminated in the adoption of the Lisbon Treaty, starting with Art 1 TEU, which links transparency to European integration and the concept of 'an ever closer Union among the peoples of Europe'.[9] The new Art 11 TEU also puts an emphasis on external transparency, that is, the necessary degree of openness of EU institutions vis-à-vis the EU citizens, their representative associations, and the civil society. One could even argue that, technically, the EU primary law still does not go as far as to fully and unconditionally endorse the principle of transparency. Rather, it wholeheartedly embraces the arguably less encompassing concept of

[6] See also Panagiotis Delimatsis, 'Transparency in the WTO's Decision-Making' (2014) 27(3) *Leiden Journal of International Law* 701 (hereafter Delimatsis, 'Transparency in the WTO').

[7] See Andrea Bianchi, 'On Power and Illusion: The Concept of Transparency in International Law' in Andrea Bianchi and Anne Peters (eds), *Transparency in International Law* (Cambridge University Press, 2013) 8 (hereafter Bianchi, 'On Power and Illusion').

[8] Vaughan Lowe, 'The Politics of Law-Making: Are the Method and Character of Norm Creation Changing?' in Michael Byers (ed), *The Role of Law in International Politics: Essays in Internatioal Relations and International Law* (Oxford University Press, 2000) 207.

[9] See also Art 10 TEU; and Cases C-39/05 P and C-52/05 P, *Sweden and Turco v Council* [2008] ECLI:EU:C:2008:374, para 34 (hereafter *Sweden and Turco v Council*).

openness. However, the CJEU has invariably regarded the aforementioned provisions as incorporating the principle of transparency.[10]

Other than the external transparency provisions in EU primary law, transparency is also a principle that permeates EU inter-institutional dealings. Internal transparency has been one of the main priorities of the new Juncker administration and has formed part of the broader discussion on better law-making and smart regulation. The better law-making inter-institutional agreement is the most recent initiative of an effort that started in the early 1990s to improve legislative performance.[11] It calls, inter alia, for public consultations for all acts and improved internal and external transparency across the legislative life cycle. Utmost transparency of the legislative process, along with consistency, simplicity, and clarity, become yardsticks for the activities of the three main EU institutions. With regard to the legislative process in particular, the three institutions are committed in respecting the principles of sincere cooperation, transparency, accountability, and efficiency.[12]

In the case of trade negotiations, Arts 218 and 207 of the Treaty on the Functioning of the European Union (TFEU) become relevant. Art 218:10 TFEU provides that, in the case of negotiation and conclusion of an international agreement, the European Parliament needs to be fully and regularly informed. This standalone obligation applies regardless of the field of action and the role foreseen by the TFEU for the European Parliament. Thus, even in Common Foreign and Security Policy (CFSP)-related agreements, the obligation to keep the Parliament informed applies.[13] An essentially similar obligation vis-à-vis the European Parliament is enshrined in Art 207:3 TFEU. Additionally, the recent better law-making inter-institutional agreement called the three institutions to ensure that each one of them can exercise its rights and fulfil its obligations under the treaties with regard to the negotiation and conclusion of international agreements.[14]

Calls for more external transparency in the EU dealings have been mainly articulated through the operationalization of Regulation 1049/2001. The adoption of the Regulation was the result of a process that started shortly before the adoption of the EU Treaty in Maastricht and Declaration No 17 on the right of access to information and was later enshrined in Art 255 EC Treaty, as amended by the Treaty of Amsterdam. The Regulation is the most important EU secondary

[10] See Joined Cases C-92/09 and C-93/09, *Volker und Markus Schecke GbR and Hartmut Eifert v Land Hessen* [2010] ECLI:EU:C:2010:662, para 68; also Case C-41/00 P, *Interporc v Commission* [2003] ECLI:EU:C:2003:125, para 39.

[11] See Inter-institutional agreement between the European Parliament, the Council of the European Union and the European Commission on Better Law-Making [2016] L123/1. The agreement entered into force on 12 April 2016.

[12] ibid, para 32.

[13] See Case C-263/14, *Parliament v Council* [2016] ECLI:EU:C:2016:435, para 68 (hereafter *Tanzania Agreement*). However, the Court clarified that, with respect to CFSP-only agreements, the information requirement does not extend to stages that are part of the internal preparatory process within the Council. Otherwise, the exclusion of the Parliament from the participation in the negotiation and conclusion of CFSP-related international agreement would be void of meaning. cf *Tanzania Agreement*, para 77.

[14] Inter-institutional agreement, para 40.

law instrument for our purposes, as it was meant to spell out that EC Treaty provision, giving meaning and further guidance as to how to balance the public and private interest with a view to enabling citizens to participate more closely in the decision-making process and guaranteeing that the EU institutions enjoy greater legitimacy and are more effective and accountable to the citizen in line with the democratic principles.[15]

In the case of the EU, transparency in its international activities relating to trade diplomacy is quintessential for constitutional reasons. Even if trade matters fall within the exclusive competence of the EU, the EU executive is bound by the TFEU to inform the European Parliament, the EU co-legislator, at regular intervals. The underlying rationale is that the Parliament must know early on what the EU negotiator (typically in trade matters, the European Commission) offers and receives in exchange at the negotiating table, as the final deal will be subject to the positive vote of the European Parliament.[16] Such early scrutiny is all the more important in negotiations for international agreements falling within the exclusive competence of the EU, as in that case the safety valve offered by the control by national Parliaments is absent.

The CJEU did not hesitate to give effect to the obligation for inter-institutional transparency and openness in favour of the European Parliament laid down in Art 218:10 TFEU.[17] In a case relating to the negotiation and conclusion of an EU agreement with Mauritius on the transfer of pirates and associated seized property,[18] the European Parliament requested the annulment of the relevant Council Decision[19] based on the fact alone that Art 218:10 was not adhered to. Even if the Court agreed that the imputed Decision fell within the scope of the CFSP, whereby an international agreement can be concluded without the consent of the Parliament, it underlined that the stand-alone procedural obligation of Art 218:10 cannot be put into question. Thus, it is incumbent upon the Council to make sure that this information requirement is met, as the Council is the dominant player under Art 218 TFEU: it authorizes the opening of negotiations, adopts negotiating directives, and authorizes the signing and conclusion of the international agreement at stake.

There is by now established case law confirming that the new Art 218 aims at simplifying and consolidating the initiation, negotiation, and conclusion of international agreements, and thus procedural obligations enshrined therein should be

[15] See also Case C-280/11 P, *Council v Access Info Europe* [2013] ECLI:EU:C:2013:671, para 32 (hereafter *Access Info Europe*).

[16] The decision by the European Parliament to vote against ratification of the ACTA in 2012 speaks volumes about its serious intentions regarding the conclusion of international—and one should add controversial—agreements by the EU.

[17] Art 218:10 TFEU provides: 'The European Parliament shall be immediately and fully informed at all stages of the procedure.'

[18] See Case C-658/11, *Parliament v Council* [2014] ECLI:EU:C:2014:2025 (hereafter *Mauritius Agreement*).

[19] Council Decision 2011/640/CFSP of 12 July 2011 on the signing and conclusion of the Agreement between the European Union and the Republic of Mauritius on the conditions of transfer of suspected pirates and associated seized property from the European Union-led naval force to the Republic of Mauritius and on the conditions of suspected pirates after transfer, [2011] OJ L 254/1.

respected absent any indication to the contrary or a special procedure established in another provision of the EU treaties.[20] In addition, para 10 of Art 218 TFEU has a special objective, that is, to ensure that the Parliament is able to perform its mission consisting of exercising democratic scrutiny of the EU's external action and, in particular, verifying that its powers were respected, notably as far as the choice of legal basis is concerned.[21] In addition, the information requirement serves the objectives of coherence and consistency, a central requirement for the EU external action under Art 21:3 TFEU.[22] In the Court's view, this information requirement is an expression of the democratic principle regarding representative democracy that constitutes the foundation of the EU.[23] Therefore, any violation of this essential procedural requirement can only lead to the nullity of the challenged measure.

Transparency in international negotiations is also important for broader political reasons: already at an early stage, transparency is important in order to address public reluctance and suspicion, and to engage with any opposition expressed regarding a particular trade deal. In this respect, in *Turco*, a seminal case relating to access to documents within the Council in the framework of a legislative procedure, the Court took a hands-on approach and readily dismissed the argument brought forward by the Council advocating a general need for confidentiality at the expense of transparency vis-à-vis the European citizens. On the contrary, the Court underscored the importance of transparency as a means not only of increasing the legitimacy of the Council's decision-making process, but also the confidence of the European citizens in the legislative process, as public access to the necessary information may allow for an open debate and the effective exercise of the democratic rights of the EU citizens.[24] The function of transparency as a confidence-building mechanism of which the EU institutions should be taking advantage in deciding when and what documents to disclose to the public was highlighted by subsequent case law.[25]

In addition, other than the straightforward obligation for this type of external transparency enshrined in Art 15 TFEU and the significance of adhering to the tenets of good governance, engaging with critical voices is vital for the successful conclusion of trade agreements, as due to their comprehensive character such agreements would be regarded as mixed agreements.[26] Mixity would then require ratification by the national parliaments. Thus, support by domestic constituents

[20] See, among others, *Mauritius Agreement* (n 18) paras 52 and 72.

[21] Indeed, as Art 218 TFEU clarifies, depending of the legal basis chosen by the Commission and/or the Council, the Parliament would need to give its consent, merely be consulted, or simply be informed.

[22] See *Tanzania Agreement* (n 13) para 72.

[23] See also Opinion of AG Kokott in ibid, para 79.

[24] See *Sweden and Turco v Council* (n 9) para 59; and *Access Info Europe* (n 15) para 33.

[25] See, more recently, Case C-615/13 P, *ClientEarth and PAN Europe v EFSA* [2015] ECLI:EU:C:2015:489, para 56.

[26] See Christophe Hillion, 'Mixity and Coherence in EU External Relations: The Significance of the "Duty of Cooperation"' in Christophe Hillion and Panos Koutrakos (eds), *Mixed Agreements Revisited: The European Union and Its Member States in the World* (Hart, 2010) 87.

would be crucial for the international agreement signed by the EU and its Member States to enter into force.

Regulation 1049/2001 establishes a general right to access to documents of the EU institutions. This right conferred on the public must be as wide as possible. In this respect, institutions must in principle ensure public access to the entire content of documents by the EU institutions. Such obligation may include, inter alia, the disclosure of the identity of those putting forward proposals in the decision-making process. Indeed, the Regulation underscores the importance of wider public access in all cases the EU institutions act in their legislative capacity, including under delegated powers. This type of document shall be made directly accessible if possible.[27] This obligation covers not only documents drawn up by the EU institutions, but also those received by them and in their possession, in all areas of the EU's activity.[28] In the specific case of trade negotiations, such obligation would cover (counter-) proposals submitted by the EU trading partners.[29] *Ratione personae*, any EU citizen and any natural person residing in the EU and any legal person having its registered office in an EU Member State can request access to documents of the EU institutions.[30] Thus, overall, the Regulation incorporates a presumption in favour of transparency and public access,[31] limiting the pervasive principle of full disclosure only in exceptional cases.

Such right, however, is not unqualified. Indeed, transparency is not an absolute requirement. According to Art 4 of the Regulation, refusal of access to a document can be allowed only in cases where disclosure could undermine the protection of one of the public (such as public security, military matters, or international relations) or private interests (such as protection of personal data, commercial interests of a natural or legal person, or court proceedings and legal advice) listed in that provision. The grounds of refusal are not mutually exclusive, meaning that the EU institution in question can take into account more than just one of the interests listed.[32] In addition, a Member State may request the EU institution at stake not to disclose a particular document originating in that Member State without its prior agreement.[33] The Court clarified early that such exceptions derogate from the

[27] See Regulation (EC) 1049/2001 regarding public access to European Parliament, Council and Commission documents [2001] OJ L 145/43, recital 6 (hereafter Regulation 1049/2001). However, Art 12 para 2 clarifies that legislative documents should be made directly accessible subject to the conditions of Arts 4 and 9.

[28] ibid, Art 2 para 3.

[29] However, such documents may be regarded as sensitive and thus fall under the scope of Art 9 of Regulation 1049/2001 (n 27). For the Art 9 protection to apply, documents should be clearly designated as sensitive (eg EU-restricted). The fact that certain documents, while sensitive, are not expressly designated as such does not prevent an EU institution from refusing access based on Art 4 alone. See Case C-399/13 P, *Stichting Corporate Europe Observatory* [2015] ECLI:EU:C:2015:360, paras 36–7.

[30] See also Art 43 of the EU Charter of Fundamental Rights.

[31] See also recital 11 of the Regulation 1049/2001 (n 27), which provides that: 'In principle, all documents of the institutions should be accessible to the public.'

[32] See Case C-404/10, *Commission v Editions Odile Jacob* [2012] ECLI:EU:C:2012:393, para 113.

[33] In the case of sensitive documents as per Art 9:3 of the Regulation 1049/2001 (n 27), they can be released only with the consent of the originator, be it an EU Member State or a third country ('originator control'). See also Case C-266/05 P, *Sison v Council* [2007] ECLI:EU:C:2007:75, para 75 (hereafter *Sison v Council*).

overarching principle of the widest possible public access to documents and thus are to be interpreted and applied strictly.[34]

Such strict interpretation does not mean that the EU institutions are bound in determining the effects of disclosure; on the contrary, the Court confirmed that, in respect of the public-interest exceptions of Art 4:1(a) of Regulation 1049/2001, the EU institutions enjoy a wide margin of appreciation when determining whether the protected interests at stake would be undermined by the disclosure of a particular document to the public. In such cases, and in the case of refusal of access to a given document, the General Court's review at first instance should be limited to verifying whether the procedural rules and the duty to state reasons have been respected, as well as whether the facts were accurately stated. Judicial review would need to assess whether a manifest error of assessment or a misuse of powers has taken place.[35]

Despite the limited review thereby suggested by the Court, based on a rigid textual interpretation of the wording of Art 4 and the fact that the exceptions are to be interpreted strictly, the Court emphasized that the EU institution still bears the burden of proof to explain how the disclosure of a particular document could *specifically* and *actually* undermine the interest protected by the Art 4 exception that it has invoked.[36] It is not sufficient that the document at stake merely concerns an interest protected by Art 4.[37] Only a reasonably foreseeable—rather than purely hypothetical—risk of the interest being undermined can trump the general obligation of transparency. According to the Court, when faced with the dilemma of disclosing or not, the EU institution at stake shall weigh the particular interest of Art 4 at issue to be protected through non-disclosure against the public interest of ensuring public access, taking into account the advantages of increased openness in a democratic system.[38]

However, the Court also suggested that a distinction is to be made between Art 4:1(a) relating to public-nature interests and Art 4:2, as in the former case refusal of access by the EU institution is *mandatory* if disclosure would undermine the interests protected by that provision.[39] It is only Art 4:2 that expressly calls for a balancing of the requirements connected to the protection of the interests listed therein against those which stem from other interests; this can lead to ensuring public access if there is an overriding public interest in disclosure.[40]

For instance, in *Turco*, where the protection of legal advice within the meaning of Art 4:2 was at stake, the Court suggested that a three-prong test is to be applied. First, the EU institution at issue must satisfy itself that the requested document

[34] ibid, para 63. [35] ibid, para 64.

[36] See Case C-350/12 P, *Council v in 't Veld* [2014] ECLI:EU:C:2014:2039, paras 63–4 (hereafter Case C-350/12 P, *Council v in 't Veld*).

[37] ibid, para 51.

[38] See *Access Info Europe* (n 15) para 32. For the specific application of this criterion to the case of legal advice given to EU institutions, see *Sweden and Turco v Council* (n 9) para 96.

[39] See also Case T-331/11, *Besselink v Council* [2013] ECLI:EU:T:2013:419, para 44 (hereafter *Besselink v Council*).

[40] See *Sison v Council* (n 33) para 46.

indeed relates to legal advice. Second, it must ensure that disclosure of the document or parts thereof which are identified as relating to legal advice threatens that institution's interest in seeking and receiving frank, objective, and comprehensive legal advice. Third, the institution should ascertain that despite this potential threat to reliable advice, there is an overriding public interest justifying disclosure notably regarding public participation, openness, legitimacy, and accountability in a democratic system.[41] In this respect, the party requesting access bears the burden of referring to specific circumstances to establish an overriding public interest justifying the disclosure of the document at stake.[42] The Court clarified recently that generally referring to the principles of transparency and democracy as empowering citizens to be informed and participate in the decision-making process would not meet the required standard, as this would not raise issues of particularly pressing concern which could have prevailed over the reasons justifying the refusal to disclose.[43] Ultimately, the Court (the General Court in first instance) will be obliged to order the production of the document at stake and examine it with a view to assessing whether access to the document could validly be refused by the EU institution at issue on the basis of the exception invoked and thus pronouncing on the lawfulness of the decision refusing access to the document at stake.[44]

Disclosure of preparatory documents of EU's trade negotiations would most likely be discussed as a potential threat to international relations. Recently, in *in 't Veld*, a seminal case in the area of transparency in the negotiation and conclusion by the EU of international agreements, the CJEU was called on appeal to decide whether documents that concern the legal basis for the conclusion of an international agreement by the EU (*in casu*, legal advice by the Council's Legal Service regarding a prospective agreement with the US making available to the US Treasury financial messaging data) can specifically and actually undermine international relations if they are made public.

In that case, the Council argued that such documents should not be disclosed. If made public, internal differences of opinion among EU institutions as to the correct legal basis to be used can be exploited by the EU negotiating partners; they can diminish the EU's credibility and effectiveness in international negotiations; and may adversely affect the EU's ability to successfully conclude an international agreement. The CJEU, just like the General Court before it, was not convinced by the arguments put forward by the Council, as it underscored the Council's failure to meet the 'specific and actual harm' standard in this particular case, although,

[41] *Sweden and Turco v Council* (n 9) paras 38–44. In *in 't Veld*, the Court clarified that this three-prong test is important and relevant not only when the institution (the Council in this case) acts in its legislative capacity, but in all areas of EU activity. See Case C-350/12 P, *Council v in 't Veld* (n 36) para 107.

[42] See Case C-612/13 P, *ClientEarth v Commission* [2015] ECLI:EU:C:2015:486, para 90.

[43] ibid, para 93.

[44] See Arts 65(b), 66:1, and 67:3 of the General Court's Rules of Procedure; also Case C-576/12 P, *Jurašinović* [2013] ECLI:EU:C:2013:777, para 27. For an application of this, see Case T-301/10, *in 't Veld v Commission* [2013] ECLI:EU:T:2013:135, paras 169ff (hereafter Case T-301/10, *in 't Veld v Commission*).

crucially, the Court confirmed that in principle the review in this case is minimal due to the wide margin of discretion enjoyed by the EU institutions. Again, the analysis of the Court clarifies that such margin of appreciation cannot lead to arbitrariness in the activities of EU institutions when the disclosure of particular documents is requested; rather, a procedure in line with good governance principles is to be followed.

In 't Veld is a landmark case in the area of external and internal transparency in the EU and the EU constitutional and external relations law, more generally. It is no coincidence that the European Commission backed the Council's arguments, while the European Parliament supported Ms in 't Veld, herself a Member of the European Parliament. Thus, the main EU institutions were divided as to the interpretation of Regulation 1049/2001 and the limits of transparency when international relations are at stake. Both the General Court and the CJEU had something to give to satisfy both sides: they both agreed with Ms in 't Veld that the Council should have provided access to certain parts of the document at stake. According to both courts, the disclosure of positions taken within institutions with regard to the appropriate choice of legal basis (an issue of constitutional significance, according to settled EU case law) cannot in principle constitute a threat to international relations within the meaning of Art 4:1(a) third indent of Regulation 1049/2001.

In addition, in this particular case, the fact that the document at issue (or a significant part thereof) was already available in the public domain through instruments of other EU institutions (in this case, a European Parliament Resolution) weighed in favour of disclosing the document. Crucially, for the purposes of the present chapter, the CJEU did not seem to be affected in its decision by the fact that the European Parliament had unlawfully, in the Council's view, disclosed this document. The Court ruled that the General Court at first instance was correct, when determining whether disclosure constituted a risk of a threat to international relations (or to any other interest mentioned in Art 4), to take into account the fact that the main content of the document at stake was already made public through the Parliament's resolution. In view of the recent TTIP leaks by Greenpeace Netherlands, it seems plausible to assume that the interpretation by the Court as to whether the official disclosure of already leaked documents would not be any different.

On the other hand, both courts clarified the contours of transparency in that they agreed that access can be refused for documents that relate to the specific content of international agreements (this would arguably include draft text and proposals by the EU) and the negotiating directives (prepared by the Council) which relate to the strategic objectives pursued by the EU in the negotiations with a third country.[45] This is all the more so if the negotiating positions of the other party or parties remain secret.[46]

[45] See Case T-529/09, *in 't Veld v Council* [2012] ECLI:EU:T:2012:215, para 39; and Case C-350/12 P, *Council v in 't Veld* (n 36) para 58.

[46] See Case T-301/10, *in 't Veld v Commission* (n 44) para 125.

According to settled case law, as the initiation and conduct of negotiations in order to conclude an international agreement fall within the domain of the EU executive, public participation in the negotiation and conclusion of an international agreement is necessarily restricted due to the legitimate interest in non-disclosure of strategic elements of the negotiations.[47] Disclosure in that case may undermine the EU's negotiating capacity and jeopardize the climate of confidence between the parties participating directly or indirectly in those negotiations.[48]

As the General Court recently noted, the mere consideration that knowledge of the negotiating directives may be exploited by the other negotiating parties suffices to establish a risk that the EU interest regarding international relations may be undermined.[49] The General Court highlighted that, with a view to ensuring the effectiveness of a given negotiation, a certain level of discretion in the negotiation of international agreements can be justified to allow the building of mutual trust and the development of a free and effective discussion among negotiators. Indeed, a climate of mutual trust is necessary for successful cooperation.[50] Such a need for confidentiality would also apply to documents which have already been communicated to the EU's trading partners. The fact that such documents were communicated to the other party to the negotiation does not mean that public access should be granted, as disclosure could indeed jeopardize the EU's interests as regards international relations.[51]

In *in 't Veld v Commission*, the General Court implied that even non-disclosure of such documents (in this case, various documents relating to the negotiations for an Anti-Counterfeiting Trade Agreement—ACTA) for a certain period after the conclusion of the negotiations could under certain circumstances be justified. Nor did the fact that a draft consolidated ACTA text was made public on the initiative of the negotiating partners justify the disclosure of all documents revealing the positions of the parties, as that text was only a draft agreement and negotiations continued at the time of disclosure.[52]

This confirms that there is a legitimate interest in the non-disclosure of strategic elements of the negotiations, leaving it for the EU institution at stake, perhaps in coordination with the other parties to the negotiations, to decide whether, despite this legitimate interest, it would still be willing to make public certain documents or parts thereof. Finally, it bears mention that neither the General Court nor the CJEU excluded the possibility that a refusal to grant public access is justified in the case of documents which, if disclosed, reveal a difference of opinion between EU institutions as to matters relating to the *substance* of the agreement (rather than the choice of legal basis, which rests on objective factors and thus does *not* fall within

[47] ibid, para 120. Interestingly, the Court deviated here from Turco, where public participation was more relevant, because the legislative procedure was at stake. However, in the case of a predominant element in favour of the EU executive, the obligation under Art 218:10 TFEU remains applicable.

[48] cf *Besselink v Council* (n 39) para 59.

[49] ibid, para 71.

[50] See Case T-301/10, *in 't Veld v Commission* (n 44) para 119.

[51] ibid, para 123.

[52] ibid, para 127.

the discretion of any EU institution) and therefore may be liable to damage the EU's interests in the field of external relations.[53]

The EU institutions may also decide to grant partial access to a document provided that the aim pursued by the institution could be achieved if the passages which might harm the public interest to be protected were merely struck.[54] In *Besselink*, for instance, the General Court examined the nature and specific content of the Council's draft negotiating directives relating to the EU accession to the European Convention of Human Rights (ECHR) to find that the Council should have granted partial access to those passages of the directives which referred to the principles governing such negotiations, certain questions to be addressed in the negotiations (without answering them), and certain objectives that are already known, such as the non-interference with the competences of the EU and the powers of its institutions.[55] The restricted nature of the partial access granted should be assessed in accordance with the principle of proportionality. And again, whether the protected interest falls under Art 4:1 rather than Art 4:2 may tilt in favour of non-disclosure.

III. CETA, TTIP, and TiSA: EU Trade Negotiations in Full Swing

A. Transparency in negotiating CETA

The EU negotiations for a Comprehensive Economic and Trade Agreement (CETA) with Canada started in May 2009 and were finalized in September 2014 on the occasion of the EU–Canada Summit. Thus, the negotiating Directives were adopted by the Council and CETA negotiations started before the entry into force of the Treaty of Lisbon, which extended the European Parliament's competences in the field of EU trade policy. CETA was the first comprehensive agreement signed by the EU with a highly industrialized Western economy and the first with another G8 country. The EU is Canada's second most important trading partner and investor, after the US. Plans for a comprehensive agreement between the two parties started as early as in 2002.[56]

It bears mentioning that trade-related negotiated mandates are typically based on a proposal ('recommendations') submitted by the Commission, which has the power to initiate EU action in a given area after assessing whether the conclusion of a given international agreement is in the EU's interest.[57] In the case of exclusive

[53] See in this respect also Opinion of AG Sharpston in Case C-350/12 P, *Council v in 't Veld* (n 36).

[54] See Case C-353/99 P, *Council v Hautala* [2001] ECLI:EU:C:2001:661, paras 27–9.

[55] See *Besselink v Council* (n 39) paras 58–60 and 91.

[56] See 'EU–Canada: Commission Agrees Design of Future EU–Canada Trade and Investment Enhancement Agreement' (3 March 2004), <http://trade.ec.europa.eu/doclib/docs/2004/march/tradoc_116065.pdf> accessed 6 April 2017.

[57] cf Opinion of AG Wathelet in Case C-425/13, *European Commission v Council of the European Union* [2015] ECLI:EU:C:2015:174, para 69.

competence like in trade matters, the Commission is not only the initiator, but also the sole negotiator. Thus, at these first stages of the process, the institutional balance tilts in favour of the Commission.

The CETA 2009 negotiating directives,[58] as amended in 2011 to allow talks on investment protection and the introduction of an Investor-State Dispute Settlement (ISDS) system,[59] were made public in mid December 2015, that is, more than a year after the draft agreement between the two parties to the agreement was agreed upon. The European Parliament's Committee on International Trade (INTA) received the basic text of the agreement, classified as confidential, a few weeks before the conclusion of the agreement in September 2014 in Ottawa.

When it comes to transparency in the EU–Canada negotiations internally (among EU institutions) as well as externally (vis-à-vis the public), CETA has been one of the least transparent agreements negotiated in recent years by the EU. This finding dramatically contradicts the importance of the trade relationship in terms of trade and investment volumes, sheer size, and substantive rule-making. The European Commission held relatively few meetings on the occasion of the sustainability impact assessment (SIA) prepared externally on behalf of the Commission.[60] Previously, the Commission launched a web-based civil society consultation in February and March 2008 based on a questionnaire.[61] It appears that, at the beginning, European civil society's interest in CETA was everything but strong. Rather, the European ban on seal products and the feed-in tariff system in Ontario drew public attention, along with the continued suspension of concessions in the aftermath of the hormones-related dispute.

In addition, initially, the EU's entire focus was on government procurement at the sub-federal level and the discussions on intellectual property. On the Canadian side, it appears that transparency-related initiatives have been much more streamlined and fully implemented upfront, as negotiations advanced.[62] The Canadian Government has even argued that CETA negotiations are the most transparent and inclusive in Canada's history.[63] In the EU, on the other hand, such checks are typically made much later at the national level, when the final text is up for ratification by the national parliaments of each EU Member State.

[58] See EU Council Doc 9036/09 EXT 2, 24 April 2009, made public on 15 December 2015.

[59] See EU Council Doc 12838/11 EXT 2, 14 July 2011, made public on 15 December 2015.

[60] For instance, see the minutes of the civil society meeting on the occasion of the Trade SIA: 'Civil Society Meeting: Trade SIA for the EU-Canada Comprehensive Economic and Trade Agreement (CETA)' (30 March 2011), <http://trade.ec.europa.eu/doclib/docs/2011/may/tradoc_147908.pdf> accessed 6 April 2017.

[61] See 'Questionnaire on a Comprehensive Economic Agreement with Canada' (7 May 2009), <http://trade.ec.europa.eu/doclib/docs/2009/may/tradoc_143107.pdf> accessed 25 August 2016.

[62] See Report of the Standing Committee on International Trade, 'Negotiations Toward a Comprehensive Economic and Trade Agreement (CETA) between Canada and the European Union' (41st Parliament, 1st Session, March 2012), <http://www.parl.gc.ca/HousePublications/Publication.aspx?DocId=5431905&File=0> accessed 6 April 2017.

[63] See Government Response—First Report of the Standing Committee on International Trade, 'Negotiations Toward a Comprehensive Economic and Trade Agreement (CETA) Between Canada and the European Union', <http://www.parl.gc.ca/HousePublications/Publication.aspx?DocId=5692254&File=0> accessed 6 April 2017.

As to public consultations relating to the ISDS system, which has been by far the most controversial aspect in both the CETA and TTIP negotiations, the European Commission organized a single, online public consultation on investment protection and ISDS clauses, which consisted of twelve questions and a general assessment of the issues at stake to the general public.[64] That consultation, however, was mostly targeted to the TTIP rather than CETA. Still, about half of the 150,000 replies received also commented on the ISDS system of CETA.[65] More crucially, the announcement of the end of the negotiations in 2014 virtually coincided with the end of the ISDS public consultation, leaving no time for a proper analysis of the comments received and, more broadly, a reflection on the necessity and utility of an ISDS system in CETA, as a separate trade agreement from TTIP.[66] As it happened, the EU confounded the necessary debate regarding the specificities, advantages, and disadvantages of including an ISDS system in a trade agreement with a third country. One would rather expect separate, targeted consultations for each of the two very significant trade agreements which the EU aspires to conclude in the very near future.

Only to cause additional headaches to the negotiators on both sides of the Atlantic, CETA negotiations suffered as a result of numerous, regular leaks in the media, with the biggest backlash caused in August 2014, when the German media outlet ARD released one-third of the CETA consolidated text ahead of the official end of the negotiations in September and only one week after negotiators reached a mutual agreement. The Canadian side in particular did not hide its irritation regarding the numerous regular leaks on the EU side, which put in jeopardy the negotiations and fueled the mounted criticism against CETA internally.

Indeed, many regarded as unfortunate the fact that the text was made public at the time that the EU and Canada decided to share the text with the EU Member States and the Canadian provinces, respectively. It also revealed, in the case of Canada, that while consultations with provinces and territories were quite satisfactory (a necessary condition to meet the EU's persistent demand to open access to procurement markets at the sub-federal level in Canada), some Canadian governmental departments were not kept abreast of the negotiations and the overall evolution of the negotiated text. It seems that a continuous criticism of the Canadian Government in both CETA and TPP negotiations has been that governmental departments were often unaware of the status of the trade negotiations.[67] On the

[64] Consultation mechanisms do not necessarily and under all circumstances act as a substitute for the political process. Their effects are particularly doubtful in case of issues that are new to the negotiating agenda and by implication the civil society and the public. See also Robert Wolfe, 'Transparency and Public Participation in the Canadian Trade Policy Process' in Mark Halle and Robert Wolfe (eds), *Process Matters: Sustainable Development and Domestic Trade Transparency* (International Institute for Sustainable Development, 2007) 21.

[65] See Wilhelm Schöllmann and Massimo Sibona, 'EU–Canada Comprehensive Economic and Trade Agreement', European Parliament, Briefing PE 573.929, January 2016, 5.

[66] See Elfriede Bierbrauer, 'Negotiations on the EU–Canada Comprehensive Economic and Trade Agreement (CETA) Concluded', European Parliament's Policy Note, PE 536.410, October 2014, 13.

[67] Michael Geist, 'Industry Canada to Foreign Affairs after CETA Leaks: Can We Get a Copy of the Text?' (7 June 2016), <http://www.michaelgeist.ca/2016/06/industry-canada-to-foreign-affairs-after-ceta-leaks-can-we-get-a-copy-of-the-text/> accessed 6 April 2017.

EU side, the Commission has greatly intensified its efforts to justify the need for a successful conclusion of CETA and the ensuing benefits only after a significant portion of the text was leaked.

Being a novelty in the EU trade agreements, the ISDS has been at the epicentre of criticism from both sides, notably by non-governmental organizations (NGOs), environmental groups, and consumer groups.[68] The Commission attempted to address this critique by underscoring the gains of the trade deal and the safety valves relating to the right to regulate, as well as with regard to the protection of the environment, safety, and health incorporated in the draft text. The fact remains that the bulk of the CETA provisions on dispute settlement, including the new two-instance mechanism for investment disputes between the parties and the joint support for a multilateral investment court, were made public with the publication of the draft agreement in the second half of 2014 and subsequently during the 'legal scrubbing' process.

This lack of proper communication and openness did not go unnoticed. For example, early on, in its resolution of June 2011 relating to the EU–Canada trade relations, the European Parliament expressed its discontent with the Commission's decision to seek the modification of the CETA negotiating mandate to authorize negotiations on investment-related issues without first waiting for the Parliament to express its view on the EU investment policy in the aftermath of the Lisbon Treaty.[69]

The source of this discomfort seems to have been the Parliament's approach vis-à-vis the normative shape of the new EU exclusive competence on investment, focusing more on the protection of the right to regulate and the avoidance of frivolous claims by investors while securing comprehensive investment protection for investors, also through ISDS provisions. The Parliament, while expressing its opposition to an ISDS system in the case of two trading partners with highly developed legal systems such as Canada and the EU, suggested that the right to regulate in sensitive policy areas such as the environment should not be hampered by any means.[70]

Furthermore, the Parliament also reminded the Commission and the Council (in a quite tactless way, one must say) that, in the end of the process, CETA cannot enter into force without the Parliament's consent. In addition, it referred to the obligation enshrined in Art 218:10 TFEU and invited the two other institutions to share all information in the stages of the procedure, keep the Parliament involved, and take its views fully into account. More recently, the Parliament appears to be happy with the final modifications and the compromise reflected in the CETA investment chapter. In any case, as regards CETA in particular, the control that the Parliament will exercise is an ex post one, in the framework of the discussions

[68] See Wanda Troszczynska-Van Genderen, 'Stakeholder, Parliamentary and Third Country Concerns about the EU–Canada Comprehensive Trade and Economic Agreement (CETA)', European Parliament, PE 536.428, December 2014, 6.

[69] As expressed in the Commission Communication, 'Towards a Comprehensive European International Investment Policy', COM (2010) 343 final, 7 July 2010.

[70] See European Parliament resolution of 8 June 2011 on EU–Canada trade relations, P7-TA(2011)0257, para 11; and European Parliament resolution of 6 April 2011 on the European international investment policy, P7-TA-2011-141.

leading to giving its consent or rejecting the trade agreement pursuant to Art 218:6(a)(v) TFEU.

The draft agreement has been on a 'legal scrubbing' stage for over a year, during which the EU managed to convince Canada to incorporate the EU's approach to ISDS, as it had already proposed in the TTIP negotiations and following the example of the ISDS contained in the EU–Vietnam free trade agreement (FTA). As noted earlier, the EU's approach incorporates a two-instance investment court and various procedural novelties that attempt to balance the public and private interests that are at stake in any investment dispute. The Commission made public the final draft text of CETA in February 2016.

A period of legal revision for internal inconsistencies in the text, but also broader reflection and uncertainty as to the correct attribution of competences, followed. Whereas the Commission was of the view that CETA is an agreement that now falls under the EU exclusive competence, Member States, and Germany in particular, did not appreciate the Commission's stance. They rather interpreted this as the Commission's effort to bypass national parliaments. The fact that the CJEU had not yet rendered its opinion as to whether the trade agreement between EU and Singapore falls under the EU exclusive competence (a case considered as a yardstick for the attribution of competences in the case of trade agreements *post*-Lisbon) added to the prevailing uncertainty.[71]

In July 2016, the Commission buckled under the pressure of the Council by formally proposing to the Council to sign and conclude the CETA as a mixed agreement.[72] As typically happens, the Council will most likely decide to apply CETA provisionally.[73] The agreement will formally enter into force after obtaining the consent of the European Parliament and ratification by the national Parliaments of the EU Member States. While this may mean that the agreement will formally enter into force later than expected, politically, ratification by the national parliaments, if successful, will give greater legitimacy to the agreement and allow for a substantive debate and sufficient control (if only belated) on the gains of concluding CETA.

[71] The European Commission requested an opinion on the extent and nature of the EU competence to conclude the EU–Singapore FTA in July 2015 based on Art 218 para 11 TFEU (Opinion 2/15). In her opinion, AG Sharpston was of the view that, despite the ever-increasing competences of the EU, the EU–Singapore FTA should still be considered as a mixed agreement. See AG Sharpston's Opinion in Opinion procedure 2/15, ECLI:EU:C:2016:992, delivered on 21 December 2016. The CJEU found that the EU exclusive competence in trade matters is extensive but still fails to cover issues such as portfolio investment or investor-State dispute settlement included in the FTA. See CJEU Opinion 2/15 of 16 May 2017.

[72] See European Commission, Proposal for a Council Decision on the signing on behalf of the European Union of the Comprehensive Economic and Trade Agreement between Canada of the one part, and the European Union and its Member States, of the other part, COM (2016) 444 final, 5 July 2016, 4.

[73] As an indication of growing recent opposition to CETA, the German Constitutional Court received a lawsuit of NGOs asking it to block the provisional application of CETA. See Chris Cottrell, 'NGOs Launch Massive Lawsuit against EU–Canada Trade Deal', *Deutsche Welle* (31 August 2016), <http://www.dw.com/en/ngos-launch-massive-lawsuit-against-eu-canada-trade-deal/a-19515611> accessed 6 April 2017. The German Constitutional Court, however, rejected the claim. See BVerfG, Decision of the second Chamber of 7 December 2016, 2 BvR 1444/16.

B. Transparency in negotiating TTIP

For the EU, TTIP is the most ambitious and strategic trade agreement ever undertaken. If successful, these negotiations will certainly shape multilateral trade rules in the not-so-distant future, but will also determine the future pace of trade liberalization, more broadly. Seen from this angle, both the EU and the US have an interest in a comprehensive and ambitious bilateral trade and investment agreement connecting the two most advanced economies in the world. Upgrading the cooperation with the US on all fronts is also the unequivocal message conveyed by the European leaders.[74]

Contrary to CETA, TTIP has been in the limelight almost since the beginning of the announcement that transatlantic negotiations would start. The most recent leaks of several draft chapters of the prospective deal by Greenpeace Netherlands did not help to dispel the growing public opposition.[75] Other than the suspicion with which it is viewed by the proponents of multilateralism in trade matters, TTIP is, legally speaking, an interesting legal construct under the EU external relations law lens. To be sure, it is not the first FTA negotiated by the EU, nor is it the first FTA that the EU will conclude after the entry into force of the Treaty of Lisbon. CETA will most likely enter into force sooner than TTIP.

The EU–Korea FTA, the EU's first FTA with an Asian country, was also concluded recently.[76] This agreement was concluded as a mixed agreement, as it included matters falling under the competence of EU Member States (eg culture-related matters). In the case of the Korea FTA, though, the Council had decided to apply the FTA provisionally as of July 2011.[77] This is the first agreement of what the Commission calls the new generation of EU FTAs. However, both the Korea FTA and CETA were concluded based on respective mandates that were addressed to the European Commission *prior* to entry into force of the Lisbon Treaty, with much confusion surrounding the normative character of the changes brought about by the then forthcoming introduction of the new Lisbon Treaty rules.[78]

However, the TTIP mandate was approved by the EU Council in 2013.[79] Thus, all related decisions and acts were adopted after the entry into force of the Lisbon Treaty. Another, less mediatized agreement also has similar characteristics—the

[74] European Council Conclusions of 16 September 2010, EUCO 21/1/10, 12 October 2010, para 7b.

[75] See Neslen, 'Leaked TTIP Documents' (n 5).

[76] Being a mixed agreement, it was first ratified by all national parliaments of EU Member States. See Council of the European Union, 'EU–South Korea Free Trade Agreement Concluded', press release (1 October 2015), <http://www.consilium.europa.eu/en/press/press-releases/2015/10/01-korea-free-trade/> accessed 6 April 2017.

[77] See Council Decision of 16 September 2010 on the signing, on behalf of the European Union, and provisional application of the Free Trade Agreement between the European Union and its Member States, of the one part, and the Republic of Korea, of the other part [2011] OJ L 127/1.

[78] As noted earlier, this has also led to the modification of the CETA negotiating directives in 2011.

[79] Council of the European Union, 'Press Release—3245th Council meeting', 10862/13, 14 June 2013. The document was declassified in October 2014: see Council Directives for the negotiation on the Transatlantic Trade and Investment Partnership between the European Union and the United States of America, ST 11103/13, 17 June 2013.

FTA with Singapore, negotiations for which were finalized in October 2014, absent political will to conclude a broader agreement with all Association of Southeast Asian Nations (ASEAN) countries. Nevertheless, the FTA with Singapore is not as prominent as TTIP in terms of trade flows: Singapore is the EU's 17th trading partner (although the EU's most important ASEAN partner).

Again, as noted earlier, the FTA with Singapore is of high constitutional significance for the evolution of EU external relations law, as the European Commission decided to go a step further and claim exclusive competence for the conclusion of this agreement based on the new Art 207 TFEU. This provision appears to suggest that common commercial policy (CCP), including investment, is an exclusive EU competence (albeit with varying decision-making procedures: qualified majority combined with unanimity when liberalization of audiovisual or public services is at stake).

The US is the EU's number one trading partner, representing over 15 per cent of extra-EU trade flows. For the US, the EU, taken together, is the second most important trading partner, after Canada. Thus, already in terms of sheer trade size, TTIP is at the epicentre of public debate regarding trade and regulatory matters on both sides of the Atlantic. In the US, a recurring discussion about the benefits of the North American Free Trade Agreement and TPP instigates suspicion against mega-regionals of this type.

In the EU, on the other hand, the debate about TTIP is even more heated due to the trauma caused by the *EC Hormones* saga, but also due to the EU-peculiar concept of public services, which some see being put in jeopardy if a trade agreement with the US is to occur. In addition, statistics show that, even in times of crisis, the EU has had a steadily positive trade balance with the US over the last decade, making the case for further integration a 'tough sell' for EU citizens anxious about their standards of living and the future of their welfare state so badly hit by the recent Great Recession that followed the global financial crisis.[80]

The negotiating directives addressed to the EU negotiator, that is, the Commission, were adopted by the Council unanimously in June 2013 pursuant to Art 207:4 TFEU.[81] However, already at the end of May, the negotiating mandate was leaked.[82] As the TTIP negotiations started drawing public attention, voices for declassifying the negotiating mandate have also increased, including from within the Commission. Nevertheless, this was not sufficient to convince the Council of the necessity of making public the mandate. Thus, requests for access to the negotiating mandate were initially rejected by the Commission.[83] For instance, a request

[80] See, for instance, Eurostat, 'US EU International Trade and Investment Statistics', Statistics in focus 2/2015, 11 September 2015.

[81] See Council of the European Union, 'Directives for the Negotiation on the Transatlantic Trade and Investment Partnership between the European Union and the United States of America', ST 11103/13 EU RESTRICTED, 17 June 2013 (declassified on 9 October 2014).

[82] See Markus Beckedahl, 'Leak: Aktueller Entwurf des Verhandlungsmandates zum EU-USA-Freihandelsabkommen' (30 May 2013), <https://netzpolitik.org/2013/leak-aktueller-entwurf-des-verhandlungsmandates-zum-eu-usa-freihandelsabkommen/> accessed 6 April 2017.

[83] However, the Commission did grant access to other TTIP-related documents. In the period January 2013–January 2015, the Commission replied to thirty TTIP-related requests for access

submitted on 17 February 2014 by Friends of the Earth Europe, the European Federation of Journalists, the European Environmental Bureau, ClientEarth, and Corporate Europe Observatory seeking access to TTIP-related documents, including the negotiating mandate, was dismissed.[84] Such a negative stance was also supported by the EU judiciary, as noted above, notably as far as the negotiating mandate was concerned.

Thus, the broader issue of external transparency remained, as public opinion has been worried by the magnitude and ambition of the two trading partners. The discussion on ISDS obviously accentuated those concerns. On the other hand, the fact that some TTIP documents such as the initial negotiating proposals by the Commission were already available did not seem to reassure certain groups. However, unfortunately, the fact that the Commission published as early as in July 2013 and then in May 2014, already under the Barroso administration, a range of initial EU negotiating position documents passed without major praise.[85] However, the Commission did not make public actual draft legal texts proposed by the Commission, exactly as promised in the letter by Bercero, the Chief EU negotiator for TTIP in July 2013, which suggested that such documents would be held in confidence.[86] However, these tentative traces of minimum transparency seem to suggest that early on the Commission did try to use transparency strategically, for both internal and external purposes.

The NGOs whose request was dismissed sought the help of the European Ombudsman who investigates complaints about maladministration by EU institutions. The Ombudsman, also triggered by other complaints of the same type, opened an inquiry in July 2014, addressing a letter to the Council and explaining why, in her view, a proactive approach to transparency (including the proactive disclosure of documents such as the negotiating mandate at stake) can enhance the legitimacy of the negotiating process. The Ombudsman also drew the Council's attention to the fact that the allegedly confidential document seemed to be easily available on the Internet.[87] Ultimately, the Council decided to adopt the proposed

to documents, giving (full or partial) access to 520 out of 807 documents assessed. See Decision of 6 January 2015 of the European Ombudsman closing her own-initiative inquiry OI/10/2014/RA concerning the European Commission, point 25 (hereafter Ombudsman Decision of 6 January 2015).

[84] See European Commission, 'Decision of the Secretary General on Behalf of the Commission Pursuant to Art 4 of the Implementing Rules to Regulation (EC) No 1049/2001' (SG.B.4/MF/mbp-sg.dsg2.b.4(2014)2378490) (9 July 2014), <http://www.foeeurope.org/sites/default/files/reply2-dg-trade-090714.pdf> accessed 6 April 2017. The request was submitted by Friends of the Earth Europe, the European Federation of Journalists, the European Environmental Bureau, ClientEarth, and Corporate Europe Observatory. In November 2015, the Ombudsman found that there was no maladministration on the side of the Commission in view of the new transparency initiative regarding TTIP negotiations adopted by the Commission.

[85] See European Commission, 'EU Publishes Initial TTIP Position Papers' (16 July 2013), <http://trade.ec.europa.eu/doclib/press/index.cfm?id=943> accessed 6 April 2017.

[86] See Ignacio Garcia Bercero's letter to L Daniel Mullaney, the Chief US Negotiator for TTIP, 'Subject: Arrangements on TTIP Negotiating Documents' (5 July 2013), <http://trade.ec.europa.eu/doclib/docs/2013/july/tradoc_151621.pdf> accessed 6 April 2017.

[87] It is worth noting that, in a recent General Court decision, the Court found that the findings by the Ombudsman are not binding on EU courts; at best, they can constitute an indication

proactive approach towards more transparency and thus declassify the negotiating mandate in October 2014.[88]

This event coincided with the appointment of the Juncker administration at the Commission and a promise for more transparency in those negotiations.[89] This promise on the side of the Commission was its positive reaction to the letter addressed to it by the European Ombudsman for more transparency regarding TTIP-related documentation. As the lead negotiator, the Commission, under the Juncker lead, promised to improve transparency by making public all EU negotiating texts shared with Member States and the Parliament. Additionally, the Commission pledged to make public those documents that it has shared with the Council and the European Parliament once they are passed on to the US. In line with this promise, the Commission made public a set of EU proposals for legal texts in the TTIP negotiations in January 2015. This was also the first time that this type of document had been made public so early in bilateral trade negotiations and obviously constitutes a major milestone in the Commission's efforts for more transparency and openness.

Importantly, the Commission also promised to periodically review the classification of negotiating documents so that certain documents change status or classification and thus become accessible after a certain period of time. However, the Commission also noted the impossibility of publishing the US documents or common negotiating documents (so-called 'consolidated texts') without the explicit agreement of the US.[90]

It bears noting that the US traditional stance vis-à-vis trade negotiations is quite restrictive in terms of public access to negotiating documents. Such documents are sometimes distributed to a small circle of stakeholders, depending on the subject matter, to ensure that the US negotiating position is sufficiently inclusive. However, the US Trade Representative (USTR—the Directorate-General for Trade (DG Trade) counterpart) website will rarely upload negotiating documents for bilateral or multilateral negotiations. For example, the TPP text was finalized in October, but it was only in December that parties to the agreement made the draft text

of infringement, by the institution concerned, of the principle of sound administration. The Court reminded of the *Komninou* judgment (Case C-167/06 P, *Komninou and Others v Commission* [2007] ECLI:EU:C:2007:633, para 44), where it was noted that proceedings before the Ombudsman, whose decisions are not binding, are for the EU citizens an extrajudicial alternative remedy to an action before EU courts, which meets specific criteria and does not necessarily have the same objective as legal proceedings. The General Court further noted that interpretations of EU law by the Ombudsman cannot be such as to bind EU courts. See Cases T-424/14 and T-425/14, *ClientEarth v Commission* [2015] ECLI:EU:T:2015:848, paras 122–3. This decision was appealed and is currently pending before the CJEU (pending Case C-57/16 P).

[88] See Decision of 31 October 2014 of the European Ombudsman closing her own initiative inquiry OI/11/2014/RA concerning the Council of the European Union.

[89] See European Commission Communication concerning transparency in TTIP negotiations, C (2014) 9052 final.

[90] See Follow-up reply from the European Commission to the Ombudsman's closing decision in OI/10/2014/RA on transparency and public participation in the TTIP negotiations, <http://www.ombudsman.europa.eu/en/cases/correspondence.faces/en/59343/html.bookmark> accessed 6 April 2017.

public. Although there have been leaked documents throughout the TPP negotiations, the lack of transparency by a US official source reveals a poor record with regard to transparency.

The fact that the EU has opted for proactive transparency of key documents in the TTIP negotiations obviously creates an imbalance in the bilateral negotiations, also because the EU went as far as to publish some initial negotiating offers, including in services. On the other hand, these latter documents could have remained confidential, as the Commission did not pledge disclosure for those documents. One would assume that the Commission decided to publish these early on to collect reactions internally, but also to reassure various groups that it does not plan to jeopardize the EU's public services sector.

Another highly interesting aspect of the TTIP-related transparency initiative by the Commission related to the access of the Members of the Parliament to the TTIP documents. The Commission promised to move away from the 'reading room' approach that has been opted for at the beginning of the TTIP negotiations and led to only a few Members of the European Parliament (MEPs) having access to TTIP confidential ('EU-restricted') documents. For a long period, only MEPs with a direct 'need to know' (eg INTA's chair and vice chairs, as well as the coordinators of the political groups within INTA; or the TTIP rapporteurs of the eleven committees associated with INTA, as well as the chairs of these committees) could have access to consolidated texts and paper (but no electronic) copies of classified documents. Thus, for a long time, a total of about forty MEPs could only have access to confidential documents in a secure reading room, while another sixty could only read 'EU-limited', TTIP-related documents (mostly technical background papers).[91]

Recently, and after a year of negotiations between the Parliament and the Commission since the pledge made in the TTIP transparency initiative in November 2014, the Commission agreed to extend access to the secure reading room to all MEPs, allowing them to read TTIP consolidated texts, take handwritten notes, and use the information in their discussions with their constituents.[92] Under the new modalities, all MEPs can have electronic access to 'EU-limited' documents, while all MEPs can read paper copies of the TTIP-related, 'EU-restricted' documents in a secure reading room in the European Parliament where only note-taking is allowed.

[91] Secure reading rooms for access of MEPs to confidential information is a common practice, as the European Parliament's Rules of Procedure reveal: 'Rules of Procedure of the European Parliament' (April 2015), <http://www.europarl.europa.eu/sides/getDoc.do?pubRef=-//EP//TEXT+RULES-EP+20150428+ANN-07+DOC+XML+V0//EN&language=EN&navigationBar=YES> accessed 6 April 2017. See, most importantly, the Decision of the European Parliament of 15 April 2013 concerning the rules governing the treatment of confidential information by the European Parliament [2014] OJ C 96/1.

[92] See Paul Hutchison, 'European Parliament TTIP Document Access Deal Confirmed' (18 January 2016), <https://www.agra-net.com/agra/agra-europe/policy-and-legislation/trade-policy/european-parliament-ttip-document-access-deal-confirmed-503672.htm> accessed 6 April 2017.

Access is also given to designate Parliament's staff who are authorized by the INTA Chair on a 'need-to-know' basis.[93]

This is the first time that the Commission has enabled all MEPs to monitor the negotiations of an international agreement. More broadly, it appears that the Commission aims at higher levels of transparency in international trade dealings than was previously the case. In this sense, TTIP is totally different from the CETA negotiations. When discussing TTIP, one should also factor in two important parallel developments, the first being the establishment of national reading rooms in all Member States for the information of Members of national parliaments of Member States (to date, only one Member State has not established a reading room).

Most TTIP reading rooms were established in the first months of 2016.[94] In these rooms, members of the national parliaments have access to the EU positions and EU documents containing references to US positions, as well as consolidated texts. However, the US negotiating documents are not made public in these reading rooms. Even so, ensuring transparency early on within national parliaments in anticipation of the ratification procedure appears wise. Second, in the meantime, the Commission convinced the US of the need to establish reading rooms in US embassies in the capitals of the EU Member States whereby members of the national parliaments can read TTIP-related negotiating documents and the consolidated texts, but apparently not the US negotiating position documents.[95]

Admittedly, TTIP's transparency record internally and externally is quite unique. The Commission ensured that public consultations were held (on ISDS, on regulatory issues, or on the future of EU–US trade relations), occasionally helping the TTIP impact assessment or the work on the US–EU High Level Working Group on Jobs and Growth. A small and medium-sized enterprise (SME) survey distributed through the Enterprise European Network also allowed voices to raise their concerns about US barriers to SMEs. The Commission also held regular civil society dialogues, discussing updates and adjustments of the EU negotiating positions and the likely impact of TTIP, as well as stakeholders meetings (for instance, on chemicals), which often take place at the margins of a TTIP negotiating round. Internally, the Commission held a regular dialogue with the Council and the European Parliament's INTA.

It is quite surprising that the SIA which was outsourced by the Commission to Ecorys was conducted so late in the process, with the draft study being released

[93] See the modalities: Martin Schulz's and Bernd Lange's letter to Cecilia Malmström, 'Subject: Access to TTIP-Related Documents—Comprehensive Agreement on Operational Arrangements between the INTA Committee and DG TRADE' (10 December 2015), <https://ec.europa.eu/carol/index-iframe.cfm?fuseaction=download&documentId=090166e5a484dc57&title=D_55633_Schulz_Lange_Malmstrom> accessed 6 April 2017.

[94] For the most recent list, see European Parliamentary Research Service Blog, 'TTIP Reading Rooms in EU Member States' (15 July 2016), <https://epthinktank.eu/2016/07/15/eu-us-negotiations-on-ttip-state-of-play/ttip-reading-rooms-in-eu-member-states/> accessed 6 April 2017.

[95] See 'Procedures for Access to T-TIP Consolidated Texts in U.S. Embassies' (18 December 2014), <https://www.documentcloud.org/documents/2162271-14-12-18-us-access-rules-to-consolidated-texts.html> accessed 6 April 2017.

only weeks ahead of TTIP's 14th negotiating round. Typically, such reports should serve the purpose of establishing the rationale for *launching* rather than *finalizing* negotiations with a trading partner and therefore should be taking place early in the negotiations, occasionally determining the areas of priority for the trading partners. At the same time, we should also acknowledge that the Commission organized a public consultation on the draft SIA. Furthermore, it commissioned two economic reports (to Ecorys and CEPR) and presented its impact assessment to the Council in 2013.[96]

Harnessing public opposition against TTIP is not a given in the EU, as recent events show. Other than the ever-decreasing public support, civil society groups and other NGOs started collecting signatures of EU citizens who were willing to support the interruption of any trade negotiations with the US. A central argument is that the agreement would possibly jeopardize the status quo with regard to the supply of public services in Europe. Whereas over 3 million signatures in favour of stopping the TTIP negotiations (but also in favour of not concluding CETA) were collected, the central organs of the movement attempted, unsuccessfully, to register this initiative as a European citizen initiative (ECI) pursuant to Art 11 TEU and the corresponding Regulation 211/2011.[97]

Indeed, in September 2014, the European Commission refused to register the 'Stop TTIP' initiative because, in its view, the Council's negotiating mandate is a preparatory act that does not allow the Commission to propose a *specific* legal act to the Council, contrary to the relevant Regulation.[98] Accordingly, the persons in charge decided to launch a lawsuit against the Commission's decision before the CJEU, which the General Court accepted and thus annulled the Commission's decision. According to the General Court, the principle of democracy as enunciated in Regulation 211/2011 can coexist with the principle of institutional balance and the possibility of EU insitutions to conclude FTAs.[99] In deciding so, the General Court elaborated further on its decision in *Anagnostakis*. In that case, the General Court recalled that ECIs are intended to reinforce EU citizenship and enhance the democratic functioning of the EU through the participation of citizens in the democratic life of the EU. In the Court's view, the refusal to register an ECI is an action that impinges on the very effectiveness of the right of Union citizens to submit in the first place a citizens' initiative pursuant to Art 24 TFEU and, therefore, it is for the Commission to clearly state the reasons that justify such a refusal.[100]

[96] See European Commission, 'Impact Assessment Report on the future of EU–US trade relations', SWD(2013) 68 final, 12 March 2013.

[97] Regulation (EU) No 211/2011 of the European Parliament and of the Council of 16 February 2011 on the citizens' initiative [2011] OJ L 65/1.

[98] See the Commission's reply: Catherine Day's letter to Michael Efler, 'Subject: Your Request for Registration of a Proposed Citizens' Initiative Entitled "STOP TTIP"' (10 September 2014), <http://ec.europa.eu/citizens-initiative/public/documents/2552> accessed 6 April 2017.

[99] See Case T-754/14, *Michael Efler and Others v Commission*, judgment of 10 May 2017, paras 37, 46, 48.

[100] See Case T-450/12, *Anagnostakis v Commission* [2015] ECLI:EU:T:2015:739, paras 25–6. An appeal is currently pending before the CJEU.

A central public concern in the EU when TTIP is discussed is the protection of public services.[101] To reassure citizens and NGOs that were mobilized, the EU and US recently promised to take into account the important preferences and values that underlie the provision of public services on the two sides of the Atlantic.[102] Water, education, health, and social services are mentioned as mere examples of sectors in which important sensitivities on both sides of the Atlantic exist. This statement confirms a consistently reluctant stance that the EU has taken in its FTAs with regard to public services (a so-called 'public utilities exception') in line with the negotiating guidelines by the Council.[103] Other sensitive areas for the EU in terms of liberalization include the opening of audiovisual services to the US service suppliers. Due to traditional sensitivities associated with this sector that have already been expressed when the most-favoured-nation exemptions to the WTO General Agreement on Trade in Services (GATS) were discussed in the early 1990s, the Council recommended the overall exclusion of the sector from the transatlantic discussions.[104]

Once the negotiations started drawing public attention, the European Parliament also engaged more, signalling the type of deal and ensuing commitments that it would be unable to approve. Recall that, in the case of TTIP being an agreement falling under the EU CCP, no agreement can be binding for the EU unless the European Parliament gives its consent. In its TTIP resolution, the Parliament invited the Commission as the lead negotiator to exclude from the scope of TTIP public services to ensure that 'national and if applicable local authorities retain the full right to introduce, adopt, maintain or repeal any measures with regards to the commissioning, organization, funding and provision of public services as provided in the Treaties as well as in the EU's negotiating mandate; this exclusion should apply *irrespective of how the services are provided and funded*'.[105] Notably in the case of public health-care services, the Parliament suggested the exclusion of the sector from the negotiations due to the differing approaches between the EU and the US. By way of illustration, whereas the EU is very keen on adding in the final text a horizontal chapter on regulatory cooperation, the EU-proposed text excludes services of general interest (ie public services) from the scope of that chapter.

[101] See, generally, Markus Krajewski and Britta Kynast, 'Impact of the Transatlantic Trade and Investment Partnership (TTIP) on the Legal Framework for Public Services in Europe' (1 October 2014), <https://papers.ssrn.com/sol3/papers.cfm?abstract_id=2576079> accessed 30 August 2016.

[102] See Joint Statement on Public Services by Ambassador Froman (USTR) and EU Commissioner Malström (DG Trade), 20 March 2015.

[103] See Panagiotis Delimatsis, 'Services of General Interest and the External Dimension of the EU Energy Policy' in Markus Krajewski (ed), *Services of General Interest Beyond the Single Market: External and International Law Dimensions* (Springer, 2015) 345ff.

[104] With regard to both audiovisual services and public services, see the European Parliament resolution on the opening of negotiations on a plurilateral agreement on services (TiSA), 2013/2583(RSP), 4 July 2013.

[105] Emphasis added. See European Parliament resolution of 8 July 2015 containing the European Parliament's recommendations to the European Commission on the negotiations for the Transatlantic Trade and Investment Partnership (TTIP), 2014/2228(INI), para 2(a)vii (hereafter TTIP resolution of 8 July 2015).

The public services debate has been a constant source of friction in the continuous TTIP negotiations and has taken centre-stage with the mobilization leading to the 'Stop TTIP' movement. Currently, it seems that the European Ombudsman is happy with the existing transparency-related arrangements regarding TTIP, while the European Parliament in its TTIP resolution encouraged the Commission to ensure civil society involvement and public and political outreach, also in line with the recommendations made by the European Ombudsman.[106] Crucially, the Parliament also encouraged the Commission to intensify efforts to actively involve national parliaments and ensure that information flows towards Member States in a timely manner.[107]

Overall, it would be fair to say that the EU has been progressively improving its transparency record in the TTIP negotiations since negotiations with the US started in 2013. Importantly, the EU also drew important lessons from the criticism received by the civil society relating to the mediocre adherence to transparency in the CETA negotiations with Canada. To be sure, continuous and insisting requests for access to TTIP-related documents and the ensuing involvement of the European Ombudsman did help to accelerate the wave of transparency on the side of the Council and the Commission. The European Parliament also eventually achieved access for all MEPs to negotiating documents and consolidated texts, which should give a boost to and constitute a precedent for the level of transparency that is desirable in the EU's trade-related dealings. One should not shy away from the observation that, based on the analysis in section II, the Commission and the Council could very well rely on the judicial interpretation of Art 4 of Regulation 1049/2001 to deny disclosure of core documents, including the negotiating directives and the draft legal texts proposed to the US by the EU. However, in a significant turn—which also constitutes an important bet on the side of the Council and the Commission—the EU institutions that lead the TTIP negotiations decided to opt for more transparency and openness.

C. Transparency in negotiating TiSA

Whereas the EU claims to remain focused on the conclusion of the Doha Round, it seems that the Doha negotiating mandate is abandoned.[108] The multilateral round of negotiations that was launched with high hopes in 2001 in the Qatari capital largely failed to meet the expectations of developing and also developed countries. With so many open issues in the Doha development agenda and an ever-increasing number of WTO Members, failure at the negotiating table has become a self-fulfilling prophecy. After fifteen years of negotiations and procrastination, the WTO Ministerial Declaration in Nairobi confirmed the indifference of many key Members regarding the conclusion of the Doha Development Round.

[106] See Ombudsman Decision of 6 January 2015 (n 83).
[107] See the TTIP resolution of 8 July 2015 (n 105) points (e)–(vii).
[108] See Shawn Donnan, 'Trade Talks Lead to "Death of Doha and Birth of New WTO"', *Financial Times* (20 December 2015).

Despite the sluggish progress in the WTO negotiations, trade liberalization notably through the decrease of tariffs in goods continued apace, showing that trade liberalization occurs, but increasingly outside the WTO. The EU trade agenda, announced in October 2015, had already signalled the arrival of a new era for the WTO by suggesting that, rather than focusing on comprehensive (and thus time-consuming) negotiations on an ever-increasing array of issues, issue-based negotiations and early harvesting may be the most sustainable future for the WTO.

This approach is being tested with the negotiations for TiSA, currently negotiated by twenty-three WTO Members (taking the EU as one). Mauritius has most recently joined the bloc to become the first African country to join the discussions. TiSA covers about 70 per cent of world trade in services and has been promoted by major services-led economies globally, including the EU, the US, Japan, Canada, and the Republic of Korea. However, Brazil, Russia, India, China, and South Africa have largely distanced themselves from this initiative, but any signal by China suggesting its participation will quickly alter the dynamics.

TiSA is a US-led initiative and the stakes for the US are quite straightforward: almost 80 per cent of US exports and about 90 per cent of US imports through commercial presence would be covered by a forthcoming agreement in these negotiations.[109] Note also that, if TiSA, TPP, and TTIP are successfully concluded, only the US will be a party in all three agreements. By July 2016, nineteen negotiating rounds have taken place, showing the magnitude of the endeavour, but also the lack of remaining resources that could focus on the GATS negotiations.

The possibility for multilateralizing the negotiating process and/or the results of the negotiations was intentionally left open. For the EU, at least, it has always been important that the trade block is not accused of undermining the multilateral negotiations. Thus, it is telling that the negotiating mandate of the Council addressed to the European Commission many times refers to the need to act consistently with the GATS and adopt its basic architecture, but at the same time try to address those elements that did not seem to work at the GATS level.[110] Based on this, for instance, the EU has proposed a modularity approach for TiSA, which would ultimately allow TiSA to be incorporated in the GATS once all WTO Members join.[111] At the same time, TiSA deviates from the GATS, notably with regard to the scheduling approach: contrary to the GATS, national treatment would apply horizontally subject to the reservations/exemptions that the TiSA parties would list. This is an indirect acceptance by the EU of the limits of an exclusively positive list approach that the EU has traditionally

[109] See Juan A Marchetti and Martin Roy, 'The TISA Initiative: An Overview of Market Access Issues' (WTO Staff Working Paper ERSD-2013-11, 27 November 2013) 27, <https://www.wto.org/english/res_e/reser_e/ersd201311_e.pdf> accessed 6 April 2017.

[110] See Council of the European Union, 'Draft Directives for the Negotiation of a Plurilateral Agreement on Trade in Services', 6891/13, ADD1, 8 March 2013.

[111] See the non-paper of the European Commission, 'A Modular Approach to the Architecture of a Plurilateral Agreement on Services' (September 2012), <http://trade.ec.europa.eu/doclib/docs/2014/july/tradoc_152686.pdf> accessed 6 April 2017.

opted for.[112] However, in both CETA and TTIP, the EU already deviates from the GATS scheduling method.[113]

Secrecy has been the overarching characteristic of the TiSA negotiations, in line with the WTO tradition of confidential negotiations, whereby transparency is a principle in a suspended mode until a final deal is struck.[114] Thus, the quest for more transparency has regularly made headlines, just like leaks of TiSA negotiating texts.[115] Owing to the importance of the current negotiations and the magnitude of the economies involved, curiosity about the actual proposals and drafts on the negotiating table is mounting. This bottom-up transparency may be unsatisfactory, but it gives an indication as to the political directions chosen by negotiators. For instance, the leaked text on domestic regulation within TiSA[116] is very similar to the most recent draft text discussed within the Working Party on Domestic Regulation at the WTO.

The TTIP transparency-related strategy has also certainly affected how the EU views the issue of transparency in the TiSA negotiations. In January 2015, Commissioner Malmström urged the Council to also make public the TiSA mandate, only months after the TTIP negotiating mandate was made public. At the time, the Commission as the lead negotiator had already published the EU offer and other relevant documents in July 2014. Rather than viewing the multiple-country setting as a hurdle for increased transparency, the Commissioner argued that increased transparency would attract more WTO Members in these negotiations, while also strengthening the legitimacy of the negotiations.[117] The Council decided to make public the mandate in March 2015, two years after its adoption by the EU ministers.

Transparency-related activities relating to TiSA include factual round reports, describing the state of play, points where progress is made, and points where more work is necessary, as well as the way forward.[118] The Commission held public consultations on TiSA in 2013, whereas the Trade SIA is still a document in progress.

[112] See also Panagiotis Delimatsis, 'Trade in Services and Regulatory Flexibility: 20 Years of GATS, 20 Years of Critique' in M Bungenberg, C Herrmann, M Krajewski, and J P Terhechte (eds), *European Yearbook of International Economic Law* (Springer, 2016) 153.

[113] The EU explained the intricacies of its new approach in European Commission, 'Services and Investment in EU Trade Deals—Using "Positive" and "Negative" Lists' (April 2016), <http://trade.ec.europa.eu/doclib/docs/2016/april/tradoc_154427.pdf> accessed 6 April 2017.

[114] See also Delimatsis, 'Transparency in the WTO' (n 6) 701.

[115] Wikileaks has been quite active in this regard: see <https://wikileaks.org/tisa/> accessed 6 April 2017.

[116] See 'Trade in Services Agreement (TiSA) Domestic Regulation Annex (February 2015) WikiLeaks release: June 3, 2015' (February 2015), <https://wikileaks.org/tisa/domestic/TiSA%20Annex%20on%20Domestic%20Regulation.pdf> accessed 6 April 2017. See the most recent version, 'TISA—Annex on Domestic Regulation' (10 October 2015), <https://wikileaks.org/tisa/document/20151010_Annex-on-Domestic-Regulation/20151010_Annex-on-Domestic-Regulation.pdf> accessed 6 April 2017.

[117] See Cecilia Malmström's letter to Minister Edgars Rinkēvičs, 'Subject: Publication of the TiSA Mandate' (29 January 2015), <http://ec.europa.eu/carol/?fuseaction=download&documentId=090166e59c73127c&title=CM_signed.pdf> accessed 6 April 2017.

[118] For the most recent report of 27 July 2016, see European Commission, 'Report of the 19th TiSA Negotiation Round, 8–18 July 2016' (27 July 2016), <http://trade.ec.europa.eu/doclib/docs/2016/july/tradoc_154824.pdf> accessed 6 April 2017.

Just like the TTIP SIA, the TiSA SIA is prepared by Ecorys, which ran a stakeholder survey and organized a civil society dialogue.[119] Furthermore, the Commission has held regular updates on TiSA talks. In its resolution of February 2016,[120] the European Parliament urged the Commission to intensify its public outreach efforts and not only include civil society groups and stakeholders. On substance, the Parliament pointed out the EU sensitivities with regard to public services, labour rights, data protection, and the right to regulate. Finally, the Parliament also called the Commission to give all negotiating documents to all MEPs and, additionally, to involve and consult national parliaments, as well as local and regional authorities.

The latter recommendation seems to make sense. As things stand, TiSA would most likely be a mixed agreement, even if in the end the results of the negotiations take the form of revised schedules (although this appears unlikely, as a whole revamping of the GATS appears to be envisaged in the TiSA negotiations). This is so based on the CJEU Opinion 1/94 (WTO Opinion),[121] but also on the more recent Opinion 1/08 (GATS Opinion),[122] which clarified that certain aspects of the GATS trigger mixity when it comes to the EU's versus Member States' competences. Arguably, the Lisbon Treaty did not change this, as certain sectors still fall under the Member States' competences or are shared competences at best (eg transport services).

To sum up, it appears that, despite its importance and the potential for a real breakthrough in plurilateral/multilateral trade negotiations, TiSA appears to be overshadowed by the TTIP negotiations. At the same time, transparency at the EU level at least is satisfactory for the most part, although in this case the EU can only influence the disclosure of a small fraction of negotiating documents. However, some caution is needed here, notably if conclusion of the TiSA is indeed achieved this year. National parliaments and regional or local authorities are not sufficiently informed; rather, they are kept in the dark as far as the level of ambition in and repercussions of TiSA are concerned.

IV. Conclusion

It is commonplace that a clear link exists between the legitimacy of any government and governmental authority and its level of transparency in terms of processes, deliberative mechanisms, and output. Demands for more transparency in the functioning of governments and actors in the domestic and international affairs, more broadly, are quasi-universal, as lack thereof has become synonymous with abuse of

[119] The final draft SIA was made public in May 2017 and is available at <http://www.trade-sia.com/tisa/wp-content/uploads/sites/7/2014/02/TiSA-Draft-Final-Report-May2017.pdf> accessed 12 May 2017.

[120] See European Parliament resolution of 3 February 2016 on Negotiations for the Trade in Services Agreement (TiSA), P8 TA(2016)0041. The first EP resolution on the opening of the TiSA negotiations was adopted on 4 July 2013, P7 TA(2013)0325.

[121] Opinion 1/94, *WTO Agreements* [1994] ECLI:EU:C:1994:384.

[122] Opinion 1/08, *GATS* [2009] ECLI:EU:C:2009:739.

power.[123] Excessive transparency upfront, on the other side, may delay negotiations and hamper efficiency and timely conclusion of such negotiations.
Indeed, transparency may cause delays in the negotiations or prompt trade negotiators to posture by taking uncompromising positions and thus causing more frequent breakdowns in negotiations.[124] This is particularly so if one assumes that the state representatives have considerable reputational concerns and therefore will choose to be on the 'safe side'. As it is assumed that domestic constituencies monitor such international developments, this may result in the state representative being more careful in its articulations if they are made in public. Thus, decision-making becomes overly politicized.[125] Finding ways to ensure that gains from an open and participatory decision-making process will be reaped without undermining the capacity to reach decisions in a representative but still efficient manner becomes essential.

In this quest, one should not forget that transparency is a multifaceted concept. Internal and external transparency do not always weigh equally, nor should they be taken into account on equal footing when assessing the transparency of a given procedure. Regarding external transparency, it is clearly asymmetrical and therefore an organization may have limited incentives (other than perhaps reputation costs)[126] to disclose information absent any explicit decision to this effect by the principals. This partly explains the sequence of events that led from the intervention of the European Ombudsman to the disclosure of various documents and a new transparency-related strategy by EU institutions.

As explained above, trade agreements have traditionally been covered with a heavy cloak of secrecy. The European Commission only recently made a considerable effort (also at the inter-institutional level) to increase transparency in EU trade negotiations. This was welcomed by the European Parliament, but also civil society circles: if an agreement is finalized, it becomes virtually impossible to change the text, notably in case of multi-party negotiations. Therefore, early involvement and diffusion of information is crucial with a view to increasing legitimacy and avoiding unnecessary friction during the compliance stage.

The Juncker administration understands transparency as a key instrument to increase public trust in the dealings of the Commission. The inter-institutional

[123] Bianchi, 'On Power and Illusion' (n 7). This may not be applicable to all IOs across the board. See also Steven R Ratner, 'Behind the Flag of Dunant: Secrecy and the Compliance Mission of the International Committee of the Red Cross' in Andrea Bianchi and Anne Peters (eds), *Transparency in International Law* (Cambridge University Press, 2013).

[124] See David Stasavage, 'Open-Door or Closed-Door? Transparency in Domestic and International Bargaining' (2004) 58 *International Organization* 668. See also Robert Baldwin, 'Trade Negotiations within the GATT/WTO Framework: A Survey of Successes and Failures' (2009) 31 *Journal of Policy Modeling* 515.

[125] Anne-Marie Slaughter, *A New World Order* (Princeton University Press, 2004) 220.

[126] Reputation costs should not be underestimated: public support for a given trade agreement can increase because of more transparency, as the absence of secretive decision-making creates confidence that due process is adhered to. Transparency can also reduce public support, as certain events or news (eg the introduction of an ISDS system) may be perceived by the public in ways that cannot be modified subsequently.

agreement of 2016 on better law-making is telling in this respect. However, the political climate in the most advanced economies is currently not very trade-friendly: the current US administration will be sceptical about any trade deal that preaches additional liberalization. Can, then, transparency be a remedy for this general mistrust of international agreements on both sides of the Atlantic? The key appears to be to convince stakeholders and civil society that the new generation of trade agreements is more balanced. For that, substantial efforts will need to be made.

One could also argue that regardless of the link with mutual trust, transparency is deeply embedded in our values and democratic principles both horizontally (among institutions) and vertically (between institutions and EU citizens). The case law analysed above confirms the bite of Regulation 1049/2001 on public access to documents, but, more importantly, corroborates the role of the EU courts as guardians of the EU values and fundamental principles of democratic systems. In addition, one should not hesitate to admit the learning-by-doing element in the process of transitioning towards more transparency in EU trade matters. Thus, while for some the reading rooms approach was an unfortunate idea, I would submit that the final outcome described above has been the result of a quite smooth inter-institutional cooperation between the Commission and the European Parliament on the basis of good faith, above all. This should be viewed as good news.

As we will start graduating from this transitioning phase, new ideas will inevitably be discussed. For instance, it appears opportune to accompany the conclusion of international (trade) agreements with a transparency report, which would enumerate at the very least the types of initiatives that have been taken to offer opportunities for comment, open debate, stakeholder participation, contestation, and so on. In addition, when seeking to consult the public, such consultations should focus on the specificities, advantages, and disadvantages of a given agreement. For instance, instead of having one consultation regarding the ISDS system, one would rather expect separate, targeted consultations for each of the two very significant trade agreements (CETA and TTIP) that the EU aspires to enforce in the very near future.

11

CETA, TTIP, TiSA, and Their Relationship with EU Law

Stefan Mayr

I. Introduction

CETA and TTIP are comprehensive EU trade agreements of a new generation; TiSA is a plurilateral agreement on trade in services, building largely on the GATS. While TiSA figures a little less prominently in the public debate, CETA and TTIP have triggered a broad and highly controversial discussion. Particularly contentious issues include the establishment of an investor-to-state dispute settlement mechanism, be it in the form of typical investor-state arbitration or under the new label of an Investment Court System, and the competence to conclude the various agreements. In the light of the fierce criticism in some Member States, the Commission seems to fear that the qualification as mixed agreements, requiring ratification by all twenty-eight Member States, could seriously delay or eventually even impede the agreements' entry into force.

Against this background, the Commission has asked the Court of Justice to issue an opinion on the scope of EU external competences in connection with another recent trade agreement—the EU–Singapore Free Trade Agreement (EUSFTA)—in July 2015.[1] While the Court's opinion is principally without prejudice to the allocation of competences in the context of other trade and investment agreements, its significance will undoubtedly go beyond the EUSFTA. As the Commission points out in its Proposal for a Council Decision on the conclusion of CETA, the latter has 'identical objectives and essentially the same contents' as the EUSFTA and the Union's competence 'is the same in both cases'.[2]

Despite the fact that Opinion 2/15 is still pending, the Commission has meanwhile decided to push forward with the conclusion of CETA. However, its initial announcement to propose the conclusion of CETA as an EU-only agreement was

[1] Request for an opinion submitted by the European Commission pursuant to Art 218(11) TFEU (Opinion 2/15) [2015] OJ C 363/18. At the time of writing, the case is still pending.

[2] Proposal for a Council Decision on the conclusion of the Comprehensive Economic and Trade Agreement between Canada of the one part, and the European Union and its Member States, of the

staunchly opposed by many Member States. As a consequence, the Commission later proposed to conclude CETA as a mixed agreement,[3] emphasizing, however, that this political concession is 'without prejudice' to its views expressed in the *EUSFTA* case and that once the Court issues its opinion, 'it will be necessary to draw the appropriate conclusions'.[4] Only recently, Advocate General Sharpston has issued her extensive and nuanced opinion in the Singapore case, arguing that the envisaged agreement 'can be concluded only by the European Union and the Member States acting jointly'.[5] Whether the Court will follow the Advocate General's opinion remains to be seen. In any case, as the issue of competence and mixity is of particular importance, it will be dealt with in some detail in this chapter (see section IV).

However, the relationship of CETA, TTIP, and TiSA with EU law is not just about competence and mixity. Further aspects that will be explored in (more or less) detail include the status and legal effects of the agreements in EU law (section II), some procedural aspects with regard to the negotiation and conclusion of agreements under the common commercial policy (CCP) (section III), the provisional application of the agreements (section V), and potential conflicts with regard to the autonomy of the EU legal order (section VI).

II. Status and Legal Effects of the Agreements within EU Law

A. Binding effect, treaty incorporation, and hierarchy

CETA, TTIP, and TiSA are agreements within the meaning of Art 216 TFEU. Hence, irrespective of their labelling as (trade) agreements, partnerships, etc, they are binding upon the institutions of the EU and on its Member States.[6] While reflecting 'the most basic tenet of the law of treaties',[7] that is, the principle *pacta sunt servanda*, it is important to emphasize that the relevant provision in Art 216(2) TFEU addresses the effects of an agreement in EU law, not in international law.[8]

As a matter of international law, *pure* or *EU-only* agreements, concluded solely by the EU, cannot create international obligations for the Member States.[9] *Mixed*

other part, COM (2016) 443 final, 4. Similar considerations are likely to apply to TTIP and other FTAs of the new generation.

3 Eventually, CETA has been signed as a mixed agreement on 30 October 2016.

4 COM (2016) 443 final (n 2) 4.

5 Opinion 2/15, *EUSFTA* [pending], Opinion of AG Sharpston, para 570 (hereafter *EUSFTA*).

6 cf Art 216(2) TFEU.

7 Iain MacLeod, Ian D Hendry, and Stephen Hyett, *The External Relations of the European Communities* (Oxford University Press, 1996) 123 (hereafter MacLeod et al, *External Relations*).

8 Piet Eeckhout, *EU External Relations Law* (2nd edn, Oxford University Press, 2011) 325 (hereafter Eeckhout, *EU External Relations Law*).

9 *Pacta tertiis* principle, cf Art 35 Vienna Convention on the Law of Treaties between States and International Organizations or Between International Organizations 1986 (not yet in force). However,

agreements are, however, principally binding on both the EU and the Member States under international law. In the absence of a—sufficiently precise[10]—declaration of competence vis-à-vis the other contracting parties, the EU and its Member States are therefore 'jointly liable ... for the fulfilment of every obligation arising from the commitments undertaken'.[11] While the exact consequences of this joint international responsibility—especially with a view to the prevailing 'executive federalism'[12]—remain somewhat unclear,[13] there is no doubt that the EU and the Member States are under a specific duty of cooperation, resulting from the principle of loyalty, enshrined in Art 4(3) TEU.[14]

From an EU law perspective, suffice it to say that the Court has consistently held that from its coming into force, the provisions of an international agreement of the EU form an *integral part* of EU law.[15] This means that the EU adheres to a model of automatic treaty incorporation: an agreement duly concluded by the Council requires no further act of transposition.[16] In the hierarchy of norms, the prevailing opinion places international agreements between primary and secondary EU law.[17] However, international agreements not only prevail over provisions of secondary EU legislation, but—as all norms of EU law—also enjoy primacy over the national laws of Member States.[18] A different question is whether an agreement has direct effect and may therefore be directly invoked by private parties before courts and

according to Art 216(2) TFEU the Member States are under an obligation in relation to the Union to comply with EU international commitments; cf Case 12/86, *Demirel v Stadt Schwäbisch Gmünd* [1987] ECLI:EU:C:1987:400, para 11 (hereafter *Demirel*).

[10] With a view to the dynamics and complexity of the division of competences, an 'article-by-article (or, even better, a clause-by-clause) analysis informing treaty partners clearly and in detail which entity will be exercising which rights and performing which obligations', as suggested by Peter M Olson, 'Mixity from the Outside: the Perspective of a Treaty Partner' in Christophe Hillion and Panos Koutrakos (eds), *Mixed Agreements Revisited* (Hart, 2010) 331, 336, appears rather unrealistic, especially with a view to comprehensive agreements such as CETA or TTIP (*if* these are to be qualified as mixed agreements, cf the detailed analysis in section IV).

[11] Case C-316/91, *Parliament v Council* [1994] ECLI:EU:C:1994:76, para 29.

[12] Pieter-Jan Kuijper, 'International Responsibility for Mixed Agreements' in Hillion and Koutrakos, *Mixed Agreements Revisited* (n 10) 208, 213.

[13] MacLeod et al, *External Relations* (n 7) 159, consider it 'unlikely that the Community and the Member States can be held to be jointly and severally liable for all obligations in the agreement so that an aggrieved third party would be entitled to seek full satisfaction from any of the Member States or the Community'.

[14] eg Opinion 1/94, *WTO Agreement* [1994] ECLI:EU:C:1994:384, para 108 (hereafter *WTO Agreement*). A violation of the duty of cooperation by a Member State was found in Case C-246/07, *Commission v Sweden* [2010] ECLI:EU:C:2010:203. Cf also Christophe Hillion, 'Mixity and Coherence in EU External Relations: The Significance of the "Duty of Cooperation"' in Hillion and Koutrakos, *Mixed Agreements Revisited* (n 10) 87; and Marcus Klamert, *The Principle of Loyalty* (Oxford University Press, 2014) 183ff.

[15] Case 181/73, *Haegeman v Belgium* [1974] ECLI:EU:C:1974:41, para 5; more recently, eg, Case C-135/10, *Società Consortile Fonografici* [2012] ECLI:EU:C:2012:140, para 39 (hereafter *SCF*).

[16] Eeckhout, *EU External Relations Law* (n 8) 327; and Mario Mendez, *The Legal Effects of EU Agreements* (Oxford University Press, 2013) 62ff.

[17] eg Jan Wouters, Dominic Coppens, and Bart De Meester, 'The European Union's External Relations after the Lisbon Treaty' in Stefan Griller and Jacques Ziller (eds), *The Lisbon Treaty* (Springer, 2008) 191–2 (hereafter Wouters et al, 'External Relations after Lisbon Treaty').

[18] eg ibid, 187; Allan Rosas, 'The Status in EU Law of International Agreements Concluded by EU Member States' (2011) 34 *Fordham International Law Journal* 1310; and Francesca Martines,

authorities. Basically, such direct effect depends on the 'nature and broad logic' of the agreement, as well as the characteristics of the individual provisions.[19]

In principle, these basic considerations also apply to mixed agreements, but only insofar as they come within EU competences. Aspects remaining within exclusive Member State competence form no integral part of EU law.[20] In this regard, it is also important to note that the Court claims exclusive 'jurisdiction to define the obligations which the [Union] has assumed and those which remain the sole responsibility of the Member States'.[21] Similarly, in areas of shared competence, the Court determines whether the EU has exercised its powers or whether an area is largely covered by EU law, thus excluding national courts from determining the effect of the relevant provisions of the agreement.[22]

B. Direct effect

The direct effect doctrine is an essential characteristic of the EU legal order and, by empowering individuals to protect their own rights, continues to have a 'beneficial impact ... on the European integration process as a whole'.[23] However, in public international law, the contracting parties are free to determine which effect the provisions of an agreement are to have in their internal legal orders, including whether individuals may rely on an agreement before domestic courts and authorities. Accordingly, the Court has consistently held that only '[i]f that question has not been expressly dealt with in the agreement, it is the courts having jurisdiction in the matter and particularly the Court of Justice ... that have the task of deciding it'.[24]

When the Court gets to decide on the issue of direct effect, it basically applies a two-tier test. To be directly effective, a provision must generally be unconditional

'Direct Effect of International Agreements of the European Union' (2014) 25 *European Journal of International Law* 133.

[19] cf Case C-363/12, *Z v A Government department* [2014] ECLI:EU:C:2014:159, paras 84–5 (hereafter *Z v A Government department*).

[20] eg Joined Cases C-300/98 and C-392/98, *Dior and Others* [2000] ECLI:EU:C:2000:688, para 48 (hereafter *Dior and Others*); and Case C-431/05, *Merck Genéricos* [2007] ECLI:EU:C:2007:496, para 34. For a different reading of the Court's case law, cf Christine Kaddous, 'Effects of International Agreements in the EU Legal Order' in Marise Cremona and Bruno de Witte (eds), *EU Foreign Relations Law: Constitutional Fundamentals* (Hart, 2008) 296.

[21] eg Case C-240/09, *Lesoochranárske zoskupenie* [2011] ECLI:EU:C:2011:125, para 31 (hereafter *Lesoochranárske*).

[22] *Lesoochranárske* (n 21) paras 32–3. For a critical assessment, eg, Marcus Klamert, 'Dark Matter—Competence, Jurisdiction and "the Area Largely Covered by EU Law": Comment on Lesoochranárske' (2012) 37 *European Law Review* 340.

[23] Bruno de Witte, 'The Continuous Significance of *Van Gend en Loos*' in Miguel P Maduro and Loïc Azoulai (eds), *The Past and Future of EU Law* (Hart, 2010) 13. Remarkably, this aspect was already mentioned in the Court's seminal decision in Case 26/62, *Van Gend en Loos* [1963] ECLI:EU:C:1963:1, 13: 'The vigilance of individuals concerned to protect their rights amounts to an effective supervision in addition to the supervision entrusted ... to the diligence of the Commission and of the Member States' (hereafter *Van Gend en Loos*).

[24] Joined Cases C-120/06 P and C-121/06 P, *FIAMM* [2008] ECLI:EU:C:2008:476, para 108 (hereafter *FIAMM*); cf already Case 104/81, *Kupferberg* [1982] ECLI:EU:C:1982:362, para 17; Case C-149/96, *Portugal v Council* [1999] ECLI:EU:C:1999:574, para 34 (hereafter *Portugal v Council*); and Case C-366/10, *ATAA* [2011] ECLI:EU:C:2011:864, para 49 (hereafter *ATAA*).

and sufficiently precise.[25] With regard to an international agreement, this condition is met where the provision relied on 'contains a clear and precise obligation which is not subject in its implementation or effects, to the adoption of any subsequent measure'.[26] In addition, the Court assesses the potential direct effect of an agreement in the light of its 'nature and broad logic'.[27]

In CETA, the parties have explicitly rejected the possibility of granting private rights to citizens: Art 30.6.1 CETA provides that '[n]othing in this Agreement shall be construed as conferring rights or imposing obligations on persons other than those created between the Parties under public international law, nor as permitting this Agreement to be directly invoked in the domestic legal systems of the Parties'. Arguably, a major problem with this 'anti-citizen clause'[28] is that it reinforces the asymmetry vis-à-vis foreign investors who have the right to submit investor-state arbitration claims to the Tribunal established under Chapter Eight.[29] And even though this eventually leads to 'discriminat[ion] against other citizens affected by FTA rules and practices',[30] it is likely that TTIP—in line with recent EU FTA practice[31]—will contain a similar clause.

As regards TiSA: unless the contracting parties determine its legal effects explicitly, it seems reasonable that the Court should treat TiSA, which largely builds on the GATS, like WTO law. It is thus important to recall that the Court—based on concerns about political room for manoeuvre and judicial reciprocity—has principally rejected any direct effect of WTO law.[32] However, WTO law has exceptionally been recognized as a standard for legal review where an EU act either explicitly refers to precise provisions of a particular WTO agreement or was adopted in order to comply

[25] See already *Van Gend en Loos* (n 23) 13; as regards provisions in agreements, eg, Case C-344/04, *IATA and ELFAA* [2006] ECLI:EU:C:2006:10, para 39 (hereafter *IATA and ELFAA*); and Case 308/06, *Intertanko and Others* [2008] ECLI:EU:C:2008:312, para 45 (hereafter *Intertanko and Others*).

[26] *Demirel* (n 9) para 14; see also Case C-213/03, *Pêcheurs de l'étang de Berre* [2004] ECLI:EU:C:2004:464, para 39; *Lesoochranárske* (n 21) para 44; and *SCF* (n 15) para 44. However, merely 'programmatic' agreements (or provisions) do not meet the requirements in terms of clarity and unconditionality, cf *Z v A Government department* (n 19) paras 88–90.

[27] eg *IATA and ELFAA* (n 25) para 39; *Intertanko and Others* (n 25) para 45; and *ATAA* (n 24) para 54.

[28] Ernst-Ulrich Petersmann, 'Transformative Transatlantic Free Trade Agreements without Rights and Remedies of Citizens?' (2015) 18 *Journal of International Economic Law* 579, 602 (hereafter Petersmann, 'Transformative Transatlantic FTAs'); see also Chapter 2 by Petersmann in this volume.

[29] cf Armand de Mestral, 'When Does the Exception Become the Rule? Conserving Regulatory Space under CETA' (2015) 18 *Journal of International Economic Law* 641, 652; and Daniel Thym, 'The Missing Link: Direct Effect, CETA/TTIP and Investor-State Dispute Settlement', *EU Law Analysis* (7 January 2015), <http://eulawanalysis.blogspot.co.at/2015/01/the-missing-link-direct-effect-cetattip.html> accessed 7 April 2017).

[30] Petersmann, 'Transformative Transatlantic FTAs' (n 28) 603.

[31] eg Art 17.15 EUSFTA; cf also Panos Koutrakos, *EU International Relations Law* (2nd edn, Hart, 2015) 258.

[32] eg *Portugal v Council* (n 24) paras 36–47; *Dior and Others* (n 20) para 44; Joined Cases C-27/00 and C-122/00, *Omega Air and Others* [2002] ECLI:EU:C:2002:161, para 93; Case C-377/02, *Van Parys* [2005] ECLI:EU:C:2005:121, para 39; and *FIAMM* (n 24) para 111. Cf already Joined Cases 21–24/72, *International Fruit Company NV and Others* [1972] ECLI:EU:C:1972:115, paras 20–8, rejecting direct effect of the GATT 1947 upon consideration of 'the spirit, the general scheme and the terms' of the agreement; cf also Case C-280/93, *Germany v Council* [1994] ECLI:EU:C:1994:367, paras 105–12.

with a particular obligation assumed by the EU under WTO law.[33] The Court finds it clearly undesirable that direct effect be granted to WTO law within the EU legal order, while major trading partners reject WTO law as a standard for domestic legal review. Recalling that TiSA is being negotiated among many of the most powerful trading partners of the EU, it appears consistent that the same reciprocity thinking would be applied in the TiSA context, thus largely excluding any direct effect.

Likewise, even in the absence of Art 30.6.1 CETA, the Court might well have rejected the agreement's direct effect with regard to its nature and structure. Moreover, limits to the direct applicability of treaties in Canadian constitutional law would again have raised serious reciprocity concerns.[34] A different question—albeit even more hypothetical in view of actual government preferences—is whether the contracting parties could have actively given direct effect to CETA or some of its provisions. Prima facie the Court's case law does not preclude such an alternative approach. The Court acknowledges the contracting parties' discretion as regards the determination of the effect of the provisions of an agreement in their internal legal orders.[35] In principle, the Court thus only comes into play if an agreement remains silent on the issue. From an EU law perspective, the contracting parties could therefore at least have decided to give direct effect to unconditional and sufficiently precise provisions in CETA.

C. Indirect effect

Even if an international agreement lacks direct applicability, it may be given *indirect effect* by way of consistent interpretation.[36] As outlined above, agreements form an integral part of the EU legal order and have primacy over provisions of EU secondary legislation as well as national laws of the Member States. As a consequence, 'such provisions must, so far as possible, be interpreted in a manner that is consistent with those agreements'.[37] While consistent interpretation 'is not often applied for the simple reason that most agreements have direct effect',[38] it may be a useful

[33] Seminal decisions in Case 70/87, *Fediol v Commission* [1989] ECLI:EU:C:1989:254, para 19; and Case C-69/89, *Nakajima v Council* [1991] ECLI:EU:C:1991:186, paras 31–2; cf, eg, Pieter-Jan Kuijper and Marco Bronckers, 'WTO Law in the European Court of Justice' (2005) 42 *Common Market Law Review* 1313, 1323–8 (hereafter Kuijper and Bronckers, 'WTO Law in the ECJ'). See also the rather recent statement of the Court with regard to the exceptions stipulated in the decisions mentioned, Joined Cases C-404/12 P and C-405/12 P, *Council and Commission v Stichting Natuur en Milieu and Pesticide Action Network* [2015] ECLI:EU:2015:2, paras 48–51.

[34] cf Karen Knop, 'Here and There: International Law in Domestic Courts' (2000) 32 *NYU Journal of International Law and Politics* 501; Louis LeBel and Gloria Chao, 'The Rise of International Law in Canadian Constitutional Litigation: Fugue or Fusion? Recent Developments and Challenges in Internalizing International Law' (2002) 16 *Supreme Court Law Review* 23; and Armand de Mestral and Evan Fox-Decent, 'Rethinking the Relationship between International and Domestic Law' (2008) 53 *McGill Law Journal* 573.

[35] eg *ATAA* (n 24) para 49.

[36] eg Frederico Casolari, 'Giving Indirect Effect to International Law within the EU Legal Order: The Doctrine of Consistent Interpretation' in Enzo Cannizzaro, Paolo Palchetti, and Ramses A Wessel (eds), *International Law as Law of the European Union* (Nijhoff, 2012) 395.

[37] Case C-61/94, *Commission v Germany* [1996] ECLI:EU:C:1996:313, para 52.

[38] Eeckhout, *EU External Relations Law* (n 8) 356.

instrument in the context of agreements like CETA, TTIP, and TiSA. In this regard, it is noteworthy that the Court has recognized particular instances where an interpretation in conformity with WTO law is actually required.[39] Thus, at least to this extent, EU secondary legislation and national laws are likely to be subject to interpretation in conformity with CETA, TTIP, and TiSA. However, while mitigating the lack of direct effect to a certain extent, indirect effect remains an 'incomplete substitute'.[40]

Finally, it is needless to say that the potential effects of CETA, TTIP, and TiSA are not limited to their legal effects before domestic courts. Other actors at the domestic level may aim to comply with obligations assumed under the agreements or at least take into account the risks of non-compliance, especially where dispute resolution (or investor-state arbitration) makes potential violations costly.[41]

III. Negotiation and Conclusion of Agreements

A. Special regime for common commercial policy

Article 218 TFEU provides the general framework for the negotiation and conclusion of agreements between the EU and third countries or international organizations. However, in the area of CCP—which is relevant for agreements like CETA, TTIP, and TiSA—the procedure set out in Art 218 TFEU is subject to the special provisions laid down in Art 207 TFEU.

According to Art 207(3) TFEU, the Commission—as the future negotiator—initiates negotiations by making recommendations to the Council. The Council may then authorize the necessary negotiations and issue negotiating directives, setting out its expectations or limits for the planned negotiations.[42] During the negotiations, the Commission regularly reports to a special committee appointed by the Council and also to the European Parliament.

[39] eg Case C-53/96, *Hermès* [1998] ECLI:EU:C:1998:292, para 28; and Case C-76/00 P, *Petrotub and Republica* [2003] ECLI:EU:C:2003:4, paras 49–64. Cf Kuijper and Bronckers, 'WTO Law in the ECJ' (n 33) 1328–30; Christian Heidfeld, *Die dezentrale Durchsetzung des WTO-Rechts in der Europäischen Union* (Nomos, 2012) 270–303; and Jan-Peter Hix, 'Indirect Effect of International Agreements: Consistent Interpretation and Other Forms of Judicial Accommodation of WTO Law by the EU Courts and the US Courts' [2013] *NYU Jean Monnet Working Paper Series* 76–82 (hereafter Hix, 'Indirect Effect of International Agreements').

[40] Hix, 'Indirect Effect of International Agreements' (n 39) 11.

[41] cf Jacques Bourgeois and Orla Lynskey, 'The extent to which the EC legislature takes account of WTO obligations: jousting lessons from the European Parliament' in Alan Dashwood and Marc Maresceau (eds), *Law and Practice of EU External Relations* (Cambridge University Press, 2008) 202. Cf also Recital 4 of Regulation No 765/2012 amending Council Regulation No 1225/2009 on protection against dumped imports from countries not members of the European Community [2012] OJ L 237/1, stating that the proposed amendment to the regulation 'should be read in the light of the Appellate Body's clarifications' in its Report in *European Communities—Definitive Anti-Dumping Measures on Certain Iron and Steel Fasteners from China*, WT/DS397/AB/R, 15 July 2011.

[42] cf the partially declassified CETA negotiating directives and the 2011 modification including investment protection in the negotiations (15 December 2015), <http://www.consilium.europa.eu/

B. Majority requirements in the Council

Generally, Art 207(4) TFEU requires a qualified majority in the Council for initiating negotiations as well as concluding agreements in the field of CCP. Unanimity, which gives a veto right to every single Member State, is only required in exceptional cases. One such exception is merely factual and concerns the conclusion of mixed agreements.[43] Other exceptions are stipulated in Art 207(4) TFEU, according to which unanimity is generally required for agreements in the fields of trade in services and the commercial aspects of intellectual property, as well as foreign direct investment (FDI), 'where such agreements include provisions for which unanimity is required for the adoption of internal rules'. However, while the scope of this provision seems quite broad at first, its effects are marginal at best. This is because—since the Lisbon Treaty—unanimity is only exceptionally required for the adoption of the respective internal rules.[44]

What is more, Art 207(4) subpara 3 TFEU requires the Council to act unanimously for the negotiation and conclusion of agreements in the field of trade in cultural and audiovisual services, where these agreements risk prejudicing the Union's cultural and linguistic diversity (lit a) and in the field of trade in social, education, and health services, where these agreements risk seriously disturbing the national organization of such services and prejudicing the responsibility of Member States to deliver them (lit b). With regard to CETA, TTIP, and TiSA, the second alternative could be of some relevance. Article 207(4)(b) TFEU reflects the importance attached by many Member States to these particular services of general economic interest.[45] Consequentially, the risk assessment is *primarily* a prerogative of the individual Member State.[46] In the light of the fragmentary nature and sometimes uncertain scope of the reservations for many public services in CETA, a Member State could argue that unanimity in the Council is required according to Art 207(4)(b) TFEU. However, a more detailed analysis shows that CETA contains relatively broad reservations in the three sectors mentioned. Hence, it is doubtful whether the other Member States (or eventually the Court) could be persuaded that the conditions for unanimity are actually met.

en/press/press-releases/2015/12/15-eu-canada-trade-negotiating-mandate-made-public/> accessed 7 April 2017.

43 cf Allan Rosas, 'The European Union and mixed agreements' in Alan Dashwood and Christophe Hillion, *The General Law of E.C. External Relations* (Sweet & Maxwell, 2000) 201–2 (hereafter Rosas, 'The European Union and Mixed Agreements').

44 eg Arts 64(3) and 113 TFEU. Cf Wolfgang Weiß, 'Art 207 AEUV' in Eberhard Grabitz, Meinhard Hilf, and Martin Nettesheim (eds), *Das Recht der Europäischen Union* (CH Beck, 2016) para 46 (hereafter Weiß, 'Art 207 AEUV').

45 cf Wouters et al, 'External Relations after Lisbon Treaty' (n 17) 183.

46 Markus Krajewski, 'The Reform of the Common Commercial Policy' in Andrea Biondi and Piet Eeckhout (eds), *EU Law After Lisbon* (Oxford University Press, 2012) 307 (hereafter Krajewski, 'The Reform of the CCP').

C. The role of the European Parliament

The Lisbon Treaty has substantially improved the role of the European Parliament in the area of CCP. Prior to Lisbon, the Council did not even have to consult the Parliament before concluding an agreement in the area of CCP.[47] Now the Council can only conclude an agreement in this field after obtaining parliamentary consent.[48] While this has certainly been an important improvement with regard to the democratic legitimacy of the EU's external trade policy, the Parliament's role may again be limited with regard to future amendments of the important annexes to agreements such as CETA, TTIP, and TiSA. When concluding an agreement, the Council may 'authorise the negotiator to approve on the Union's behalf modifications to the agreement where it provides for them to be adopted by a simplified procedure or by a body set up by the agreement . . .'.[49]

In this regard, it is important to highlight that, according to the conditions set out in Art 30.2 CETA, the CETA Joint Committee 'may decide to amend the protocols and annexes of this Agreement'. The parties then may approve the decision of the CETA Joint Committee 'subject to their internal requirements and procedures'. Hence, where the simplified procedure for amending annexes to the agreement applies, the European Parliament only has to be informed of the changes intended.[50] In principle, this means that quite far-reaching treaty amendments could be made without parliamentary consent.

However, at least in the CETA context, the scope of this simplified amendment procedure is limited in two important ways. First, Art 30.2 CETA provides that it does not apply to a number of the more sensitive annexes, ie Annexes I, II, and III and the annexes to Chapters Eight (Investment), Nine (Cross-Border Trade in Services), Ten (Temporary Entry and Stay of Natural Persons for Business Purposes), and Thirteen (Financial Services).[51] Still, this leaves a number of important annexes subject to Art 30.2 CETA, for example, the annexes to the chapters on government procurement or intellectual property. Second, however, in its Proposal for a Council Decision on the conclusion of CETA, the Commission only suggests to include the simplified amendment procedure for Annex 20-A on geographical indications identifying a product's place of origin.[52] Thus, in the context of CETA, the Commission will only be competent to approve decisions of the CETA Joint Committee on modifications to Annex 20-A. Amendments to other annexes or protocols, however, require a regular amendment to the agreement, including parliamentary consent at EU level. What is more, if CETA, TTIP, or TiSA are qualified

[47] cf Art 300(3) EC. Exceptional requirements for parliamentary consent were contained in subpara 2, for example, for agreements establishing a specific institutional framework by organizing cooperation procedures.

[48] cf Arts 218(6)(a)(v) and 207(2) TFEU.

[49] Art 218(7) TFEU.

[50] Art 218(10) TFEU.

[51] There is an exception for Annex 10-A, containing a List of Contact Points of the Member States of the European Union.

[52] COM (2016) 443 final (n 2) 11.

as mixed agreements, amendments (in practice[53]) also have to be accepted by the Member States, in accordance with their respective constitutional requirements.

IV. The Issue of Competence and Mixity

A. Political background

The question of mixity has been a recurring theme in the above considerations and is, without doubt, of utmost legal and political relevance. In view of the controversy regarding the extent and nature of the EU's competence to conclude comprehensive trade and investment agreements, the Commission has asked the Court to issue an opinion in the context of the EUSFTA in July 2015.[54] As pointed out in the introduction, the significance of Opinion 2/15 will go beyond the Singapore agreement. With regard to CETA, the Commission has explicitly set out that both EUSFTA and CETA have 'identical objectives and essentially the same contents',[55] and that the EU's competence is the same in both cases. Moreover, in principle, similar considerations are likely to apply to TTIP and other FTAs of the new generation.

However, despite the significance of the EUSFTA opinion, the Commission has chosen to proceed with the conclusion of CETA. Based on a political compromise, 'the Commission has decided to propose the conclusion of CETA as a mixed agreement'.[56] The Commission emphasizes, however, that this is without prejudice to its views expressed in the case of the EUSFTA, that is, that 'the Union has exclusive competence to conclude EUSFTA alone and, in the alternative, that it has at least shared competence in those areas where the Union's competence is not exclusive'.[57]

This course of action may satisfy the Member States which insist that EUSFTA, CETA, and TTIP are to be concluded as mixed agreements. Yet, it leaves the underlying competence issue unresolved and also raises the question of to what extent mixity may be at the discretion of the institutions, even if it were not legally required.[58]

While the seminal *EUSFTA* case is still pending in the Court, Sharpston AG has recently issued her extensive and nuanced opinion, arguing that the envisaged FTA 'can be concluded only by the European Union and the Member States acting jointly'.[59] However, before discussing whether CETA, TTIP, and TiSA are to be concluded as mixed agreements, it seems useful to generally reiterate some basics regarding EU external competence.

[53] MacLeod et al, *External Relations* (n 7) 163.
[54] At the time of writing, the case is still pending.
[55] COM (2016) 443 final (n 2) 4.
[56] ibid.
[57] ibid.
[58] cf Eeckhout, *EU External Relations Law* (n 8) 216–17.
[59] *EUSFTA* (n 5) Opinion of AG Sharpston, para 570.

B. EU external competence

1. *Fundamental structure*

The division of competences between the EU and its Member States is essentially characterized by the so-called *principle of conferral*. According to Art 5(2) TEU: 'the Union shall only act within the limits of the competences conferred upon it by the Member States in the Treaties to attain the objectives set out therein. Competences not conferred upon the Union in the Treaties remain with the Member States.' This principle also applies with regard to external action.[60]

Hence, for present purposes, we can distinguish three main types of competences, namely, exclusive competences of the Member States, exclusive competences of the EU, and shared competences.[61] Moreover, in the field of external competences, a further distinction can be drawn between express and implied powers. This is also reflected in Art 216(1) TFEU, which provides that:

> The Union may conclude an agreement ... where the Treaties so provide or where the conclusion of an agreement is necessary in order to achieve, within the framework of the Union's policies, one of the objectives referred to in the Treaties, or is provided for in a legally binding Union act or is likely to affect common rules or alter their scope.

Thus, when analysing EU external competence, it is necessary to differentiate between the existence of external competence and its exclusivity. However, as Craig has pointedly observed, 'the reality is that it will be rare, if ever, for the EU to lack power to conclude an international agreement'.[62] The 'real' question, then, is whether the EU has the power to conclude an agreement alone or whether a mixed agreement is required.

2. *Exclusive competence of the EU*

a) Express competences

In areas of exclusive EU competence, 'only the Union may legislate and adopt legally binding acts', while the Member States—irrespective of whether the EU has actually exercised its power—may do so 'only if so empowered by the Union or for the implementation of Union acts'.[63] Article 3(1) TFEU includes a list of subject-matter areas that fall expressly within exclusive EU competence. With regard to CETA, TTIP, and TiSA, the relevant provision is Art 3(1)(e), conferring on the EU exclusive competence in the area of CCP. Early on, the Court has recognized the external dimension of this exclusive EU competence which thus also includes the

[60] eg Opinion 1/13, *Convention of the civil aspects of international child abduction* [2014] ECLI:EU:C:2014:2303, para 74.

[61] Art 2 TFEU furthermore establishes the category of supporting, coordinating, and supplementary competence, in which EU action does not supersede Member State competence (Art 2(5) TFEU).

[62] Paul Craig, *The Lisbon Treaty* (Oxford University Press, 2010) 165 (hereafter Craig, *The Lisbon Treaty*).

[63] Art 2(1) TFEU.

power to conclude agreements.[64] However, the exact scope of the competence has to be determined in the light of the relevant treaty provisions.[65]

b) Implied competences

i) Development in the Court's case law

Before its codification in Arts 216(1) and 3(2) TFEU, the doctrine on implied powers has been gradually developed by the Court of Justice in its case law. It is important to note, however, that the provisions introduced by the Lisbon Treaty do not 'capture all the nuances from that jurisprudence'.[66] Thus, a brief outline of the Court's case law will contribute to a better understanding of these provisions and the underlying doctrine on implied powers.

In its European Road Transport Agreement (*ERTA*) judgment, the Court first recognized the possibility of implied external powers 'flow[ing] from ... provisions of the Treaty [which do not expressly confer external competence] and from measures adopted, within the framework of these provisions, by Community institutions'.[67] The Court held that when the Community acted to implement a common policy 'for the attainment of the objectives of the Treaty, the Member States cannot ... assume obligations *which might affect those rules or alter their scope*'.[68] In *ERTA*, the scope of the implied external power thus coincided with the scope of the potentially affected common rules.[69]

In *Kramer*, the Court went one step further and held that the Community could have implied external power in an area which had hitherto not been subject to internal measures implementing the relevant policy.[70] In its Opinion 1/76, the Court referring to *Kramer* underlined that even if 'internal Community measures are only adopted when the international agreement is concluded', an exclusive implied external power exists 'in so far as the participation of the Community in the international agreement is ... necessary for the attainment of one of the objectives of the Community'.[71] However, in Opinion 1/94, the Court advanced a more limited reading and stated that '[s]ave where internal powers can only be effectively exercised at the same time as external powers ... internal competence can give rise to exclusive external competence only if it is exercised'.[72]

In Opinion 2/91, the Court had already clarified that implied powers are not per se exclusive.[73] In particular, if both an agreement and Community law stipulate

[64] Opinion 1/75, *Local Cost Standard* [1975] ECLI:EU:C:1975:145, 1363.

[65] cf Art 2(6) TFEU.

[66] Craig, *The Lisbon Treaty* (n 62) 162.

[67] Case 22/70, *Commission v Council* [1971] ECLI:EU:C:1971:31, para 16 (hereafter *ERTA*).

[68] ibid, para 22 (emphasis added).

[69] ibid, paras 30–1. The Court did not scrutinize in detail any specific impairment, but held that 'any steps taken outside the framework of the Community institutions would be incompatible with the unity of the Common Market and the uniform application of Community law'.

[70] Joined Cases 3, 4, and 6/76, *Kramer* [1976] ECLI:EU:C:1976:114, para 30/33.

[71] Opinion 1/76, *Inland Waterway Vessels* [1977] ECLI:EU:C:1977:63, para 4.

[72] *WTO Agreement* (n 14) para 89. Cf also Opinion 2/92, *OECD* [1995] ECLI:EU:C:1995:83, para 32 (hereafter Opinion 2/92, *OECD*).

[73] Opinion 2/91, *International Labour Organization* [1993] ECLI:EU:C:1993:106, para 18 (hereafter *International Labour Organization*); and Opinion 1/03, *Lugano Convention* [2006] ECLI:EU:C:2006:81, para 115 (hereafter *Lugano Convention*).

minimum standards, exclusivity cannot be founded on the respective Community provisions.[74] The reason is that Member States' commitments in such a case arguably neither affect common rules nor alter their scope. However, this raises the question of under what circumstances the Community actually acquires exclusive external competence. In the 'open skies' cases, the Court set out three situations in which it recognized exclusivity:[75] first, where an agreement falls within the scope of the common rules or at least within an area largely covered by such rules;[76] second, if internal legislative acts contain provisions relating to the treatment of nationals of non-member countries or expressly confer on the institutions powers to negotiate with non-member countries;[77] and, third, where the Community has achieved 'complete harmonization' in a given area.[78] However, in Opinion 1/03, the Court held that those three situations are 'only examples, formulated in the light of the particular contexts with which the Court was concerned'[79] and emphasized that the general rationale behind exclusive competence 'is primarily to preserve the effectiveness of Community law and the proper functioning of the systems established by its rules'.[80]

ii) Codification in the TFEU

According to Art 3(2) TFEU, the EU has exclusive competence to conclude an agreement 'when its conclusion is provided for in a legislative act of the Union or is necessary to enable the Union to exercise its internal competence, or insofar as its conclusion may affect common rules or alter their scope'. While the provision in Art 3(2) TFEU *largely* codifies the Court's case law on exclusive implied external powers, Cremona has convincingly argued that it 'conflates the two separate questions of the existence of implied external competence and the exclusivity of that competence'.[81] Reading Arts 3(2) and 216(1) TFEU together may suggest that all implied powers would be exclusive. However, as Cremona emphasizes, such a reading is hard to defend in policy terms, as it 'would entail a potentially large expansion of exclusive competence'.[82]

3. Shared competence

Shared competence is defined in Art 2(2) TFEU. Basically, in an area of shared competence, the Member States may legislate, adopt legally binding acts, or conclude international agreements '*to the extent* that the Union has not exercised its

[74] *International Labour Organization* (n 73) paras 18–21.
[75] eg Case C-468/98, *Commission v Sweden* [2002] ECLI:EU:C:2002:626, paras 77–80.
[76] *ERTA* (n 67) para 30; *International Labour Organization* (n 73) para 25; and *Lugano Convention* (n 73) para 126.
[77] *WTO Agreement* (n 14) para 95.
[78] *WTO Agreement* (n 14) para 96; and Opinion 2/92, *OECD* (n 72) para 33.
[79] *Lugano Convention* (n 73) para 121.
[80] ibid, para 131.
[81] Marise Cremona, 'Defining Competence in EU External Relations' in Alan Dashwood and Marc Maresceau (eds), *Law and Practice of EU External Relations* (Cambridge University Press, 2008) 61.
[82] ibid, 62.

competence'.[83] Protocol (No 25) On the Exercise of Shared Competence underlines that pre-emption is limited, stating that 'when the Union has taken action in a certain area, the scope of this exercise of competence only covers those elements governed by the Union act in question and therefore does not cover the whole area'. This type of shared competence has also been labelled as *concurrent* competence.[84] Principal areas of this type of shared competence are listed in Art 4(2) TFEU and comprise, for example, the internal market, environment, transport, and energy. The main difference with regard to areas of exclusive competence is that a shared competence only bars Member States from autonomously taking action or entering into agreements once (and insofar as) the EU has actually exercised its competences. The exact scope of the EU's particular competences—and hence the 'practical divide between Member State and EU competence'[85]—has to be determined in the light of the relevant Treaty provisions and EU legislation within these areas.[86]

Article 4(3) and (4) TFEU contains a different type of shared competence, also labelled as *parallel* competence.[87] In the areas of research, technological development, and space, as well as development cooperation and humanitarian aid, the exercise of the EU's competence does not prevent Member States from autonomously exercising theirs.

With regard to CETA, TTIP, and TiSA, it is important to note that 'at the political level in the EU there is a tendency to consider that, unless an agreement falls wholly within the exclusive competence of the EU, mixity is required'.[88] However, legally, the situation is more complicated. A distinction has to be made between cases of obligatory mixity and facultative mixity. While in the former type of case the conclusion of a mixed agreement is legally necessary, it is (only) legally possible in the latter.[89] Moreover, in some cases, mixity may even be legally objectionable. Arguably, this would be the case, if an agreement fell entirely within exclusive EU competence. As mentioned above, the Commission claims such exclusive competence in the context of EUSFTA (and implicitly also CETA).[90] Concluding a mixed agreement in such a case could then be seen as a distortion of the powers laid down in the Treaty.[91]

[83] Emphasis added. Moreover, the Member States, at least in theory, 'shall again exercise their competence to the extent that the Union has decided to cease exercising its competence'.

[84] eg Armin von Bogdandy and Jürgen Bast, 'The Federal Order of Competences' in Armin von Bogdandy and Jürgen Bast (eds), *Principles of European Constitutional Law* (2nd edn, Hart and CH Beck, 2009) 290 (hereafter von Bogdandy and Bast, 'The Federal Order of Competences').

[85] Craig, *The Lisbon Treaty* (n 62) 171.

[86] cf Art 2(6) TFEU.

[87] cf von Bogdandy and Bast, 'The Federal Order of Competences' (n 84) 294.

[88] Eeckhout, *EU External Relations Law* (n 8) 214.

[89] Rosas, 'The European Union and Mixed Agreements' (n 43) 206.

[90] In the alternative, the Commission claims that the EU has at least shared competence in those areas where its competence is not exclusive, COM (2016) 443 final (n 2) 4.

[91] cf Eeckhout, *EU External Relations Law* (n 8) 216–17, considering at least in some cases a violation of Art 4(3) TEU. However, it should be considered whether a proposal to conclude a mixed agreement in an area of exclusive EU competence may be constructed as an empowerment in the sense of Art 2(1) TFEU.

C. CETA, TTIP, and TiSA: Mixed or EU only?

1. Outline

The analysis so far has shown that the division of external competences between the EU and the Member States is rather complex and the scope of particular competences often not readily apparent. In addition, it has been set out that mixity—depending on the actual contents of an agreement—may be legally necessary, legally possible, or legally objectionable.

Only recently, Advocate General Sharpston published her opinion in *EUSFTA*, reaching the conclusion that the agreement with Singapore 'can be concluded only by the European Union and the Member States acting jointly'.[92] Against this background, the following section explores whether CETA, TTIP, and TiSA are likely to be cases of obligatory mixity, facultative mixity, or no mixity at all. As regards CETA, a number of competence issues (similar to those in the EUSFTA context) have been identified in the literature, for example, regarding the inclusion of portfolio investment in the chapter on investment and investment protection or the termination of existing bilateral investment treaties (BITs) of Member States with contracting parties.[93] Other aspects considered problematic include commitments in the area of transport and the establishment of a framework for the mutual recognition of professional qualifications.[94] Additionally, with regard to EU Member States which are not members of the European Monetary Union, provisions on the safeguarding of the national balance of payments or external financial position may also raise competence issues.[95]

After a brief summary of the main findings of the Advocate General in *EUSFTA*, the following analysis will focus on the EU's particularly controversial competence in the field of investment. In the light of both, the AG's recent opinion and the current literature, it will first determine the scope of the EU's express exclusive competence in the area of CCP, which is the main legal basis for agreements like

[92] *EUSFTA* (n 5) Opinion of AG Sharpston, para 570.

[93] eg Franz C Mayer, 'Stellt das geplante Freihandelsabkommen der EU mit Kanada (Comprehensive Economic and Trade Agreement, CETA) ein gemischtes Abkommen dar?' (28 August 2014), <https://www.bmwi.de/Redaktion/DE/Downloads/C-D/ceta-gutachten-einstufung-als-gemischtes-abkommen.pdf?__blob=publicationFile&v=4> accessed 7 April 2017 (hereafter Mayer, 'CETA ein gemischtes Abkommen?'); and Stefan Mayr, '"Mixed" oder "EU-only"—Sind die Investitionsschutzbestimmungen im CETA von der Außenhandelskompetenz der EU "gedeckt"?' [2015] *Europarecht* 575 (hereafter Mayr, '"Mixed" oder "EU-only"').

[94] Mayer, 'CETA ein gemischtes Abkommen?' (n 93) 16–19; consenting, for example, Andreas Fischer-Lescano and Johan Horst, 'Europa- und verfassungsrechtliche Vorgaben für das Comprehensive Economic and Trade Agreement der EU und Kanada (CETA)' (October 2014) 5–6, <http://www.eesc.europa.eu/resources/docs/04-gutachten_ceta_171014_final-fischer-lescano.pdf> accessed 25 August 2016.

[95] cf Christoph Ohler, 'Die Umsetzung der Gemeinsamen Handelspolitik nach dem Vertrag von Lissabon' in Thomas Eilmansberger, Stefan Griller, and Walter Obwexer (eds), *Rechtsfragen der Implementierung des Vertrags von Lissabon* (Springer, 2011) 424–5 (hereafter Ohler, 'Die Umsetzung der Gemeinsamen Handelspolitik nach dem Vertrag von Lissabon'). With regard to the provision in Art 28.5 CETA, it has to be noted that according to Arts 143 and 144 TFEU, the EU has the competence to investigate and to grant mutual assistance, but no legislative competence.

CETA, TTIP, and TiSA. Subsequently, it will explore whether and to what extent the EU might have acquired complementary implied powers. Finally, the outcome will be 'mapped' against the contents of the agreements and the consequences for the conclusion of the agreement will be discussed.

2. *Brief overview: The opinion of the Advocate General in* EUSFTA

On 21 December 2016, AG Sharpton issued her opinion in *EUSFTA*. After analysing the Treaty rules on the allocation of competences to the EU and the nature of those competences, the AG meticulously determines the precise division of powers between the EU and the Member States chapter by chapter.

In summary, she finds that the EU enjoys exclusive external competence with regard to matters such as: trade in goods; trade and investment in renewable energy generation; trade in services and public procurement (with the exception of transport services); FDI; the commercial aspects of intellectual property rights; competition; trade and sustainable development (insofar as the provisions relate primarily to commercial policy); the conservation of marine and biological resources; and trade in rail and road transport services. However, with regard to other parts of the EUSFTA, the AG considers the EU's external competence to be shared with the Member States. These include the provisions on trade in air transport services, maritime transport services, and transport by inland waterways; the provisions on types of investment other than FDI (eg portfolio investment); the provisions on public procurement insofar as they apply to transport services; the provisions relating to the non-commercial aspects of intellectual property rights; and the provisions laying down fundamental labour and environmental standards. What is more, she finds that the competence to agree to dispute settlement and mediation mechanisms is ancillary to the respective substantive competences and thus partly exclusive and partly shared. Finally, the AG states that the EU has no external competence to terminate bilateral agreements such as BITs concluded between certain Member States and Singapore. This power remains exclusively with those Member States.[96]

On this basis, the AG argues that the EUSFTA 'can be concluded only by the European Union and the Member States acting jointly'.[97] The underlying rationale is twofold: insofar as the EU has no competence to act, Member State participation is evidently required if the principle of conferral is to be taken seriously. However, according to the AG's opinion, this is only the case with regard to the rather isolated aspect of the termination of existing Member State BITs. Other than that, the EU either has exclusive competence or shares competences with the Member States. In the areas of shared competence, Art 2(2) TFEU grants the EU a so-called 'right of pre-emption', that is, the right to choose whether and to what extent the EU actually exercises its shared competences.[98] Hence, if the EU chooses

[96] *EUSFTA* (n 5) Opinion of AG Sharpston, para 570. [97] ibid. [98] ibid, para 61.

not to exercise a particular shared competence, this competence remains with the Member States 'and it follows that they ... will be competent to negotiate, sign and conclude an international agreement whose subject matter falls within that area of shared competence'.[99] The AG acknowledges that this is a political choice which is, however, legally channelled in the detailed procedures set out in Art 218 TFEU:[100] as the negotiation and conclusion of an agreement require a number of separate Council decisions[101] (usually taken by a qualified majority[102]), it is eventually 'the Member States acting in their capacity as members of the Council which authorise the appropriate EU institution to act'.[103]

3. Competence with regard to investment

a) Express competence for FDI

Over the last decades, the exact scope of the EU's competence in the area of CCP has time and again given rise to controversy. While the Court initially gave the competence for CCP a broad reading, emphasizing its dynamic character,[104] it later arguably switched to a more restrictive approach.[105] However, in order to strengthen the EU as a player in the global economic context, the Lisbon Treaty, again, amended the provisions on CCP significantly. Article 207(1) TFEU reads as follows:

> The common commercial policy shall be based on uniform principles, particularly with regard to changes in tariff rates, the conclusion of tariff and trade agreements relating to trade in goods and services, and the commercial aspects of intellectual property, foreign direct investment, the achievement of uniformity in measures of liberalisation, export policy and measures to protect trade such as those to be taken in the event of dumping or subsidies. The common commercial policy shall be conducted in the context of the principles and objectives of the Union's external action.

The provision now makes explicit reference not only to trade in services and commercial aspects of intellectual property,[106] but also newly adds FDI to the CCP.

[99] ibid, para 73. [100] cf also above, section III.

[101] eg authorizing the opening of negotiations, adopting negotiating directives, and authorizing the signing and conclusion of an agreement.

[102] For exceptions requiring unanimity, see Art 218(8) TFEU.

[103] *EUSFTA* (n 5) Opinion of AG Sharpston, para 74.

[104] eg Opinion 1/78, *Natural Rubber* [1979] ECLI:EU:C:1979:224, paras 44–5 (with regard to then Art 113 EEC Treaty) (hereafter *Natural Rubber*).

[105] eg *WTO Agreement* (n 14) paras 42–7. Cf Stefan Griller and Katharina Gamharter, 'External Trade: Is There a Path Through the Maze of Competences?' in Stefan Griller and Birgit Weidel (eds), *External Economic Relations and Foreign Policy in the European Union* (Springer, 2002) 70–1. In her opinion in *EUSFTA* (n 5), AG Sharpston doubts 'that it is particularly useful to debate whether or not the common commercial policy is "dynamic". What matters is that Article 207(1) TFEU should be interpreted in a manner that both respects the wording of that provision and guarantees that the European Union is able to conduct an effective common commercial policy in an international commercial environment that is permanently evolving' (para 99).

[106] Pre-Lisbon trade in services and commercial aspects of intellectual property were subject to a special regime in (then) Art 133(5) and (6) EC.

While the inclusion of FDI clearly marks a significant shift of competence, its exact scope has yet to be determined.[107]

b) The limits of Art 207(1) TFEU

The clear wording indicates that Art 207(1) TFEU extends to the category of FDI, but not to other categories of investment, for example, portfolio investment. While there is no definition of either FDI or portfolio investment in the Treaty, there is broad agreement on the essentials characterizing both types of investment in the literature.[108] Direct investment is basically considered to aim at establishing lasting economic links and a strategic long-term relationship, granting the direct investor control or a significant degree of influence over the investment. This is arguably evidenced when a direct investor owns at least 10 per cent of the voting power.[109] Portfolio investment, on the other hand, is not based on the investor's expectation of gaining influence on the management of the enterprise; it is characterized by its more short-term and often speculative nature.[110] In view of this distinction and the clear wording of the provision, prevailing opinion argues that Art 207(1) TFEU does not confer exclusive competence on the EU with regard to portfolio investment.[111] The inclusion of FDI but not portfolio investment in Art 207(1) TFEU thus arguably indicates that the Member States, while assigning new powers to the EU, at the same time sought to secure a certain level of their influence. Such a gradual 'retreat' is by no means exceptional,[112] albeit only a 'second best solution' with

[107] Michael Waibel, 'Competence Review: Trade and Investment' (2013) para 31, <https://www.gov.uk/government/uploads/system/uploads/attachment_data/file/270992/bis-14-511-trade-and-investment-competence-review-independent-review-legal-research-by-michael-waibel.pdf> accessed 7 April 2017.

[108] eg based on the nomenclature annexed to Directive 88/361/EEC of 24 June 1988 for the implementation of Art 67 of the Treaty [1988] OJ L 178/05, which according to the Court has indicative value for the interpretation of the concept of direct investment; cf Case C-446/04, *Test Claimants in the FII Group Litigation* [2006] ECLI:EU:C:2006:774, para 180. Further definitional sources are the *IMF Balance of Payments and International Position Manual* (6th edn, IMF, 2013) 110ff and the *OECD Benchmark Definition of Foreign Direct Investment* (4th edn, OECD, 2008) 17.

[109] Similarly, AG Sharpston considers that 'the fact that the direct investor owns at least 10% of the voting power of the direct investment enterprise may offer evidentiary guidance but is certainly not determinative', *EUSFTA* (n 5) para 322.

[110] cf also European Commission, 'Towards a Comprehensive European International Investment Policy', COM (2010) 343 final, 2–3.

[111] cf Christian Tietje, 'Die Außenwirtschaftsverfassung der EU nach dem Vertrag von Lissabon' (2009) 83 *Beiträge zum Transnationalen Wirtschaftsrecht* 16 (hereafter Tietje, 'Die Außenwirtschaftsverfassung der EU nach dem Vertrag von Lissabon'); Marc Bungenberg, 'Außenbeziehungen und Außenhandelspolitik' [2009] *Europarecht Beiheft 1* 195 (hereafter Bungenberg, 'Außenbeziehungen und Außenhandelspolitik'); August Reinisch, 'The Division of Powers between the EU and its Member States "after Lisbon"' in Marc Bungenberg, Joern Griebel, and Steffen Hindelang (eds), *Internationaler Investitionsschutz und Europarecht* (Nomos, 2010) 106–7 (hereafter Reinisch, 'The Division of Powers'); Ohler, 'Die Umsetzung der Gemeinsamen Handelspolitik nach dem Vertrag von Lissabon' (n 95) 431; Krajewski, 'The Reform of the CCP' (n 46) 302; and Frederico Ortino and Piet Eeckhout, 'Towards an EU Policy on Foreign Direct Investment' in Andrea Biondi and Piet Eeckhout (eds), *EU Law after Lisbon* (Oxford University Press, 2012) 315 (hereafter Ortino and Eeckhout, 'Towards an EU Policy on Foreign Direct Investment').

[112] eg Art 133(5) and (6) EC, introduced by the Nice Treaty, contained a special regime with regard to trade in services and commercial aspects of intellectual property, before the Lisbon Treaty led to the inclusion of both areas in the general regime in Art 207(1) TFEU.

regard to ensuring the effective representation of EU interests at the international level.[113]

A different question is whether the scope of the EU's exclusive competence for FDI is limited to the regulation of market access and promotion of investment issues or whether the competence also extends to the post-establishment protection of investors and their investments. Proponents of a restrictive approach, for example, emphasize that according to Art 206 TFEU the EU aims at contributing to 'the progressive abolition of restrictions on international trade and on foreign direct investment', which arguably 'suggests that foreign direct investment is only part of the common commercial policy as far as restrictions to foreign direct investment are concerned'.[114] However, the wording of Art 207(1) TFEU does not support such a narrow reading. What is more, as AG Sharpston rightly observes, market access limitations are 'merely one type of restriction', while other restrictions might, for example, result from 'discriminatory treatment; the lack of security, predictability and transparency in the regulation of international trade and foreign direct investment; or the existence of unfair trade practices'.[115]

Then again, some commentators argue that in accordance with Art 345 TFEU—which provides that the Treaties 'shall in no way prejudice the rules in Member States governing the system of property ownership'—at least standards of protection against expropriation fall within Member States' competence.[116] A number of Member States have put forward similar arguments in *EUSFTA*. However, the AG—arguably in line with the Court's narrow reading of the provision in Art 345 TFEU[117]—rejects this line of reasoning, arguing that EUSFTA 'does not infringe the Member States' prerogative (that is, the exclusive competence) to choose their system of property ownership'.[118]

c) Implied competence for portfolio investment?

i) Implied exclusive competence

The analysis has thus far shown that Art 207(1) expressly grants the EU a far-reaching exclusive competence with regard to FDI, but not with regard to portfolio

[113] Also, the Court has consistently held 'that the resolution of the issue of the allocation of competence could not depend on problems which might possibly arise in administration of the agreements concerned', Opinion 1/08, *GATS* [2009] ECLI:EU:C:2009:739, para 127; cf also *WTO Agreement* (n 14) para 107; and Opinion 2/00, *Cartagena Protocol* [2001] ECLI:EU:C:2001:664, para 41 (hereafter *Cartagena Protocol*).

[114] cf Markus Krajewski, 'External Trade Law and the Constitution Treaty: Towards a Federal and More Democratic Common Commercial Policy?' [2005] *CML Rev* 91, 113–14 (hereafter Krajewski, 'External Trade Law and the Constitution Treaty').

[115] *EUSFTA* (n 5) Opinion of AG Sharpston, para 331.

[116] cf Sven Leif Erik Johannsen, 'Die Kompetenz der Europäischen Union für ausländische Direktinvestitionen ach dem Vertrag von Lissabon' (2009) 90 *Beiträge zum Transnationalen Wirtschaftsrecht* 16–17; and Krajewski, 'External Trade Law and the Constitution Treaty' (n 114) 114.

[117] cf Cases C-105–7/12, *Essent and Others* [2013] ECLI:EU:C:2013:677, para 36 and the case law cited.

[118] *EUSFTA* (n 5) Opinion of AG Sharpston, para 341.

investment. This raises the question of whether and to what extent the EU has an (exclusive or shared) implied competence with regard to portfolio investment.

Already in its 2010 Communication on the EU's international investment policy, the Commission had argued that the treaty provisions on capital and payments read together with the third ground under Art 3(2) TFEU—according to which implied external competence shall be exclusive, insofar as the conclusion of an agreement may affect common rules or alter their scope[119]—give the EU an implied exclusive competence also for portfolio investment.[120,121]

However, many commentators have disagreed with the Commission's reasoning and questioned its conformity with the law of EU external competence.[122] For example, Ortino and Eeckhout point out that it is 'difficult to see on what basis the EU could claim a general competence to conclude international agreements on the protection of portfolio investment'.[123] They convincingly argue that, while Arts 64(2) and 66 TFEU give the EU some substantive competences in the field of portfolio investment, these provisions 'clearly do not cover all aspects of such investment'.[124] In a similar vein, Weiß rejects the argument that such a general and exclusive competence can be deduced from Art 63 TFEU, simply because this provision (also) covers the movement of capital between Member States and third countries.[125] What is more, Krajewski argues that including FDI in Art 207(1)

[119] Arguably, the other alternatives stipulated in Art 3(2) TFEU do not support the Commission's claim to an exclusive competence either. In particular, there is no indication why concluding an international agreement would be necessary to enable the Union to exercise its internal competence in the field of portfolio investment. In any case, it would be for the Commission 'to provide evidence to establish the exclusive nature of the external competence of the EU on which it seeks to rely', Case C-114/12, *Commission v Council* [2014] ECLI:EU:C:2014:2151, para 75.

[120] The Commission states that the articulation of investment policy should be consistent with the chapter on capital and payments, 'which provides that, in principle, all restrictions on payments and capital movements, including those involving direct as well as portfolio investments, both between Member States and between Member States and third countries, are prohibited' and that 'to the extent that international agreements on investment affect the scope of the common rules set by the Treaty's Chapter on capital and payments, the exclusive Union competence to conclude agreements in this area would be implied', COM (2010) 343 final (n 110) 8. Cf also European Council Conclusions of 25 October 2010 on a comprehensive European international investment policy, para 7, where the Council 'supports the definition of a broad scope for the new EU policy in [the field of international investment] as suggested by the Commission, to be further elaborated *in full respect of the respective competences of the Union and its Member States* as defined by the Treaties' (emphasis added); European Parliament Resolution of 6 April 2011 on the future European international investment policy (2010/2203(INI)).

[121] Consenting, eg, Frank Hoffmeister and Güneş Ünüvar, 'From BITS and Pieces towards European Investment Agreements' in Marc Bungenberg, August Reinisch, and Christian Tietje (eds), *EU and Investment Agreements* (Nomos, 2013) 66–7. Cf also Christoph Herrmann, 'Die Zukunft der mitgliedstaatlichen Investitionspolitik nach dem Vertrag von Lissabon' [2010] *Europäische Zeitschrift für Wirtschaftsrecht* 207, 209.

[122] eg Ortino and Eeckhout, 'Towards an EU Policy on Foreign Direct Investment' (n 111) 315; and Krajewski, 'The Reform of the CCP' (n 46) 302.

[123] Ortino and Eeckhout, 'Towards an EU Policy on Foreign Direct Investment' (n 111) 317. The background to this is that the Court carefully defines the scope of substantive competences in implied powers cases, cf also Eeckhout, *EU External Relations Law* (n 8) 115.

[124] Ortino and Eeckhout, 'Towards an EU Policy on Foreign Direct Investment' (n 111) 317.

[125] Weiß, 'Art 207 AEUV' (n 44) para 46.

TFEU would have been superfluous if far-reaching implied powers—covering both FDI and portfolio investment—had existed prior to Lisbon.[126]

In *EUSFTA*, the Commission refines its line of reasoning. Based on a novel and rather creative reading of the third ground under Art 3(2) TFEU, suggesting that 'common rules' in the absence of secondary legislation also include Treaty provisions, the Commission argues that the EU has exclusive competence over portfolio investment on the basis of Art 3(2) read together with Art 63(1) TFEU.[127] The AG, however, rejects the Commission's approach, arguing that in the light of the Court's decision in *ERTA* and the subsequent case law, 'it is clear that the Commission's broad interpretation of "common rules" cannot be accepted'.[128] The AG emphasizes that Art 3(2) TFEU lays down *additional* grounds for the EU to have exclusive external competence in areas not covered by Art 3(1) TFEU and that such competence 'must therefore stem from some *other basis* than the Treaties themselves'.[129] However, since there is no secondary legislation under Arts 63(1) and 64(2) TFEU and thus no 'common rules', the requirements of the third ground under Art 3(2) TFEU are not met.[130] What is more, the AG argues that the Commission's reading of Art 3(2) TFEU implies that the EU has the right to conclude agreements that affect the Treaties or alter their scope. However, as the AG rightly points out, EU primary law 'can be changed only by amending the Treaties in accordance with Art 48 TEU'.[131]

ii) Implied shared competence

However, AG Sharpston accepts the Commission's (alternative) proposition that the investment chapter—insofar as it applies to types of investment other than FDI—entirely falls within the shared competences of the EU and the Member States. She basically argues that the free movement of capital aspect of the internal market 'has both an internal and an external component' and that an agreement that aims at 'reciprocal liberalisation between the EU and a third country ... falls within the framework of that policy'.[132] On this basis, the AG finds that concluding an agreement may be necessary, within the meaning of the second ground under Art 216(1) TFEU, in order to achieve that objective.[133] Bearing in mind that the AG considers dispute settlement and mediation mechanisms ancillary in nature, her finding is also decisive for the competence to agree to such mechanisms.

[126] Krajewski, 'The Reform of the CCP' (n 46) 302. Moreover, he opines that the Commission's reasoning 'ignore[s] the express intention of the drafters of the Lisbon Treaty' (ibid).

[127] *EUSFTA* (n 5) Opinion of AG Sharpston, paras 270–8.

[128] ibid, 352.

[129] ibid, 353 (emphasis in the original).

[130] In Case C-205/06, *Commission v Austria* and Case C-249/06, *Commission v Sweden* [2008] ECLI:EU:C:2008:391, Opinion of AG Maduro, para 3, the AG pointed out, the EU had not yet made use of its competences under Arts 64(2) or 66 TFEU. Similarly, Ortino and Eeckhout find that there are no common rules which an agreement covering portfolio investment may affect or alter the scope of (Ortino and Eeckhout, 'Towards an EU Policy on Foreign Direct Investment' (n 111) 317); cf also Mayer, 'CETA ein gemischtes Abkommen?' (n 93) 12–13.

[131] *EUSFTA* (n 5) Opinion of AG Sharpston, para 354.

[132] ibid, para 369.

[133] ibid, para 370.

In other words, the allocation of competences for such mechanisms is the same as the allocation of substantive competences.[134]

A different question is whether the EU has actually exercised its right of pre-emption with regard to these shared competences. In this context, Regulation 912/2014[135] has to be mentioned: the regulation addresses the conduct of investment disputes and the apportionment of financial responsibility between the EU and the Member States in the context of international (investment) agreements to which the EU is party. However, Art 1 provides that 'the adoption and application of this Regulation shall not affect the delimitation of competences established by the Treaties'. Moreover, a joint declaration by the European Parliament, the Council, and the Commission attached to the Regulation reads as follows: 'The adoption and application of this Regulation are without prejudice to the division of competences established by the Treaties and shall not be interpreted as an exercise of shared competence by the Union in areas where the Union's competence has not been exercised.' In her opinion, the AG, referring to Art 1 of Regulation 912/2014, explicitly states that 'the rules on the apportionment of financial responsibility between the European Union and its Member States ... do not affect the allocation of competences under the Treaties'.[136] While it is open whether the Court will similarly accept such 'interpretative guidance', the declaration clearly reflects the delicacy of the competence issue.[137]

The analysis has shown that the Commission's claim to a general and exclusive competence in the field of portfolio investment is probably going too far. However, in line with the reasoning of AG Sharpston in *EUSFTA*, the EU's shared competence might well cover all relevant aspects of portfolio investment. If so, the extent to which the EU actually exercises its shared competence is principally subject to a political choice which is, however, legally channelled in the detailed procedures set out in Art 218 TFEU.

4. *Consequences for CETA, TTIP, and TiSA*

CETA Chapter Eight contains provisions on investment, investment protection, and investment arbitration. According to Art 8.2.1 CETA, this chapter applies particularly to measures adopted or maintained by a Party in its territory relating to an investor of the other Party or a covered investment. Thus, the scope of the chapter basically depends on the scope of the terms 'investment', 'covered investment', and 'investor'. According to the definition in Art 8.1 CETA, 'investment means every kind of asset that an investor owns or controls, directly or indirectly, that has the

[134] ibid, paras 523–35.

[135] Regulation (EU) No 912/2014 of 23 July 2014 establishing a framework for managing financial responsibility linked to investor-to-state dispute settlement tribunals established by international agreements to which the European Union is party, OJ [2014] L 257/121.

[136] *EUSFTA* (n 5) Opinion of AG Sharpston, para 531.

[137] cf also Regulation (EU) No 1219/2012 of 12 December 2012 establishing transitional arrangements for bilateral agreements between Member States and third countries, OJ [2012] L 351/40. Article 1 of this regulation similarly states that the regulation addresses the status of Member State BITs under EU law '[w]ithout prejudice to the division of competences established by the TFEU'.

characteristics of an investment, which includes a certain duration and other characteristics such as the commitment of capital or other resources, the expectation to gain profit, or the assumption of risk'.[138] Arguably, this broad 'asset-based' conception of investment covers both FDI and portfolio investment.[139] With regard to EU investment agreements, a broad definition of investment, including FDI as well as portfolio investment, is one of the main arguments advanced in favour of mixity.[140]

As mentioned above, the underlying rationale for obligatory mixity lies in the principle of conferral as laid down in Art 5(1) and (2) TFEU, while facultative mixity reflects a political choice. This is, however, not to be confused with the choice of the proper legal basis for EU external action, which is subject to a 'main-purpose test'. The Court has consistently held that:

> If examination of a Community measure reveals that it pursues a twofold purpose or that it has a twofold component and if one is identifiable as the main or predominant purpose or component, whereas the other is merely incidental, the measure must be founded on a single legal basis, namely that required by the main or predominant purpose or component ... By way of exception, if it is established that the measure simultaneously pursues several objectives which are inseparably linked without one being secondary and indirect in relation to the other, the measure may be founded on the corresponding legal bases.[141]

However, it has been rightly pointed out that this line of reasoning only applies if the question of EU competence 'as such is beyond doubt',[142] that is, if the necessary competence has been conferred upon the EU either explicitly or implicitly. If, however, Member States have retained competence for specific components of an agreement or the Treaties contain a *lex specialis*,[143] the EU 'cannot declare that

[138] Forms that an investment may take according to this definition include, inter alia, an enterprise, shares, stocks, and other forms of equity participation in an enterprise; bonds, debentures, and other debt instruments of an enterprise; a loan to an enterprise; intellectual property rights; other moveable property, tangible or intangible; or immovable property and related rights.

[139] The scope of the investment chapter is, however, also subject to a number of limitations. First, the term 'covered investment' only comprises investments which are made in accordance with the applicable law at the time and which are directly or indirectly owned or controlled by an investor of the other Party. Second, the term 'investor' means a Party, a natural person, or an enterprise of a Party, other than a branch or a representative office. In this regard, it is important to underline that the definition of an 'enterprise of a Party', requires, inter alia, *substantial business activities* in the territory of that Party and particularly aims at excluding *mailbox companies* from profiting from investor-state arbitration. However, these limitations on the scope of the investment chapter have no influence on the competence issue under EU law. According to the second alternative, an enterprise of a Party is 'an enterprise that is constituted or organised under the laws of that Party and is directly or indirectly owned or controlled by a natural person of that Party or by an enterprise mentioned under paragraph (a)'.

[140] eg Tietje, 'Die Außenwirtschaftsverfassung der EU nach dem Vertrag von Lissabon' (n 111) 16; Bungenberg, 'Außenbeziehungen und Außenhandelspolitik' (n 111) 209; Reinisch, 'The Division of Powers' (n 111) 106; Ohler, 'Die Umsetzung der Gemeinsamen Handelspolitik nach dem Vertrag von Lissabon' (n 95) 431–2; Krajewski, 'The Reform of the CCP' (n 46) 302; and Mayr, '"Mixed" oder "EU-only"' (n 93) 596.

[141] eg *Cartagena Protocol* (n 113) para 23. The Court also emphasizes that the choice of the legal basis for an international agreement will be assessed in the light of its context, aim, and content (*Cartagena Protocol*, paras 22 and 25).

[142] Case C-13/07, *Commission v Council* [2009] ECLI:EU:C:2009:190, Opinion of AG Kokott, para 113 (hereafter *Accession of Vietnam to WTO*).

[143] eg Art 207(5) TFEU, which provides that '[t]he negotiation and conclusion of international agreements in the field of transport shall be subject to Title VI of Part Three and to Art 218'.

it is competent for the entire act by way of a main-purpose test'.[144] As a consequence, AG Kokott opined that '[i]ndividual aspects of an agreement for which the Community has no competence internally "infect" the agreement as a whole and make it dependent on the common accord of the Member States … Just as a little drop of pastis can turn a glass of water milky, individual provisions, however secondary … can make it necessary to conclude a shared agreement'.[145] While the Court—upon the Commission's withdrawal of its application—did not decide on the substantial questions raised in the particular case, the rationale behind the oft-cited *Pastis metaphor* is principally convincing.[146]

The above analysis has shown that the allocation of investment competences requires some differentiation. While FDI clearly falls within the EU's exclusive external competence, the power to terminate existing BITs belongs exclusively to the Member States concerned. In contrast, portfolio investment, at least to a large extent, falls within the shared competences of the EU and the Member States. In this regard, it remains to be seen whether the Court in *EUSFTA* will follow AG Sharpston, who has argued that the EU's shared competence covers all relevant aspects of portfolio investment, despite some Member States insisting that they have retained exclusive competences in this area. In any case, the Court's decision will have far-reaching consequences. Only to the extent that agreements like EUSFTA, CETA, and TTIP cover matters falling within Member States' exclusive competence, mixity is obligatory. If, however, such agreements cover only matters falling within EU exclusive and shared competences, mixity is principally subject to a political choice and thus facultative. Also TiSA—building largely on the GATS—has a clear investment dimension, that is, GATS mode 3 (*commercial presence*), which basically corresponds to FDI. As *all* modes of trade in services fall fully within the scope of Art 207 TFEU, TiSA *insofar* comes within exclusive EU competence. The question of mixity may, however, arise with a view to certain commitments in the area of transport, which remains one of the principal areas of shared competence.[147] Subject to more detailed analysis of the exact scope of competence and commitments, TiSA would thus appear to be an example of *facultative* mixity.

V. Provisional Application

A. Overview

The possibility of provisionally applying an agreement, pending the completion of procedures for its conclusion, is frequently used by the EU in the context of mixed

[144] *Accession of Vietnam to WTO* (n 142) Opinion of AG Kokott, para 113.

[145] ibid, para 121.

[146] It has to be noted, however, that the Court has held that 'individual clauses of an altogether subsidiary or ancillary nature' may not trigger mixity; cf *Natural Rubber* (n 104) para 56.

[147] cf Arts 207(5) and 4(2)(g) TFEU.

agreements, as ratification by all Member States may seriously delay an agreement's entry into force.[148] Nonetheless, the announcement of the (intended) provisional application of CETA has sparked yet another political controversy.[149]

Legally, the question of the provisional application prima facie appears quite clear-cut. According to Art 218(5) TFEU, the Council, on a proposal of the negotiator, may, *if necessary*, adopt a decision authorizing the provisional application of the agreement before its entry into force.[150] Parliamentary consent is not required. However, according to an inter-institutional agreement between the Commission and the Parliament, information shall be provided to Parliament 'in sufficient time for it to be able to express its point of view if appropriate, and for the Commission to be able to take Parliament's views as far as possible into account'.[151]

Article 30.7.3 CETA stipulates details on the provisional application of the agreement. If a party does not intend to provisionally apply the entire agreement, it notifies the other party accordingly and offers to enter into consultations. The other party may either object, in which case the entire agreement shall not be provisionally applied, or provide a notification of those provisions that it does not intend to apply provisionally in turn. If no further objections are made, the provisions which are not subject to a notification shall be provisionally applied. A party may also terminate the provisional application by written notice at any time.

B. Termination

On the occasion of the adoption by the Council of the decision authorizing the signature of CETA, a number of Member States have issued statements regarding the termination of provisional application of CETA. For example, Germany and Austria 'declare that as Parties to CETA they can exercise their rights which derive from article 30.7(3)(c) of CETA'.[152] The declaration seems to imply that each individual Member State (as a party to the mixed agreement) could actually terminate the provisional application of CETA. However, this is somewhat misleading. First, partial termination of the provisional application (ie limited to the territory of the Member State) is neither provided for in the CETA nor feasible within the

[148] eg the Free Trade Agreement between the European Union and its Member States, of the one part, and the Republic of Korea, of the other part [2011] OJ L 127/6, has been provisionally applied since 1 July 2011. Cf also Rosas, 'The European Union and Mixed Agreements' (n 43) 208.

[149] eg ClientEarth, 'Commission's CETA proposal violates EU Law' (6 July 2016), <http://www.clientearth.org/commission-proposal-provisional-application-ceta-violates-eu-law/> accessed 7 April 2017.

[150] cf also Art 25 VCLT.

[151] Framework Agreement on relations between the European Parliament and the European Commission [2011] OJ L 304/47. See point 24 in conjunction with Annex III, para 7.

[152] EU Council Doc 13463/1/16, 27 October 2016, 14. Also, the German Federal Constitutional Court in a recent decision emphasized the importance of Germany having the option to terminate the provisional application of CETA, albeit as a measure of last resort, cf Decision of 13 October 2016, 2 BvR 1368/16 and Others, para 72.

European single market and customs union.[153] Thus, the question arises whether an individual Member State could terminate the provisional application of CETA *in toto*. Here, a statement issued by the Council on the same occasion appears instructive. It reads: 'If the ratification of CETA fails permanently and definitively because of a ruling of a constitutional court, or following the completion of other constitutional processes and formal notification by the government of the concerned state, provisional application must be and will be terminated. The necessary steps will be taken in accordance with EU procedures.'[154] Hence, an individual Member State can cause the termination of the provisional application, but it cannot on its own terminate the provisional application vis-à-vis Canada. Rather, the termination of the provisional application would require a decision by the Council, adopted by a qualified majority.[155]

C. Exceptions

Regarding the scope of the provisional application of CETA, it is remarkable that the Commission had initially proposed the provisional application of the *entire* agreement. This clearly reflected the Commission's view that CETA comes fully within EU competence, but was somewhat at odds with its proposal to conclude CETA as a mixed agreement. Arguably, the provisional application of the entire agreement would have reduced mixity to a somewhat 'empty shell', as in international law provisional application means that an agreement is binding and enforceable.[156] However, in contrast to the Commission's sweeping approach, the relevant Council Decision substantially limits the provisional application of CETA. For example, only selected provisions of Chapter Eight (Investment) shall be provisionally applied, 'and only in so far as foreign direct investment is concerned'.[157] Conversely, all other provisions of the Investment Chapter—including those on the treatment of investors and of covered investments, on expropriation, and on the resolution of investment disputes between investors and states—are not to be applied on a provisional basis, pending the agreement's ratification. Further exceptions are, for example, stipulated for particular provisions of Chapter Thirteen (Financial Services).[158]

[153] cf also David Kleimann and Gesa Kübeck, 'The Signing, Provisional Application, and Conclusion of Trade and Investment Agreements in the EU' (2016) 58 *EUI Working Papers RSCAS* 20.

[154] EU Council Doc 13463/1/16, 27 October 2016, 14.

[155] The legal basis could either be Art 218(5) or 218(9) TFEU (both applied by analogy); procedurally, both provisions contain simplified procedures, prescribing no active participation by the European Parliament.

[156] As to the legal effects of provisional application at the international level, see Rene Lefeber, 'The Provisional Application of Treaties' in Jan Klabbers and Rene Lefeber (eds), *Essays on the Law of Treaties* (Nijhoff, 1998) 90.

[157] cf EU Council Doc 10974/16, 5 October 2016. The provisions which shall be provisionally applied in the context of the Investment Chapter are Arts 8.1–8.8, 8.13, 8.15, with the exception of para 3 thereof, and 8.16.

[158] cf EU Council Doc 10974/16, 5 October 2016.

VI. Autonomy of EU Law

A. The preservation of the 'very nature' of EU law

Finally, the question arises whether the establishment of an investor-to-state dispute settlement mechanism in CETA and TTIP might come into conflict with the autonomy of EU law.[159] This question is of particular relevance, since Belgium has stated that it will ask the Court of Justice for an opinion on the compatibility of the Investment Court System with the European treaties.[160]

According to Art 19(1) TEU, the Court 'shall ensure that in the interpretation and application of the Treaties the law is observed'. The exclusivity of the Court's jurisdiction is reflected in Art 344 TFEU, which provides that the Member States 'undertake not to submit a dispute concerning the interpretation of application of the Treaties to any method of settlement other than those provided therein'.[161] In Opinion 2/13, the CJEU emphasized that '[i]n order to ensure that the specific characteristics and the autonomy of that legal order are preserved, the Treaties have established a judicial system intended to ensure consistency and uniformity in the interpretation of EU law'.[162] An essential characteristic of this system is the preliminary ruling procedure, which sets up a judicial dialogue between the CJEU and the courts and tribunals of the Member States.[163]

Against this background, the Court reacts with a certain scepticism where an international agreement subjects the EU to an external judicial control mechanism. While acknowledging that the EU's capacity to conclude international agreements 'necessarily entail[s] the power to submit to the decisions of a court which is created or designated by such agreements as regards the interpretation and application of their provisions', it has consistently emphasized 'that an international agreement may affect [the Court's] own powers *only if* indispensable conditions for safeguarding the essential character of those powers are satisfied and, consequently, there is *no adverse effect on the autonomy of the EU legal order*'.[164]

[159] See, in particular, Opinion 1/91, *European Economic Area I* [1991] ECLI:EU:C:1991:490 (hereafter *EEA I*); Opinion 1/92, *European Economic Area II* [1992] ECLI:EU:C:1992:189 (hereafter *EEA II*); Opinion 1/00, *ECAA* [2002] ECLI:EU:C:2002:231 (hereafter *ECAA*); Opinion 1/09, *Patents Court* [2011] ECLI:EU:C:2011:123 (hereafter *Patents Court*); and Opinion 2/13, *ECHR II* [2014] ECLI:EU:C:2014:2454 (hereafter *ECHR II*).

[160] The commitment to submit this question to the Court of Justice is part of a domestic compromise struck (in particular) with the regional government of Wallonia, in order to secure the signature of the agreement in October 2016; cf Statement by the Kingdom of Belgium on the conditions attached to full powers, on the part of the Federal State and the federated entities, for the signing of CETA, EU Council Doc 13463/1/16, 27 October 2016, 28–30.

[161] cf *EEA I* (n 159) para 35; and Case C-459/03, *Mox Plant* [2006] ECLI:EU:C:2006:345, para 123. For a detailed analysis, see Erich Vranes, 'Gemischte Abkommen und die Zuständigkeit des EuGH—Grundfragen und neuere Entwicklungen in den Außenbeziehungen' [2009] *Europarecht* 44, 72ff; and Erich Vranes, 'Die EU-Außenkompetenzen im Schnittpunkt von Europarecht, Völkerrecht und nationalem Recht' (2011) 133 *Juristische Blätter* 11, 17.

[162] *ECHR II* (n 159) para 174.

[163] ibid, para 176.

[164] ibid, paras 182–3 (emphases added).

In its case law, the Court has identified three conditions that must be met in order to safeguard the autonomy of the EU legal order.[165]

First, the decisions of an international court 'must not have the effect of binding the EU and its institutions, in the exercise of their internal powers, to a particular interpretation of the rules of EU law'.[166] The Court underlines that empowering an existing or establishing a new international court which is responsible for the interpretation of an international agreement and whose decisions are binding on the EU institutions, including the Court, 'is not, in principle, incompatible with EU law'.[167] However, the autonomy of the EU legal order is at stake if an international court is called upon to interpret and apply EU law,[168] or if the decisions of such a court might produce 'spillover effects',[169] namely, if an agreement replicates provisions which are *in substance* provisions of EU law and aims at securing their uniform application within its territorial scope.[170]

Second, the allocation of powers between the EU and its Member States has to remain unaltered.[171] Problems may particularly arise in the context of mixed agreements, for example, if an international court is competent to determine whether the EU and/or its Member States are the responsible contracting party (and thus the respondent) in a specific dispute. In Opinion 1/91, the CJEU held that such a determination by the international court would be likely to have an impact on the allocation of competences between the EU and its Member States and was therefore incompatible with the autonomy of the EU legal order.[172]

Third, an agreement may not change the essential character of the powers of the Union and its institutions.[173] Hence, an agreement may not interfere with the Court's 'exclusive task of reviewing the legality of acts of the [EU] institutions'.[174] Moreover, the third condition is relevant, where an agreement confers powers on the Court or the Commission vis-à-vis contracting parties which are not members of the EU.[175] For example, the CJEU found it 'unacceptable' that it should deliver preliminary rulings which are 'purely advisory and without any binding effects', as this would 'change the nature of the function of the Court of Justice as it is conceived by the … Treaty'.[176]

[165] cf Inge Govaere, 'Beware of the Trojan Horse: Dispute Settlement in (Mixed) Agreements and the Autonomy of the EU Legal Order' in Hillion and Koutrakos, *Mixed Agreements Revisited* (n 10) 192–9 (hereafter Govaere, 'Beware of the Trojan Horse'); Steffen Hindelang, 'The Autonomy of the European Legal Order' in Marc Bungenberg and Christoph Herrmann (eds), *Common Commercial Policy after Lisbon* (Springer, 2013) 190–2 (hereafter Hindelang, 'The Autonomy of the European Legal Order'); and Juliane Ahner, *Investor-Staat-Schiedsverfahren nach Europäischem Unionsrecht* (Mohr Siebeck, 2015) 215–37 (hereafter Ahner, *Investor-Staat-Schiedsverfahren*).

[166] *ECHR II* (n 159) para 184; see also *ECAA* (n 159) para 13.

[167] *ECHR II* (n 159) para 182; and *EEA I* (n 159) para 40.

[168] *Patents Court* (n 159) para 78.

[169] Hindelang, 'The Autonomy of the European Legal Order' (n 165) 190.

[170] *EEA I* (n 159) paras 40–6.

[171] *ECAA* (n 159) para 12.

[172] *EEA I* (n 159) paras 30–6.

[173] *ECAA* (n 159) para 12.

[174] ibid, 24.

[175] ibid, 18–21.

[176] *EEA I* (n 159) para 61; cf also *EEA II* (n 159) para 32; and *ECAA* (n 159) para 25.

B. Implications for investor-state arbitration in CETA and TTIP

CETA Chapter Eight contains provisions on investor-state dispute settlement in the form of the so-called Investment Court System (ICS).[177] The EU's proposal for TTIP contains similar provisions.[178] In the literature, the discussion of whether such agreements may come into conflict with the autonomy of EU law is equally broad and controversial.[179] A detailed analysis goes, however, beyond the scope of this chapter, which will thus focus on some crucial aspects in the context of CETA.

In view of the three conditions outlined above, an obvious question is whether the CETA Tribunal may bind the EU and its institutions, in the exercise of their internal powers, to a particular interpretation of the rules of EU law. Principally, it is not unusual that investment tribunals *apply* domestic law.[180] For example, CETA Chapter Eight defines 'covered investment', inter alia, as investment 'made in accordance with the applicable law [of the host state] at the time the investment is made'. This indicates that the content and scope of the rights which correspond to the different categories of assets have to be determined by reference to domestic law (which in the case of CETA may include EU law).[181] Also, more generally, material standards of treatment of foreign investment (eg non-discrimination) may *in substance* overlap with guarantees under EU law.

Article 8.31.2 CETA clearly states that the Tribunal 'shall not have jurisdiction to determine the legality of a measure, alleged to constitute a breach of this Agreement, under the domestic law of a Party'. In determining the consistency of a measure with CETA, the Tribunal may, however, 'consider ... domestic law

[177] For a detailed analysis, see Chapter 5 by Schill in this volume. Cf also the relevant disciplines in the Draft FTA between the EU and Vietnam, <http://trade.ec.europa.eu/doclib/docs/2016/february/tradoc_154210.pdf> accessed 7 April 2017.

[178] cf also Investment s 3 Art 9-12 TTIP-EU.

[179] eg Govaere, 'Beware of the Trojan Horse' (n 165) 187; Nikos Lavranos, 'Is an International Investor-to-State System under the Auspices of the ECJ Possible?' (16 December 2011), <http://ssrn.com/abstract=1973491> accessed 7 April 2017; Markus Burgstaller, 'Investor-State Arbitration in EU International Investment Agreements with Third States' (2012) 39 *Legal Issues of Economic Integration* 207; Angelos Dimopoulos, 'The Compatibility of Future EU Investment Agreements with EU Law' (2012) 39 *Legal Issues of Economic Integration* 447; Claus Dieter Classen, 'Der EuGH und die Schiedsgerichtsbarkeit in Investitionsschutzabkommen' [2012] *Europarecht* 611; Hindelang, 'The Autonomy of the European Legal Order' (n 165) 187; Stephan Schill, 'Luxembourg Limits: Conditions for Investor-State Dispute Settlement under Future EU Investment Agreements' [2013] *TDM* (March 2013), <https://www.transnational-dispute-management.com/article.asp?key=1943> accessed 7 April 2017 (hereafter Schill, 'Luxembourg Limits'); Christoph Herrmann, 'The Role of the Court of Justice of the European Union in the Emerging EU Investment Policy' [2014] *Journal of World Investment and Trade* 570 (hereafter Herrmann, 'The Role of the Court of Justice'); Stephan Schill, 'Editorial: Opinion 2/13—The End of Dispute Settlement in EU Trade and Investment Agreements?' [2015] *Journal of World Investment and Trade* 379 (hereafter Schill, 'Editorial'); Steffen Hindelang, 'Repellent Forces: The CJEU and Investor-State Dispute Settlement' [2015] *AVR* 68 (hereafter Hindelang, 'Repellent Forces'); Ahner, *Investor-Staat-Schiedsverfahren* (n 165) 204ff; and Laurens Ankersmit, 'The Compatibility of Investment Arbitration in EU Trade Agreements with the EU Judicial System' (2016) 13 *Journal for European Environmental & Planning Law* 43.

[180] cf Art 42(1) ICSID.

[181] Andrew Newcombe and Lluís Paradell, *Law and Practice of Investment Treaties: Standards of Treatment* (Wolters Kluwer, 2009) 92–3.

of a Party as a matter of fact'. And the provision continues: 'In doing so, the Tribunal shall follow the prevailing interpretation given to the domestic law by the courts or authorities of that Party and any meaning given to domestic law by the Tribunal shall not be binding upon the courts or the authorities of that Party'.[182] Arguably, the proposition that the Tribunal can apply domestic law *as a matter of fact* without interpretation appears somewhat simplistic. However, with regard to the autonomy of the EU legal order, it is important to note that the provision explicitly precludes any formally binding interpretation of EU law by the Tribunal.

Even if material standards of investment protection and EU law overlap, the Court is thus—de jure—under no obligation to adapt its own interpretation of EU law to the interpretation of the Tribunal in respect of CETA.[183] A different question, however, is whether the factual pressure to conform to the arbitral decisions might pose a threat to the autonomy of the EU legal order.[184] Similarly, there may be cases where the compliance with an award factually amounts to 'selective non-application'[185] of the relevant EU law. One prominent example discussed in the literature concerns EU State aid law and reminds of the situation in the *Micula* case:[186] first, the foreign investor has to repay state aid according to an EU ruling. Then, an arbitral tribunal finds that this EU ruling and/or its implementation by a Member violate investment protection standards and orders the EU or the Member State to pay damages. The crux is that '[b]y way of the damages award, the investor would end up in the same position it would have been in had it kept the original State aid'.[187] However, in the CETA context, this scenario is subject to Art 8.9.4 CETA, which provides:[188]

> For greater certainty, nothing in this Section shall be construed as preventing a Party from discontinuing the granting of a subsidy or requesting its reimbursement where such measure is necessary in order to comply with international obligations between the Parties or has been ordered by a competent court, administrative tribunal or other competent authority, or requiring that Party to compensate the investor therefor.

Moreover, a footnote clarifies that 'competent authority' in the case of the EU is the Commission. Consequently, if the Commission (in accordance with EU State aid law) rules that a Canadian investor has to repay State aid, neither this decision

[182] cf also Investment s 3 Art 13 TTIP-EU.

[183] cf Angelos Dimopoulos, 'The Involvement of the EU in Investor-State Dispute Settlement: A Question of Responsibilities' [2014] *CML Rev* 1671, 1699; and Schill, 'Editorial' (n 179) 385.

[184] Hindelang, 'Repellent Forces' (n 179) 74.

[185] Hindelang, 'The Autonomy of the European Legal Order' (n 165) 194.

[186] *Ioan Micula and Others v Romania*, ICSID Case No ARB/05/20, Award, 11 December 2013. An application for annulment according to Art 52 ICSID remained unsuccessful: see *Ioan Micula and Others v Romania*, ICSID Case No ARB/05/20, Decision on Annulment, 26 February 2016.

[187] Hindelang, 'Repellent Forces' (n 179) 74–5.

[188] For a discussion of Art 8.9 CETA on Investment and regulatory measures, cf Stefan Mayr, 'Same Same But Different? Öffentliche Dienstleistungen und das neue Investment Court System der EU' [2016] *juridikum* 231, 237–40. Cf also Investment s 2 Art 2.4 TTIP-EU.

as such nor its proper implementation will trigger an obligation to compensate the investor. Article 8.9.4 CETA aims to avoid the inconsistency outlined above, albeit in a rather casuistic manner. Thus, while the particular State aid scenario arguably poses no factual threat to the autonomy of EU law in the CETA context, other similarly problematic situations may occur.[189]

With regard to the allocation of powers between the EU and its Member States, Art 8.21 CETA is arguably of great importance. The provision contains detailed rules for the determination of the respondent in disputes with either the EU or its Member States. Generally, the question of who acts as respondent is to be decided EU-internally.[190] However, if the investor has not been informed of the determination within due time, the investor may identify the respondent on the basis of Art 8.21.4 CETA. According to this 'fallback rule', the Member State shall be the respondent if the measures identified in the notice requesting a determination of the respondent 'are exclusively measures of a Member State'. If, however, the measures identified 'include measures of the European Union', the EU shall be the respondent. What appears significant in terms of autonomy is that, according to Art 8.21.6 CETA, neither the EU nor the Member State 'may assert the inadmissibility of the claim, lack of jurisdiction of the Tribunal or otherwise object to the claim or award on the ground that the respondent was not properly … identified on the basis of the application of paragraph 4'. In Opinion 2/13, the Court stated that the European Court of Human Rights, in ascertaining the plausibility of a request of the EU or the Member States to intervene as co-respondents, 'would be required to assess the rules of EU law governing the division of powers between the EU and its Member States as well as the criteria for the attribution of their acts or omissions, in order to adopt a final decision in that regard which would be binding both on the Member States and on the EU'.[191] The Court concluded that '[s]uch a review would be liable to interfere with the division of powers between the EU and its Member States'.[192] In the light of this ruling, it appears doubtful whether the investor involvement in the determination of the respondent actually conforms to the autonomy principle.[193]

Finally, the Court has consistently held that the dialogue between the CJEU and the courts and tribunals of the Member States is an essential characteristic of the judicial system established by the treaties. The Court thus takes issue with an international court that 'affect[s] the powers of the courts and tribunals of Member States in relation to the interpretation and application of European Union law, [or] the power, or indeed the obligation, of those courts and tribunals to request a preliminary ruling from the Court of Justice and the power of the Court to

189 For further examples of potentially problematic scenarios, see Ingolf Pernice, 'Part III: Study on International Investment Protection Agreements and EU Law' in Directorate-General for External Policies of the Union (ed), *Investor-State Dispute Settlement (ISDS) Provisions in the EU's International Investment Agreements*, vol 2 (EU, 2014) 146–9.

190 Art 8.21.3 CETA. 191 *ECHR II* (n 159) para 224. 192 ibid, para 225.

193 Investment s 3 Art 5 TTIP-EU does not contain such a 'fallback rule' allowing the investor to identify the respondent, and thus raises no similar autonomy issues.

reply'.[194] In this context, it is important to note that CETA does not require the use of local remedies, let alone their exhaustion, prior to the submission of a claim to the Tribunal.[195] CETA, however, avoids parallel claims. Article 8.22.1(f) and (g) requires an investor to withdraw or discontinue any existing proceedings or waive its right to initiate any claim or proceeding with regard to a measure alleged to constitute a breach referred to in its CETA claim.[196] Bearing in mind that 'the tasks attributed to the national courts and to the Court of Justice respectively are indispensable to the preservation of the very nature of the law established by the Treaties',[197] the question arises whether Art 8.22 CETA undermines the system of direct cooperation established by Art 267 TFEU.[198] Eventually, the Court would have to decide whether the ICS mechanism—giving the Tribunal jurisdiction to decide a significant number of claims brought by individuals in the field of investment—'deprive[s] courts of Member States of their powers in relation to the interpretation and application of European Union law and the Court of its powers to reply, by preliminary ruling, to questions referred by those courts and, consequently, would alter the essential character of the powers which the Treaties confer on the institutions of the European Union and on the Member States'.[199]

To sum up: The autonomy of the EU legal order sets limits to conferring jurisdiction on an international court outside the institutional and judicial framework of the EU. In view of the Court's case law, the establishment of an investor-state dispute settlement mechanism appears not per se incompatible with the autonomy principle. The compatibility rather seems to depend on the particular institutional design of an agreement like CETA or TTIP.[200] In the context of CETA, potential problems could arguably arise with regard to the determination of the respondent by an investor and the so-called 'no u-turn' approach.

VII. Conclusion

CETA, TTIP, and TiSA raise a plethora of intricate legal questions touching on the fundamentals of the EU legal order and illustrating the complex interplay between the EU and its Member States and also between EU institutions. Among

[194] *Patents Court* (n 159) para 77.

[195] cf more generally Christoph Schreuer, 'Calvo's Grandchildren: The Return of Local Remedies in Investment Arbitration' (2005) 4 *The Law & Practice of International Courts and Tribunals* 1.

[196] The Commission calls this the ' "no u-turn" approach': see Concept Paper, 'Investment in TTIP and Beyond—the Path for Reform' (5 May 2015) 10.

[197] *Patents Court* (n 159) para 85.

[198] On the possible involvement of the CJEU in investor-state arbitration, see Christoph Ohler, 'Die Vereinbarkeit von Investor-Staat-Schiedsverfahren mit deutschem und europäischem Verfassungsrecht' [2015] *Juristen Zeitung* 337, 345; cf also Herrmann, 'The Role of the Court of Justice' (n 179) 570ff.

[199] *Patents Court* (n 159) para 89.

[200] Schill, 'Luxembourg Limits' (n 179) 11–16; and Catharine Titi, 'The European Union's Proposal for an International Investment Court: Significance, Innovations and Challenges Ahead' [2016] *TDM* (25 May 2016) 30, <https://www.transnational-dispute-management.com/journal-advance-publication-article.asp?key=1619> accessed 7 April 2017.

the three agreements, CETA is clearly the 'frontrunner'. The negotiations were officially concluded in September 2014 and the draft text was also made public at that time. Quite uniquely, substantial amendments were made during the so-called legal scrubbing phase. Eventually, the agreement was signed on 30 October 2016. Meanwhile, as the negotiations on TTIP and TiSA are still ongoing, both agreements are much more of a 'moving target'. In this context, the above analysis has shown that CETA is not simply a 'blueprint' or 'template' for TTIP. While the key issues are similar, even minor differences in the wording may have a major impact, for example, with regard to the autonomy of the EU legal order.

The issue of competence and mixity has proven to be particularly contentious. The Commission eventually has proposed to conclude CETA as a mixed agreement. However, it made clear that this proposal is only a political concession 'without prejudice' to the views expressed by the Commission in the Singapore case. While the Court's decision is still pending, AG Sharpston only recently issued her extensive opinion, arguing that the EUSFTA 'can be concluded only by the European Union and the Member States acting jointly'. Prima facie, this result seems clearly in favour of the position advanced by the Member States and the Council; however, a closer look reveals the AG's nuanced reasoning. Against this background, the current analysis concludes that mixity is likely to be obligatory in the cases of CETA and TTIP and possibly facultative in the case of TiSA (eg with regard to transport). However, it also points out that mixity is only a 'second best solution' with regard to ensuring the effective representation of EU interests at the international level, where it is important to act as a unified and reliable partner.

Finally, the concluding section considers the controversial question of whether the establishment of an investor-to-state dispute settlement mechanism in CETA and TTIP might come into conflict with the autonomy of the EU legal order. While the material compatibility of the ISDS mechanism in Chapter 9 EUSFTA falls outside the scope of Opinion 2/15, Belgium has announced that it will submit a request on the issue in the CETA context. A tentative analysis of the Court's case law suggests that the establishment of an investor-state dispute settlement mechanism is not per se incompatible with this basic principle. However, the actual compatibility depends on the particular institutional design of an agreement like CETA or TTIP. In the context of CETA, potentially problematic aspects concern the determination of the respondent by an investor and the so-called 'no u-turn' approach.

PART III

CETA, TTIP, AND TISA

New Challenges for Politics, Law, and Legitimacy?

12

On the Expected Economic Effects of Trade Liberalization and the Transatlantic Trade and Investment Partnership

Christoph Moser

The EU and the US are currently negotiating a regional trade agreement (RTA).[1] While this book offers numerous insights into the legal challenges of the Transatlantic Trade and Investment Partnership (TTIP), this chapter aims at providing the *big picture* on international trade, RTAs, and TTIP *from an economist's perspective*.

It seems fair to state that there is widespread consensus among economists that international trade is positive. What are the *main theoretical arguments in favour of international trade*? Let's focus on four workhorses of international trade. Each of these theoretical models offers another main theoretical channel that leads to welfare gains due to trade. To start with probably the best known (but not always well understood) economic principle in trade: the *comparative advantage*. We consider two countries that produce two goods. According to David Ricardo, both countries will profit from opening up to international trade as long as they specialize in those goods, where they are relatively more productive. An important take-away of this simple model is that both countries will profit from trade, even if one country is more productive in producing both goods. For both countries, the consumption basket is larger with trade than in autarky. It is the comparative advantage that matters in international trade, not the absolute advantage. *Differences in technology* determine the comparative advantage in the *Ricardo model*. In contrast to that, *differences in factor endowment* characterize the second trade model. In the *Heckscher-Ohlin model*, gains from trade stem from the fact that countries are differently endowed with certain production factors. Countries will profit from specializing in the products that use their abundant production factor more intensively. In this kind of framework, changes in the relative prices for the produced goods can lead to

[1] Note that the term RTA is often used for trade agreements like TTIP. In this chapter, the terms RTA, free trade agreement (FTA), and preferential trade agreement (PTA) are used interchangeably and always refer to trade agreements that grant preferential access to member countries.

On the Expected Economic Effects of Trade Liberalization and the Transatlantic Trade and Investment Partnership (TTIP). Christoph Moser.

distributional effects within a country that participates in international trade. Note that the first two kinds of models predict that countries specialize in different goods that they consequently trade (inter-industry trade). The third model offers a mechanism why countries exchange goods even in narrowly defined industries (intra-industry trade). The so-called 'New Trade Theory' pioneered by Paul Krugman is able to explain this intra-industry trade.[2] There are two main new ingredients in the *Krugman model*. First, the model acknowledges that there is a *fixed cost of production* to be covered by a firm in order to produce a certain good. Higher production allows this fixed cost to be spread over more units of production, lowering the average costs of production and the price charged on this good. Second, consumers are happy to choose from a wide range of different goods, even goods that are very similar in nature ('*love of variety*'). Opening up to international trade leads to a larger market, more firms, and more differentiated products in equilibrium. While the fourth trade model builds on the third model, the theoretical framework differs in one crucial dimension. The 'New New Trade Theory' (or heterogeneous firm model) proposed by Marc Melitz allows firms to differ in their productivity.[3] Some firms are more productive than others, even in the very same industry. When an economy moves from autarky to trade, the *Melitz model* predicts a reallocation of resources from less productive firms (that partly exit the market) to more productive firms that increase their market share and profits. The reallocation leads to an increase in productivity at the industry level and to welfare gains.

All of these trade models predict an increase in welfare for countries participating in international trade. Furthermore, the empirical evidence on international trade is also overwhelmingly positive. At the same time, it is important to bear in mind that not everybody is equally affected by trade liberalization. There will always be *winners and losers* from trade liberalization.

What kind of trade liberalization should be pursued from an economist's perspective? Ideally, all (or a large number of) countries should lower their trade barriers simultaneously vis-à-vis each other. Such *multilateral trade liberalization* has traditionally been hammered out under the aegis of the General Agreement on Tariffs and Trade (GATT) and the World Trade Organization (WTO). But the last round of the multilateral trade liberalization, the Doha Round, has stalled and an increasing number of countries now liberalize trade on a bilateral or regional level. These so-called RTAs are booming and controversial at the same time. What are the main reasons behind this scepticism? Economic theory (going back to a static model by Jacob Viner in the 1950s) suggests that RTAs can have negative welfare effects for countries within the trade agreement and countries outside the agreement.[4] The main concern is that relatively more efficient exports from countries outside the new trade agreement are diverted away to relatively less efficient exports from

[2] See Paul Krugman, 'Increasing Returns, Monopolistic Competition, and International Trade' (1979) 9 *Journal of International Economics* 469–79.

[3] See Marc Melitz, 'The Impact of Trade in Intra-industry Reallocations and Aggregate Industry Productivity' (2003) 71 *Econometrica* 1695–725.

[4] cf Jacob Viner, 'The Customs Union Issue' (Carnegie Endow Int Peace, 1950).

new RTA partner countries (*trade diversion*). If this were to be the dominant force, insiders and outsiders would be worse off due to the new agreement. For insiders, product prices will tend to rise and outsiders will face lower export demand. At the same time, lower trade barriers very likely boost trade within the free trade area (*trade creation*). The excellent literature review by Freund and Ornelas summarizes the empirical literature on RTAs.[5] Trade creation dominates trade diversion and there is on average positive net trade creation. This makes overall negative welfare effects from RTAs very unlikely. But a closer look also reveals that there are agreements with considerable trade diversion from time to time.

What should we expect from the TTIP? On the one hand, the trade volume between the US and the EU is already large in absolute terms. On the other hand, we would expect in a hypothetical world without any trade frictions much larger trade flows between these two countries.[6] In a similar vein, Egger and others argue that the trade flows between the EU and the US seem relatively low compared to their economic size and relative to other trading partners.[7] These arguments hint at substantial potential for a deep trade agreement between these two economic powerhouses. Since tariffs are on average already very low, the bulk of remaining trade frictions are *non-tariff barriers to trade* (NTBs). Most observers agree that NTBs should be central to any potential agreement on TTIP.

The empirical studies on TTIP differ on how to approximate for non-tariff barriers to trade. The main idea is to either collect as much data as possible on these types of barriers (bottom-up approach) or to infer from a theoretical trade model how large trade costs have to be in order to be consistent with observed trade flows (top-down approach). Since non-tariff barriers to trade are hard to identify and measure, it does not come as a surprise that the later approach implies higher trade costs due to NTBs and, hence, also higher potential gains from eliminating these barriers.

What is even harder to come by is a concrete idea of what TTIP might look like. At the time of writing, many chapters have not been negotiated or are not public yet. This makes any definitive quantitative assessment of the economic effects of TTIP illusive. Each economic study needs to take a stance on the likely (or less likely) *scenarios of TTIP*.

In what follows, I would like to highlight the main findings of two carefully executed economic studies that have been recently published in *Economic Policy*, a peer-review academic journal. This summary mainly focuses on the *expected economic effects of TTIP on EU* Member States and other European states. Based on the assumption of an ambitious trade agreement, Egger and others expect bilateral trade to increase by 80 per cent between the US and the EU.[8] This boost in trade

[5] cf Caroline Freund and Emanuel Ornelas, 'Regional Trade Agreements' (2010) 2 *Annual Review of Economics* 139–67.

[6] See, for instance, Gabriel Felbermayr and Mario Larch, 'Transatlantic Free Trade: Questions and Answers from the Vantage Point of Trade Theory' (2013) 4 *CESifo Forum* 3–17.

[7] cf Peter Egger, Joseph Francois, Miriam Manchin, and Douglas Nelson, 'Non-Tariff Barriers, Integration and the Transatlantic Economy' (2015) 30 *Economic Policy* 539–84 (hereafter Egger et al, 'Non-Tariff Barriers').

[8] cf ibid.

flows leads in their estimation framework to a gain in annual consumption of over 2 per cent in the EU. These gains from trade tend to be more pronounced in the smaller economies within the EU. Based on a substantial reduction in trade costs, Felbermayr and others also expect a positive effect of TTIP on the EU.[9] Their preferred estimation yields an expected increase in income per capita of 3.9 per cent in the EU in the long run. While there is once more some heterogeneity in the welfare gains within the EU, the authors stress that all Member States would profit from such an agreement. We conclude that both studies find economically sizeable effects from this trade policy. This at least holds true as long as a deep trade agreement eventually materializes.

The *economic consequences of TTIP for non-TTIP member countries* (outsiders) look less rosy. Felbermayr and others envision that non-TTIP countries stand to lose about 1 per cent in income per capita in the long run.[10] Egger and others mention that the nature of reduction in NTBs (discriminatory vs non-discriminatory) due to TTIP is decisive for the sign and magnitude of third-country effects, leaving also the door open for substantial losses for third countries.[11] Countries that are geographically close and well integrated with the EU or the US are among the biggest potential losers of non-TTIP countries. Countries like Switzerland and Turkey or Mexico might lose most in terms of preferential margins,[12] because they are currently linked through other preferential trade agreements with the EU and the US. In the case of Switzerland, Swiss firms would face stronger competition from American firms in the European market due to TTIP. Canada, another country with potentially negative effects from TTIP, would be able to cushion these effects, if the Comprehensive Economic and Trade Agreement (CETA) between the EU and Canada were to be ratified by both RTA partners in the near future. Provided that both RTAs are in force, Canadian companies would be granted similar market access to the EU as American firms. So far, so good. But Canadian firms would still face stronger competition from European firms on the US market.

From a public policy perspective, it seems warranted to *caution against any strong claims for a positive impact of RTAs on employment*. Economic theory is largely silent on the employment effects of trade liberalization. In most theoretical models, any distributional effects of trade are confined to relative income effects, the labour market is still assumed to be perfect, and unemployment does not occur as an equilibrium outcome. Furthermore, the empirical literature on unemployment and trade openness is very scant.[13] Hence, any quantitative claims of job growth due to TTIP seem to be at best plagued with uncertainty and at worst speculative.

[9] Gabriel Felbermayr, Benedikt Heid, Mario Larch, and Erdal Yalcin, 'Macroeconomic Potentials of Transatlantic Free Trade: A High Resolution Perspective for Europe and the World' (2015) 30 *Economic Policy* 491–537.

[10] cf ibid. [11] cf Egger et al, 'Non-Tariff Barriers' (n 7).

[12] cf Marco Fugazza and Alessandro Nicita, 'The Direct and Relative Effects of Preferential Market Access.' (2013) 89 *Journal of International Economics* 357–68.

[13] For a notable exception, see Gabriel Felbermayr, Julien Prat, and Hans-Jörg Schmerer, 'Trade and Unemployment: What Do the Data Say?' (2011) 55 *European Economic Review* 741–58.

This word of caution does not imply that positive effects of TTIP on the European labour market are not possible. They are. I would rather like to change the focus of this trade policy question. Let me briefly lay out the reason for that. As an empirical economist, we always seek to carefully identify whether a certain treatment variable has a causal effect on the outcome variable. In our context, we are interested in the causal effect of TTIP (treatment) on job growth in the EU (outcome). To simplify matters, let's assume that TTIP is already in force and we have labour market data (like employment) for several years before and after the treatment happens. Ideally, we would like to compare changes in EU employment with TTIP relative to changes in EU employment without TTIP. Obviously, in our example, we can only observe the outcome variable for one state of the world, here the trade agreement, but not at the same time without one. So, the natural question of the relevant comparison arises. *What is the correct counterfactual?* Is it reasonable to compare job growth with TTIP to job growth in a world identical to this world except for TTIP? Rather, no. Other countries continue to sign RTAs, and even other mega-RTAs like the Trans-Pacific Partnership (TPP) are under negotiation. It seems overly optimistic that a failure to negotiate and sign a substantial trade agreement with the US allows Europe to preserve the status quo. Signing such an agreement might not add thousands of new jobs, but signing such an agreement ensures that European firms stay competitive in the world economy. Signing a comprehensive and deep RTA with the US is likely to secure existing European jobs.

13

The Struggle for and against Globalization

International Trade Agreements and the Democratic Question

Sonja Puntscher Riekmann

I. Introduction

With the notable exception of the Multilateral Agreement on Investment (MAI) negotiated among OECD countries at the end of the twentieth century, never before in history have international trade agreements encountered such fierce opposition as ACTA, CETA, TTIP, and TPP.[1] For two decades, hundreds of trade agreements—whether bi- or multilateral—were negotiated, concluded, and ratified[2] with little further much ado, but now things are different. Public protest has become vociferous on both sides of the Atlantic, while political parties of various colour, parliaments, and even some governments follow suit. Why is that so? My conjecture is that growing numbers of citizens are captured by sentiments of unease about their capacity to democratically voice their opinion, to claim their rights, and advocate their interests in a world increasingly framed by international trade agreements that are more or less stealthily negotiated among anonymous bureaucracies. Once these agreements are concluded and reach parliaments for ratification, it seems all but impossible to call for changes. Advocates and detractors of pertinent agreements appear deaf to the others' arguments: whereas the former incessantly praise their socio-economic advantages, the latter decry the dangers for national sovereignty, democracy, and the possibility to defend specific ways of life. 'Why They're Wrong' is the title story of *The Economist* in its issue of 1 October 2016, providing a 'Special report in defence of globalisation' of which international trade agreements are an integral part. Independently of their accuracy, such reports no longer reach, let alone convince, the civil protest movements of

[1] My thanks go to Gabriele Spilker for very valuable comments. The usual disclaimer applies.

[2] Andreas Dür, Leonardo Baccini, and Manfred Elsig, 'The Design of International Trade Agreements: Introducing a New Dataset' (2014) 9(3) *Review of International Organizations* 353–75. For example, between 2000 and 2014, 309 preferential trade agreements were signed.

The Struggle for and against Globalisation: International Trade Agreements and the Democratic Question. Sonja Puntscher Riekmann.

world regions whose citizens perceive themselves as losers of free trade. Whatever its origin and impact on receiving societies, migration as much as capital movement, tax avoidance, and financial crash exacerbate feelings of loss and disenfranchisement. Populist parties thriving on nativist, xenophobic, and protectionist discourse are thus also expressions of social cleavages.[3] There is, indeed, empirical evidence for unequal distribution of gains and losses stemming from trade, but also for quite different state responses to cope with it.[4] Given that trade agreements of the last two decades no longer just lower or abolish tariff barriers, but regulate a number of policy fields, citizens suspect important shifts of power. This raises questions of democratic representation and control as citizens ask who represents whom in pertinent negotiations and to whose advantage.

In this chapter, my assumption about the democratic deficit of international trade agreements is developed by the following arguments: first, international trade agreements are perceived as changing the traditional power structures and the political economy of states partaking; in particular CETA and TTIP are said to usher in a new era of trade agreements as they no longer just dismantle tariff barriers, but create new regulatory communities and establish forms of dispute settlements circumventing the ordinary judiciary of states; second, in the EU, the perception of power shift is heightened by a lack of ex ante clarification about whether competence to negotiate and conclude such agreements is the exclusive right of the EU or whether it is shared with the Member States; third, international trade agreements are negotiated in diplomatic secrecy and reach the parliamentary arena or the public at large when they are well advanced or already concluded; ratification by national parliaments is meant to be largely a rubber-stamping exercise. Amendments are de facto ruled out as they would entail the return to the cumbersome process of negotiation, whereas public communication is either avoided or steeped in largely positive rhetoric; if opposing forces succeed in rendering content and procedure salient, it may lead to contestation and even to the failure of agreements. These arguments will be dealt with in greater detail in the next sections. In my concluding remarks, I advocate the strengthening of representative democracy and as a corollary greater responsiveness of elected officials as a possible way out of the malaise.

II. Shifting and Reclaiming Powers

While international trade agreements are part and parcel of the modern capitalist world since the nineteenth century, they have not experienced a linear development,

[3] See, among others, Swen Hutter, Edgar Grande, and Hanspeter Kriesi (eds), *Politicising Europe: Integration and Mass Politics* (Cambridge University Press, 2016); and Hanspeter Kriesi and Takis S Pappas (eds), *European Populism in the Shadow of the Great Recession* (ECPR Colchester Press, 2015).

[4] Cullen S Hendrix, 'Protectionism in the 2016 Elections: Causes and Consequences, Truths and Fictions' (2016) *Policy Brief* 16–20 (Peterson Institute for International Economics, Washington DC).

but ups and downs depending on historical contexts and varying national preferences oscillating between liberalization and protectionism.[5] However, more recent agreements show an important shift concerning issues and powers: first, agreements are no longer about simply lowering tariffs between contracting parties. They now also touch upon non-tariff provisions for foreign direct investment (FDI) and protection of investments, competition policy, public procurement, standards of production, intellectual property rights, labour, environment, agriculture, information technology, and services. While this shift already began within the WTO and numerous preferential trade agreements, their implications for national policy-making have only more recently become publicly acknowledged and thus unleashed contestation. In particular, on both sides of the Atlantic, public fears about national preferences being thwarted by trade agreements are voiced so forcefully that governments and business representations are compelled to hitherto unheard of justification. Contestation regards institutions and procedures providing for joint regulatory frameworks and investor-state dispute settlements (ISDS). While the latter are not a new invention[6] as they were installed to protect investors against states with doubtful rule of law and expropriation policy, they are now seen as an instrument of powerful multinational corporations to curb a state's capacity to democratically decide on regulations in specific policy fields that may run counter to corporations' interests.[7]

In line with this argument, contesting parties purport that inequality between contracting states not only maximizes the power of states with large market size, but that it also gives multinational corporations a leverage for social and environmental dumping and for tax evasion from their country of origin. While such a shift of power is already taking place as a consequence of so-called global value chains that allow for the production of intermediate goods in countries with lower wages and taxes as well as perhaps less strict safety rules,[8] it may be furthered by joint regulation among states having different standards. Whereas pertinent research on these power shifts and their impact on national political economy is still in its infancy, they have entered public discourse in several countries. With regard to CETA, relevant arguments became prominent also in a judicial case brought before the German Federal Constitutional Court (FCC) by some 125,000 citizens (endorsed by another 377,000 signatories depositing their protest at the doorstep of the German Federal Chancellery on the day of the ruling) who claimed that the international trade agreement is to disempower the German Parliament.[9] Therein,

[5] Andreas Dür, *Protection for Exporters: Power and Discrimination in Transatlantic Trade Relations 1930–2010* (Cornell University Press, 2010).

[6] As a matter of fact, ISDS have existed since 1968.

[7] Pia Eberhardt, Blair Redlin, and Cecile Toubeau, 'Trading Away Democracy: How CETA's Investor Protection Rules Threaten the Public Good in Canada and the EU' (Amsterdam, Berlin, Brussels, Montreal, Paris, Ottawa, and Vienna, 2014), <https://corporateeurope.org/sites/default/files/trading-away-democracy.pdf> accessed 7 April 2017. This document is supported by eleven NGOs and labour interest groups from Canada and selected EU Member States.

[8] Bart Los, Marcel P Timmer, and Gaaitzen J de Vries, 'How Global are Global Value Chains? A New Approach to Measure International Fragmentation' (2015) 55(1) *Journal of Regional Sciences* 66–92.

[9] 'Verfassungsbeschwerde und Antrag auf eilige Verfügung' (29 August 2016), <https://www.ceta-verfassungsbeschwerde.de> accessed 7 April 2017.

the plaintiffs claim that CETA entails the submission to international arbitration courts, the deprivation of citizens of their lawful judge, an ultra vires act of the EU in concluding such agreement, the further transfer of sovereignty to the international level, and hence the violation of the 'identity' of the German constitution. The German party 'Die Linke' added to this a so-called 'Organstreit proceeding' (dispute between constitutional organs) to assert the right of the Bundestag to legislative discretion.

While the German FCC in a first ruling rebutted the preliminary injunction,[10] it did not decide on the principal matter which will occur at a later stage. What it did, though, was to formulate three important reservations that epitomize the title of this section: it hedged the power shift. Unsurprisingly, complainants hailed the judgment as partial victory. The Court requires from the German Government to ensure that 'a Council decision on provisional application will only apply to those parts of CETA that lie indisputably within the scope of competences of the European Union', that until a decision in the principal proceedings is rendered, 'sufficient democratic legitimacy with regard to the decisions of CETA Joint Committee' is guaranteed, and finally that the 'interpretation of Art.30.7 sec. 3 lit. c CETA allows Germany to unilaterally terminate the provisional application'.[11] With regard to the third aspect, many seem to fear that once the treaty is in force provisionally, it will create a new reality and thus render nullification difficult even in a case where one or more participants were unable to master ratification.

III. Whose Is the Power to Negotiate and Approve International Trade Agreements in the EU?

With regard to the issue of power shift, the EU is a special case. Since the ratification of Maastricht and even more so the big bang enlargement of 2004, the question of 'Who is in charge? Who is responsible?' has morphed into a more fundamental one about national sovereignty vs supranational encroachment. Indeed, euro-scepticism is the epitome of this conflict. However, the negotiation and conclusion of international trade agreements are complicated by the need to decide the allocation of power in accordance with the agreement's content. Thus, the power is with supranational institutions (Commission, Council, and Parliament) if the agreement falls under Art 207(1) TFEU, whereas the power is to be shared with the Member States if it is a 'mixed agreement' and thus needs ratification by national parliaments. However, such distinction is all but easy and prone to contention. It is, moreover, difficult to decide it ex ante. By way of example: The German FCC

[10] German Federal Constitutional Court, 2 BvR 1368/16, 2 BvR 1444/16, 2 BvR 1823/16, 2 BvR 1482/16, 2 BvE 3/16.

[11] German Federal Constitutional Court, Press Release No 71/2016 of 13 October 2016, <https://www.bundesverfassungsgericht.de/SharedDocs/Pressemitteilungen/EN/2016/bvg16-071.html> accessed 7 April 2017.

already in its 2009 judgment on the Treaty of Lisbon held that portfolio investments (foreseen by CETA) are not to be considered as FDIs pursuant to Art 207(1) TFEU and thus would need ratification by Member States.[12]

Until July 2016, the Commission, however, considered CETA as the exclusive EU prerogative according to the mandates it had received from the Council in 2009 and 2011.[13] Despite a letter signed in June 2014 by twenty-one chairs of relevant committees in national parliaments asking for a mixed agreement, a claim reiterated in the bi-annual report of COSAC in May 2015 as well as in the COREPER,[14] it was only after public protest and subsequent disputes with a number of heads of states and governments that the president of the Commission Jean-Claude Juncker gave in: ' "I would like to see the clear legal proof that this is not an EU only competence. To say that it was my personal preference to make sure that national parliaments had no say in this is absurd", he said, noting that every government is perfectly free to ask their national parliaments how the government should vote'.[15] Finally, on 5 July 2016, the Commission formally proposed to the Council the signature and conclusion of CETA, while recognizing 'the need for proposing it as a mixed agreement, in order to allow for a speedy signature'.[16] In the light of the opposition of the region of Wallonia, voices were raised against the Commission's indulgence, who is still awaiting—at the time of writing—a legal opinion by the CJEU regarding a similar agreement with Singapore (EUSFTA). If the Court's opinion were to confirm the Commission's stance that EUSFTA falls into the exclusive power of the EU, it would certainly unfold its bearing on CETA and TTIP. As so often in EU-related political controversies, 'judicialization' seems to show the way out of the quagmire.

IV. Democracy, Secrecy, and Salience

Democracy and secrecy are a contradiction *in subiecto*. By definition, democracy thrives on public deliberation in representative organs, the media, and civil society. All the more so if the outcome of deliberations are legislative acts binding the whole of a society. While traditionally foreign policy has by and large been the prerogative of state administrations, for two decades parliaments have struggled for an equal footing with their executives. This holds particularly true in the EU, where supranational law enjoys supremacy and direct effect. Owing to its scope and depth of impact, international trade law is also increasingly considered in need of enhanced

[12] BVerfGE 123, 267–437, para 379.

[13] EU Council Doc 9036/09 RESTREINT UE; EU Council Doc 12838/11 RESTREINT UE.

[14] Wilhelm Schöllmann, 'Is CETA a Mixed Agreement?' (European Parliamentary Research Service, 1 July 2016), <http://www.europarl.europa.eu/RegData/etudes/ATAG/2016/586597/EPRS_ATA%282016%29586597_EN.pdf> accessed 7 April 2017.

[15] Daniela Vincenti, 'EU Leaders on Collision Course with Commission over CETA' (EurActiv, 29 June 2016, updated: 30 June 2016), <https://www.euractiv.com/section/trade-society/news/eu-leaders-on-collision-course-with-commission-over-ceta/> accessed 7 April 2017.

[16] Press Release of the European Commission, 'European Commission Proposes Signature and Conclusion of EU–Canada Trade Deal' (5 July 2016), <http://europa.eu/rapid/press-release_IP-16-2371_en.htm> accessed 7 April 2017.

democratic legitimacy: that is, not only for parliamentary consent, but for more appropriate representation of potentially conflicting interests, better deliberation of pros and cons, and a more promising influence of interest groups beyond those traditionally taken into account by state diplomacy. These claims are, however, contested by administrations mainly on grounds of necessity: international (trade) agreements require strategic prudence in disclosing one's position to the other side. Hence, confidentiality is paramount. And, indeed, also Regulation (EC) 1049/2001 regarding public access to European Parliament, Council and Commission documents not only refers to the virtues of openness to strengthen the principles of democracy and respect for fundamental rights, but also stipulates exceptions in case of undermining the protection of the public interest as regards—among other matters—'international relations' (Art 4(1)). In political science, the dilemma stemming from the need to maintain an advantageous position vis-à-vis negotiation partners on the one hand and to satisfy domestic constituencies on the other has been theorized by the concept of a two-level game:[17] it allows to pit the two levels against each other in order to maximize one's room for manoeuvre and attain desired outcomes. Such a game, however, does not guarantee success as the derailment of the Anti-Counterfeiting Trade Agreement (ACTA)[18] or the current inconclusiveness of CETA and TPP ratification demonstrate.

Success or failure largely depends on whether relevant issues are or have the potential to become salient. While ACTA, CETA, TTIP, and TPP are instances of unprecedented salience, secrecy of negotiations and documents perhaps adds to it. Secrecy of documents which are, as it seems, almost inevitably leaked fuels one-sided interpretation and criticism. Members of Parliaments queuing before entering locked rooms in which they are allowed to study drafts of CETA without the possibility of making copies leaves an awkward impression about the standards of Western democracies. This has been recognized also by leading politicians advocating greater transparency,[19] whereas the Court of Justice of the European Union (CJEU) judgment in the appeal case *Council v in't Veld* of 2014 raised hopes about a more general transparency in international negotiations. In that case, the Court decided 'that the Council was justified in refusing access to those parts of document 11897/09 that related to the specific content of the proposed agreement and the strategic objectives which the European Union pursued in the negotiations'. However, the Court also came to the conclusion 'that the Council did not provide any evidence to establish how the disclosure of the remainder of that document would have given rise to such risks' and dismissed the appeal in its entirety.[20]

[17] Robert D Putnam, 'Diplomacy and Domestic Politics: The Logic of Two-Level Games' (1988) 42(3) *International Organization* 427–60.

[18] Andreas Dür and Gemma Mateo, 'Public Opinion and Interest Group Influence: How Citizen Groups Derailed the Anti-Counterfeiting Trade Agreement' (2014) 21(8) *Journal of European Public Policy* 1199–217.

[19] 'Schulz on TTIP: There Will Be No Secret Negotiations' (EurActiv, 6 May 2014, updated: 8 May 2014), <http://www.euractiv.com/section/trade-society/news/schulz-on-ttip-there-will-be-no-secret-negotiations/> accessed 7 April 2017.

[20] Case C-350/12 P, *Council v in 't Veld* [2014] ECLI:EU:C:2014:2039, paras 23–4.

The recent row over CETA could become a text book example for the difficult relations between international trade negotiations and democracy. CETA was indeed in danger of being derailed by the negative vote of the regional parliament of Wallonia which represents some 3.6 million citizens. However, the treaty negotiated by the EU and Canada had become utterly salient in a number of EU member countries: the Austrian chancellor and leader of the Social-Democratic Party had posed the question to party members who delivered a negative vote on the treaty. Yet, he decided to ignore the vote first in the light of the aforementioned judgment of the German FCC and second because he was granted additional clarifications about social rights in a separate document with legal force. The governments of the Netherlands, Slovenia, Bulgaria, and Romania, albeit for different reasons, had teetered for some time, but eventually gave up resistance after lengthy discussions and some concessions. Thus, all the blame was on Wallonia, which was seen as threatening 'to scupper the ability of the world's biggest trading bloc to make good on its word … Dalia Grybauskaite, Lithuania's president, said the 28 EU leaders had become "hostages" to internal Belgian politics'.[21] It was an extraordinary fact that the Canadian Trade Minister had to enter direct talks with the President of the region of Wallonia mediated by the President of the European Parliament. Despite a last-minute compromise, Wallonian politicians from the right to the left were proud of their opposition: 'concessions have only been gained because of the obstinacy of the Walloons', said Christophe Collignon, a member of the centre-left Socialist Party. 'We are giving a little bit of an example to Europe.'[22]

However, also in the US, TPP, the twelve-nation Pacific Rim trade pact, has become so salient that 'chances of the trade deal receiving US congressional approval are now slim'.[23] Moreover, the issue became prominent in the 2016 presidential election with both candidates, Hillary Clinton and Donald Trump, opposed to the deal. Public pressure induced Clinton who originally had been in favour of the agreement to change course.

Opposition to CETA is considered a rehearsal for the even more controversial TTIP to be signed by the EU and the US. While its conclusion and signing appears ever more illusionary, its saliency is also demonstrated by the most successful European Citizens Initiative in terms of signatures: Organizers were able to collect 3.5 million signatures from all twenty-eight EU Member States, of which all but five reached the necessary quorum. Nevertheless, the Commission rejected the registration of 'STOP TTIP' as a citizens' initiative on the grounds of the following arguments. First, the Council decision authorizing the Commission to open negotiations is to be considered a preparatory act that does not fall within the scope of the Regulation (EU) No 211/2011 which defines the conditions for the registration of a citizens' initiative; second, inviting the Commission 'to propose a

[21] Arthur Beesley and Jim Brunsden, 'Canada–EU Trade Accord Teeters on Verge of Collapse', *Financial Times* (21 October 2016).

[22] ibid.

[23] Jeevan Vasagar and Jamil Anderlini, 'Singapore Deputy PM Warns on US Retreat from Asia', *Financial Times* (24 October 2016).

"decision" not to adopt a legal act' is also beyond the Commission's powers. The same holds true for asking the Commission to 'submit proposals for Council decisions not to authorise the signature of or not to conclude CETA'.[24] Yet, this was not the end of the story, as the proponents of the European Citizen Initiative (ECI) have filed a complaint with the CJEU as well as an application for preliminary injunction to stop negotiations. Even if both were rejected on formal grounds, proponents announced that they will continue by organizing the ECI outside EU procedures. However, also with regard to CETA, public pressure was not without consequences: besides separate declarations on the rights of states to legislate in social and environmental affairs, the contested dispute settlement was transformed into a permanent court consisting of fifteen judges evenly distributed between contracting parties and non-nationals.

V. Conclusions

Clearly, negotiations of international trade agreements can no longer take place behind closed doors. They have reached a degree of salience that forces negotiators to publicly justify goals and outcomes. This renders procedures more difficult, but it can also be interpreted as a victory of democracy. Protest is the result of societal cleavages that negotiators can hardly ignore if they want to attain public support and prevent derailment of negotiations. International trade agreements obviously produce winners and losers.[25] To absorb the shocks created for the latter is therefore one of the tasks for states partaking in such agreements. As comparative studies show, states react quite differently as regards shock absorbing, some EU members investing more in social expenditures than others and significantly more than the US.

The second task is to ensure the discretionary powers of parliaments to define policies responsive to the preferences of their electorates. While this may be difficult for the EU polity that consists of twenty-eight members whose constitutional rights are different and moreover may include also veto powers for national sub-units, the most coherent solution would indeed be to further empower the European organs to negotiate, conclude, and ratify international trade agreements. This would require greater responsibility and responsiveness of the European Parliament, the Commission, and the Council towards European citizens. Such endeavour would, however, presuppose a new constitutional approach to European integration. While this is not very likely to happen in the foreseeable future, relaunching the debate on European representative democracy is an urgent matter for several reasons. First, European organs need to regain trust by shedding the odour of anonymous Brussels that is open to the lobbying of powerful interests only. Second, and as a corollary, they need to demonstrate more convincingly that they represent European

[24] European Commission, COM (2014) 6501 final.

[25] See also the data in the Economist Special Report (1 October 2016).

interests in international negotiation fora. This would, however, imply procedures allowing for citizens to voice their interests. Third, they should as representatives of European citizens elaborate European programmes to close the gap between winners and losers of international trade. While this is a tall order, shunning it can become costly in terms of reducing international trade and of fuelling the success of populist forces inside and outside parliaments.

14

Three Salient Issues of the New Comprehensive Free Trade Agreements

Stefan Griller

I. Opening Up the Markets by Reducing Technical Barriers to Trade, and Other Standards

Proposition 1: By incorporating WTO standards on technical barriers to trade (TBTs), CETA, TTIP, and TiSA[1] inevitably and substantially affect domestic policies, including public policy priorities such as consumer or environmental protection standards. Such effects are at the heart of removing barriers to trade. It is pointless to deny, but equally pointless to severely criticize that, given that in this respect there is no substantive change envisaged if compared to WTO standards.

In other words: we might still be concerned about some effects on national (and EU-) law making, but more regarding WTO standards than regarding possible changes. Consequently: in this regard, there is no strong case to rally against the Comprehensive Trade Agreements.

The trade creating and the resulting positive welfare effects of FTAs in principle are undisputed.[2] Against this premise, the crucial issue is whether the expected advantages are sufficient to outweigh the disadvantages, if there are any. The difficulty here is at least twofold: first, it is not easy to quantify the resulting advantages from the FTAs, meaning *additional* advantages compared to those achieved at WTO level. This is due to the incorporation of the substance of the respective WTO law on TBT elimination (Arts 4.2 and 5.4 CETA), while the added value which may mainly flow from regulatory cooperation (chapter 21 CETA) is far from being clear and remains to be seen, especially given the voluntary character

[1] This statement is based on the pertinent CETA wording, given the respective uncertainties for TTIP and TiSA. However, the situation regarding these later agreements seems to be comparable, as far as information is available.

[2] cf Chapter 12 by Moser in this volume.

Three Salient Issues of the New Comprehensive Free Trade Agreements. Stefan Griller.

of that cooperation.[3] With all due respect, and without questioning the overall positive effects, coming up with concrete figures on the trade creating effects is courageous, but yet not more than educated guessing, already regarding CETA, and even more so regarding TTIP without any respective final text; arguably, any *concrete* figures are beside the point, even if the overall positive tendency remains undisputed. Second, the contended disadvantages, especially the loss in regulatory discretion to protect public goods (health, safety, consumer protection, the environment, etc), seem to impact on a categorically different level,[4] and are at least equally difficult to quantify. Thus, it is at this point in time highly uncertain to weigh advantages and disadvantages.

However, regarding the latter, it might be fair to counter some of the criticism announcing all sorts of deterioration in protecting legitimate values like public health, environment, and so forth—the chlorinated chicken example,[5] hormones, etc. Clearly, these arguments are unfounded insofar as the claim is that CETA, etc would force the EU to introduce lower standards, and that this is a fresh threat. What is true, however, is that substantive restrictions are already there, resulting mainly from WTO obligations. Thus, the real issue is: do we want to do away with them? As long as we do not,[6] we should not blame the mega-regionals for eventual difficulties. Inasmuch as the WTO standards are the target of the critique, that should be disclosed, for the sake of clarity. That would then be another debate.

To illustrate the point: the TBT Agreement requires Member States to ensure that 'technical regulations shall not be more trade-restrictive than necessary to fulfil a legitimate objective', among which we find the prevention of deceptive practices, protection of human health or safety, animal or plant life or health, or the environment.[7]

According to Art 2 of the Agreement on the Application of Sanitary and Phytosanitary Measures (SPS Agreement), 'Members have the right to take sanitary and phytosanitary measures necessary for the protection of human, animal and plant life or health', provided that such measure is 'applied only to the extent necessary to protect ... life or health, is based on scientific principles, and is not maintained without sufficient scientific evidence', except as provisional measures. Restrictive measures must be based on a proper *risk assessment*.[8] In that assessment, the Member must take into account, inter alia, 'available scientific evidence', and

[3] See Art 21(6) CETA and, reaffirming this, the Joint Interpretative Declaration on the Comprehensive Economic and Trade Agreement (CETA) between Canada and the European Union and its Member States.

[4] Even if it would be feasible to quantify 'external costs' caused by reduced protection for the consumer, for the environment, etc, it is a primarily political debate whether such costs are worth bearing for the sake of trade creation.

[5] See Friends of the Earth Europe, 'A Rotten Deal: Why TTIP Threatens EU Food Safety Standards for Poultry' (March 2015), <http://www.foeeurope.org/rotten-deal-110315> accessed 7 April 2017 (hereafter Friends of the Earth Europe, 'A Rotten Deal').

[6] This author shares the overall thrust of the critical appraisal presented by Mitsuo Matsushita, Thomas J Schoenbaum, Petros C Mavroidis, and Michael Hahn, *The World Trade Organization: Law, Practice, and Policy* (Oxford University Press, 2015) 503ff (hereafter Matsushita et al, *The WTO*).

[7] Agreement on Technical Barriers to Trade (TBT Agreement) Art 2.2.

[8] The WTO Agreement on the Application of Sanitary and Phytosanitary Measures (SPS Agreement) Art 5.

must apply the appropriate level of protection consistently (by avoiding 'arbitrary or unjustifiable distinctions in the levels it considers to be appropriate in different situations'). In cases where 'relevant scientific evidence is insufficient, a Member may provisionally adopt sanitary or phytosanitary measures on the basis of available pertinent information', and it has to 'seek to obtain the additional information necessary for a more objective assessment of risk' and review the measure within a 'reasonable period of time'.[9]

As a result, restrictive measures have to pass a proportionality test. Moreover, the SPS Agreement is strict in the sense that only in the absence of sufficient information to perform a risk assessment justifying a measure, that measure might, based on pertinent (ie factual) information, only be applied provisionally. It is certainly wrong and misleading that the precautionary principle would be banned under the two agreements (and by importing them, also under the mega-regionals), as is sometimes argued. The contrary is true,[10] as the Appellate Body (AB) stressed in *EC—Hormones*.[11] However, it is also true, but should not surprise, that WTO law justifies not any, but only, the specific variation of the precautionary principle the parties agreed upon.

Suffice it to put some flesh on these bones by referring to the already mentioned hormones case.

According to the AB's findings in this case, the listing of factors that may be taken into account in the risk assessment is not a closed list. The risk that is to be evaluated 'is not only the risk ascertainable in a science laboratory operating under strictly controlled conditions, but also risk in human societies as they actually exist, in other words, the actual potential for adverse effects on human health in the real world where people live and work and die'.[12]

The AB also spelt out what it considers to be a rational relationship between an SPS measure and a risk assessment. Accordingly, the risk assessment could set out both the prevailing view and diverging views. The very existence of diverging views presented by qualified scientists might indicate the state of scientific uncertainty. While in most cases governments would base their measures on 'mainstream' scientific opinion, it is also legitimate to 'act in good faith on the basis of what, at a given time, may be a diverging opinion coming from qualified and respected sources. By itself, this does not necessarily signal the absence of a reasonable relationship between the SPS measure and the risk assessment, especially where the risk involved is life-threatening in character and is perceived to constitute a clear and imminent threat to public health and safety.'[13] This means that it is still a prerogative of the

[9] SPS Agreement Art 5.7.

[10] For more details, cf Matsushita et al, *The WTO* (n 6) 491ff.

[11] WTO, Appellate Body Report, *EC Measures Concerning Meat and Meat Products (hormones)* (16 January 1998) WT/DS26/AB/R, WT/DS48/AB/R, paras 120–5, esp in para 124 (hereafter WTO, *EC Measures Concerning Meat*, 16 January 1998). See also WTO, Appellate Body Report, *US Continued Suspension of Obligations in the EC Hormones Dispute* (16 October 2008) WT/DS320/R/AB/R, paras 674ff (hereafter WTO, *US Continued Suspensions*, 16 October 2008).

[12] WTO, *EC Measures Concerning Meat*, 16 January 1998 (n 11) para 187.

[13] ibid, para 194.

Member to determine the level of protection within its jurisdiction, yet on the condition that this is, as sketched out, evidence based. If scientific evidence is insufficient to perform a proper risk assessment, the measure can still hold on a provisional basis. In that sense, the system is 'science-centred', putting much emphasis on the rational force of a scientific approach.

However, the EC at the time, for whatever reason, had *not* invoked Art 5.7 SPS Agreement (provisional measures) which led, after the AB had held that a proper risk assessment had not been performed, to the verdict that the ban of hormone-treated meat was illegal. This resulted in arbitration allowing US retaliation by suspending tariff concessions and related obligations in a maximum amount of US $116.8 million per year.[14]

It was only thereafter that the EC (EU) initiated a proper risk assessment, and, in 2003, came up with results that arguably justified the upholding of the ban of hormone-treated meat. This was done by repealing the former by another directive which arguably was on better grounds. However, the US (and others) disagreed, and continued with their (authorized) retaliation measures, which led the EU to initiate another dispute settlement round.[15] To cut a long story short: until today, no full settlement could be reached. It was only in 2009 and 2013 that the parties to the dispute agreed to put it provisionally to rest, by the EU opening up an autonomous *erga omnes* zero tariff quota for (non-hormone treated) quality beef, and the US consequently suspending their sanctions.[16] However, the definitive WTO settlement is still outstanding.

To be precise: what happened is that the EU had, according to WTO dispute settlement decisions, violated the SPS Agreement, and decided to accept retaliatory measures in order to continue with that policy until a WTO conform solution could (hopefully) be reached. Probably that could have been avoided by respecting the SPS obligations from the beginning, be it by performing a proper risk assessment at the outset or by invoking the right for provisional measures as long as such an assessment had been incomplete.

It cannot be denied that the hormones case—and other cases in the same vein[17]—demonstrate substantive limits on the Members' discretion to protect public goods

[14] WTO, Decision by the Arbitrators, EC Measures Concerning Meat and Meat Products (hormones), Decision by the arbitrators (12 July 1999) WT/DS26/ARB.

[15] WTO, *US Continued Suspensions*, 16 October 2008 (n 11).

[16] cf Council Decision 2014/44/EU on the conclusion of the revised Memorandum of Understanding with the United States of America Regarding the Importation of Beef from Animals Not Treated with Certain Growth-Promoting Hormones and Increased Duties Applied by the United States to Certain Products of the European Union [2014] OJ L 27/1.

[17] To mention only the so-called *GMO* or *Biotech* case: WTO, *EC Measures Affecting the Approval and Marketing of Biotech Products* (29 September 2006) WT/DS291/R, WT/DS292/R, WT/DS293/R. The Panel held that the EU and its Member States had violated the SPS Agreement by the general de facto moratorium on approvals of biotech products, inter alia, by the lack of a proper risk assessment as required under that agreement. It is probably worthwhile recalling that the Panel in this case also found illegal safeguard measures taken by six EC Member States (ie Austria, Belgium, France, Germany, Italy, and Luxembourg). This had been a very detailed and controversial scrutiny, referring even to the EC-internal discussion on the framework of the Community-wide approval of GMO products and the Member States' efforts to rely on the EC-intern safeguards rules.

like health, etc for the sake of fair and open trade. What is does not prove, however, is that WTO standards would eliminate the right to determine the level of protection a Member would like to choose for its jurisdiction.[18]

All that is already there. We live with it and may even conclude that WTO law, in the field of trade in goods, today comes close to what, inside the EU, is known as a ban on restrictions which might, however, be justified for reasons of general interest, and on the grounds of a proportionality test.

What can we learn for CETA, TTIP, and TiSA? If we agree that the new agreements do not go much beyond what we do already know under WTO law, then we might still be concerned, but more regarding WTO standards than regarding possible changes.[19]

II. The 'Right to Regulate'

> Proposition 2: the relationship between the removal of technical barriers to trade and standards on the one hand side and investment protection standards on the other hand, under the new agreements, is poorly balanced, unclear, and creates fresh problems.

In the 2009 EU Council mandate for the CETA negotiations by the Commission, we find a more or less clear commitment to reduce TBTs beyond WTO standards, without any reservation. The 2011 amendment to that mandate is much more cautious and reflects some of the respective concerns. When it comes to investment protection, the mandate requires that the provisions of the agreement 'shall be without prejudice to the right of the EU and the Member States to adopt and enforce, in accordance with their respective competences, measures necessary to pursue legitimate public policy objectives such as social, environmental, security, public health and safety in a non-discriminatory manner'. Similar passages can be found in the 2013 mandates for the TTIP and TiSA.

The relationship between investment protection and the relevant provisions on the removal of TBTs is not obvious. This results mainly from the novel merger of

But see also, to demonstrate the flip side of the coin, for example, WTO, Appellate Body Report, *EC Measures Affecting Asbestos and Asbestos-containing Products* (12 March 2001) WT/DS135/AB/R, esp paras 170ff.

[18] Illustrated with regard to the chlorinated chicken case (see Friends of the Earth Europe, 'A Rotten Deal' (n 5)): evidence-based concerns on the threat of damages to health, etc justify a ban, even if this should be a minority position within the relevant scientific community. Suspicion of such a threat can, in the absence of sufficient evidence which would allow for a proper risk assessment, justify a provisional ban on the basis of pertinent information which should be accompanied by efforts to perform a proper risk assessment as soon as possible. In the absence of any such threat, a ban might not be justified. However, consumer protection might still allow for specific labelling provisions enabling any consumer to decide on his or her preferences.

[19] In addition, however, we probably have to pay attention that more specific concerns arise in areas like data protection and intellectual property rights, where changes to the WTO regime appear more substantive and less balanced. Cf, in this respect, Chapters 6 and 7 by Cottier and Berka in this volume.

an already comprehensive trade agreement with investment protection provisions which are normally to be found in specific agreements. Traditionally, these provisions are not primarily designed for a fully fledged balancing exercise with 'non-economic' policy preferences, and far from being subordinate to such preferences.

First, the issue cannot be solved by simply pointing to the respective general provisions which are explicitly safeguarding 'non-economic' tasks like public health or environmental protection. These provisions are, at least in principle, beyond doubt,[20] which is not to say that hard cases might never arise; however, this is 'normal' and inevitable, as already sketched out. The more intricate issue is the relationship of these general safeguard clauses with the investment protection chapter (Chapter 8). Second, this chapter includes its own safeguard clauses which fuels the assumption of a different realm of protection standards. Most important is, in this respect, Art 8.9 CETA reaffirming the 'right to regulate' of the parties, underlining the legality of the pursuit of legitimate policy objectives, such as the protection of public health, safety, the environment, or public morals, social or consumer protection, or the promotion and protection of cultural diversity. At first sight, it seems reassuring, in this context, that Art 8.9 para 2 explicitly clarifies that a modification to a party's laws, in a manner which negatively affects an investment or interferes with an investor's expectations, including its expectations of profits, does not amount to breach of an obligation. Consequently, eventual damages (monetary damages under Art 8.39 CETA) claimed on these grounds appear to be excluded.

However, two caveats have to be added, the first of which is less, and the second more likely to materialize. One issue is the arguable separation between the right to regulate and the duty to fair and equitable treatment (FET, Art 8.10 CETA). The argument may run as follows. Even if a modification to the party's law—say, in the interest of the protection of the environment or human health—does not per se constitute a breach of the agreement, it might nevertheless violate the right to FET. At first sight, that may appear far-fetched, but Art 8.10 para 4 includes a special protection for a 'legitimate expectation' which might counter the mentioned exception of mere 'expectations of profits' from any protection. A second issue could be even more dangerous, and that is the protection against 'measures having an effect equivalent to nationalisation or expropriation' (Art 8.12 CETA). Any such measure would trigger the obligation of 'payment of prompt, adequate and effective compensation'.[21] The obvious argument could be that even a perfectly legal modification of domestic regulation leading to an equivalent effect to expropriation would justify a claim for damages.

[20] eg the mentioned provisions incorporating WTO standards on the protection of 'non-economic' tasks; as well as ch 23 on Trade and Labour, and ch 24 on Trade and Environment.

This is what the Commission rightly and repeatedly emphasizes, for example, in its Explanatory Memorandum attached to the proposal to the Council to sign the CETA: 'Proposal for a Council Decision on the signing on behalf of the European Union of the Comprehensive Economic and Trade Agreement between Canada of the one part, and the European Union and its Member States, of the other part', COM (2016) 444 final, 5 July 2016, 3.

[21] Art 8.12 para 1 lit d CETA.

Both avenues could provoke the result that a measure which, under the general safeguard clauses on the protection of the environment, health, and so forth, is perfectly legal, could nevertheless at the same time create an obligation to compensate the affected investor, or would otherwise result in the adjudication of damages.[22] It would not only be cynical, but beside the point, claiming that, in such circumstances, the 'right to regulate' would nevertheless remain intact. Such 'right' would be an empty shell if the legislator is under the constant pressure of eventual compensation. If the concern has its merits, CETA would jeopardize the principle that normally, the claimant would first have to establish the illegality of a measure, and only on that grounds could go for damages, and that only in very exceptional cases (like expropriation) legal restrictions might require compensation.

To elaborate the point a bit further: the European Court of Justice (ECJ), for example, is very cautious when it comes to non-contractual liabilities, and even more so in cases of law-abiding actions. It emphasizes in its standing jurisprudence that the EU legislator enjoys broad discretion in assessing the provision of compensation for certain harmful effects resulting from legislation.[23] More specifically, the right to property and the freedom to pursue a trade or profession are considered by the Court as 'general principles' that 'do not constitute absolute prerogatives, but must be viewed in relation to their social function'. It has thus held that, 'the exercise of the right to property and to pursue a trade or profession freely may be restricted ... that is on condition that those restrictions in fact correspond to objectives of general interest pursued by the Community [today: Union] and that they do not constitute, with regard to the aim pursued, a disproportionate and intolerable interference which infringes upon the very substance of the rights guaranteed'.[24] While that could, at least in principle, give rise to non-contractual liability in cases of disproportionate and intolerable impairment of the right to property and the freedom to pursue a trade, the ECJ is eager to make the caveat clear, which so far blocked any success worth noting in claiming damages for legislative measures. As the Court constantly holds:

> ... an economic operator cannot claim a right to property in a market share which he held at a given time, since such a market share constitutes only a momentary economic position,

[22] A similar, but probably less 'systemic', concern might arise from the opposite scenario: what about measures found to be in breach with the obligations on the reduction of TBTs? Would every such violation entitle to go for damages under the investment protection provisions? At first sight, that seems to be excluded by Art 8.10 para 6 CETA stipulating that the breach of another provision of the agreement does not establish a breach of that article on investment protection. But would the establishment of such a breach not more or less inevitably inform the interpretation of the FET, tilting the balance at least in hard cases in favour of the investor? Also here we cannot be sure about what the investment tribunals will find.

[23] eg Joined Cases C-120/06 P and C-121/06 P, *FIAMM* [2008] ECLI:EU:C:2008:476, para 181, with further references (hereafter *FIAMM*). From the more recent jurisprudence, and in the same vein, cf, eg, Case C-611/12 P, *Giordano v Commission* [2014] ECLI:EU:C:2014:2282 (hereafter *Giordano v Commission*).

From the rich academic debate on the entire subject, see only Anna-Zoe Steiner, *Die außervertragliche Haftung der Europäischen Union nach Art. 340 Abs. 2 AEUV für rechtswidriges Verhalten* (Mohr Siebeck, 2015) with further references.

[24] *FIAMM* (n 23) para 183.

> exposed to the risks of changing circumstances ... The Court has also stated that the guarantees accorded by the right to property or by the general principle safeguarding the freedom to pursue a trade or profession cannot be extended to protect mere commercial interests or opportunities, the uncertainties of which are part of the very essence of economic activity.[25]

In its more recent jurisprudence, the ECJ mentions, in this respect, Art 52(1) of the EU Charter of Fundamental Rights allowing for limitations that 'are prescribed by law and that, in accordance with the principle of proportionality ... are necessary and genuinely meet objectives of general interest recognised by the European Union or the need to protect the rights and freedoms of others'.[26]

To cut a long story short: while arguably the cited CETA provisions could be read along these lines, we cannot be sure that CETA Investment Tribunals, which by definition have to apply only the CETA, but not the domestic law of the parties,[27] would do so. Quite to the contrary, we have to admit that any prediction of such jurisprudence is, on the grounds of the CETA wording, risky. Furthermore, in the past, the record of investment tribunals in thoroughly balancing investors' rights against non-economic regulatory public interest is mixed, to put it mildly.[28] That might change, and some recent decisions seem to confirm this, but the wording is too vague to be sure. In that sense, it would be exaggerated to conclude that CETA establishes a well-balanced relation between public policy interests to issue legislation which imposes limits to economic activities on the one hand, and investors' interests on the other. All depends on the future jurisprudence of the investment tribunals, while their discretion to favour investment protection remains considerable.

This leads us to the third of the salient issues addressed in this short chapter: the role of the investment protection tribunals.

III. Investment Protection Tribunals

> Proposition 3: The dispute settlement system foreseen for investments is complex, and it creates unbalanced advantages for investors. In addition, it remains dubious if it meets the ECJ's conditions for international adjudication as established in its recent jurisprudence. It would be better to opt for integrating national courts into the system.

[25] ibid, 185, with further references. [26] eg *Giordano v Commission* (n 23) para 49.

[27] Art 8.31 CETA. Under this provision, domestic law may be considered as a matter of fact, but not of law.

[28] This is not the place to elaborate on that very intricate issue. Cf, with further references, the telling controversies in Marc Bungenberg, Christoph Hermann, Markus Krajewski, and Jörg Philipp Terhechte (eds) *European Yearbook of International Economic Law* (Springer, 2016); specifically the contributions by Kate Miles, 'Investor-State Dispute Settlement: Conflict, Convergence, and Future Directions' 273ff (hereafter Miles, 'Investor-State Dispute Settlement'), on the one hand, and by Stephan W Schill, 'In Defense of International Investment Law' 309ff (hereafter Schill, 'In Defense of International Investment Law'), on the other; both with abundant further references, including the mentees of the Philip Morris, Vattenfall, and Clayton&Bilcon Award cases.

Much has been written on the deficiencies of the 'system' of investment protection which has evolved over the last decades, with investment protection tribunals at its centre, mostly established under the vast number of bilateral investment protection agreements.[29] We note some substantive improvements that could be achieved recently, and would again be developed further in CETA, not least by introducing more independence to the arbitrators, improved transparency, and an Appeals Tribunal, all that accompanied by the commitment to go for a multilateral investment tribunal and appellate mechanism. However, the asymmetry that such agreements include only obligations for the states, but not for investors, remains. The following remarks are not entering into this debate. Instead, a more principled argument shall be submitted. It dwells on the awkward relationship between investment tribunals, domestic jurisdiction, and the lack of direct effect of 'rights' under the agreements.

Investment protection agreements with specific tribunals as a centrepiece are born out of distrust vis-a-vis the national legal system of the 'recipient state' of the investment. The tribunal not being subordinate to the legal order of that state is seen as a guarantee against all sorts of deficiencies like lengthy procedures, arbitrary jurisdiction, undue influence by the host state, or a corrupt judiciary. Allegedly, it is this type of reassurement which motivates potential investors and is therefore considered beneficial not only for them, but also for the state where they are eventually investing.[30]

While this might be an appropriate approach for enhancing investment in developing or less developed countries without a functioning and reliable court system, or without proper individual rights protection, this is less obvious for investment protection between partner states with a functioning court system based on related principles, especially on the rule of law, and individual rights protection, like the US, Canada, and the EU.[31] Between such states, the obvious alternative would be to make the investors' rights—in fact: anybody's rights—flowing from the agreement directly enforceable within the respective legal orders.[32] In cases of breaches of the agreement, they could go for any domestic legal remedy. Why should partners each disposing of a reliable judiciary distrust each other to the extent that the respective jurisdiction would be unacceptable for individual rights protection, and thus make such remedies even inaccessible for them? And if a certain remedy should

[29] eg Chapter 4 by Tietje and Crow in this volume; Miles, 'Investor-State Dispute Settlement' (n 28) 287ff, 298ff; both with further references.

[30] However, see for a very critical account of this concept, Muthucumaraswamy Sornarajah, 'International Investment Law as Development Law: The Obsolescence of a Fraudulent System' in Bungenberg et al, *European Yearbook of International Economic Law*, 209ff.

[31] Bluntly, this is, between partners with a developed court system, the alternative, Schill, 'In Defense of International Investment Law' (n 28) 313ff is searching for. His criticism on 315f is partly far-fetched, and can partly easily be addressed by respective provisions in the agreements themselves, provided that they are directly enforceable. It is not that the world of investment protection tribunals is the best available, while that of domestic law is inevitably rotten.

[32] For an in-depth and balanced account, cf Marco Bronckers, 'Is Investor-State Dispute Settlement (ISDS) Superior to Litigation Before Domestic Courts? An EU View on Bilateral Trade Agreements' (2015) 18 *Journal of International Economic Law* 655–77.

not be available in one of these jurisdictions, why not create it under the agreement, and thus avoid asymmetry?

However, to the detriment of such ideas, distrust against domestic judiciaries meets with distrust against unbalanced unilateral compliance. We have to note that Art 30.6 CETA excludes expressly any provision to be directly invoked in the domestic legal systems of the parties. This meets with and comes from the tradition developed under GATT and later WTO law, which is not at all common for international agreements in general. With regard to WTO law, most important WTO members like the US, the EU, and Japan do exclude direct applicability.[33] Arguably, there is no compelling legal argument for that result, but more the concern that granting direct applicability within one's own legal system would create an undue advantage for individuals from the partner's jurisdiction.[34] Such concern is understandable if the other party denies direct applicability. Under this logic, direct applicability is only available on the basis of reciprocity, and if that cannot be taken as granted, direct applicability has to be denied.

It is this unfortunate alliance between two different kinds of distrust which results in a robust impediment against efficient legal remedies within the respective legal orders. Consequently, any individual beneficiary under WTO law and under CETA would have to rely on his (or her) home government to introduce dispute settlement under the respective agreement, and even if he succeeds in motivating his government to sue the trading partner allegedly breaking the rules, and to go for retaliation, he cannot be sure that eventual 'damages' would be passed on to him.

But there is one big exception to all these restrictions: under CETA—as well as under bilateral investment agreements in general—investors are the only individuals benefiting from executable awards which may be handed down from specific investment tribunals.[35] Neither consumers nor enterprises, which are equally supposed to benefit from reducing barriers to trade, are in a similar position. They would have to motivate, as mentioned, their government to bring the matter to dispute settlement under ch 29 CETA. However, that remedy is available for the parties to the agreement only, not for individuals. Note the difference: for investors, this is an *additional* option.

Altogether, this results in an imbalanced legal enforcement mechanism clearly favouring investors over all other citizens and enterprises.

Suffice it to add that its compatibility with EU law as applied by the ECJ[36] is dubious. Without, for reasons of limited space, fully developing the argument, this is so because of the restriction that 'any action by the bodies given decision-making

[33] Matsushita et al, *The WTO* (n 6) 31ff.

[34] See for this debate and the position of this author Stefan Griller, 'Enforcement and Implementation of WTO Law in the European Union' in Fritz Breuss, Stefan Griller, and Erich Vranes (eds), *The Banana Dispute: An Economic and Legal Analysis* (Springer, 2003) 247ff, with further references (hereafter Griller, 'Enforcement and Implementation of WTO Law in the EU').

[35] Art 8.41 para 4 CETA.

[36] Opinion 2/13, *ECHR II* [2014] ECLI:EU:C:2014:2454 (hereafter *ECHR II*). For a full discussion, cf only Benjamin Kneihs, 'Der (Nicht-)Beitritt der Union zur EMRK und seine Konsequenzen für Österreich in der Union' in Stefan Griller, Arno Kahl, Benjamin Kneihs, and Walter Obwexer (eds),

powers … as provided for in the agreement envisaged, must not have the effect of binding the EU and its institutions, in the exercise of their internal powers, to a particular interpretation of the rules of EU law',[37] specifically 'in relation to the scope *ratione materiae* of EU law, for the purposes, in particular, of determining whether a Member State is bound by fundamental rights of the EU'.[38] But how could that be achieved if an investment tribunal enacts a directly executable award striking the balance between the right to property and the freedom to pursue a trade or profession, and limits to those rights as imposed by EU or national legislation? It is hard to see how the tribunal could, in its decision, avoid to (at least implicitly) express on the 'correct' balance of the fundamental rights of the investor and those of, say, the consumers, whose health should be protected by a restrictive measure of the legislator. Doing so, however, it would enter a field where the ECJ is claiming its own responsibility to strike that balance.[39] And if such a collision cannot be avoided, it renders CETA in open conflict with the EU Constitution. Similar concerns arise with the requirement that regarding an international agreement forming an integral part of EU law, as would be the case after the conclusion of the mega-regionals, it must be the ECJ which 'has exclusive jurisdiction in any dispute between the Member States … and the EU regarding compliance'[40] with that agreement. How could that be achieved if CETA empowers its investment tribunals to decide exactly on that compliance with CETA? Also in this regard it is not easy to argue in favour of the compatibility with EU law as read by the ECJ.

On these grounds, considerable concerns remain. Contrasting to the choices taken in CETA, several options for improving trade agreements between developed partners like the EU, Canada, and the US would be available, which alone or in combination would reduce or even avoid the mentioned asymmetries, but also the concern on the compatibility with the EU legal order.

The first is to expressly determine those provisions of the agreement which should be directly applicable within the respective jurisdictions. Second, that could, if need be, be accompanied by detailing those remedies which must be provided.[41]

20 Jahre EU-Mitgliedschaft Österreichs (Verlag Österreich, 2015) 257ff; and Ana Maria Guerra Martins, 'Opinion 2/13 of the Court of Justice in the Context of Multilevel Protection of Fundamental Rights and Multilevel Constitutionalism' (2016) 71(1) *Zeitschrift für öffentliches Recht* 27ff; all with further references. Also, this author is not fully convinced by the ECJ's restrictive approach.

Cf, regarding CETA and TTIP specifically, Erich Vranes, 'CETA und TTIP: Kerninhalte und EU-Kompetenzen' in Hans-Peter Folz, Hubert Isak, and Andreas Kumin (eds), *Beiträge zum Österreichischen Europarechtstag 2015* (Facultas, 2017) 177ff, whose account includes the jurisprudence leading to the ECHR opinion, and points more in the direction of the compatibility of the CETA ISDS provisions with that jurisprudence, than the above text.

What we do not and need not address in the above text is whether the ECJ's verdict on ECHR accession might be too restrictive given the specific primary law provisions explicitly calling for and enabling that step, for respective primary law provisions are lacking for concluding CETA, TTIP, or TiSA. Therefore, the restrictions invoked by the ECJ remain valid here, even if they might not be fully applicable for ECHR accession.

[37] *ECHR II* (n 36) para 184. [38] ibid, para 186.

[39] cf only in the above text near n 25. [40] *ECHR II* (n 36) para 204.

[41] This is far from being novel, and even present within the WTO agreements. Cf, eg, Arts X(3)(c) GATT, VI(2) GATS, and 42 TRIPS—and for a discussion of the issue, see Griller, 'Enforcement and Implementation of WTO Law in the EU' (n 34) 294ff.

Beneficiaries of such a system would be all individuals (consumers, enterprises, investors, etc) with regard to their individual rights created under the agreement. And, finally, that might, in order to harmonize jurisprudence across the systems, be combined with a multilateral dispute settlement system including investment issues, where recourse could be sought after a decision of the national instance, or the exhaustion of national remedies. It would be even better if the WTO system could be further developed to that end. This author is not so naive that he would suggest that could be achieved overnight. But if these ideas are constantly sidelined, when it comes to international trade negotiations, unbalanced results will be more likely.

Altogether, this author is concerned that we cannot expect much progress from the new agreements, but instead, as things stand today, we can expect additional difficulties. This is not what one would wish for to conclude after studying brand new agreements.

15

A New Generation of Trade Agreements

An Opportunity Not to Be Missed?

Verena Madner

I. Introduction

'Trade is not an end in itself. It is a tool to benefit people.' This statement would come as no surprise in a publication of the anti- and alter-globalization movement. Here, however, it is a quote from the European Commission, concluding the EU's new trade and investment strategy. The strategy, entitled 'Trade for All',[1] was presented in 2015. It pledges to make EU trade policy more responsible and it explicitly targets the heated public debate over the ongoing transatlantic trade negotiations. The Commission promises to listen and respond both to the widespread critique of secrecy in trade policy as well as to concerns over negative impacts on regulatory standards and public services. Yet, at the same time, the strategy leaves no doubt that comprehensive bilateral trade agreements stay high on the EU trade policy agenda. The Commission heralds a trade policy that is based on transparency and on European values like sustainable development; a trade policy that will safeguard the European social model at home and address the concerns of those who are afraid to be left behind by globalization.

Against the backdrop of this highly ambitious rhetoric, I will take a general look at the debate over CETA, TTIP, and TiSA[2] and then target three sites of contestation, namely: estimated gains from trade; the impact of trade agreements on public services; and the aspiration to enshrine commitments to sustainable development in trade agreements.

[1] European Commission Communication, 'Trade for All: Towards a more Responsible Trade and Investment Policy', COM (2015) 497 final, 19 October 2015 (hereafter European Commission, 'Trade for All').

[2] For obvious reasons, CETA currently provides the best point of reference for further discussion, since we can rely on a text that reflects the final results of negotiations. With regard to TTIP and TiSA, there is still considerable uncertainty. In any case, these agreements share an ambitious approach to comprehensive trade liberalization.

II. Opposition against TTIP & Co: Ignorance, German Angst, or a Genuine Concern?

CETA and TTIP are comprehensive EU trade agreements of a new generation. Negotiations on these agreements reflect a high level of ambition to advance the level of trade liberalization beyond current WTO commitments.[3] The same is true for the plurilateral TiSA negotiations. As the 'low-hanging fruits' of tariff reductions have mostly been reaped in previous multilateral efforts, the focus of these agreements is now on regulatory divergences as possible barriers to trade. Their broad agenda reaches beyond borders and includes provisions on technical barriers to trade and rules on government procurement, on domestic regulation, on regulatory cooperation, and on investment protection.

Regarded individually, there is nothing genuinely new about any of these provisions: rules and standards regarding technical barriers to trade, domestic regulation, or government procurement are incorporated from or modelled after WTO law.[4] Procedures for cooperation and dialogue between regulators in the US and the EU have long been established.[5] And last but not least: provisions on investment protection and on Investor-State Dispute Settlement (ISDS) have been included in bilateral investment treaties (BITs) for decades and have been booming over the past fifteen years. Yet, what is new about the current EU trade agreements are the combination of these elements within one agreement, the economic power of the trading partners involved, and the high level of ambition with regard to scope and content of the agreements.

The shift of negotiation efforts towards bi- and plurilateral EU trade agreements involves a strategic move to overcome the stalemate in WTO negotiations. It aims at both hedging and promoting a comprehensive liberalization agenda with a view to future multilateralization.[6] In this vein, the European Commission strongly and persistently emphasizes that TTIP and CETA are a chance to forge gold standards for global trade.[7] It is this blueprint character of comprehensive trade agreements that has become a decisive driver for the unprecedented opposition to trade negotiations and a major building block in the case of civil society organizations against the new generation of EU trade agreements.

3 cf, with regard to CETA, the negotiating directives that have been made public in 2015, <http://data.consilium.europa.eu/doc/document/ST-9036-2009-EXT-2/en/pdf> accessed 7 April 2017.

4 See, eg, Art 4.2 CETA on TBTs or the CETA provisions on domestic regulations. The CETA chapter on procurement is building on the GPA.

5 eg the US–EU Transatlantic Economic Council. On this and on further US–EU efforts for regulatory cooperation prior to TTIP negotiations, see Jonathan B Wiener and Alberto Alemanno, 'The Future of International Regulatory Cooperation: TTIP as a Learning Process Towards a Global Policy Laboratory' (2015) 78(4) *Law and Contemporary Problems* 103. The account given by the authors lacks, however, any appreciation of the power issues involved in these processes.

6 For an insightful analysis of this strategy, see Werner Raza, 'Politics of Scale and Strategic Selectivity in the Liberalisation of Public Services—the Role of Trade in Services' (2016) 21(2) *New Political Economy* 204–19.

7 See, eg, European Commission, 'Trade for All' (n 1).

III. Sites of Contestation

A. Economic benefits: little to gain and much to lose?

When it comes to determining the economic benefits of trade agreements, empirical studies typically show a wide array of estimations. For anybody but an economist, to closely follow track of this battle over numbers[8] is a futile task to undertake. What is obvious, though, is that due to the underlying complex assumptions, any quantitative prediction on the economic effects of a trade agreement will inevitably include a high level of uncertainty. This is particularly true for estimates regarding the removal of non-tariff barriers to trade and even more so if the outcome of negotiations is still open, as is, for example, the case with TTIP. Studies on the benefits of comprehensive trade agreements like CETA and TTIP will thus yield rather unreliable results, especially in a long-term perspective.[9] Ultimately, the spread of results is dependent on the type of economic modelling that is applied. Different predictive models each come with specific limitations and caveats.[10] Effects on employment and adjustment costs due to unemployment, for example, are difficult to handle and tend to be neglected in most standard models.[11] Estimates on the removal of non-tariff barriers to trade inevitably relate to the issue of regulatory divergence and public preferences. How to measure in monetary terms, for example, the social costs that will result from reducing or adjusting standards in public health, environmental, or consumer protection remains an open question. However, the aforementioned methodological limitations and challenges are rarely an issue in public discussions and there is no meaningful public debate on the adequacy of quantitative estimates for policy advice in general.

Yet, remarkably, studies on the economic effects of TTIP and CETA—though based on completely different methodologies—report rather small effects of these agreements on gross domestic product.[12] However, for the most part of the political debate, gains from the agreements have been widely overstated. The Commission, for example, promoted the proposed transatlantic trade deals as a 'no-brainer', a

[8] For an illustrative account on the war over trade models, see the short contribution by Dani Rodrik, 'The War of Trade Models' (4 May 2015), <http://rodrik.typepad.com/dani_rodriks_weblog/2015/05/the-war-of-trade-models.html> accessed 18 May 2017.

[9] In public debate, however, these methodological limitations are rarely mentioned and there is no broad public debate on the adequacy and usefulness of quantitative estimates on trade effects for policy advice.

[10] For a critical assessment of several studies on the economic impacts of both CETA and TTIP, see Werner Raza, Jan Grumiller, Lance Taylor et al, 'ASSESS_TTIP: Assessing the Claimed Benefits of the Transatlantic Trade and Investment Partnership' (Österreichische Forschungsstiftung für Internationale Entwicklung, Policy Note, October 2014), <http://www.oefse.at/fileadmin/content/Downloads/Publikationen/Policynote/PN10_ASSESS_TTIP.pdf> accessed 7 April 2017 (hereafter Raza et al, 'ASSESS_TTIP'); and Werner Raza, Bernhard Tröster, and Rudi von Arnim, 'Assess CETA: Assessing the Claimed Benefits of the EU–Canada Trade Agreement (CETA)' (Kammer für Arbeiter und Angestellte für Wien, Studie, 2016), <https://wien.arbeiterkammer.at/service/studien/eu/Assess_CETA.html> accessed 16 December 2016.

[11] See Chapter 12 by Moser in this volume.

[12] See Raza et al, 'ASSESS_TTIP' (n 10).

boost for jobs and growth, and TTIP as the greatest prize still to be won.[13] And while it is generally acknowledged among economists that trade liberalization will inevitably produce winners and losers,[14] Brussels remained silent on the distributional effects of CETA and TTIP. Contrary to the emotive language adopted in its 'Trade for All' strategy, the Commission has not presented a plan for the potential losers of trade liberalization. It is safe to assume that not giving the full picture of the impacts of the comprehensive trade policy carries the risk that in the long run, rather than to regain credibility and public support for EU trade policy, the European public's trust will be further undermined.

B. Public services: safeguarding European values?

Public services are core to the shared values of the Union and they take a special role in promoting social and territorial cohesion.[15] Yet, the balance between Member States' political autonomy to organize and finance public services and the requirements of internal market and competition is rather delicate. CETA is not only about liberalizing disciplines on market access, performance requirements, national treatment provisions, etc, but also includes provisions on investment protection. With regard to services, the EU considers CETA the most comprehensive trade agreement it has ever concluded. In terms of sectoral coverage, it is also the first EU trade agreement that follows a 'negative list approach'. CETA therefore also sparks concerns—especially of municipalities, trade unions, and civil society organizations—regarding the freedom of Member States to pursue public policy objectives. In contrast, the European Commission emphasizes repeatedly that CETA, like other trade deals, comes with solid guarantees, which protect policy space for public services.

A detailed analysis and assessment of the agreement and the complex interplay of commitments, exceptions, and reservations in its annexes reveals that policy space with regard to public services is by no means unaffected by CETA.[16] While CETA contains reservations both for existing and future measures also with regard to public services, the fragmentary nature and the ambiguous scope of some of these exceptions for public services can cause considerable uncertainty.

A few examples will illustrate these findings: the scope of the carve-out for services that are not 'supplied on a commercial basis, or in competition with one

[13] See, eg, Cecilia Malmström and Jonathan Hill, 'Don't Believe the Anti-TTIP Hype—Increasing Trade Is a No-Brainer' (16 February 2015), <https://www.theguardian.com/commentisfree/2015/feb/16/ttip-transatlantic-trade-deal-businesses> accessed 7 April 2017.

[14] See Chapter 12 by Moser in this volume.

[15] See Art 14 TFEU, Art 36 CFR, and Protocol No 26 annexed to the Treaty on the Functioning of the European Union.

[16] Verena Madner, Stefan Mayr, and Dragana Damjanovic, 'The Impact of the Comprehensive Economic and Trade Agreement (CETA) on the Legal Framework for the Provision of Public Services in Austria' (Study commissioned by the Chamber of Labour Vienna, Executive Summary, 2015), <https://media.arbeiterkammer.at/wien/PDF/studien/Ceta_studie_2015_Kurzfassung_Englisch.pdf> accessed 7 April 2017.

or more service suppliers'—which has been modelled after the GATS,[17] is highly uncertain and has not yet been clarified by WTO jurisprudence. The so-called public utilities clause,[18] which is often presented as a general exception for public services, only covers specific restrictions, namely, public monopolies and exclusive rights, but does not allow for other restrictions, for example, market access requirements such as economic needs test or requirements with regard to the legal form of enterprizes that deliver public services. The exception that is of relevance for in-house procurement and inter-municipal cooperation is extremely succinct and laconic ('procured by a covered authority internally'),[19] hence it remains to be seen whether in case of a trade dispute the provision will be interpreted as to cover all in-house constellations provided for by the new EU procurement directives. EU reservations in CETA provide for safeguards with regard to education, health, and social services, which receive public funding or state support in any form, and are therefore not considered to be privately funded. However, it is important to stress that these sector-specific reservations have no bearing on the obligations in the field of investment protection. Claims to compensation for alleged violations of investment protection standards can thus also have repercussions in the health, educational, or social sector.

The inclusion of an investor-to-state dispute settlement mechanism (ISDS) that is linked to a broad, asset-based definition of 'investment' is particularly controversial. ISDS has sparked considerable criticism and concern not least with regard to the possible impact of claims for compensation on regulatory activities ('regulatory chill'). Against this background, CETA establishes a new approach to ISDS that is undoubtedly superior to previous trade and investment treaties: the so-called Investor Court System, comprising a permanent tribunal and an instance of appeal, has been implemented. With regard to content, CETA explicitly 'reaffirms' the parties' right to regulate and attempts to define investment standards (eg fair and equitable treatment, indirect appropriation) more precisely. However, the casuistic nature of these definitions gives rise to new questions of interpretation and the (to a certain extent unavoidably) vague language of investment protection standards still leaves considerable room for interpretation to investment tribunals. It is also by no means clear that the right to regulate will effectively provide states with policy space beyond what dispute settlement tribunals consider in conformity with investment protection standards.

What is more, the crucial question with regard to the inclusion of ISDS in CETA has not yet been answered satisfactorily: why is there at all a need to grant special rights to foreign investors? All the more so, given the quality of judicial review in both Canada and the EU?

With a view to the quality of ISDS provisions in hundreds of EU Member States' BITs with developing and emerging countries, the opposition to ISDS in TTIP and

[17] Ch 8, Art 8.2, 1(b) CETA.
[18] Annex II Schedule of the European Union CETA.
[19] Annex 19–7, 1(d) CETA.

CETA has been qualified as hypocritical.[20] It is most certainly true that the transatlantic agenda to improve ISDS was not least spurred by the realization that BITs can bite developed states too. Hypocrisy does not, however, delegitimize all protest against ISDS, given that parts of the civil society organizations that now voice concern over ISDS have already previously been campaigning against ISDS.

C. Sustainable development

The EU commits itself to a high level of environmental protection and claims to uphold and promote its values in its relation with the wider world, contributing, inter alia, to the sustainable development of the Earth.[21] The Commission declares that the inclusion of chapters on trade and sustainable development reflects the core value of sustainability and aims at maximizing the potential of increased trade and investment for environmental protection. However, CETA does not, by far, deliver on the level of ambition that is reflected in this rhetoric; neither does the CETA chapter on trade and environment include any meaningful enforcement provisions nor does it provide for access to justice of individuals. Disputes over trade and environment provisions are excluded from state-to-state dispute settlement and will be handled by a special panel that cannot issue binding decisions or provide for sanctions. Whereas foreign investors may lodge claims for compensation with domestic courts or in ISDS procedures, domestic investors, civil society groups, and individuals may in general not invoke CETA directly in the domestic legal system of the parties. CETA is thus creating a problematic asymmetry that can hardly be perceived as maximizing environmental protection. Furthermore, ISDS gives rise to concerns that regulatory activities that aim at addressing climate change and contributing to meet the targets agreed upon in the Paris Agreement may actually be subject to regulatory chill.

IV. Framing the Debate over Trade Policy: Conclusions

Opposition against TTIP, CETA, and TiSA is far from being homogenous, let alone an all-progressive, left-wing movement. Trade unions, civil society organizations like ATTAC, farmers' associations, representatives of small and medium-sized enterprises, and nativists à la Trump are allies *nolens volens*. It may, therefore, well be that the fight against TTIP & Co is at the same time fuelled by the desire to 'take back control' in order to uphold consumerism and market fundamentalism and by the 'Polanyian' desire to re-embed the economy in society.[22] Yet, political

[20] See, eg, Joseph H H Weiler, 'European Hypocrisy: TTIP and ISDS', *EJIL: Talk!* (21 January 2015), <http://www.ejiltalk.org/european-hypocrisy-ttip-and-isds/> accessed 7 April 2017.

[21] Art 3 TEU.

[22] Contrary to what has recently been claimed in a contribution from political science. See Leif Johan Eliasson and Patricia García-Duran, 'Why TTIP Is an Unprecedented Geopolitical Game-Changer, But Not a Polanyian Moment' (2016) *Journal of European Public Policy*, <http://www.tandfonline.com/doi/pdf/10.1080/13501763.2016.1254275?needAccess=true> accessed 7 April 2017.

contestation over values and trade-offs from trade liberalization is not centre stage of the public debate. Proponents of trade agreements, not least the European Commission, have been staging the debate over the new agreements as a struggle between reason and insight into complex technicalities on the side of proponents and ignorance and irrationality on the side of opponents.[23] Traditional media often choose to replicate the framing that has been offered by supporters of comprehensive EU trade agreements, rather than enabling a differentiated understanding of the EU trade agenda and its underpinnings. And although transparency is an indispensable prerequisite of political debate and democratic deliberation, publishing negotiating texts is obviously neither sufficient nor adequate in order to stimulate an informed public debate about where to go with trade policy.

Thus, so far, Brussels has failed to address adequately the concerns that have been voiced by civil society.[24] What is even more, the inherently political nature of the dispute over EU trade policy has been disregarded. There are different (although not necessarily mutually exclusive) explanations for this lack of political contestation: one reading may be that the failure of the EU to provide for the political[25] is inextricably linked to the supposedly 'non-partisan' nature of the European Commission and to the institutional structure of European governance overall. A somewhat different explanation is that trade policy—like other fields of EU policy—reflects power asymmetries. Framing the debate over TTIP, CETA & Co as a matter of technical expert discourse ('it's the economy, stupid') may thus serve the interest of groups that benefit from having the debate staged as a no-brainer rather than as a political contestation over values reflected in trade policy.

The case of comprehensive trade agreements like CETA and TTIP illustrates that there is still a wide gap between the rhetorical promise of a trade policy that is regarding trade not as an end in itself and the actual reality of EU trade policy on the ground. Shaping globalization according to European values and visions while having honest and difficult conversations at home[26] is still a long way to go for Europe.

Their claim does not adequately take into account the odd alliance against TTIP and it fails, inter alia, to take notice of the movement advocating for an 'Alternative Trade Mandate' ('The Alternative Trade Mandate: What Trade Policy Should Be About' (EPSU European Public Service Union, 25 February 2014), <http://www.epsu.org/article/alternative-trade-mandatewhat-trade-policy-should-be-about> accessed 7 April 2017).

[23] See, eg, European Commission, 'The Transatlantic Trade and Investment Partnership (TTIP): The Top 10 Myths about TTIP—Separating Fact from Fiction' (2015), <http://trade.ec.europa.eu/doclib/docs/2015/march/tradoc_153266.pdf> accessed 7 April 2017.

[24] Some of these have been briefly revisited above.

[25] On the political deficit of the Union, see Joseph H H Weiler, 'In the Face of Crisis: Input Legitimacy, Output Legitimacy and the Political Messianism of European Integration' (2012) 34(7) *Journal of European Integration* 825–41.

[26] Cecilia Malmström (EU Commissioner for Trade on the day CETA was signed), 'CETA Shows that Europe Can Shape Globalisation' (31 October 2016), <http://www.euractiv.com/section/trade-society/opinion/ceta-shows-that-europe-can-shape-globalisation/> accessed 7 April 2017.

16

Conclusions

Stefan Griller, Walter Obwexer, and Erich Vranes

This final chapter synopsizes principal conclusions presented in the chapters of this book (section I) and highlights themes that have recurred in these contributions (section II).

I. Summary of Conclusions

Part I has served to provide the backdrop for the analyses in this volume. In the first chapter, Stefan Griller, Walter Obwexer, and Erich Vranes have examined the extent to which mega-regional trade agreements constitute new orientations for EU external relations. Since, from the viewpoint of the EU, CETA, TTIP, and TiSA are the most important instruments in the context of mega-regional initiatives that are meant to transform the international economic order and to promote more far-reaching geopolitical goals, this introductory chapter has focused on these three initiatives, placing them in the broader context of other mega-regional initiatives such as TPP and the RCEP. Griller, Obwexer, and Vranes have explained the main motivations underlying the worldwide move to bilateral, regional, and mega-regional trade agreements in the course of the last ten to fifteen years, pointing out that if the main mega-regional trade agreements negotiated today were to enter into force, then most important goods, services, and investment transactions would be covered by regional agreements in the near future. This introductory chapter has also expounded main functions of mega-regional trade agreements, which are meant to spill over into other trade relations due to their economic pull and the negotiating leverage of the EU and the US and to possibly even rekindle multilateral process in the WTO. Having also sketched out the principal (geo-)political implications of today's prime mega-regional projects, the authors have indicated that the re-orientation attempted with these initiatives calls for a re-evaluation in view of the problematic experiences made during the negotiations on CETA and TTIP, in particular.

In the second chapter of Part I, Ernst-Ulrich Petersmann recalls that the failure of the WTO Doha Round has not prevented the successful conclusion of a series of other agreements in the WTO context. As pointed out by him, the WTO system still remains the most successful multilateral trading system in history, covering more than 90 per cent of trade today. Initiatives such as CETA, TTIP, TPP, and RCEP are regarded by Petersmann as reactions to the failures of the consensus-based and single-undertaking practices of the WTO: if consensus-based negotiations within the WTO continue to fail, then the parties to mega-regional trade agreements such as CETA, TTIP, TPP, and RCEP—which together account for almost 80 per cent of world gross domestic product—could decide to create a new 'WTO 2020' on the basis of their treaties. In his contribution, Petersmann explicates changing and competing conceptions of international economic law and underlying principles of justice, in order to evaluate the CETA, TTIP, and TiSA initiatives against this background. According to him, these projects reflect trends of legal fragmentation and methodological disagreements over how to liberalize and regulate trade. While Petersmann argues that, from an economic viewpoint, these initiatives are likely to be beneficial (although the precise gains and their distribution among economic actors remain contested), he points to a series of problematic developments: Petersmann, inter alia, expresses sincere doubts as to whether the CETA and TTIP projects are consistent with the EU's mandate to protect the fundamental rights of its citizens also in external relations. Likewise, he questions whether the EU has complied with its directive to be guided, in its international relations, by the principles that have inspired its own creation. Furthermore, Petersmann submits that the Commission and EU politicians have not convincingly justified the necessity of denying EU citizens the judicial remedies that are to be granted to foreign investors under CETA and TTIP. Likewise, he criticizes that EU politicians continue to deny citizens the right to invoke individual rights to be derived from free trade agreements (FTAs) with non-European countries. In his vigorous critique, Petersmann cautions that such 'disempowerment' of citizens risks estranging them from the EU by undermining the protection of public goods and 'public reason'.

Part II of this volume has been devoted to an examination of selected sectoral issues in CETA, TTIP, and TiSA. In the chapter 'The Contents of CETA, TTIP, and TiSA', Erich Vranes has attempted to provide an overview of the trade disciplines envisaged in these treaty projects, focusing on CETA, but taking into account available information and negotiating materials on TTIP and TiSA. As large parts of these exceptionally extensive treaty initiatives deal with trade issues, the focus of this contribution has been on essential structures and contents. As explained in this chapter, while CETA is meant to create a free trade area in line with WTO law, it also has 'WTO-plus' dimensions, clearly reaching beyond WTO law in terms of substance and depth of commitments. While outlining the main trade in goods and services disciplines of CETA, this chapter has also pointed to some fundamental issues that have remained unclear in this agreement, such as the interplay between market access and non-discrimination disciplines in the services context. It has also stressed essential structural differences, such as the divergent scopes of application, substantive disciplines, and scheduling approaches under the WTO GATS agreement on the one hand and CETA on the other. Moreover, this contribution has dealt with the framework for regulatory cooperation established in CETA, trying to explain why it is, despite many non-binding rules, regarded as so controversial by many commentators. This chapter has then turned to an analysis of available TTIP and TiSA materials, contrasting these initiatives with the contents and structures of WTO law and CETA.

In their chapter 'The Reform of Investment Protection Rules in CETA, TTIP, and Other Recent EU FTAs: Convincing?', Christian Tietje and Kevin Crow have first underlined that the current debate on the investment disciplines in such FTAs is to a large extent fostered by non-governmental organizations, which has led to a focus in the academic and broader public debate that tends to disregard other developments in international economic law that may have considerably greater systemic impacts. Tietje and Crow argue that a central dilemma of this debate consists in the vagueness of international investment law, a characteristic that is inherent and even necessary, to some extent, in international investment law as in law in general. As is shown in this chapter, current attempts to more clearly define central investment standards aim to secure more policy space for states that enter into investment agreements. This must be seen against the background that textual ambiguity tends to increase the powers of international arbitrators, whose awards—if perceived as being inadequate—cannot as easily be corrected as court rulings in domestic systems, as international arbitration awards rest on international rules that cannot unilaterally be adapted by one state only. Examining reform efforts in recent agreements, Tietje and Crow argue that these textual modifications do not change the functioning of the system, as they merely reflect already existing arbitral practice and do not further restrict the interpretative powers of arbitrators. What is needed, according to these authors, is a considerably more fundamental reform consisting in the introduction of counterclaims by states against investors, which would transform international investment law into a more symmetrical system.

The dispute settlement disciplines in mega-regional trade agreements have been examined also in the contribution by Stephan W Schill, who treats CETA and TPP as indicators of how mega-regionals more generally are likely to deal with concerns that international judges and arbitrators appear to be empowered to independently shape international law in the fields of trade and investment, thereby also undermining the multilateral trading system and balances struck between economic and non-economic concerns. As regards inter-state dispute settlement, Schill submits that CETA, just as TPP, largely builds on the WTO dispute resolution system, thereby minimizing friction with the latter. As dispute settlement under these mega-regionals is to take place on an ad hoc basis, the ensuing jurisprudence is likely to be less coherent, which is why WTO rulings, which must be taken into account under these mega-regionals, will remain relevant. Moreover, the small degree of institutionalization of the dispute settlement systems under CETA and TPP will facilitate their eventual integration into the WTO system in the long run. Overall, Schill argues that—despite attempts by the contracting parties to better control inter-state dispute settlement—there is little that is remarkable in the developments regarding this type of dispute settlement in these agreements. Things are quite different as regards ISDS. As Schill highlights, ISDS is suffering from a legitimacy crisis due to its implications for democracy, the rule of law, and the protection of fundamental rights. CETA and TPP react to these concerns by only selectively judicializing disciplines, by creating carve-outs from investment protection (such as the exemption of audio-visual services from CETA), by requiring attempts for amicable settlement and consultations before adjudication, and by, for example, promoting alternative dispute resolution, transparency, and public hearings. While Schill regards this as promising for efforts to globally reform ISDS, he also points to a wider transatlantic gap regarding the institutional structures for ISDS. According to him, the EU's preferred option of permanent *sui generis* ISDS institutions is entangled with legitimacy problems of its own, not least the fact that a permanent multilateral court may even be further removed from democratic processes. Finally, Schill argues that the cures for today's concerns regarding ISDS had already been present in the CETA draft of 2014 (ie before the ISDS reform during the legal scrubbing phase), as this version had already provided for increased transparency, stricter ethics rules, a joint interpretation mechanism, and clarifications of central disciplines and exceptions.

In the next chapter, Thomas Cottier has examined the progress and opportunities missed in intellectual property protection under mega-regional trade agreements, using CETA and TPP as the most important points of reference for the EU and the US, respectively. As Cottier underlines, the new standards developed under these and other mega-regional trade agreements will also benefit other WTO Members due to the most-favoured nation clause enshrined in the TRIPs agreement, thereby contributing to a common law of intellectual property rights protection. As mentioned by Cottier, one would expect recent mega-regional projects to address systemic problems that exist under WTO law today, such as the insufficient international regulation of parallel trade, the relationship between intellectual property rights and competition law, and investment protection and trade. However, these issues are inadequately dealt with in most recent free trade and mega-regional trade agreements. After an extensive overview of the main provisions in CETA and TPP, Cottier also warns that conflicts of norms may arise for countries that are parties to more than one preferential agreement. In wide-ranging conclusions, Cottier argues that future agreements, including TTIP, should establish a proper balance between exclusive rights and the public domain. Furthermore, trademarked products should be subject to international exhaustion, and linkages should be established to investment law, competition policy, technical barriers to trade, regulatory cooperation and coherence, and human rights, so as to allow arbitrators to take into account relevant rules. Also, negotiations should aim at solving problems of legal fragmentation. In a related vein, the status of WTO law and TRIPs should be made clearer in future FTAs; alternatively, the jurisdiction of the WTO dispute settlement system should be extended to other FTAs. Finally, Cottier argues that, in order to prevent conflicting obligations, future negotiations on intellectual property standards should move back to the WTO.

In the following chapter, Walter Berka has dealt with data protection in CETA, TTIP, and TiSA. While emphasizing that the flow of data is the backbone of trade, Berka also underlines that these three agreements are particularly problematic in view of considerably diverging attitudes towards data protection on both sides of the Atlantic. As explained by Berka, the US approach to privacy protection has traditionally focused, in a piecemeal manner, on the protection of personal privacy against government surveillance, trusting in self-regulation and contractual agreements. By contrast, the EU aims to protect personal data through an overarching framework, in which data protection constitutes a fundamental right that tends to trump over commercial interests. In view of this conceptual divide, there is a need for international rules on the level of protection and the balance to be struck between data protection and economic interests. Regarding CETA, Berka argues that this agreement arguably has not restricted the application of national data protection measures, even if they interfere with data flows. The situation is quite different under the TiSA proposals that have become available so far, as these seem to attribute greater weight to the free flow of information than to privacy. According to Berka, a similar development towards a minimum standard of privacy protection can also be inferred from TPP. As pointed out by Berka, the international regulation of these issues might be moving on to other arenas such as the 'EU–US Privacy Shield' and the 'Umbrella Agreement', and may also be influenced by future Asian initiatives. In view of these developments, Berka concludes that the question might arise as to whether a new design of data protection is preferable also in Europe.

In his contribution 'CETA, TTIP, TiSA, and Financial Services', Christoph Ohler has argued that financial services are, in principle, well suited for trade liberalization given that capital is a highly mobile factor. Moreover, trade in financial services especially profits from technological advances. However, as shown in Ohler's contribution, a series of hurdles still remain to be overcome in this field. These have their root in the fact that the interplay between trade and regulatory issues has not been addressed in a satisfactory manner on the international level so far. Thus, trade in financial services is impeded by an insufficient international coordination of divergent national regimes for the regulation and supervision of financial institutions. According to Ohler, this interface problem between trade and regulatory cooperation is due, first, to the persisting mutual distrust among states in this field and, second, to the lack of sufficient coordination between international trade fora such as the WTO and regulatory institutions such as the Basel fora. This problem is further exacerbated by unilateral regulations enacted, for example, by the EU and the US which have an extraterritorial thrust and therefore risk giving rise to conflicting obligations. As Ohler has pointed out, while the WTO still constitutes an inadequate forum for addressing the link between trade and regulatory issues in the field of financial services, combining the procedural and substantive approaches used in CETA and the TTIP draft would be more promising. However, as rightly stressed by Ohler, there remains the problem that such issues could only be convincingly resolved on a truly *multi*lateral basis.

In the chapter 'Human Rights, Labour Standards, and Environmental Standards in CETA', Lorand Bartels has shown that CETA contains various types of obligations regarding these issues and has emphasized that international obligations to implement existing domestic laws and regulations may prove significant, as is underlined by recent dispute settlement in the Central America FTA context. Likewise, current international practice has shown that obligations to 'seek to ensure' high standards of protection can lead to international consultations, triggered by one contracting party, if the other party manifestly violates such obligations. On the other hand, Bartels has stressed that—although the substantive standards on labour, environmental, and human rights protection in CETA tend to be in line with recent EU and Canadian agreements—the implementation of relevant standards has been watered down in CETA to some extent. The same holds true for the human rights clause in the 2016 EU–Canada Strategic Partnership Agreement, which cross-refers to CETA and hardly lives up to established practice in EU agreements with other third countries.

In his contribution 'TTIP, CETA, and TiSA Behind Closed Doors: Transparency in the EU Trade Policy', Panagiotis Delimatsis has recounted the struggle for increased transparency in the negotiations on CETA, TTIP, and TiSA from the viewpoint of the EU in particular. Having reminded us that transparency is both a constitutional and political requirement in the EU, Delimatsis has juxtaposed the quite intransparent negotiations on CETA and TiSA on the one hand and TTIP on the other. Whereas transparency has increased slightly during the negotiations and the legal scrubbing phase of CETA, transparency in the TiSA negotiations is still regarded as insufficient by Delimatsis. Regarding TTIP, Delimatsis has argued that the significant turn towards more transparency in the TTIP negotiations is particularly noteworthy, not least in view of the fact that the disclosure of core documents—such as negotiating directives issued by the EU Council and draft legal texts proposed by the EU to the US—may not be legally required according to European Court of Justice (ECJ) case law.

In the chapter entitled 'CETA, TTIP, TiSA, and Their Relationship with EU Law', Stefan Mayr has extensively examined the many facets of this complex interrelationship. Mayr has, inter alia, highlighted that, from an EU law perspective, the contracting parties to CETA could indeed have awarded direct effect to unconditional and sufficiently precise provisions in CETA, as the ECJ can decide on the (non-)existence of such effect only if an agreement remains silent on this issue. Furthermore, Mayr has submitted that while the European Parliament is indeed involved in the conclusion of agreements such as CETA, TTIP, and TiSA, future amendments, for example, of annexes to such agreements through simplified amendment procedures could be effected without approval of the European Parliament, which only needs to be informed of such modifications. If such agreements were concluded as mixed agreements, however, then amendments would have to be accepted by the Member States. Regarding the intricate issue as to whether CETA, TTIP, and TiSA have to be concluded as mixed agreements in the first place, Mayr has argued that CETA and TTIP should be regarded as obligatory mixed agreements. As regards TiSA, Stefan Mayr has submitted that while TiSA in principle falls under the EU's common commercial policy and is to that extent covered by an exclusive EU competence, the question of mixity may, however, arise with a view to commitments in the area of transport. Finally, this chapter has argued that the establishment of investor-to-state dispute settlement as envisaged in CETA and TTIP may come into conflict with the autonomy of EU law and the ECJ's competence to interpret and apply EU law.

In Part III of this volume, comprising four short contributions and a chapter on conclusions, fundamental questions surrounding these mega-regional trade agreements have been discussed by an economist, a political scientist, and two lawyers. From an economic perspective, Christoph Moser has argued that the widespread consensus among economists that international trade is positive is supported also by robust empirical evidence. While trade liberalization should ideally be pursued on a multilateral basis, overall negative effects from regional trade agreements are, however, rather unlikely, with the exception of some agreements that may occasionally cause considerable trade diversion. Regarding TTIP, Moser submits that substantial economic benefits—which are difficult to predict precisely—are to be expected, if TTIP were to take on the form of a deep trade agreement focusing on non-tariff barriers to trade. Yet, such an agreement would be likely to negatively affect non-participating countries, especially states that are geographically close to, and well integrated with, the EU and the US. As also pointed out by Moser, quantitative claims of job growth generated by a future TTIP agreement are highly uncertain. However, since other countries will continue to enter into (mega-)regional trade agreements, concluding a TTIP-type agreement would ensure that European enterprises remain competitive, which is likely to safeguard existing European jobs.

In the second short contribution to Part III, political scientist Sonja Puntscher Riekmann reminds us that democracy and secrecy are a contradiction in terms. It is the secrecy of negotiations which augments the growing feeling of many citizens that they may not be able to democratically voice their opinion in a world that is increasingly governed by FTAs, the negotiations of which can only insufficiently be influenced by parliaments. FTAs are perceived as changing established power structures; this holds true especially for deep integration agreements such as CETA and TTIP, which are not confined to 'classic' trade issues such as tariffs, but lay down disciplines influencing many fields of domestic regulation. As pointed out by Puntscher Riekmann, many citizens have arguably started to more clearly become aware of this impact of international trade agreements as the negotiations on CETA and TTIP, in particular, advanced. These negotiations, which have been overshadowed by extraordinarily numerous political and constitutional problems related to democratic legitimacy, may therefore become textbook examples for the difficult relations between trade and democracy.

From a lawyer's perspective, Stefan Griller has made three propositions in his chapter. First, he argues that the incorporation of WTO rules on technical barriers to trade and other standards in mega-regional trade agreements will substantially affect domestic regulatory autonomy. But, as Griller points out, since this effect already exists under WTO law as it stands today, the incorporation of such standards into mega-regional trade agreements is no real reason to rally against these agreements. Second, focusing on the CETA agreement, Griller submits that the relationship between CETA's disciplines on technical barriers to trade and standards on the one hand and its provisions on investment protection on the other is poorly balanced and creates new problems. In particular, Griller argues that there is a risk that mere commercial interests or opportunities that might lawfully be affected by modifications of national law (namely when such modifications are justified under CETA's general exception clauses) might nonetheless receive protection under the investment chapter. Third, similarly to Stefan Mayr's contribution, Griller argues that the investor-state dispute settlement system—even though it has been improved in CETA—still creates unbalanced advantages for investors and would not be in line with the ECJ's jurisprudence on the permissibility of the creation of international tribunals whose rulings might affect EU law. According to Griller's contribution, it would be preferable to explicitly grant direct effect to certain provisions of agreements such as CETA and to integrate national courts into the system.

In the fourth short contribution, Verena Madner has examined three issues against the backdrop of the EU's 'Trade for All' strategy, arguing first that the gains to be expected from CETA and TTIP have arguably been overstated in the political debate, with the EU also remaining silent on the distributional effects of such mega-regional trade agreements, which risks further undermining public trust in the EU's trade policy. Second, Madner expresses doubts as to whether domestic policy space for regulating public services is secured under CETA. Like other contributors, she questions why foreign investors are to be granted special rights in the highly developed systems of judicial review of Canada and the EU. Third, Madner submits that the CETA disciplines on sustainable development fail to live up to the EU Commission's rhetoric, as they do not provide for sufficient means of enforcement. Finally, this contribution argues that Brussels has, by framing the debate on CETA, TTIP, and other similar initiatives as technical expert discourses, so far failed to adequately address the concerns voiced by civil society.

II. Recurrent Themes in this Book

In view of the extraordinarily broad range of issues covered by CETA, TTIP, TiSA, and other mega-regional initiatives more generally, the contributions to this book have had to address a wide spectrum of subjects. Nonetheless, some recurrent themes have become discernible in several chapters. These shall be briefly recapitulated in this concluding section.

As in the academic debate more generally, many contributors to this volume have underscored that these mega-regional trade agreements and the related turn to bilateralism and regionalism risk further augmenting the fragmentation of international economic law. This threat concerns the system of international economic governance in institutional as well as substantive terms, as the potential for insufficient international coordination, legal conflicts, and political tensions is likely to increase. Several chapters have, in this context, referred to the potential repercussions on the WTO system. One concern is that the WTO may be further undermined as the central multilateral negotiating system. Another worry is that economic issues will be regulated bi- or plurilaterally, although they could be more, and perhaps only, adequately dealt with in a multilateral setting. Several contributors have therefore accentuated the view that relevant negotiations should move back to the WTO. One should add that such a return to the WTO may become more likely in the short or medium term, if further impasses surface in the negotiation or ratification of mega-regional trade agreements. As has been indicated in the introductory chapter, such stalemates are indeed not only unlikely regarding TPP and TTIP. They may also affect TiSA, RCEP, or CETA, the latter of which still needs to be ratified by the national and regional parliaments in the EU Member States. Should such deadlocks multiply, then a return to the WTO may not only be preferable, but even unavoidable, in many fields.

Even if all of these agreements were to enter into force, the multilateral WTO system would not, however, be automatically undermined in terms of substantive disciplines to the extent that the aforementioned mega-regional projects reconfirm WTO law and often add further disciplines that are meant to be WTO-consistent. Still—and despite mandates for dispute settlement bodies established under regional agreements to follow WTO jurisprudence—the risk of divergent rulings persists under such a fragmented system. This risk is all the more acute as dispute settlement mechanisms typically enjoy considerable interpretative leeway under the commonly rather vague norms in international trade and investment agreements.

In terms of 'WTO-plus' features of mega-regional initiatives and CETA and TTIP in particular, one of the topics most discussed in the academia and the wider public is the mechanism of regulatory cooperation. While it is generally held that the most important economic benefits to be derived from mega-regional trade agreements concluded between industrialized countries would stem from regulatory cooperation, various contributions to this book have emphasized that such effects are difficult to estimate in economic terms, on the one hand. On the other, it is all but clear whether, after many failed or feeble attempts at broader transatlantic regulatory cooperation, further non-binding initiatives as those envisioned under CETA and TTIP would be more successful. The hurdles are high and not only legal in nature, as they appear to be rooted in different regulatory philosophies reflecting divergent societal preferences, different traditions, and sometimes distrust and lack of political will or leadership.

Also in terms of substance, the efforts to decrease the vagueness of investment disciplines and thereby to protect domestic policy spaces have been called into question in this book, especially on the basis that these attempts appear to merely codify existing practice and raise new questions in the context of comprehensive trade and investment agreements. As regards modifications, laid down in CETA, to traditional investment dispute resolution, it has been pointed out that while these are noteworthy, the final outcome seems problematic, since the cures sought would have been achieved already under the 2014 version of CETA.

Another focal point in the academic debate and also in contributions to this book is the controversial distribution of competences in the EU's external economic relations. Whereas until recently this used to be a highly technical issue debated only in relatively small expert circles, the fact that the unclear and controversial division of competences between the EU and its Member States overshadows and indeed greatly impedes their capability to act in international relations has become evident, in particular in the process of signing CETA, for political observers, trading partners throughout the world, and even the interested public at large.

These uncertainties arguably accentuate apprehensions of EU citizens who appear to increasingly wonder who is in control in the 'multilevel system' of EU governance, which is perceived as progressively being transcended by international economic developments and external influences, making responsibilities obscurer still. A rapidly growing number of citizens are evidently anxious that they may not be able to democratically influence negotiations on potentially highly transformative international agreements and the process of international economic governance. As has also been pointed out, citizens may therefore feel progressively estranged from European integration, which is seen as being closely entwined with, and contributing to the speed of, globalization. Several contributors have therefore also called for enhanced transparency and democratic feedback in the negotiation of international agreements. The adoption of 'interpretative instruments' of vague import and status may work as a questionable one-time 'remedy' to disperse anxieties as in the case of CETA, but certainly not as a lasting cure. The fact that the fears associated with CETA, TTIP, and the process of globalization more generally have arguably been factors contributing to the Brexit vote should be more than a resounding wake-up call.

In sum, and paraphrasing Sonja Puntscher Riekmann's contribution to this book, the negotiations of the mega-regional trade agreements analysed in this volume constitute textbook examples not only as regards the problematic relationship between trade and democracy, but also as regards the intricate distribution of competences in the EU's external relations, the complex interactions between bilateralism, regionalism, and multilateralism, the reform of international trade and investment law, and the intricate, and arguably irresolvable, tensions between economic and non-economic concerns. In view of the experiences made by many actors and the public at large in the process of the negotiation of these treaty projects, international trade and investment agreements will arguably, for a considerable time at least, not be discussed, negotiated, and concluded in the same manner again.

Index

The manufacturer's authorised representative in the EU for product
safety is Oxford University Press España S.A. of El Parque Empresarial
San Fernando de Henares, Avenida de Castilla, 2 - 28830 Madrid
(www.oup.es/en or product.safety@oup.com). OUP España S.A. also acts
as importer into Spain of products made by the manufacturer.
Printed and bound by CPI Group (UK) Ltd, Croydon, CR0 4YY
14/09/2026
02216306-0011